KIERKEGAARD'S PSYCHOLOGY

Kresten Nordentoft

Translated by
BRUCE H. KIRMMSE

DUQUESNE UNIVERSITY PRESS: PITTSBURGH

Distributed by Humanities Press, Atlantic Highlands

Originally published as *Kierkegaard's Psykologi* by G.E.C GAD, Copenhagen, 1972.
Copyright © 1972 by Kresten Nordentoft

Library of Congress Cataloging in Publication Data

Nordentoft, Kresten.
　　Kierkegaard's psychology.

　　(Psychological series; v. 7)
　　Translation of Kierkegaards psykologi.
　　Includes bibliographical references and index.
　　1. Psychology. 2. Kierkegaard, Soren Aabye, 1813-1855. I Title. II.
Series: Duquesne studies: Psychological series; v. 7)
　　BF128.D3N6713　　　　　　　　　　150'.19'2　　　77-14423
　　ISBN O-391-00661-4

CONTENTS

TRANSLATOR'S NOTE

The translation of a book of this size would not have been possible without the assistance and support of many people and institutions. There are a great many passages from Kierkegaard's works and papers translated in the present work, and, while all the translations are my own, I gladly acknowledge my indebtedness to previous Kierkegaard translators, particularly Howard and Edna Hong, whose consistently high standard has been an inspiration and a challenge. This translation was made possible by the financial support of the State Research Council for the Humanities (Copenhagen) and the research funds of Aarhus University and Connecticut College, for all of which I am very thankful. Kresten Nordentoft, the author of the present work, has been helpful and encouraging throughout, as has John Dowds, the Director of the Duquesne University Press. My parents, Herbert and Helen Kirmmse, have been very helpful in the preparation of the manuscript, as have David Desiderato, Teri Dibble, Adrienne Riley, Tamara Saunders and Joan Warren. Finally, I would like to express my deepest thanks to my wife, Judith, not only for the many hours which she spent in editing the translation and in preparing the manuscript for the press, but even more for her continuing support and encouragement.

Connecticut College
New London, Connecticut

Bruce H. Kirmmse

BIBLIOGRAPHICAL NOTE AND ABBREVIATIONS

The text contains many citations from and references to Søren Kierkegaard's works and papers and the collected works of Sigmund Freud. The page number and the volume being cited from or referred to are included in square brackets [ ] at the end of the phrase, sentence or paragraph in question. All translations from Kierkegaard which appear in the present work have been made by the translator and often differ somewhat from any published translation. The bracketed references following the Kierkegaard passages are therefore keyed to the standard Danish edition of Søren Kierkegaard's collected works, *Søren Kierkegaards Samlede Væker*, second edition, vols. I-XV, Copenhagen: Gyldendal, 1920-36. Bracketed references to Kierkegaard's works are abbreviated to the volume number and page number on which the passage in question appears, e.g., [V 25]. As almost all of Kierkegaard's published works exist in English translation, an abbreviated page and title reference to the English version has also been included in the brackets, so that the curious reader may seek out the context in which a given citation or reference appears, or may compare the published English translation with that of the present translator. Kierkegaard's work, *Stages on Life's Way*, for instance, is abbreviated SLW, and a typical bracketed reference to both the Danish edition and the standard English translation is thus: [VI 296, SLW 262]. An annotated list of the English translations and their abbreviations follows below. The list also mentions the major Kierkegaardian pseudonyms dealt with in the present study and gives an indication of the contents of each work.

CI   *The Concept of Irony*, New York: Harper and Row, 1965. First published 1841. Kierkegaard's master's thesis, a voluminous work on Socratic and modern romantic irony.

E/O   *Either/Or*, vols. I and II, New York: Anchor Books, 1959. First
I-II   published 1843, edited by SK's pseudonym Victor Eremita. Volume I, written by Aesthete A, presents the aesthetic attitude toward life in aphorisms, essays, and a novel. In this volume appear various pseudonymous figures, including the Page, Papageno, and Don Giovanni (from the essay on Mozart, "The Immediate Erotic Stages or the Musical Erotic"); Antigone (from "The Ancient Tragic Motif as Reflected in the Modern"); Marie Beaumarchais, Donna Elvira, and Margaret (from "Shadowgraphs"); Cordelia and Johannes the Seducer (from

"The Diary of a Seducer," a diaristic novel). Volume II, written by Judge William, presents the ethical attitude toward life in two lengthy "letters," and discusses Aesthete A. Among the other characters discussed is Emperor Nero.

ED
I-IV
Edifying Discourses, vols. I-IV, Minneapolis: Augsburg Publishing House, 1943-46. First published 1843-44. Kierkegaard published in his own name a series of small books of religious discourses parallel with the pseudonymous authorship. They often contain excellent illustrations of the psychology in the principal pseudonymous works.

FT
Fear and Trembling, Princeton: Princeton University Press, 1954, paperback edition 1968 (with *The Sickness Unto Death*). First published 1843 by Kierkegaard's pseudonym Johannes de silentio. About Abraham and "the knight of faith"; other figures include Sarah (from the Old Testament) and Shakespeare's Richard III.

R
Repetition, Princeton: Princeton University Press, 1946. First published 1843 by Kierkegaard's pseudonym Constantine Constantius. Half essay, half novel about "the young man" and his love story and religious development.

PF
Philosophical Fragments, second edition, Princeton: Princeton University Press, 1962. Principal work on the relation between philosophy and Christianity.

CD
The Concept of Dread, Princeton: Princeton University Press, 1957. First published 1844 by Kierkegaard's pseudonym Vigilius Haufniensis. The first of Kierkegaard's two principal works on psychology (not "genuinely" pseudonymous). contains Adam and Napoleon, among other figures. ["The Concept of Anxiety" is actually a better translation of the original Danish title, and that is the title which is employed when the book is mentioned in the present work. The new English translation of the book being prepared for the Princeton University Press will also use this "new" title.].

TCS
Thoughts on Crucial Situations in Human Life, Minneapolis: Augsburg Publishing House, 1941. First published 1845. Religious discourses.

SLW
Stages on Life's Way, Princeton: Princeton University Press, 1945. First published 1845 by Kierkegaard's pseudonym Hilarius

Bookbinder. About the three "stages," the aesthetic (cf. E/O I), the ethical (cf. E/O II), and the religious. Among the figures included in the work are William Afham and Victor Eremita (in the aesthetic symposium "In vino veritas"), Judge William (in the essay "Observations about Marriage"), and *quidam* (means "someone or other," the main character and the writer in the diaristic novel "Guilty?/Not Guilty?," a religiously-tinged "passion narrative" about a broken love affair), and Frater Taciturnus ("author" of the diaristic novel and of a long, commentative postscript ot this novel).

CUP   *Concluding Unscientific Postscript,* Princeton: Princeton University Press, 1941. First published in 1846 by Kierkegaard's pseudonym Johannes Climacus. Kierkegaard's principal philosophical work, the basis for his later reputation as an "existentialist." Contains, among other things, his settling of accounts with Hegel.

PA   *The Present Age,* New York: Harper Torchbooks, 1962. First published 1846. The English translation of the second half of a book (Danish title, *A Literary Review*) in which Kierkegaard, under his own name, reviews a contemporary novel, in order then to give his own critical analysis of "the present age," the 1840's, and its socio-psychological character.

AR   *On Authority and Revelation: The Book on Adler,* New York: Harper Torchbooks, 1966. Written 1846-47. A critical analysis of a contemporary Danish religious personality. Not published by Kierkegaard. (The Danish "book on Adler" is to be found in Kierkegaard's *Papirer* [Papers], volume VII 2).

PH   *Purity of Heart,* New York: Harper Torchbooks, 1956. First published in 1847. A religious discourse with relevance for psychology.

GS   *The Gospel of Suffering,* Minneapolis: Augsburg Publishing House, 1948. First published 1847. Religious discourses.

WL   *Works of Love,* New York: Harper and Brothers, 1962. First published 1847. Ethical-religious considerations of the concept of love. A principal work in the authorship as a whole and for the understanding of Kierkegaard as a psychologist in particular.

ChD   *Christian Discourses,* London: Oxford University Press, 1940. First published 1848.

CLA   *Crisis in the Life of an Actress,* New York: Harper Torchbooks, 1967. Published anonymously in 1848. A dazzling psychological analysis of a Danish actress in the role of Shakespeare's Juliet.

SD   *The Sickness Unto Death,* Princeton: Princeton University Press, 1968 (with FT). First published in 1849, with Kierkegaard himself appearing on the title page as "editor," and Kierkegaard's pseudonym Anti-Climacus named as "author." The other principal psychological work. In this case, the pseudonymity does not mean that Kierkegaard does not embrace the book's views fully as his own, but only that he sees himself as personally suffering from "the sickness unto death" (i.e. "despair"), while its pseudonymous "author," who makes the diagnosis, must be thought of as "recovered" from this sickness, or he would not be able to describe it properly. Anti-Climacus is Kierkegaard's "better self."

TC   *Training in Christianity,* Princeton: Princeton University Press, 1944. First published in 1850 by Kierkegaard's pseudonym Anti-Climacus. Religious preaching, analysis, and criticism of the church.

PV   *The Point of View,* New York: Harper Torchbooks, 1962. First published in 1851 and 1859. Kierkegaard's autobiographical account and his interpretation of his own authorship. The most important part was published posthumously in 1859.

SE   *For Self-Examination and Judge for Yourselves!,* Princeton:
JY   Princeton University Press, 1968. First published in 1851 and 1876 (posthumously), respectively. Continuations of TC.

AC   *Attack Upon "Christendom,"* Princeton: Princeton University Press, 1968. First published 1854-55. This volume contains numbers 1-10 of "The Instant" as well as the other polemical writings against the Danish People's Church. This violent settling-up with "the Christianity of Christendom" was Kierkegaard's last, energetic act before his death in the fall of 1855.

Starting with his twentieth year and throughout the rest of his life, Kierkegaard kept a very important diary, which not only gives information about his personal life, but also gives a great deal of commentary on the authorship and information about his ideas, his reading, etc. All this copious material was first published long after his death. Not all of these voluminous papers exist in English translation. All the bracketed references to Kierkegaard's papers in the present work are keyed to the standard Danish edition, *Søren Kierkegaards Papirer,* second edition, vols. I-XIII (in 22 tomes), Copenhagen: Gyldendal, 1968-70, and the international standard abbreviation will be used in the bracketed references: "Pap." followed by volume number, tome number (if applicable), the appropriate letter ("A" refers to journal entries, "B" to drafts of published material, "C" to notes on reading), serial number, and page number (if applicable). Thus, a typical reference to a passage in Kierkegaard's papers not in English translation would be: [Pap. VI A 221, p. 274]. This form of reference is lengthy but is the only form which enables the curious reader to locate precisely the passage in question. Three major English translations of selections from Kierkegaard's papers have appeared: *The Journals of Søren Kierkegaard,* Alexander Dru, editor and translator, London: Oxford University Press, 1938; *The Last Years: Journals 1853-55,* Ronald Gregor Smith, editor and translator, New York: Harper and Row, 1965; and *Søren Kierkegaard's Journals and Papers,* Howard and Edna Hong, editors and translators, volume 1, A-E, volume 2, F-K, volume 3, L-R, volume 4, S-Z, Bloomington: Indiana University Press, 1967-75 (a volume of autobiographical entries will follow). If a passage in Kierkegaard's papers has been translated in one of these English versions, the location of the translation will be noted following the Danish reference in brackets, using the abbreviation "Dru" for the Dru translation, "Smith" for Gregor Smith's translation, and "Hong" for the Hongs' translation, followed by the serial or page number in the translation in question. Thus, a typical reference to a passage in Kierkegaard's papers which appears in English translation would be: [Pap. II A 206, Hong 1288]. (The Dru and Smith translations do not overlap, and should a passage from the papers appear in one of these translations and also in the Hongs' translation, only the Hongs' translation will be noted, as it is far more complete and readily available.)

All citations from and references to the works of Sigmund Freud are taken from and keyed to the standard English translation, *The Standard Edition of the Complete Psychological Works of Sigmund Freud,* vols. I-XXIV, translated under the editorship of James Strachey, London: Hogarth Press, 1953-64, and the standard form in which bracketed references will appear will be "Freud," plus the volume and page number of the Standard Edition, e.g., [Freud XVIII 135].

These bracketed references (to Kierkegaard's works and papers and to Freud's works) and the abbreviations noted above are the only references which will appear in the body of the text. All other references will be found in the notes.

INTRODUCTION

"Psychology is what we need, and above all, expert knowledge of human life and sympathy with its interests. Thus, here there is a problem the solution of which must precede any talk of rounding out a Christian view of life," wrote Soren Kierkegaard in 1844 [Pap. V B 53, p. 119].

This book is an attempt to show that he honored this programmatic declaration. But the quotation also shows that psychology is no isolated, special discipline for him. On the contrary, it is enmeshed in a network of other problems from which it cannot be separated without seriously distorting the picture. This is the difficulty in understanding Kierkegaard as a psychologist, but it is probably this which, along with other things, gives him his special force. Therefore an exposition which will do justice to Kierkegaard's psychology must also deal with subjects along the way which are not psychological in the narrow sense, but literary, ethical, social, philosophical, and theological. Nor in fact is it the case — as was implied in the quotation — that for Kierkegaard psychology is the presupposition for the "Christian view of life." The situation is nearer the reverse of this, but precisely this fact points out that this "Christian view" is not narrowly theological, but contains dimensions and insights which theology rarely possesses.

It is a difficult problem to present this enormously complex, detailed, but consistently carried-out train of thought, so that the larger context and the many nuances are preserved. Nor is it very easy to read this exposition in such a way as to avoid losing the broad view. Therefore, I will give the reader a brief guide to the structure of this book (see also the Table of Contents, which can profitably be read first).

Chapter I deals with Kierkegaard's psychological method and with the place of psychology within his authorship. Some of these problems are given another, more intensive, treatment in Chapter VIII. The intervening chapters, II-VII, present Kierkegaard's psychology itself, while they simultaneously sketch the anthropological framework for this psychology.

Chapters II and III introduce the psychology by dealing with the individual's "immediate" development from the child's original, undifferentiated connection with its world to the crisis of separation and of becoming conscious, which signals the transition to a new complex of problems. In particular, it is the concept of anxiety which is introduced at this point. In Chapter II, separation anxiety is viewed "abstractly," intrapsychically; in Chapter III it is viewed "concretely," in connection with the environmental factors which complicate it.

At one point, Kierkegaard writes, with respect to this division between an abstract and a concrete mode of presenting problems: "The mathematician is satisfied with his algebra and does not wish to use dollars and cents in order to engage the participation of the sensory man. But even if the concrete is more necessary than it is for the mathematician, one does not begin right away with letting the thought become concrete, but one abstractly clarifies the thought which one wishes to demonstrate in the concrete. Thus if a musician wished to explain to someone that a dominant instrument saturated all the other music with its sound, and that it was the constitutive element of the whole, he would certainly perform the particular passage on that instrument first, until the learner was familiar with it and could recognize it amid a hundred others which sounded at once. Only then would he let the orchestra begin to make its din, asking the learner to note carefully how that instrument's sound was present everywhere" [Pap. V B 41, p. 96 f., Hong 1606].

This has also been my principle of exposition in the succeeding chapters, IV-VII, which begin "abstractly" and generally, and gradually become more and more "concrete," specific, and varied. From a psychological point of view, these are the central chapters. In Chapter IV several basic anthropological concepts are introduced in a temporarily simplified form. Problems are posed and given concrete form in Chapters V-VII, where the dominant concept is "despair." Chapter V begins by dealing with the basic concepts on a relatively abstract and general plane. These concepts are then given their definitive psychological differentiations in Chapter VI, and in Chapter VII they are illustrated concretely by means of a close reading of a number of individual problems and Kierkegaardian analyses.

Thus, where Chapters II-III deal with "innocence" (to use the theological expression), Chapter IV with "creation," and Chapters V-VII with "sin," Chapter VIII deals with "recovery." A discussion of the norms which form the basis for Kierkegaard's psychology, and of the epistemology which is its precondition, leads into the important concluding question of the practical, therapeutic implications of this psychology.

Thus, everything in the exposition is carefully interconnected, and this also means that in a certain sense new aspects of the *same* problems are continually being developed. "I dare say that the lecture will be continually haunted by the remembrance of what has already been said at other points; it will be continually criss-crossed by reflections which are designed to remind one of what has been said and of what is yet to come," Kierkegaard writes at one point, with reference to his peculiar method of presenting a particular problem, and it has also been a basic inspiration for my own presentation. "The intention is obviously not that I will continually mix all the categories of thought with each other in a tumultuous or kaleidoscopic fashion, so that the places where each thought-category should receive its more exact and detailed development do not come in their succession; the intention is simply that, if possible, every point will bear the mark of what has been said at other points, all in order to produce, if possible, an uninterrupted simultaneity in the listener . . . ; in any event, if possible, the way in which the next point is spoken of will indirectly be a discussion of that which has already been said. You yourselves will also see that it is not strange that I have chosen this as my task, because everything I intend to say is one thought . . . " [Pap. VIII 2 B 88, p. 180, f., Hong 656].

The subject of this book, then, is Kierkegaard's psychology, not his psyche. Psychological and psychiatric diagnoses of Kierkegaard as a private person have been attempted in learned works by quite a number of Scandinavian and German psychologists. Within the framework of Kretschmer's typology, he has been diagnosed as manic-depressive[1] or as schizothymic.[2] Kierkegaard's private world of conflicts has also been analysed from the psychoanalytic point of view.[3]

As different as these various psychological studies of Kierkegaard are with respect to their methods and results, they do have one thing in common: they treat Kierkegaard as the *object* of psychological investigation, not as a psychologist. By virtue of this point of view itself, the author is cut off from learning from Kierkegaard and from seeing that, as a psychologist, he was in possession of insights which indeed can bear comparison to those of his analysts. It is certainly true that as a private person Søren Kierkegaard was a suffering, perhaps neurotic, individual. More interesting, however, than applying the views of Kretschmer, Freud, Jung, or others to Kierkegaard's suffering, is an investigation of Kierkegaard's own diagnosis of suffering, and thus the discovery that his talk of anxiety and despair is not merely the literary autobiography of a neurotic, but a genuine psychological theory. Kierkegaard was not merely a suffering, sickly individual. He also had a critical, analytic distance from this sickness.

It is a relatively recent discovery that Kierkegaard's psychology can be taken seriously. The discovery was made by the so-called existential psychology, which sprung up in various places in Europe in the 1930's and which has now been thoroughly introduced into the USA. Existential psychology has used Kierkegaard profitably as a critique of the conceptions of man held by psychoanalysis and experimental psychology, which ignore the concrete and historical character of existence. In addition to this, the existential psychologists have studied Kierkegaard's psychology itself and have attempted to make use of it. American psychologists, in particular, have made important contributions. A Scandinavian technical journal could print a review article on "Kierkegaard in American Psychology" as early as 1955.[4] A first attempt at a complete presentation of Kierkegaard's psychological theories was made by Rollo May in *The Meaning of Anxiety*.[5] Of the more recent contributions, an exciting work by J. Preston Cole, *The Problematic Self in Kierkegaard and Freud*[6] is of particular note.

It is therefore with a special joy and thankfulness that I present an American edition of my contribution to this research. The book addresses itself to all psychologists—and perhaps I will be permitted to say that it especially addresses itself to the teachers and students of the Department of Psychology at Duquesne University, Pittsburgh, whom I came to know in a richly productive "summer school" in 1974. But the book also addresses itself to philosophers, theologians, students of literature, and all others who are interested in the subject. There is perhaps reason to mention that I am not myself a psychologist—at any rate only *con amore*—but an historian of literature and ideas by profession.[7]

The present book was published in Danish in 1972.[8] The American edition contains a number of revisions, including a certain amount of foreshortening and a number of minor changes. A portion of the cited material, several less important passages, and a series of references to Danish and European Kierkegaard research have been omitted. Hopefully this will only make the book more comprehensible for the American reader. Various segments of the original edition have been completely rewritten, but without any essential changes in the content; this is the case particularly for Chapters IV: 3: 1, IV: 4: 1-3, and V: 7: 1. Chapter VII: 1 is entirely new material, not included in the original edition, containing a resume of several of the main points of another book which I published in 1973 about Kierkegaard viewed in his social and political context (see the reference to this at the beginning of Chapter VII).

This book does not address itself only to Kierkegaard specialists, but to the reader who is interested in psychological and allied problems, regardless of whether he or she is an expert on Kierkegaard's authorship. It is hoped that the book will be more than an historical exposition; the wish is that it will speak to a present situation. It will, however, be helpful for the reader to have an elementary acquaintance with Kierkegaard's authorship. From a psychological point of view, there are two of Kierkegaard's works which are especially significant, *The Concept of Anxiety*, from 1844, and *The Sickness Unto Death*, from 1849 (written

1848). But Kierkegaard's authorship is very extensive. We are dealing with 40 smaller of larger books and lesser publications, which in the standard Danish edition of the collected works fill 14 heavy volumes. In addition to this is the mass of journals, notes, manuscripts, etc., which are a valuable supplement to the works, and which fill 22 volumes in the Danish edition *(Papirer)*. This very large corpus of material has been used in this investigation. *The Concept of Anxiety* and *The Sickness Unto Death* basically contain only a full resumé of Kierkegaard's psychology, a final summary of it. These two works also contain, at various points, an enormously abbreviated, formulaic intimation of Kierkegaard's presention of psychological problems, which can be illuminated much more precisely when one brings in parallel texts from the rest of the authorship.

The difference between the two principal psychological works is specifically one of terminology and subject area. They are so different in terminology that it is only upon a reflective analysis that one sees that they are dealing with the same problem. *The Concept of Anxiety* consists of five chapters, of which the first two belong together and introduce the problem-structure with which I have dealt in Chapters II and III of the present book. In *The Sickness Unto Death* this entire subject area is not dealt with, but only briefly hinted at as the presupposition for a further psychological investigation. The third and fourth chapters of *The concept of Anxiety,* on the other hand, deal with the same questions which are dealt with again, in a more clarified and definitive form, in the entirety of *The Sickness Unto Death.* This is the problem complex which I have developed in Chapters IV-VII in my presentation, but with the utilization of a mass of material which is found in other of Kierkegaard's writings. *The Sickness Unto Death* presents itself as a more comprehensible and integral work than *The Concept of Anxiety,* but is also more abbreviated and abstract. But on many points, *The Concept of Anxiety,* too, is nothing more than a skeleton of Kierkegaard's psychological insight. "In keeping with the form of this investigation, I can only very briefly, almost algebraically, hint at the individual conditions here. This is not the place for real delineation," he writes at one point in this book [IV 421 note, CD 101 note], and, later, "I do not wish to pursue this further. The main consideration for me is simply to have my schema in order" [IV 447, CD 122].

It is important to keep this "schema" before us, that is, to have an overview of Kierkegaard's psychological train of thought in its totality and continuity. But, if the exposition is not to be "schematic" in the bad sense, it must also seek out the many passages in Kierkegaard's other writings and in the journals, which often contain the "real delineation," which has not been included in *The Concept of Anxiety* and *The Sickness Unto Death*.

The reader can obtain a rudimentary orientation in the authorship by studying the bibliographic note above; in addition to a survey of the most important writings of the authorship, it contains a short description of the individual works. Also mentioned here are the most important pseudonyms (fictive "authors" of the writings) and the most important fictional, historical, and mythical names with which the reader will be confronted in this book.

This book is published with support from the State Research Council for the Humanities (Copenhagen). I give my respectful thanks.

Warm thanks also to the director of the Duquesne University Press, and particularly to Professor Amedeo Giorgi, who has overseen the publication of the book in the USA. I also thank research fellow Boje Katzenelson of Aarhus University, for friendly assistance.

Aarhus University, Denmark

Kresten Nordentoft

Chapter I

KIERKEGAARD AS A PSYCHOLOGIST

1. Kierkegaard's Method

1:1. *Autopsy and Engagement*

The nerve in Kierkegaard's psychological methodology is expressed in his own commentary to *The Sickness Unto Death,* which he published pseudonymously in 1849, though in such a way as to leave no doubt that the pseudonym and the real author were one and the same person: "This book is written as if by a physician. I, the editor, am not the physician; I am one of the sick" [Pap. X 2 A 204]. Kierkegaard is patient *and* physician, the object *and* the subject of the investigation at the same time. On the one hand, the doubleness in this implies a criticism of the ideal of "pure" scientific objectivity, and makes a claim for the involvement of the subject as a condition for adequate knowledge, but, on the other hand, Kierkegaard's double point of view does not have nihilistic epistemological consequences. The entire question of the conditions for and the possibilities of knowledge will be discussed in the concluding chapter of this book. What are at issue at this point are the methodological points of view which make it possible for Kierkegaard to formulate a psychology at all.

All science has its beginning in wonder [Pap. III A 107, Hong 3284; IV B 1, p. 127; VII 1 A 34 Hong 2292]. Therefore the amateur is a better primary observer than one who is burdened with learning, and Kierkegaard enjoys making a show of his amateur status [III 72, FT 26 and IV 310, CD 5] and his rather carefree relationship to the technical scientific literature: "In our day writing a book is the easiest thing of all when, as is customary, one takes ten older works, which all deal with the same matter, and, based upon them, puts together an eleventh which deals with the same matter . . . " [V 43 ff.]. Kierkegaard does not deny that he has learned from others, but this is not the decisive thing—cf. his thesis that "great geniuses cannot really read a book, because during the reading they will continually develop themselves more than they will understand the author" [Pap. II A 26, Hong 1288]. The most important thing is the autopsy, the primary observation and the original thinking-through of that which has been observed.

1

But not every observation or observer is equally valuable. The keenness of the observation increases with the degree of personal engagement. Frater Taciturnus sets up the following hierarchy (the discussion is of the study of facial expressions): "A curiously interested observer sees much; a scientifically interested observer sees much that is worth honoring; a concerned, interested observer sees what others do not see, but a mad observer sees perhaps the most. His observations are keener and more persevering, just as the senses of certain animals are keener than man's. Only it follows of itself that his observations must be verified" [VI 296, SLW 262-63]. In practice, it is the concerned observation which is the highest (that it, too, must be verified will be mentioned shortly): "All Christian knowledge, however rigorous in form it may otherwise be, ought to be concerned; but this concern is precisely that which is upbuilding. The concern is the relationship to life, to the reality of the personality, and thus, from a Christian point of view, to seriousness. The elevatedness of indifferent knowledge is, from a Christian point of view, far from being more serious; it is, Christianly understood, foolishness and vanity. But, again, seriousness is that which is upbuilding" [XI 133, SD 142-43, the Foreword to *The Sickness Unto Death*]. Christian and scientific concerns coincide here, because indifferent knowledge is worthless both for Christian and for scientific observation, while, on the other hand, knowledge which is engaged is *eo ipso* an essentially scientific knowledge. It ought to be added that this understanding is valid particularly for such areas of knowledge as psychology, philosophy, and theology. Indifferent, objective, value-free knowledge in these areas—statistical overviews and average figures—is nonsense [IV 368, CD 56]. Corresponding principles hold for literary interpretation: only the interpreter who is personally involved in his subject can give pith and perspective to his analysis. In connection with his interpretation of Abraham, Johannes de silentio posits the hermeneutical principle that: "only the person who labors, gets the bread; only the one who was in anguish, finds rest; only the one who descends to the underworld, saves the beloved; only the one who draws the knife gets Isaac"; disinterested knowledge understands nothing and must express itself in vague generalities [III 89 f., FT 38 f.].

1:2. *"Unum noris, omnes"*[1]

In the final analysis, all understanding is self-understanding. An "objective" understanding of one's surroundings, which is not grounded in self-understanding, is either a triviality or a demonic illusion. Only by means of self-understanding can a genuine understanding of one's surroundings come into being. Therefore, self-understanding is the *conditio sine qua non* for the areas of knowledge which are under discussion here—and therefore, Kierkegaard's psychology is based upon self-analyses.

"Instead of the great project of understanding all people, he has chosen to understand himself, which one might indeed call narrow-minded and foolish," he writes of himself in an unused foreword to *The Concept of Anxiety* [V 48]. In this same foreword he describes himself as "a straggler who has seen nothing in the world and has only taken a journey to the interior within his own consciousness" [V 53]. The background in private experience for *The Concept of Anxiety* can be studied in the journals [for example, Pap. II A 18-20, Hong 91, Dru 103; 456, Hong 1238; 512, Dru 303; 515, Hong 4415; 584, Hong 3999; 805-07; III A 64, Dru 33], and *The Sickness Unto Death* is no less personally inspired. Moreover, biographical Kierkegaard research has certainly produced a wealth of proof that there are personal motives at work everywhere in the pseudonymous authorship. Kierkegaard consciously and methodically conducts self-observation: "I sit and listen to the sounds inside me, the joyous intimations of the music and the deep seriousness of the organ; to unify them—this is a task not for a composer, but for a man, who, for want of the greater challenges of life, limits himself to the simple thing of wanting to understand himself" [Pap. IV A 93].

The worth of introspection as a psychological method has often been doubted, especially by the experimental and behavioristic schools of psychology. In its pure form, as it was used by academic psychologists in the late 19th century, the method aims at the registration and description of subjective emotional states in as objective and disinterested a mode as possible, and with the conscious abstraction from all possible accompanying circumstances and causes. It requires no careful demonstration to show that in its pure form this procedure is self-contradictory and without perspective. Kierkegaard's self-analyses are anything but disinterested, and his interest ranges far beyond the mere registration of the emotions. It is precisely the passions which must give perspective and general validity to knowledge. The method is not simply a passive registration and description, but an active analyzing. Naturally, introspection in itself cannot give insight into the significance of emotional states as the motivating factors of actions. The connection between emotion and action is understood only with the will to critical self-disclosure. We will encounter examples of Kierkegaard's self-analyses in what follows. The most classical and central example of the disclosure of motives is this finding from 1848: "I have, however, loved the world in my melancholia, because I have loved my melancholia" [Pap. VIII 1 A 641, Dru 748]. Essentially, an insight such as this constitutes the sufficient basis for a psychology such as Kierkegaard's. Self-deception is a central concept in this psychology; but to reveal self-deception is to reveal the displacement of motives. It is the interest in the *function* of emotional states which differentiates Kierkegaard from mere introspectionism. Kierkegaard has said of one of his contemporaries, the philosopher and psychologist F.C. Sibbern, that he is satisfied with describing the individual emotions, and therefore lacks "an eye for the disguised passions, for the reduplication by which one passion takes the form of another."

Kierkegaard's interest in psychology is thus personal, but not narrowly private. It is also based upon the desire for valid knowledge, and self-analysis is accompanied by a consistent effort to give a universally valid interpretation to private experiences. Even while engaged in the subjective, he also practices abstraction from the private. His "novels" are to be regarded as the objectifications of personal experiences, and in this process of objectification, the experience takes on general validity: "Everyone who has a primal experience of something also experiences, in the ideal, the possibility of this experience and the possibility of its opposite. These possibilities are his poetically lawful property. His own private, personal actuality, on the other hand, is not . . . . As soon as the artist must forsake his own actuality, his factuality, then he is no longer essentially productive . . . . A person, for example, who became productive in becoming unhappy, would have the same predilection to produce happy works as he would unhappy works, if he has really consecrated himself to the realm of the ideal. But the condition for winning the ideal is the silence with which he delimits his own personal actuality . . . " [VIII 106, PA 69-70].

What holds for the poetic production also holds for the scientific. The objective knowledge is a product of the subjective; the general understanding is a result of personal engagement. Therefore self-understanding is the *cardo rerum*[2] in Kierkegaard's way of knowledge. Self-understanding does not here mean mere introspective familiarity with one's own emotional life, but is also, and especially, an ethical self-reflection. To carry on the scientific study of man is to be ethically obligated. And when knowledge of the surrounding world is bound in a condition of dependence upon self-knowledge, it is the observer's own position which first and foremost must be verified. "It does not simply depend upon what one sees," Kierkegaard writes in a discourse from 1843, "but what one sees depends upon how one sees. This is because all observation is not merely a receiving, a discovery, but also a creation, and to the extent that it is this latter, the decisive factor becomes how the observer himself is. . . . To the extent that the object of the observation is part of the external world, the condition of the observer is a matter of indifference, or, rather, that which is essential to the observation does not concern his deeper being. On the other hand, the more the object of observation belongs to the world of spirit, the more important is the state of the innermost being of the observer" [III 308 f., ED I 67]. If the observer does not know himself, his understanding of the surrounding world will be an unreflective projection of his own characteristics.

The task of the observer is thus not simply to engage himself subjectively, but in addition — to use an expression which Kierkegaard uses at one point with respect to Socrates — "to relate oneself objectively to one's own subjectivity . . . . He is subjectivity raised to a higher power; he conducts himself with the objectivity with which a true poet wishes to be related to his own poetic creation. With this objectivity he relates himself to his own subjectivity" [Pap. XI 2 A 97, Hong 4571]. The situation of the observer is always private, and the naked, unprocessed inference from the subjective to the objective is arbitrary. Even the most trained psychologist is unable to eliminate the subjective prejudices which come along with personal fascination: "The posture of psychology is one of discovering anxiety, and, in this anxiety, delineating sin, while it is more and more anxious about the delineation which it has itself created . . . but in a treatment such as this, sin does not become what it is, but a greater or lesser approximation." This is the epistemological foundation upon the basis of which *The Concept of Anxiety* is able to insist that sin may not be dealt with by psychology, but only by dogmatics: "It is the object of the sermon" [IV 319 f., CD 13 f.]. Only when the observer obligates himself to an authority outside himself does he receive a valid standard of measure — not for his psychological knowledge of the surrounding world, for it is not in that sense that there is talk of a "Christian knowledge" — but for his own self-understanding as the precondition for an adequate understanding of the surrounding world.

That the requirement of responsible self-understanding is both existentially and scientifically valid can also be seen in Climacus' discussion of "the subjective thinker" in *Concluding Unscientific Postscript*. First (and last), one learns that this thinker must have fantasy and feeling; he must be able to talk poetically and ethically, and he must be able to think dialectically. But, especially, he must have passion. Therefore Climacus will not call him a man of science, but an artist: his art is to exist [VII 339 f. and 346 f., CUP 312 f. and 319 f.]. His task is *"to understand himself in existence."* He must both think about existence and exist himself at the same time, and he must therefore be aware of the position of the observer: "Thus, in all his thoughts he must also think that he himself is an existing being." But this does not mean that his thought is purely and simply private. On the contrary, it means that the concrete, private-personal point of departure keeps his thinking from losing itself in generalities which evade the problems. Indeed, language itself, thoughts and concepts as the mediums of thinking, certainly hinders thinking from becoming immediately concrete, because intellectual activity *in itself* is an abstraction from reality—the reality which it is supposed to grasp. This contains a problem in epistemological theory which we will discuss further on. But the fact that conceivability is by definition abstract in relation to reality, and is thus unreal, does not imply that it ignores the problem of reality: "In a certain sense, the subjective thinker speaks just as abstractly as the abstract thinker, for the latter speaks of sheer humanity and sheer subjectivity, while the former speaks of the single person (*unum noris, omnes*). But this one person is an existing person, and the difficulty is not avoided" [VII 340-42, CUP 314-16].

Unum noris, omnes is one of Kierkegaard's favorite expressions, a key principle in his psychological method. It comes from Terence, but Kierkegaard changes the wording and puts his own meaning into it: to know oneself is the only decisive precondition for knowing others. In *The Concept of Anxiety* it is stated that this principle expresses the same thing as the Greek "know thyself," "if one understands the observer himself as *unum,* and does not search curiously for *omnes,* but seriously clings fast to the One who is really All" [IV 385 note, CD 70-71 note; the expression is also used in VII 562, CUP 507; Pap. VII 1 A 70, Hong 3327; X 2 A 390, Hong 2952; X 3 A 656, Hong 2958].

The presupposition for the validity of this way of thinking is that the One "really is All." In Kierkegaard's opinion this is a valid assumption, because man is defined precisely by his difference from animals in being able to relate himself to himself. "Every person must fundamentally be assumed to possess that which is fundamental to being a person" [VII 345, CUP 318]. If one denied this, the consequence would be "that at various times *fundamentally* different people have been produced, and the universal unity of mankind is abolished" [Pap. IV C 78, Hong 3657]. For "every person possesses in himself, when he looks carefully, a more complete expression for everything human than the *summa summarum*[3] of all the knowledge he acquires by that method [i.e., by learned studies]" [Pap. V B 53, p. 112]. "Therefore, what holds here in a profound psychological decision is *unum noris omnes.* When the possibility of sin is shown in one, it is shown in all, and all that is left to the ideal arena of observation are considerations of more and less" [Pap. V B 49, p. 110].

This idea is not an expression of any epistemological idealism; it does not imply that the surrounding world, as in Fichte, is a product of the subjective power of imagination. Neither does it mean that all people *factually* resemble one another, even less that they resemble Kierkegaard, nor that his psychological writings only describe facets of his own being. The anthropological principles which constitute the conceptual basis of his psychology put forth a claim for a unity common to all human existence, but psychology itself is the science "which, however, above all, has the right almost to intoxicate itself with the foaming multiplicity of life" [IV 327, CD 20]. And if psychology does not do this, it is not its own fault, but that of its practitioners.

1: 3. *Observation of Others*

The primary method in Kierkegaard's psychology is self-understanding and self-observation, but he tests his knowledge and broadens the scope of his psychology by observing others. That this is the order of priorities is clear from what has already been cited, and thus it is also inconceivable that the observation of others by itself could form a sufficient basis for his psychological reasoning. It is upon the basis of self-understanding that he establishes his method and his points of view, and these can then be confirmed by observations in the field, i.e., in drawing rooms and on the streets and byways. His methods for the observation of others may seem a bit primitive in comparison to modern psychology. As will shortly be shown, he understands something quite different by psychological experiment than does modern experimental psychology. It is more natural to compare his method with that of the psychoanalyst, but here to Kierkegaard is the amateur thinker who is more interested in observational method than in professional, clinical technique. Thus the interpretation of dreams plays no role in his psychology, but a single remark on the significance of dreams indicates where his interests lie: "People must have lived far more simply in the days when they thought that God revealed His will in dreams. . . . When one thinks of the great cities and the manner in which people live there, it is no wonder that dreams are attributed to the devil or to demons. In addition, the small significance which our times attributes to dreams is connected with the intellectualism which continually stresses consciousness, while those simpler times piously believed that the unconscious life in man was both the most predominant and the most profound part of life" [Pap. X 2 A 258, Hong 781].

The above quotation is not especially characteristic, though; it expresses a view of dreams and of the unconscious which reminds one of romanticism and of Jung. Kierkegaard's psychological observations tend in other directions, however. The method is one of empathetic insight and the uncovering of deep dimensions: "The external, then, is indeed the object of our observations but not of our interest; thus the fisherman sits and stares unwaveringly at the river, while the river does not interest him at all, but rather the movements down on the bottom. The external thus indeed has significance for us, not as the expression of the internal, but as a telegraphic report that something deep within has been concealed." It is Aesthete A who is speaking. He observes faces and his look "is one of desire, and yet so careful; is unnerving and compelling, but yet so sympathetic; is patient and cunning, but yet so honest and benevolent, that it lulls the individual into a pleasing sort of dullness in which he finds a pleasure in pouring out his sorrows which is like the pleasure of being bled." The point in his method is the ability to identify himself with the person whom he observes, "because our passion is of course not a curiosity which satisfies itself with external and superficial things, but is a sympathetic anxiety which searches the heart and its hidden thoughts, conjuring forth with sorcery and spells that which has been hidden" [I 175-77, E/O I 172-74].

For Victor Eremita it is not sight, but hearing, which is the most important sense when it is a case of "revealing hidden things." His interest in the contradiction between what one sees and what one hears puts him upon the track of the incongruence between the internal and the external [I vii f., E/O I 3f]. The method is especially useful when it is a case of observing what Kierkegaard calls demonic encapsulation, for it is precisely involuntary revelations which characterize this state. A more detailed discussion of this comes later in this volume; here, it is sufficient to allude to *quidam's* warning against awakening a resistance to communication on the part of the person observed. If one is to profit from the method of free association, one must allow the analysand to take the initiative, but one must also be ready to analyse resistance when it occurs: "I have studied it in my campaign against an encapsulated person, and therefore I know it. One must never force oneself in upon an encapsulated person, or one loses him, but just as a gout-ridden person is fearful of drafts, so can one touch him with a chance allusion which one does not pursue at all. Or one can waylay him when he chances to unburden himself. One can immediately judge the degree of his encapsulation by the difficulty he has in stopping himself. He regrets that he has said anything; he wishes to dispel the impression; one remains silent; now he becomes suspicious of himself, that he has not succeeded; he wants to change the topic of conversation; it is not successful; one remains silent; he is angry about the silence; he betrays more and more, if by nothing else than by his eagerness to conceal. But when one knows this, one does one's exercises regularly. And the art is to talk a little about the matter (for total silence is unwise), and thus to keep a consuming passion upon the supple reins of conversation, so that, like a rider, one can steer with a thread . . . " [VI 231, SLW 207-08].

Adroitness in empathetic insight and a silence which causes that which is hidden to "dart out and chatter with itself" are also the main points in the observational methods of Vigilius Haufniensis. But Vigilius is not merely writing upon the basis of empirical observations. He himself formulates his examples, which do not need to have "the authority of factuality." He psychologizes at home at his desk, and the examples which he will use are "immediately available, by virtue of his general practice." But the foundation is the observation of reality, and if his conclusions need verification, he can quickly find "a tolerable individual who is fit for the experiment." "His observation must have the stamp of freshness and the interest of actuality when he takes the caution to verify his observation." Then follows a sketch of such a verification experiment; the reader is asked to suspend the ethical for a moment. The observer experiences empathetically "every mood, every mental state, which he discovers in the other," and thereby seeks to pull the other along "into the more extreme interpretation, which is his own creation by virtue of the idea . . . . Now quiet, silence, and obscurity are important, so that one can find out his secret. Next, one practices what one has learned, until one is capable of disappointing him. Next one creates the passion poetically and appears before him in the more than natural dimensions of passion. If this is done properly, the individual will feel an indescribable relief and satisfaction, just as a mad person does when one has found and poetically grasped his *idée fixe*, and then carries it further" [IV 360 f., CD 49 f.].

Vigilius' statement is ambiguous. There is no doubt that his principal view of psychology is identical with Kierkegaard's, but his experiment is clearly a fiction. On the whole, the passages on the psychological observation of others which are cited here are taken from the pseudonymous authorship, and Vigilius is in this particular respect — though scarcely in others — a genuine pseudonym, a fictive form with whom Kierkegaard does not wish to be identified. "The sketch of an observer which I have dashed off in *The Concept of Anxiety* will probably disturb some people . . . . I stand in an altogether poetic relation to my works, and therefore I am pseudonymous. Each time the book develops something, the corresponding individuality is delineated. Now Vigilius Hauf. delineates a number of these, but I have also dashed off a sketch of him himself in the book" [Pap. V A 34, Dru 484]. In this sketch Vigilius is characterized as the aesthete-type, the pure-blooded psychologist who has no considerations other than the experiment. The nearest parallel is Johannes the Seducer, whose art also rests precisely upon his formidable talent for empathetic insight and for developing the germ which lies hidden in Cordelia's soul into an intense passion, whose course he directs. "The Diary of the Seducer" is the standard example in Kierkegaard's authorship of what psychology may not be used for.

There is thus reason to believe that Kierkegaard has reservations about the art of psychological experimentation which is under discussion here. This naturally does not exclude the possibility that he himself may have practiced it—though scarcely to any great extent. Vigilius' experiment is fully as fictional in character as the sketch of the Seducer's sovereign psychological mastery of the girl, and there is every reason to believe that in both cases we are dealing with thought experiments. It is my belief that the direct observation of other people does not play so great a role in the shaping of Kierkegaard's psychological writings as he might have us believe from his sketches of observational situations and methods. The strong emphasis upon empathetic understanding and identification with the person observed also indicates that disciplined and thoroughly reflective self-observation is the most essential tool Kierkegaard had with which to gain psychological insight.[4]

1:4. *The Formation of Theories*

Kierkegaard thus wants very much to emphasize his realism and his fidelity to reality. Isolated psychological data is worthless [IV 359, CD 49], and the psychologist must therefore "be able to create regularity and wholeness out of what is only partially or erratically present in the individual" [IV 360, CD 49]. "The *conditio sine qua non* for observation to be significant in the deeper sense is the ability to employ its category. When the phenomenon is present to a certain degree, most people notice it, but are incapable of explaining it, because they do not have the category. When they have it, then they are in possession of a key which opens up every place in which a trace of the phenomenon is to be found" [IV 435 note, CD 113 note]. In this way, abstraction is introduced, and as will gradually become clear, Kierkegaard's capacity for abstraction is highly developed. Psychology's task is not merely to observe, but just as much to articulate itself, to formulate theories. When he has found his fundamental concepts and has assured himself regarding their utility, he no longer reasons from the individual observation to the generalization, but from the abstract to the concrete, from the category to the individual case. It is particularly in *The Sickness Unto Death* that Kierkegaard is no longer in doubt as to the structural strength of his ideas: "The forms of despair may be found out abstractly by reflecting upon the moments of which the self, as a synthesis, consists" [XI 160, SD 162]. But here, also, abstraction admits of verification: "And if one will look around at actuality psychologically, one will occasionally have the opportunity to assure oneself that that which is intellectually correct and thus which shall and must suffice, does suffice, and that this classification encompasses the entire actuality of despair" [XI 182 f. note, SD 183 note]. Thus is posited a complex of epistemological problems, the significance of which will become clearer after we have seen how Kierkegaard's psychological thinking develops (cf. Chapter VIII).

2. "The Idea of Representation"

2: 1. *The Psychological Experiment*

What has been said in this connection has been said primarily with regard to *The Concept of Anxiety, The Sickness Unto Death,* and the passages in the rest of the authorship which supplement the reasoning in these two writings. But the word psychology also appears in other contexts in Kierkegaard's work. On its title page, *Repetition* is characterized as "An Essay in Experimental Psychology," and "Guilty?"/"Not Guilty?" is subtitled "Psychological Experiment." Many other writings could with equal justification have had comparable genre designations. Nevertheless, there is a certain difference in method and intention between the psychology in these literary texts and that in the two books which are the particular objects of this investigation.

Kierkegaard's portrayals of people are never realistic in the literary sense, but consciously stylized. As a novelist, he is not interested in naturalistic illusion and creating portraits which are faithful to reality. Frater Taciturnus criticizes literary realism in the introduction to the passion narrative "Guilty?"/"Not Guilty?"; in the present age, poetry has "seized upon the expedient of wishing to seem like actuality. They wish to have a little psychology, a little observation of so-called actual people, but when this science or art follows its own desires, when it looks away from the incomplete expressions of mental states which actuality offers, when it slips away in order to compose, in solitude, an individual from its own knowledge, and to find in this individual an object for its observations — then many people become weary. In actuality it is indeed the case that passions, mental states, etc. are only present to a certain degree. Psychology can find joy in this fact, too, but it also takes another sort of joy in seeing a passion carried out to its most extreme limit" [VI 203, SLW

18ᴬ]. The method is to conjure forth, by means of experiment, forms and figures which one does *not* find in actuality. Kierkegaard abstracts from the composite and indistinct essence of everyday humanity. The simplification takes place methodically and consciously, with the intention of distilling out a specific form of a problem, which then can aid in shedding light back upon that which is more general, as is attempted, for example, in the "Epistle to the Reader" by Frater Taciturnus, in which he comments upon his work. The novel itself, however, consists of "psychological experiments and unreal constructions" [*ibid.*]. Comparable situations are present in Kierkegaard's other "novels," "The Diary of a Seducer" and *Repetition.*

The inspiration behind Kierkegaard's consciously unrealistic psychology of the novel stems from his studies in the intellectual life of the Middle Ages, and the "three great ideas" of this period, Don Giovanni, Faust, and Ahasuerus, who represent three aspects of life beyond the pale of Christianity, portraying, respectively, sensual genius, intellectual doubt, and hopelessness [Pap. I A 150, Hong 795]. They are abstractions from concrete psychological reality: "The Middle Ages are, on the whole, the idea of representation, in part consciously, in part unconsciously; the whole is represented in a single individual, though in such a way that it is only a single facet which is determined as the whole, and which then becomes revealed in a single individual, who is therefore both more and less than an individual" [I 80, E/O I 86]. It is this method which Kierkegaard has adapted for use in his literary experiments. The characters in his novels are personifications of abstract concepts and phenomena in approximately the same sense as are the characters in a medieval morality play. The difference is only that Kierkegaard's method is not naively moralizing, but analytic. As contrasted with that of the Middle Ages, the abstraction from concrete actuality is conscious; the quotation about the idea of representation continues: "Thus, alongside of this individual stands another individual who just as completely represents another facet of life's content, thus the Knight and the Scholastic, the Cleric and the Physician. The grand dialectic of life is here made continually apparent in representative individuals, who most often confront one another as opposed pairs. Life is always present only *sub una specie,* and the grand dialectical unity, which, in unity, possesses life *sub utraque specie,*[5] is not perceived. Therefore, the oppositions most often stand beyond one another in indifference. The Middle Ages had no understanding of this. In this way the idea of representation is realized unconsciously, and it is only upon later reflection that the idea in this is seen" [I 80, E/O I 86; cf. Pap. I A 122, Hong 4387; 145, Hong 1670; 150 Hong 795; 226, Hong 2699; and I C 113, p. 295, Hong 2703].

Therefore, when Kierkegaard uses the psychology of types in his "novels," it is done with the conscious presupposition that it is a matter of methodical abstraction from the complexity of actuality. The nearest analogy to this method is thus hardly the medieval morality play, but the modern psychological experiment — except that Kierkegaard's experiments are performed at the writing desk, not among the brass instruments and rat cages of the laboratory. The method in "the novels" consists of isolating a particular phenomenon and making it the object of analysis under conscious abstraction from the concrete attendant circumstances. Johannes the Seducer is such a one-sided abstraction, and the point in the literary interpretation of his diary must lie precisely in the complex relation in which it stands to the aesthete's other papers in *Either/Or*, the literary whole of which the diary is only a part. Thus the experiment here consists of an abstraction from the aesthete's world of conflicts. In the experiments in the other novels, the subject of the experiment — "the young man" in *Repetition*, and *quidam* in "Guilty?"/"Not Guilty?," cf. also the three women in "Shadowgraphs" in *Either/Or* — is exposed to a particular influence, an erotic frustration, and the novel then describes the conflict which arises from the collision between the presuppositions of the character-type and the peculiarity of the influence. In these conflict studies of abstract individuals in artificially contrived situations, Kierkegaard is far from the one-dimensional psychology of the medieval morality play, but the abstraction itself is the same.

2:2. *Psychology and "The Stages on Life's Way"*

That which all Kierkegaard's literary-psychological experiments have in common, then, is that they describe extreme, isolated, and unrealistic cases. The intention with these is not to give direct psychological illumination to reality but to place the ethical and religious problems of reality in relief. "The exception also thinks the universal when it thinks carefully about itself; it works for the universal when it works through itself; it explains the universal when it explains itself . . . it shows everything far more clearly than the universal itself" [III 289, R 152-53]. These experiments are thus of *literary and ethical-religious* interest, but only occasionally are they of any independent psychological interest, in the narrow sense. It is this which separates them from *The Concept of Anxiety* and *The Sickness Unto Death*.

"The novels" refer especially to Kierkegaard's doctrine of the stages: the aesthetic, the ethical, and the religious, and to the differentiations which are operative within this framework. The doctrine of stages itself could perhaps with some justification also be designated as psychological, but the most important criteria of differentiation here are the ethical-religious concepts and the relationship of the individual to them. In *The Concept of Anxiety* and *The Sickness Unto Death*, the differentiations are psychologically motivated. Even if the criteria here are also the individual's relationship to categories such as guilt, sin, the evil and the good, faith and eternity, these concepts are not (only) viewed ethically-religiously, but (also) as psychological realities and motivational factors. This gives us the second important difference between the doctrine of stages and psychology, namely, that in the doctrine of stages there is never any question of a transition between the various conditions; the doctrine of stages is not a doctrine of development, but a purely ideal thinking-through of the various possibilities and spheres of existence, which are not placed in any causal relationship to one another. In psychology, on the other hand, there are motivated transitions between the various conditions.

Kierkegaard's psychology is a broadening and deepening of that which goes under the name of the aesthetic way of life in *Either/Or,* parts I and II. It is precisely in this first pseudonymous work that the common point of departure is to be found, both for the doctrine of the stages, which later finds development in, particularly, *Stages on Life's Way* and *Postscript,* and for the psychology which is later developed in *The Concept of Anxiety* and *The Sickness Unto Death.* While the ethical and the religious stages can be seen as a deepening, a differentiation, and a partial revision of Judge William's views, the psychology can be seen as a continuation of some of the analyses of the aesthetic person which are undertaken by Judge William and Aesthete A.

In addition to *The Concept of Anxiety* and *The Sickness Unto Death,* I thus reckon parts of *Either/Or* plus a series of passages from other books and from the *Papirer* as psychological texts. These texts also sketch people as types, as striking examples of the condition under discussion, not rounded, individualized "whole" portraits à la Henry James, but prototypical forms, sometimes "representations." But the psychology differs from that of the literary experiments in that it now attempts to be realistic — not in the sense that the examples and the representations always "resemble" actual people as a matter of course, but in the sense that the intention is to give a *psychological* illumination of that which is universally human. Psychology must be credible, and it is not necessary to support it "with learned quotations, that in Saxony there was a peasant girl, of whom a doctor observed, that in Rome there lived an emperor, of whom an historian relates, etc., as if it were so that such things occur only once every thousand years. What interest does psychology have, then? No, it is everything; it occurs every day, if only the observer is there" [IV 360, CD 50].

If Kierkegaard nevertheless does in fact illustrate his argument with the help of the emperor in Rome (Nero) or other historical, literary, or mythical figures, it is only because they are prototypes of the universal.

Chapter II

"WHEN THE CHILD IS TO BE WEANED . . ."

1. Separation

One of the key concepts of Kierkegaard's psychology is *the crisis*. The crisis is the fundamental anthropological condition, which comes into being when the individual is removed from an original, symbiotic life-context. It is this *process of separation* which will be studied in this chapter and in the succeeding one, which more concretely points out the empirical factors which precipitate this process. What is said about childhood, the dawning of sexuality, upbringing, etc., is of interest in itself, but also has the purpose of referring beyond the immediate context toward an understanding of the manifest crisis, just as that which will later be said about psychological phenomena and conditions in the adult individual is derived in one or another way from the conception of crisis and thus from the analysis of the phenomenon of separation.

Fear and Trembling — the book about Abraham's sacrifice and faith — dramatically illustrates the phenomenon of separation and concludes in a radical reflection upon ethical and religious problems. Only as an exception can Abraham, who is the exception, illuminate the universal. The fact that the condition which is described is nonetheless a shared human condition is alluded to in the book's prelude with four short variations upon the theme of separation. The third of them reads as follows:

"When the child is to be weaned, then the mother too, is not without sorrow that she and the child are to be separated more and more; that the child, which lay at first under her heart, and later rested against her breast, will no longer be so near. So they grieve the same short sorrow together. Lucky the one who kept the child so close and had no further need of sorrow" [III 76, FT 29].

As the theme of separation is struck here, it is an unspecific symbol of a fundamental motif in the book and in Kierkegaard's thought. The story of Abraham demonstrates a separation which is more radical than that alluded to in the vignette. Kierkegaard does this same thing when, in another context, he goes from a symbolic to a concrete understanding of the separation which precedes and psychologically conditions the crisis.

16

"For, in relation to God, the bird and the lily are like the child of the tender age at which it is still practically one with the mother. But when the child has become bigger, even if it remains in the parents' house, ever so close to them, never out of the right sight, there is nevertheless an infinite distance between the child and the parents. And in this distance lies the possibility of being able to be presumptuous. Even if the mother grasps the child, even if she encircles it in her arms in order by her closeness to guard it completely against every danger, nevertheless, in the possibility of being able to be presumptuous, the child is still infinitely far from her. It is an enormous distance, an enormous remove. For is it not true that he who lives in his wonted place, but far from his only desire, lives in the distance? The child is like this, even though at home with his parents, yet he is remote by means of this possibility of being able to be presumptuous. And thus is man, in the possibility of being able to be presumptuous, infinitely removed from God, in whom nevertheless he lives, moves and has his being. But if, from this distance and in this distance, he ever comes to be as near to God as the bird and the lily do in their continuing wish to do only what God wills, then he has become a Christian" [X 78, ChD 65-66].

The quotation — from *Christian Discourses* (1848) — circumscribes the whole of Kierkegaard's psychological topic, from eternity to eternity, or at least from unity to unity, or, to use other words, from the *beginning* of *The Concept of Anxiety:* "In the state of innocence, Man is not determined as spirit, but is mentally determined in immediate unity with his natural condition" [IV 345, CD 37], to the *conclusion of The Sickness Unto Death:* "in relating itself to itself, and in willing to be itself, the self grounds itself transparently in the power which posited it. And this formula again, as has often been noted, is the definition of faith" [XI 272, SD 262]. Kierkegaard's psychology lies between these two quotations.

2. Anthropological Anxiety and Original Sin

We begin at the beginning: the tiny baby in immediate unity with its natural condition, and the dissolution of that unity which comes into existence together with the possibility of being able to be presumptuous, to rebel, to be disobedient. In *The Concept of Anxiety* Kierkegaard sketches this universal human development with Adam as the paradigm. "Therefore, what explains Adam explains the race, and vice versa" [IV 333, CD 27]. Just as Adam begins in Paradise, so does every subsequent individual begin in innocence [IV 366, CD 54], and "innocence is *something,* . . . a quality, it is a *state,* which can very well endure" [IV 341, CD 34]. If this state is terminated, it happens by means of a fall into sin: "As Adam lost innocence by guilt, so does every individual man lose it" [IV 339 f., CD 32].

Adam is Man, the prototype. This is also the case, be it noted, with respect to original sin: "His sin is original sin" [IV 337, CD 30], and "no explanation which will explain Adam but not original sin, or will explain original sin but not Adam, is of any help" [IV 332, CD 26].[1]

How can Kierkegaard maintain that the first man's sin, Adam's sin, was original sin?[2] He explains it by saying that Adam, just as any individual, participates in the life of the race" [IV 332 f., CD 26 f.]. Adam has a history, and by means of this history he has psychological significance for posterity, just as every other individual has [IV 337, CD 30], but he himself has no history prior to his creation, while the later individual participates in and is marked by the human past, "inheritance." Original sin is not simply identical (as the Danish word might imply) with the determining factors of inheritance and environment. Original sin is a dogmatic concept which, however, dogmatics must not explain, but only presuppose [IV 324, CD 18]. The psychological concept which corresponds to original sin is anxiety.

"The consequence, or the presence, of original sin in the individual is anxiety, which differs only quantitatively from Adam's" [IV 357, CD 47]. Adam's original sin also showed itself as anxiety. Thus, anxiety (original sin) is primary and independent of inheritance and milieu. It is present by virtue of the fact that man is a contradiction, a synthesis, and it becomes visible when the elements of the synthesis separate from one another. Man is an individual who participates in the race, and he is a synthesis of body and soul, of temporality and eternity. When the original unity of these contraries is gradually dissolved, anxiety becomes visible as the precondition necessary so that the inherited and environmental factors can have psychological significance, and thus anxiety shows itself as the *condition of possibility* for the fall into sin and the entire psychological development. "Descent" in itself means nothing with respect to psychological matters. Descent is not "capable of producing an individual; because an animal species even if it has preserved itself for a thousand and another thousand generations, never brings forth an individual" [IV 338, CD 31]. And it is only because man, as opposed to the animal, is anxious, that inheritance and environment come to play a role. Anxiety is the middle term, the condition of possibility which enables "the fact of generation" and "the historical situation" to have psychological consequences [IV 368 and 379, CD 56 and 66]. These consequences are not in themselves original sin, but they are that which "signifies what original sin means strictly speaking" [IV 367, CD 56].

This distinction between a fundamental anthropological anxiety and the concrete psychological complications which are conditioned by that fundamental anxiety and which give it its specific form is decisive for Kierkegaard's arrangement of his material. In Chapter I, Parts 5 and 6 of *The Concept of Anxiety*, Adam's innocence and the fall into sin are treated. In Chapter II, the same development is dealt with in "the later individual." Adam is of course the prototype of man but, because he has not descended from anyone and does not partake of any social or familial context, it is only the fundamental, anthropological anxiety and the intrapsychic development which corresponds to this which can be illustrated by means of his example. The complications in the form of inherited or environmental conditions are illuminated in Chapter II. Kierkegaard has naturally chosen this method of presentation quite deliberately, partly to show that it is the anthropological anxiety which is fundamental, and partly in order to be able to say that in "the later individual" there is a concrete reciprocity between the fundamental anxiety and the anxiety which is conditioned by circumstances.

In the pages which follow we will more closely examine Kierkegaard's understanding of anthropological, primary anxiety and its significance in the development of the individual. The environmental complications will be dealt with in the next chapter.

It may seem strange that in *The Concept of Anxiety* Kierkegaard does not expressly say that that which he is describing is the same as that which he elsewhere calls "the two ages of immediacy," namely childhood and youth [XIII 608, PV 81]. In conformity with the science of his period, he does not speak of firmly delineated phases of development, but only hints that it is relevant to associate it with childhood. A closer investigation of his thought will show clearly enough that, *psychologically understood,* "innocence" or "immediacy" are his designations for the development from the age of infancy to that of puberty, or perhaps to the identity crisis and re-adjustment process of a delayed puberty. But Kierkegaard's parsimony in indicating definite ages can remind us that many of the phenomena which he discusses here are also of significance for the understanding of the psychology of the adult.

3. "The Child's 'Me' "

3: 1. *Adam and the Erotic Stages of Immediacy*

Adam must be understood, then, as an abstraction from the development of the concrete individual. In the sketch of him, immediacy is seen from one, essential side, while for the time being the interplay with other factors is ignored. But Adam in *The Concept of Anxiety* is also to be seen in another sense as a conscious, experimental abstraction from given, factual reality. Adam is a representation (cf. above, Chapter I: 2), and is thus the consciously one-sided personification of a particular idea. The notion of the idea of representation was put forth in Aesthete A's essay on "The Immediate Erotic Stages or the Musical Erotic" in *Either/Or*. And it is precisely in this essay that the most important complement to the sketch of Adam is to be found.

It is not made explicitly clear in *The Concept of Anxiety* that this is so, but the two essays correspond with one another on essential points. Just as the three figures with which the aesthete illustrates the stages of immediacy—the Page in *The Marriage of Figaro,* Papageno in *The Magic Flute,* and Don Giovanni in the opera of the same name—are mythical figures, so, too, is Adam. It is true that Kierkegaard stresses that the story in Genesis is not to be taken as a myth [IV 350, cf. 335 f.; CD 41, cf. 29 f.], but this claim is purely polemical in motivation, and is directed against the speculative conception of myth, and most probably that of D.F. Strauss. In fact, Kierkegaard himself subjects the account to the mythical point of view, and allows himself, as an interpreter of myth, to interpret the literal unliterally [IV 351, CD 42].

The portrayal of Adam's innocence in *The Concept of Anxiety* (Chapter I, Part 5) can be divided into three phases, which correspond to the three erotic stages in the Mozart essay in *Either/Or*. To the first stage (the Page's) corresponds a general description of the state of innocence in *The Concept of Anxiety*. To the second stage (Papageno's) corresponds a passage on the child's anxiety. And to the third, erotic stage (Don Giovanni) corresponds the sequence which immediately precedes Adam's "fall into sin" [IV 345-49, CD 37-40]. We will investigate these important relationships more closely, because it is only by seeing the Mozart essay and other related Kierkegaard texts as commentaries to the delineation of Adam that we can see the real significance of that very short and pregnant passage in *The Concept of Anxiety*. A bit of philology in relation to these texts is the precondition of our being able to see the breadth of Kierkegaard's psychological thinking.

"Innocence is ignorance. In the state of innocence, Man is not determined as spirit, but is mentally determined in immediate unity with his natural condition. Spirit is dreaming in the person" [IV 345, CD 37]. Thus runs the prelude to the description of Adam's development. For a closer understanding, it is surely helpful to note that this incredibly compressed starting point for Kierkegaard's analysis is so compressed precisely because he could presuppose that the notion was familiar to the contemporary reader. In fact, Kierkegaard's formulation is not original. It is almost word-for-word identical with some introductory observations in a book to which he himself refers later in *The Concept of Anxiety,* namely the German philosopher Karl Rosenkranz' *Psychologie*.[3] The similarity does not mean that Kierkegaard is simply plagiarizing this German pupil of Hegel, but it shows that Kierkegaard is taking his point of origin in views which were well-known in his time, while he continues his analysis in a completely original way. Rosenkranz' introduction to psychology is therefore a welcome commentary on Kierkegaard. The spirit "in immediate unity with its natural condition" and the mind as the spirit which is still "dreaming," which reaches beyond its unity with itself, is "the beginning of psychology." In the embryonic state, which is Rosenkranz' real point of beginning, the child is immediately *one* with the mother. The whole of its "natural condition" is its corporeality. But already in birth the process of separation begins. The infant separates itself from something else, and the separation receives its first, unarticulated emotional expression in the scream. Later the child becomes an object for itself; it receives language and speaks of itself in the third person ("August wants this"). Then finally it comprehends itself as I and comes into possession of reason. At a later point, Rosenkranz discusses the entirety of this developmental process as "the necessarily occurring bipartition (Entzweiung)" of the spiritual and the corporeal.[4]

This, then, is also Kierkegaard's point of departure and the problem which he proposes to study. In the more detailed psychological analysis of this subject, he can no longer find help in Rosenkranz. Kierkegaard's analyses began as early as 1837, before he read the German philosopher's book. This can be seen from the two journal entries, Pap. I C 125 and 126 [Hong 4397, 4398], which are preparatory studies to the essay on Mozart, and thus perhaps the most important rudimentary beginnings of the passage about Adam's anxiety in *The Concept of Anxiety.*

Kierkegaard was to go to the opera one evening in January 1837 and hear Mozart's *Magic Flute,* and for this occasion he formulated an aesthetic-psychological theory "about the Page in *Figaro,* Papageno in *The Magic Flute,* and Don Giovanni." The next day he wrote another entry which is a continuation of this: "Something about the four stages of life, also with respect to mythology." Thus, in the first entry there are three, in the second, four, stages, but what they have in common is the emphasis which is placed upon the first stage, that of the Page, "the stage in which the child has not separated itself from its surroundings ('me')." Here one also gets a rather precise dating of this first stage: it is the pre-school age.[5] The Page represents "the first stage of development; it is indefinite, awakening desire in unconscious conflict with its surroundings; it is the play of colors from which a pure color gradually develops; it is the still unposited I, but the becoming I with its sensitive antenna. Just as all coming-into-being is polemical, so, too, is life itself. At its first stage it is not conscious, but in continual approximation of consciousness. In a way it identifies itself with the world (the child's 'me'), but precisely because it is a life, a development, it is an endless approaching to conscious desire . . . " [Pap. I C 125, Hong 4397]. For Kierkegaard, the fact that the child says "me" expresses that it cannot "differentiate" itself from objects, and that the child has for a long time been so slightly separated from its surroundings that stressing the passive side, it says, for example, 'me hit horse' " [Pap. I A 75, p. 53, Dru 22; cf. Pap. I A 319, Hong 4395]. But this primary identification (as it is called in psychoanalytic terminology) is always in the process of being abolished. "The I is not given, but the possibility for it is, and to this extent it is a conflict. It is sketched in indistinct and fluid contours, just like the naiads which the ocean . . . produces, only to produce new ones in the same instant . . . . [I]n this way the innumerable elements exist with and supplant one another in childhood in order to be taken up into the presence of the eternal I, so that in childhood is given atomistic multiplicity, and in the I is given the One in the Many . . . . [I]t is, to use an expression from dogma, the original righteousness, which the Catholic dogmatists believe is granted to man in—if I may call it so—super-abundance. But the nearer life, in its endless approach, comes to self-consciousness, the more visible the conflict becomes . . .")Pap. I C 126, Hong 4398].

It is this original righteousness and this developing I, with its sensitive antenna, which is described in *The Concept of Anxiety* under the rubric of innocence. But a second phase of the same development is delineated in *Either/Or* as the first of immediacy's stages, represented by the Page in *The Marriage of Figaro*. In both cases it is a case of the "dreaming" state where "the difference between myself and my Other . . . is an implied Nothing" [IV 346, CD 38]. This state can be illuminated from two sides. In the essay in *Either/Or* it is primarily separation which is discussed; in *The Concept of Anxiety* it is primarily individuation. These two things are closely connected, however, because the sense of identity arises precisely when the primary identification is broken down and the individual differentiates himself from his surroundings. It is particularly in his study of the Page and Papageno that Aesthete A provides a phenomenology of separation and differentiation, and this, then, is the background for the phenomenology of individuation which is presented in *The Concept of*

Anxiety. In both texts an original unity and its fission are described; with the aesthete it is the development of the division between the individual and the surrounding world which is studied; in Vigilius Haufniensis' account, special attention is given also to the dissolution of the individual's own unity with himself.

3: 2. *The Theme of the Essay on Mozart*

Before use can be made of the essay on the immediate erotic stages, however, it is necessary to make clear what it deals with. Formally it deals with Mozart's operas, but its real subject is sensuous desire and its metamorphoses. One could easily borrow a title from C.G. Jung and call the essay *The Transformations and Symbolisms of the Libido.* The three Mozart figures who appear are abstractions and representations fully as much as was Adam, except that here the abstraction takes another direction. The most striking abstraction in the Mozart essay is the abstraction from the concept of consciousness. The real subject of the essay is desire, the blind natural instinct in its impersonal boundlessness, "the immediacy of sensuality" [I 73, E/O I 80]. Don Giovanni is not a completed individual, but "the natural force, the demonic which no more tires of seduction or finishes with it than the wind tires of blowing, the sea of billowing, or a waterfall of plunging down from the heights" [I 85, E/O I 91]. In Don Giovanni is concentrated "the sensuous-erotic as a principle, as a power, as a kingdom" [I 54, E/O I 62], as "power, life, movement, continual unrest, continual succession" [I 62, E/O I 70]. This desire is immediate, and according to Kierkegaard's theory of media can only be presented musically. Immediacy is "the indefinable" and "the obscure, the unexplained," which language cannot adequately express [I 60 f., E/O I 68 f.]. The essay gives an experimental description of this natural instinct as it would develop itself *if* there were no consciousness to set a limit to this expansion. Don Giovanni is the representative of this pure, boundless, sensuous desire, which is not hampered by any form of reflection, but is only intensified by the very exclusion of the realm of spirit (more about this later). It is Kierkegaard's primary goal to conjure this idea forth experimentally, in part in order to illuminate the idea in Mozart's opera, and in part, of course, also in order to characterize the essay's "author," Aesthete A, as a wishful thinker. The aesthete, however, has no real illusions about immediacy, but is aware that his idea is an unreal abstraction. In this essay, too, consciousness is the limiting case which brings the adventure to a sudden end, though this is not the aesthete's subject, but the boundary of his sphere of interest [I 82, 107 f., 120 f., E/O I 88, 111 f., 123 f.].

The Page and Papageno together constitute the ingredients, as it were, of the Don Giovanni experiment, but there is an essential difference between them and Don Giovanni. The Don Giovanni has no factual, individual existence; he is a life-force which never occurs in its pure form, but is always delimited and hampered by consciousness. Neither may the Page and Papageno be conceived of as concrete individuals, but as personifications of this same life-force, the sensual desire, in its earlier phases of development. But they are less abstract than Don Giovanni. He is the definitive sexual desire in its frictionless, intensified development, statically sustained in the aesthetic eternity of music, in a sort of artificial or artificially prolonged, timeless childhood, a chronic innocent. He does not exist in concrete actuality. Neither, most certainly, do the Page and Papageno, but the desire they represent is not of a specifically sexual sort. It is not the genitally-fixated desire of the sexually mature person, but the child's universal, non-fixated appetite for life. The difference is that desire at these stages occurs in a more or less spontaneous form, unhampered by consciousness. The Page is not "a child" or "the child," but he represents prototypically a certain phase of the early development of the individual the development in which the child's primary identification with his surroundings has not yet been replaced by any distinct sense of identity and perception of the schism between the I and the surrounding world, while, however such a perception is latently and obscurely present all the while.

Kierkegaard's interpretation of Mozart's theatrical figures as symbols for three phases of psychic development is more carefully defined in the essay as meaning that these are not, strictly speaking, three distinct stages, but rather metamorphoses within one and the same stage, that of immediacy. Kierkegaard emphasizes the continuity between them, not the break, because the qualitative break lies beyond the Don Giovanni stage and dissolves it. Therefore it is also written of the Page, Papageno, and Don Giovanni, that one must "not think of different levels of consciousness, because even the last stage has not yet come to consciousness; I am still dealing only with the immediate in its complete immediacy" [I 65, E/O I, 73]. These words do not contradict the interpretation of the Mozart essay as a description of the phases of psychological development, but, on the contrary, confirm it.' According to Kierkegaard's terminology, the child has, indeed, no consciousness. Consciousness means something other and something more than the ability to sense and to experience. But it is precisely sensing and experiencing which are the child's essential relation to the world. The child is not "conscious of its existence as such," Kierkegaard writes at another point [III 125, FT 72; cf. IV 146, ED III 80], and in the journal it is stated, with more precision: "How is the child's consciousness determined? It is really not determined at all, which can also be expressed by saying that it is immediate. *Immediacy* is precisely *undeterminedness.* There is no relationship in immediacy, for as soon as there is a relationship, immediacy is broken" [Pap. IV B 1, p. 145]. This language contains an important point which we will illuminate more closely in a later section on the concept of consciousness (Chapter IV: 3: 1). According to the draft from 1837, the talk of an "immediate development," in connection with the Mozart characters means "that precisely as a striving, it has not yet come to consciousness of its relation to the world, but, like a magnet, seeks its satisfaction" [Pap. I C 125, Hong 4397].

Kierkegaard speaks of the Page and Papageno as "mythical" figures [I 60 ff., E/O I 68 ff.]. This means that he does not wish to have his symbolic figures confused too much with Mozart's actual theatrical characters, whose spoken lines and ages will, on closer inspection, show themselves not too well-suited to this free interpretation which Kierkegaard gives them. Further, it also means that Kierkegaard's figures must not be understood as concrete individuals. Kierkegaard's Mozart essay is not a piece of empirical child psychology. The characters are personifications, not persons. They "represent" desire as a principle, but with a conscious abstraction from any distinct social milieu and its conflicts [I 101, E/O I 106]. They are prototypes in the same way that Adam is in *The Concept of Anxiety,* and the surrounding world exists for him only as the object of desire, and otherwise not at all. Thus, in other words, what is being prototypically studied here is an intrapsychic, fundamental psychological (anthropological) phenomenon, and not — not yet — an empirical psychological development, but its conditions of possibility. It is a case of an analytic process of abstraction from the complex, impenetrable, empirical world, but this abstraction is also the precondition for coming to an adequate conception of concrete complexity.[6]

3: 3. *The First Stage*

How, then, shall this phenomenon, desire, be understood, and what does it mean that the Page in *The Marriage of Figaro* is the personification of this desire? Kierkegaard writes "that it is of great significance that the part of the Page is arranged musically for a woman's voice. It is as if that which is contradictory in this stage is alluded to by that contradiction. The desire is so indefinite, the object differentiated so slightly, that that which is desired reposes androgynously within the desire, just as, in plant life, male and female repose upon the same flower. The desire and the desired are united in this unity, that both are of the neuter gender" [I 68, E/O I

76]. Kierkegaard apparently contradicts this picture of sexless symbiosis when he writes immediately thereafter in reference to the mythical Page, that it is "equally essential that he [i.e., the Page] be in love with the Countess and with Marcelina. Femininity, in fact, is his object, and this is something which both women have in common" [I 69, E/O I 76]. If one is to harmonize both of these statements, this can certainly only be done if one assumes that the relation here described is that of a little child to its mother ("femininity"), and that the point is that the child does not differentiate clearly between itself and the mother [cf. Pap. I C 125, Hong 4397].

The assumption that the object of the Page's desire in his mother—or, expressed more cautiously, the maternal—can look like an interpolation made in the wish to have Kierkegaard be more "psychoanalytic" than he is. It is *not* the doctrine of the Oedipus complex for which he is setting the stage. It could seem more reasonable to imagine the Page as a 12 to 14 year-old boy who is gradually beginning to take an interest in girls. But not only is this idea in disagreement with the journal entries from 1837, but also with the description of the Page in *Either/Or*. The adjective "erotic" does not denote anything specifically sexual here, but an unspecific sort of attraction.[7] And, indeed, the Page's desire was neuter in gender. If one imagines the Page as a grown boy, it becomes impossible to understand the symbiotic relation between the desire and its object. It is an absolute, passive, sensuous satisfaction of need which is depicted, and this satisfaction corresponds to primary identification. It is the little child's indistinct, "magical" world, which is experienced in accordance with the laws of the primary process.[8] "In desire it is always that which is desired which arises from the desire and manifests itself in a confusing daybreak. This is the situation in which the sensuous exists: it is placed at a remove by clouds and fogs; it is brought closer by its reflection in them. Desire possesses that which is to become its object, but it possesses it without having desire it, and so it does not possess it . . . . That which is desired hovers over desire and sinks down into it, although this movement does not take place by means of desire's own power of attraction, or because of desiring. That which is desired does not disappear or wrest itself from the embrace of desire, because precisely this would awaken desire." The individual exists, as does Adam in *The Concept of Anxiety,* in immediate unity with its natural condition: "Thus desire, which at this stage is only present in a premonition of itself, is without movement, without unrest, rocked but softly by an inexplicable inner motion; as the life of the plant is imprisoned to the earth, so is desire sunken in a quiet, present-tense, longing, deep on contemplation, and yet cannot exhaust its object, essentially because, in a deeper sense, there is no object" [I 66 f., E/O I 74 f.]. The unity is thus still undisturbed, although it is destined to be abolished. Transcendence is latently present in the present-tense, or, as it is also called, substantial, longing in which the first stage is imprisoned [I 72, E/O I, 78-79].

The condition is clearly the same as that which is called innocence in *The Concept of Anxiety*. "In this condition there is peace and repose, but at the same time there is something else, which is not discord and struggle, for there is, of course, nothing with which to struggle . . . " [IV 346, CD 38]. In order to maintain the parallel between the two texts, however, we must look more carefully at the Page, who is described in more detail than is the corresponding phase of Adam. It could be surprising that the Page's stage is denoted as melancholy, but this melancholia is just the expression of this stage's transience and of its teleological destination: "The sensuous awakens, though not to movement, but to still quiescence, not to joy and gladness, but to deep melancholia. Desire has not yet awakened, it is sadly suspected . . . . This is the contradiction which is painful, but which is also captivating and bewitching with its sweetness, the contradiction which, with its sadness and its melancholia, echoes throughout this stage. Its sorrow does not come from there being too little, but sooner from there being too much. . . . [That which is desired] exists for desire without being desired, and desire therefore becomes melancholy, because it cannot come to the point of desiring. . . . When desire has not awakened, it is charmed and captivated by what it desires; indeed, it is almost frightened by it" [I 66 f., E/O I 74 f.]. The condition contains "within itself the contradiction which is peculiar to melancholia and sadness, . . . the ambiguity which is the sweetness in melancholia" [I 68, E/O I 75].

Does not this contradict the hypothesis of the Page as the representative of the earliest part of childhood? A melancholy infant! And yet this is surely Kierkegaard's meaning. Even though the expression is peculiar, it essentially and understandably explains the situation at hand in the given context. There is also mention of the melancholia of the first stage in the two journal entries from 1837. The little child experiences the world in its "atomistic multiplicity," but "because life has not yet come to self-consciousness, has not yet gotten its center of gravity in itself, this multiplicity exerts a pressure" [Pap. I C 126, Hong 4398], which is due to the fact that "at this level the individual has not differentiated itself and therefore really has no standard of measure to use"; "the peculiarity of this level's melancholia" is therefore to be found in the fact that "the whole fullness of life presses down and, so to speak, overwhelms" [Pap. I C 125, Hong 4397]. Melancholia, then, is here a sign, a symptom, of an unconscious need to differentiate oneself, to take note of resistance, even frustration, to get an identity, to be liberated from the primary symbiosis. It is the expression of the fact that it is man's destiny to become spirit. "In the state of innocence, man is not merely an animal, for then, if for even a single moment in his life he were merely an animal, he would never become man," it says in *The Concept of Anxiety* [IV 348, CD 39].

When the object of desire cannot be put at a distance as an object, it bewitches and captivates, "indeed it almost frightens," the aesthete wrote. According to *The Concept of Anxiety,* in the state of innocence there was nothing to struggle with: "But what effect does nothing have? It gives birth to anxiety. This is the deep secret of innocence, that it is, at the same time, anxiety. Dreaming, the spirit projects its own actuality, but this actuality is nothing, and this nothing sees innocence outside itself. Anxiety is a determination of dreaming spirit, and as such belongs to the sphere of psychology. In wakefulness, the difference between myself and my Other is posited; in sleep, the difference is suspended; in dreaming it is a nothing which is vaguely intimated. The actuality of spirit shows itself continually as a form which tempts its possibility, but is gone as soon as possibility grasps after it, and is a nothing, which can only cause anxiety. It can do no more, so long as it only shows itself" [IV 346, CD 38].

The fact that this anxiety has in itself the same lack of object and the same ambiguous power of attraction as the Page's melancholia, becomes clear when Kierkegaard, in a direct continuation of the above quotation, sets forth his famous distinction between anxiety and fear—the concept of anxiety "is completely different from fear and similar concepts, which refer to something definite, while anxiety is the actuality of freedom as a possibility for possibility" [*ibid.*]—and it is also made clear in his no less significant definition of anxiety as ambivalent fascination: "anxiety is *a sympathetic antipathy and an antipathetic sympathy* . . . . Linguistic usage fully confirms this; one speaks of sweet anxiety, sweet unease; one speaks of a strange anxiety, a shy anxiety, etc.," [*ibid.*].

A modern reader does not have difficulty in seeing how decisively significant these definitions are. The distinction between object-fixated fear and diffuse, objectless anxiety reappears in both Heidegger and Freud (though only as a loan from Kierkegaard in the former), and thereby in what is most likely the majority of modern theories of anxiety. The definition of anxiety as sympathetic-antipathetic is no less decisive. It is also basic to the whole of Kierkegaard's psychology, which is why concepts such as ambivalence, ambiguousness, and doubleness also become key terms in the rest of this presentation (the term "ambivalence" itself first took on its character, at the beginning of the present century, from Eugen

Bleuler). But because the reader who is oriented to the psychology and phenomenology of the 20th century perceives the significance of these concepts so easily, he perhaps overlooks how much conceptual precision and stringent analytical self-understanding must have been the precondition for formulating them for the first time.[9]

The similarity between Vigilius Haufniensis' depiction of innocence and Aesthete A's depiction of the first phase of immediacy is unmistakable. And yet, the reasoning in the two texts is not entirely the same. In the aesthete's account, it is the surrounding world which is the contourless object of anxiety; with Vigilius, it is the individual's own future identity. The queer expression, that "anxiety is the actuality of freedom as a possibility for possibility" must mean (if it is not a typographical error!) that the object of anxiety is the individual's concrete identity, apprehended vaguely as a future possibility. It is this which is the meaning of the famous statement that anxiety's object is "nothing" [IV 347, CD 39]. The statement does not mean that there is in fact no object, nor, as it has been understood by existential philosophy, that the object is non-being, death, but it means that the object has not yet come into existence for the individual, because the individual has not yet won any identity — and the object is the identity. The parallel in Aesthete A is the statement that "in the deeper sense, there is no object," that is, no definite point of orientation. In the aesthete's account one must understand by "object," first and foremost the object of sensual desire. With Vigilius, the discussion is of the object of a sort of spiritual instinct, the need for individuation. But, as has been made clear, the aesthete also discusses this striving for individuation, this striving which is given in the fact that man is man and not an animal, namely, where the aesthete writes of the melancholia and sadness of the first stage. The need for differentiation from the primary identification with the environment (the mother?) is only another expression of the need to become an individual. In *Either/Or,* it was melancholia which was the expression of this need. In *The Concept of Anxiety* it is anxiety. And, furthermore, here, too, there is mention of an unclear notion of "the difference between myself and my Other" as characteristic of this condition. The transition to the next phase of development takes place gradually as this difference becomes clearer.

Is Adam, then, a child under six, a child who says "me," an infant who is nursed? Well, Adam is just as little a concrete individual as are the Page and Don Giovanni. The delineation of him takes its point of departure in the original unity, but Vigilius does not dwell upon this, because his task is to show the teleology of the condition. We are referred, by means of anxiety, out beyond the unity and the lack of identity, forward to fission

and the coming-to-consciousness. The second phase of this development is
illustrated by Aesthete A by means of Papageno in *The Magic Flute*.

4. Individuation and Anxiety

4:1. *The Second Stage*

It is evident, from Kierkegaard's journal entries of 1837, that the first
efforts of childhood are replaced by a developmental phase which, using
the Freudian expression, one could call the period of latency: "a
tranquility, an idyllic well-being. It is the boy's satisfaction in family and
school (Church and State), it is the second stage . . . . Here is the real
equilibrium, here is divinity conjoined with the world."

It is the same "second stage" which is represented by Papageno in Pap. I
C 125 [Hong 4397] and in *Either/Or*. It is true that Papageno is one of the
most physically busy stage figures we know, but mentally he is at rest; "the
heart beats healthily and happily" [I 72, E/O I 79], and "melancholia
never gets to take on form as it did at the previous level," which is
connected to the fact that Papageno's appetite for life is goal-oriented and
extroverted, "just as the perpendicular direction of plant life is replaced by
the horizontal direction of locomotion" [Pap. I C 125, Hong 4397]. Desire
gets an object, that is, it now really comes into existence for the first time.
The child's "me" is beginning to become an "I" as it comes to relate itself
distinctly to its environment. "This is a dialectical definition which must be
firmly maintained: desire exists only when the object exists; the object
exists only when desire exists; desire and the object are a pair of twins,
neither of which can come into the world the least second before the other"
[I 71, E/O I 78]. It is the separation which allows desire to have a bit of air,
to "break forth," so that it breathes "freely and healthily, while earlier it
was unable to breathe because of [the close presence of] the desired"; this
takes place — to recall a partially symbolic expression used earlier — when
the child is weaned: "[T]he object of desire flees bashfully, as modest as a
woman; a separation comes between them; the object of desire disappears
et apparat sublimis, [10] or, at any rate, outside of desire" [I 67, E/O I 75].
"The consequence of the separation is that desire is wrested out of its
substantial repose in itself, and as a consequence of this, the object no
longer belongs to the category of substantiality, but disperses itself into a
multiplicity" [I 71, E/O I 78-79]. This separation and differentiation
causes no conflict for the time being, but simply signifies the liberation of
forces. The world is taken into possession. Desire is not fixated upon any
distinct object, but flutters about like a butterfly. "Only occasionally is a

deeper desire suspected, but this suspicion is forgotten. In Papageno, desire goes out to make discoveries . . . . It finds no real object for this discovery, but it discovers the manifold when it seeks in it for the object it wishes to discover . . . . If one remembers that desire is present at all three stages, then one can say that at the first stage it is present as *dreaming,* at the second as *seeking,* at the third as *desiring"* [I 72, E/O I 79].

On the previous pages I have been concerned with the dreaming stage, as it is discussed, among other places, in *The Concept of Anxiety* by Vigilius Haufniensis. But in his continuation of this discussion, Vigilius, too, discusses the indefinite searching which follows upon the melancholia of the first stage: "The anxiety which is posited in innocence is thus, first of all, not guilt, and second of all, no heavy burden, no suffering of the sort which does not admit of harmonization with the bliss of innocence. When one observes children, one finds anxiety more distinctly adumbrated as a searching after the fabulous, the monstrous, the puzzling . . . . This anxiety is so essentially a part of the child that he will not be without it; even if it causes him anxiety, still it captivates him with its sweet unease" [IV 346-47, CD 38].

In the Page, anxiety was present only latently, in the form of a contourless, anxiety-producing melancholia. But anxiety is not manifest in the older child either. (For the time being it is only purely intrapsychic, normal development which is under discussion, while the complications caused by the environment will be dealt with later). It is not noticed as anxiety, but is converted into restless activity, fascinated searching and discovery. Anxiety is not a feeling here, but an unconscious motivational factor. In the depiction of Papageno, there is no discussion of anxiety, but it is present in the analysis of Don Giovanni, and Don Giovanni is to be understood, at any rate in this respect, as a continuation of the interpretation of Papageno. Where Papageno is seeking and discovering, Don Giovanni is discovering and conquering [I 72, cf. 77, E/O I 79, cf. 83]. And Don Giovanni's anxiety corresponds to the anxiety described in children in *The Concept of Anxiety,* except that the level of activity is higher. In both cases anxiety is the unconscious driving force behind the conquests, without which the joy of discovery and the desire would not exist; "There is an anxiety in him, but this anxiety is his energy. It is not an anxiety which is subjectively reflected in him; it is a substantial anxiety . . . . When one throws a stone so that it skims the surface of the water, it can skip along for a while in little hops, but as soon as it stops skipping, it instantly sinks into the abyss. In the same way, he dances upon the abyss, jubilant in his brief respite" [I 126, E/O I 128-29].

Kierkegaard has also described this substantial anxiety of immediacy in another connection, namely, in his newspaper series from 1848 about "The Crisis and a Crisis in the Life of an Actress." Here we are moving definitively from childhood to youth. The first portion of the serial describes the sixteen-year-old actress in the role of Juliet (in Shakespeare's piece). The aesthetic-psychological analysis actually deals with the Royal Theatre's primadonna, Johanne Luise Heiberg. Her name is not mentioned, however, for Kierkegaard is not interested in this particular person, but is ideally concerned with the analysis of "an actress in her first beginning" [X 372, CLA 72], and he thus delineates her according to his aesthetic formula for immediacy. She is happy, youthful, soulful, in inner harmony with herself, and yet moved by an inner, inexhaustible unrest, "an elemental tirelessness, like the wind's, like the sounds of nature" [X 373-76, CLA 73-76] — just like Don Giovanni. This unrest in the midst of certainty is her anxiety, and this anxiety has the same property as Don Giovanni's: it is convertible. The anxiety is the precondition for her work on the stage. In the genius, anxiety is restlessly converted into achievement: "Every tension can act in a double fashion: this is dialectic's own dialectic. It can make the effort manifest, but it can also do the opposite — it can conceal the effort, and not only conceal it, but continually convert it, transform and transfigure it into lightness. The lightness is thus invisibly rooted in the effort of tension, but this is not seen, not even suspected; only lightness is revealed . . . . Thus it is with the young actress; in the tension of the stage, she is in her element. It is precisely there that she is as light as a bird; it is precisely the weight which gives her lightness, and the pressure which enables her to swing so high. There is not a trace of anxiety; in the wings, perhaps, she is anxious, but on the stage she is as happy and as light as a bird that has gotten its freedom, for only now, under pressure, is she free and has received freedom. What shows itself as anxiety at home in the study or in the wings is not weakness, but precisely the opposite; it is elasticity which makes her anxious precisely because she bears no burden; in the tension of the theatre this anxiety transfigures itself absolutely happily into power" [X 377 f., CLA 77-78].

Thus, when it is properly administered, anxiety is an active motivating factor behind maximum achievement. This positive function as the precondition for great accomplishments is emphasized by modern "Third Force" psychologists, and Kierkegaard's description of Fru Heiberg's happy theatrical transformation of anxiety into "peak experience" is probably the best illustration of the idea. For Kierkegaard, however, this is not the most important function of anxiety. Of much more decisive significance is the fact that it can also be converted in other directions, such as happens in the crisis. For the present we shall see what role anxiety plays in the transition from innocence to the fall into sin, from ignorance to the coming-to-consciousness.

4: 2. *The Third Stage*

When Kierkegaard sets up three "stages" of immediacy, it can easily lead to some rather heavy-handed, crude notions of what he imagines this developmental process to be. In the Mozart essay, the sequence was thus: dreaming desire searching desire desiring desire. Don Giovanni is the symbol of the last form, and this formulation therefore accentuates the instinctual culmination, which also plays a role in Adam's desire for the forbidden unknown in *The Concept of Anxiety*. But Kierkegaard also treats this entire development in other texts, which more closely illuminate other facets of the process and show the continuity between the stages, which, according to the Mozart essay, are indeed only metamorphoses within one and the same stage.

Therefore it will cause no amazement that Kierkegaard's terminology can fluctuate from one text to another, but in a meaningful way. In *The Concept of Anxiety* and even more clearly in the Mozart essay, the adjective "dreaming" was emphasized as characteristic of the first stage. But this characteristic can also be stretched to cover the whole of "childhood's life and the life of youth," which Kierkegaard calls "a dream life" in one of his religious discourses. The definition of dream life is teeming with significance and sheds light upon the whole of "immediacy." The fact that it is dream life must quite expressly not be understood with superficial literalness, because the child has, of course, just awakened, "his senses open for every impression, the child [is] sheer life and movement, sheer attentiveness all day long." The child's "inwardness" is wide-awake "extroversion." But it is precisely this openness which Kierkegaard calls the child's dream life: "[H]e dreams himself sensuously together with everything, almost to the point of confusing himself with the sense-impression." One recognizes Papageno's stage here. In the youth, however, a metamorphosis has taken place. It is no longer sensation, but fantasy, which moves him. As the child is, so also is the youth "awake as rarely any adult is, his spirit without rest day and night, moved in passion." The youth, however, is "more introverted" than the child, but only on the plane of fantasy. Just as the child confounds himself with his sense impressions, the youth confounds himself with the productions of fantasy. They become his provisional identity, which is precisely a sort of lack of identity: "[H]e dreams, or it seems to him as though everything about him dreamt of him." In this sense, both the child and the youth are without identity. But at the same time, the religious discourse demonstrates that it is the fantasy stage of the youth which forms the transition to the crisis of identity which is discussed in *The Concept of Anxiety* as the fall into sin [X 131 f., ChD 113 f.].

Kierkegaard has made notations in a number of contexts about this fantasy stage which anticipates the crisis. In *Repetition* one reads of the pubescent youth's search for a life role, an ideal or an idol, in a mercurial, narcissistic identification with the hero of the stage. The youth goes to the theatre "in order to see and hear himself as a Doppelgänger, to disperse into all his possible differences from himself, and yet in such a way that every difference is also *one* self. It is naturally at a very young age that such a desire makes itself heard. Only fantasy has awakened from its dream of the personality; everything else still sleeps soundly. In such a fantastic self-perception, the individual is not an actual form, but a shadow, or, rather, the actual form is invisibly present, and therefore is not satisfied with casting one shadow, but the individual has a multiplicity of shadows, which all resemble him, and each of which, momentarily, has an equal claim to be himself. The personality has not yet been discovered; its energy heralds itself only in the passion of possibility" [III 217 f., R 42-43].

This, then is the "third stage" of immediacy, but viewed from a slightly different angle than that of the Don Giovanni analysis in the essay on Mozart. The stage is a culmination and a transition to a radically different problem complex. The concept of the "fantastic self-perception" is enormously important for the understanding of Kierkegaard's psychological insights. And the delineation of the youth's search for an identity is follows in *The Concept of Anxiety* by the delineation of Adam's development in the corresponding phase. But in preparation for the reading of this essential text, the "third stage" of immediacy must be illuminated in a bit more detail, on the basis of the aesthete's analyses in *Either/Or* of two representatives of other aspects of this stage: Cordelia and Don Giovanni.

4: 3. *Cordelia's Anxiety*

One of the most beautiful girls in Danish poetry is named Cordelia Wahl. In the gallery of "pale, bloodless, tenacious, nocturnal forms" [I 9, E/O I 23] and abstract human constructions which populate the pseudonymous universe, she lights up as the only tolerably human person. Furthermore, in relation to the rest of Kierkegaard's characters she can be experienced as almost luxuriant. And yet, although Cordelia is not *only* a marionette, a pawn in Kierkegaard's psychological chess game with

himself, she is all the same a guinea pig in a psychological experiment—
"The Diary of a Seducer"—which is carried through more cynically than
anything else in Kierkegaard. And therefore she also reveals, despite her
humanity, the characteristics which are typical for her "stage."
Kierkegaard depicts in her the metamorphosis from child to adult.[11]

Pale she is, but not bloodless, nor even tenacious. And as for
nocturnality, it is precisely on the night of the seduction that she
culminates fully—while Johannes the Seducer, febrile, ethereal, and pale,
hurries out to the assignation to be seduced, swearing nervously that his
soul is strong and healthy and happy [I 478 f., E/O I 439]. I do not believe
him. There is something fundamentally unerotic about this image-
worshipper who flees from reality, whose divinity is untouched virginity [I
467 f., E/O I 429]. Never at any time does he ever come into genuine
contact with Cordelia, but keeps her, even in the most intimate situations,
at the distance of irony and observation, misunderstanding and
admiration. And when they finally meet in the embrace, it signifies the
end of the relationship.[12] Johannes is related to Cordelia as Pygmalion is to
his beloved [I 471, cf. 414, E/O I 433, cf. 384]. As the product of his
fantasy, she has no meaning for him as the girl she in fact is, but as—so to
speak—the mythical Cordelia, the idea of Cordelia. Cordelia is the essence
of the Page, Papageno, and Don Giovanni, the feminine parallel to the
development which was viewed in three stages in the Mozart essay. While
Johannes is Kierkegaard's (or Aesthete A's) experiment and, as such, is an
atypical abstraction, Cordelia is Johannes' experiment, and, as such, is
prototypical. In the novel she is the object of a very peculiar form of
influence from Johannes, but that which is peculiar, let it be noted,
consists precisely in the fact that what he nurtures in her is her typicality in
its ideal purity. "I keep a strict and austere watch over myself, so that
everything which is in her, all of her divine, rich nature, will be developed"
[I 409, E/O I 380]. His method is a refined form of maieutic instruction. It
has similarities with Kierkegaard's own maieutic method, but they differ
on the decisive point, because Kierkegaard's method tends toward making
one conscious and independent, while the Seducer's method tends toward
the moment in which Cordelia is an obedient tool for his manipulations.
Of course, his method does indeed lead into the crisis [cf. I 323 ff., E/O I
304 ff.], but at the same instant she ceases to occupy him. The Seducer's
maieutic method results in the conflict and the fall into sin which
Kierkegaard's indirect communication presupposes. The achievement of
independence for Cordelia, which the Seducer successfully attempts, is
illusory in the essential sense that she is prevented from becoming aware of

the kind of relationship they have — before it is too late. But it is a genuine achievement of independence, in the sense that it really is *she* who develops herself, while he is only the catalyst, the occasion. If he is able to direct her in so sovereign a fashion, it is only because he is developing and cultivating the traits which she already has in latent form. "She herself must be developed in herself. . . . She must owe nothing to me, because she must be free. Only in freedom is there love; only in freedom is there diversion and eternal amusement. Although I direct my intentions in such a way that she will sink into my arms as if by natural necessity, although I strive to bring things to the point where she gravitates toward me, even so, it is also important that she does not fall like a heavy body, but as spirit gravitating toward spirit" [I 382, E/O I 356]. It can be seen that the Seducer's concepts of freedom and spirit are not quite identical with Kierkegaard's. It is the natural necessity in her which he develops, and it is this development he calls freedom. But in this area he is the perfect psychologist and pedagogue, that is, seducer; his instruction is highly pupil-oriented: "Now, I am a rather old practitioner, and yet I never approach a young girl as other than nature's *Venerabile,*[13] and I learn first from her. To the extent, then, that I can have any formative influence upon her, it is by teaching her again and again what I have learned from her" [I 416, cf. 390, 400, 411 f. and 441; E/O I 386, cf. 364, 373, 382-83, and 407].

In approximately four months the seventeen-year-old Cordelia goes through the development from pure immediacy to the fall into sin which in the other texts seems to take quite a bit more time. This has its literary explanation. In part, the foreshortened perspective gives the novel an artistic concentration, and, in part, no self-respecting aesthete can prolong an adventure for more than half a year [I 390; II 212; E/O I 364; E/O II 201]. However, Johannes also has a psychological explanation ready: "A young girl is not developed in the sense that a boy is. She does not grow; she is born. A boy begins to develop himself right away and takes a long time for this; a young girl is born slowly and born adult . . . . She does not awaken successively, but at once, but on the other hand, she dreams so much longer, when people are not so unreasonable as to call upon her too early" [I 350, E/O 327].[14]

As intimated here and elsewhere, Cordelia is not a completely ordinary example. "Even to find an example of pure, immediate femininity is a great event" [I 364 f., E/O I 340]. But precisely because she is so uncorrupted and inexperienced, she will ideally and prototypically demonstrate the development. Her environmental background is sketched, but it is as neutral as possible. She lives in isolation from the world and only faintly presupposes "the idea of life's pains, of its darker side" [I 356, E/O I

333], which gives her a certain proud elevation in relation to her surroundings, but everything is undisturbed and unconscious. "She has fantasy, soul, passion, in short, all substantialities, but does not possess them in subjective reflection" [I 362, E/O I 338], and therefore, in a deeper sense, she is without a history, and is in immediate unity with her natural condition: "Straight she was, and proud, secretive and full of ideas; she was like a fir tree, a shoot, a thought, which shoots up toward the sky from deep within the earth, unexplained, inexplicable to herself, a whole with no parts. The beech tree wears a crown; its leaves tell of what has transpired under them. The fir tree has no crown, no story, is mysterious to itself. Thus was she. She was concealed from herself in herself; she grew forth out of herself; there was a resting pride in her which was like the dearing flight of the fir tree, even though it is firmly fastened to the earth. There was a sadness poured over her like the cooing of the wood dove, a deep longing which lacked nothing" [I 348, E/O I 325-26].

This is the mythical Cordelia of the first stage, the Page's stage, phenomenologically timeless, not concretely seventeen years old. The description recurs in *The Concept of Anxiety.* "She was preoccupied not with herself but *in* herself, and this preoccupation was an infinite peace and repose within herself"; but, according to Vigilius, there is also something else in this peace and repose, something which is not discord and struggle: "Quiet peace reigned over her, and a little sadness" [I 350, E/O I 328]. Cordelia's substantial sadness and her unobjectified longing are her anxiety, the germ of the dissolution of her unity. Her development in the novel can be described with the help of the concepts of unity and doubleness. And it is Johannes' task, then, to foster the development of her latent inner contradiction.

The first phase in this development is erotically neutral, and consists of making Cordelia conscious in relation to the surrounding world. She learns to understand herself in pointed opposition to the bourgeois milieu with its conventions. Johannes entertains her aunt with talk of market prices and rural economics, and Cordelia is offended by this trivial conversation. She becomes bitter and indignant. "That is the first, false wisdom: we must teach her to smile ironically," and this happens with the help of "the repulsions of misunderstanding" [I 371, E/O I 347]. Johannes manages to get her to hate him and to be bored with Edward, the colonial commissioner whom he for a time foisted upon Cordelia as a suitor [I 372 f., E/O I 347 f.]. In this contradictory situation she becomes angry that Johannes treats her like a child [I 374, E/O I 349], but he gradually captivates her with his irony about the badness of people [I 382, E/O I

356], and he thus produces "the indescribable, enchanting anxiety, which makes her beauty interesting." Her situation is ambivalent, but not yet of an erotic character; she hates, fears, loves him. "Now, for the first time, I have produced this conflict in her soul," and his mockery "tempts her to assume a haughty independence from other people" [I 384 f., E/O I 359]. Ambiguity is introduced in this polemical differentiation from the environment, but is still erotically neutral. Only with the help of tiresome Edward is the erotic negatively intimated, as a consciousness of something she abhors and a presentiment of something she desires [I 384 f., E/O I 358]. At this point Johannes and Cordelia become engaged, but in the beginning only disdain and feelings of independence are stimulated by their confrontations with other, young, engaged, bourgeois couples at his uncle's house. Johannes arranged this "in order to ruin her taste for this love-smitten heavy-handedness" [I 403, E/O I 375].

With this the phase of individuation is brought to completion, and the erotic education begins. It must still be insisted upon that in principle Johannes is only the maieutic attendant, who helps the germ within Cordelia's being to develop and to bloom. "She moves within the melody of her own soul; I am only the occasion that she moves" [I 404, E/O I 376]. " . . . I will always admit that a young girl is a born teacher, from whom one can always learn, if nothing else, then how to deceive her" [I 411, E/O I 382-83].

Johannes makes himself the object of her desire, and encourages that desire by retreating. And at the same time that the desire is encouraged, anxiety and ambiguity are also developed. The erotic education takes place in two phases. The "first war with Cordelia," "the war of liberation," must awaken sensuality, while "the second conflict," "the war of conquest," must intensify anxiety and concentrate attention upon the object of desire. In the first war, he retreats and teaches her to conquer in pursuing him, while at the same time he acquaints her with the power of love, "its restless thoughts, its passion, what longing and hope and impatient expectations are" [I 408 f., E/O I 379 f.]. The plan is put into effect by the alternate use of fiery love letters and ironically cool conversations [I 410 f., E/O I 381 f.], for, in order to stimulate the ambivalence and to train fantasy, "her soul must be moved and agitated in all possible directions, not however in bits and in sudden gusts, but totally. She must discover the infinite, learn that it is that which is closest to a person" [I 416, E/O I 386]. At the same time, the exercises in indignation at the kissing engaged couples at the uncle's house are continued, and Johannes ascertains with satisfaction that she possesses wit and mockery [I 418, E/O I 388]. Her mental condition is characterized as "pantheistic daring"; her gaze is full of rash expectation, but she is still "dreaming and prayerful, not proud and commanding. She seeks the marvelous outside of herself" [I 426 f., E/O I 395], just like the dreaming youth in the religious discourse. She still lacks definite, goal-oriented effort. She is in the transition to the final phase, in "naive passion" [I 440, E/O I 406], but not as yet in possession of initiative. But the time has come when her fantasy has reached its highest point. "When she becomes familiar with this tumult, then I will add the erotic, then she is what I want and desire. Then my job, my task is finished. Then I will take in all my sails. I will sit by her side and will speed ahead under her sails. And truly, when this girl comes to be erotically intoxicated I will have enough to do to sit by the rudder in order to moderate the speed so that nothing happens prematurely or in an ugly fashion" [I 417, E/O I 387-88]. It is the war of conquest which begins, Cordelia's Don Giovanni phase, in which she is the one taking the initiative and pursuing Johannes, who now withdraw, shams distraction, stops writing letters, leaves her to herself [I 452, E/O I 416]. "Her passion then becomes distinct, energetic, conclusive, dialectical; her kiss total, her embrace complete" [I 441, E/O I 406]. Her first goal is to break off the engagement as an expression of disdain for things bourgeois; her next goal is the embrace. Her passion is no longer naive and unmoved, but even in this emotion she is beautiful, "not torn apart into moods, not dispersed into elements. She is always an Aphrodite arising, except that she does not rise up in naive loveliness or immaculate calm, but moved by the strong pulse of love, even while she is unity and equilibrium . . . . She must not be held too long upon this pinnacle, where only anxiety and unrest can keep her and prevent her from falling" [I 456, E/O I 419].

This is the stage immediately before the fall into sin, where unity is at the point of bursting, but has not yet burst. But the energy behind the passion is anxiety, because fear and love belong together, and behind love broods "the deep, anxiety-filled night, from which the flower of love springs forth. Thus does the *nymphaea alba* [white water lily] repose with her cup upon the surface of the water, while thought is filled with anxiety at plunging down into the deep darkness where it has its root" [I 455, E/O I 418-19]. Johannes' insight into anxiety is the secret in his seducer's art, Kierkegaard writes in a note in a draft of *The Concept of Anxiety,* where it very importantly says that "The Diary of a Seducer" can "serve as preparation to extremely serious, and not merely superficial, investigations" [Pap. V B 53, p. 26].

Thus Cordelia's anxiety is intensified in tempo with her sexual development. The Seducer wishes to enjoy her at this bursting point; here lies her aesthetic idea, the interesting, the tension-filled unity of oppositions. Her development up to this point is without real breaks, and even the breaking of the engagement is not a breakthrough, but the last intensification of tension within the unity. The aesthetic culmination on the night of seduction, with which the book concludes, is her fall into sin, where she finally becomes conscious of herself in her ambivalent lack of freedom. But the consciousness and the break lie beyond the Seducer's sphere of interest, which does not include women's tears and women's prayers [I 479, E/O I 439]. One hears of the crisis in Aesthete A's introduction to the diary, where some letters from Cordelia are cited; here she is conscious; she has gained the power of speech, and she uses it to formulate her love-hate. The ambivalence has finally broken forth into open conflict [I 323 ff., E/O I 304 ff.].

So much for Cordelia. I cannot leave her with the same carefree cynicism as her seducer, but will try to preserve her memory as I return to her masculine colleagues, Don Giovanni and Adam. The fact that they are masculine implies that they are less lovely and more highly determined by spirit, but otherwise it is the same development with which we are dealing.

4:4. *Don Giovanni and the Commendatore*

We have approached the empirical level with Cordelia, and yet the analysis showed that she is more an "idea" or a prototype than a distinct, concrete individual. This becomes even clearer when we deal with Don Giovanni, the principal figure in the essay on Mozart.

If Aesthete A's essay on Don Giovanni were published in our time, it would be easy to prove the author's great dependence upon psychoanalytic ideas. As this is not the case, I will mention the most important points of similarity, though not in such a way that any decisive emphasis is placed upon this comparison, because the whole question of the relation between Freud and Kierkegaard will be taken up in another and certainly more crucial connection.

One must not associate Kierkegaard's three erotic stages with Freud's three infantile phases (the oral, the anal, and the phallic), but rather perhaps from the sequence of the Page — Papageno — Don Giovanni to the sequence of infantile phase — latency period — puberty. Much more important, however, is the similarity with Freud's "topographical" subdivision of the personality into "the id," "the ego," and "the super-ego," which corresponds quite well to desire, reflection, and "spirit" in the Mozart essay. What happens when the Commendatore damns Don Giovanni (when the spirit excludes sensuality) is at some points not very different from what happens when the ego and the superego repress the libidinous id impulses — as we will see in the next chapter. Here I will first point to the similarity between desire and the id. Desire, it will be remembered, was not narrowly defined as sexual instinct (cf. the Page and Papageno), but neither is Freud's libido [cf. e.g. Freud XVIII 90-92].

The libido has its seat in "the id" or (to use Freud's earlier terminology) in the unconscious. At one point, Freud summarizes his theory on the special properties of the unconscious thusly: its nuclei are the representatives of instinct, that is, the wish-impulses; the unconscious knows no negation or doubt, but is characterized by its lack of oppositions; it is ruled by the pleasure principle and by primary process thinking, which give it its "mobility of cathexis" (cf. Don Giovanni and the 1003 girls!), and therefore it also has no knowledge of the concepts of time and reality, which, like negation and doubt, belong to secondary process thinking (the reality principle) and thus to the conscious, linguistic sphere ["The Unconscious," Freud XIV 187 f.]. Language is the boundary between "the id" and "the ego," for the unconscious can only become conscious with words [The Ego and the Id, Freud XIX 20-23]. "The ego represents what may be called reason and common sense, in contrast to the id, which contains the passions. All this falls into line with popular distinctions which we are all familiar with; at the same time, however, it is only to be regarded as holding good on the average or 'ideally' " [ibid., p. 25].

It can therefore be of interest that Aesthete A likewise refrains from remaining on the popular plane, but in fact includes in his essay all of Freud's detailed definitions of the special characteristics of the unconscious. As the incarnation of sensuous genius, as "power," "omnipotence," and "life" without "shrewd sobermindedness" [I 94 f., E/O I 99 f.], Don Giovanni can be characterized as a personification of "the id," at any rate in some sections of this multi-dimensional essay of which he is the hero. This similarity has already been made clear (above, Chapter II: 3: 2), and I will only make it a bit more precise here. The division between the worlds of language and non-language, the word and music, the concrete and the abstract, is everywhere in the essay. When the sensuous genius is characterized as "the most abstract idea which admits of being thought" [I 45, E/O I 55], abstract means poor, while concrete means rich [I 43, E/O I 52].[15] Language is "the most concrete of all media" [I 44, E/O I 53], that is, the most expressive and full of nuances; but this is precisely the reason why it cannot adequately express the idea of the sensuous, that which is uncompounded and massively wordless. This idea can only be reproduced in music, because music quite certainly (as opposed to architecture and sculpture) develops itself in time, but only "in an unreal sense. It cannot express the historical in time" [I 46, E/O I 55; cf. also Schopenhauer's theory of music as the adequate aesthetic medium for "the will," i.e., instinct]. Music is a non-linguistic realm which lies beyond and delimits the world of language on all sides [I 59 f., E/O I 67]. Don Giovanni is the first-born of this kingdom. Sensual desire has not "come to words" [I 46, E/O I 55], and Kierkegaard draws attention in this connection to the fact that Mozart's *Don Giovanni* is an *opera seria*, thus, without spoken lines [I 66, E/O I 74; nor will Kierkegaard grant lines to the Page in *Figaro*]. Don Giovanni's home is the mythical locality which the Middle Ages called *"Venus*-Berg. That is where sensuousness has its home; there it has its wild joys, for it is a kingdom, a state. In this kingdom language has no home, nor is there shrewdness of thought, nor the patient acquisitions of reflection; the only sounds are the elemental voices of the passions, the play of desires, the wild shouting of intoxication; there is nothing but pleasure, in an eternal tumult" [I 82, E/O I 88].

Don Giovanni's desire is therefore stereotyped and expressionless; its unrest "does not make it any richer; it is always the same. It does not develop itself, but storms forward uninterruptedly, as if in a single breath" [I 62, E/O I 70]. His love is absolutely faithless; "it loves not One, but All"; it is a monotonous repetition, and it is devoid of the doubt, unrest, and concern which characterize all mentally determined infatuations. It is "absolutely victorious," but this characteristic is its poverty. Don Giovanni's love is timeless and without nuances, it "exists in the moment; in the same moment everything is over, and the same thing repeats itself infinitely"; its object is "completely abstract femininity." Unable to differentiate or individualize, it loves not the person in the woman, but the sex, "the general quality which she has in common with every woman." And the music which is his medium is correspondingly "too abstract to express the differences" [I 87-90, E/O I 93-95]. Therefore, he is not so much seducer as deceiver. "To be a seducer always requires a certain reflection and consciousness, and as soon as these are present it is proper to speak of cunning and schemes and clever plans. Don Giovanni does not have this consciousness . . . . Therefore, he does indeed deceive, but not in such a way that he plans his deceptions in advance. It is the power of sensuality itself which deceives those who are seduced . . . . He lacks the time before, in which he lays his plans, and the time after, in which he becomes conscious of his actions, and thus he cannot be a seducer. A seducer ought therefore to possess a power which Don Giovanni does not possess, however well equipped he may otherwise be — the power of the word" [I 92, E/O I 97-98].

But it must be added that this detailed definition of the content of what Kierkegaard later called "man's lower nature" [XI 231, SD 225] is not especially characteristic of his psychological thinking, which generally moves in other and (in his opinion) more important channels. What is most characteristic for Kierkegaard in the Don Giovanni essay is not the description of the lower nature as such, but the analysis of the process whereby the individual wrests himself from his substantial lack of identity, and the definition of the relation of the lower nature to the rest of man.

A more detailed understanding of what is meant by the statement that Don Giovanni is negatively determined of and by spirit, will be given in the next chapter. It is sufficient here to point out that, according to Kierkegaard's interpretation, Mozart's opera does not exclusively deal with Don Giovanni as "the incarnation of the flesh" [I 80, E/O I 87], but also as the conflict between this principle and its antithesis. In the total view, the "definitive endeavor of the opera [is] . . . extremely moral" [I 111, E/O I 114], and even if the moral sphere naturally is not the Aesthete's affair, he does not completely ignore it in his interpretation. For the attentive listener, the overture to *Don Giovanni* is "the hidden workplace, in which the forces in the piece with which one has become familiar, more themselves with primal energy, where they wrestle with one another with all their strength" [I 123, E/O I 126]. In view of the fact that it is in this same essay that Kierkegaard puts forth his theory of the idea of representation, it does not seem unreasonable to understand this wrestling as an intrapsychic conflict between different authorities in *one* person. "The grand dialectic of life is here [that is, in the mythical figures of the Middle Ages] made continually apparent in representative individuals, who most often confront one another as opposed pairs. Life is always present only *sub una specie,* and the grand dialectical unity, which, in unity, possesses life *sub utraque specie,*[16] is not perceived. Therefore, the oppositions most often stand beyond one another in indifference" [I 80, E/O I 86; cf. above, Chapter I:2]. Don Giovanni's antithesis is the Commendatore, the only person in the opera who exists beyond his charmed circle, and who is therefore superior to Don Giovanni [I 107 f., 116, 120; E/O I 111 f., 120, 123]. "He can exercise no power over the Commendatore; he is consciousness [I 121, E/O I 124], while Don Giovanni is unconscious instinct. But these antitheses do not simply confront one another in indifference. The relationship between them is complementary as is clear from the musical analysis of the overture. The Commendatore's attributes are his "thunderous tone" and "his serious, solemn voice" [I 121, E/O I 123], and it is precisely thunder and seriousness which are the background without which Don Giovanni could not exist. Two forces battle for mastery in the overture, the dark and the light, seriousness and levity, and the latter breaks forth musically as the flash of lightning from a thunder cloud. "There is an anxiety in that gaze; it is as if anxiety were born in that profound darkness—thus is the life of *Don Giovanni*" [I 126, E/O I 128]. The anxiety and the sensual energy which it drives forward are a product of the conflict between the flesh and the spirit, which is also intimated in this rhythmic sound-picture of the sexual climax: "as lightning comes forth from the dark of the thunder cloud, so does he break forth from the depth of seriousness, faster than the speed of lightning, less stable than lightning, yet just as steady; hear how he plunges down into the multiplicity of life, hear how he dashes himself against its firm walls, hear these light, dancing violin tones, hear the signal of joy, hear the jubilation of desire, hear the festive happiness of enjoyment; hear his wild flight, rushing past himself, always faster, ever more unceasingly, hear the boundless desire of the passions, hear the sighing of love, hear the whispering of temptation, hear the seducer's whirlwind, hear the stillness of the moment—hear, hear, hear *Mozart's Don Giovanni*" [I 97, E/O I 102].

Just as the Commendatore is the background for Don Giovanni's power, so is he also that which delimits it. The Commendatore is no more an individual than is Don Giovanni, but a force. If one maintains the thesis that the two characters are the representatives of psychic forces, one could perhaps call the Commendatore the super-ego (it is a better word than conscience, which has another, less unambiguously moral meaning for Kierkegaard): "[H]e is spirit," and his voice is "transfigured to something more than a human voice; he no longer speaks, he judges" [I 120 f., E/O I 123-24]. The Aesthete only describes the conflict between them metaphorically in his analysis of the overture: "The struggle is not a struggle of words, but an elemental rage" [I 124, E/O I 126]. But the outcome of the conflict is given beforehand: the coming-to-consciousness. Don Giovanni is the first-born in the kingdom of sensuousness, but that this kingdom is also "the kingdom of sin has not yet been said, for it must be maintained in aesthetic indifference in the moment in which it has shown itself. Only when reflection enters does it show itself to be the kingdom of sin, but then Don Giovanni is killed, then the music is silent, then one sees only the despairing defiance which impotently protests but which can find no consistency, not even in the music" [I 82, E/O I 88-89].

Or, as it is written in Genesis 3: 7: "Then they both lifted up their eyes and they knew that they were naked. And they bound fig leaves and made themselves skirts"—while in their innocence they had not been ashamed of their nakedness (Genesis 2: 25).

4: 5. *Adam*

The themes touched upon above are summarized (though not simply in the form of a resumé) in the delineation of Adam in *The Concept of Anxiety,* which is built upon the biblical account of the fall into sin. It is a matter of an intrapsychic development, described in a conscious, provisional abstraction from the concrete circumstances of life. It is a case of a dual tendency, which is due to the fact that the individual finds himself in a magnetic field between the original unity and the instinct of individuation. It is, in other words, a case of anxiety, and in connection with anxiety it deals in addition with an inner conflict of psychic forces and tendencies within the individual. And it is a case of the development which, from a psychological point of view, makes possible the fall into sin.

Adam's development toward the fall into sin is described as a rising course with three phases (which should not be confused with the three "stages" in the Mozart essay; that which we will now investigate is Adam's development within the "third stage," Adam in the Don Giovanni phase, so to speak — which is thus described in three tempos): (a) "the pinnacle of innocence," (b) "ignorance concentrated," and (c) "innocence brought to its extremity" [IV 348 f., CD 40, 41]. Next comes the fall into sin, which psychology cannot explain, "but it can reach this far, and above all, it can point to it again and again in its observation of human life" [IV 350, CD 41]. Thus the sketch makes a claim of universal validity. For the time being it is sufficient to say that we apparently must not understand the fall into sin as meaning primarily a particular transgression, a particular immoral act. To the extent that this is the case, it is accidental; it does not cause the person to become guilty, but is the occasion by which the person discovers that he is guilty. I say "apparently," because it is precisely on this point that *The Concept of Anxiety* is a bit unclear; but this will be discussed later.

(a) The beginning-point is the picture of innocence and its anxiety, which was discussed above; the unity, the mental-physical synthesis, in which the spirit quite certainly is present, but "as something immediate, as something dreaming": the Page's melancholia, the child's anxiety, the latent inner contradiction in Cordelia, the vague searching of the youth in *Repetition.* This beginning position is presented structurally in *The Concept of Anxiety.* No description is given of the contents of the concepts of body, mind, and spirit, but what is studied are the relations between these three temporarily undescribed quantities. And, as will be sent later, the spirit is not a static, existing authority, but precisely a function, an expression of the relation between the two elements of the synthesis, not a third element on a par with them.

We remain with Adam for the present. When it is written that the spirit is only present as dreaming, this means that the relationship between the physical and the mental has not yet come into existence as a relationship: the two elements are identical. And what is delineated is the process in which this original synthetic structure is decomposed. A relation, a polarization, arises, but in the state of innocence this opposition is latent. The structure becomes unstable. The spirit is the relation. "To the extent that it is now present, it is in a way an enemy power, because it continually disturbs the relation between the mind and the body, which indeed has a continuing existence, and yet does not have a continuing existence, to the extent that it first receives this from the spirit. On the other hand, it is a friendly power, which indeed wishes exactly to constitute the relation." Thus the situation is characterized by the unclarified antithesis between two tendencies, unity and separation. To this formal dual-tendency corresponds psychology's "ambivalence": "What then is the person's relation to this ambiguous power, how does the spirit relate itself to itself and to its preconditions? It relates itself as anxiety. The spirit cannot do away with itself; nor can it conceive of itself so long as it has itself outside of itself; nor can the person sink down into vegetative existence, for it is exactly as spirit that he is defined; he cannot flee from the anxiety, because he loves it; he cannot really love it, because he flees from it." We will not inquire concretely here about content-definitions, and read the passage, for example, as a disguised description of the child's ambivalent feelings about his parents. This is not a matter of a concrete psychological description of feelings and experiences, but of the formal substratum upon which concrete feelings can arise. What is under discussion is not a particular condition in a particular individual, but an emotional potential in Adam, "man." Only the formal definitions of relations are decisive; the unity is in the process of becoming a duality. It is the condition of the possibility of experience and action which is described, not any particular emotional state. "Now innocence is upon its pinnacle. It is ignorance, not an animal brutality, but an ignorance which is determined by spirit, which is precisely anxiety, because its ignorance is about nothing. There is no knowledge of good and evil, etc., here, but the whole actuality of knowledge projects itself in anxiety as the enormous nothing of ignorance" [IV 348, CD 40]. It is sheer plastic indefiniteness; the lack of an object is exactly the sign of the absence of firm points of orientation in the unstable equilibrium between two poles.

(b) But as we have seen, it is not possible to remain standing on a "pinnacle." In the next phase of the development we are reminded that it is a psychological essay we are reading. A definition of content is introduced, but only in order to maintain the formal structure, or, rather, lack of structure. The structuring which is intimated merely emphasizes the absence of firm relations. It is an evolving consciousness which is depicted: "Innocence still exists, but only a word is needed and the innocence is concentrated. This word can naturally not be understood by innocence, but it is as though anxiety has taken its first prey: instead of nothing, it has gotten a mysterious word. Thus, when it says in Genesis that God said to Adam: 'only of the tree of knowledge of good and evil must you not eat,' it is of course obvious that Adam did not really understand these words, for how should he understand the difference between good and evil, when this differentiation indeed only came with the enjoyment [of the fruit] . . . . The prohibition causes him anxiety, because the prohibition awakens within him the possibility of freedom. What had gone past innocence as anxiety's nothing has now come into him himself, and is here another nothing, an anxiety-producing possibility of *being able*. He has no notion of what it is that he is able to do, and to interpret his situation otherwise is of course to presuppose — as most interpreters do — what comes later, the difference between good and evil, it is only the possibility of being able which is present as a higher form of ignorance, as a higher expression of anxiety, because, in a higher sense, it both does and does not exist; because in a higher sense he loves and flees from it" [IV 348 f., CD 40].

The definition of contents is the prohibition. But Kierkegaard scrupulously avoids telling what it is that is forbidden, and to this extent the presentation is still purely formal.[17] Anxiety gets an object with the prohibition; a determination of direction arises within the physical-mental unity, but it is a relation between things which are empty of content, which therefore simply means that the poles are moved farther away from one another and the potential is intensified, without there being any break in the unity. The prohibition is a point upon which attention can fix, but an indefinable point of fixation, which only exercises an attractive force, without splitting up the synthesis into its component parts. What is depicted is an intrapsychic conflict in its evolution. Thus, immediately after this, we find out that the entire dialogue between God and Adam dealt with in Genesis must here be understood as Adam's conversation with himself. In Genesis the prohibition and the punishment come from without, but Kierkegaard has them come from within. "Innocence can of course speak very well, to the extent that it possesses, in language, the expression for all spiritual things. To this extent, one need only assume that Adam has conversed with himself. The imperfection in the story, that someone else speaks to Adam about what he does not understand, then disappears. However, it does not follow from the fact that Adam was able to speak that he was able to understand what was spoken." Adam possesses language immediately, "in a fashion which, in its imperfection, resembles the way in which children learn to recognize animals from an ABC book" [IV 350, CD 42]. When Kierkegaard has to explain the meaning of the serpent which tempts Adam to disobey the prohibition, he also makes it into a symbol of something intrapsychic: "The myth lets what is internal take place externally" [IV 351, CD 42]; no meaning can be associated with it as a phenomenon in the external world, and Kierkegaard thinks that this interpretation is in agreement with the New Testament (James 1: 13 f.) teaching "that God tempts no one and is tempted by no one, but everyone is tempted by himself" [IV 352, CD 43].

Thus, when it is written that the prohibition, which before went right past innocence, now has "come into him himself," then it is tempting to understand it as the coming-into-being of a moral, censuring authority within Adam's psyche, a super-ego which is depicted. This version, however, is probably too narrow. It is true that Adam himself pronounces the prohibition, but this prohibition acts not only restrictively, but destructively in relation to the unambiguousness. The prohibition acts against its intentions, so to speak. Alternatives to the original unamibguousness arise. "The prohibition awakens the possibility of freedom in him . . . the anxiety-producing possibility of *being able.*" If one recalls the fragment from *Christian Discourses* which was cited in the introduction to this chapter, it further becomes clear that the prohibition awakens the possibility of disobedience and rebellion, "the possibility of being able to be presumptuous" [X 78, ChD 65], in which the individual is at an infinite distance from the mother and (what means the same thing in *this* connection) God. Thus, the distance is increased, the unity is further destructured, and the *telos* of the development is the total lack of relation and disorientation of the fall into sin — and, thereupon, the establishment of a new structure, that of faith or despair. But this will be discussed later.

(c) "After the words of prohibition come the words of judgment: then you shall surely die. What this means, to die, Adam naturally does not understand at all, but on the other hand, if one assumes that this was said to him, there is nothing to prevent him from having a notion of something frightful . . . . In this case, the fear only becomes anxiety, for Adam has not understood what has been said, and thus has only the ambiguousness of anxiety in this instance. The infinite possibility of being able, which the prohibition awakened, now draws closer when this possibility indicates a possibility as its consequence. Thus is innocence brought to its extremity.

It is in anxiety in relation to that which has been forbidden and in relation to the punishment. It is not guilty, and yet there is an anxiety, as though it were lost. Psychology can go no further . . . " [IV 349, CD 40-41].

The definition of content is made more precise, but again it is not the definite content which attracts the attention, but the effect the notion has upon the relationship. Anxiety does not become unambiguous fear of particular reprisals (castration, to think of Freud), but preserves its ambiguousness by means of the relation to an unknown possibility. And it does not lead to the repression of forbidden impulses, but to fascination for the forbidden and unknown possibility (the repression of that which is forbidden comes in the next chapter). A new determination of direction is introduced into the de-structured synthesis when a particular direction is forbidden. It must be presupposed that we are still dealing with an intrapsychic development, in spite of the expression: "if one assumes that this was said to him." It is Adam himself who "says" it to himself, without understanding what it means. A new structure is coming to be formed within him, a consciousness of time: "[T]his possibility indicates a possibility as its consequence."

Kierkegaard leads his Adam to this concentration point of the diffusion. If the reader objects that he is unable to recognize himself in this description, the answer must presumably be that that was not the intention. *The Concept of Anxiety* is not a novel, and Adam is not placed in a concrete context with a milieu. His development is not "realistic," but on the other hand, the delineation claims to demonstrate the unstable structure which constitutes the background for an understanding of every concrete development from original unity toward the crisis of restructuring.

This development is seen in purity as an ideal type in Adam and in the other forms which have been discussed up to this point. That this is an ideal type and not an attempt at realism is stated by Kierkegaard himself, for example, in a parenthetical passage in *The Sickness Unto Death,* which sums up the most important features of the delineation of immediacy which has been given here: "The immediate person (to the extent that immediacy can actually occur entirely without any reflection at all) is merely mentally determined; his self, and he himself, are a something within the compass of temporality and worldliness, in immediate coherence with 'the other' (τὸ ἕτερον [to heteron]) and having only an illusory appearance of containing something eternal. Thus the self coheres immediately with 'the other,' wishing, desiring, enjoying, etc., but passively; [18] even in desiring, this self is something dative, like the child's me.' Its dialectic is: the pleasant and the unpleasant; its concepts: good luck, bad luck, fate" [XI 184, SD 184]. When one adds to this the fact that *The Sickness Unto Death* also says that immediacy is anxiety [XI 157, SD 158] (the noun, not the adjective is used; immediacy is not "anxious," but "anxiety"), then one will understand that the ideas developed here are also presupposed in this book.

How this conception is modified and refined in and by the concrete context of a surrounding world will be shown in what follows.

Chapter III

THE INDIVIDUAL AND "THE RACE"

1. The Historical and Biological Concretion

Among the first rudiments of *The Concept of Anxiety* is a little group of journal entries from 1837, which sketch a "Theory of Presentiments" [Pap. II A 18, Hong 91]. Kierkegaard has not yet discovered the expression "anxiety," but is satisfied with using the adjective "anxiety-producing" with respect to presentiment. His plan is to "go about pointing out subjective susceptibility, not as something sickly and unhealthy, but as a normal part of the constitution" [Pap. II A 32, Hong 3551].

The word susceptibility is good, for the normal, anthropological anxiety I have discussed up to this point is precisely not so much a definite feeling as a potential for experience. This normal anxiety has been depicted in the previous chapter primarily as an intrapsychic phenomenon which arises when the individual differentiates himself from the original, substantial unity with himself and his surroundings, and discovers alternative possibilities. However, it is only by virtue of his formidable powers of abstraction that Kierkegaard is able to depict this development as purely intrapsychic. From a concrete, psychological point of view the interplay with the surrounding world cannot be ignored. Kierkegaard strongly emphasizes this by saying that "the essential thing in human existence [is] that man is an individual and as such is at once both himself and the whole race, such that the whole race participates in the individual and the individual in the whole race." The view which is here under criticism is that which would dissolve the race numerically "into a one times one" [IV 332, CD 26], the "Pelagianism which lets every individual play his little story in his private theatre, unconcerned about the race" [IV 338, CD 31]. "No individual is indifferent toward the history of the race, no more than the race is toward any individual's" [IV 333, CD 26]. The meaning is the same as when Judge William says that in the choice, one finds oneself "as this particular individual, with these capacities, these tendencies, these instincts, these passions, affected by these particular surroundings as this particular product of a particular environment" [II 271, E/O II 255].

Kierkegaard's psychology is thus not so "spiritual" that it ignores the concrete and the substantial. As he takes account of the fact that the individual is a product of the race, so also is he inclined to respect the fact that man is a biological being, that he has a body. In view of Kierkegaard's personal aversion to "this sweat-soaked, stuffy wrapping of porridge, which is the body and the body's tiredness" [Pap. VI A 103], it is not surprising that in his psychology he often prefers to choose the "internal" side of problems and to make light of the other aspects. But what is interesting, precisely against this background, is that in *The Concept of Anxiety* Kierkegaard does not merely describe the body as a wrapping, but as an integrated link in the total human organism. The physical and the mental constitute the basis of the human synthesis, to which the spirit relates itself, and "a disorganization of one part makes itself visible in the rest." The demonic, which is in itself a spiritually-determined state of conflict, therefore expresses itself not only spiritually, but "belongs to all spheres, to the somatic, the psychic, the pneumatic" [IV 430, CD 109]. What Kierkegaard is formulating here can without exaggeration be called the fundamental principle of the reasoning behind psychosomatic medicine, i.e., that a series of somatic illnesses have their origins in psychic conflicts, and must therefore not be looked at in isolation, but dynamically and holistically. Kierkegaard expresses himself in brief: "The body is the organ of the mind and thus, in turn, of the spirit. As soon as this servant relationship is ended, as soon as the body revolts, as soon as freedom conspires with the body against itself, then unfreedom is present as the demonic," and therefore, even though it is not a somatogenic condition, the power of the demonic can have both somatic and psychic consequences: "An overwrought sensibility, an overwrought irritability, nerves, hysteria, hypochondria, etc., are all nuances of this, or could be" [IV 446, CD 121-22].

The thought is noteworthy, but plays no further role in Kierkegaard's psychology. And yet, it is precisely corporeality which is essential for him. When he speaks of the body in *The Concept of Anxiety* he means first and foremost something defined by sexuality. The fact that, according to *The Concept of Anxiety,* sexuality can be called a conflict-causing factor, does not mean that the conflicts of which Kierkegaard is speaking in this connection can be called somatogenic, because they are not provoked by sexuality, but by the contradiction between sexuality and consciousness. Corporeality, then, is not the explanation of but an important occasion for the spiritual crisis. This is shown perhaps most clearly by the fact that sexuality is a problem first and foremost at the point where it is not yet fully developed, but is present only as an anxiety-producing possibility: in childhood and puberty. It is particularly in connection with "the state of innocence" and its relation to "the race" and "a particular environment" that Kierkegaard sets forth his psychological theory of the significance of sexuality. But in order to understand the development of innocence we must take hold of the whole of his understanding of the subject.

2. Sexuality

2:1. *The Exclusion of Sensuality*

In the broadest sense the historical environment with which Kierkegaard operates in his psychology is Christian culture. Normal, anthropological anxiety is the universal potential which can take on different forms in different individuals and cultures. In ancient Greek culture, which Kierkegaard conceives, so to speak, as world history's period of innocence,[1] a sense of security reigned, "but just this is the reason that there was also an anxiety, which admittedly the Greek did not notice, despite the fact that his plastic beauty trembled in it . . . . Therefore sensuality is not sinfulness, but an unexplained riddle, which causes anxiety; therefore naivete is accompanied by an inexplicable nothing, which is the nothing of anxiety" [IV 370 f., CD 58].

The situation is different within "the Christian difference" [IV 380, CD 66]. Here anxiety has a double significance. "With anxiety, sin came in, but sin, in turn, brought anxiety with it" [IV 358, CD 47]. A difference is being made between primary anxiety, which was discussed in the previous chapter of the present book, and secondary anxiety, which is conditioned by historical events. "Anxiety, then, means two things. The anxiety in which the individual, by a qualitative leap, posits sin; and the anxiety which has come in and comes in with sin, and also comes into the world quantitatively, each time an individual posits sin" [IV 359, CD 49].

In order to show the purely psychological significance of this, it is necessary to discuss Kierkegaard's view of the relationship between anxiety, sexuality, and Christianity. His thesis is, first, that "sensuality's situation corresponds to that of anxiety" [IV 370, CD 58]; second, that sensuality corresponds to Christianity; and consequently, third, that Christianity corresponds to anxiety. When one knows in addition that, from a psychological viewpoint, anxiety corresponds to sinfulness, one can conclude from this that sinfulness corresponds psychologically to Christianity.

The fact that "Christianity has brought sensuality into the world" is a claim which is put forth in the Don Giovanni essay in *Either/Or* [I 50, E/O I 59]. Christianity and its enmity to the flesh is here being viewed exclusively historically and psychologically. One hears nothing about whether or not this is true Christianity, or whether Christianity might possibly have something other to do than to bring sensuality into the world by excluding it. But Christianity has in fact had this effect: "This is something one will see when one considers that when one posits one thing, one also posits, indirectly, the thing which one excludes. In order that sensuality be negated at all, it must first come into view properly, it must be posited by the action which excludes it in positing the opposite. Sensuality was first posited as a principle, as a force, as a system in itself, by Christianity, and to this extent Christianity has brought sensuality into the world. If one wishes to understand correctly the statement that Christianity has brought sensuality into the world, it must be understood to be identical with its contrary, that it is Christianity which has chased sensuality out of the world, excluded sensuality from the world . . . . [B]ecause in order for the spirit, which is itself a principle, to exclude, there must be something which shows itself as a principle, even if it only shows itself *qua* principle at the instant it is excluded. The fact that sensuality has existed in the world before Christianity would naturally be an extremely foolish objection to what I am saying, because it of course follows of itself that that which is to be excluded is always prior to that which excludes it, even if, in another sense, it only comes into being at the moment it is excluded" [I 51, E/O I 59-60].

In Greekness sensuality was mental; it was "not antithesis, exclusion, but harmony and concord"; "it was . . . not an enemy, which must be subjugated, not a dangerous rebel, which must be held in check; it was liberated to life and joy in the beautiful individuality" [I 52, E/O I 60]. But intensification and demonization are the consequences of exclusion. Don Giovanni is the product of Christianity, and his desire is "absolutely healthy, victorious, tiumphant, irresistable, and demonic. One must therefore not overlook the fact that this is not a matter of desire in a single individual, but of desire as a principle, spiritually determined as that which the spirit excludes" [I 77, E/O I 83-84]. The word demonic does not automatically mean the same as in *The Concept of Anxiety*. That sensuality becomes demonic here means that it is repressed, dis-integrated, and that it therefore develops itself lawlessly and uncontrollably in secret. It is precisely in being excluded that sensuality gains a power which it could never have in Greekness, where the mental was "in concord with the sensual" [I 86, E/O I 92]. The aesthete dates this dis-integration at the close of the Middle Ages; I will not concern myself with this dating, but with the psychological process which is depicted in this historical costume. The chivalric eroticism of the early Middle Ages recalls that of the Greeks, and the conflict between flesh and spirit is still only latent here.

" . . . [K]nighthood is still only a relative antithesis to spirit, and only when the antithesis developed a deeper split, only then did *Don Giovanni* appear, as the sensual, who is opposed to the spirit unto death." This takes place in the later Middle Ages, "while the spirit more and more withdraws its shares from the joint stock company, in order to act on its own." Kierkegaard is evidently thinking of the monastic movement. "When the spirit, determined solely and alone as spirit, gives up this world, feeling not only that the world is not its home, but not even its theatre, and it withdraws itself to the higher regions, then it leaves the world behind as the arena for the power with which it has always lived in strife, and to which the spirit now yields its territory. Thus, when the spirit gives up its hold on the earth, then sensuality reveals itself in all its power; it has nothing against the change; it also sees the profit in being separated, and is happy that the Church does not manage to keep them together, but severs the bonds which bound them" [I 81 f., E/O I 87-88].

But the fact that the bonds have been severed does not mean that every relation has been negated. On the contrary, it means that it is now that the relationship first becomes problematic. Conflicts are not the business of the aesthete, and yet we have already seen that the enmity between flesh and spirit is represented in his essay by the oppositional relation between Don Giovanni and the Commendatore. Thus, not even Aesthete A succeeds in keeping these two forces separated from one another by the distance of indifference. In *The Concept of Anxiety* it is revealed that the conflict is permanent, and that spirit, alias "Christianity," continually brings sensuality into the world in its attempt to repress it out of the world.

2:2. *Integrated Sensuality*

It can certainly be objected that the conception which is summarized here is not Kierkegaard's own, but must be attributed to the pseudonym alone. This is apparently refuted even by the Ethicist in *Either/Or*. Aesthete A says that "when the spirit is posited, everything which is not spirit is excluded. But this exclusion is the definition of spirit" [I 57, E/O I 65]; on the other hand, Judge William maintains the principle of harmonic integration in his writings to the aesthete. The aesthetic, the ethical, and the religious are "the three great allies" in his view of life; none of them can be done without, because they reciprocally presuppose one another [II 160, E/O II 150]. He will not hear of any antithetical relationship between these three things. Aesthetic, immediate, erotic love is not annihilated by ethics and Christianity, but it is exactly by means of them that it takes on significance and duration, when it "is taken up into a higher concentricity" [II 52, E/O II 47]. To take a phrase from

Kierkegaard's master's thesis, one could say that the Judge's ideal is *"the spirituality* in which sensuality is an *included element,"* while his criticism is directed against *"the naked sensuality* in which spirit is a *negated element"* [XIII 392, CI 307]. The sensual must not be isolated, but must be integrated in the personality in continuity with life's other voices; it must be coordinated with the ethical and the religious. This harmony of course presupposes an ethical takeover of the aesthetic — a decision — but William stresses that not even the decision itself involves any break with the erotic, or any pain or anxiety [II 65, 99; E/O II 59, 91].

The difference between the views of the aesthete and the ethicist is that the aesthete is speaking psychologically and historically about the conflict which has in fact arisen between flesh and spirit, while the ethicist is saying that there need not and ought not be any such conflict. I have difficulty seeing that they really contradict one another on this particular point. Moreover, it cannot be denied that in these matters the ethicist is a good deal more superficial than his partner in the discussion. But the nucleus of his argument is the distinction he makes between sexuality and selfishness; they can coincide, but they do not have to: "It is true that the Christian God is spirit and Christianity is spirit, and that an enmity is posited between flesh and spirit, but the flesh is not the sensual, it is the selfish; in this sense even the spirit could become sensual; for example, if a person took his spiritual gifts in vain — then he would be fleshly" [II 55, E/O II 50].

With this excursus into *Either/Or* we have outlined the problem-complex of the relationship between sensuality and Christianity as it reveals itself in *The Concept of Anxiety*. Vigilius attempts to take note of both Aesthete A's and the Judge's points of view, the psychological and the ethical.

2:3. *Sin Makes Sexuality into Sin*

It is easy to see that the idea in Aesthete A's essay on the erotic is akin to, though not identical to, Freud's view. When sensuality is excluded by spirit, it is transformed into a demonic power. When the libido is repressed from consciousness it is converted into anxiety or anxiety-equivalent symptoms. The aesthete and Freud are apparently both in agreement and in disagreement. They are in pointing out exclusion, but disagree about its consequences, because according to the aesthete it is precisely the excluded sensuality which becomes a powerful, healthy, triumphant, even if therefore a demonic sexual instinct, while according to Freud the excluded sensuality disappears as manifest sexuality and reveals itself in the anxiety and the symptom. Where, according to the one view, sexuality is intensified by exclusion, according to the other it is stunted by repression. However, that view, too, is represented in Aesthete A, who wrote that exclusion not only results in an emancipation and an intensification of sexuality, but that it is exactly this intensification which is the precondition for its problematic position in the enmity between flesh and spirit. It is this side of the matter which is carefully studied by Vigilius in *The Concept of Anxiety*. The exclusion of the sensual does not merely mean that sexuality is stimulated, but it is just this stimulation which causes anxiety about sexual matters to be steadily intensified: "When the sensuality in propagation is increased, anxiety is also increased" [IV 370, CD 58]. But thereby both flesh and spirit are impoverished, and therefore it is Vigilius' business to counter "Christianity's" tendency to discriminate against sensuality and sexuality.

In no fewer than ten places in *The Concept of Anxiety* one can find the statement (or variants of the statement) that sensuality is not sinfulness. There is thus reason to assume that Kierkegaard wants to emphasize this. But in almost every place the claim is followed by a "but," and the question is then whether this reservation means that Kierkegaard denies his own statement at the same time that he makes it, or whether it means that he is commenting upon it without denying its validity. I believe that the latter is the case, and that the comments are to be understood primarily from the point of view we have seen put forth in the aesthete's essay in *Either/Or*, while this psychological view, in its turn, takes on ethical consequences. I understand the text such that the phenomenon which interests Kierkegaard psychologically is the process by which spirit excludes (ignores, represses, perhaps condemns) sexuality and *eo ipso* strengthens its significance and contributes to the dis-integration of the human synthesis. Sensuality, thus emancipated, has psychological influence upon the development of the individual. The individual *understands* it as sinful, and therefore it awakens anxiety; and when Kierkegaard maintains that sensuality is not sinfulness, it is in order to reduce this anxiety. The sensuality which he designates as sinful is that which is detached and isolated, and his efforts are therefore directed at paving the way for a new acceptance and integration of it. The means is not to surround sexual life with taboos, but to acknowledge its just claims. If, in spite of this, Kierkegaard refrains from starting an anti-Victorian campaign for liberation or from describing sexuality purely and simply as an unproblematic source of joy, it is in part because he sees such a view as psychologically unrealistic, and in part because he both regards anxiety about sexual matters as harmful, and also assigns to this critical attention to sexuality an important positive function in the development of the individual. *Quod erat demonstrandum.*

The passage in *The Concept of Anxiety* which most explicitly recalls the reasoning in the aesthete's essay — that the spirit withdraws its shares from the joint stock company, etc. — is the following: "In Christianity the religious has suspended the erotic, not simply due to an ethical misunderstanding of it as sinful, but as something which is indifferent, because there is no difference in spirit between man and woman. The erotic is not ironically neutralized here, but suspended, because it is Christianity's tendency to lead the spirit further. When, in being modest, the spirit becomes anxious and timid about clothing itself in generic differences, the individual suddenly jumps free, and instead of saturating his generic difference ethically, he seizes an explanation from the highest sphere of the spirit. This is one side of the monastic view, whether it is more precisely defined as ethical rigorism or as predominantly contemplation" [IV 376 f., CD 63-64].

Correctly understood, these lines contain an important part of the view we are discussing. It is made unambiguously clear that it is a misunderstanding to see the erotic as sinful. But apart from this, the quotation is not an ethical remark but an analytic psychological statement. That which is described is a process of repression or sublimation, in which the erotic is excluded as something indifferent. Some Kierkegaard interpreters have wanted to read these words as a normative expression of Kierkegaard's ethical views. This is an obvious misunderstanding. Kierkegaard is clearly in agreement with "Christianity" that sexuality ought to be something indifferent, i.e., that it ought not, in anxiety-laden abstinence, lay special claim to an individual's emotional life, but he does not think that this can be achieved by suspending it, but only by "penetrating it ethically." "People think that it is so easy to conquer sensuality," says Judge William in *Stages* with reference to the exceptional existence which wants to forsake ordinary life: "Yes, and so it is, when one does not excite it by wanting to annihilate it"; according to the Judge, from this point of view — that annihilated sensuality is unconquerable — one understands "psychologically correctly the catastrophe of Faust, who just by wanting to be sheer spirit, finally succumbs to the wild rebellion of sensuality" [VI 192 f., SLW 174-75].

That sensuality only becomes a power factor in its exclusion is not said quite as directly in *The Concept of Anxiety* as in *Either/Or,* but this is clearly the underlying thought. "After Christianity has come into the world and redemption has been posited, sensuality has been placed in an antithetical light, which was not present in heathendom, and which serves precisely to strengthen the principle that sensuality is sinfulness" [IV 380,

CD 66]. Thus Christianity furthers this ethical misunderstanding even though it does not directly give it formal confirmation.

That which determines the exclusion of the sensual is modesty. For Kierkegaard, modesty is not simply something "good," but something which has many meanings that can change from harmful to helpful, and thus it is first and foremost a psychological phenomenon which requires analysis. Modesty is one important side of the anxiety of innocence; here, especially the anxiety of puberty. It is a common anthropological phenomenon, present in and with the intrapsychic disposition of conflict and the need for individuation. "Therefore, modesty's anxiety can awaken of itself," but, just like anthropological anxiety, it can take on different forms in different situations. Modesty is a spontaneous defense instinct, a bashfulness for things of the libido. "There is an anxiety in modesty, because the spirit has been determined at the extremity of the difference of which the synthesis is composed, so that the spirit has not only been determined by the body, but by the body with a generic difference. . . . The real significance of modesty is that the spirit, as it were, cannot recognize itself as the extremity of the synthesis." "The sexual is the expression for this enormous contradiction (Widerspruch),[2] that the immortal spirit is defined as a sexual being. This contradiction expresses itself as a deep shame, which hides and dares not understand this," [IV 374 f., CD 61-62].

Modesty hides, and the more it hides, the more power is acquired by that which is hidden. In the Greeks, sensuality is not excluded by spirit and therefore is not sinful, but is "an unexplained puzzle, which causes anxiety" [IV 371, CD 58]. Thus, the sensual is not without psychological significance, but its form is other than in Judaeo-Christian culture, where the sexual has taken on power in being isolated as a special taboo area. The consequence of Adam's fall was "a double one, that sin came into the world, and that the sexual was posited, and the one must be inseparable from the other" from a psychological viewpoint. Kierkegaard maintains the ethical distinction between sensuality and sin. But psychologically and historically viewed, sensuality and the consciousness of sin accompany one another; the consciousness of sin concentrates attention upon the sexual and makes it into something sinful. "Were he [i.e., Adam] not a synthesis of mind and body, borne by spirit, the sexual never could have come in with sinfulness." "Sinfulness, then, is not sensuality, not at all, but without sin, no sexuality . . . " [IV 353, CD 44]. Psychologically speaking, the spirit is the principle of exclusion and delimination (modesty), which causes the individual to identify sensuality with sin. "With Adam's sin, sinfulness came into the world, as did sexuality, which came to mean

sinfulness to him. The sexual was posited" [IV 372, CD 60]. The thought is
the same as that in the Don Giovanni essay: by means of the spirit,
sensuality is posited as a principle and a power. Adam's sin caused "the
degradation of sensuality to mean sinfulness, and it will continue to be so
degraded as long as sin continues to come into the world" [IV 364, CD 52-
53]. The formulation remains for the present purely psychological. But
because sexuality *means* sinfulness for the individual, it has become an
isolated area, which in isolation emancipates itself and gains power. This
happens by means of moral discrimination: "By eating of the fruit of
knowledge came the difference between good and evil, but also the sexual
differentiation as an instinct" [IV 382, CD 68-69]. But, when the morally
conscious individual thus segregates sensuality into a special area which is
not saturated ethically, but is suspended, then, precisely by this
segregation and suspension, it *becomes* sinful, in Kierkegaard's opinion.
"We do not say that sensuality is sinfulness, but that sin makes it so" [IV
379, CD 66].

Sin, then, from a psychological point of view, is a product of morality,
or of the consciousness of sin. That sin is posited means that moral
distinctions arise, and, consequently, that sensuality is rejected as
unworthy and sinful. Thereby it becomes sinful.

From this view Kierkegaard draws an important and simple conclusion
for his psychological understanding of the immediate person (the child and
the youth) and for his views on the upbringing of children. We will come
back to this. But first I wish to illuminate a bit more closely Kierkegaard's
view of the sexual question.

2: 4. *"Love's Victory"*

"Christianity" has not reduced, but increased, sinfulness in the world.
Kierkegaard takes note of this perception. Instead of suspending and
perhaps condemning the sensual, he seeks to draw the entire problematic
forth into the light and to recognize sexuality as a legitimate reality. "The
whole question of the significance of the sexual, and its significance in the
individual spheres, has undeniably been poorly answered hitherto, and
above all it has been rarely answered in the proper tone. It is a cheap trick
to make jokes about it. To admonish is not difficult. Nor is it difficult to
preach about it such that one omits what is difficult. But to speak truly
humanly about it is an art" [IV 373, CD 60; . Kierkegaard himself
intimates that his own view is not simply identical with the view attributed
to "Christianity" in the book, when he discusses the latter: "[T]his view
which they call Christian or what you will" [IV 386, CD 72]. The intention
is to deprive sexuality of its compelling power and liberate the individual in

relation to it, that is, to make it into something indifferent, not into something which, against the individual's will, dominates the mind with anxiety, but into something to which the individual can freely relate himself. Kierkegaard regards it as unrealistic to ignore "this enormous contradiction" or to attempt to set up moral barriers. Kierkegaard's "determination of spirit"[3] does not mean conquest by exclusion or sublimation, but by bringing into consciousness and by integration. "Here, as everywhere, I must request that I be spared from all mistaken conclusions, as if, for example, the real problem were to abstract from — i.e., in the external sense to annihilate — the sexual. As long as the sexual has been posited as the extreme point of the synthesis, all abstraction from it does no good whatever. The task is naturally to gain it as a part of the determination of spirit. (Here lie all the moral problems of the erotic.) The realization of this is love's victory in a person, in which the spirit has conquered such that the sexual is forgotten and is only remembered in oblivion. When this has happened, then sensuality has been transfigured in spirit, and anxiety has been expelled" [IV 386, CD 71-72]. If one does not simply maintain that Kierkegaard puts forth two irreconcilable statements in this passage, then "the determination of spirit" and "love's victory" can only mean that the sexual has not been annihilated, but has been taken up and made into an expression of love, and therefore no longer exists as an excluded taboo area.

Sinfulness is not sensuality, but denied sensuality which, in denial, has become isolated [cf. Pap. V B 53, p. 122, Hong 3964; IV 389 note, 399 f.; CD 74-75 note, 82-83]. But the reason that sensuality is denied and isolated is modesty's anxiety, and for Kierkegaard this is an inescapable reality. Sexuality is bound up with anxiety. Kierkegaard's explanation seems to be that the feeling of identity is temporarily abolished in sexual union [IV 377, CD 62]. But the point is that even if this anxiety is present in the sexual, it does not mean that the sexual is to be condemned, even though sexual anxiety is the reason that it is seen this way. Where this confusion does not take place, sexual anxiety is converted into joy, "and therefore the poets are right in speaking of sweet anxiety" [IV 377 f., CD 64]. Conversely, the anxiety can also be converted into aggressiveness: "If the erotic is not pure, then anxiety is an anger, and if anxiety is not present at all, then the erotic is brutish" [Pap. V B 53, p. 121, the draft of *The Concept of Anxiety*].

2:5. *Sexuality and the Development of Consciousness*

In spite of his radical criticism of the attitude of "Christianity" and moralism toward the sexual, Kierkegaard does not deny the reality of modesty, nor does he begin a campaign for sexual liberation. Modesty is the most concrete expression of that which makes man into man and differentiates him from the animal, namely, the ability to relate himself to himself. Modesty is man's critical consciousness of himself as a sexual being, an expression of the consciousness of conflict which means that his development is no longer a pure, instinctual unfolding, but "history." Here, then, lies the most important function of sexuality. It is the occasion by which man becomes aware of himself, and this means the end of immediacy. "In the animal, sexual differentiation can be developed instinctually, but man[4] cannot have it thus, precisely because he is a synthesis. At the instant that spirit posits itself, it posits the synthesis, but in order to posit the synthesis, it must first saturate it in its differentiation, and the extremity of the sensual is precisely the sexual. Man can only reach this extreme at the instant that the spirit becomes actual. Before that time he is not an animal, but not really a man either. The instant that he becomes man, he does so only by becoming an animal as well. Sinfulness, then, is not sensuality, by no means, but without sin no sexuality, and without sexuality no history . . . . Only in the sexual is the synthesis first posited as a contradiction, but in addition, as every contradiction, it is also posited as a task, whose history begins in the same instant" [IV 353, CD 44]. Sexuality and modesty thus serve the development of consciousness which occurs when the original synthetic unity collapses into its component parts and a new synthesis must be established, that is, in the fall into sin, when man must be confronted with himself.

With this we are again led beyond innocence and forward to the crisis. Before we venture forth into it, however, we must still make a couple of tentative approaches.

2:6. *Sensuality and its Selfish Form*

The present work attempts to read Kierkegaard's testimony as a very carefully thought-out view. But it can also be interpreted as simply a contradiction-filled, self-contradictory expression of an unclarified private ambivalence. Sensuality is not sinfulness, but . . . ; it does not help to abstract from sensuality, but the problem is to forget it . . . Is this dialectical precision and nuance, or are these the symptoms of a fruitless struggle against his own prejudice by a puritan who is filled with anxiety about life? In any case, Kierkegaard's formulations have given rise to other interpretations than the one attempted here. The problem lies in the distinction he makes between sexuality and sensuality, thus between sensuality as such (natural, instinctive love) and its egoistic form. It has been claimed — as an objection against Kierkegaard — that his distinction is meaningless, an empty assertion whose only purpose is to prevent the idea from having ascetic consequences, but which must result in a life-denying asceticism, because the idea is never really carried through. Those who know a bit of Kierkegaard's journals from his last years cannot simply dismiss this objection. There is therefore reason to consider it more carefully.

The distinction is put forth again very clearly in one of Kierkegaard's later works, *Works of Love* from 1847. [5] In the old days, Kierkegaard writes here, people thought that Christianity had something against love, instinct, and sensuality; but it was an overwrought misunderstanding; Christianity does not excite sensuality by condemning it: ". . . it has no more taken offense from an instinct which man did not, of course, give himself, than it has wished to forbid men to eat and drink. By the sensual, the fleshly, Christianity understands the selfish. Nor is strife between spirit and flesh thinkable, unless there is a rebellious spirit on the side of the flesh with which the spirit is contending. In the same way, of course, strife between spirit and a stone, or spirit and a tree, is unthinkable. Thus self-love is the sensual. This is precisely the reason that Christianity is suspicious of love and friendship, because inclination in passion, or passionate inclination, is really another form of self-love" [IX 66 f., WL 65].

Thus the distinction is put forth, but what does it mean? Kierkegaard says two things: first, that the satisfaction of the sexual need is just as legitimate as all other satisfactions of fundamental needs, and second, that erotically determined love is suspect, not because it is instinctually determined, but because it is egoistic ("a rebellious spirit on the side of the flesh"). Does Kierkegaard contradict himself in saying this? In practice it is the essence of the erotic to assume a selfish form. In itself the instinct is ethically neutral, and when Kierkegaard expressly avoids casting suspicion upon it, his obvious intention is not to condemn eros, but to help make us conscious of the difference between narcissistic self-affirmation, mutual flattery, dependence, and the like, on the one hand, and love of one's neighbor on the other. [6] Both forms are rooted in the same "need" (which will be discussed later). "Christianity never wishes to make changes in external things; it wishes to abolish neither instinct nor inclination; it only wants to make the infinite transformation in what is internal." It is this viewpoint of wholeness, the idea of integration, which is crucial, here as elsewhere. The infinite transformation is to "change all love into a matter of conscience. It is therefore an incorrect view of Christianity to think that it is only a single form of love which, as an exception, Christianity wants to make a matter of conscience. One cannot under any circumstances make any single thing a matter of conscience; one must either make everything a matter of conscience, as Christianity does, or nothing at all . . . . [T]o limit the relationship of conscience to a single thing is to deny the relationship of conscience completely" [IX 162, WL 140].

If one wishes to speak of a development in Kierkegaard's conception of the sexual, it is misleading to characterize it as a development from relatively tolerant to a relatively strict point of view, which segregates the sensual and the sexual into an area reserved for particular condemnation. It is more accurate to say that a moralistic and casuistic conception, which still plays a certain role in *The Concept of Anxiety,* is abandoned more and more in the later authorship. In *The Concept of Anxiety,* detached and isolated sexuality is characterized as sinful; the moral, casuistic conception of sin here occupies Kierkegaard from a purely psychological point of view, because the rebellion against a given moral norm is of great psychological interest, and because it is precisely in that rebellion that the individual becomes conscious of himself. "The Carpocratian view of reaching perfection via sin is true on this point. It has its truth in the moment of decision, when the immediate spirit posits itself as spirit by means of spirit; on the other hand, it is blasphemy to think that this view should be realized in the concrete" [IV 411, CD 93]. In order to protect himself from this blasphemous consequence, and in general to combat the speculative evaporation of ethical distinctions, Kierkegaard operates with a sort of ethical norm, and views certain — not further specified — forms of sexual behavior as sinful.

On the other hand, in *The Sickness Unto Death*—the book most concerned with sin—Kierkegaard's interest in characterizing particular action as sinful falls to an absolute minimum. Sin is despair, and the antithesis of sin is not virtue, but faith. Traditional morality is not dissolved by this, but is understood in its relative validity. Kierkegaard does not ignore "murder, theft, fornication, and the like," but he does not wish to accentuate what is inessential by "beginning to describe the individual sins" [XI 218 f., SD 212-13; cf. below Chapter V: 7: 2 and 7: 3].

In the last years before his death Kierkegaard says quite a bit about sensuality, sexuality, et al., which can, and is calculated to, awaken offense. At some points his pronouncements are so sensationally offensive, that one should at leass avoid being deceived by special pleading. One is free to take a position; it is a matter open to discussion. It is impossible in this book to discuss "the late Kierkegaard." In his last years the ascetic tendency and the hostility to sexuality became apparent to the point of the grotesque and the obscene, and everyone, not only Kierkegaard himself, can see that this is a radical deviation from the view one finds in the "classical" authorship with which I am dealing in this book. But it is important to note that it is also a matter of a radically different *posing of the problem,* conditioned by the political, social, and ecclesiastical developments of the period. This is a chapter or a *book* by itself—but not the present book. It is then no longer a case—in the years after circa 1852—of the role of sexuality and love in the personal development of the single individual, but of the relationship between Christianity and bourgeoisified "Christendom," between the preaching of Jesus and the official institutions and the society which has exploited this for its own advantage. In this context, the negative remarks on sexuality play a sometimes striking, but nonetheless objectively subordinate role. What is important in this connection is that not even here is it sensuality "as such," but its selfish form which is the target: idyllic egoism, Biedermeier Denmark's self-certainty, the sacrosanct notion of *the home,* the clerical-erotic, Christian-familial miasma as the climate which fostered the most luxuriant growth of self-deception and hypocrisy, and the atmosphere of diluted bourgeois morality which guaranteed the growth of all these phenomena. Nor is the concept of sin atomistic or moralistic here. In the 1854 journal Kierkegaard writes that the sins which Christianity sees as the most frightful, "for example, cunning, ingenious evil, subtleness" are admired by the bourgeoisie, who, on the other hand, are offended at "what Christianity regards as the most forgivable," namely, "theft and everything related to security of property" plus—let it be noted—"the sins of the flesh." Kierkegaard continues: "And if one should root about in the consciences of the numberless throng, one's mood would be like that of a person who goes through old attics where all sorts of oods and ends are lying about, as in the trunk in *Love Without Stockings,*[7] so that in a certain sense one might say that when the conscience becomes the storehouse for this sort of stuff and nothing else, one might almost as well have no conscience at all . . . . [T]hey are like the person who possesses an instrument which is designed for one particular purpose, but who uses it for something quite different and does not really know what it is to be used for—so it is only in an unreal sense that he can be said to possess that instrument" [Pap. XI 2 A 6 f., Hong 4049 and 3362].

3. The Child and his Environment

3: 1. *"The Sins of the Fathers"*

One must understand Kierkegaard's deterministic view of the individual's immediate development upon the basis of the interpretation of the relationship between anxiety and sensuality which is discussed here. That it is immediate is another expression for the fact that it is determined by alien forces. The individual participates in the history of the race, and thereby in its anxiety. "Life proclaims loudly enough what Scripture teaches: that God visits the sins of the fathers upon the children unto the third and fourth generation. It is of no avail to wish to talk oneself out of this frightful statement with the explanation that it is Jewish doctrine. Christianity has never claimed to give every single individual the privilege of starting afresh in the external sense. Every individual begins in an historical nexus and the consequences of nature hold as much as ever. The difference consists only in the fact that Christianity teaches one to raise oneself above these surplus factors, and it judges, of the person who does not do this, that he will not do this" [IV 379, CD 65].

In *The Concept of Anxiety* Kierkegaard puts forth an odd theory about how anxiety is inherited from generation to generation. In conception and birth, that is, when the new individual comes into being and enters the world, anxiety culminates in the mother, and is thereby propagated and increased. "The procreated individual is more sensual than the original one" [IV 378, CD 65]. The notion is curious and seems like an alien element in Kierkegaard's thought, a bit of hereditary biological speculation, which readily calls to mind Freud's theory of the birth trauma, as profound as it is unverified. The background for Kierkegaard's theory, though, is not so much natural science as the Old Testament [Psalms 51: 7; cf. IV 343, CD 35], and when Kierkegaard recasts this inspiration into a sort of theory of heredity, it is probably the strongest expression of the role he ascribes to the growth of anxiety and original sin. We find ourselves on the speculative fringe where Kierkegaard and Freud reveal themselves as spiritually akin, who each in his own way attempts an explanation of a problem which, indeed, neither of them can fathom in the final analysis: that the sins of the fathers are visited upon the children, that anxiety is propagated. Their respective theories must be understood as rationalized expressions of their bewilderment. In practice these theories do not play a great role. The main thing for Kierkegaard is the functional point of view, that "the surplus of anxiety and sensuality which every later individual has in relation to Adam, can naturally be something greater or lesser in each particular individual" [IV 378, CD 65].

3: 2. *Anxiety About Sin Produces Sin*

The significance of this "surplus" is perhaps best understood with the help of a couple of entries from Kierkegaard's journals about the environmental effects which determine the development of the child. Childhood is the receptive age, in which impressions root themselves deeply in the unconscious layers of the personality: "The frightful situation is when an individual's consciousness has been subjected from childhood onward to a pressure which all the elasticity of the soul and all the energy of freedom cannot cast off. Sorrows in life can certainly oppress the consciousness, but if the sorrows first come at a more mature age, they do not have the time to assume this natural form; they remain an historical element, not something which extends beyond consciousness itself. He who is subject to such a pressure from childhood onward is like a child who has been removed from the womb with forceps, and who always has the memory of the mother's pain" [Pap. IV A 60, Hong 267]. The most notable expression of the idea is this entry from 1849: "It is frightful to see the recklessness and indifference and certainty with which children are brought up, because by the time he is ten years old, every person is essentially what he will become; and one will find that nearly everyone has an infirmity from their childhood, which they do not conquer even by their seventieth year, and also that all unhappy individuals are usually influenced by some incorrect childhood impression" [Pap. X 1 A 468, Hong 1171].

Kierkegaard's remarks in this area have a particularly practical, pedagogical intention. His interest is upbringing, with special regard to the role played by sexual matters. It is especially on this point that it becomes clear why he so strongly insists that sensuality is not sin. The reasoning is expressed in a short formula in *Works of Love*: "Scripture says that sin takes its opportunity in the command or in the prohibition. Precisely the fact that something is commanded or forbidden thus becomes the opportunity, not that the opportunity produced the sin, for opportunity never produces anything. The opportunity is like a middleman, a mediator, merely helpful in the transaction, only causing to be arranged something which, in another sense, already existed, namely as possibility. The command, the prohibition, tempt, just because they wish to compel evil; and now sin takes the opportunity, it *takes* it, because the prohibition *is* the opportunity" [IX 337 f., WL 276 cf. Romans 7: 8 ff.]. Or, in other words: "If one said to a child that it was a sin to break a leg, what anxiety he would live in, and probably break it more often, and he would regard even to be close to doing so as a sin . . . . As if a man who had been very debauched, in order to scare his son away from the same thing, came to regard the sexual instinct itself as a sin, and forgot that there was a difference between himself and the child, that the child was innocent, and therefore must necessarily misunderstand" [Pap. VI A 105, Hong 4009].

The prohibition is the opportunity, not the cause, Kierkegaard's determinism is not unambiguous; the prohibition does not always have to

combat the intention, but it will often do so. The result of the influence
cannot be predicted with certainty, because it is dependent upon the
individual reaction. Kierkegaard explains this in *The Concept of Anxiety,*
in a contemplation of "the power of example," where he gives an account
of "the psychological middle term, by which it comes about that the
example has an effect." The middle term is the child's subjective anxiety,
which causes him to react individually. It is not automatically assumed
that a corrupt environment corrupts the child, or that good society makes
a child good. Kierkegaard here speaks expressly of the Christian
environment, that is, of "an historical environment in which it can appear
that sensuality can signify sinfulness," whereby the anxiety of the innocent
individual is intensified. The child does not understand what sin really is,
but this is exactly why the prohibition tempts. "The possibility of freedom
proclaims itself in anxiety. A warning can cause an individual to succumb
in anxiety . . . and this in spite of the fact that the warning naturally was
calculated with the opposite in mind. . . . Speech and silence can produce
the opposite effect from that intended." The rigorous, puritanical
upbringing in which the individual "from his earliest awakening is
positioned and influenced such that sensuality becomes synonymous with
sin for him," will in all likelihood defeat its intention, not necessarily
because the child *wants* to be rebellious, but because the inner conflict
comes to a head "in the most painful form of collision," and the result can
thus be *"that the individual becomes guilty, not out of an anxiety of
becoming guilty, but of being regarded as guilty"* [IV 379-81, CD 66-67].
Shortly before this point, Kierkegaard has put forth the parallel theory
that the sensuality and anxiety which is hereditarily propagated can cause
it to happen that *"anxiety about sin produces sin"* [IV 379, CD 65]. What
we are dealing with here is an intensification of modesty's instinctual
defenses which is made clear earlier in the book, where the same conflict is
spoken of as "the phenomenon in which one seems to become guilty simply
out of anxiety for oneself" [IV 358, CD 48]. Thus it is a case of an
intrapsychic opposition between the individual's awakening moral
consciousness and the power of instinct, a confirmation of the theory that
modesty's anxiety can awaken of itself. But Kierkegaard's opinion is that
the development of this inner conflict is closely connected psychologically
to the attitude of the environment toward the realm of instinct.[8] Here,
then, as earlier, the idea is that sin is a product of guilt feelings. It is quite
consistent, however, that this does not lead Kierkegaard to combat the
consciousness of sin in every form and at all costs. The guilt feeling which
he here speaks of as the cause of sin, is not a genuine acknowledgement of
guilt, but an implanted emotion which is connected to the fact that "the

individual confuses himself with his historical knowledge of sinfulness, and in the blanch of anxiety he simply subsumes himself *qua* individual under the same category" [IV 381, CD 67]. Or, as it is also written with regard to this identification process: the emotion arises by means of "a misunderstood historical appropriation of the historic saying *de te fabula narratur,*[9] where the point of the saying, the originality of the individual is omitted . . . " [IV 379, CD 66].

3: 3. *Upbringing*

Kierkegaard drew the pedagogical consequences of these views as early as 1837, in one of the earliest drafts to *The Concept of Anxiety,* where he warns against having ill-timed suspicions of children, because it is precisely suspicion which can call forth the child's anxiety and thereby the action of which the child — innocently — was suspected [Pap. II A 18, Hong 91]. An echo of this journal entry can be heard in the confessional discourse from 1845, where Kierkegaard writes of the "godly debauchery" of the moralists. With his talk of sin the moralist awakens anxiety in innocent souls, and thereby adds a new sin to his own great catalogue of them, "for the ungodly imposition upon others of the dark passions is indeed also a new sin!" [V 227 f., TCS 34-35].

One should give children a reasonable sexual education instead of dirty stories, prohibitions, or secrecy, Kierkegaard maintains in the draft to *The Concept of Anxiety:* "[A]s many a young life was corrupted because a joke made it foolish and made jest of the sexual, and many a young life was corrupted because rigorism made it morose and made the sexual into sinfulness, so, too, were many young lives wasted because of complete silence. It is also certain that it is often a foolish prudishness which refrains from speaking about these things . . . . Psychology does not need to be embarrassed, and I obligate myself right now to sketch ten sorts of innate mental dispositions which will make it clear what enormous conflicts can be occasioned from such an order of things . . . . It is therefore high time that someone silenced the sort of immortality which wants to chatter naively about these things" [Pap. V B 53, p. 118].

However, puritanical prudishness and condemnations of sexuality are not the only causes by which the sins of the fathers are visited upon the children. Thrashings can have the same effect. "Most people lack the self-esteem to be able to assert themselves directly vis-a-vis others, so their self-esteem requires that they have some people who must obey them unconditionally, whom they have entirely in their power, so that they, too, can feel themselves to be rulers. These, then, are the children. God have mercy upon the cruelty and egoism which family life conceals in this respect, for it is, alas, only all too certain that it is more often the parents than the children who need an upbringing" [Pap. XI 2 A 176, Hong 2627]. This little analysis of the mechanism behind authoritarian upbringing is from 1854 (thus from Kierkegaard's "anti-life," "misanthropic" period), but the observation itself is much older. A similar point of view can be found in a long journal entry from 1837 about the raising of children, where he puts forth, among other things, the idea that one must develop the child's desire to question, and that the one who does the upbringing must himself learn from the child. The child must be motivated to appropriate that which is to be learned, and one must therefore not merely give the child "a purely atomistic knowledge, which does not enter into any deeper relationship to children and their existence, which *does not get appropriated* in a mental way and which is thereby deprived of any possible standard by which it could be measured" [Pap. II A 12, Hong 265].

It is in any event the relationship between parents and children which most interests him. The art of raising children consists in paying careful attention to the child, following its development attentively, though in such a way that the care shown allows the child to develop itself to the point where, spiritually speaking, it is capable of walking alone [IV 435, CD 112]. Attention gradually becomes focussed upon the psychological effects and the intention of child-rearing. If Kierkegaard's thoughts have significance, it is not because of positive solutions, for they become increasingly rare in his journals, but because of the clear-cut way in which he casts the entire problem. As time went by, his views became increasingly laden with dilemmas. The ideal method of upbringing does not exist. Every form of upbringing is suspect, so to speak, because it always implies a potential encroachment upon the child. The task, then, is to give the child the best possible chance to liberate himself from the deprivation of sovereignty over the self, which upbringing necessarily entails.

In the *Concluding Unscientific Postscript,* Kierkegaard poses a question about upbringing in and for Christianity. What is most striking is the criticism of the strict religious upbringing, which is characterized as the rape, compulsion, and spiritual mistreatment of the child, which normally results only in subjugation and anxiety—the intensified anxiety of either depression or exhilaration. The child cannot comprehend Christianity in the decisive sense, and one must therefore not force him to understand something which it is only possible for him to misunderstand. "The religiosity of childhood is the universal, abstract, and yet inwardly fantasy-laden fundament upon which all religiosity rests; becoming a Christian is a decision which belongs to a much later age" [VII 581 f., 589 ff.; CUP 523, 529 ff.].

But cannot the upbringing, then, provide the conditions of possibility for this decision? The child must have the possibility to relate himself freely to his background. The dilemma in all upbringing is that one cannot determine the child to be free. The only thing one can do is to give the child the possibility of freedom, the possibility to chose Christianity or non-Christianity himself. Kierkegaard discusses how this can take place in *On Authority and Revelation: The Book on Adler*. The point is that the "mild" bourgeois-Christian upbringing does not leave the child any possibility of choice either, because it understands itself unproblematically and harmoniously, as being without alternatives, Kierkegaard makes a novelistic sketch of a bourgeois family, harmonious, cultivated, well-off, for whom Christianity is an undoubted matter of course which follows throughout the whole of life like pageantry. The children in this family receive the best education, and while they "grow thusly in knowledge and insight, they unconsciously appropriate the cultivated essence of the parents." In Kierkegaard's opinion, the children are being subjected to a deception. Such a child "will probably never come to discover that he is deceived; he has been initiated into and formed by that in which his life is to remain." His life is unfree because it is without alternative possibilities. He is prevented from placing his background at a distance from himself.

As a contrast to this, a strictly religious form of upbringing is described, one in which the child at his most impressionable age receives a strong impression of his parents' deep, serious religiosity, which imprints itself upon the child's soul and modifies his character. This upbringing is problematic and filled with risk, and it does not automatically lead to the child's becoming Christian either. But, because the effect upon the child is obvious, marked, and controversial in relation to the norms of society, it gives the child an opportunity to distance himself from his own background: "[H]is life must lay before him such that he cannot avoid a catastrophe; he must come to a decision about whether he will become a Christian or whether he will really abandon Christianity."

That this latter is also a possibility, an alternative which Kierkegaard takes seriously, is emphasized by the fact that he places the strictly irreligious upbringing beside the strictly religious as a valid method of child-rearing: "*Either* he must be kept, from his early childhood and as long as he is in custody, distant from every relationship to Christianity, allowing him to grow up without any sort of Christian knowledge, so that he can receive a decisive impression of Christianity at a mature age and choose for himself; *or* the parents must take the responsibility from his earliest childhood to instill in him a decisive impression of Christianity by means of a strict Christian upbringing" [Pap. VII 2 B 235, p. 220-29, AR 179-88].

Kierkegaard does not give any unambiguous answer to the question of upbringing. The discussion continues in various places in the journals, with attacks upon both the strict Christian and the facile bourgeois-Christian methods without ever really fastening upon an answer. In many places it can appear as if the atheistic upbringing is the only one he can accept [see, e.g., Pap. VIII 1 A 663, Hong 1215; X 1 A 521; X 2 A 389, Hong 3035; X 2 A 454 f., Hong 1173; X 3 A 505 f., Hong 398].

What is decisive in this argument is that one cannot force the child into freedom or into Christianity. One can, by means of a manipulative upbringing, prevent the child from making himself independent in relation to the impressions of childhood. But one cannot determine him to be free. The motto to the handbook of child-rearing which Kierkegaard never managed to write could therefore be an entry in the journal from 1846, which reads in its entirety: "No compulsory school graduates one into Eternity" [Pap. VII 1 A 71, Hong 1250].

Chapter IV

THE ANTHROPOLOGICAL MODEL

1. From Child to Adult

With the fall into sin, the condition of existence to which Kierkegaard's psychology everywhere refers becomes manifest. In an edifying discourse he describes it as follows: "It was of the tree of knowledge of good and evil alone that man was not to eat, in order that knowledge would not come into the world, bringing grief with it: the pain of loss and the dubious happiness of possession, the frightfulness and the difficulty of separation, the unrest and the concern of thought, the distress and commitment of choice, the judgement and condemnation of the law, the possibility and the anxiety of perdition; the suffering and the expectation of death. If this had not happened, if the prohibition had not been disobeyed, then everything would have remained as it was, so very good . . . then heaven would not even have reflected itself in earthly life, so that no presentiment should arise from the depths of innocence; then no echo would have called forth longing out of its secret hiding place. . . . And there would have been no difference between good and evil, for this distinction was, of course, precisely the fruit of knowledge; and no one would have asked *where* everything came from; nor would the Lord's voice have wandered in the garden of Eden and asked for Adam, nor would Adam have hidden himself in the garden and in his own interior; but everything would have been manifest. . . . The gates of Eden were closed; everything was transformed; man became afraid of himself, afraid of the world around him. He worriedly asked what is the good, where is the perfect to be found, where does it have its source, if it exists. . . . What happened in the beginning of time repeats itself in every generation and in the individual. The effect of the fruit of knowledge is not to be stopped. With knowledge, doubt became more passionately internal, and knowledge, which should serve to guide a person, bound him in suffering and contradiction . . . " [IV 25-27, ED II 27-30].

This is the condition. That which happened at the beginning of time and which repeats itself in the generation and in the individual is that the person became man, that is, received consciousness. Without consciousness man would not have known loss or possession, would not have experienced separation as a difficulty, would not have known of thought and unrest, worry and choice, law and morality; and he would not have been able to forsee perdition and death or to be anxious about them, for he would not have known of time, because everything would have been the present. The consciousness of time and distance are the conditions for presentiment and longing, just as they are the conditions for moral distinctions and religious rumination, and also for the possibility that Adam could conceal himself in his own interior.

Adam was also anxious before the fall into sin, but he did not know his own anxiety and simply acted by virtue of it. But because that which has occupied us in the two previous chapters has been precisely approaches to consciousness, this can also aid in the understanding of what follows. It goes without saying that psychologically seen the fall into sin is not one sudden event, and the transition from innocence to consciousness which is under discussion must not be understood too heavy-handedly. But that which will be described in this and the following chapters is the psychology of the adult person.

"Childhood is the paradigmatic part of life, adulthood is its syntax" [Pap. II A 41, Hong 266]. It is clear from the presentation of immediacy and its stages that Kierkegaard *could* have written a psychology of a sort that would recall Freud's, a psychology that explains the adult's conflicts genetically, as a result of the child's. But the syntactic part of life is not a simple, mechanical reproduction of the paradigmatic portion, but a new structure, and despite his knowledge of the traumas of childhood and his assertion that every man is essentially what he will become by the time he is ten years old, Kierkegaard only occasionally uses a retrospective viewpoint, as a supplement to the functional analysis of the psychology of the adult. The determination is not unambiguous, because it can be reacted to differently, and these reactions are not automatically determined by the past, but, from a functional point of view, by the individual's current notions of his present and future. In this respect, Kierkegaard has been seconded by a good number of Freud's critical disciples. The clash between "orthodox" and "revisionist" psychoanalysts has concerned this point, among other things.

2. Anthropology and Psychology

2:1. *The Idea of Creation*

It is neither possible nor defensible to separate Kierkegaard's psychology, in the narrower sense, into a special area of his thought which admits of observation in isolation. On the contrary, his psychology is enmeshed in a more comprehensive anthropological pattern, which implies ethical, philosophical and theological questions. This larger pattern must accompany any attempt to reproduce the psychology. The psychology must be presented in its context. This is necessary and reasonable, not only out of a regard for Kierkegaard, but also out of a regard for the present-day psychologist who might be interested in concerning himself with him. In the past centuries psychology has done its best to emancipate itself from its philosophical and theological origins, in order to establish itself as an independent branch of knowledge, and the only place where these separated disciplines now appear together is probably in the catalogues of used book dealers. There is probably no one who will deny that this development has been gainful for psychology's status as a field. But that it has also been harmful and productive of illusions — because philosophical and ethical prejudices and consequences in psychology can never be eliminated, but at best ignored, and thereby render commonplace — is a discovery which quite a few psychologists are making today. A psychologist or psychoanalyst who abstains from philosophizing about the anthropological and ethical implications of his science very easily risks turning himself into a blind tool for the forces of "the times," which, unacknowledged, are just as omnipotent as the psychic forces he studies in his laboratory or consulting room.

The title of this chapter is "The Anthropological Model." The title of the next chapter is "The Conflict Model." The point is not to discuss two different models, but one and the same model, viewed from two different points of view, which to begin with may be called the ethical and the psychological viewpoints.

The fact that the conflict model and the anthropological model are one and the same makes it difficult to keep the two ways of viewing them separate. Fundamentally, it is an abstraction to do so, but because it is an abstraction which Kierkegaard carries out methodically and consciously, the attempt must also be made here. The model is the Kierkegaardian model of the personality, according to which man is a synthesis of unlike quantities. This synthesis-structure is a potential, and the possibilities it contains are, in brief, two: completion or despair. Completion is the ethical ideality; despair the psychological reality and the negation of contemplation. It is therefore that the distinction between the two points of view — the ethical and the psychological — is an abstraction, for, concretely understood, the ethical is never completed without an admixture of despair. In reality, the idea that the synthesis-structure contains the possibility of completion must be labelled as a theological postulate which cannot be verified empirically, but which nonetheless is of the greatest relevance for psychology. The postulate is that the synthesis-structure is created ("posited") by God, given to man as a good and perfect gift, and the perfection of the gift is precisely that it is not finished, but given for living use, according to the word of scripture: be ye therefore perfect. Teachers will know that it is better for a child to be given a lump of modelling clay which he can shape himself, than a marble statuette, with which he cannot really do anything. And the model which man has had given to him is capable of being modelled: it is unfinished and shapable. The matter can also be expressed by saying that the gift is a task or problem[1] which contains the possibility of its own solution.

This gift and this problem or task will be discussed in this chapter. The ethical task is the completion, the realization, of the possibilities which God has implanted in the synthesis. The synthesis is not, like modelling clay, an indifferent mass which can be shaped arbitrarily. It has its own inherent laws which must be respected. The possibility, which is contained in it, is to shape it in God's image — according to the words of scripture: be ye therefore perfect, even as I your Father in Heaven am perfect. God's perfection is his transparency, his total congruency with himself, his absolute spontaneity in love of man. Man's ethical task is thus transparency [cf. e.g., X 54 f., ChD 43 f.].

It is important to make it clear that in Kierkegaard the concept of "the ethical" is not as a rule used as the name for a set of principles for the regulation of mankind's mutual relationships, but as the name for the individual person's life task and problem. This linguistic usage stems from *Either/Or,* where an important point in the Judge's ethical view is precisely that one does not posit any unambiguous and normative doctrine of duty, but a requirement that one choose, that is, realize, oneself existentially: ". . . [W]hen a person fears transparency, then he always flees from the ethical, for this is really what the ethical wills" [II 274, E/O II 258].

It is also important to maintain that the idea of transparency is only the abstract formula for the notion of a concrete fullness. To be transparent is to develop the possibilities of one's credited life in accordance with the laws of one's being. The idea of God's individually-determined will of creation for every indivdiual person involves the idea that the standard of measure for the individual's ethical development does not lie outside the individual himself in a set of norms or ideals, but is implanted in the individual himself, in his possibility of becoming "the whole person."

Another expression for the idea of creation is the idea of equality. "Every person must fundamentally be assumed to posses that which is fundamental to being a person" [VII 345, CUP 318]. It is this idea which forms the basis for Kierkegaard's thesis of *unum noris, omnes*. The idea of equality is ethical, to the extent that it implies that every individual person has the same fundamental task: to fulfill his created destiny as an individual. There is no talk of an equality of content, but one of form, which is established in order to respect individual talents and to counter every tendency toward the standardization of psychic life. Every person has "the same essential thing as his task," but "everyone understands it a bit differently and in his own way," for there "are many ways which lead to one truth, and everyone walks his own. From this comes the individuality, when that which is essential becomes the property of the individual, and this individuality is conditioned and discovered thereby [i.e., by each individual's coming to the essential by his own path]" [V 230 f., TCS 37 f.]. But the idea of equality is also anthropological, for the task could not be set if it were not possible for man to realize it. "Every human life is founded religiously," is one formulation of this idea [IV 312, CD 94]. It is not an empirical definition, which says that all people are active practitioners of religion, but an anthropological definition, which says that every person becomes conscious of himself in concern for himself, because his existence takes place upon conditions of ambiguity, in time, in hope or fear. It is in this awareness, then, that the equality lies, and in it lies the possibility of realizing oneself. Kierkegaard here calls this possibility the religious. "If every person does not essentially participate in the absolute, then everything is over" [IV 423, CD 102].

2: 2 *Ethics, Christianity, Psychology*

I characterized this idea of creation as an abstraction. It contains the assertion that the synthesis-structure implies the possibility of total self-actualization. This assertion is of fundamental importance, but it is not empirically verifiable, because in actuality we only know the more or less abused synthesis, the more or less uncompleted life, the corrupted edition. That which is abused or uncompleted is the area of investigation for psychology. But to the extent that the boundaries of this area are drawn with the help of the standard of measure or the ethical idea of completion, psychology is thus in the final analysis based upon or dependent upon a non-empirical postulate. This is in itself completely normal and necessary. Without a concept of what is healthy, no psychologist or doctor could speak of sickness, because the two are categories of reflection. This problem is made conscious in Kierkegaard. Without a concept of the goal and definition of human life, it would be impossible to speak of a failure in relation to it. It is with this failure that psychology concerns itself.

Ethics wishes to make every person "into the true, into the whole person, the person κατ' ἐξοχὴν [kat exochen]"; [2] and "the more ideal the ethics, the better," it says in the introduction to *The Concept of Anxiety,* where this whole line of reasoning is summarized. Ethics is "an ideal science," which "wants to bring ideality into actuality." Kierkegaard here calls it "the first ethics" or "πρώτη φιλοσοφία [prote philosophia]." [3] Its essence is immanence, "or in Greek, recollection." The essence of the Kierkegaardian ethics is not recollection, but repetition; but repetition is the modern parallel to the Greeks' idea of recollection (this will be discussed later). And just as Greek ethics presupposes that "virtue is realizable," so does the Kierkegaardian ethics presuppose "that man possesses the preconditions."

In saying this, Kierkegaard makes it clear that ethics is an abstraction, and ideal fiction. That from which it abstracts is the actuality of sin. "Ethics hereby develops a contradiction, in that it makes the difficulty and the impossibility clear" — and doing this is its most genuine function. Even with its uncompromising ideality, ethics finally makes itself superfluous and impossible. "Now everything is lost for ethics, and ethics has helped to lose everything." Just as the law, according to Paul (but otherwise different from him, because the law for Paul is the prohibitive, Jewish norm), ethics is "a chastiser who, when he commands, only condemns and does not sustain with his command" (cf. Galatians 3: 24). Therefore, one is also unable to "write an ethics without having quite different categories up one's sleeve." These categories are the dogmatic categories. With the help of ethics, "sin reveals itself not as something which only accidentally belongs to an accidental individual, but . . . as a precondition which extends beyond the individual," that is, as original sin. Dogmatics "makes everything even more despairing, i.e., it abolishes the difficulty," which is to say that dogmatics is the doctrine of sin and of the forgiveness of sins (and not of anything else).

With dogmatics a second science begins, *"secunda philosophia,"* which, in contrast to that strictly speaking ideal science, begins in actuality. And here ethics again has a function. "The new ethics" presupposes original sin, "and its ideality does not consist in making ideal requirements, but in the penetrating consciousness of actuality, of sin's actuality, though, be it noted, not with metaphysical rashness or psychological concupiscence."

The added warning against "psychological concupiscence" expresses Kierkegaard's continuing reservations about psychology, which as a science can never have to do with sin, but only with its possibility. This drawing of boundaries does not prevent Kierkegaard from writing psychology, but, rather, is precisely what renders him capable of doing so.

But just as Paul's criticism of the attitude of the law did not prevent him from admonishing the Christians to put aside the deeds of darkness and walk in love, so does ethics serve Kierkegaard as something other than only a chastiser. In sin, that is, in man's wasting of his possibility for becoming the "true" and "whole" person, the ideality of ethics is put out of action, and the "new ethics" therefore begins with actuality and its untrue and riven person. This is where "the movement's difference" is to be found. But it does not imply that the new ethics loses sight of the true and whole person, because, on the contrary, in addition to requiring a penetrating awareness of the actuality of sin, the new ethics also "sets up ideality as a task and problem, though not in the downward movement from above, but upward, from below": "It begins with the actual in order to lift it up into ideality" [IV 320-26, CD 14-19].

The theological aspects of this line of reasoning cannot be ignored, not even in a presentation of Kierkegaard's psychology. To speak theologically without at the same time speaking of man's existential situation is to make theology into irrelevant metaphysics. But conversely, it is also impossible to speak psychologically without at the same time speaking theologically, because theology and psychology have a common topic. They concern themselves with man's betrayal of the ethical task and problem, the completion of existence.

The distinction between the two sorts of ethics which is put forward in *The Concept of Anxiety* is fundamental to Kierkegaard's authorship. In general, however, he reserves the expression "ethics" or "the ethical" for that which has here been called "the first ethics." Roughly and schematically, the distinction's scope can be suggested as follows:

Ethics	Christianity
edification	judgement/forgiveness of sins
religiousness A	religiousness B
subjectivity is truth	subjectivity is untruth
"Ideality in requiring ideally"	"Ideality in the penetrating awareness of actuality"
Either/Or II, Fear and Trembling, Repetition, edifying discourses	*Philosophical Fragments, The Concept of Anxiety, The Sickness Unto Death*

This diagram is of course quite banal, because it only outlines in a violently simplified fashion what Kierkegaard himself and a series of Kierkegaard researchers have tried to do with subtlety. I add two more columns:

Ethics	Psychology
transparency	obscurity
self-realization	despair
repetition	blocking
becoming	stagnation
simplicity	unambiguousness/double-mindedness
love	selfishness

Many more key terms could be added, but this is only for orientation about what will gradually be explained in more detail. The two columns under the heading *Ethics* are one extended column: ethics speaks edifyingly of self-realization, etc., it makes ideal requirements, and it presupposes that subjectivity is truth and is therefore capable of completing its task. The two columns *Christianity* and *Psychology* also complete one another, and both are determined by the opposition to ethics, because they both possess the penetrating awareness that man does not in fact realize the requirements of ethics. Christianity calls this failure sin; psychology calls it despair. Christianity (preaching, etc.) judges this failure and promises — as part of the judgement — the forgiveness of sins; psychology analyzes it. And psychology is in the service of dogmatics, i.e., in the service of the forgiveness of sins [IV 327, CD 21]. Both speak of the same thing, but each in its own tone. Psychology cannot bring about the forgiveness of sins or faith in it, but it can establish the understanding which can be requisite if a person is to associate any meaning with the proclaimed message of dogmatics, which commands man to believe in the forgiveness of his sins. But the relationship between the two columns, *Ethics* and *Christianity/Psychology* is not the simplistic situation in which the latter annuls the former as an abstract ideal fiction. The relationship is dialectical, because that for which the Christian message, supported by prior psychological understanding, is to prepare the way, is precisely the realization of the ethical.

The concept of ethics thus implies a conception of the personality. It is this which is here called "the anthropological model." It is claimed that the human synthesis contains the condition of possibility for authentic self-realization. But the *same* synthesis also contains the condition of possibility for despair, and from this perspective it is here called "the conflict model."

In this chapter I will aim at a *provisional* understanding of some of Kierkegaard's most important anthropological definitions, and upon the basis of this, discuss the possibilities of ethical realization which it is claimed that they imply. This is only to isolate some of the most relevant aspects, that is, the aspects which reveal that the anthropological model is also the conflict model. The possibility of sin is always hinted at, and it will be demonstrated in more detail in Chapter V. This is not an exhaustive presentation of the "ethical stage," "religiousness A," etc. The nature of the matter prevents any sharp and systematic separation of the two models or perspectives. In psychopathology textbooks the author often succeeds in arranging his presentation such that he deals first with pathology, then with therapy, first the sickness, then the method of cure. Very often the reason is that there is no comprehensible or obvious relationship between the method of cure and the peculiarity of the sickness. One knows only that the treatment diminishes the symptoms, but in many cases one does not know why, or whether the sickness itself is actually being treated at all. The textbook author can therefore arrange his presentation clearly, so that he first describes the symptoms and the course of the illness, and then the pills and the shock therapy. The situation is quite different when the sickness — here, despair — is a sickness of the spirit which must be healed by spirit. Then the discussion of the sickness is simultaneously a discussion of the cure, and vice versa. But this does not mean that there is not something special to be said about the way to the cure (see the final chapter).

3. The Self

3: 1. *Consciousness and Concern*

In the prelude to *The Sickness Unto Death* Kierkegaard puts forth his definition of the human self. The definition is fundamental, but it is also so compressed and abstract that it is necessary when we analyze it to take our point of departure in other Kierkegaardian texts which illuminate the idea in a bit more detail.

One of the texts in Kierkegaard which clearly anticipates the definition of the self in *The Sickness Unto Death* is a fragment from 1842-43, which gives an account of the concept of consciousness. We have seen that according to Kierkegaard's terminology the child is not conscious. The child lives in his experiences, adventures, and sense impressions, and it is just this extroversion which is the child's lack of consciousness. Perhaps, in order to avoid misunderstandings, we should recall that this is a sketch of the child's "typical" mode of being, and not a bit of empirical child psychology (cf. Chapter II). When Kierkegaard discusses childhood as "immediacy" or "innocence," these words can give the modern reader the impression of a much more naive understanding than the one which Kierkegaard in fact displays. The preceding chapters have shown that immediacy is far from being an uncomplicated condition. "Pure" immediacy in Kierkegaard is more a concept, an intellectual construction which is employed for analytic purposes, than the name of a factual condition in man.

Thus, when Kierkegaard says that the child is not conscious, it is clear from this that he uses the word consciousness in a special sense. In the philosophical fragment *Johannes Climacus or, de omnibus dubitandum est* from 1842-43, Kierkegaard has his pseudonym complain that philosophy talks of "sense consciousness, perceptive consciousness, understanding, etc., in spite of the fact that they might better be called sensing and experience, because consciousness is much more than this." Consciousness arises as doubt about the validity of that which is immediately experienced. Sensing and experiencing cannot in themselves give occasion for doubt, but only for the registration of data. "In immediacy, the most false and the most true are equally true; in immediacy, the most possible and the most impossible are equally actual. As long as this confusion continues without collision, consciousness does not really exist, and this enormous falsification does not cause any difficulties." But "it is exactly in the collision that consciousness arises, just as consciousness presupposes the collision" [Pap. IV B 1, p. 147-49].[4] In consciousness, the sensed and the experienced are put into relation with something else, and consciousness is the function which compares, it appears from the draft of this same fragment: "Thus, when I have seen an egg and now see something which resembles an egg, and refer what I now see to what I have seen, then I have seen ideally, because the fact that I have it in memory is a category of ideality; it no longer exists. Indeed, even if I place two objects next to one another, there is ideality in consciousness, because the ideality is the relationship I posit between them. Therefore, as soon as I bring a reality into relation with an ideality, I have doubt. The converse is also the same, when I bring an ideality into relation with a reality" [Pap. IV B 12].

This last example, however, is omitted from the final version of the fragment, most likely because it fails to reveal one important side of the concept of consciousness, namely, that the observer is personally and critically involved in the observed relationship. Consciousness is the relationship which arises when comparisons are made between dissimilar things, because what has been given in sensing and experience is no longer simply registered, but is made the object of criticism as to its validity and truth value for the person who experiences it. The possibility of doubting the validity of what is immediately present is given as a part of human speech, for "speech is ideality" and not identical with actuality. It is therefore in the coming-to-consciousness fostered by lanaguage that it becomes possible to ask about the truth value of what has been sensed.

Immediacy, i.e., the naive faith in the reality of what is sensed, can be abolished by means of mediacy, i.e., language. In itself, as a grammatic and phonetic system, language is also naive, and it can therefore be employed, as by the child, without bringing to consciousness the contradiction between language and the actuality which language designates. For the naive user of language, language is identical with actuality. "As long as this exchange takes place without mutual contact, consciousness exists only as possibility" [Pap. IV B 1, p. 147].[5] Language is the condition of possibility for coming-to-consciousness, but it is not in itself a sufficient condition to enable the question of the validity of immediate experience to arise (cf. above, Chapter II: 4:5, on Adam's relation to language: in it he possesses the expression for everything spiritual, and can pronounce the difference between good and evil, but "it does not follow from this that he can understand in a deeper sense what has been said" [IV 350, CD 41]). The development of consciousness also presupposes an opportunity, a collision: "How does the question of truth come forth? By means of untruth; because at the instant that I ask about truth, I have already asked about untruth. In the question about truth, consciousness is brought into relation with something else, and what makes this relation possible is untruth."

Thus in the Climacus fragment, Kierkegaard understands consciousness to mean the contradiction which has been made conscious between given things, or the act in which incongruent things are put in relation to one another, but in such a way that the questioner himself is involved in the question. The mere registration of contradiction is no more consciousness than immediacy is, but it is a condition for coming-to-consciousness. Climacus calls this reflection: "Reflection is *the possibility of a relationship;* consciousness is *the relationship whose first form is the contradiction.*" The categories of reflection are dichotomous, i.e., in reflection is registered the relation between the two given things. In consciousness a third thing is implicated, the registering person himself, who is subjectively engaged in the contradiction. "The categories of consciousness . . . are *trichotomous,* which language also proves; for when I say, I am conscious *myself* of *that sense-impression,* then I am making a triad. Consciousness is spirit. . . . This can also be expressed as follows: reflection is *disinterested.* Consciousness, on the other hand, is the relation, and thereby the Interest, which is expressed with full doubleness and pithy ambiguousness in the word *interesse.*[6] All knowledge is therefore disinterested (mathematical, aesthetic, metaphysical knowledge); it is only the precondition of doubt . . . for doubt is a higher form than all objective thinking, because it presupposes it, but it has a surplus, a third thing, which is interest or consciousness" [Pap. IV B 1, p. 146-48].[7]

The text from which these quotations are taken is, as has been noted, an early fragment, and one ought not to assume that this line of reasoning is preserved unchanged in Kierkegaard's later writings. In general his terminology fluctuates in a rather confusing fashion, but nonetheless there is both continuity and consistency in the line of his reasoning. In spite of the difference in terminology, the Climacus fragment can thus illuminate the meaning of the anthropological definition with which Anti-Climacus begins *The Sickness Unto Death.*

"Consciousness is spirit," it went in the fragment. Anti-Climacus continues: "Spirit is the self." Man is a dichotomous creature, "a relationship between two." The poles of the dichotomy may be given different sets of names: infinity-finitude, the eternal-the temporal, freedom-necessity. But these definitions are not decisive for the present. What is devisive is — and here the similarity with the Climacus fragment is clear — that *qua* a dichotomous synthesis, "man is not yet a self." That which constitutes man as a self is the trichotomous relationship.

In a relationship between two factors, the relationship itself is but a "negative unity," merely the expression of the fact that the poles of the dichotomy stand in a mutual relationship. This corresponds to what the Climacus fragment called the relationship of reflection. "If, on the other hand, the relationship relates itself to itself, then this relationship is the positive third factor, and this is the self." This trichotomous definition, then, is the point of departure for Anti-Climacus' deliberations. The self is not a pure and simple, substantial, existing thing, but is the *function* of referring what exists to itself: "The self is a relationship which relates itself to itself, or is *that* which is in the relationship which *is that* the relationship relates itself to itself. The self is not the relationship, but *that* the relationship relates itself to itself" [XI 143, SD 146].

This is clearly the same as that which was also characterized as "a third thing" in the Climacus fragment, namely, the *interest* (inter-esse, to be between). The self is interestedness in itself.

The terminology of the Climacus fragment is changed in Kierkegaard's later writings. The words "reflection" and "consciousness" gradually take on another meaning, and consciousness is no longer used as a synonym for interest. Nor does Kierkegaard use the word interest in the same sense later on. But the situation which is described by these words continues to occupy him. Thus one reads in one of the edifying discourses what when man deliberates upon himself, his relation to the world arises as something other and more than "a mere knowledge about this world and about himself as a part of it, for such a knowledge is no relationship, exactly because in this knowledge he is himself indifferent to the world, and this world is indifferent to his knowledge of it. Only at the moment that concern awakens in his soul about what the world means for him, and he for the world, what everything in him by virtue of which he belongs to the world, means to him, and he, in these things, means to the world, only then does the inward man announce himself in this *concern*" [III 334 f., ED I 100-01].

"Concern" is the edifying discourse's translation of the Climacus fragment's "interesse," and it is the name of the situation which Anti Climacus describes when he says that "the relationship relates itself to itself."[8] With these concepts one must not think primarily of an ethical requirement which Kierkegaard makes of the individual, to deliberate upon his own life. This requirement is indeed only possible because the individual in fact already relates himself to himself in a form of self-involvement. Therefore, the notion of a "pure" immediacy is also misleading. "All immediacy, in spite of its illusory security and peace, is anxiety." it says in *The Sickness Unto Death,* where one also finds a significant parenthesis which modifies the discussion of immediacy: "The immediate (to the extent, then, that immediacy can occur in actuality entirely without reflection) is only mentally determined . . ." [XI 157 and 184, SD 158 and 184].

Even the apparently immediate, "thoughtless" person is, strictly speaking, reflected in the sense of being self-concerned, of referring to himself. The adult is not purely and simply spontaneously extroverted, even when he seems to be. This is seen perhaps most clearly in a series of religious discourses with the common title "The Concerns of the Heathen" (from *Christian Discourses,* 1848). In these discourses Kierkegaard naturally avoids using the philosophical-psychological terminology. He does not speak of immediacy, and yet it is clearly this concept which is presupposed. However, immediacy is not attributed to man here at all, but to the animals. The lily of the field and the bird of the sky have none of the concerns which characterize human existence. They are never in doubt, because they function with a miraculous, instinctual certainty, or, in the words of the discourse, because they "always will what God wills and always do what God wills." When the bird "agrees with itself one morning when it awakens, saying 'today you must travel,' then it travels many, many hundreds of miles, and thus, yes it is curious, thus it was exactly this which God had willed that it should do. . . . [I]t knows no other way than the one along which it travels this time; it takes no note of the way for the sake of the next time, no note of the time for the sake of the next time; it considers nothing in advance and nothing afterwards" [X 76 f., ChD 64]. The bird — as the representative of non-human nature — is without consciousness of time and therefore without plans or reflections. It knows no alternatives to the concrete things which it is and does. It is, as Kierkegaard says also here, ignorant of itself.

With this the bird differentiates itself from man. When Kierkegaard writes of "The Concerns of the Heathen" in these discourses, he means man as man — not merely man in pre-Christian society, but also "the heathen who are found in Christendom" [X 23, ChD 16]. Man as "heathen," man as he "naturally" is, has the concerns which the bird does not have. He is knowing about himself, about his social status, and about time. In the original sense of the word, he is re-flected, self-mirroring, occupied with himself in whatever he does. He makes *comparisons* and mirrors himself comparatively in his surroundings, or he self-concernedly projects his own present and past out into anxiety's future in order thus to compare himself with himself. As characteristic examples of the "concerns" which are prompted by comparison, these religious discourses discuss the superfluous worries about financial matters and slavery to money, envy and ambitious rivalry, feelings of social inferiority and social pride, unbelief and superstition, anxiety about the future, irresolution which cripples one's ability to act, sloth or futile hyperactivity.

We will return later to these more concrete, psychological expressions of the function of comparison and of the fundamental self-concern ("interesse") to which they testify. What is decisive first of all is that man *qua* man thus relates himself to himself — even when he is not conscious of it, but is apparently turned outward toward the world. However, this fundamental human relation to oneself can assume many different forms. In *The Sickness Unto Death,* these forms are discussed as "the degrees of consciousness about the self." Later we will examine these forms which the fundamental relationship may empirically assume. The higher degrees of intensity of reflection are found in individuals who consciously and unceasingly occupy themselves intellectually or emotionally with their own problematic selves — such as various of Kierkegaard's pseudonymous novelistic heroes do. The lower forms are those in which the person concerns himself with himself, without making it clear to himself that he does so. The individual's attention is here turned completely in the direction of his surroundings — but this implies at the same time that attention is turned away from the fact that the self-concern of the self *is brought along* even in this outward movement toward the world. The individual does not discover this himself, for this form of self-concern does not express itself as articulated thought about the self, but expresses itself "immediately" in his actions and mode of existence.

But this form of "immediacy" is nonetheless an unreal immediacy, different from the unconcern of the animal. It is clear from another of Kierkegaard's edifying discourses[9] that the normal situation for man is *not* one in which he absolutely does not "know himself." What is normal, on the contrary, is that everyone learns to know himself, "discovers what abilities are entrusted to him," and understands to assert himself according to his merits — "and in this way what we call a person's self is also just like the value of money, and he who knows himself, knows to the last penny how much he is worth, and knows how to sell himself so that he gets his entire worth." He knows himself as an object of comparison for others; he values himself as an article of trade by applying the value norms of the social environment as a measure of his own worth, and in this way he relates himself to himself, concerned about who he is. And should he not know himself like this to a sufficient degree, the discourse continues, then his more experienced fellow men will teach him the wrongness of not utilizing his possibilities, "that he does not assert himself for what he actually is; that he does not know that people take one for what one presents oneself to be, that he has not known how to make himself significant, and thereby to give life significance for himself." This is, of course, not the requirement which Kierkegaard makes of man, but his criticism of the fashion in which the bourgeois form of life exploits and forms man's potential, which is his fundamental relationship to himself. This situation means that man in general "knew himself in relation to something else, but did not know himself in relation to himself" [V 102 f., ED IV 29-30].

The ethical requirement which Kierkegaard makes of man is that he must "know himself in relation to himself." When, for example, Kierkegaard discusses the heathen, in "The concerns of the Heathen," it is because he sets up another category vis-a-vis the heathen, namely, the Christian. "The Christian" differentiates himself from the bird and the lily with the same traits as "the heathen." They share the common human characteristic, namely, a knowledge of oneself, of time, and thereby of alternative possibilities. "The Christian," as man, is also re-flected in relation to himself. But he realizes the goal which "the heathen" does not know, because "the heathen" is riven in his concerns and his reflection. "The Christian" realizes the unconcern of the bird, the bird's "simplicity," but he does it upon the terms of consciousness.

This is the ethical-existential task and problem which Kierkegaard sets up as a goal for man, and which he thinks is the central message in his authorship: "[O]ne does not reflect oneself into Christianity, but one reflects oneself out of other things and becomes, more and more simply,

Christian" [XIII 529, PV 144]. This is the "Christian motion" which Kierkegaard, in *On My Activity as an Author,* thinks his authorship as a whole describes. But this motion presupposes that man begins in reflection. The word reflection has a slightly different meaning than in the Climacus fragment from 1842-43, which we took as our point of departure. In that work "reflection" stood for the disinterested, scientific registration of antitheses, while "consciousness" meant the subjectively interested comparison of incongruent things. In the sense in which the word reflection is later used, it means precisely the concerned comparison: the individual's comparison of himself with the world which surrounds him (his noticing of himself as different from others, thus, e.g., his noticing of his own social status, his own abilities and characteristics, and the like, compared with those of others), his comparative notions of himself in the present and past or future, and the self-concern which reveals itself in these comparisons.

Man's relation to himself is thus a fact—and only after that, and precisely because of that, is it also a task or problem. The task is not the nostalgic, sentimental attempt to hang on to the lost original state. "Innocence is not a perfection, which one should wish to have again, for as soon as one wishes for it, it is lost, and then there is a new guilt, that of wasting time with wishing" [IV 341, CD 34]. But the task is to make the loss and its implications conscious to oneself. Because man is man, he cannot simply realize the spontaneity of the bird and the lily. Because, with the concept of "the self," the concept of "the selfish" is also given [IV 384, CD 70]. That man is a self also involves the fact that he is self-concernedly egoistic. But man can become conscious of himself in this self-concern, and in this coming-to-consciousness he can give up the self-concern and "come to the simple." it will perhaps be useful to emphasize that this unconcern is not synonymous with indifference vis-a-vis the world and the environment. It is *self*-concern from which the "simple Christian" has died away, not love of one's neighbor. But this dying away and this simplicity are at the same time a concrete fulfillment of the true potential of the self, and this fulfillment is only possible by virtue of the consciousness about the self: "The more consciousness, the more self; the more consciousness, the more will; the more will, the more self. A person who has no will at all is no self, but the more will he has, the more self-consciousness he also has" [XI 160, SD 162].

And yet it is clear that the self cannot liberate itself from its self-concern merely by virtue of its relation to itself or by virtue of its autonomous consciousness of this. This would be a futile, circular movement, an attempt to pull oneself up by one's own bootstraps. It is therefore of decisive significance that Kierkegaard's anthropological model also has another dimension besides the self's selfish relation to itself. It is this other dimension which we will now examine.

3:2. *Dependence and Freedom*

Thus according to Anti-Climacus, the self is a relationship which relates itself to itself. But the anthropological model has yet another dimension. Man is God's creature, or, an Anti-Climacus' words, man's self is "derived" or "posited by an Other." The human self is not purely and simply an autonomous, self-contained and exclusively self referential identity (as it was understood by part of German idealistic philosophy, especially by Fichte). Its relation to itself is only possible by virtue of its relation to something which is different from itself. The most definitive, compact definition of the self in Kierkegaard is thus this: "Such a derived, posited relationship is man's self, a relationship which relates itself to itself, and, in relating itself to itself, relates itself to an Other."

This definition has many important consequences. We will gradually become acquainted with them, and will see that it is an error to understand Kierkegaard's "self" as a solipsistic abstraction. The consequence of this definition to which Kierkegaard immediately draws attention in *The Sickness Unto Death* is that the self, thus understood, is dependent upon something other than itself. "This formula is namely the expression for the whole of the relationship's (the self's) dependence, the expression of the fact that the self cannot of itself come to or be in equilibrium and rest, but can do so only when, *in* relating itself to itself, it relates itself to that which has posited the entire relationship" [XI 144, SD 147].

For Kierkegaard, the notion of human autonomy is just as unreasonable an illusion as the notion of a free will in the indeterministic sense. To be a self is not only to relate oneself to oneself, but also to relate oneself to "that which has posited the entire relationship," that is, God or the Eternal. The relationship to oneself and the relationship to the eternal are two sides of the same relationship.[10] Man always relates himself to God, and man's existence is always determined by this relationship, regardless of whether man acknowledges this relationship or not. This—superficially viewed, very curious—assertion about the unavoidability of the relation to God is the theological expression for a view which has important psychological consequences. The meaning is that man does not become free in an illusory attempt to emancipate himself from every relationship of dependence, but by acknowledging to himself his real dependence, that is his createdness by God, and, thereby, his relationship to the authority which liberates him. "Dependence upon God is the only independence" [VIII 316, GS 197]. The clearest presentation of the idea is perhaps in a journal entry from 1846: "That which is absolutely the greatest thing which can be done for a being, greater than anything one could make it into, is to make it free. It is exactly here that omnipotence is required. This seems odd, as it is precisely omnipotence which has the capacity of making dependent. But if one will think about omnipotence, one will see that it is precisely in this concept that there must also lie the definition of being able to retreat into oneself again in an expression of omnipotence, in such a way as to allow that which omnipotence leaves behind to be independent. Therefore it is the case that one person cannot make another completely free, because he who has power is himself entrapped by it, and therefore always comes into an incorrect relation to the person whom he wants to liberate. In addition to this is the fact that all finite power (talentedness, etc.) contains a finite self-love. Only omnipotence can take itself back while it gives away, and this relationship is, of course, exactly the independence of the recipient. God's omnipotence is therefore his goodness. For it is goodness to give away entirely, but in such a way that, by omnipotently taking oneself back again, one makes the recipient independent. . . . It is only the wretched and worldly notion of the dialectic of power which believes that it is greater and greater in proportion to the degree to which it can compel and create dependence. No, this was better understood by Socrates, that the art of power is exactly to make free. But this never admits of achievement in the relationship between man and man; even though it always needs to be emphasized again and again that this is the highest thing, only omnipotence is truly capable of it. Therefore if man has the least bit of independent, prior existence vis-a-vis God (in the material sense), then God could not make him free. Creation out of nothing is again omnipotence's expression for the capability of making independent. He to whom I absolutely owe everything, he has indeed made me independent. He to whom I absolutely owe everyting, while he, however, equally absolutely has retained everything, he has indeed made me independent. If, in order to create man, God himself lost a bit of his power, he would be unable to make man independent" [Pap. VII 1 A 181, Hong 1251].

God is thus the sovereign giver, the agape-God who gives life and creates man in his image. At the same time, he is the maieutic practitioner who does what Socrates himself could not: gives man freedom. Both aspects enter into Kierkegaard's idea of creation, and thereby into his idea of what man has been determined to be. The determination is to fulfill God's will as creator: to become oneself, or, what is the same thing, to become free. But freedom presupposes that one acknowledges one's dependence. If one does not become free in relation to the Almighty, one makes oneself unfree in relation to other powers which one does not know.

This is a basic idea or a basic formula in Kierkegaard's psychology, but the ethical-anthropological line of reasoning corresponds to the psychological analysis. As a part of the ethicist's choosing of himself (according to Judge William's account) he also chooses God or his own God-createdness: "I choose the Absolute, which chooses me; I posit the Absolute, which posits me" [II 230, E/O II 217]. The same theme is found in a number of Kierkegaard's edifying discourses on the bird and the lily. A discourse from 1849 on "Obedience" can be taken as an example. Obedience is a synonym for freedom in an acknowledged dependence, or, as Kierkegaard also calls it here, in necessity. The discourse begins by setting forth an idea, with whose psychological significance we will later become acquainted, the idea that man not only can and ought to choose, but that he in fact always does choose, regardless of whether he knows it or not: not to choose God is to choose the world and disdain God. But one can learn obedience from the bird and the lily, who always and unconditionally do God's will, i.e., are always in agreement with their own being, developing themselves according to the way in which they have been determined, surely and simply, untroubled by the concerns which cause man to ask about the meaning of the development: " 'Whence?' he would ask, or 'why?' he would say, or 'what good can it do?' he would say, and so he did not develop the whole of his possibility, but got his just desserts when, crippled and ugly, he perished before the moment." But the bird and the lily are the teachers. Kierkegaard lets the reader object that they, of course, merely make a virtue of necessity, for, because of the way in which they were created, they cannot be otherwise than obedient, in contrast to man, who possesses the possibility of rebellion, deviation from the self, the alternative. Here, then, lies the problem, the determination, which is to *become* what the bird and the lily *are* — oneself, or to come into agreement with one's own created being: "You, too, are subject to necessity, of course; God's will is done anyway, of course, so strive to make a virtue of necessity by doing God's will with unconditional obedience" [XI 39 f., ChD 340-41].

Freedom, then, is not insight into necessity, as in Hegel, but the choice of necessity, the individual's passionate acceptance of his own received life. But this acceptance stipulates the completion, obedience in relation to the task, which is to become oneself.

3:3 *Development*

What does it mean to be oneself? According to the edifying discourse, it must involve, among other things, that one develops one's created possibilities, just as the obedient lily "bursts forth in all its loveliness" [XI

37, ChD 339]. Kierkegaard was not much interested in botany, and therefore the metaphor is not carried through, but the idea of the organic and comprehensive, harmonically beautiful personality development, which is a part of the philosophy of life of Goethean humanism, is also essential for Kierkegaard, not only when he lets Judge William recite his teaching about "the equilibrium between the aesthetic and the ethical in the composition of the personality" [II 277, cf. 148-50; E/O II 260-61, cf. 139-40], or when Vigilius Haufniensis lets "the significance of life" be the transformation of existence into "a beautiful, artistically composed whole" [Pap. V B 53, p. 120, the draft to *The Concept of Anxiety*], but also when Anti-Climacus defines the self as the unity of antitheses, "the synthesis in which the finite is the delimiting, the infinite the expanding." Seen thusly, despair becomes synonymous with one-sidedness, a lack of balance between the possibilities of the self, psychic disintegration. Kierkegaard's view in these areas is not the expression of some rigorous either/or, but of an inclusive and dialectical both/and. Just as "finitude's despair is to lack infinity," so is "infinity's despair . . . to lack finitude." Where finitude's one-sidedness is narrowness and prudishness, infinity's one-sidedness is boundless fantasy. The person in finite despair is unoriginal, glib and conventional in his life style, "as worn down as a rolling stone, as current as a coin in circulation," filled with anxiety about daring off the well-marked paths of the acceptable, which might make him become aware of himself, while the person in infinite despair is lost in abstract, sentimental emotionalism, in irrelevant perceptions of things far from reality, and in fantastic and non-committal plans — "Thus the will does not continually become concrete and abstract to the same degree, so that, the more it is infinitized in intention and resolution, the more and more present and contemporaneous it becomes to itself in that little bit of the task which can be done right away, now. . . . " Kierkegaard's idea does not repose at one or another moderate location midway between the extremes, but is found in the integration of the extremes into a harmonic function of the whole. To one-sided infinity corresponds "the despair of possibility," which runs wild in phantasmagoria and mirages, in sanguine expectations or in depressive notions of anxiety, while the opposite one-sidedness, "the despair of necessity" is stuck fast in triviality or in fatalistic hopelessness, and is strangled by spiritual suffocation. But "the personality is a synthesis of possibility and necessity. Its existence is therefore like breathing (respiration); there is a breathing-in and a breathing-out" [XI 161-74, SD 162-75].

The criticism of psychic one-sidedness and the idea of the organic harmony of the abilities and functions of the personality is also expressed in the definition of the self as the synthesis of body, mind, and spirit. Spirit is the making conscious of antitheses, but in the mature personality, the word is synonymous with the integrated function of the self, the organizing, not the sublimating, principle. The view is summarized in *Works of Love* as follows: that "Man, even though he is spirit from the moment of birth, only later becomes conscious of himself as spirit, and thus has lived out a portion of his life in a sensuous-intellectual way prior to this. But this first portion must not then be cast away when the spirit awakens, any more than the awakening of the spirit proclaims itself in a sensuous or a sensuous-intellectual way in opposition to the sensuous or the sensuous-intellectual" [IX 239, WL 199].

In the *Postscript,* Johannes Climacus puts forth this point of view with polemical reference to the psychology inspired by Hegel, which immediately suggests a one-sided spiritualism when, in its scientific description, it ascends "from the lower to the higher" by setting up the step sequence "soul, consciousness, spirit" and by declaring the spirit, i.e., the intellect, as the highest step. "Scientifically . . . it can be quite correct, abstractly and dialectically, in accordance with the determination of psychology, to ascend from the psychic-somatic, to the psychic, to the pneumatic," but this order of rank must not be made ethically normative, for "ethically understood, it is every individual's task to become a whole person." Kierkegaard rejects the notion of the supremacy of thought, and asserts the harmony of thought, fantasy, and feeling. Under all circumstances, one-sidedness is an erroneous development, and it is just as sad when a person loses his fantasy and feeling as when he loses his understanding. Disintegration will revenge itself: "Thought disregards fantasy, then fantasy disregards thought in return, and the same with feeling." The idea is the harmonious interplay of all three functions: "[T]o unite life's elements in contemporaneity, that is precisely the task." In connection with this, Climacus carries on an energetic defense of poetry, and the conclusion runs: "The true is not higher than the good and the beautiful, but the true and the good and the beautiful belong essentially to every human existence, and are united for an existing individual not in thinking this, but in existing" [VII 333-38, CUP 307-12].

Kierkegaard's reasoning is not particularly original here. The triad of feeling-fantasy-thought is well-known in the German and Danish philosophy of the period, and the idea of the harmonic relation among the good, the true, and the beautiful is almost a cliché in Danish and German, Goethe-inspired, post-romantic intellectual life. Criticism of the one-sided intellectualism of Hegelian speculation was also carried on by others. Kierkegaard, then, is thus solidly anchored in one of the most positive traditions of his time, the personality philosophy of cultivated humanism. It is an important side of his thought which is all too easily overlooked when he is labelled as "the father of modern existentialism." Kierkegaard holds the idea — or the ideology, if you will — of the fully developed, *whole* personality in common with the bourgeois life-view of his times.

What separates him from this tradition is that he spends very little time celebrating its beautiful, harmonic ideal, but invests his analytic energy in the question of why this ideal is never realized.

3: 4 *Becoming*

This balanced view is not Kierkegaard's most important point of view, or in any event it is not his only one. He gives passion a higher priority than well-roundedness. It is well if passion and well-roundedness can be united, but harmony without passionate energy is simply a laxity which "dabbles in everything." The section of the *Postscript* which deals with harmonic integration therefore ends with a defense of passionate one-sidedness as being in "second place" [VII 338 f., CUP 312 f.].

Passion is something Kierkegaard "requires" of man. But it is important to note that he only requires it because it is already there. Human existence *is* passion, because it is existence in uncertainty and contradiction, or to use an expression which says the same thing: it is existence in becoming, in time, not in eternity. The requirement is therefore not a requirement to make oneself passionate — that would only be affectation. But it is a requirement to live the passion, because it is an essential part of existence. One cannot make oneself passionate — but one can forget passion, for example, by means of all too much evasive chatter about well-rounded harmony.

Well-rounded harmony is a straightforward and positive ideal. In Kierkegaard it is an ideal for which "the ethicist" Judge William in particular stands up. William is rescued in the snug harbor of marriage, and does not seem to be in doubt at any time that it is God the Creator's individually-determined will for him that he should be and continue to be a judge in the royal and municipal courts. The "bourgeois" self is not to be the decisive one, however, not even in *Either/Or*. That God is the Creator does not simply mean that, in the good Lutheran manner, he assigns a person his place in the social context and commands him to do his duty and develop himself within his limitation. The Judge's bourgeois nature is an accidental expression of his self — even though Kierkegaard, in 1843, gladly acknowledges his loyalty to the society in which William functions.

But according to Kierkegaard's concepts, the self is not a static substance nor is it identical with an allotted role in life which is

unambiguously laid down in advance. "The self is not the relationship, but
that the relationship relates itself to itself," it was stated in *The Sickness
Unto Death* [XI 143, SD 146]—not a given constant, but a function, an
act. "In the life of the spirit there is no stasis (nor, really, any condition;
everything is actuality). . ." [XI 231, SD 224-25].

The whole of *The Sickness Unto Death* is built up around the concept of
the self. The fundamental antithesis in the book is between faith and
despair, and this means between willing to be oneself and willing to do
away with oneself. The true self is the self which grounds itself
transparently in the power which posited it. The false self is the self which
the individual "himself has thought up" [XI 151, SD 153]. In the book
different variations are played upon this fundamental antithesis. The
question which a modern reader may ask is how it is possible to
differentiate like this between a true and a false self. Psychoanalysis,
behaviorism, and social psychology must reject this concept of a "true" self
as metaphysical and unscientific. What are Kierkegaard's criteria for
saying that one self is more true than another, the one role more correct
than the other?

The completely adequate, Kierkegaardian answer to this question is
most probably its rejection on the grounds that it inquires impersonally
and objectively about the self in general and the truth in general, not
about this particular person's, the inquirer's own self and its truth or
untruth. When a question is put like this, it is merely meaningless
reflection, and Kierkegaard cannot come to the aid of his reader with a
clever and ready answer. He must criticize the question instead.

This does not mean, however, that all discussion of this and all inquiry
about this has been made impossible. Kierkegaard's line of reasoning is
historically akin to the conception of the personality shared by
romanticism and bourgeois idealism. A single example will be sufficient to
demonstrate this here. In a little fragment, "On Affectation," from 1837,
Kierkegaard's older friend, the poet and philosopher Poul Møller, differentiated between the true and the affected self in a fashion which
prefigures Kierkegaard's distinction between faith and despair. "To the extent that a man has affectation in his life, he does not determine himself
with complete moral freedom; his actions do not have their source in the
true self, which is his free moral will. His will is determined by one or
another merely natural purpose, by which he is induced to construct an
alien person or to take upon himself à false role, which is not the one
assigned to him in life." Poul Møller was a witty and insightful observer of
human pretensions, and Kierkegaard speaks gratefully of him as his
teacher. But Poul Møller's mention of the "the true self" is part of a

metaphysical understanding of existence which was so self-evident for him and his contemporaries, that he merely needed to mention it: "To the extent that the finite person's pure self-determination is the will which has been sanctified by religiosity, he acts in complete harmony with the entire world of reason; he is what he is to be, and his life can attain no higher truth. But this truth is nothing other than morality, and all deviation from it is immorality."[11] For Kierkegaard's contemporaries, existence is a reasonable, cosmic order, and the task of the individual is thus to acknowledge this order and to put himself in order by placing himself in agreement with it.

When Kierkegaard says that the human self is a derived self, "posited by another," and says that the truth of the self is its transparent agreement with "the power which posited it," he is expressing himself in a manner which was self-evident for his contemporaries. All the same, there is an important difference between Kierkegaard and the period's official understanding of life. Where, for the general view of the period, the eternal, super-individual order — Poul Møller's "entire world of reason" — was an indubitable and commonly acknowledged, reliable presupposition, for Kierkegaard it becomes deceptive and unreliable — not in itself, but because it is inaccessible to the person who must understand his own life in relation to it. That which is presupposed is real, but it is hidden, unknown, and not the object of any possible cognition. The difference between Kierkegaard and the traditional cultural metaphysics is one of security and *a priori* certainty.

Therefore, when the modern reader asks Kierkegaard how he comes to know which particular self, which role or life style is the true one, the answer is that he does not know. The idea of the hiddenness of the eternal becomes serious for him, and because the eternal reveals itself to man as that which is yet to come, this future is the unknown — the object of anxiety. Man has a destiny for his life, but a destiny which cannot be laid out in advance or known before it is lived. The idea of the hiddenness of one's destiny is to be found in some of Kierkegaard's contemporaries, perhaps, but it is Kierkegaard who makes it into a problem.

God, as Creator, is also the practitioner of maieutics who makes man free, lets man go from his hand so that man himself can choose his situation. *"God created man in his image,"* one reads in an edifying discourse which deals with the glory of the creature. But the point is that this image cannot be maintained in an unambiguous and straightforward sense, because "God is spirit, is invisible, and the image of invisibility is of course invisibility once more: thus does the invisible Creator reproduce himself in the invisibility, which is the determination of spirit, and God's image is precisely invisible glory. If God were visible, then no one could resemble him or be in his image; for *no* image of the visible *exists,* and of everything visible, there is nothing, not even a leaf, which resembles anything else or is its image; for, if that were the case, then the image would be the object itself. But, as God is invisible, it is impossible for anyone to resemble him *visibly"* [VIII 326 f., GS 210-11]. In this way Kierkegaard here formulates his rejection of idealism's notion of the eternal — the world of ideas which lies behind things like a pattern or an unambiguous ideal norm, which merely requires that man acknowledge it and bring himself into agreement with it. The eternal does not admit of being known or pinned down, but is only negatively present to man.

God is invisible. He is "the Unknown," the boundary of the human ability to comprehend, "the absolutely different, which has no characteristics by which it is to be known," and which therefore cannot be pinned down [IV 238, PF 55]. And "no anonymous author can conceal himself more cunningly, and no practitioner of maieutics can withdraw more carefully from a straightforward relationship than does God. . . . Is this not behaving toward the individual man as a deceptive author who does not write the outcome anywhere in large type or give it in advance in a forword? And why is God so deceptive? Precisely because he is the truth, and in so being the truth wants to prevent man from falling into untruth" [VII 229, cf. 231 and 464; CUP 218, cf. 219 and 424].

Here, too — in the *Postscript* — the discussion is of God as the Creator. And the anthropological definition which corresponds to this theological definition of God is that the self is becoming. "To be continually in becoming like this is the deceptiveness of the infinite in existence," it is written earlier in the book [VII 74, CUP 79]. The invisible God or the deceptive infinity — "the negativity of the infinite in existence" [VII 73, CUP 78] — is the standard of measure for the human self. And the task with which one is presented, to become oneself, is not the movement from one fixed point to another. Kierkegaard does not operate with concepts such as point of departure-goal, question-answer, beginning-conclusion, but with the idea of the absence of a result, inconclusiveness, a renewal of what is given: "The fact that the existing subjective thinker is striving does not, however, mean that in the finite sense he has a goal toward which he is striving, a point at which he would be finished when he reached it; no, he strives infinitely, is constantly in becoming . . ." [VII 79, CUP 84].

Therefore, when Kierkegaard writes in *The Sickness Unto Death:* "The self, however, at every moment that it exists is in becoming, because the self κατὰ δύναμιν [kata dynamin][12] does not actually exist; it is only that which is to come into being. To the extent, then, that the self does not become itself, it is not itself; but not to be oneself is precisely despair" [XI 161, SD 163]—then it means that the self is not a static thing which admits of unambiguous description, not a form or a garment which is given in advance and simply waits for the individual to crawl into it, but a concrete, unpredictable coming-into-being which cannot be exhausted and pinned down in a linguistic description. The positive meaning of being oneself cannot be formulated in universal statements of definite content and cannot be verified by universal norms. A given, static role which is always seeking an unambiguous identity by one or another means would be better as a description of despair.

This will be discussed further in the chapters which follow. For the present, the idea of the self as a becoming will be illuminated a bit more closely.

4. "To Acquire One's Soul in Patience"

4: 1. *The Doctrine of Anamnesis and Maieutics*

"To the extent, then, that the self does not become itself, it is not itself," we read in *The Sickness Unto Death*. But how can the self "become itself"? Does this not presuppose precisely that in another sense it *is* itself? The idea must be that the self is always itself already, but that this self is an uncompleted self. Thus, when the self must "become itself" it means that it must become a completed, true self. But what does this task involve, and is it possible at all?

This is the problem which Kierkegaard discusses in a number of different contexts. A point of departure for understanding this can be found by considering the Socratic problem which Kierkegaard raises on the first page of *Philosophical Fragments*. Can man "learn the truth"— when it is not a case of external facts, but of the truth of the self?

Kierkegaard reproduces the problem and Socrates' answer as follows: "To the extent that the truth is to be learned, it must of course be presumed not to exist, thus when it is to be learned, it is sought after. Now here is the difficulty to which Socrates draws attention in the *Meno* (§80, conclusion), as if to a 'pugnacious proposition' that it is impossible for a man to seek what he knows, and equally impossible for him to seek what he does not know; for what he knows, he cannot seek, because he knows it; and what he does not know he cannot seek, because, of course, he does not even know what he is to seek. Socrates thinks his way through this difficulty by claiming that all learning and seeking is only remembering, so that the ignorant person only needs to be reminded in order to gather his thoughts upon what he knows. The truth is thus not brought into him, but was in him" [IV 203, PF 11].

The Socratic answer — the Greek doctrine of anamnesis — is not simply Kierkegaard's answer to this problem. All the same, it is an answer with which he is intensely occupied, and which he reinterprets and uses as the basis for his own thinking. The Socratic version was that the truth is reached by remembering (anamnesis), because it already "was" in the individual before he gathered his thoughts upon it and thereby made conscious the implicit truth. This means that the distinction between what the individual "knows" and what he does not "know" is not an absolute distinction. For in remembering the individual comes to know that which "was in him" without his knowledge.

This Greek idea comes to play a central role in Kierkegaard's deliberations about the self and about how man can become himself. But this does not mean that he simply accepts the Greek line of reasoning at face value. In *Philosophical Fragments* it even looks as though he flatly rejects it. The book takes its point of departure in Socrates, but only in order to demonstrate all the more clearly the antithesis between Christianity and the metaphysical idealism, which can be derived from the Greek idea of anamnesis. The Greek notion assumes that man is in possession of the truth and of the conditions for its realization. In opposition to this, Christianity maintains that man, as sinner, stands outside of the truth and lacks the conditions which would make it possible to attain it. Only a condition which lies beyond man can rescue man out of his untruth. This condition is Jesus Christ and the preaching about him. This is why one must differentiate between idealism, on the one hand, represented by the Greeks and the German idealistic philosophy, and characterized by the assumption that man in and of himself has access to an adequate and complete perception of the truth, and, on the other hand, Christianity, represented by Kierkegaard himself, and characterized by the assertion that subjectivity is *untruth*.

In the next chapter we will study carefully what this conception of Christianity means concretely for anthropology and psychology. But it does not mean simply that Kierkegaard rejects the idea that man *qua* man possesses the possibility of mobilizing an authentic understanding of himself. Before one differentiates between idealistic speculation and Kierkegaardian Christianity, one must differentiate between speculation's epistemological interpretation and Kierkegaard's ethical-existential interpretation of their *common* assumption, that man is *the truth* and possesses the condition for realizing it.

This latter complex of problems becomes clear in *Concluding Unscientific Postscript* where Kierkegaard says *both* that "subjectivity is untruth" *and* that "subjectivity is truth." One could explain the matter briefly by pointing out that the conception of Socrates in *Philosophical Fragments* is different from that in the *Postscript*. In the latter book, Kierkegaard himself points out that the *Fragments* simplified the way in which the problem was posed by making Socrates into the representative for the doctrine of anamnesis. By this means he could make plain the difference between the "heathen philosophy" and Christianity, but this was achieved in part at the expense of another important difference, namely, that between the consequences which Socrates and Plato, respectively, draw from the doctrine of anamnesis. In the *Postscript,* Kierkegaard now wishes to rehabilitate Socrates and distance himself from Plato. Both of them take their point of departure in the proposition that knolwedge is remembering. But they understand this in different ways, Socrates existentially, Plato speculatively. For Socrates, therefore, this proposition does not mean that remembering is literally the source of knowledge. The doctrine of anamnesis is reinterpreted by the Kierkegaardian Socrates in such a way that it comes to mean "that existing — the process of appropriation into inwardness, in and by means of existence — is the truth" [VII 191 f., CUP 184]. This is the expression of the understanding of existence which Kierkegaard calls "religiousness A," according to which subjectivity is the truth and as such is capable of realizing the existential authenticity which Socrates personifies in the *Postscript*.

The notion that man has access to the truth is also the premise of Plato and modern German idealistic philosophy, but in this case another consequence is drawn. Speculation supposes that man, by means of contemplation (remembering or, in Hegel, the speculative clarification of the forms in which the spirit makes its appearance), has access to an adequate understanding of the essential truth "behind" the phenomena. In the Kierkegaardian Socrates-figure, it is assumed that man, via self-understanding, has access to the realization of existential truth in his own life. Speculation takes for granted that the knowing subject conforms in principle with the known object (the eternal, the spirit, God, and so forth). With Kierkegaard's Socrates, understanding involves the fact that the individual is in a paradoxical relationship to the object, and that he can therefore only know it as the unknown and the ambiguous. It is in the light of this non-understanding that the "subjective existing thinker" understands himself. He is thrust back from knowledge of the eternal in and for itself, into knowledge of himself, as that which has been ambiguously determined by this eternal.

But in this way subjectivity is truth. This "Socratic" thought is made further problematic in the *Postscript,* when Kierkegaard adds that subjectivity is untruth—as we will see in the next chapter. But it is not simply rejected at face value. In any case, the Socratic idea from *Philosophical Fragments,* that the truth is in the individual himself and must be retrieved from this individual, plays a central role. This is precisely the core of Kierkegaard's idea of creation. It can also be seen, among other places, in his considerations of the concept of communication.

Kierkegaard has presented his conception of "The Dialectic of Communication" in a series of connected entries in the journal from 1847 [Pap. VIII 2 B 79-89, Hong 648-57]. Here it is not a matter of the communication of facts, but of the communication of "the ethical." As we have seen, "the ethical" is not primarily the designation for a set of moral norms, but first and foremost for the idea of the completion of the self as an existential task. Therefore, ethical communication cannot be the communication of knowledge, a set of instructions about ethical rules for life, but an existential communication, whose purpose is to "lure the ethical forth out of the individual, because it is in the individual." The point of view corresponds to that which was attributed to Socrates in *Philosophical Fragments,* to the extent that it implies that the individual himself possesses the truth, though in an undeveloped, latent form. Kierkegaard then refers to the same Socratic, deliberation as in the *Fragments,* and justifies his line of reasoning with reference to Socrates, who "said he could not give birth, but could only be a midwife. That is, every person is in possession of the ethical." But at the same time with this and parallel to it, he refers to the Christian idea of creation, according to which God has given all men the knowledge that is necessary in order to realize the ethical [Pap. VII 2 B 81, Hong 649]. Therefore, ethical instruction begins by assuming that he who is to be instructed has knowledge of the ethical.

This does not mean that an explicit knowledge of ethics is innate in man. A clear understanding of what the concepts good and evil involve does not exist for the individual before he himself chooses the good or the evil. Judge William has already made this clear in *Either/Or:* "The good exists in my willing it, and except for this it does not exist at all. This is the expression of freedom. The same is the case with the evil; it exists only in my willing of it." On the other hand, this does not mean that the individual sovereignly creates morality and moral concepts, but it means that the understanding of the ethical as something actual only comes into existence in action. The individual may perhaps know the difference between good and evil verbally without acting, but in actuality, this difference first comes into being in its moral or amoral engagement. "as long as he has not chosen himself, this difference is latent" [II 241 f., E/O II 227-28].

Therefore, when the journal entries on communication, from 1847, say that the ethical "begins with a knowing," it is exactly a latent knowledge which is meant, a potential for understanding. Ethical communication "requires realization" of the potential and it therefore assumes that every person is potentially in possession of the ethical [Pap. VIII 2 B 81, Hong 649].

Thus the idea is Socratic, as is the idea of the maieutic instruction which is to help this understanding come forth. Kierkegaard's doctrine of maieutic communication will be discussed later in this book. Maieutic communication is the "art of midwifery," which does not impart a "truth" to the other individual from without by propounding facts or views, but which helps the other himself to "give birth" to the truth which he has within himself, but has not yet collected his thought upon. Socrates' questions serve this purpose, for "the ultimate idea of all questioning is . . . that the one who is asked must have the truth, and come to it by himself," it says in *Philosophical Fragments* [IV 207, PF 15]. In the *Fragments,* as has been mentioned, Kierkegaard wishes to demonstrate the antithesis between the Socratic (or Platonic) doctrine of anamnesis and Christianity. The one presupposes that man "has the truth," and the other that he has forfeited it in sin. Nonetheless, Kierkegaard also defends "the Socratic theory of recollection" here against the objections raised against it by skepticism and sophistry [IV 231 f., PF 47 f.]. Kierkegaard himself does not accept this theory of recollection. But he accepts the maieutic communication which is connected with it: "for between man and man the Μαιεύεσθαι [maieusthai][13] is the highest relation; to give birth is indeed the property of the gods" [IV 205, PF 13]. The idea is the same as in an entry which was cited earlier: God, as Creator of man, is the only real practitioner of maieutics; the liberating effect of maieutics in the mutual relationship between human beings will always be limited: "[E]ven though it always needs to be emphasized again and again that this is the highest thing, only omnipotence is truly capable of it" (cf. above, Chapter IV: 3: 2). The idea is naturally that maieutics "between man and man" is to contribute to liberate and actualize the potential which is laid down in man as he is created.

Maieutic instruction or communication is built upon the assumption that there is a potential to be realized in the person who is to be instructed. If man is to become himself, therefore, he must in another sense be himself. The assumption need not have anything to do with the doctrine of recollection or the pre-existence of the soul in the literal sense [cf. IV 204, cf. PF 12]. In an early journal entry from 1840, which expressly refers to the anamnesis doctrine of the Greeks, Kierkegaard has pointed out what it is which takes on significance for his own reasoning. The human spirit is a "unity of necessity and freedom," and this means "it does not have to determine itself to become something by means of an infinite development, but through development, to determine itself to be what it is." Further, the human spirit is a "unity of the result and the striving," which implies that "it does not bring forth something new by means of development, but, through development, it acquires what it has" [Pap. III A 5, Hong 2274]. This is a fundamental idea in Kierkegaard. Thus Judge William says that the individual who chooses himself becomes "not something other than what he was before, but he becomes himself" [II 192, E/O II 181].

4:2. *To Own and to Acquire*

Kierkegaard maintains this existential version of the idea of anamnesis until *The Sickness Unto Death,* where the self, "in every minute that it exists, is in becoming, because the self κατὰ δύναμιν [kata dynamin] does not actually exist; it is only that which must come into being" [XI 161, SD 163].

The self, then, is not purely and simply any particular existing thing, which can be drawn forth out of concealment and made manifest as a definite, concluded totality. The self is the process of coming-into-being. In the journal entry from 1840 the self is a "unity of result and striving." With Judge William it is "the goal of man's striving," but also the "beginning" of this striving [II 279, E/O II 263].

The most precise formulation of this situation is certainly to be found in one of Kierkegaard's edifying discourses from 1843, "To Acquire One's Soul in Patience." The fact that Kierkegaard writes "soul" instead of self in this text is due to the fact that he is building upon a Biblical citation about "acquiring the soul" (Luke 21:19). For the rest, however, the discourse is more of a philosophical-anthropological text than a sermon.

The discourse asks first whether man himself owns his soul (his self) when he is born, or whether he comes "naked into the world." The problem is posed as a clear analogy to the Socratic question which introduced *Philosophical Fragments:* "However, if a person owns his soul, then he does not need to acquire it, and if he does not own it, how then can he acquire it, for the soul itself is the ultimate precondition which is assumed in every act of acquiring, thus also in the acquisition of the soul. Should there exist, then, such a sort of ownership, which is precisely what designates the precondition of being able to acquire this very ownership?"

The answer here does not lie in a reference to remembering. But the problem is, as with Socrates, that that which is to be acquired is also the precondition for being able to acquire it. The answer must therefore be that the self at once both owns and does not own, or that it owns potentially, but not actually: "He who comes naked into the world owns nothing, but he who comes into the world in his soul's nakedness, owns at least his soul, that is, as something which is to be acquired." And, "that which guarantees that the soul's acquisition is not a disappointment is precisely the fact that it is already owned" [IV 60-64, ED II 68-73].

Where the journal entry from 1840 stated that the human spirit is a unity of result and striving, the edifying discourse says that the soul can at not a "thing" or a static core of the personality which is to be found by itself "behind" life's manifestations: "[T]hat which is to be acquired is in patience, not concealed within it as if it were something that someone who patiently peeled the leaves off of patience would find hidden inside, but it is in patience in the sense that it is patience itself into which the soul spins itself [like a cocoon — trans.], and thereby acquires both it and itself" [IV 71, ED II 81].

Therefore the soul's property relationship differs from the property relationships of material things. If one owns a thing, one cannot simultaneously be in the process of acquiring it, and if one is in the process of acquiring it, one does not own it [IV 63, ED II 71]. If the thing belongs to one owner, it cannot simultaneously belong to another [IV 66, ED II 72]. It is otherwise with the self. In one sense it is owned by the individual himself from birth, for in order for him to acquire it, it must be "within" him; but the problem is that he is "outside of himself," and to that extent he does not own it [IV 71, ED II 81]. Who owns it then? Kierkegaard answers that it is owned by "the world," but he adds that this "being owned by the world" is identical with "owning the world." Owning the world is a goal which many people covet, without understanding that this is exactly what they did originally. The (adult) person who absolutely and unreservedly "owns the world," belongs to what he owns, and is lost in it in the same absolute way as an infant. "The world can only be owned in such a way that it owns me." It does not offer itself to man as property without simultaneously guaranteeing itself lordship over him. Only if the individual owns himself can he own "something" without being a slave to his property.

How then does man come into possession of himself, how does he avoid becoming the property of his property? "In the first instant," from birth, man is thus "lost in the life of the world, he owns the world, which means that he is owned by it." To take an expression from Freud, one could say that it is the "oceanic" primal condition which Kierkegaard is describing, in which man "owned the world in himself, as the beating of the waves possesses the unrest of the sea and the depths of the earth in itself, and it knows no other heartbeat than the infinite beat of the sea." Here we recognize the description of the first stage of innocence, where the I and the Not-I are indifferentiated, but where there is all the same a continual approach to consciousness and conflict [cf. above chapter II: 3: 1 and 3: 3]. In the undifferentiated unity of the I and the not-I, the difference is latent, however, and this difference is the self. While man is one with the world from the beginning, he is still "different from the world, and he perceives a counter-striving which does not follow the movements of the life of the world." And if he wants to "acquire his soul, then he must allow this counter-striving to become more and more distinct and thereby acquire his soul; for his soul is exactly this differentness." This differentness is his possibility. We know the idea. The identity comes into being in the act of separation in which man becomes conscious of himself as different from the surroundings. In innocence the spirit is dreaming, but its possibility reveals itself in the differentness as anxiety, which drives man forward toward the crisis of individuation—if he does not forfeit the possibility and disappear again "like the beat of the waves in the life of the world."

This possibility of acquiring oneself is thus not given as a part of the fact that "the world" owns the self. Nor is it given as a part of the fact that the self owns itself, because the self does so only potentially, not really. The lawful owner of the self (the soul) must thus be a third, alternative authority, who owns it without making it his slave, but owns it in such a way that "the person himself can acquire it as his lawful property. This owner can therefore be none other than the eternal being, than God himself" [IV 64-67, ED II 74-77].

This, then, is the condition for the possibility that the self can acquire itself. In this acquisition, that which is to be acquired is also the precondition for acquiring it. The goal of the process is nothing other than the process itself. The self is neither a fixed point of departure nor a fixed goal. The process which is the precondition for acquiring the self is identical with the self, because the self is becoming. In all other acquisition, the means is one thing, the object another. "If it were also the case for the person who would acquire his soul, that the condition disappeared in the face of the thing conditioned, then that person would be the most deceived of all men; for the condition was precisely the possession of the soul which made the soul's acquisition possible" [IV 69, ED II 78]. In a later book, *Training in Christianity,* Kierkegaard similarly says that the truth is "the way," not "the result." The merely scientific truth exists as a fixed answer to fixed questions, and the process of research is subordinate in relation to the finished result. Existentially, on the other hand, the process is identical with the truth and the result: "The truth is the way" [XII 229-32, TC 202-04].

Kierkegaard's discourse on acquiring the soul also has affinity to his concept of repetition. This is made explicitly clear in the edifying discourse [IV 71, ED II 81-82], and a more detailed conceptual analysis would confirm this. In Danish, "repetition"[14] means to "take (something) again." In this connection it must suffice to point out the fact that Kierkegaard draws the parallel between his own concept of repetition and the classical concept of anamnesis: "for *repetition* is the decisive expression for what *'recollection'* was to the Greeks." Understood in the Greek fashion, this is a matter of the uncovering of the truth by means of retrospective self-reflection; in this connection it is relevant to recall Freud's psychotherapeutic method. The antithesis of this is thus the Kierkegaardian acquisition of the subjective truth which relates itself to the future: "Repetition and recollection are the same movement, only in opposite directions; for what is recollected, has been, is repeated backwards; while on the other hand, the real repetition is recollected forwards" [III 193, R 3-4].[15]

This is also the reason that the self is never "finished," and can never be described definitively and exhaustively. This view does not involve a rejection of an anthropological or psychological understanding of the self, but it itself expresses such an understanding, namely, that the reason that one cannot speak *adequately* about the self as an object of scientific observation is that it is not a statically given, material thing, but develops itself in time and relates itself to the future, so that it is always on the path of coming-into-being and has never in a definitive sense *come* into being. In *The Concept of Anxiety,* Vigilius writes of the self (the represented or experienced self, self-consciousness): "This self-consciousness is not contemplation, for he who believes this has not understood himself, when he sees that he himself at the same time is in becoming, and thus cannot be a completed object for contemplation" [IV 453, CD 128].

That which is to be susceptible of unambiguous and scientific description must be something finished and unchangeable, and that is not the self. The edifying discourse formulates the matter in a reflection upon the relationship between knowing and acquiring the soul. It is a new aspect of the main theme of the discourse, to own and to acquire. "A man may therefore know his soul in order to acquire it . . ."; the word "may"[16] cannot mean "has to" or "ought to" here. An ascertainment or an assumption is expressed here, namely, the assumption of a potential for understanding. The idea is the same as previously: ". . . but this knowledge is not the acquisition, for in this knowledge he indeed assures himself of the fact that he is in the grasp of an alien power. . . ." Even if it were possible — but because of the temporal dimension it plainly is not — to know the soul entirely before it is acquired, "This possession in knowledge would still only be a possessing which, just like that first ownership, was the precondition for being able to acquire the soul in patience. Therefore, every knowledge which will not stand in relation to an acquiring is incomplete and lacking, because he of course does not yet know what he will become; because he becomes it only in the acquiring; and even in the company of an acquiring, knowledge is lacking, because 'we do not yet know what we will become' "[IV 73 f., ED II 84-85].[17]

This, then, is Kierkegaard's variant of the idea of anamnesis. The potential of understanding is not realized by means of retrospective meditation, but in a forward-looking engagement. The self is becoming.

4: 3. Anthropological Model and Conflict Model

The edifying discourse from 1843 which has been examined here was written shortly after *Either/Or* and is closely connected with the ethical views that the pseudonym Judge William develops in connection with the concept of the existential choice. In the choice the individual acquires himself, appropriates the self as it were. But as the representative of "the ethical stage," the Judge is and remains a pseudonym. Some very essential aspects of Kierkegaard's thought are expressed in the Judge's writings, but the idea is not carried out completely in all its problematic consequences. There are decisive dimensions of Kierkegaard's thought which are made light of, or harmonized, or not mentioned at all. The difference between the Judge and Kierkegaard's later pseudonyms can be defined, among other ways, as follows: that William presents the choice as a stage which he himself as left behind him, by and large, [II 172, E/O II 162], even if he also hints that the choice is not only a conclusion but also a new beginning: "Thus when the individual knows himself, he is not finished; on the contrary, this knowledge is highly fruitful and it is from this knowledge that the true individual comes forth" [II 279, E/O II 263].

But it is the later pseudonyms who first begin to carry out the business of looking forward, and pose the question of whether an authentic repetition is possible at all — without giving any unambiguous answer (*Repeition* and *Fear and Trembling,* from 1843). This is the direction from which Kierkegaard approaches the problem of sin, which first becomes conspicuous and explicit in the writings from 1844 and thereafter (*Philosophical Fragments* and *The Concept of Anxiety*). The Judge's analyses of "the aesthetic" despair and the demonic are substantial enough, but he himself, as a fictional person, sits safe and sound, and this also characterizes his style and the way in which he deals with the problem. His anthropology, or the anthropology which belongs to "the ethical stage," contains the possibility of self-completion, and it is this anthropology with which we have here become acquainted, with the assistance of the edifying discourse, among other things. And yet it is precisely this anthropology which also contains the possibility of sin. And even if this possibility is not dealt with in detail in the ethical edifying discourse about acquiring the soul, then it is at least suggested.

According to the discourse, the soul (the self) belongs to three different authorities. It belongs to the world "as unlawful property," to God "as true property," and to itself "as the property which is to be acquired." Therefore, the self is "in contradiction and is a self-contradiction" [IV 67, ED II 76]. It is "the contradiction of the temporal and the eternal," and this is the pre-condition for the self's ability to acquire itself [IV 64, ED II 72].

With these phrases, the discourse anticipates the definition of the self in *The Sickness Unto Death* as "a synthesis of infinity and finitude, of the temporal and the eternal, of freedom and necessity, in short, a synthesis" [XI 143, SD 146]. And perhaps the expression "contradiction" is more precise than the expression "synthesis." In the discourse, it is clear that "finitude," "the temporal," and "necessity" are what characterize the self's boundness to "the life of the world," the undifferentiated unity of the I with the not-I. But this boundness also contains the possibility of liberation through the difference or the contradiction: from the beginning, the self is "indeed under an alien power. If the soul were free in any other way, then it would not be the self-contradiction in the contradiction between the external and the internal, the temporal and the eternal" [IV 72, ED II 83].

This "self-contradiction in the contradiction" is thus the possibility of liberation, corresponding to the synthesis structure in *The Sickness Unto Death*. But according to *The Sickness Unto Death,* the synthesis structure is also the possibility of unfreedom or despair. The edifying discourse gives a provisional hint of the explanation. The contradiction, the unconcluded process of coming-into-being, and the openness toward the ambiguous and unsecured future which corresponds to this process, are what make possible the ethical completion of the self. But in this contradiction also lies the anxiety about this possibility: "And is it not anxiety-producing to walk that path on which one sees the goal now and indeed at every moment, but never sees it reached, unlike the wanderer who finally reaches the goal, unlike the bearer of burdens who makes his way to the destination . . ." [IV 62, ED II 70].

In this dizziness freedom succumbs and grasps finitude in order to support itself, it says in *The Concept of Anxiety*. In this process of coming-into-being it is revealed that the anthropological model is also a conflict model, and that the possibility of freedom is also the anxiety about freedom and the flight into unfreedom. Kierkegaard calls this despair and sin.

Chapter V

THE CONFLICT MODEL

1. The Vicious Circle

According to Kierkegaard's own conceptual categories, the edifying discourse about acquiring the soul in patience is not really Christian, but philosophical, which means that it depicts man according to his ideal possibility and with the tacit assumption that this possibility admits of being realized. It deals with inwardness, not with the exclusion of inwardness, with the ideal, not with actuality. Kierkegaard himself explains this in a retrospective look at this and other discourses, in which he also draws attention to this idea's affinity to the notion of anamnesis: "[T]he return of metaphysical recollection into the eternal is always possible" [VII 257, cf. 259 with note; CUP 241, cf. 243 with note].

Kierkegaard's authorship is constructed so as to sketch a sequence of different stages or interpretations of existence which mutually correct and in some respects exclude one another. The ideas which I have sought to illuminate with the help of the edifying discourse belong to the sphere of understanding called "religiousness A," the human-religious, or the ethical-religious. The Christian interpretation of existence, "religiousness B," could appear to be a single, sustained denial of the human understanding of life. The fact that existence is given to man and that man is created, is indeed not denied. God is love — but man is not. Subjectivity is untruth. Man is not a splendidly equipped being who realizes himself in authenticity, but a sinner capable of nothing. In sin man has cut himself off from his own delivery from impotence, and his only possibility is God's forgiving grace in Jesus Christ. Man's only possibility of salvation lies in the unlikely and singular historical event, in which God sent his son to earth 1800 years ago, but in the same event it was revealed and made plain that man is disqualified as a bearer of truth. What does this mean?

In the relationship of the Christian understanding of existence to the human-religious version of life like the relationship of water to fire or like oil to fire? Does "religiousness B" represent exclusively a sovereign call to believe in Christ as redeemer and savior or to be offended by him, or does it also involve a deepened understanding of the concrete conditions of man's life? If the latter is the case, how then does the absurdity relate to this understanding? Does the Christian point of view mean that the ethical-anthropological line of reasoning is to be rejected as invalid speculation, destined to be lost sight of, or does it mean the reverse, that it is only now that the ethical-anthropological view receives its decisive amplification?

The prelude to *Philosophical Fragments* is the place where Kierkegaard first clearly and concisely allows the fundamental ideas of the Socratic and the Christian points of view to confront and delimit one another. The presupposition of Socratic instruction was that the individual himself possesses the truth in an accessible form, and needs only to gather his thoughts upon it. The Christian understanding of the situation, on the other hand, is that the individual does not possess the truth, "not even in the form of ignorance," but is outside of the truth, "not approaching it like a proselyte, but taking leave of it" [IV 207, PF 16]. Now we have already demonstrated at a number of points that Kierkegaard was to a great extent inspired by the Greek idea of anamnesis, and it is quite in keeping with this fact that in *Philosophical Fragments* the two views are not defined simply as totally antithetical. To the idea of anamnesis corresponds the idea of creation, and it is partly of Greek inspiration. "Insofar, then, as the learner exists, he is of course created, and to this extent God must have given him the precondition for understanding the truth" [IV 208 f., PF 18]. Kierkegaard then also mentions that if nothing further is added, one has not come beyond the Socratic stage. Thus, the Christian anthropology does not differ from the Socratic by maintaining that man is created without the precondition for realizing the truth, but by asserting that man has forfeited this precondition in the fall into sin. The truth is no longer accessible to self-reflection and self-acquisition, but is inaccessible, for the individual "is polemical against the truth, which is expressed in the fact that he himself has forfeited and continues to forfeit the precondition." One could perhaps draw a—somewhat risky—parallel to psychoanalytic terminology and say that, Socratically, the truth is pre-conscious (accessible), while Christianly, it is unconscious (inaccessible), and only becomes accessible again by means of the help of someone else. One should not stress this analogy, however, because it becomes misleading as soon as it is insisted upon. It is really only correct to the extent that both "the sinner" and "the neurotic" are assumed to be bound in a vicious circle, which neither can leave by his own efforts, because each has excluded and continues to exclude himself from understanding the truth about himself, which is the precondition for leaving that circle. In sin man has lost freedom, at any rate in one sense. It is true that the fall into sin occurred by means of the individual himself, that it is self-inflicted, (according to

Kierkegaard, not according to Freud), and to this extent "it might seem that he was free; for to be with oneself is of course freedom. And yet he is of course unfree and bound and excluded; for to be free of the truth is of course to be excluded, and to be excluded by oneself is of course to be bound. But since he is bound by himself, he cannot release himself or deliver himself . . . ," because "he uses the power of freedom in the service of unfreedom, which he indeed freely entered into, and in this way, the combined power of unfreedom grows and makes him the slave of sin" [IV 209-11, PF 18-21].

Sin, then, is a vicious circle, a consistency into which the individual locks himself, and from which he is unable to break free by his own efforts. We will later see how "the consistency of evil" [XI 245, SD 238] manifests itself psychologically, and how Kierkegaard justifies the idea that no one is stronger than himself and therefore cannot vanquish himself, because he exhausts his power in struggle with himself and is thereby paralyzed. Only a few of the formulations will be cited here in order to provide some provisional orientation concerning this fundamental theme. Aesthete A betrays insight into the essence of sin when he explains, in connection with Johannes the Seducer, what it means "to run wild in oneself": "[H]e quickly notes that it is a circular course from which he cannot escape . . . . He has many exits from his den, but to no avail. Every time his anxious soul thinks it sees daylight coming in, it turns out to be another entrance, and thus he is always searching for an exit, like a terrified animal, pursued by despair, and always finds an entrance by which he goes back into himself. . . . His punishment has a purely aesthetic character, for even to say that conscience is awakening is too ethical an expression for him; for him, conscience only takes on the form of a higher consciousness which expresses itself as an unrest, which does not accuse him in any profound sense, but keeps him awake, granting him no rest in his fruitless unrest" [I 323, E/O I 304-05].

He cannot break out of the circle by his own efforts, but only with the help of a relation to a power which stands outside of its consistency. What is paradoxical, however, is that the relationship to this power, which is what makes liberation possible, is the same relationship which makes unfreedom possible, for this relationship is unavoidable. Sin is— theologically expressed—man's vain attempt to deny the relation to the power who posited him, and it is vain precisely because of the unavoidability of the relation. In other words, that which was previously called the anthropological model now reveals itself as a potential conflict model. Man is created, and his task is to complete his life in obedience to the will of the creator. To do this is to be free, and the created synthesis contains this possibility of freedom. Omnipotence is the only force which has the power to make free. But liberation is not the automatic consequence of creation. It is precisely freedom which implies that the possibility of rebellion or disobedience is also present in the synthesis. The rebellion against omnipotence and its will is the opposite of liberation, for in rebellion one merely makes oneself more and more dependent upon the power from which one seeks to wrest oneself. It is this unfree dependence which takes form in the seducer's life, not as a conscious conflict of conscience, but as uneasiness and restlessness. His rebellion against the Creator's will contains its own punishment; the punishment is inescapable, because the relation to God is inescapable. The relationship of conscience — the relation to God — reveals itself, but camouflaged as ordinary existential unrest. In unfreedom, the relationship to omnipotence, which makes one free, takes on the form of a relation to other powers, which binds one. In Kierkegaard's view, this is not authoritarian religion, for the will of the Almighty is, indeed, precisely the liberation of man, and a self-realization which is in agreement with this will would therefore be the opposite of what one normally means by an authoritarian posture. But, in contrast to many ideologues of anti-authoritarianism, Kierkegaard does not think that man's will is a "free" will, a *liberum arbitrium,* which gives man the possibility of autonomous, assumption-free self-determination [IV 354, 420; CD 44-45, 100; II 188, E/O II 178; cf. Pap. IV C 39, Hong 1241; X 2 A 243, Hong 1260, where this idea is placed in direct connection with anxiety]. The line of reasoning thus aims at liberation from self-inflicted slavery.

What has here been expressed theologically, is also true psychologically, with respect to unknown forces within the individual himself: "Therefore, in despairing . . . man is freely in the clutches of an alien power, freely, or with freedom, slaving unfreely under its domination; or he is freely-unfreely in his own clutches. If one wishes to call the alien power the dominator, then the despairing individual slaves freely and self-inflictedly for this dominator. And if one wishes to say that he is unfreely in his own clutches, then he enslaves himself, is his own slave. This is the misrelationship. The true relationship of freedom is this: freely to be in the power of the good, of freedom, or in the power of that in whose power one can only exist by being free, and, by existing in whose power, one becomes free" [Pap. VIII 2 B 170, p. 267].

The quote is from the preliminary studies for *The Sickness Unto Death.* But the line of reasoning itself is put forth as early as *Either/Or,* in the passage about the seducer's vicious circle. In his denial of the eternal, man binds himself in an unacknowledged, uncomprehended, masked dependence upon the unavoidable relation which is denied. (It is useful at this point to point out that words like the eternal, the spirit, the good, freedom, and God often appear in Kierkegaard as synonyms or near-synonyms.) In what follows I will discuss this line of reasoning as the *theme of revenge* in Kierkegaard's psychology. Judge William expresses it in the following formulation, which also hints at the real psychological relevance of the theological-anthropological statement: "The spirit does not let itself be mocked; it revenges itself upon you; it binds you in the chains of melancholia" [II 220, E/O 208].

2. Revision of the Socratic Definition of Sin

2:1. *Cognition, the Will, and the Lower Nature*

When one has to describe a circle, even a vicious circle, it can be difficult to know where to begin. Everything is connected to everything else. In a certain sense, everything is decisive, for if one part of the circle were lacking, there would be no circle. However, it will perhaps be useful to take our point of departure in a text which, in addition to revealing something of what Kierkegaard thinks, also can reveal something of what he does not think: "[I]f . . . a man does not do the right in the same second that he knows it — well, first of all that knowledge cools off and loses steam. Then comes the question, what does the will think of what is known? The will is something dialectical, and under it, in turn, is the whole of man's lower nature. If the will does not like what is known, it does not follow that the will goes out and does the opposite of what cognition had understood, for such strong antitheses are probably quite rare in occurrence. But the will lets some time pass; it becomes an interim called 'but we will wait and see until tomorrow.' During all this, cognition becomes more and more obscure, and the lower nature conquers more and more. Oh, the good must be done immediately, immediately as soon as it is known . . . but the lower nature's strength consists in dragging things out. Gradually the will comes to have nothing against this, and almost winks at it. And when cognition has become sufficiently obscured, then cognition and the will can understand one another better. In the end they are entirely in agreement, for cognition has now gone over to the side of the will, and acknowledges that this is just the way it wants it" [XI 231, SD 225].

The quote is from the chapter of *The Sickness Unto Death* which has the heading "The Socratic Definition of Sin." Now I cite several lines from *T'.e Id and the Ego,* where Freud uses a Platonic metaphor to compare th: I with a rider whose task is to rein in the superior powers of the horses — and Freud adds: "The analogy may be carried a little further. Often a rider, if he is not to be parted from his horse, is obliged to guide it where it wants to go; so in the same way the ego is in the habit of transforming the id's will into action as if it were its own" [Freud XIX 25, cf. XXII 77].

If one ignores (provisionally) the ethical side of the matter and keeps to the purely psychological aspects, one will easily discern the factual agreement behind the different terminologies in these two quotes. What Kierkegaard calls "cognition," Freud calls "the ego": the conscious intention. The agreement is to be found in the fact that both of them speak of the antithesis between the I's conscious intention and the "lower" forces in man, which have the effect of preventing the intention from being realized in action. The I, which is assumed to direct these forces, is in actuality directed by them and merely administers the impulses which stem from them.

To gain a more accurate impression of this idea in Kierkegaard and Freud, it may perhaps be useful to mention a third thinker who has systematically worked out the idea of the power of the "lower" forces over the conscious processes of thought and action: Arthur Schopenhauer. It is well known that Schopenhauer anticipated psychoanalysis, which Freud willingly admits; but, he adds, it is not a matter of influence: "I read Schopenhauer very late in my life" [Freud XX 59-60].[1] This same is true of Kierkegaard, who only became acquainted with Schopenhauer's writings in 1854, but was surprised, on the other hand, "to find, in spite of complete disagreement, an author who affects me so much" [Pap. XI 1 A 144, Hong 3877].

If Schopenhauer, in his principal work, *The World as Will and Representation* (1819),[2] can be said to have anticipated Freud, it is not only because he attributes a much greater significance to the sexual instinct than did his contemporaries (excepting Aesthete A and Vigilius Haufniensis), or that at one point he explains the origin of madness in a way which strikingly recalls the psychoanalytic doctrine of repression, but it is due especially to the entire conception of man which forms the background for these theories. Schopenhauer introduces the most important psychological chapter, "On the Primacy of the Will in Self-Consciousness,"[3] with this declaration: "The will, as the thing-in-itself, constitutes the inner, true, and indestructible nature of man; yet in itself it is without consciousness."[4] The difference between Schopenhauer and certain of his romantic contemporaries, who also spoke of the unconscious as the deepest and most decisive entity, is that for the pessimist Schopenhauer, the unconscious will is not a manifestation of the divine, but a blind, animal, egoistic, searching and desiring "attachment of life,"[5] an unchangeable, incorrigible, invincible, primitive natural instinct,

which penetrates man's feelings and determines his actions. The intellect is
the antithesis of the will, but scarcely its opponent, for even if the intellect
can govern the will and give it representations and fantastic images with
which to work, in the final analysis it is the will which is the master and the
intellect which is the servant. The will can forbid unpleasant
representations and prevent painful thoughts from gaining access to
consciousness, and therefore it is the will which retains the power. The will
is "the strong blind man carrying the sighted lame on his shoulders."[6] Man
is in the grip of the will and the egoistic impulses, and his thinking is
therefore wishful thinking: "What opposes the heart is not admitted by the
head."[7] The will constitutes "the real core, the being-in-itself, of man."[8] It
is tireless, spontaneous, and automatic, and as such reveals itself
everywhere, in willing and deciding, in "striving, wishing, shunning,
hoping, fearing, loving, hating, in short, all that directly constitutes our
own weal and woe, desire and disinclination."[9] It is one and indivisible,
solid, without nuance, and incapable of modification, and its function is
the simple one of pronouncing its monotonous "approval and
disapproval,"[10] from which there is no appeal, about the ideas which the
secondary, complicated intellect painfully devises. Therefore, it is only one
of the will's usual tricks of illusion which has misled the rationalistic and
idealistic philosophers to regard thinking as the primary and superior
element in man, and the will as its servant. In fact, things are just the
reverse. This thesis thus contains the explanation of the many examples of
self-deception, displacement of motives, and errors which are cited by
Schoepenhauer.[11]

This summary is probably enough to reveal the similarity, not only to
the relationship between "the ego" and "the id," but also to the
relationship between "cognition" and "the lower nature" in *The Sickness
Unto Death*—in rough outlines. Here I am ignoring Freud for the time
being; his psychology is naturally infinitely more complicated than
Schopenhauer's, even though it is not without similarities to it. Instead, it
can be illuminating to sum up the relationship between Schopenhauer and
Kierkegaard: [12]

Kierkegaard	Schopenhauer
Cognition	The Intellect
The Will	
The Lower Nature	The Will.

In the quotation from *The Sickness Unto Death* with which we started it
was indeed not only cognition and the lower nature which were mentioned,

but also the will, which mediated the relationship between them. The point of the above diagram is therefore in part the empty box in Schopenhauer's section, and in part the two different meanings of the word "will." For neither of them does "will" mean the conscious intention to act. In Schopenhauer, "the will" is expressly unconscious, and it has the same function as "the lower nature" in the Kierkegaard quotation above. [13] One can point to a rather exact Kierkegaardian parallel to Schopenhauer's concept of the will: Don Giovanni's monotonous, unbroken, unconscious, eternally victorious desire, in the essay about the musical erotic stages (cf. above, especially Chapter II: 4: 4). But this detailed description of the content of desire, of instinct as such, in the form of Don Giovanni, is precisely the expression of a sort of psychological reasoning which Kierkegaard more and more abandons in the later authorship. In the cited passage from *The Sickness Unto Death,* one literally gets only the simple formula "the lower nature" and the only more detailed definition of it is that it stands "under" the will (but influences it, however), that "its strength consists in dragging things out," and that it does not love "decisions and consequences" [XI 231 f., SD 225]. This rudimentary description can of course be supplemented. In an earlier section of the same book Kierkegaard compares man with "a house, consisting of cellar, ground floor, and second floor," and the cellar area and the ground floor are constituted by "the sensual and the sensual-mental" or "the mental-physical synthesis," while the spirit makes man capable of "occupying the second floor." [14] According to this description, the categories of the sensual are "the pleasant and the unpleasant" [XI 175 f., SD 176]. In connection with this one can recall the "wishing, desiring, enjoying" immediacy, whose conceptual categories are good fortune, misfortune, and fate [XI 184 SD 184, cf. above, conclusion of Chapter II]. Finally, in order to get a commentary on "the lower nature," one could also mention *The Concept of Anxiety,* where there is indeed discussion of a physical-mental synthesis. One can ascertain that the word "mind" [15] in Kierkegaard does not designate a special, immortal part of man, but belongs to the same "natural" sphere as the body. And one may also assume, in *The Concept of Anxiety,* that "the body" is almost always the designation for sex. But Kierkegaard does not come much nearer to the matter than this. Apart from the Don Giovanni essay, there is no lengthy, coherent description which admits of comparison with Schopenhauer's.

This absence of a specification of content does not, however, have to be seen as a flaw in Kierkegaard's line of reasoning. The explanation is that Kierkegaard was not so much interested in the substantial as in the structural, and therefore it is not "cognition" or "the lower nature" which is emphasized as such, but the relationship between them, and this means the analysis of "the will." This analysis is by no means lacking in pithy insight. The will is not a substantial or metaphysical "essence," but an ambivalent link in the transaction between understanding and action, a mediator, an ambiguous middle term between cognition and the lower nature; in brief: "[T]he will is something dialectical." Schopenhauer has no concept parallel to this. What is peripheral in Kierkegaard, which is mentioned only in order to note in which dimension the analysis is taking place, is the central concept in Schopenhauer. On the other hand, what stands in the center of Kierkegaard's area of attention has apparently entirely escaped Schopenhaurer's notice.

"Middle terms! Middle terms! Let someone provide a middle term which has an ambiguousness which saves the idea . . . ," exclaims Vigilius in *The Concept of Anxiety* [IV 382, CD 68]. His middle term is anxiety. Anti-Climacus' is the will. However, in order to get hold of the relationship between these two concepts and their psychological significance, we must first look at the little chapter in *The Sickness Unto Death* in which we find the passage about cognition, the lower nature and the dialectical will.

2:2 *Sin is Produced Ignorance*

In the piece on "The Socratic Definition of Sin" in *The Sickness Unto Death,* Kierkegaard does what he has also done in other connections: taking a point of departure in Socrates, he undertakes a critical revision of the Socratic conception, and thus comes to the Christian understanding, or, perhaps better, he thus brings the Christian understanding into a meaningful perspective.

The Socratic definition of sin is one which has been derived from the principle of virtue as insight: "Sin is ignorance" [XI 224, SD 218]. It is this principle which is discussed, revised, and deepened in *The Sickness Unto Death,* while at the same time, it is retained as a prior understanding. The customary and obvious understanding of Socrates is of course that his principle is an expression of a "rational determinism" which presupposes a free and conscious will, determined by reason, which governs actions in life.[16] This line of reasoning of course cannot satisfy Kierkegaard, any more than it could satisfy Freud or Schopenhauer. In his *Introductory Lectures on Psycho-Analysis* Freud found occasion to draw attention to the difference between the Socratic doctrine and psychoanalytic theory, which indeed also builds upon the idea of neurosis as the result of a sort of ignorance; but this ignorance is not a simple not-knowing, for it is due to a repression, and therefore can only be rendered accessible and become knowledge when an inner transformation has taken place in the sick person. For, just as there is more than one form of ignorance, so is there also more than one form of knowledge. And only the knowledge which is due to an inner transformation can result in a transformation: "Knowledge is not always the same as knowledge: there are two different sorts of knowledge, which are far from equivalent psychologically" [Freud XIV 281].

Kierkegaard has too much respect for Socrates as a judge of character, however, simply to attribute to Socrates the conception that intellectual knowledge of the good is identical to, or leads automatically to, its realization. Therefore, he allows Socrates to employ a distinction which strikingly recalls Freud's distinction between knowledge and knowledge: "[T]o understand and to understand are two things" [XI 229, cf. 227; SD 223, cf. 220]. Naturally, Socrates the ironist is not blind to the contradiction which arises when a person says one thing and does another; he explains this by saying that the understanding this person proclaims is imagined. A psychological process of rationalization such as that which was cited above about the cognition which cools off and loses steam and, after an interim, allows itself to be lured to the will's side, can be interpreted Socratically, "for, Socrates would say, if this happens, it simply shows that such a person has not really understood what is right" [XI 232, SD 225].

As a commentary on this Socratic psychology, Kierkegaard says, on his own account, that "then the definition is indeed correct." The true understanding of that which is ethically correct would quickly make the individual into "a reflex of his understanding — ergo sin is ignorance" [XI 230, SD 223-24]. But Kierkegaard has an addition to make, His criticism of Socrates (as he himself interprets him) is not to the effect that his conception is wrong, but that it is vague, that it "leaves indefinite the matter of a detailed understanding of ignorance, its origin, etc." If sin is to be identical with ignorance — "which in one sense cannot be denied" — this must not be understood straightforwardly, but so that sin is "a produced, a later ignorance." And attention must thus be concentrated upon "the activity in man by means of which he has worked to obscure his cognition." Ignorance is therefore not an "original ignorance," but "the result" of the process of obscuration. (Some of these crucial statements are formulated as questions, but in such a way that Kierkegaard's answer is not in doubt) [XI 225, SD 219].

Sin is ignorance, but an ignorance which the sinner himself produces by distorting or deleting what he knows (just as, according to Freud, the neurosis is caused by an ignorance which the neurotic produces by repression). As has been made clear, this obscuration is not brought about by cognition or by the lower nature, but by the middle term between them, the dialectical will, which, as the ambiguous link in the transaction, determines the relationship between them. Socrates has ignored this entire portion of the problem, and it is in this that his superficiality lies. Socrates explains the contradiction between word and action by means of his ironic distinction: "[W]hen one does what is wrong, he has not understood what is right." The Christian understanding presupposes the Socratic, but it does so with the decisive addition, that when man has not understood what is right, it is "because he does not want to understand it, and this in turn, because he does not want to do what is right." And in this way, "sin thus lies in the will, not in cognition" [XI 232 f., SD 225-26].

Kierkegaard assumes of the individual, that "when he began to obscure cognition, he was clearly aware of it" [XI 225, SD 219]. The context shows that this must not be understood as meaning that he who obscures his cognition like this begins with the conscious intention of obscuring it. On the other hand, that of which he is aware at the beginning of the process is his moral purpose. That is what is meant when it is stated here: "Sin is precisely consciousness" [XI 226, SD 220]. Only by means of the law do I become acquainted with sin, Paul says (Romans 7: 7). Only where man is aware of the distinction between good and evil can there be talk of sin. But Kierkegaard's interest is not only (although it is this, too) the misrelationship between a particular, conscious moral objective and the individual action which results from it. This misrelationship can still be said to belong on the plane of the moral understanding, where it is meaningful to speak of virtue and vice. But it is rooted in a much deeper misrelationship, which can only be understood when one speaks of sin and faith instead. It is this deepening which Kierkegaard undertakes in his authorship, and therefore his revision of the Socratic definition of sin is also connected with the Christian understanding of sin as a vicious circle. In sin man obscures his cognition and distorts the potential for understanding which ought to make him capable of realizing the ethical task of life. The formula for this line of thought was that sin lies in the will. What does this mean?

2: 3. *Original Sin*

If "sin, however, does not lie in the fact that man has not understood what is right, but in the fact that he does not want to understand it, and in the fact he does not want to do it," a judgement is hereby expressed upon man, and the proper reaction to this is not an attempt to "conceive Christianity" intellectually, but the reaction of either faith or offense. The only explanation of it is just as intellectually inconceivable: "that it is revealed" [XI 232 f., SD 226].

Once this has been stated, we can go on to see how it is that Kierkegaard can explain the fact that sin lies in the will. He does indeed explain it, and this explanation does not conflict in any way with the assertion that it cannot be intellectually conceived. The assertion of the inconceivability of this position does not involve any demand that all thinking activity and understanding be suspended; if that were the case, Kierkegaard could not have written a book such as *The Sickness Unto Death*. That which he explains is *not* the fact that it is sin when the will causes an obscuration of cognition. That is something which he *believes*, that is, from revelation he derives the fact that it is a dogmatic postulate which exists to be believed or to give offense. What Kierkegaard does explain is that revelation's assertion may *not* seek to support itself by appealing to any psychological proof of the fact that the individual is guilty in what he does, i.e., that the individual himself is the cause of his own actions. Therefore, the assertion about guilt must be added as an unverifiable postulate of the Christian message. This, however, does not imply that the psychological understanding of the matter is an integral matter which can be isolated by itself, and that the theological assertion is a statement which can be appended or deleted at will. On the contrary, the statement that sin lies in the will is a double statement, and its theological and psychological aspects are inseparable. Without the Christian revelation that sin lies in the will and in defiance, the psychological understanding of the will's process of evasion would be just as unthinkable as the theological postulate would be without the corresponding understanding of the concrete situation of the individual person [XI 232, SD 226]. The point of coincidence is the dogma of original sin, which contains both statements.

The line of reasoning depicted here could also be presented in a bit more detail with reference to *The Concept of Anxiety*. For the present, however, it must suffice to cite a journal entry from 1850 which summarizes the matter in a concise formula. What is paradoxical with original sin is that man becomes guilty by means of it; the phrase "original sin"[17] has been "formed by means of the juxtaposition of qualitatively heterogenous categories. To 'inherit' is a natural category; 'guilt' is an ethical category of the spirit," and therefore the juxtaposition is logically unreasonable and accessible only to faith, which respects another standard of measure than the human [Pap. X 2 A 481, Hong 1530]. Thus the Christian category also has a psychological meaning. It is this aspect of dogmatics which the young Kierkegaard emphasizes rather undogmatically when he says: *"Every dogma is nothing other than a more concrete extract* of ordinary human consciousness" [Pap. II A 440, Hong 3273].

Sin, then, lies in the will. Arthur Schopenhauer can remind us that this word does not always have to designate a consciously motivated intention of action. With Schopenhauer it means the opposite. And when he exemplifies his theory of the will by relating how one can vainly seek to convince one's partner in a discussion by means of arguments until one discovers "that he *will* not understand; that we therefore had to do with his *will*, which pays no heed to the truth . . . ,"[18] then this language can give us an idea of how we ought to interpret Kierkegaard, when he writes: " . . . it is because he does not want to understand it, and this, in turn, because he does not want to do what is right."

The line of reasoning, of course, is not the same. But when Kierkegaard, in making his assertion that sin lies in the will, adds the decisive phrase that "this corruptedness of the will extends beyond the individual's consciousness [XI 233, SD 226], he is making a statement which, isolated from its context, could have been included in *The World as Will and Representation*. Kierkegaard's explanation of this statement lies in the dogma of original sin, which in turn explains "the *prius*[19] in which sin presupposes itself" [XI 226, cf. 230; SD 220, cf. 224]. This is the reason that psychology cannot prove (or disprove) that the individual bears the guilt for (or is the cause of) his own actions.

Kierkegaard notes in this connection that the Socratic definition of sin gives no information "with respect to the distinction between being *unable* to understand and *unwilling* to understand" [XI 232, SD 226]. This is the information supplied by Kierkegaard: sin lies in the will. And yet it is precisely the idea of original sin which makes dialectical the relationship between being willing and being able. In the consistency of sin man cannot will, and even the most strenuous act of will, even the most persistent intention, is incapable of dissolving the vicious circle, for the corruptedness of the will extends beyond the consciousness of the individual. Sin lies in the will, but the will as such cannot abolish sin. "Faith is not an act of the will," it says in *Philosophical Fragments* [IV 255, PF 77]. In *The Concept of Anxiety,* where it is affirmed that "sin is evasive . . . as a presupposition which extends beyond the individual," the formulation of the problem was circumscribed precisely by its opposition to classical ethics and its implicit presupposition, "that virtue can be realized" (cf. above, Chapter IV: 2: 2). In his retrospective view of the authorship, Climacus writes of *The Concept of Anxiety* that its subject, sin and original sin, is a deepening of the idea of the teleological suspension of the ethical: "Thus anxiety is the psychic state of the person who has teleologically suspended the ethical, who is in that despairing liberation from having to realize the ethical" [VII 256, CUP 240]. And the suspension consists precisely in the fact that the individual, far from being able to begin to realize the ethical, is on the contrary more and more hindered in doing so the longer he remains in this condition: "The situation is not that of the relation of possibility, but of impossibility, to actuality" [VII 253, CUP 238].

The circle is closed.

2:4 ". . . in order to bring about obscurity"

Thus the chapter on the Socratic definition of sin deals with "the relationship of cognition and the will to one another" [XI 225, SD 219]. This is not an isolated part of *The Sickness Unto Death*, but points beyond itself to other contexts. We know from *The Concept of Anxiety* that original sin manifests itself psychologically in anxiety. Nothing is said of this in the text with which we now are dealing, but the connection between anxiety and the dialectical will, which brings about "the activity in man by which he labors to obscure his cognition" appears gradually as one follows Kierkegaard's tacit references to his other writings. He has also discussed the relation of cognition and the will to one another at an earlier point in *The Sickness Unto Death:* "In all obscurity and ignorance there is a dialectical interplay of cognition and will . . . . ," and the effects of this interplay can be seen in other areas than the one which merely concerns the relation between an individual intention and its implementation. The ignorance which is spoken of here is not merely ignorance of a particular, partial purpose of which the individual gradually loses sight, but an ignorance of the individual's self-understanding in the wider sense. And with this we also make a connection to the vicious circle of despair which the despairing person himself creates by excluding himself from the potential understanding which he otherwise had the possibility to acquire, because he already possesses it. Despair is described in its everyday dress: "Most often, the condition of the despairing person is quite certainly one of semiobscurity concerning his own condition, though this occurs with many overtones." It is made completely clear that this ignorance is a produced ignorance. The despairing person has an unclear sense of crisis, which he seeks to ward off by explaining it away or by distractions or by work, but, be it noted, without willingness to understand or admit to himself his motives for his busyness; he "seeks to keep himself in obscurity about his condition, though not in such a way that it becomes quite clear to him that he is doing this in order to bring about obscurity. Or perhaps he is even conscious that he is doing this in order to submerge his soul into obscurity, and does so with a certain cleverness and calculation, with psychological insight, but he is not clearly aware in a deeper sense of what he is doing, of how despairingly he behaves, etc." [XI 181, SD 181].

The key term is the repeated "in order to," which contains the explanation of why the process of obscuration is put in motion, in that the term contains a reference to the temporal dimension in Kierkegaard's psychology, and thus to anxiety, which, like the will, is the dialectical middle term by means of which original sin manifests itself.

However, in order to examine the internal dialectic of despair in more detail, we must first look at its origin.

3. "The Hysteria of the Spirit"

The precondition for the description of the crisis in which despair comes into being is the development of childhood and youth, which we have analyzed above in Chapter II. If Kierkegaard had been a faithful disciple of Hegel, the development would have been described as a regular dialectical course, which at its completed goal would have contained the integration of the contradictions and the harmonic interplay of the moments which had been taken up into ("aufgehobene") it. But Kierkegaard's description results in disintegration and conflict instead. This is the destination of the development, so to speak, and it is in this crisis that the spirit first reveals itself as spirit. Where the Hegelian psychologist allows the contradictions to be reconciled into a richer whole, Kierkegaard allows them to develop to the point of explosion. The idealistic, harmonic, growth-oriented point of view is the idea of speculation. Kierkegaard's idea, or the problem he collides with, is the idea of latent contradictions which culminate in a manifest conflict in which they block one another and either stop the development or place it upon a compulsive, one-track course. [20]

In Kierkegaard one can differentiate between a primary identity crisis and its secondary effects. A textual basis for this distinction can be seen, among other places, in the pseudonymous commentary upon the novelistic figure *quidam* in *The Stages on Life's Way*. Throughout the novel he is in a crisis of youth, a condition of melancholia and encapsulation, but it is clear from the appended commentary that this crisis is of a temporary, transient character. The youth who suffers from the crisis does not understand his own condition, but it is said of him that the crisis can either be the passage to a renewal and a personal maturation, if he persists and works through the crisis on its own terms — or it can also be the transition to "the consolidated encapsulation." The latter will be the case if he interrupts the "developmental process of encapsulation" in an arbitrary fashion, breaking out of the condition of ferment and unrest which characterizes him in oRder to find an easy way out of the crisis. He will not succeed, for then the crisis condition will merely be hidden away "in his interior as an *idée fixe"* [XI 451, SLW 389].

The primary crisis is thus an unstable transition, teeming with possibilities, and "the consolidated encapsulation" is one of the forms which the reaction to this crisis *can* take. The primary crisis is the dizzy, chaotic, unstructured phase, in which the individual is thrown back upon himself, becoming painfully aware of the fact that he relates himself to himself. This is the phase of unstable ambiguousness. Genuine, firmly frozen despair consists of the forms of self-understanding which come into being as the reactions to this primary phase, as psychic sediments and fossil formations, which are supposed to conceal ambiguousness.

The primary crisis can thus be described as an identity crisis which arises in the vacuum that follows upon the dissolution of primary identification. The human synthesis is "in its proper relation as it comes originally from God's hand," it says in *The Sickness Unto Death:* "Where, then, does despair come from? From the relationship in which the synthesis relates itself to itself, when God who made man into the relationship, lets it slip from his hand, as it were, that is, when the relationship relates itself to itself" [XI 146, SD 149]. The crisis is man's attempt to structure the amorphous or contradiction-filled vacuum and to find new bases to replace the substantial relations, the "God" of the state of innocence, who now lets man go and makes himself unrecognizable. "But a relationship which is itself precisely by means of the fact that God lets it slip from his hand, as it were — or is itself at the instant in which God lets it slip from his hand, as it were — this relationship can become a misrelationship in the same instant. To despair is the misrelationship coming into being," it says in Kierkegaard's draft of the book [Pap. VIII 2 B 168, p. 260, Hong 68]. The crisis is thus the transition in which the original unitary structure is dissociated. The individual's conscious relation to himself arises in place of substantial relations, and with this comes the consciousness of contradictions.

It is still the idea of created man which is maintained here. However, man's development does not take place uninterruptedly like the lily's or the bird's, but in crises and breaks. The synthesis, which is originally in the proper relation, is the condition of possibility for obedience (the completion of life in agreement with the being created by God), but it is also the condition of possibility for misrelationship and disobedience. In the crisis man does not exist as an obedient and simple self, but as an ambiguous being in conflict with himself and in rebellion against his "determination."

We have a very important insight into the psychology of the crisis in Judge William's piece in *Either/Or II* in a famous passage which begins: "What is melancholia then? It is the hysteria of the spirit." It was the Judge who formulated the proposition that the spirit does not permit itself to be mocked, but revenges itself with melancholia (above Chapter V: 1). A more detailed explanation of this theme of revenge runs like this: "A moment comes in a person's life when immediacy has ripened, as it were, and when the spirit requires a higher form in which it will grasp itself as spirit. As immediate spirit man coheres with the entire earthly life, and now the spirit wishes to gather itself together and come out of this diversion, so to speak, and to transfigure itself into itself. The personality wants to become conscious of itself in its eternal validity. If this does not take place, the movement is stopped and pushed back. Then melancholia enters in." The last two sentences of course direct attention especially to the psychoanalytic teachings of a later era, which wished to explain psychopathological conflicts, and particularly hysteria, as the consequences of instinctual inhibitions and repressions. The similarity is not diminished in the continuation of the quotation: "One can do much to forget it: one can work; one can use more innocent means than a Nero. The melancholia remains there. There is something inexplicable in melancholia. He who has sorrow or worry, he knows why he sorrows or is worried. If you ask a melancholic what his reasons are for this, what it is which is weighing upon him, he will answer 'I do not know; I cannot explain it.' Herein lies the infinity of melancholia. This answer is quite correct; as soon as he knows why, it is abolished, while on the other hand, the sorrow of a person who sorrows is not abolished by the fact that he know why he sorrows" [II 204 f., E/O II 193].

The similarity between the Judge's description of the hysteria of the spirit and the Freudian doctrine of neurosis lies in two points. For the first, they agree that the cause of the crisis condition they are discussing is to be found in a suppression. The Judge speaks of a movement which is stopped or pushed back, Freud of a repression of an instinctual impulse out of an area of consciousness.

The fact that repressed libidinous energy—alias sensual immediacy which has been excluded by the spirit—is the conflict-causing factor is not the judge's view, but is the view of Aesthete A in the Don Giovanni essay, a view which is carried further by Vigilius in *The Concept of Anxiety* (above, Chapter III: 2). The aesthete says that the process of exclusion in which sensuality is isolated and made into an alien area results in anxiety-laden conflict between sensuality and spirit, while the ethicist says that the repression of the spirit's process of individuation results in melancholia. What the two of them have in common with each other and with the Freudian doctrine of repression is that they report about a given process of psychic exclusion (exclusion/suppression/repression) which results in an "abnormal" psychic condition (conflict/melancholia/neurosis). On the other hand, they disagree about what it is that is excluded. Here Freud seems to make common cause with the aesthete when he maintains that it primarily libidinous impulses which are the object of repression, while the ethicist thinks that it is "the spirit"; "for, of course, you scarcely assume, as many doctors do, that melancholia is rooted in the body (and, strangely enough, in spite of this, the doctors cannot cure it)," he writes to his aesthetic friend. "[O]nly the spirit can cure it, for it is rooted in the spirit, and when the spirit finds itself, then all the petty sorrows disappear, all the causes which, in the opinions of various people, produce melancholia, which make them unable to situate themselves in the world, which are the reasons that one comes into the world both too early and too late, which keep one from finding one's place in life . . . " [II 206, E/O II 194]. To this extent, one could, purely provisionally, put forward a formula which suggests both the similarity and the difference between Kierkegaard and Freud, by allowing the following re-writing of the Judge's words to cover Freud's doctrine of repression: "The flesh does not permit itself to be mocked; it revenges itself upon you; it binds you in the chains of neurosis." It is thus a case of a sort of reversed, mirror-image parallel. But even though the formula contains a part of the matter, it is obviously simplified and serves only for provisional orientation. According to Freud's opinion, it was only with the pure (and, in pure form, very rare) actual neuroses that the explanation was to be found in the corporeal alone, chiefly in sexual frustration, while the explanation of the psychoneuroses must be sought in other places, namely in the conflict between the libidinous and the "moral," which resulted in repression.

The other point of similarity between the Judge's description of melancholia and Freud's doctrine of neurosis concerns the question of why suppression or repression takes place. The Judge touches upon this question with his distinction between sorrow and melancholia, but comes no closer to the matter than this. The agreement with Freud is in the fact that the melancholic person does not know the cause of his melancholia; it is not conscious to him, but when it is, the melancholia is abolished, and is thus differentiated from sorrow, which stands in a reasonable and objective relationship to an objective cause. Nor was *quidam*, in *The*

Stages on Life's Way, capable of seeing through his own melancholia, but knew only its occasion. In the draft of the portrait of him it says that "the melancholic person can name many worries which have held him bound, but he cannot name the one which binds him" [Pap. V B 148, p. 246]. And in the published work itself: "Psychology knows well that, although the encapsulated person can tell much and with ease about what *has made* him encapsulated, he does not and cannot tell what *makes* him encapsulated." Kierkegaard's explanation of that which the encapsulated person cannot explain himself is thus suggested here; the explanation lies in his future-oriented posture, which he himself does not understand: "This is the most abstract form of encapsulation, when it is the anticipation of a higher life in the condensation of possibility. Therefore he never says what his encapsulation contains, but only that it is present" [VI 450 f., SLW 388-89].

Kierkegaard and Freud are in agreement about seeking the real cause of melancholia (despair) and neurosis, respectively, in a location other than that which the crisis-ridden person himself can propose. But while Freud concentrates his attention upon repressed, past conflicts, Kierkegaard particularly poses the question of the future which determines the present condition of the despairing individual. During a discussion of the child's anxiety in *The Concept of Anxiety* he refers directly to Judge William's description of "the hysteria of the spirit," where it says that this hysteria has "the same significance as melancholia at a much later point" [IV 347, CD 39]. The meaning is not that melancholia is to be regarded straight-forwardly as a product of the child's traumas, but that the child's anxiety and the melancholia of the crisis are forward-looking attitudes, anticipations. And yet the child's anxiety and the adult's melancholia are not the same, of course. The child's anxiety — when his development is not complicated by any spiritual rape — is a positively fascinated dreaming and seeking after the fabulous unknown, a sweet anxiety which only functions as the unnoticed motive force behind the development. The object of anxiety is possibility, it is explained at the point in *The Concept of Anxiety* where Kierkegaard presents his theory of time. As possibility appeared to innocence, so does that which is to come appear to the older individual, and "the possible corresponds completely to that future" [IV 397 f., CD-82]. The entire theory about the significance of time could therefore also have been developed earlier in the book, it is written, but at the point where it is brought up it leads forward to the sections which deal with adult psychology [IV 400 note, CD 83 note]. The child's forward-directedness does indeed correspond to that of the adult, but the difference between them is also important. The anxiety of innocence only promotes activity, while the anxiety of the crisis acts as a blockage. After the fall into sin, anxiety is no longer equally pleasing and unpleasing, but the antipathetic relationship preponderates over the sympathetic. It is thus this alien possibility — alien because the expectation is colored by the present state of crisis in the expectant person — which blocks the development and compels the individual to attempt to evade it (cf. the next section).

The evasive manoeuvre is here called suppression. The idea is closely connected with the phenomenon which according to Anti-Climacus was called obscuration. It is precisely this sketch of "the hysteria of the spirit" by Judge William which illustrates the notion of the crisis-ridden person, who "labors to submerge his soul in obscurity" i.e., the thesis of produced ignorance, which is sin, and the assertion about sin being in the will: "Melancholia is sin, is really the sin *instar omnium,*[21] for it is the sin of not willing deeply and passionately, and this is the mother of all sins" [II 205, E/O II 193].

In what follows I will call this evasive manoeuvre *the theme of escape,* just as I used the phrase theme of revenge above with respect to the notion that escape revenges itself. Properly regarded, both themes are maintained in the Judge's formula about the spirit which does not permit itself to be mocked, but revenges itself with melancholia; for the attempt to mock the spirit is of course the attempt to escape from (evade) it, that is, to suppress or obscure the challenge which it represents.

4. Time

"Since man now is consciousness, he is the place at which the eternal and the temporal continually come into contact, where the eternal breaks into the temporal." The statement is from one of Kierkegaard's edifying discourses about the bird and the lily. The fact that man is determined by the eternal means psychologically that he is aware of time. Man can — these are the symptoms of his determination — be bored or worried or have expectations, while time never seems long to the bird, because it is unable to distance itself from that which is momentary. "Therefore, man has a dangerous enemy which the bird does not know — time, an enemy, yes, an enemy or a friend, from whose persecutions or company man cannot withdraw, because he has the eternal in consciousness, and must therefore measure it." The eternal is the standard of measure with whose help time becomes a reality for man, and the fact that man is determined by the eternal means that he develops himself in time and relates himself to the future: "By means of consciousness he discovers a world which the most well-traveled bird does not know, the future. And when this future is taken back into the moment by means of consciousness, then a concern is discovered which the bird does not know . . . " [VIII 330, GS 214-15].

Consciousness is consciousness of time, and consciousness of time is the condition of possibility for the crisis. This possibility is the special feature of man, "the proof of his divine origin . . . for if there were no future, then there would be no past, and were there neither future nor past, then man would be bound in slavery like the animal, whose head is bowed to the ground and whose mind is captive in the service of the instant," one reads in Kierkegaard's first edifying discourse, "The Expectation of Faith" [III 29, ED I 18]. The discourse then deals with how man "can conquer the future" by means of faith, i.e., with a confidence which makes his present life "healthy and strong." But, Kierkegaard thinks, if this life in the present is to be other and more than a pillow upon which one whiles away one's existence, it must presuppose a continuing struggle and an eternal victory over the future. "The struggle with it is the most ennobling. He who struggles with the present struggles with an individual thing, against which he can use the whole of his might. Therefore if a person had nothing else with which to struggle, it would be possible for him to go through his entire life victoriously, without, however, learning to know himself or his own strength. He who fights with the future has a more dangerous enemy. He cannot remain in ignorance about himself, for he fights with himself. The future does not exist, it borrows its power from him himself. And when it has stolen it from him, then it reveals itself outside of him as the enemy he must encounter. Let a man be as strong as he wants to be, no man is stronger than himself. Therefore we often see them in life: people who won every battle, who then became impotent when it was a future enemy with whom they had to deal; their arms became paralyzed. . . . Thus when a man struggles with the future, he learns that, however strong he is, there is one enemy who is stronger, and that is himself; there is one enemy he cannot conquer by himself, and that is himself" [III 30 f., ED I 19-20]. The future is a reflection of the past and the present, "everyone forms it, all according to how he himself is formed" [III 33, ED I 22]. But this reflection acts retroactively upon the present, i.e., upon the individual's present self-understanding and actions.

In the discourse on the expectation of faith Kierkegaard himself states that this conception of time is one side of his theory of anxiety: "If you have anxiety, it is because you wish; for anxiety is the form of the wish" [III 24, ED I 12]. In *Either/Or* the aesthete states more precisely that "anxiety always contains in itself reflection upon time, for I cannot be anxious about the present, but only the past and the future" [II 153, E/O I 153]. The temporal aspect is already hinted at in the fact that Kierkegaard's theory of anxiety, as has been mentioned, was originally a

"Theory of Presentiments" [Pap. II A 18, Hong 91]. In 1839 he draws this diagram in his journal:

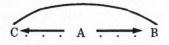

$$C \longleftarrow \cdots \quad A \quad \cdots \longrightarrow B$$

"A" is the present, "B" the future, and "C" the past. But the presentiment does not arise when I turn from "A" to "B," for then I see nothing at all. Presentiment does not lie in the directing of the eye toward the future, but "in the reflection of the directing of the eye toward the past." Thus, when I turn myself toward "C," the disposition to perceive "B" is developed [Pap. II A 558, Hong 3553].

The relationship to the future, i.e., the individual's expectation and interpretation of his own future, is determined by the past. But Kierkegaard is more interested in prospective than in retrospective determination. As early as his first draft of the theory, from 1837, he noted that the expectation of faith or mistrust is an active but ambiguous motivating factor: "There is usually a certain presentiment which precedes everything which is to happen . . . , but just as this can have a deterrent effect, so can it also have a tempting effect, when the idea awakens in a man that he is predestined, as it were; he sees himself as though he were transported somewhere by consequences upon which he had no influence" [Pap. II A 18, Hong 91].

The temporal aspect is of enormous importance, and Kierkegaard employs it often, both for the description of the nadir of existence lived by his aesthete and in edifying contexts. The unhappiness of "the unhappiest person" is described in *Either/Or* in temporal categories — in a tour de force of conceptual equilibrium, which builds up a scale of intricacy in relation to the past and the future, ending in this absurd climax: "He cannot love, for love is always in the present tense, and he has no present time, no future, no past. And yet he is a sympathetic nature, and he hates the world only because he loves it. He has no passion, not because he lacks it, but because he has the opposite passion in the same instant. He has no time for anything, not because his time is taken up with anything, but because he has absolutely no time at all. He is impotent, not because he lacks strength, but because his own strength makes him impotent" [I 231, E/O I 224].

In a commentary upon *Either/Or*, Kierkegaard has remarked that "that upon which Part One continually shipwrecks is time" [Pap. IV A 213, Hong 907]. He operates most graphically with the category of time in the "Diapsalmata," the aphoristic self-surrender of Aesthete A, a phenomenological analysis of a neurotic's *Eigenwelt* — a Dasein analyst would probably say. The author of the "Diapsalmata" lives in a continual attempt to escape from his present and future by means of flight into the unambiguousness of the past, in continual longing for childhood and what was uncomplicated and pre-reflective, longing for memory, death, and dreamless sleep, the protective dark of the bed and the grave: "Why was I not born in a miserable tenement, why did I not die as a little child? Then my father would have put me in a little coffin, taken me under his arm, carried me out to the grave one Sunday morning, thrown the earth upon the coffin himself, said half-aloud a couple of words comprehensible only to himself . . . " [I 27 f., E/O I 39]. Only in the moment of longing for the past, of happy memory, can he encapsulate himself with his inner schism and talk to himself undisturbed. "Then I sit thoughtfully like an old grizzled man, and explain the pictures in a soft voice, almost a whisper, and at my side sits a child who listens, even though he remembers everything before I say it" [I 30, E/O I 41]. The past is his possibility of finding forgetfulness and security, and therefore he always seeks regression. When he is confronted with the present and the future, the schism in him, which could be mastered in remembrance, becomes an acute conflict which freezes him fast. He is only occupied with himself; his surroundings exist only as the object of his mockery and loathing, and the conflict takes place upon the inner stage. Here he struggles with his own fantasy and with the bloodless forms to which he himself gives life and existence. He is "bound in chains which are formed of dark imaginings, of anxiety-producing dreams, of resltess thoughts, of fearful presentiments, of unexplained anxieties" [I 21, E/O I 33]. He attempts to live facing backward, because his experience of time is blocked by anxiety. Time is not experienced as succession and going forward, but as a frozen condition of stasis: "I used to mount my horse easily and healthily and heartily. When I rode slowly through the woods it was as though I flew. Now when the horse is lathered almost to the point of collapse it seems to me that I have not gone anywhere . . . . My soul has lost possibility. If I were to wish for anything, I would not wish for wealth or power but for the passion of possibility, the eternally youthful, fiery eye, which everywhere sees possibility" [I 29, E/O I 40]. But anxiety is the form of the wish, and therefore he cannot break through the time barrier, but is unceasingly cast back into himself: "Time goes. Life is a stream, people say, etc. I cannot notice it; time stands still and I with it. All the plans I make fly straight back into my face; when I spit, I spit in my own face" [I 11, E/O I 25]. This blocking, then, is the reason for his escape. The future is an anxiety-producing vacuum which he seeks to avoid and is only forced into it unwillingly, driven only by the past to which he vainly seeks to return: "What will come? What will the future bring? I do not know. I suspect nothing. When a spider hurls himself down into the consistency of his nature from a firm point, then he continually sees empty space in front of him, where he can find no footing, however much he twitches. So it is with me; there is an empty space in front of me; what drives me forward is a consistency which lies behind me" [I 9, E/O I 24].

When one reads of the pseudonyms' or of Kierkegaard's experiences of time, one can get the impression that it is a matter of especially unusual phenomena without universal relevance. The idea is here, as elsewhere, that the exception illuminated the rule—as it is expressed at one point: "The genius manifests . . . most clearly what in less original people is lived in such a way that it cannot easily be placed in its category. The genius generally differs from every other man only in that he consciously begins within his historical presuppositions as primitively as Adam" [IV 412, CD 93-94]. Therefore, the experience of time which is characteristic of Kierkegaard himself and of his aesthetes is fundamentally the same as that which is also present in the lives of people who experience things less intensely.

"What is anxiety?" Kierkegaard asks in a discourse on the worry of self-torment: "It is the next day" [X 95, ChD 80]. The discourse deals with "the heathen," and here this means the common citizen, Everyman. He relates himself to time just as much as the self-analyzing aesthete, except that he does not make this clear to himself, but his worry and his officiousness proclaim it. "Earthly and worldly worry are made possible precisely by the fact that man was composed of the temporal and the eternal, that man became a self. But when he became a self, the next day came into existence for him. And it is fundamentally here that the battle is fought . . . . The next day, that is the grappling iron, by the help of which the enormous mass of worries gets hold of 'the individual's' light ship—if it succeeds, he is at the mercy of that power" [X 88, ChD 74-75]. The future determines the present and takes from it its content and fullness. "What today is like means nothing to him one way or the other, happy or sad, fortunate or misfortunate, he can come neither to use nor enjoy it, for he cannot get away from the invisible writing on the wall: Tomorrow" [X 95, ChD 80]. And despite the fact that the heathen lives less consciously than the aesthete, it is the same experience of time which is revealed in his worry: "With whom, then, does the heathen struggle in his anxiety? With himself, with an imaginary thing; for the next day is an impotent nothing unless you youself give it your strength. And if you give it all of your strength, then you come to know as the heathen did, in a frightful way, how strong you are—for what an enormous power the next day has! The next day, which the heathen goes toward with horror in his soul, struggling against it as a person who is dragged to the place of his execution, laboring against it in vain . . . ." It is thus from this anxiety-laden future that the heathen seeks to escape: "He is so anxious about the next day that he casts himself into wild narcosis in order to forget it—and to forget how anxious he is" [X 94 f., ChD 80-81].

The edifying theme of the discourse is—here as elsewhere—to become present to oneself in the concrete. The same is also the case in the section of *The Concept of Anxiety* where Kierkegaard explains man as "a *synthesis of the temporal and the eternal*" [IV 391, CD 76]. However, the entire conceptual definition results in the psychological theory of prospective motivation, with which we by now have already become acquainted in other texts, and it is probably best understood in this perspective: "For freedom, the possible is the future, and for time the future is the possible. In the individual life, anxiety corresponds to both. Exact and correct linguistic usage therefore links together anxiety and the future. Sometimes one does indeed speak of having anxiety for the past, which seems to conflict with this. However, upon closer inspection it can be seen that one only says this in such a way that the future becomes visible in one fashion or another. The past about which I am to have anxiety must stand in a relationship of possibility to me. If I have anxiety with respect to a past misfortune, then it is not insofar as it is past, but insofar as it can be repeated, i.e., become future" [IV 398, CD 82].

To Kierkegaard's prospective psychology belongs the thesis that "in a certain sense the future means more than the present and the past; for in a certain sense the future is the whole of which the past is a part, and the future can mean the whole in a certain sense. This is due to the fact that the eternal first means the future, or that the future is the incognito in which the eternal, incommensurable as it is for time, nevertheless wishes to preserve its intercourse with time" [IV 395 f., CD 80]. In the crisis, "the future [is] the possibility of the eternal (of freedom) in the individual in the form of anxiety. When freedom's possibility reveals itself to freedom, freedom succumbs" [IV 397 f., CD 81].

Kierkegaard has sought to clarify this transition, which is exactly the transition from the primary crisis to consolidated despair, by means of a dramatic suggestive metaphor. In *The Sickness Unto Death* he compares the crisis with an attack of dizziness; despite the fact that the two phenomena must not be confused, dizziness is nevertheless "teeming with analogies to despair" [XI 146, SD 149]. What this analogy means is clear from *The Concept of Anxiety*: "One can compare anxiety with dizziness.

He whose eye comes to look down into a yawning chasm becomes dizzy. But what is the reason; it is as much in his eye as in the abyss. For suppose he had not stared down. Thus anxiety is the dizziness of freedom, which begins when the spirit wants to posit the synthesis, and then freedom peers down into its own possibility, and grasps finitude in order to support itself. Freedom succumbs in that dizziness." Here, anxiety is that which is absolutely ambiguous and problematically indefinable, the individual's own future, presented as a projection of the present unstructuredness of the crisis, containing "the possibility of every concretion." This represented future acts retroactively upon the present: "This in turn is something overwhelming, which determines the individual's ambiguous sympathetic and antipathetic situation." In this condition the individual "swoons" — "from a psychological point of view, the fall into sin always occurs in impotence" [IV 366 f., CD 55].

5. Ambiguousness and Unambiguousness

5:1. *The Position of Ambiguousness*

This section will be a sort of exegesis of the theme that freedom becomes dizzy and succumbs and grasps finitude with which to support itself. The internal dialectic of consolidated despair will be circumscribed quite provisionally with the help of several formulae, and at the same time an affinity between Kierkegaard's psychology and his interpretation of existence will be adumbrated.

The human self never exists as achieved or accomplished or simply as unambiguously attainable actuality, but only as possibility. The self is becoming, and the opposite of becoming is stagnation. If we wish to define more precisely the elements of the "becoming-stagnation" antithesis, we can do so by translating "becoming" as *simplicity* and "stagnation" as *unambiguousness,* and by introducing as a helping device a third concept, *ambiguousness,* which relates to both of the other concepts. A basic pattern in Kierkegaard's thinking can be sketched with the help of these terms.

Simply the fact that anxiety is a basic concept in Kierkegaard's psychology is enough to make it clear that ambiguousness is a basic concept for him as well. Furthermore, it is visible everywhere. But the ambiguousness of anxiety is fundamentally the same as the ambiguousness of existence of which Climacus speaks in the *Postscript,* e.g., when he connects it with Plato's doctrine of eros and defines existence as "that child who is born of the infinite and the finite, the eternal and the temporal, and who is therefore continually striving." It is the same doubleness and the same infinite striving which also entered into Anti-Climacus' definition of the self: " . . . no matter how much the subject contains infinity within himself, by being an existing individual, he is in becoming" [VII 81, CUP 85].

That existence is ambiguousness is thus not a statement about any objective property of the world, but a statement about man in the world. Ambiguousness is man's experience of the world, because he is not capable of experiencing the world independently of subjectivity and independently of time. The attempt of philosophy to do so is an illusion: "Precisely because abstract thinking is *sub specie æterni,* [22] it ignores the concrete; it ignores temporality, the becoming of existence, and the suffering of the existing individual which is due to his being a composite of the eternal and the temporal which has been placed in existence" [VII 288, CUP 267].

At a couple of points in the *Postscript* Kierkegaard utilizes the Platonic dualism as the point of departure for the formulation of his own dualistic thinking about existence. Existence is an "intermediate condition," and man is an "intermediate being"; and to exist is "not to be in the same sense that a potato is, nor yet in the same sense that the idea is. Human existence has an idea in itself, but nevertheless is not idea-existence. Plato put the idea in second place as the middle term between God and matter, and as an existing individual man may well participate in the idea, but is not himself the idea" [VII 318 f., CUP 294-95]. Kierkegaard can thus determine man's position in a fashion which is in agreement with the classical European dualistic model of the world, which puts man on an intermediate step in the cosmic hierarchy, in a tragic double position: "Placed on this isthmus of a middle state," as it is written in Alexander Pope's *Essay on Man.*

What the majority of the thinkers who acknowledge the dualistic picture of man's situation have in common is that they seek to conquer the doubleness it contains. [23] To the extent that the point of departure is taken in man's existence as an intermediate being, the model of the world is dualistic. But to the extent that it succeeds in conquering or approaching an "eternal" standpoint, it is monistic. Consequently, there is a movement from dualism to monism, from ambiguousness to unambiguousness, from tension to harmony, from a wealth of antitheses to mediation and congruence between idea and existence, the merging of thought and being, the reconciling of eternity and temporality, so that the poles of the duality are covered over or viewed in a perspective which makes the contrast comprehensible and manageable, and makes existence understandable and acceptable. "To vindicate the ways of God to man," it says in Pope's *Essay* (with a pious expression which Kierkegaard would have called blasphemous). But the objective of the theodicists is only one variant of this tendency. Another variant is Hegel's philosophy, which can be properly characterized as an historical theodicy. As is well known, in the *Postscript* Kierkegaard directed his fire against Hegel's attempt at reconciliation: "The idea of the system is the subject-object, the unity of thought and being; existence, on the other hand, is precisely the differentiation between these" [VII 111, CUP 112].

Kierkegaard differentiates himself so thoroughly from the dualistic-monistic tradition that his reference to Plato's metaphysics must be called lip service. Dualism is merely the terminology with the assistance of which he formulates man's position in the situation of ambiguousness. The point about his dualism is therefore that it is consistently maintained, and that it is a statement about man and not about the cosmos. "To make man's being into a unity in this life is the tendency to indolence, even if one demonstrates a primary state in which disunity and doubleness were present" [Pap. X 3 A 186, Hong 77]. The emphasis is upon the maintained duality, not upon infinitization as such; " . . . to become oneself is to become concrete. But to become concrete is neither to become finite nor to become infinite, for that which is to become concrete is of course a synthesis" [XI 161, SD 162].

5: 2. *Unambiguousness and Double-Mindedness*

The point of departure is thus ambiguousness or duality. Besides the antitheses of nature-spirit and finitude-infinity (temporality eternity), Kierkegaard occasionally employs other, more or less parallel pairs of concepts, such as being-thinking, life-death, positivity-negativity, and the good-the evil. The point in this context is polarity itself, not the more detailed definition of the poles, but the tension between them. This duality means two things. First of all, it is the condition for every human existence, the postulated presupposition for the authentic realization of existence, and second of all, it is the condition of possibility for despair. Kierkegaard's view, then, is that this condition must be maintained. The possibility of despair (ambiguousness) must unceasingly be present, but its actuality, despair itself, must unceasingly be rejected.

But despair is precisely the attempt to ignore the possibility of despair, i.e., to repress the tension. Except that despair's attempt does not succeed, because the repression does not conquer or abolish the antitheses, but merely removes them from consciousness. Despair is the desperate—i.e., the impossible—attempt to conquer ambiguousness and to "will one thing," and therefore despair is identical with double-mindedness: "[O]r what is it to despair other than to have two wills! For, whether he, the weak person, despairs over the fact that he cannot wrest himself from the evil, or whether he, the presumptuous person, despairs over the fact that he cannot quite wrest himself from the good, they are both double-minded. Both have two wills. Neither of them truly wills one thing, however desperately they seem to will it. Whether it was a woman who was brought to despair by wishing, or a man who despaired in defiance; whether a person despaired because he got his will, or despaired because he did not get his will, every despairing person has two wills, one which he vainly wishes to follow entirely, and one which he vainly wishes to be rid of entirely" [VIII 159, PH 61]. The quotation is from the great confessional discourse upon the phrase "Purity of Heart is to Will One Thing." It summarizes a theme in *The Concept of Anxiety* and *The Sickness Unto Death* with which we will later become acquainted. The despairing person wishes to find unambiguousness, and his very attempt to do so is despair; but because the attempt consists of denying ambiguousness, it is doomed to failure, and the result is simply an intensification of despair, i.e., double-mindedness.

5:3. *Simplicity and Unambiguousness*

The concept of unambiguousness is not given the significance in Kierkegaard's linguistic usage which is assigned to it here, but the concept of simplicity, on the other hand, is. While unambiguousness is the goal which the despairing person vainly pursues, simplicity is the genuine answer to ambiguousness. While, according to the discourse about purity of heart, "the evil" is "disunited with itself, divided against itself," the good is identical with simplicity: *"Truly to will one thing can thus only mean to will the good"* [VIII 163, PH 66]. Or, to cite another discourse, the one earlier cited with respect to obedience: "For if you are unconditionally obedient to God, then there is nothing ambiguous in you, and if there is nothing ambiguous in you, then you are sheer simplicity for God" [XI 43, ChD 344].

The question is thus whether, in Kierkegaard's view, simplicity succeeds in doing what despair's attempt to reach the unambiguous did not succeed in doing; to conquer ambiguousness. If this is the case, it could seem to contradict that which was asserted above, namely, that Kierkegaard demands that the duality be maintained. But according to the discourse on obedience, simplicity does succeed. We thus have need of a more precise definition, and the discourse also gives us this. Kierkegaard says that the simple or the obedient person cannot be tempted, for Satan can only tempt ambiguousness, and "the person who hides himself in God with unconditional obedience is unconditionally secure." But immediately after this he says that man "by being man" is situated in "an enormous danger," placed between two struggling forces, good and evil, God and the world, "a danger, let it be noted, of the sort which certainly cannot be guarded against by trying to forget it" [XI 45, ChD 345]. There is no unambiguous chronological relationship between the danger and security. Security is a security according to the terms of danger. But one must also distinguish between security and guaranteed safety. Security is the way of life of simplicity, and it is unsafe. The demand of despair, on the other hand, is for guaranteed safety: unambiguousness is the vain attempt to evade the danger. One of the pseudonyms expresses it as follows: "Every attempt to block one's receptivity of the fact that one is in danger is an aesthetic deviation, which tends not toward poetry, but toward the aesthetic, which is callous in its relation to actuality" [VI 492, SLW 424].

This is a theme which is to be found throughout Kierkegaard's psychology, but it is also active in his criticism of speculative philosophy. The formula which "despair" and "speculation" share is unambiguousness, or more accurately, the attempt to establish unambiguous positions which are designed to make it possible to keep ambiguousness at a distance, to put it behind one in a definitive sense. According to Kierkegaard, the attempt is in principle a vain one; ambiguousness is always unacknowledged and present. But this lack of acknowledgement does not hamper this position from performing satisfactorily in a social and cultural context. In the *Postscript* it is principally the socially accepted, well-established, and to this extent "successful" philosophical and religious attempts to become "finished" in an unambiguous conclusiveness which are discussed, while in the psychological writings the accent is upon the analysis of the latent, sometimes manifest, but always more or less repressed conflict, which is the driving force in the attempt to establish a safe position as a defense of guaranteed safety. But the fact that unambiguousness and double-mindedness are in fact two sides of the same thing — that unambiguousness covers over double-mindedness and functions as compensation for subjective uncertainty — can be seen, among other ways, from the fact that speculation and the attempts to obtain objective certainty are not only torn to shreds in the *Postscript* because they ignore the ambiguous terms of existence, but are also diagnosed in *The Concept of Anxiety* as forms or symptoms of "anxiety for the good," the demonic element which is most characteristic of the forms of despair. Here it is not especially Hegel's speculation, but the right-wing Hegelian speculative attempts to "marshal a new, an exhaustive, an absolutely correct proof, combined from all previous proofs of the immortality of the soul" or for God's existence, which are mentioned as examples. The speculator defends himself against his own insecurity and his lack of conviction; he "saves . . . and tranquilizes his soul" with the help of the proof and the intellectual efforts of marshalling it. The proof is a parrying manoeuvre, and as such it conceals the problem—the speculator's own double-mindedness, his anxiety for the good—instead of revealing it. Therefore, the intention is not realized: "To the same degree that the excellence of the proof increases, certainty seems to decrease" [IV 448-50, CD 124-26].

Climacus' criticism of Hegel's philosophy in the *Postscript* is similarly "unobjective," in the sense that it does not only concern the system as such, but also the speculative thinker as a person, because by virtue of, or in the shelter of, the system he is able to place himself beyond the antitheses, and to make his disciples capable of doing the same thing. By excluding negativity, with its many meanings, systematic speculation tends toward unambiguous positivity. The religious person who consolidates himself in his salvation does the same thing. The sort of religious certainty which does not maintain that the relationship to the absolute can only be determined negatively and without the possibility of verification, is an illusion and a stagnation in the unambiguous: "As soon as certainty's form ceases to be uncertainty, as soon as uncertainty does not continually keep the religious person suspended in order to grasp certainty, as soon as certainty fills up the religious person, as it were, yes, then he is naturally on the way to becoming [mere] substance" [VII 497, cf. 445; CUP 453, cf. 407].

Kierkegaard's concept of security is thus dialectical. Security can be the symptom of a "successful" repression, an unacknowledged despair, but security can also be a sign that a conflict is actually vanquished in simplicity, because it has been maintained as a possibility. To express this with a quotation from *The Sickness Unto Death*: ". . . all characteristics in relation to despair are dialectical . . . . Security and tranquility can mean despair, exactly this security, this tranquility, can be despair. And it can mean that despair has been conquered and that peace has been won" [XI 156, SD 157]. This line of reasoning could be exemplified with many references to Kierkegaard's philosophical and theological polemics. I mention only the section of the *Postscript* which deals with keeping "the wound of negativity open" [VII 73, CUP 78]. "Precisely because the negative is present in existence and is everywhere present (for existence is constantly in a state of becoming), it is therefore important to remain constantly aware of this as the only means of salvation" [VII 69, CUP 75].

This line of reasoning is just as essential to Kierkegaard's psychology as to his philosophical writings. Unambiguousness is escape from ambiguousness; driven by internal insecurity, it seeks a positive safety, in which the negativity and the conflict are left behind, past, and excluded as possibilities. But it is precisely the excluded possibilities and the need to keep them excluded which gives this form of existence its narrowness, for unambiguousness must defend itself against what has been excluded and against the alternative in order to maintain its position.

The simple person surrenders himself defenselessly to existence. Simplicity is infinite becoming, openness and continuing renewal while persisting in ambiguousness. It admits its own double-mindedness to itself and persists in this consciousness. Therefore it is never "finished." It is sympathetic, receptive, and transparent; it is "silence, obedience, and joy," confidence surpassing all understanding and in spite of all appearances. It is defenseless invulnerability and knowing naiveté: "No, there is only one thing which wins and more than wins, which from the beginning has infinitely conquered all cunning: the simplicity of the Gospel, which simply lets itself be deceived, as it were, and yet simply continues to be the simple. And this too is what is edifying about the simplicity of the Gospel, that evil cannot gain over it the power to make it clever, or to make it want to be clever. Truly, evil has already won a victory, and a very considerable one, when it has moved simplicity to want to be clever — in order to make itself secure. Because only simplicity is secure, and eternally secure, in allowing itself simply to be deceived, no matter how clearly it sees through the deception" [XI 294, ChD 374]. Here it is a matter of a deceptive and hypocritical surrounding world: "For in the infinite sense only one deception is possible, self-deception," as it is expressed in *Works of Love* [IX 269, WL 223]. But this is also the case when it is a matter of the deception of existence, of ambiguousness, of the objective uncertainty: simplicity surrenders itself unconcerned and full of confidence; it places itself at the mercy of life.[24]

Unambiguousness secures itself, and it is very unwillingly deceived. It wishes to have joy without its conditions; it loves the destination but not the road, security more than the truth. Therefore it grasps finitude with which to support itself: "All we people, we are more or less intoxicated. But with us it is as with a drunken man who is not so completely drunk that he has lost consciousness. No, he has just the consciousness of the fact that he is a little drunk, and this is precisely why he takes pains to conceal it from others, and if possible from himself. What does he do, then? He looks for something with which he can support himself. He walks right alongside the houses and walks so straightly without getting dizzy — a sober man. But he would not dare to walk across a great plaza, for then what he himself knows well enough in private would become obvious — that he is drunk

Things are the same, spiritually understood, with us people" [XII 453, JY 129]. In this section I have only attempted to circumscribe—purely provisionally—what I have previously labelled the theme of escape: man's escape from ambiguousness to unambiguousness, from anxiety to safety. We will gradually approach a more precise psychological understanding of this. The dialectical connection of the theme of escape to the theme of revenge has been suggested previously; the spirit does not permit itself to be mocked, because the eternal (the infinite and, for man, the ambiguous) which one casts away returns in disguised forms as double-mindedness.

6. Escape and Revenge

6:1. *Freud and Kierkegaard*

In the preceding pages I have pointed out similarities and differences between Freud and Kierkegaard on various points. It is now appropriate to discuss the relation between them a bit more systematically. I will sketch a central dialectic in psychoanalysis with the help of the Kierkegaardian themes I have called the theme of escape and the theme of revenge. Freud had no knowledge of Kierkegaard, and thus we must rule out any influence. The intention is thus something else, namely, to point out a particular conflict structure which Freud (and some of the post-Freudians) has in common with Kierkegaard. But the intention is also to use the comparison as part of a more precise depiction of Kierkegaard on the points where he deviates most markedly from the Freudian conception and provides an alternative to it. There is, however, reason to mention that the discussion of Freud is not concluded with the present section, which only provides the premises for a continued dialogue between these two great psychologists in the latter portions of the book.

I return to Judge William's description of "the hysteria of the spirit." In the preceding pages a parallel was drawn between this and Freud's doctrine of repression, but instead of repression I chose the expression "suppression" in order to note the difference. It is now possible—in relation to both repression and suppression—to pose three questions in order to gain a more detailed knowledge of: 1) the consequences of suppression; 2) the object of suppression; and 3) the cause of suppression. Judge William gave a clear answer to the first of these three questions ("if the movement is stopped, if it is suppressed, melancholia enters") and, not quite so precisely, the second question as well (it is the movement of "the spirit" or "the personality" which is suppressed). It is Kierkegaard's theme of revenge which is formulated with these two answers: when the spirit is mocked, it revenges itself with melancholia. The third question, on the other hand, concerns the theme of escape, and the Judge gave no clear answer to it. But the answer is given in Kierkegaard's analyses of the temporal dimension and of anticipatory anxiety, and these analyses were begun as early as the journals from the end of the 1830's. A representative answer to the question of the cause of suppression is the one cited in *The Sickness Unto Death:* ". . . it does not become entirely clear to him that this is why he is doing it, that he does it in order to bring about obscurity."

The similarity between Freud and Kierkegaard lies in their answers to questions 1 and 3, the difference in their answer to question 2. 1): Just as suppression results in melancholia (the hysteria of the spirit), so does repression result in neurosis (particularly hysteria). It is the theme of revenge. 3): Just as the individual stops the movement *in order to* avoid the anxiety which would be connected with carrying it through, so does repression arise in an attempt to avoid an anticipated danger situation. It is the theme of escape. But 2): While the object of suppression is "the spirit," or the individual's own potential future, the objects of repression are certain past conflicts and traumas, especially of the sexual variety.

Thus the relationship can be put into a diagram, but like all diagrams this too is lacking and full of contradictions, and therefore requires comment. (I point out that in this chapter we have not yet directed our attention to Kierkegaard's conflict psychology in the narrow sense, but are remaining with general formulations.) I have noted earlier that the antithesis between Kierkegaard's "the spirit does not permit itself to be mocked" and Freud's "the flesh does not permit itself to be mocked," is less absolute than that arrangement might suggest. The same thing can be seen when attention is directed to the temporal dimension. It was written above that the object of suppression for Kierkegaard is something in the future (more closely defined, the individual's present expectation of the future), while the object of repression for Freud is something past. But this antithesis was modified immediately preceding the above statement when it was said that the repression arises in order to make the individual capable of avoiding an anticipated danger, that is, something in the future or expected. This sounds indeed like an inconsistency, and it is surely explained best by means of a sketch of how Freud's theories developed historically.

As a prelude to this sketch, yet another schematic resumé will be undertaken: [7]

	Revenge	Escape
Freud	Repression → Neurosis or: Frustration → Anxiety	Anxiety → Repression
Kierkegaard	Suppression→ Melancholia (cf. Obscuration→Despair, Unambiguousness → Double-Mindedness)	Anxiety → Suppression (Obscuration) (cf. Ambiguousness → Unambiguousness)

The point here is that while, with Kierkegaard, the themes of revenge and escape stand from the very beginning in a dialectical connection which is so intimate that it is really an abstraction to keep them separated, with Freud, it is a case of two different theories which were formulated 20 to 30 years apart. The correct formulation of Kierkegaard's conception is that escape revenges itself (the revenge consists in the fact that the escape is unsuccessful):

anxiety → suppression (obscuration) → despair (melancholia)

or, in a more complex formulation:

ambiguousness → unambiguousness/double-mindedness.

These are the formulae with which we will work; they have been given a provisional explanation above (especially ambiguousness and anticipatory anxiety), and they will be exemplified in more detail later on (especially the dialectic of unambiguousness/double-mindedness, which is what constitutes despair).

For Freud, on the other hand, the dialectic between escape and revenge was not clear from the beginning; only in the course of the 1920's does the formula:

anxiety → repression → neurosis

coincide with his conception. Before that time it is by and large only the theme of revenge which occupies him, though it had a number of modifications which point forward, and these will be discussed here.

6: 2. Freud's Theories of Anxiety

One finds two different theories of anxiety in Freud. The first can be expressed (slightly simplified) in the formula: frustration, inhibition or repression of the libido → anxiety as the product. In the second theory of anxiety, the formula is turned around, so that the sequence becomes: anxiety → repression. This latter theory was put forth in the book *Inhibitions, Symptoms and Anxiety* from 1926. For the time being, we will only cite here a summary, self-revising statement from 1932: "it was not the repression that created the anxiety; the anxiety was there earlier; it was the anxiety that made the repression!" [*New Introductory Lectures on Psycho-Analysis,* Freud XXII 86].

This change in Freud's view is well-known.[25] It is also clear from the above that this shift is the precondition for a meaningful comparison of Freud and Kierkegaard. However, Freud's second theory of anxiety is no sudden impulse. On the contrary, it was prepared over many years, and in order to understand what this change involves, it will therefore be useful to outline some of the main characteristics of the movement of Freud's thought from the beginning in the 1890's, to the first great synthesis from 1916-17, and forward to the new breakthrough of the 1920's.

The simplest formula for that which I here call the Freudian theme of revenge is the early observation that different forms of sexual frustration cause anxiety. At this point, the formula "the flesh does not permit itself to be mocked" is really appropriate, because the idea is that the libidinous energy which does not find release in staisfying sexual activity, is re-formed into anxiety, which is thus a biochemical product of the frustration. This, then, is the explanation of actual neuroses (anxiety neuroses). The first decisive step in the direction of a more differentiated understanding is taken at approximately this time with the beginning of the study of psychoneuroses (especially hysteria and compulsive neurosis), or the neuropsychoses of defense, as they are are also called in the first publications from the 1890's. In Freud's earliest terminology, the word "defense" was synonymous with repression, and repression, as is well known, was the fundamental discovery which provided him with the explanation of psychoneuroses. His next step was thus the exploration of the newly-discovered unconscious area, the tabooed sexuality, et al.; the intention was to understand what particular content of consciousness constituted the object of repression, and in addition to study the hidden and circuitous routes by which the repressed material manifests itself. The symbolism of dreams is thus one of these disguised forms of manifestation, the neurotic symptom is another, and the involuntary revelations of wit is a third. They require interpretation, that is, they must be explained retrospectively in the light of their origin in the repressed material, which is predominantly of the sexual sort. Thus does Freud deepen the question of the object of repression. On the other hand, for the time being he laid no stress upon the question of why repression takes place, but was provisionally satisfied with a relatively rudimentary and unproblematically adopted theory of the conscious I, whose interest is self-preservation, exercising censorship upon unacceptable impulses and recollections in the name of respectability and, so to speak, on behalf of social morality.

In the older theory, the question of the consequences of repression is answered clearly enough, as far as it goes, in saying that the consequence is the formation of the neurotic symptom, which functions as a camouflaged expression of the repressed conflict material. On the other hand, in the beginning, Freud does not seem to posit any connection between the symptoms and anxiety. In the actual neuroses, anxiety is the principal symptom, while with the psychoneuroses we find other symptoms: compulsive rituals, phobias, hysterical paralysis, etc. Gradually, however, Freud discovers a dynamic-psychological coherence between anxiety and the other symptoms. This discovery is very significant, even though it, too, was later revised. In the resumé in the *Introductory Lectures on Psycho-Analysis* from 1916-17, anxiety is inserted as a sort of middle term between repression and the formation of symptoms. It is not the simple sexual frustration, but also the repression itself which results in anxiety. Every passion can be transformed into anxiety, when the content of the notion with which it is connected becomes the object of repression. Anxiety is thus one of the symptoms of psychoneurosis, but at the same time it assumes a special position in relation to the other symptoms. Freud puts forward the supposition that "in an abstract sense" it can be said that "in general symptoms are only formed to escape an otherwise unavoidable generating of anxiety. If we adopt this view, anxiety is placed, as it were, in the very centre of our interest in the problem of neurosis" [Freud XVI 404].

From being a sign of something else, which it is therefore important to ignore or see through [cf. e.g., *Totem and Taboo,* Freud XIII 24-25 and 97], anxiety has now become an independent, dynamic factor which requires attention. The "centre" in which it is placed is more precisely defined as the point between the repression and the symptom. Where Freud earlier operated with two causal connections without mutual connection — frustration → anxiety and repression → symptom — he now operates with the continuity of repression → anxiety → symptom. The connection between the first two of these links is explained causally, now as earlier: instinctual impulses and the passions connected to them are converted into anxiety by means of inhibitions and repressions. This is the Freudian theme of revenge, his answer to the questions of the object of and the consequences of repression. But in addition to this, there is now introduced, with more emphasis than previously, the question of the cause of repression. The question does not yet concern the repression itself, but the symptom-formation, and the anwer lies in the formula "to escape." The symptom is not merely a sign of something else, but it functions actively as the defense against or the escape from this other thing— anxiety. With this the theme of escape is clearly sounded. The escape route goes from the passion of the anxiety to the anxiety-reducing symptom-formation. And this broadening of the theory is connected to the fact that Freud goes beyond the mere natural-scientific, causal-genetic way of presenting the problem, in which one works with the concepts of cause and effect in a straightforward sequence, and in which causality is understood in analogy with that which can be observed and verified in biological processes. This sort of an explanation can be applied to the transition of repression → anxiety. But the transition of anxiety → symptom is explained with the help of another analogy, namely, with realistic anxiety, and this explanation is not objectively causal, but phenomenological; the active factor is not described as an objectively ascertainable quantity (damned-up instinctual energy), but as a subjective quality of experience (anxiety). Realistic anxiety is the normal reaction to threatening external dangers, which lead to a more or less appropriate attempt to avoid the dangerous situation. The individual experiences anxiety in a threatening situation, and this experience results in an escape or defense reaction. Something similar takes place with respect to neurotic anxiety: "Just as the attempt at flight from an external danger is replaced by standing firm and the adoption of expedient measures of defense, so too the generation of neurotic anxiety gives place to the formation of symptoms, which results in the anxiety being bound" [Freud XVI 405]. The symptom is thus a defense in itself, not against the instinctual energy as such, but against the anxiety which is the product of the repression of this libido. Such "systems of defense . . . against the possible generation of anxiety" [Freud XVI 410] form a part of every neurotic process.

The chapter on anxiety in Freud's *Lectures* is a crossroads in his understanding of that emotion, because it at once summarizes his earlier theory of anxiety and anticipates the later. There is mention of anxiety as the psychophysiological product of a process of energy transformation; it is the theme of revenge from the first theory of anxiety, and it deals with a scientifically verifiable process described in simple causal categories by an external observer, while on the other hand, it is not recognizable to the person who experiences the anxiety. But beyond this, anxiety also reveals itself as the dynamic motivation factor in the formation of symptoms, when it is observed phenomenologically, i.e., from the standpoint of the person who is experiencing it; not only does one inquire about what unconscious processes have caused the experience of anxiety, but the inquiry also concerns the significance this experience has for the person experiencing it in the acute situation. This significance can be expressed with the formula: I must find myself a way out of this experience—"to escape an otherwise unavoidable generating of anxiety." This is the theme of escape.

The fact that the mode of observation is phenomenological does not, however, imply that Freud is now interested only in the sort of qualities of experience of which the neurotic himself is capable of giving an account or of seeing through clearly Phenomenology does not become identical with introspection, because the experience of anxiety we are concerned with does not manage to become manifest and capable of being registered before the defense against it sets in. The two phases can be held separate from one another methodically, but as experiences they can only be differentiated when the anxiety-reducing, defensive symptom-formation is retarded or absent, for only in such cases does anxiety manage to manifest itself clearly as an experience.Normally, the defense against this anxiety sets in prior to or at approximately the same time that the anxiety becomes conscious, and the person experiencing it thus does not understand what is taking place. Kierkegaard and Freud are in agreement about his. The idea is expressed, among other places, in the cited sentence from *The Sickness Unto Death:* " . . . it does not become entirely clear to him that this is why he is doing it, that he does what he does in order to bring about obscurity. Or perhaps he is even conscious that he is doing this in order to submerge his soul into obscurity, . . . but he is not clearly aware in a deeper sense of what he is doing, of how despairing he is. . . ." Nor does Kierkegaard's phenomenological, finalistic method of observation ("in order to") imply that he is abandoning himself to the immediate, introspective, registering of the experience alone. He also advances hypotheses which make it possible to operate with the context of understanding which generally escapes the attention or consciousness of the experiencing individual. Fully as much as Freud, Kierkegaard makes the claim of knowing more about the despairing person than this person himself normally knows. Therefore we will later on work with a distinction between descriptive and diagnostic statements about despair.

Back to Freud. In the later period—especially in 1923 and thereafter, when ego psychology was introduced with *The Ego and the Id*—attention is directed more single-mindedly to the intentionality which is attributed to the I in its attempts to direct the instinctual impulses and to avoid the anxiety which is connected with them—but with the addition that the I is a partially unconscious area. This shift does not imply that the natural-scientific view of causality disappears from view in the second theory of anxiety. The explanation of the origin of anxiety is now also sought in certain psychophysiological processes. According to the new view, anxiety is not (primarily) a product of libido frustrations in the narrow sense, but of traumatic situations which overwhelm the psyche with stimuli. Birth is the first and prototypical anxiety-producing trauma, but similar trauma situations arise throughout life, especially, however, in the early years of childhood, when the child is totally dependent upon the mother's care, which is why even a short period of loneliness can be enough to call forth intense anxiety. Gradually the child learns to master this anxiety, or, rather, to avoid it.

It is at this point that the decisive transformation of the theory of anxiety lies. But the transformation is only the further development of the point of view in the *Lectures*. In that book anxiety was thus viewed in part as the product of repression, and in part it was placed in a dynamic functional context as the motive for the formation of anxiety-equivalent symptoms. The new thing which happens in *Inhibitions, Symptoms and Anxiety* is that this anxiety is now assumed to come in advance of repression and to be the cause of it, instead of coming after it and being its product. Thus an even more fundamental significance is attributed to anxiety than previously. In anxiety, which is now called signal anxiety, the individual (the child) anticipates a threatening danger, namely, a repetition or a variant of the traumatic (anxiety-provoking) situations experienced earlier. What is decisive is that the I itself produces this anxiety, and that it is not a question of any unambiguously predictable or localizable danger as is the case with fear or realistic anxiety, but of an indistinct, future possibility of danger. "Anxiety has an unmistakable relation to *expectation*: it is anxiety *about* ["*vor*" = literally "before"] something," Freud writes, as if he had recently read *The Concept of Anxiety* (which, as far as is known, he had not): "It has a quality of *indefiniteness and lack of object*" [Freud XX 164-65], which differentiates it from fear. The danger which is anticipated like this is an instinctual danger, it says. The reaction thus consists in the repression of the instinctual impulse. But in contrast to the situation with realistic anxiety, the defense against the indefinite instinctual danger is pathogenic.

The cause of repression is explained in essentially the same way as the cause of the symptom in the *Lectures:* it is in order to avoid anxiety. Nor, in *Inhibitions, Symptoms and Anxiety* is the danger which is avoided by means of repression simply instinct, but it is the anxiety-provoking experience which the staisfaction of the instinct is expected to bring about. The object of repression is the instinctual impulse, Freud says, but the object of anxiety is something far more indefinite and overwhelming, and it is this indefiniteness which makes the defensive reaction against it neurotic: "The essence and meaning of a danger-situation" is "the subject's estimation of his own strength compared to the magnitude of the danger and in his admission of helplessness in the fact of it" [*Inhibitions, Symptoms and Anxiety,* Freud XX 164-67 *et passim*]. In formulations such as this, Freud has suggested that the object of pathogenic anxiety is in actuality not sexuality or other specified "objects," but, in a comprehensive and unlimited sense, the obliteration of the individual and the identity— even though he does not often express it like this. But this nevertheless seems to be the final view behind the many attempts to formulate the matter in more conceivable and tangible terms. "What it is that the ego fears from the external and from the libidinal danger cannot be specified; we know that the fear is of being overwhelmed or annihilated, but it cannot be grasped analytically" [*The Ego and the Id,* Freud XIX 57].

It probably lies in the nature of the matter that the object of the anxiety experience cannot be indicated more definitely and unambiguously than in the cited passages, inasmuch as the object is precisely that which is indefinite and hostile. According to Freud, the expectation of anxiety always has one or another form of connection with the instinctual impulses, and it results in the repression of them. But the object of anxiety is not so much the impulse itself as the danger which it is expected that the satisfaction of that impulse will entail. There is reason to point out here that it is possible to interpret Freud's later theory of anxiety as a theory of separation anxiety. Freud discusses a series of typical anticipations of danger situations, especially anxiety about loss of the object (the mother), anxiety about the loss of the object's love, castration anxiety (i.e., anxiety about punishment), and anxiety about the reprisals of the super-ego (i.e., guilt feelings). These forms of anxiety can all be understood as separation anxiety, and thus not primarily as instinctual anxiety, because the danger is not the satisfaction of the instinct, but the danger of separation from (loss of) the surroundings and their love, in which the satisfaction is expected to result.[26]

If one wishes to put this in relation to Kierkegaard, it is not enough to recall the process of separation and individuation which was examined above in the chapter on what happens when the child is weaned—even though this development, too, could undoubtedly be illuminated more thoroughly with the help of the psychoanalysts. In Kierkegaard, however, there is less emphasis upon the notion of definite danger situations, reprisals, prohibitions, and threats, than upon the analysis of the separation from the substantial unity and from identity-lessness, and the understanding of the indefinite, contourless, and unknown something which is the object of separation anxiety. The shortest formula for Freud's second theory of anxiety is: anticipation → reaction. This formula can also be applied to Kierkegaard's psychology of innocence. But the child's reaction to the anticipation is not suppression or obscuration, but the actualization of that which an anticipation (fantasy) is still only possibility (anxiety about sin brings forth sin; the possibility of being able calls forth the action; the prohibition occasions the transgression by pointing it out as a possibility). On the other hand, Kierkegaard ascribes the reaction to anticipation — which consists of suppression or obscuration — to the crisis, after "the fall into sin." From this it appears that there is a factual disagreement with Freud, which I will discuss later. For the present, what matters is the reaction pattern itself. Freud's second theory of anxiety can be summarized as follows: anticipation of danger (signal anxiety) → reaction (repression of instinctual impulse) → neurosis; , or, anticipation → escape → revenge.

The thing is that signal anxiety cannot be designated as a "revenge" as anxiety could according to the older theory of anxiety. Signal anxiety is an innate potential of experience, which *can* but does not always need to lead to pathogenic repressions. It is these pathogenic repressions, then, which "revenge" themselves.

The corresponding Kierkegaardian formula is thus: anticipation (anxiety about "ambiguousness") → reaction (suppression or obscuration, which is supposed to bring about "unambiguousness") → despair; or, anticipation → escape → revenge.

It is noted that the words "ambiguousness" and "unambiguousness" in this schematic arrangement cover some situations which have been, and some which will be, explained in more detail elsewhere.

6: 3. *Escape Revenges Itself*

In order to gain a somewhat broader perspective on this interpretation, I am setting up a diagram which summarizes and broadens what has been said up to this point regarding the dialectic of escape-revenge (see page 153). The fact that there is a conflict structure which is common to Freud and to the revisionist tendencies within psychoanalysis which have been called "the non-libido schools"[27] is neither new nor surprising. The revisionist analysts acknowledge their heritage and their indebtedness. Karen Horney introduces her critical revision of Freud's psychology in *New Ways in Psychoanalysis*[28] by declaring that the theory of motivation itself, the dynamic model of the personality, and the doctrine of psychic defense are central to psychoanalysis, while the doctrine of instincts and drives is designated as a handicap for its further development in theory and practice. One can find similar views in Erick Fromm.[29]

What is new is simply that Kierkegaard has been put into this context.

On the pages which follow, however, Kierkegaard's thought will only be referred to sporadically, because the intention is not to demonstrate similarities and differences in details, but merely to outline a background, which will hopefully serve to make his conception more commensurable with that of the present.

"Ultimately all such [defensive] measures are designed to secure the ego and to save it from experiencing 'pain,' " Anna Freud writes in summarizing Freud's theories. [30] In an otherwise very critical commentary on Alfred Adler's psychology, Freud remarks that he regards Adler's term " safeguarding [Sicherung],' for instance, [as] a better term than 'protective measure [Schutzmassregel],' which is the one I employ; but I cannot discover any difference in their meaning" [Freud XIV 53]. Variations of the anxiety-security antithesis recur as a common theme in the various schools ot psychoanalysis. [31] In Alfred Adler[32] the antithesis is called inferiority feelings-compensation, and the idea is, in brief, that inferiority is a universal human condition, simply because man begins his life as a helpless, dependent being. In normal development, inferiority is conquered and is replaced by the feeling of fellowship, but Adler finds the explanation of neurotic development in the fact that for some people, because of various constitutional and especially environmentally-conditioned causes, the feeling of inferiority becomes an insurmountable problem — which the person then seeks to conquer in direct or disguised efforts to gain power over his surroundings. In this way the neurotic life-style is developed. It can express itself in various sorts of conflict-prone and asocial behavior, but which can always be understood as stemming from the need to avoid feelings of having failed. A continuing, confused and tense relationship obtains between the unconquered feelings of inferiority and the compensatory, neurotic life-style. For all the psychologists with whom we are dealing, there is a close dialectical relationship between the categories "unsolved, camouflaged problem" and "camouflage" on the schematic diagram of the opposite page.

In Karne Horney[33] the fundamental need of the neurotic is more generally defined as a demand for existential security. The fundamental neurotic problem is an all-encompassing, diffuse "basic anxiety" which arose in childhood as the result of unfortunate environmental conditions. This fundamental mood is what dictates the neurotic's attempt to obtain security with the help of various "safety devices," which have the particular result of the establishment of role behavior which is adhered to compulsively, and which are supposed to secure for the neurotic the love, respect, admiration, fear, indifference, etc., of his surroundings, all according to what the individual neurotic thinks will best serve his need for security.

	ESCAPE				REVENGE	
	Negative Emotion	From or Around — Negatively-Charged (Feared) Impression	Intended Direction of Escape — Evasive Manoeuvre	Intended Direction of Escape — Positively-charged Impression	Actual Direction of Escape — Unsolved, Camouflaged Problem	Actual Direction of Escape — Camouflage
Common Denominator	Anxiety	Insecurity	Defense, Escape	Security	Insecurity	Symptom
Freud	Signal Anxiety	Helplessness, Annihilation, Displeasure	Repression or other Defense	Feelings of Pleasure, Security	Conflict Between Ego and Id/Super-ego	Neurotic Symptom
Adler	Inferiority Feelings	Inferiority	Compensation	Superiority, Feelings of Power	Inferiority Feelings	Neurotic Life-Style
Horney	Fundamental Anxiety	Insecurity	Safety Devices	Security	Insecurity, Anxiety	Neurotic Roles
Fromm	Loneliness, Meaninglessness, Anxiety	Isolation, Individuation, Freedom	Establishment of Affiliations	Security, Relatedness	Loneliness, etc.	Neurotic Interpersonal Relations
Kierkegaard	Anxiety	Ambiguousness	Suppression, Obscuration	Unambiguousness	Double-Mindedness	Unambiguousness

In Erich Fromm's principal work, *Escape From Freedom*[34] — which is the only one of his books which can come under discussion in this connection — the fundamental antithesis is formulated less unambiguously, but for the sake of this survey it can be called loneliness-fellowship ("relatedness"). Loneliness thus includes both Adler's feeling of personal insignificance and inferiority and Horney's fundamental anxiety. Fromm does not view this antithesis from an individual-psychological point of view as the product of the family constellation and the history of the child's emancipation from the adult, but historically and sociologically as the product of the history of emancipation whose developmental phases are demarcated by words such as renaissance, reformation, capitalism, individualism, and liberalism. Loneliness is the reverse side of the freedom medal of modern western society, and freedom is the object of the lonely person's anxiety. Just as the inferior person seeks power and the anxious person seeks security, so does the lonely person seek his salvation in unfree forms of fellowship, i.e., he seeks compulsive forgetfulness of his painful situation by binding himself in authoritarian or conformist interpersonal and social relations.

Although the perspective here is very different from Freud's, the fundamental dialectic, the anticipation-reaction dynamism, is still psychoanalytic. By this I do not mean the Fromm's concept of freedom is identical with the anxiety-laden conflict of which Freud speaks, or with the inferiority or insecurity which is the object of anxiety in Adler and Horney. The different definitions of the content of the negatively-charged impression can be ignored for the present, while we remain with the shared idea of negative motivation: the neurosis (et al.) is thought of as having arisen as the result of an attempt to avoid a present and/or anticipated painful condition (emotion), which forces the individual into definite reactions in forms of behavior and responses (however, we do not find any explicit account of the anticipation — the temporal dimension — in these psychologists). The explanation is phenomenological and teleological-functional; the description concerns the subjective experience of the situation (not the objectively active, psychobiological forces), which motivate the escape reaction, and the maneouvre is put into motion *in order to* get away, forget, "in order to bring about obscurity" [XI 181, SD 181] or "to avoid danger, anxiety and displeasure" [Freud XXIII 235]. It is by means of this theory of negative motivation that psychoanalysis differentiates itself from other sorts of need psychology, and its distinguishing characteristic is thus that it does not see its principal task in meeting or satisfying the neurotic's need for protection and security, but in helping him to acknowledge the pathogenic nature of the need. This view implies that the neurotic's need, his "goal" ("positively-charged impression," in the schematic diagram) is determined reactively by the negative emotion (impression) as its antithesis; therefore, this goal is not a realizable possibility, but an unrealistic, compensatory, representation of a wish, whether one thinks of it as a more or less conscious representation or merely as the goal of a sort of reflexive effort. This goal is of course akin to what the respective psychologists understand by normality, health, and the like, but the similarity is only superficial. Freud thinks that the ability to have the feeling of pleasure is what characterizes the psychically healthy person; Adler thinks that a natural conquest of the feeling of inferiority is characteristic of the mature personality; Horney thinks that the healthy person is also secure with himself and his surroundings; and Fromm thinks that the healthy individual is capable of participating positively in fellowship. All the same, there is a difference between this condition of health and the goal which directs the neurotic's actions, and it does not merely consist in the fact that the neurotic's goal is beyond his abilities. This is the difference which I have sought to express in Kierkegaard by differentiating between unambiguousness and simplicity: the despairing person seeks the unambiguous (safe), as his goal and in a certain sense he reaches his goal. This differentiation, used in conjunction with Kierkegaard's terminology, here makes a point which is not made as clearly in the other psychologists: that in a certain sense the despairing person really achieves the security for which he is striving, but in such a way that the unambiguousness covers over the original, unsolved problem, double-mindedness (anxiety), which cunningly corresponds to unambiguousness in the despairing person.

The parallels with which I here operate are purely formal. They do not concern the definitions of content. But the parallel is there all the same, *mutatis mutandis*. The security, feeling of pleasure, feeling of power, peace of mind, and unambiguousness which the neurotic demands are "blind," while the healthy person's ability to enjoy, his self-confidence, his simplicity, etc., are sighted. The neurotic (the despairing person) is only capable of reaching his goal, of having his need satisfied, at the expense of or with the help of the exclusion of the negative emotion or the impressions or expectations connected with it—that is, by letting the wound of negativity grow over, as was written in the *Postscript*. But this means that, correctly viewed, he is still incapable of reaching his goal, because that which he wants to exclude is something which, properly speaking, cannot be excluded: "it comes back," to use an expression from *The Sickness Unto Death,* which will later be cited in its context [XI 147, SD 150]. This does not mean that the evasive manoeuvre (the escape, the defense) does not work as intended. It actually gives protection against the danger, and the neurosis always functions in one way or another (understood somewhat differently with each of the five psychologists) as a safety device. That is why it is so capable of resistance. The neurotic draws an advantage from it, and it is this advantage which makes the condition "demonic." But the evasive manoeuvre is nevertheless always in principle unsuccessful and pathogenic. The defense never succeeds as intended. It is always ineffective, inadequate in relation to the danger which it seeks to avoid; it always causes complications, and it is this unsuccessfulness which causes the conflict which constitutes the neurosis: "Whatever the ego does in its efforts of defense, whether it seeks to disavow a portion of the real external world or whether it seeks to reject an instinctual demand from the internal world, its success is never complete and unqualified. The outcome always lies in two contrary attitudes, of which the defeated, weaker one, no less than the other, leads to psychical complications" [Freud XXIII 204]. In the escape manoeuvre, one always leaves an unsolved problem behind one; one keeps it in by keeping it out, but it is precisely as something unsolved and unnoticed that it continues to exist and to exert influence. The neurosis can thus be defined as the contradiction between the existence of this problem and the individual's denial of it—as the contradiction between the real and the apparent, the disguised and the disguise.

It would not be difficult to let Kierkegaard contribute to this little symposium. But this would anticipate the course of things. For the present I will let the above sketch stand as a framework for orientation, while I gradually approach Kierkegaard's special elaboration of the dialectic.

6:4. *Freud's Conflict Model*

Before we go on to discuss some disagreements between the psychologists who have here been brought together in a common formula, it will perhaps be of interest to ask whether the suggested, partial parallel between Kierkegaard and Freud can be confirmed in other areas.

At the beginning of this chapter I cited a passage from Freud's *The Ego and the Id* about the relationship between these two authorities: the ego is to the id as the rider is to the horse, but it is usually the horse who determines the speed and the direction, while the rider's mastery is illusory (above, Chapter V: 2: 7). This view was compared, among other things, with the view of the relationship between "intellect" and "will" in Schopenhauer, but it was also noted that Freud's psychology cannot reasonably be represented by so simple a formula as Schopenhauer's. The reason for this has already become clear. In Freud's earlier periods his basic anthropological view is approximately as simple as Schopenhauer's, although his psychology is naturally much more refined and differentiated than Schopenhauer's. But man consists of the conscious and the unconscious, and it is the unconscious which governs. This is the view summarized in the quotation about the horse and rider. In a certain sense, *The Ego and the Id* from 1923 involves only the undergirding of this basic view — doubt about the mastery of rationality and consciousness over the irrational — with new arguments; this is because the main thesis of the book, and the reason for the terminological shift, is that the differentiation between conscious and unconscious has revealed itself to have been based upon a simplification; "the ego," too, reacts in part unconsciously, guided by powers of which it itself has no knowledge.

However, the situation is not merely that the I is under the power of the irresistible instinctual impulses. "The ego" is not determined one-sidedly by "the id," but it is located in a field of tension between mutually conflicting forces. The real broadening of the theory which takes place in *The Ego and the Id* is certainly the one which is expressed in the description of the three "dependencies of the ego." I cite here Freud's resumé in the *New Introductory Lectures:* "We are warned by a proverb [sic!] against serving two masters at the same time. The poor ego has things even worse: it serves three severe masters and does what it can to bring their claims and demands into harmony with one another. These claims are always divergent and often seem incompatible. No wonder that the ego so often fails in its task. Its three tyrannical masters are the external world, the super-ego and the id. When we follow the ego's efforts to satisfy them simultaneously — or rather, to obey them simultaneously — we cannot feel any regret at having personified this ego and having set it up as a separate organism. It feels hemmed in on three sides, threatened by three kinds of danger, to which, if it is hard pressed, it reacts by generating anxiety" [Freud XXII 77].

This, then, is Freud's conflict model. According to *The Ego and the Id,* the I is the psyche's mediating institution, central coordinator, communications bureau, and service organ, so to speak, but as such it is almost without independent power. Freud compares it with a constitutional monarch, who in spite of his prestige is bound by the decisions of parliament, and whose sovereignty is therefore more formal than factual. In its role as mediator between the contradictory forces, it often succumbs to the temptations of opportunism or the falsification of reality, because in the conflict with the three strict masters it is "the actual seat of anxiety" [Freud XIX 55-57].

It is thus difficult to claim that Freud lacks the eye for middle terms which Vigilius Haufniensis so energetically required of the psychologist. He also seems to be in agreement with Kierkegaard that the middle term is anxiety. Freud formulates this idea of anxiety as the middle term in a spatial metaphor: anxiety arises because of the I's position "between" antagonistic powers. At the conclusion of the previous chapter, I examined Kierkegaard's edifying discourse about "Acquiring One's Soul in Patience." It contained the suggestion that it is precisely the anthropological model — the precondition enabling man to acquire his soul patiently — which is also the precondition enabling him to forfeit it. The self is in contradiction and is a self-contradiction, because, in addition to belonging to itself, it also belongs to two foreign powers who struggle for mastery over it: God and the world. Anxiety comes into being in this contradiction, the discourse intimates (above, Chapter IV: 4: 3). The personality model in this discourse is the same as the one Kierkegaard uses in his principal works. Man is a synthesis of antitheses, a composite of finitude and infinity, of temporality and eternity, freedom and necessity — "in brief, a synthesis" [XI 143, SD 146]. Therefore, the contradiction (the ambiguousness) is the fundamental anthropological condition, which is the condition of possibility for various reactions, but which always manifests itself as anxiety.

This does not mean that Kierkegaard's view is simply identical with Freud's, but perhaps they can mutually illuminate one another. The difference is perhaps not only that Freud operates with three, and Kierkegaard with two, opposed things. Freud's three foreign powers certainly admit of being reduced to two, for he has made it clear elsewhere that in the process of psychic maturation "the super-ego" takes over the role as replacement for the demands which are made by "the external world"; in any case, these two authorities both pull in the same harness. One cannot assert an identity of content between "the world" (temporality, finitude, necessity) and "the id," and especially not between God (the eternal, infinity, freedom) and the fault-finding, restrictive, and jealous Yahweh who in Freud takes the name of "the super-ego." All this, however, does not change the shared notion of an I which is placed in the contradiction between mutually conflicting powers, and which reacts to the conflict with anxiety and falsifications of reality. The most important difference — in the psychological respect — seems to be, on the other hand, that according to Kierkegaard the self is not only "a relationship between two," but the self is "*that* the relationship relates itself to itself" (above, Chapter IV: 3: 1).

And yet neither does this difference have to be total. It is possibly due only to the fact that Kierkegaard formulates precisely something which Freud seeks to express falteringly and incoherently, something which he has scarcely thought through or formulated as a whole. That the relationship relates itself to itself, is of course to say that man is not only capable of forming an impression of himself, a self-perception, but finds this activity unavoidable (this will be further discussed later on). Man imagines himself in the past, present, and (perhaps especially) the future, and it is to this impression that he reacts. When anxiety is called a middle term in *The Concept of Anxiety,* it is a middle term in time, between possibility and actuality, impression and action, anticipation and reaction [IV 354, cf. 381-83; CD 44-45, cf. 67-68]. But this middle term is the same one which was under discussion when it was stated in a spatial metaphor that anxiety came into being in the contradiction between the world and God, between the temporal and the eternal. And the formula which ties together these dimensions — and thereby demonstrates the metaphorical character of the spatial dimension — is the passage cited earlier: "that the eternal first means the future, or that the future is the incognito in which the eternal, incommensurable as it is for time, nevertheless wishes to preserve its intercourse with time" (above, Chapter V: 4). The "spatial" dimension in Kierkegaard (that the self is a composite of temporality and eternity) is thus psychologically the same dimension as the temporal dimension (that man imagines himself in a prospective projection), and the result in both cases is the same: anxiety — and the attempt to avoid anxiety by means of the obscuration of actuality.

It cannot be denied that Freud does not express himself like this. The question is only whether he could have expressed himself in this way. To the best of my knowledge, Freud did not attempt to coordinate the theory of anxiety which is expressed in spatial metaphors in *The Ego and the Id* (the conflict between "the id," "the external world," and "the super-ego" → anxiety in "the ego") either with the first theory of anxiety or with the second, which was put forward three years later in *Inhibitions, Symptoms and Anxiety.* But the coordination could be made with the assistance of Kierkegaard's psychological dissolution of the "spatial" dimension into the temporal dimension, and Freud's idea must be that in signal anxiety "the ego" anticipates the conflict between the three foreign powers, and reacts to this anticipated conflict with repression.

Thus we are back to the escape-revenge dialectic and the temporal dimension. Before we leave the spatial metaphors from 'The Ego and the Id, there is, however, reason to mention that Freud's conflict model is *also* his ethical-anthropological model. The I's position between antagonistic forces is the condition of possibility for the neurotic process, but also for recovery. In general, "the ego" is the pawn and slave of the foreign powers, but the relationship can also be reversed. This is the famous credo of psychoanalysis: "Its intention is, indeed, to strengthen the ego, to make it more independent of the super-ego, to widen its field of perception and enlarge its organization, so that it can appropriate fresh portions of the id. Where id was, there ego shall be. It is a work of culture—not unlike the draining of the Zuider Zee" [Freud XXII 80].

Freud's "draining" is of course not the same as Kierkegaard's "transparency." What is paradoxical with Freud is of course that he, with his knowledge of man's abysmally deep irrationality, still confesses faith in *ratio,* in the autonomous reason, "our god λόγος [Logos]" [*The Future of an Illusion,* Freud XXI 54, cf. XXII 171].[35] Kierkegaard's paradox, as is well known, is another: not to give up thinking, but to let thinking "discover something which it cannot itself think" [IV 230, PF 46]. And this "something" is precisely the paradox, which was never invented in any man's heart: the God-man, whose paradoxicality consists in the fact that he, who alone is cut off from the paradoxical dialectic of sin, nevertheless addresses himself to the sinner in order to give the sinner the condition of possibility for grounding himself transparently in the power which posited him: "Only the omnipotent can take itself back while it gives itself away, and this relationship is indeed precisely the independence of the recipient" [Pap. VII 1 A 181, Hong 1251].

6: 5. *Retrospective or Functional Analysis*

After this excursus we can return to the escape-revenge diagram. "Revenge" is the contradiction which is due to the fact that the neurotic's solution of his problem is only an apparent solution. However, this formulation is rather abstract, to say the least, as long as we have not dealt with how the contradiction manifests itself in experience and behavior. But, when we turn to this question, it is no longer possible to assign one common denominator to Freud, the neo-Freudians, and Kierkegaard, for here—in the more detailed understanding of the relationship between escape and revenge—the differences reveal themselves.

We can isolate this disagreement by first recalling that Kierkegaard's interest was in the future, while Freud's interest was in the neurotic person's past. The disagreement is not dissolved by demonstrating that, in his second theory of anxiety, Freud is also operating in prospective categories and speaks of the anticipatory function of signal anxiety. Kierkegaard and Freud are in agreement that "the child is father of the man." But the center of Kierkegaard's interest is nonetheless the function of separation anxiety in the present crisis of the adult. The anticipation-reaction pattern, which according to Kierkegaard is characteristic of this crisis, is assigned by Freud almost exclusively to early childhood. The prospective-functional point of view, which is crucial in Freud's second theory of anxiety, is employed in the understanding of the origin of the neurosis in childhood, but the adult's nuerosis is seen by and large as a fixated product of this early conflict, a disguised and distorted, symbolic reproduction of the early development. That which is regarded as contemporary in the adult's crisis is (broadly speaking) only the disguise, not the conflict itself, for it is, just because it is past, fixated and represeed, accessible only to a retrospective reconstruction in analysis.

What is profound about Freud is this idea of neurosis as the result of the fact that a part of the personality has been split off, excluded, and thereby stopped at an undeveloped, infantile stage. The idea that the reconstruction and reactivation of this segment of forgotten or unlived life is supposed to lead to a new integration is no less profound. The dubious point is the question of whether this reconstruction of the past is possible, of whether it does not more likely have the character of a construction, and also the question of whether the reconstruction, if it were possible, serves its purpose, or whether it does not lead methodically around the crux of the matter, the patient's here and now. Freud did not draw particularly major consequences from his revised theory of anxiety. The therapeutic effort continues to aim at the uncovering of the early, oedipal conflict material, which Freud studied under the auspices of the first theory of anxiety. Of course, analysis also concerns itself with the I and its defenses, but chiefly only to the extent that these defenses function as hindrances to the recognition of the real thing, namely, the instinctual conflicts.

One could label as consistent this failure to draw conclusions, namely, if one is a convinced Freudian and thinks that one must not throw the baby (the analysis of early childhood, et al.) out with the bath water (the first theory of anxiety). Or one could call it inconsistent, namely, if one finds that the consequence of these doctrines — the doctrines of anticipatory anxiety and of escape from the anxiety-producing possibility of danger with the help of defense mechanisms — must be that the retrospective analysis of conflict becomes more or less inessential, or perhaps directly self-contradictory and misleading, because it leads attention away from what factually takes place in the personality here and now. Ego psychology, which involves the notion that the I is not simply identical with "the conscious," but is itself governed a good deal of the time by unconscious motives, can seem to tend in the direction of making id psychology untrustworthy. Freud's second theory of anxiety, and the fully formed doctrine of the I's defense mechanisms contain the germ of a denial of the theory about the infantile sexual conflicts, or in any case, of a denial of the thesis about the sickness-inducing significance of these conflicts in the long run — which of course cannot be confirmed directly by the study of children, but which depends upon inference from the reports of adult neurosis patients. One can observe sexual behavior and the like in children, but one cannot observe what long-term significance it has, and, furthermore, one can observe so many other things which can seem so much more essential and alarming. It is obvious to assume that the wealth of psychoanalytic material which illuminates infantile conflicts is in large measure the product of the patients' need to project their present anxiety- and guilt-laden conflicts back onto the relationship to their parents in early childhood, for which it would be difficult for them to be held responsible, either by themselves or others — a mechanism which is eagerly helped along by Freudian analysts, whose theory is confirmed in this way. As is well known, Freud discovered early in his career that most of the patients' reports of seductions in early childhood, which formed the basis for some of his central theories of the etiology of neurosis, were free inventions. This discovery came close to overthrowing the whole of psychoanalysis, but Freud held firmly to his ideas, and soon after came to the doctrine of infantile sexuality, the Oedipus conflict, et al. [cf. *inter alia,* Freud XIV 17-19].[36] If he instead had turned to analyze more closely his patients' motives in inventing these reports and in believing in them themselves, or his own motives in finding another, related, but less verifiable explanation of the etiology of hysteria to replace the one he had to reject, it is possible that psychoanalytic research would have taken a course other than the one it did. One can understand (with good reason, in one sense) the fact that Freud's psychology is much more differentiated and complicated that that of the neo-Freudians as proof of the fact that he is much more original and aware of the problems than they. But one can also interpret this as the expression of an abstruse over-problematizing, which is due to the fact that he threw himself into the study of the instinct world almost without regard to the ego functions, and one can, if one is an adherent of this view, think that the revisions of the theory which took place in the 1920's are far from sufficient.

It is, among other things, objections such as these which lie at the root of much neo-Freudian and phenomenological criticism of Freud. The critics have attempted to draw what they saw as the full consequences of Freud's self-revisions, by asserting — with greater or lesser reservations — that the neurotic conflict is only to be adequately understood when it is seen as contemporary, regardless of the fact that it (naturally) is connected to situations in the individual's childhood. In all this, Freud's critics are in fundamental agreement with Kierkegaard.

But this difference in point of view naturally implies that there are also other disagreements. One of them concerns the conception of the relationship between defense and symptom.

6:6. *Defense and Symptom*

According to Freud, the defense mechanism (repression, etc.) is in all its essentials a phenomenon of the past, while the symptom is the present representative of the conflict which the defense mechanism has caused. The two things are kept sharply separated, and we are warned against thinking that the symptom is identical with the sickness itself. Freud calls the symptom a compromise-formation, and the idea is that it is the fixated, stereotyped, so to speak institutionalized and dramatized way in which the struggle between the repressed instinctual impulses and the repressed powers of the I take on form. But even though the symptom must thus not be confused with the conflict which constitutes the sickness, it does not stand in any accidental relationship to it, but is an expression of it, even if a distorted expression which is only transparent to analysis. The symptom is symbolic in the same sense as the dream, and it is interpreted according to the same principles, i.e., with the help of the distinction between the manifest and latent content. The symptom not only renders visible the unconscious wish, but precisely the conflict between the wish and the attempt to deny its existence.

Thus the symptom is first and foremost an expression. As an expression it is camouflaged; however, the real camouflaging of the instinctual impulse is not brought about by the symptom but by the defense mechanism. This does not mean that Freud completely ignores the fact that the symptom can have an independent function. This view is expressed in his doctrine of secondary gain and gain from illness. In the defense mechanism itself, the neurotic achieves a so-called primary gain, which consists of a reduced feeling of anxiety. With the formation of the symptom, he can achieve a secondary gain in the form of a quite strongly modified instinctual release, and in addition, by virtue of his general condition, he can achieve a gain from illness in the form of exemption from responsibility and work, in the form of the possibility of calling forth the sympathy of his surroundings, or the attainment of social support (money neuroses) and the like. However, these ideas do not play any great role in Freud. For him the symptom is first and foremost a symbol which demands analysis, and only in a derived and subordinate sense is any independent and contemporary function ascribed to it.

In the neo-Freudians these views are changed, and the tendency is in the direction of equating defense with symptom. Freud's doctrine of neurosis is

worked out upon the basis of specific symptom neuroses, where the point is
that the symptom is one thing and the conflict is something which is quite
different and which lies much deeper. On the other hand, the neurotic
cases which constitute the background for the neo-Freudian theories are
especially those which are not characterized by any such specific and
localizable symptom. And even if such a symptom were present, the neo-
Freudian puts much less emphasis upon it, and more upon the
comprehensive, unspecifiable symptomatology, which Adler has
characterized as the neurotic life-style. It is the stamp of the neurotic's
total personality which attracts the attention of the analyst—the neurotic's
behavior and reactions, his physical posture and his psychic attitudes, his
evaluations as they are expressed in his relationship to himself and to
others, his ideals and aversions as they reveal themselves in dreams or in
straightforward statements, his emotional life, and his world of
experience. It is particularly the Dasein analysts who have sought to
develop methods for the description and clarification of the patient's
subjective universe of experience; but the distance from the neo-Freudian
analysis of life-style to the phenomenological analysis of "being-in-the-
world" is not insurmountably great. This life-style is thus the symptom, but
it is also the defense; that is, the fundamental character of the life-style is
defensive. This is not to say that the symptom is unambiguously
transparent. Adler, Horney and Fromm, who place particular emphasis
upon describing the neurotic person's behavior in relation to other people,
show how this defensive character can find expression in both activity and
passivity, in aggressive and accommodating postures, in sadism and
masochism, in dominating and in self-effacing behavior, etc. Horney, in
particular, has her strength in the analysis of neurotic conflict disguises,
mixtures of motives, reaction-formations, et al., which make the basic
conflict unrecognizable. But in every case, the life-style, viewed as a
totality, is understood at once as the means to the conquest of the conflict
(inferiority feelings, anxiety, loneliness) and as the sign that it has not been
conquered. It is this dialectic which makes the neurosis into a vicious circle
(Horney uses the expression): the symptom grants protection, but, because
it is inadequate—which is due to the fact that it involves an escape from
the fundamental problem instead of a confrontation with it—the defense
continually fails, and it thus has to be intensified with the investment of
continually increasing quantities of energy into the symptomatic-defensive
life-style.

This section is not intended to give a detailed account of Kierkegaard's
relation to the psychoanalytic theories discussed, but only to sketch some of
the principal outlines for the purpose of orientation. For the present it

must be sufficient to say that for Kierkegaard, symptom and defense also coalesce into a life-style, which is the sign of an inner conflict, but which is also the defensive posture with which the despairing individual seeks to entrench himself against the conflict. The most characteristic expression of this life-style is "encapsulation." In place of this word I have used the word "unambiguousness" up to this point. This is due to the fact that Kierkegaard uses the term encapsulation in a somewhat more specialized way than that in which I use the term unambiguousness. Unambiguousness is therefore a more comprehensive concept, even though it covers the same situations. Unambiguousness was earlier defined, in contrast to simplicity, as the life-style which seeks to exclude ambiguousness in an unambiguous way. The point was that this exclusion is done in vain, and that unambiguousness therefore covers over a latent psychic ambiguousness, double-mindedness. It is thus at the same time the method of defense which is employed to keep ambiguousness out, and the symptom of the fact that it has entered.

7. Sin is a Condition

7:1. *Science and its Limits*

When one speaks of Freud and the neo-Freudians one can proceed immediately and directly to the problems of psychology. With Kierkegaard this is not possible. There are historical reasons for this. In our century psychology is an independent scientific institution. It has its own university departments, its own education and its own labor market, its own objectives and functions in society, its own international organizations, journals, research centers, congresses, and its own language; and it has its own academic subdisciplines and its own rival "schools." In brief, it has "become itself," though perhaps not in the sense in which Kierkegaard uses that expression. In becoming itself, it has also become divided against itself. But from the point of view of the history of science, the institutional independence of psychology is surely a more important fact than the schisms and the expansion which have accompanied this independence.

Psychology has not been alone in experiencing this development. This development has been conditioned by the total development of the whole of western, industrial society, its greatly accelerating economic growth, its rapid expansion, its differentiation and multiplication of needs, and its scientific ideal, which serves this development by demanding specialization, effectiveness, and exactitude (verification). In addition, this society's crises and conflicts, its divisive, oppressive transformation of needs, its rapid and planless revolutionizing of society, social values, institutions, and milieus, and its accumulation of human and social problems, have given psychology a series of problems to solve — problems which are perhaps beyond its abilities.

Therefore we observe that the most original psychologists transcend psychology and seek its connectedness with forms of knowledge other than the narrowly psychological. In a certain sense, however, this is what all psychologists have done, but most of them have done so without themselves understanding what this meant. For in a certain sense, psychology's coming to "independence" is of course an illusion. It is not psychology as such, but science in general which has made itself independent, i.e., wrested itself loose from its philosophical and theological traditions. In this sense, psychology's independence is only a special case of the independence of science, and its "scientificization" is only its assumption of the scientific creed and the new values and norms which are ordinary in capitalistic society: exactitude, effectiveness, adaptation, the ability to function and to achieve maximally in this society and upon its terms, and the ability *not* to pose "irrelevant" questions about its values and norms or its fundamental economic and political processes.

As long as this society could, with a certain reasonableness, regard its own dynamic as an undoubtedly progressive movement, as man's triumph over nature and his liberation from the prejudices and limitations of past times, psychology could also make itself "independent" in natural conformity with "progress." It could spurn its own past and its former "unscientific" problems with a good conscience and scientific self-consciousness. Only when the progressiveness of bourgeois capitalist society becomes clearly visible as problem-filled and perhaps life-destroying in its consequences, does a need arise for scientific self-reflection and for criticism of science's overly narrow sphere of experience, its artificially restricted horizon.

Guilt and sin are among the "unscientific" problems which progressive science can *treat* — but only as scientific problems, as psychic phenomena. For Kierkegaard these problems are not a part of psychology. And yet his psychology is only possible when it is precisely the reality of these problems which is respected. The *feeling* of guilt is a psychological problem, but guilt is not. This distinction is difficult to manage, and Kierkegaard has also had difficulties in formulating his view, as we will see. But the fact that he embarks upon differentiating at all is connected, among other things, with the fact that he lives, thinks, and writes in a tradition which historically precedes the scientific and social development whose inheritors (and victims?) we are today. Or, rather, he lives in a period in which this development is in its earliest beginning.

In the 1840's, Denmark was a small, socially and economically retarded argricultural country with an old capital, rich in traditions, a relatively high academic culture, and with beginning tendencies toward urbanization and a liberal market economy. In the political sphere, "enlightened" absolutism was replaced by parliamentary democracy in 1849, and in the economic sphere, the country was in a period of slow growth,. in a transition from mercantilism and feudalism to private enterprise capitalism. However, these tendencies only made their striking breakthrough at the end of the century. Kierkegaard, at the same time, was extremely attentive to these coming changes, and if he is often experienced in the 20th century as a pronouncedly "modern" thinker, it is connected with his great awareness of the epoch-making changes and of the radically "new" sorts of problems which were coming along.

However, all these were just *beginning* tendencies. And therefore the scientific tradition and the intellectual milieu is different from what we are familiar with today. Specialization and "becoming independent" had not yet succeeded, though they were certainly on the way. This can be noted, for example, in the discussions of Hegel's philosophy, where the question was whether philosophy had here become independent of theology, so that there was a genuine secularization, or whether it was precisely the unity of philosophy and theology which had been preserved and strengthened in Hegel's synthetic thinking. In any case, Hegel and most of the learned men of the period thought in terms of much larger wholes than we are accustomed to doing. Psychology was not an autonomous science, but in Hegel, a couple of paragraphs in the system. In the places in Denmark where psychology was taught as a discipline — at the pastoral seminary and at the country's only university (at that time) — the teachers were theologians and philosophers. The typical intellectual of the period was many-sided, but he scarcely viewed his versatility as fragmentation, for it was a versatility which could be contained within a vision of the whole. The intellectual life of the period, in Germany and Denmark, was well-stocked with personalities who, without difficulty and without self-contradiction, were, for example, at once poets, aesthetic critics or theoreticians, philosophers, psychologists, theologians, and in some cases natural scientists — not because they were specialists in all these areas, but because they did not experience any discord between their various activities.

In this respect, Kierkegaard is a child of his times. And yet, one of his serious objections against the thinkers of his period is that they thought in syntheses which attempted to encompass too much. In the introduction to *The Concept of Anxiety,* we see him calling for order in the kingdom of science. Where romantic and hegelian speculation, in its universal vision of the totality, thought of everything together in wholes and tended toward the abolition of all differences and the volatilization of all distinctions, Kierkegaard demands distinctions, conciseness and specificity. On the other hand, he is also connected, in a fruitful way, to his contemporaries' sense for coherence and wholeness. He does not think everything into a unity, for example; he distinguishes carefully between psychology and theology, between the feeling of guilt and guilt itself. But on the other hand, he thinks of all these *different* concepts *together* or simultaneously, so that psychology finds its limitations in the extra-scientific ("dogmatic") problems, and extra-scientific problems receive their concrete interpretation in psychological analysis. Both aspects of the problem in their mutual relations are thought through simultaneously.

7: 2. *Guilt, Sin and the Qualitative Leap*

In order to come to Kierkegaard's most important and dominant definition of the concept of despair, I must first point out an oft-repeated assertion in *The Concept of Anxiety,* which, however, is contradicted in *The Sickness Unto Death.* The assertion must therefore be called misleading. It is to the effect that sin is an action and not a condition. On the other hand, it is clear from *The Sickness Unto Death* that sin is a condition and not (only) an action (cf. above Chapter III: 2: 6). One must naturally assume that Anti-Climacus' correction is the expression of Kierkegaard's definitive view, and the task becomes only to show what it involves, theologically *and* psychologically. We can begin with *The Concept of Anxiety.* Vigilius, or rather, the Christianity he formulates, wants to make man responsible for his actions. If this becomes a problem for him, it is because he is at the same time a psychologist, who as such is setting the stage for a causal explanation of these actions, which apparently runs counter to the idea of individual guilt. Therefore, he operates throughout the book with a distinction between, on the one hand, the psychological condition, anxiety, which is the condition of possibility for sin, and on the other hand, sin as an actuality, as a definite, completed action [IV 319, CD 14]. "Here sin naturally means something concrete; for one never sins on the whole or in general" [IV 422, CD 101]. Sin is the individual, immoral action, and if we are to be able to say that man becomes guilty in this action, we must also be able to speak of a prior state of innocence. Between that state and the action, therefore, lies a qualitative leap. The state is the possibility of sin, the approximation, which psychology can explain. But the action, in which the sin becomes actualized, lies on the far side of the leap, which psychology cannot explain.

It is difficult to understand some of Vigilius' formulations of this idea other than as meaning that there is an inexplicable break in causality within the psychological development itself. It looks as if Kierkegaard wants to have his cake and eat it too; in part he wants to explain the action as a product of the condition; in part he will not let go of the idea of freedom all the same, and therefore he must assert that the psychological explanation is merely *almost* sufficient, while the development is in actuality discontinuous, and the chain of causality is broken. This view seems self-contradictory. It has also been criticized by Kierkegaard researchers. From a psychological point of view we must reject the notion of a sudden, inexplicable twitch which breaks off the coherence and the development. And from an ethical-existential point of view, we must object that the assertion about the qualitative leap is enervated in practice by Kierkegaard's penetrating analyses of the leap's psychological preconditions. Kierkegaard says in the book about anxiety that one must not explain original sin [IV 324, CD 18], and yet the first chapter deals with anxiety "as explaining original sin retrogressively, in the direction of its origin" [IV 329, CD 23].

The Concept of Anxiety here contains what is undoubtedly a real unclarity because some of the book's formulations may be read as the expression of a radical indeterminism, which is supposed to make it possible to speak psychologically about the individual as the cause of, and therefore as guilty in, his own actions. If this is Kierkegaard's intention, a good deal of what he says in addition to this is inconsistent. But it is exactly this inconsistency which can suggest that this is not Kierkegaard's intention, despite the formulations mentioned. The qualitative leap is indeed quite expressly not a psychological or a quasi-psychological theory, and the boundary which Kierkegaard sets for psychology's sphere of activity [IV 343, CD 35] does not have to mean that psychology is denied the right to describe a course of psychological causation. Kierkegaard is not an indeterminist, and his real meaning cannot be that a leap takes place within the psychological development. What he does speak of is a spring from a psychological to a non-psychological way of viewing this development. To the extent that psychology is to speak about the question of guilt, it must tend toward dismissing it, because it cannot unambiguously establish that the actor himself is the cause of his action: ". . . he who becomes guilty through anxiety, he is of course innocent; for it was not he himself, but anxiety, an alien force, which grasped him, a force which he did not love, but which made him anxious"; on the other hand, neither can psychological analysis provide any unambiguous proof of the actor's innocence: "and yet he is guilty, for he sank into anxiety, as if he loved it even though he feared it. There is nothing in the world more ambiguous than this . . ." [IV 347, CD 39]. What psychological analysis can and must do is to put forward the question of guilt in all its opacity. On the other hand, it cannot come to a decision in the matter, "because the purely empirical observation can never be finished" [IV 366, CD 54]. In the question of freedom and of guilt, one cannot simply appeal to experience [IV 345, CD 37]. Kierkegaard's view also builds upon an epistemological argument; we shall later return to this. Here it will only be emphasized that everywhere in the authorship Kierkegaard maintains the dialectically unclarified element in the question of "guilty?/not-guilty?." If he is nonetheless able to speak of guilt as an ethical reality, he is thus not building upon the indeterminist notion of a free choice, which, on the contrary, is labelled "a nuisance-idea" [IV 354, CD 45]. The assertion of ethics is that man is guilty even in the actions of which he himself cannot be proven to be the cause (and it is precisely this which makes it possible for Kierkegaard to employ determinism as a working psychological hypothesis). Only if one becomes "guilty by means of fate" [IV 405, CD 87], is there any meaning in speaking of guilt. This is why Judge William speaks of repenting oneself back into the race — "and if it were the father's sin, which the son had inherited, he repents that as well" [II 233 f., E/O II 221]. If guilt is only to be substantiated by referring to actions of which the individual himself can be proven to be the source, it can never be substantiated.

Even if one rejects, as does Climacus in the *Postscript*, the notion of "comparative" guilt, according to which guilt consists of certain more or less immoral individual actions, and one instead deepens the notion of guilt into the idea of the totality of guilt — even in this case the question of guilt remains ambiguous in the final analysis, "because when guilt is explained as being a part of existence, this of course seems to make the existing person innocent; it seems as if he might be able to place the guilt upon whomever has brought him into existence, or upon existence itself." The total guilt is not only a guilt for individual actions (although, be it noted, it is a guilt for this as well), but it is the precondition for such guilt in individual matters. To this extent it is inexplicable, as it is not motivated by the person's conscious intention, but by his — psychologically speaking, blameless — failure vis-a-vis the task of existence. The individual relates to the task, begins to realize it, but in the attempt to do so, he does not reach his goal. Instead, he discovers more and more profoundly that, rather than ascending to the ideal in Icarus fashion, he is on the contrary removing himself from it, because he began from an incorrect starting position. The guilt, then, is a consequence of this, a consequence of the fact that the individual does not know at the outset what the essence of the task of existence is or how it is to be realized, but only becomes more and more acquainted with his task through his flawed attempts to realize it. Guilt is unavoidable for the person who makes the attempt, for it arises from the very situation that the understanding of the task of existence is not given in advance of action, but only comes into being in and with ethical engagement. Guilt, thus, is not due to the fact that the individual wills what is wrong, but it comes into being in the attempt to take the task of existence seriously, or rather: it *is discovered* in this attempt. For the guilt which is discovered by this means is naturally also present where it has not been discovered. But this fundamental (ontological) guilt is thus not due in the literal (psychological) sense to the individual himself. And to this extent it seems reasonable enough that "the existing individual should be able to place the guilt upon existence or upon whomever has placed him in existence, and thus be without guilt" [VII 517 f., CUP 470]. For the existing individual who has discovered the totality of guilt, however, there is no doubt that he is guilty, and even the attempt to cast off guilt from himself would only be a new proof of its reality [VII 519, CUP 471].

It can easily be seen that there is an insistent theodicy problem just beneath the surface of Kierkegaard's line of reasoning. He is naturally fully aware of this. The *Postscript* is "such an extremely dialectical defense of Christianity, that it may seem to many people that it is an attack," he notes in his diary [Pap. X 2 A 163, Dru 994]. Therefore he is also aware that he does not discuss the problem of theodicy in his books, but is satisfied with the Christian message "by virtue of the absurd"—unto faith or offense. Absurdity and faith by virtue of the absurd come into being when Kierkegaard rejects theodicy [cf. *inter alia* Pap. IV C 33, Hong 41; concerning Leibniz] without rejecting the problem which gave rise to it: original sin. In a discourse from 1845 it is written that he who considers his sins will discover "that sin has an inner connectedness in itself"—"an unfathomable connection." This insight can give occasion to speak generally "on the generality of sin, not in him, but in the entire race." He who speaks thusly escapes from the problem, "for he has become an observer. And there are probably many who wish to hear his observations." These observations are those of theodicy: "the question becomes one of justifying God to the world, not the concern about justifying oneself to God" [V 224 and 226, TCS 230-33].

Kierkegaard continues this line of reasoning in the *Postscript* and speaks of the individual's consciousness of guilt. For the existing individual, who discovers the totality of sin, no doubt is possible with regard to guilt. Guilt's own dialectic prevents the existing individual from carrying on his own dialectic about the question of guilt. But a dialectically ambiguous and undetermined element returns at another point, in the question of whether the existing individual persists with sufficient stamina in his consciousness of his guilt. The expression for the total consciousness of guilt is "guilt's eternal recollection" — not a single outburst of grief, but a continuing recollection. However, no one can persist in such an eternal — i.e., in this context, a ceaseless — remembering of guilt, Kierkegaard writes: it would perhaps lead to madness or death. Thus, just as the doctor (in a concentration camp?) keeps the prisoner alive at a minimum of existence in order to keep him from dying of hunger, so, too, must the guilt-conscious existing individual "seek to find the minimum of forgetfulness which is needed in order to endure. . . . But because it is impossible to come to absolute certainty in this dialectic, he will, in spite of all his efforts, have his consciousness of guilt completely determined by the fact that he would never dare say, with relation to his eternal salvation, that he had done all he could in order to persevere in the recollection of guilt" [VII 525-27, CUP 477-78].

I do not need to explain that this consequence of Kierkegaard's thoughts on guilt is absurd. Kierkegaard's critics· have said it very precisely. A Danish theologian has objected that in Climacus the consciousness of guilt lives its own sham life and feeds upon its own uncertainty, sundered from every ethical situation. It is self-reinforcing and results in a ceaseless circular course of self-observation and self-concern without connection to reality.[37]

This is quite correct. However, the only thing which Kierkegaard's valiant critics overlook is that this is not a relevant objection against Kierkegaard, for it is precisely what he himself wishes to demonstrate. The whole thing can be expressed with the help of a journal entry from 1843: "[T]herefore, the person who believes in the atonement is greater than the greatest penitent. Penitence continually becomes ensnared in itself; for if it is to be the greatest and the only thing in a person, that which saves him, etc., then it again becomes subject to the dialectical consideration of whether it is quite deep enough, etc." [Pap. IV A 116, Hong 3078]. It is this thought which Climacus implements in grand style. He demonstrates psychologically what the consequences of thinking about guilt must be, when guilt is not simply ignored, on the one hand, but on the other hand is not brought to a halt by the Gospel message which calls guilt "sin" and which penetrates the impenetrable with the promise of the forgiveness of sins. Man must discover and hold fast to guilt, and therefore he unavoidably ends in a fatiguing vicious circle. Climacus' description has a parallel in *The Concept of Anxiety,* where it is confirmed that the feeling of guilt can culminate in a mad spinning of dialectics, "because the repentance becomes dialectically ambiguous with respect to that which it is supposed to annul, an ambiguousness which is only annulled by dogmatics in the atonement, in which the category of original sin becomes clear" [IV 426, CD 105]. We will return to the purely psychological side of the matter later. Guilt leads to such consequences because it is the individual himself who must persevere in the idea. Sin, on the other hand (the Christian category) is not to be discovered by the existing individual himself, but he "comes to know it from without" [VII 524 note, CUP 475 note]. With this, the tantalizing dialectic is broken, for the individual no longer has to judge himself guilty, but *is* judged and forgiven, and must simply receive (and the consciousness of guilt is the condition in which the individual can take note of this; this is why Kierkegaard accentuates guilt in the *Postscript*). The idea is formulated clearly enough in Climacus, and I need only note it by following up a reference to an earlier section of Kierkegaard's book, where the matter is expressed such that thinking about guilt culminates in the enthusiastic attempt to endure in the misrelationship between the finite and the infinite with the pathetic cry to God: "I cannot understand you, but I will love you; you are always right. . . ." On the other hand, where "a category of sin" has been made the basis of things, the situation does not culminate in teeth-gnashing pathos, but in "abolishing the misunderstanding" [VII 254 f., CUP 239-40].

Climacus' explorations in the problem of guilt are nothing other than a problematization of that which was called "the first ethic" in *The Concept of Anxiety* (cf. above, Chapter IV: 2: 2). Vigilius Haufniensis is also aware that a total guilt must underlie the fact that man can be guilty in his individual actions [IV 471 f., CD 144]. Sin, like guilt, is naturally total in the sense that it cannot be substantiated psychologically in any unobjectionable fashion. It can only be substantiated by means of the Gospel message, i.e., it is not substantiated. But this does not mean that the word "sin" is without content, a meaningless term. Vigilius attempts to fix the meaning of the word; Anti-Climacus does define it. If Vigilius speaks of sin as discrete individual actions, and not as the condition from which they spring forth, it is due to his psychological interest in the significance of the fall into sin as the occasion for coming to consciousness, including the consciousness of guilt. He shares this interest with Anti-Climacus in *The Sickness Unto Death*: "The sins of the flesh are the self-centered willfulness of the lower self; but how often it happens that one devil is driven out with the help of another, and the latter situation becomes worse that the former. For this is the way things go in the world: first a man sins out of wretchedness and weakness, and then . . . he despairs over his weakness and becomes either a pharisee, who desperately pushes things to a certain legalistic righteousness, or he despairingly plunges himself into sin again" [XI 218, SD 213]. But Anti-Climacus does not regard the individual action, "the sins of the flesh," as sin in any qualified sense. The whole of Vigilius' argument must therefore seem superfluous and self-contradictory. Various observations upon the child and guilt are among the evidence which shows that Kierkegaard himself has abandoned this position. As early as *Fear and Trembling* it is noted that the existence of the child is sin, even if he is not himself aware of it [III 125, FT 72], and Climacus seems to correct Vigilius quite openly when he calls the notion of the child's innocence sentimental and undogmatic: "The child does not have the consciousness of sin, and is thus a sinner without the consciousness of sin" [VII 583, CUP 524]. The consequence of this is naturally that the fall into sin does not consist of the individual's becoming guilty by means of one or another individual action, e.g. of a sexual sort, but in becoming aware of himself as guilty, perhaps by means of a particular action which serves as the occasion.

Sin, in its qualified sense, is thus not an action, but a state. Even in *The Concept of Anxiety* there is occasional mention of "the state of sin" [IV 358, CD 48] — even though this is in conflict with the line of reasoning in the rest of the book — and there is also mention of the fact that "the state itself is a new sin" [IV 425, CD 104]. The point of departure for this book, and the sphere in which many of the psychological analyses take place, is the legalistic concept of sin, but the book itself prepares for the transition to *The Sickness Unto Death,* where one reads that despair is a state [XI 152, 174, et al.; SD 154, 175, et al.], that despair is sin [XI 213, SD 208], and that "the state of being in sin is a worse sin than the individual sins; it is sin" [XI 245, cf. 243; SD 237, cf. 236]. But here he has abandoned the moralistic, particularistic conception of guilt as an individual action: "And this is one of the most decisive determinations for the whole of Christianity, that the antithesis of sin is not virtue, but faith" [XI 219, SD 213].

The qualitative leap is thus no longer an inexplicable transition from possibility to actuality, from the motivation of action to action, from anticipation to reaction, but a transition, first from the comparative conception to the total conception of guilt, and then from total guilt, which the individual himself must "discover" and in which he must attempt to persevere with "the eternal recollection of guilt," to the Christian doctrine of sin, which man is exempted from conceiving, and in which he must therefore believe — or be offended.

7: 3. *The Possibility of Offense*

It has been made clear that Kierkegaard really leaves open the possibility of offense for those who wish to choose it. How obvious it would have been — particularly for a psychologist with his understanding of the first part of the compound Danish word for original sin,[38] i.e., an understanding of the consequences of nature and the historical nexus, of man as a product, of anxiety as a power which commandeers the will against the will's own wishes — for Kierkegaard to have used "existence itself" as the explanation of guilt, i.e., to make guilt and sin into purely psychic phenomena, which only deserve a reductive analysis. If he does not do this, it is because he is a religious thinker, in the final analysis a Christian dogmatist. It is offense's own business if it wishes to say that the Christian cross is Kierkegaard's vicious circle, his neurosis. He himself does not say this, but he is staisfied to let the possibility of offense remain open — unto faith or offense. Only when the ontological concept of guilt is replaced by the dogmatic concept of sin does it become possible to speak of the forgiveness of sins, which "in turn will get rid of sin as completely as if it had drowned in the sea" [XI 238, SD 231]. The question of offense concerns whether one could avoid the costly and risky circuitous route via the consciousness of guilt, the acknowledgement of sin, and the forgiveness of sins, and instead simply abolish the consciousness of sin — and with it sin as well; combatting sin has always been the intention of qualified offense (from Feuerback to Marcuse), even if other expressions are used, and something other than the sins of the flesh is understood by sin. Kierkegaard has indeed taught us that it is precisely anxiety about sin which brings forth sin, and this analysis could be deepened (and has been in our century). Has Kierkegaard himself drawn the conclusions of this insight, and would not a further development render superfluous both the consciousness of guilt and the forgiveness of sins? Kierkegaard has only his absurd answer to this question: that "Christianity remains with this, that it must be believed, and not conceived, that *neither* it must be believed, *or* one must be offended by it . . ." [XI 236, SD 229].

This does not imply that enmity is declared upon all intellectual activity. By taking psychology into the service of dogmatics, Kierkegaard has not, it is true, secured himself any proof of the correctness of his assertion, but he has kept the assertion about sin and the forgiveness of sins from hovering inexplicably in the air as an empty abstract sound. Therefore the psychological reduction of guilt can also be argued against psychologically. Guilt is a phenomenological fact. The spirit does not permit itself to be mocked, and if the relationship of conscience does not manifest itself as a relationship of conscience, it will take form in other, impenetrable ways.

The reductive analysis of guilt is therefore a repression of it. The task is to make it manifest, and Kierkegaard's working through of the problem serves this purpose. Man's task is not to forget guilt unambiguously, but to persist in the consciousness of it: " . . . the religious person knows no means against remorse which does not take remorse into account; the religious person, on the contrary, uses the negative as the essential form. The consciousness of sin is thus a definite component part of the consciousness of the forgiveness of sins. The negative is not done with once and for all, and then on to the positive; but the positive is always within the negative . . . " [VII 514 f., CUP 467]. Only when this consciousness is persisted in can man give up the feeling of guilt, not by forgetting the guilt, but in the faith that it has been forgotten: "Then a man reposes in the forgiveness of sins, when the thought of God does not remind him of sin, but of the fact that it is forgiven, so that the past is not a memory of how much he did that was wrong, but of how much he has been forgiven" [Pap. VIII 1 A 230, Hong 1209].

The merely reductive view of guilt is of course that which is ordinarily attributed to psychoanalysis—perhaps not entirely with justification. Not even for Freud is the idea that the consciousness of guilt can be the object of repression an entirely foreign thought. But he has not drawn the consequences of this notion. In *Totem and Taboo* Freud makes his ambitious attempt to illumine what he calls in a later comment on the book the "obscure sense of guilt to which mankind has been subject since prehistoric times," and which "in some religions has been condensed into the doctrine of primal guilt, of original sin . . ." [Freud XIV 292]. It is of course not the dogma, but original sin as a "natural category" which occupies him.[39] Freud's scientific myth (that is his term for it, Freud XVIII 135) about the source of religion, which is the psychoanalytic parallel to the interpretation of the fall into sin in *The Concept of Anxiety,* can be summarized as follows: people originally lived in a primitively organized primal horde, dominated by a power-hungry and jealous father, who appropriated all the clan's women unto himself and forbade his sons to have sexual intercourse with them. It is quite true that Freud is not here concentrating as Kierkegaard does on the possibility of freedom which the prohibition awakens in the sons. But the result is the same: the prohibition is transgressed. The sons conspire against the father, murder and consume him collectively—but then are struck by remorse. In this way, Freud reports in *Totem and Taboo,* the feeling of guilt came into the world, and with it social organization, morality, and religion. The sons must bring about a social order which can hamper a recurrence of the primal crime, they must take upon themselves voluntary restrictions with respect to instinctual gratification (the prohibition against incest), and they must above all repress the guilt-laden memory of the murder of the father by elevating the murdered father into a god. Civilization, morality, and religion build upon repression [Freud XIII 141-57, cf. XXIII 80 ff. and 86 ff.]. This is of course the same famous thesis as in *Civilization and its Discontents*. The striking thing about *Totem and Taboo* is simply that the original repression is here plainly not a repression of an instinct, but a repression of the guilt feeling based upon the murder of the father — which then results in instinctual repression and the repressive society. The repression of guilt and its expression, the deification of the person murdered, never completely succeeds, and it must therefore be continually repeated. In Freud's opinion, all later religions are a more or less successful attempt at this, and consist in representations and sacrificial ceremonies, which all at once or alternately express the conscious wish of subservience to the father god and the unconscious wish to triumph over him and to overthrow him violently (communion, for example, where one eats the god and at the same time receives forgiveness for doing so). I will later examine Kierkegaard's interpretation of the ancient Jewish sacrificial ritual, which is to be understood precisely as an ambiguous and continually repeated attempt to atone for the guilt; Freud's analysis in *Totem and Taboo* can perhaps serve to emphasize the meaning of Kierkegaard's statement in connection with this: "The atonement is first posited with sin, and its sacrifice is not repeated" [IV 411, CD 93]. But in spite of the fact that Freud elsewhere points out the similarity between religion and neurosis (*The Future of an Illusion*), and in spite of the fact that he concludes in *Totem and Taboo* that the explanation of the origin of religion, morality, society, and art is the same ambivalence conflict which forms the basis of all neuroses, namely the Oedipus conflict, whose core is of course exactly the tabooed and counter-cathected wish to kill the father and have sexual intercourse with the mother — in spite of all this, he has not therefore drawn the conclusion that the fundamental task of psychoanalysis must be to annul the primal repression of guilt. Freud restricts himself to what are — according to the view adumbrated above — secondary instinctual repressions.

This is due perhaps not only to the fact that as a scientist he is only interested in the first half of the Danish compound word for original sin, but also to the fact that as an ethicist, as a "moralist," he cannot accept the notion that original sin means that man must repent for the sins of his fathers, because man could be *guilty* of something which "extends beyond the consciousness of the individual" — to cite Anti-Climacus' formulation again. It is also precisely this view which contains "the possibility of offense" [XI 233, SD 226]. But it also contains — according to

Kierkegaard—the possibility of recovery as well, because it is only with the help of this view that guilt manifests itself as sin (and not merely as suffering), and thus can be forgiven (cf. below Chapter VII: 4, for more on this subject).

8. "The Formula for All Despair"

8: 1. *"Anxiety about the Good"*

We have heard that sin (= despair) is a state. The question now is how we are to understand that state in more detail. I will again use Freud as an approach and begin with the question of what it is, in Freud's opinion, that an individual attempts to avoid in the process which leads to neurosis. In the section on Freud's theories of anxiety, there was mention of displeasure, insecurity, helplessness, and straightforward annihilation as that which the individual sought to avoid, and in the immediately preceding section it was suggested that it was perhaps the feeling of guilt which the individual sought to avoid. But the matter can also be expressed another way. There is important therapeutic experience which shows that the analysand regularly puts up resistance against the treatment at one or another point. The resistance appears when significant progress in breaking down the patient's symptoms has occurred. One only speaks of resistance as occurring in cases where the patient consciously declares himself in agreement with the treatment, while the resistance manifests itself without the patient being completely clear about what is happening, e.g., when his memory is blocked at certain painful points, or when he in one way or another breaks "the fundamental rule of analysis" which requires complete honesty. The resistance is the form of defense which appears in the analytic situation itself; it is directed against the helplessness or anxiety which threaten as a result of the therapist's successful attempt to break down the patient's other, established defense mechanisms. In resistance, the patient is fighting to retain his primary gain. The analysis of the resistance is therefore an analysis of his motives to persist in the neurosis and to oppose recovery. The phenomenon of resistance is a compressed and contemporaneous edition of the phenomenon of defense, but with the essential difference that the defense here is not directed against this or that instinctual impulse in order to ward off this or that traumatic situation, but is directed against recovery itself. In the *Lectures* Freud uses the famous expression that "whenever a neurotic is faced by a conflict he takes flight into illness" [Freud XVI 382]. The statement is an early formulation of the idea which is later shaped into the second theory of anxiety, but which naturally was dimly present to

Freud all the while. It describes the sequence of anticipation-reaction and the dialectic escape-revenge, and it notes that the sickness gives protection against the conflict (the primary gain). The same formulation could be used to describe the phenomenon of resistance, but with the change that the word conflict could then be exchanged for — or be more closely defined as— recovery. The little child who reacts with defense mechanisms in signal anxiety does not reflect upon the nature of the critical situation, but forgets it as quickly as possible with the help of repression. The adult analysand, on the other hand, is aware of the situation and of his own critical condition. He comes to the analyst with his sickness and with the express wish to be healed. When he then defends himself (offers resistance) in the analytic situation, it is an unconscious defense quite clearly directed against an anticipated conflict or an anxiety-laden possibility — namely, that which threatens when the old defense is analyzed away, though a better expression for the same thing is perhaps that the defense is directed against recovery or against emancipation from the neurosis. "The crux of the matter is that the defensive mechanisms directed against former danger recur in the treatment as *resistances* against recovery. It follows from this that the ego treats recovery itself as a danger." And, further, "thus we see that there *is* a resistance against the uncovering of resistances, and the defensive mechanisms really do deserve the name which we gave them originally, before they had been more closely examined. They are resistances not only to the making conscious of the contents of the id, but also to analysis as a whole, and thus to recovery" [*Analysis Terminable and interminable,* Freud XXIII 238].

Even though in this same connection Freud reminds us that analysis must not ignore "the id" because of all this, it is to remarks such as those above that neo-Freudian and existentialist-oriented revisionists can attach themselves. Thus one can add the word "recovery" to the schematic diagram above in Chapter V: 6: 3, next to Freud's name, in the column labelled "negatively-charged (feared) impression." Indeed, one could also place the word "freedom" in the same column, cf. a footnote in *The Ego and the Id* about "the effectiveness of analysis [which] . . . does not set out to make pathological reactions impossible, but to give the patient's ego *freedom* to decide one way or the other" [Freud's emphasis, Freud XIX 50 note].

Much has been said concerning the relation between Freud and his successors when one notes that Freud places his concept of freedom in a footnote, while his successors place it on the title page. The title of Erich Fromm's book *Escape from Freedom* is a variant upon formulae such as the ones just cited. When, on the other hand, Fromm changes the title of the British edition of the same, famous book to *Fear of Freedom,* it could sound as though it were a conscious allusion to Kierkegaard's formula "anxiety about the good," especially in view of the fact that Kierkegaard defines "the good" more closely as "freedom" [IV 419 note, CD 99-100 note].[40]

It is quite obvious that Kierkegaard's description of anxiety about the good in *The Concept of Anxiety* is akin to Freud's description of the resistance to recovery. The question is merely one of the broadness of the scope of this idea. I will attempt to demonstrate that "anxiety about the good" is a central and dominant formula for Kierkegaard's concept of despair, both in *The Concept of Anxiety* and in *The Sickness Unto Death.*

This is not so clearly evident from *The Concept of Anxiety.* Here "anxiety about the good," alias "the demonic," appears as the heading of one particular section of the book, and the concept is kept carefully separated from the other concepts which are described. A long series of widely differing phenomena are discussed in the section on anxiety about the good: from hysteria to religious ritualism, from prostitution to metaphysical speculations, from nervous irritability to hypocrisy and superstition, from indolence to madness — all as expressions for one and the same anxiety. It is confusing reading, and Kierkegaard also reminds the reader that he "is taking the concept of the demonic in a broad sense, thought, be it noted, no broader than the concept extends" [IV 445, CD 121], and that examples of the demonic are to be found "in all possible spheres and to all possible degrees" [IV 433, CD 111]. When Kierkegaard adds to this the assertion that: "Whether the demonic means something frightful in the single individual, or whether it is only present like a spot on the sun, or like a little white dot in a corn, the total and the partial demonic have the same characteristics, and the tiny portion is anxious about the good in the same sense as the person who is totally encompassed by it" [IV 445, CD 120-21] — when Kierkegaard adds this, one cannot avoid the suspicion that one is dealing with a diagnostic category which is so encompassing as to be meaningless.

However, the suspicion does not have to be correct. The section about "anxiety about the good" is far from easy to understand, and yet the error is hardly that the category is too broad, but that it is not broad enough. The kaleidoscopic overabundance of the section indicates that Kierkegaard has not thought the idea through fully in *The Concept of Anxiety,* but has come very near to doing so, and this is why the content is on the verge of toppling over the category and exploding the framework. "Anxiety about the good" appears in *The Concept of Anxiety* as one category among others, which, for their part, are each of them rather homogeneously arranged with respect to content. They deal with "the anxiety of spiritlessness," "anxiety determined dialectically in the direction of fate," "anxiety which is dialectical in the direction of guilt," and "anxiety about the evil." Anxiety about the good integrates itself into this series of conditions, which have in common the fact that they are all consequences of sin [IV 387 and 419, CD 73 and 99]. But the section "Anxiety About the Good" differentiates itself with its heterogeneous contents, and this indicates that this formula is not parallel, but superior in relation to the other sections, a definitive formula which also contains the diagnosis of the phenomena which are discussed under the other headings. However, Kietkegaard was not entirely clear about this in 1844. The situation can be expressed as follows, that the anxiety of spiritlessness, and anxiety of fate and guilt, and the anxiety about the evil are partial, descriptive definitions of content, while "anxiety about the good" is the diagnostic formula which encompasses them all. This becomes clear— though not explicitly so—in *The Sickness Unto Death*, and it is from the perspective of that book that one if first able to understand the idea which is still being directly denied in *The Concept of Anxiety*, even though it is present, in undeveloped form, in that book as well. Where *The Concept of Anxiety* is a detailed, partially unclear upwelling of ideas, *The Sickness Unto Death* is a compressed and explanatory book.[41]

8:2. *"Despair about the Eternal"*

In *The Sickness Unto Death* Kierkegaard notes the necessity of making a correct diagnosis of the sickness one is treating. Before the physician can treat the sickness, he must know it, and he must be especially clear as to "whether the supposedly sick person is actually sick, or whether it is perhaps the supposedly healthy person who is actually sick." The physician cannot simply rely upon the patient's statements, but must first make his own investigations, and in certain cases he will not simply restrict himself to the superficial symptoms, but will employ "methods in order to make the sickness become manifest." The psychologist must use a similar method with respect to despair. His analysis must penetrate behind appearances, for his task is not simply to remove the symptom, but to find the reason for the despair. Here a difference between somatic illness and the pneumatic illness, the sickness unto death, reveals itself: "The situation with despair is not as it is with a sickness, where the feelings of poor health are the sickness" [XI 154-56, SD 155-57]. The sick person can easily have a knowledge of being sick without therefore recognizing his sickness or its explanation, or he can be sick without having any knowledge of being sick. But a recognition of the sickness is a precondition of becoming healed.

Freud would doubtless agree with Kierkegaard in all this. The difference between them is that each seeks the explanation in his own place. Freud found it in the traumas of the past. If one views *The Concept of Anxiety* through Freudian glasses and with a feeling that there are "psychoanalytic" insights in the book, it can almost seem inconsistent that the causal connection between the first section of the book and the later sections is not established any more directly than it is. As should be clear at this point, it would also have been a rather natural thing for Kierkegaard to have given a genetic interpretation. Kierkegaard described the retrospective method of analysis in 1837 with this formula: "One must run backwards over the same course by which one has come forward, just as one learns from the elves in the musical piece (the piece on the elf-king), where the bewitchment is ended only when the music is played exactly backwards (retrogressively)" [Pap. II A 65, Hong 3996]. This notion is put forward again *en passant* by Judge William [II 179, E/O II 169], and Vigilius Haufniensis refers to the same theme: "Therefore they say in an old proverb, that when one dares to mention the word, the witchery of the magic disappears . . ." [IV 436, CD 113]. But, characteristically enough, the explicit reference to the past is omitted here, and when the idea finally appears in *The Sickness Unto Death,* the meaning has been changed: "The despairing individual is ignorant of the fact that he is in despair; he is, compared to the person who is conscious of this, simply one negation further removed from the truth and salvation. . . . But in order to reach the truth, one must go through every negativity; for here it is the same as in the folk tale, which tells how to break a certain kind of spell: the piece must be played through backwards in its entirely or the spell is not broken" [XI 176 f., SD 177]. In *The Sickness Unto Death* there is no mention of a retrospective, but of a functional-prospective method.

In place of Freud's distinction between the apparent contemporaneity and factual pastness of the neurosis, Kierkegaard develops a distinction between despair's occasion and its actual cause. The occasion, which makes the unacknowledged despairing person aware of his condition, is "that *over* which he despairs," while the cause is what one despairs *about* (i.e., with respect to), he says, and he gives a pithy re-definition of a well-worn religious term, conversion: "One despairs *over* that which anchors one firmly in despair: over one's misfortune, over earthly things, over the loss of one's fortune, etc.; but one despairs *about* that which, correctly understood, releases one from despair: about the eternal, about one's salvation, about one's own strength, etc. . . . And this is the obscurity which consists in the fact that particularly in all lower forms of despair and in almost every despairing person, the individual sees and knows so passionately what it is that he despairs *over,* but it escapes him what it is he despairs *about.* The precondition for recovery is always this conversion" [XI 195 note, SD 194 note].[42]

Therefore the analysis is functional. Even though the crisis is conditioned by the past, it is not the straightforward consequence of circumstances, but is a consequence of man's present attitude toward the given circumstances. Or in other words, in contrast to the situation in somatic illness, it is here important "that every actual moment of despair is to be traced back to possibility; every moment he is in despair, he *is* *inflicting it upon* himself; it is always the present time; there is nothing which becomes actualized in the present because of its relation to a bygone past; in every actual moment of despair, the despairing person retains the entire past as a possibility in the present" [XI 147, SD 149-50].

The schism between the "over what" and the "about what" of despair is a schism between a descriptive and a diagnostic point of view. In the one case we are dealing with the despairing person's own experience and explanation of the condition. In the other case we are dealing with Kierkegaard's understanding of it. As a rule, the despairing person is "not aware of what is happening behind him, so to speak" [XI 195, SD 194-95]; "he is facing backwards, and what he says must be understood in reverse: he stands and points at that which is not despair, explaining that he is in despair, and yet, it is quite true that despair is taking place behind him, which he knows nothing about" [XI 185, SD 185]. Therefore, the psychologist has another understanding of despair, which "in its concept is always *about* the eternal, while what one despairs *over* can vary greatly."

"The formula for all despair" — namely, the diagnostic formula which summarizes the many phenomenologically different forms — is thus: "Despair about the eternal and over oneself." I will explain the latter segment of the formula in the following section. Here we will restrict ourselves to the first part. "Despair about the eternal" is clearly the same as "anxiety about the good," for just as despair's "about what" is more closely defined in *The Sickness Unto Death* as "*about* that which, correctly understood, releases one from despair; about the eternal, about one's salvation, about one's own strength, etc." [XI 195 note, SD 194 note], so is the object of anxiety defined in *The Concept of Anxiety* as follows: "The good naturally means freedom's re-integration, redemption, salvation, or whatever one wishes to call it" [IV 428, CD 106]. But it is only when we have the assistance of Anti-Climacus that it becomes possible to see that this diagnosis is universal.

It can easily be seen how these formulae correspond to the definition of consolidated despair which was given earlier in the formula unambiguousness/double-mindedness. The despairing person fortifies himself against ambiguousness in an unambiguous position, but the unsuccessfulness of the fortifications reveals the despairing person's double-mindedness. Now it is added that the ambiguous possibility ultimately is always the possibility of recovery—"or whatever one wishes to call it." The possibility of recovery (the good, the eternal, freedom, etc.) manifests itself to (is experienced by) the despairing person as ambiguousness, as "a nothing which the individual both loves and fears." But the fact that the possibility is ambiguous means that it deters the individual who seeks unambiguousness; and yet that which deters is nothing other than a reflection of the individual's own double-mindedness, because one always forms the future as one is formed oneself: "As long as we are only dealing with that which is expected, sin still has the power in man, and naturally conceives of that which is expected as hostile" [IV 358, CD 48]. And yet the point of Kierkegaard's description of the despairing or the demonic person is that he is still unable to avoid having a relationship with that which he detests or defends himself against or despairs "about." The dialectical ambiguousness of this condition lies in this relationship; that is, there is a doubled-mindedness behind the despairing person's attempt to establish himself unambiguously in his rejection or abandonment of recovery. (This will be further illuminated in the next chapter.)

8:3. *The Applicability of the Formulae*

If one wanted to maintain that Kierkegaard's expressions "anxiety about the good" and "despair about the eternal" are names for the most definitive view of neurosis, a view to which Freud found his way by many circuitous routes, namely, the idea of resistance against recovery, a Freudian would immediately raise the same objections which he raises against the neo-Freudians, that the simplicity of Kierkegaard's terms are a kind of simplification. Freud's many circuitous routes were not travelled in vain, and the insight they gave him was in no way rendered superfluous by the idea that "ultimately" the defense can be said to be directed against recovery.

I will not directly rebut this objection. But if it is nonetheless maintained that Kierkegaard, in one important respect, speaks more clearly and adequately about things than Freud does, this judgement is based upon the qualitative criterion that what is decisive in judging a given intellectual structure must be its central and fundamental formulations and their applicability. The advantage of the Kierkegaardian formulations is precisely their applicability, that is their latitude, their flexibility, and their capacity for specificity, which is not simply synonymous with vagueness, but which is connected to the fact that they have been formulated at a higher level of abstraction that Freud's. It is not necessarily wrong to speak of neurosis, as Freud often does, as a consequence of the fact that a sexual impulse was repressed because of the danger of the unpleasurable experiences which the satisfaction of that impulse was expected to cause, but it involves the introduction of qualifications in the definition of neurosis, which cause one to come to a conclusion before the matter has been thought through all the way to the bottom. To speak, as Adler does, of neurosis as a product of a frustrated will to power is again to specify — that is, to determine the content — of the definition. And it is only when one has abstracted from these more or less overly hasty and mutually exclusive determinations of content that it becomes possible to bring forth by means of analysis the dialectic which lies hidden in the background, as we have attempted to do here. To speak, as Kierkegaard does, of despair as a despair about the eternal or as an anxiety about the good is on the other hand to refrain from all qualifications of the definition of the concept itself, in order then to be able to operate with determinations of content in the concrete cases. Freud's and Adler's central definitions *are* qualified; Kierkegaard's *admits* of qualification — and it becomes qualified.

Now it will certainly be asked whether "the good," from which the despairing person recoils, is not after all a positive thing of definite content, thus parallel with libidinous satisfaction and its effects, which is the object of anxiety in Freud. It is not the "noogenetic neurosis" we are dealing with in Kierkegaard — which, according to Viktor E. Frankl (if I understand him correctly) is due to the fact that the neurotic lacks a moral view of life, and which is healed when the physician provides him with one? It could appear that this were so. One could split hairs and say that for Freud the libidinous satisfaction is "the good," and that the difference between him and Kierkegaard is merely the fact that each of them operates with his own central value concept, Freud with a "fleshly" one, and Kierkegaard with a "spiritual" one. But this is a sloganistic arrangement of things. The difference between them is not a difference between immoral and moral (such a formulation would be unjust to both of them), but first of all a difference between a definition of the object of anxiety which has its contents predominantly defined, and a definition which is predominantly formal. "The good does not admit of definition at all. The good is freedom" [IV 419 note, CD 99 note]. This is to say that the good does not admit of an unambiguous definition of contents; the word does not universally describe or prescribe a particular sort of behavior or moral conduct, but it is defined purely formally by its relation to its antithesis, unfreedom. It is important to insist upon this—before we go on to the definitions of content.

In spite of the fact that "the good" does not admit of definition *in abstracto* in any unambiguous way, any more than does the eternal,[43] it can very well take on reality for the despairing individual, and come into being for him as something which has firm contours, something to which anxiety relates itself in a definite way. Kierkegaard can therefore say in this connection: "Yet the object of anxiety is something definite, its nothingness is actually something, when the difference between good and evil is posited *in concreto*" [IV 419, CD 99]. The object is the good, freedom, recovery. One can imagine the objection against Kierkegaard to the effect that it is all very well with his level of abstraction and his ability to formulate things definitively, but that it is hardly reasonable to assume that the despairing person always has this definite object for his anxiety, that he always has the possibility of recovery in view, in order then to evade the issue with cunning. One can imagine something like this in the psychoanalytic situation, where the patient comes with the conscious wish to be healed, and then unconsciously makes resistance against the analysis. But then it is precisely the situation which makes it possible to say that the anxiety has recovery as its object. And Kierkegaard does not speak of any such physician-patient situation. His description of the demonic, which evades the good, can at the most be valid for certain highly-reflective, crisis-conscious types, who test themselves with self-analysis, and who discover in this self-analysis their own ambivalent relationship to recovery.

At first this objection can sound very correct. If it is correct, it greatly restricts the range of Kierkegaard's observations, and makes central portions of his psychology into a bit of "interesting" psychological autobiography without universal relevance. Nor does one need to be in doubt as to who the model was for the anthropology with which we here concern ourselves—Søren Aabye Kierkegaard. The fundamental postulate which one must accept here, as elsewhere, if one is to be able to view his psychology as other and more than a disguised and philosophically-staged autobiography, is that the same thing which takes place on a high and relatively clarified level of consciousness in a reflective observer repeats itself in less distinct variations in the less reflective and less conscious person. *Unum noris, omnes,* is the assertion.[44] But this assertion is not to the effect that every despairing person experiences the possibility of recovery or freedom as an ambiguous-hostile possibility in the same conscious way as did Kierkegaard himself, or in the same way that psychoanalytic patients can do in the situation of analysis. Nor, in *The Concept of Anxiety,* in the very section about "Anxiety about the Good" (alias the demonic), is there mention of individuals who constantly have the possibility of recovery in view, or the good in mind, but of people who *inter alia* can be characterized by their hostile or evasive reactions to attempts to change their condition. A constant perception of "the good" as something which must be avoided at all costs is only present at the rarest and most intense stages of despair. In other cases, the manifest perception of anxiety can be something else—fate, guilt, or "the evil"—but these perceptions must be understood as inadequate and markedly "hostile" phenomenological concretizations of, or replacements for, the unspecified "good," which in principle is always the object of anxiety or despair. Or anxiety can be so indistinct, so "hidden and disguised" [IV 403, CD 86], that it does not leave behind distinct notions, but merely manifests itself diffusely in the individual's behavior. Even the person who is spiritless is nevertheless anxious about the good (although this is not said directly in *The Concept of Anxiety*) and is in despair about the eternal (which is directly said in *The Sickness Unto Death,* because this is the formula for all despair). But he does not recognize his own anxiety or its object, and is thus determined by it without himself knowing it (cf. below, Chapter VII).

The criteria which Kierkegaard employs when he must divide the unitary despair into a series of different despairs will be investigated in the next chapter. But in order to understand them we must first examine the second part of the formula for all despair, which was: "Despair about the eternal and over oneself."

9. "The Self the Individual Knows"

9:1. *"The Self is the Relationship to Itself"*

Thus, despair is always despair "over oneself." This formulation forces us to ask once again what it is that Kietkegaard understands by the self, and to pose this question in a different manner than in the previous chapter, for the side of the question which is to be discussed now was only hinted at there: the self is not simply a relationship between two given antithetical elements, but the self is "*that* the relationship relates itself to itself" [XI 143, SD 146]. There was also mention of the self as created, and, as a part of this, possessing the condition of possibility for the authentic realization of the ethical task. But the ethical-anthropological model was the same as the conflict model: "Despair is the misrelationship in a relationship of a synthesis, which relates itself to itself. But the synthesis is not the misrelationship; it is only the possibility, or, in the synthesis lies the possibility of the misrelationship." By this Kierkegaard wishes to insist that despair is not a necessary and unavoidable consequence of "human nature as such." What is unavoidable is not the misrelationship, but the relationship, also called the eternal in man: " . . . to despair is a category of spirit, and is related to the eternal in man. But he cannot become quit of the eternal, no, in all eternity no; he cannot cast if off once and for all. Nothing is more impossible; at every instant in which he does not have it, he must be casting it or have cast it away from himself — but it comes back; that is, at every instant that he is in despair, he is inflicting despair upon himself. For the despair is not a consequence of the misrelationship, but of the relationship which relates itself to itself. And one can no more be quit of the relation to oneself than one can be quit of oneself, which is incidentally one and the same thing, for the self is indeed the relationship to itself" [XI 146 f., SD 148-50].

What does it mean to say that a person's self is identical with his unavoidable relationship to himself? The hint of an answer was given above, where it was written that the relationship is first a fact, and only thereafter a task (cf. above Chapter IV: 3: 1), or where there was mention of the psychological consequences of the notion of the unavoidability of the relationship to God (cf. above Chapter V: 1). It is these themes which will be pursued here. One could also call the relationship to oneself the representation of oneself. The self is thus the represented self, the self-image or self-perception, to use an expression from modern psychology. The fact that man is created as a synthesis means that he unavoidably forms such a representation of himself. When Kierkegaard says that the synthesis does not automatically in itself bring about despair, he is thinking of consolidated despair. His meaning is apparently that despair (the misrelationship) always does in fact arise, "when God, who made man into the relationship, lets man slip out of his hand, as it were, that is, when the relationship relates itself to itself" (cf. above Chapter V: 3). But this despair, the primary crisis, can be both the transitional phase to faith and to consolidated despair. When despair has appeared, then it does not follow of itself that it continues, for its continuation is not simply a consequence "of the misrelationship, but of the relationship which relates itself to itself. That is, every time the misrelationship manifests itself, and in every second it exists, it has to go back to the relationship," i.e., to the self-perception. Therefore, continuing despair is not a static phenomenon, "a simple consequence of the fact that he at one time inflicted it upon himself," but a condition which the despairing person at every moment "*inflicts upon* himself" [XI 147, SD 149]. In saying this Kierkegaard is not denying his own idea of the consistency of evil, but is pointing to the self's perception of itself as a point of departure for the understanding of despair, because the despairing person's self-perception confirms itself and, thereby, the misrelationship.

9: 2. The Genesis of Self-perception: the Standard of Measure and Fantasy

The self-perception is the sum of the individual's representations of himself, and his experience and evaluations of himself. Such a representation does not arise merely by virtue of the individual's relationship to himself, but by virtue of his relationship to something other. The idea is already partially known to us. In Kierkegaard one can differentiate between a negative and a positive "other" as the factors which help bring about this self-perception. The negative factor is the mere distancing of the self from a surrounding world which is indistinct in other respects; the positive factor is the relationship to definite things in this surrounding world. To the extent that one can imagine "pure" immediacy, it is situated "in immediate coherence with the other (τὸ ἕτερον) [to eteron]"; its self is "a dative like the child's me" [XI 184, SD 184], or, in other words: "Immediacy really has no self; it does not know itself, and thus cannot recognize itself . . ." [XI 186, SD 186]. Thus the identity or the self-perception arises in "the act of separation, in which the self becomes aware of itself as essentially different from the surrounding world and externality and their influences upon itself" [XI 188, SD 188]. Thus it is here a matter of the development of the individual, which I have examined in Chapter II, about the child who is weaned. The process of separation involves an approximation to self-consciousness. This arises when the spirit posits itself, i.e., when the individual's representation of himself as a unity, in distinct opposition to the other, comes into being.

That which is to be illuminated here is the synthetic function by means of which the individual forms for himself a whole picture of himself. The negatively active factor was the separation itself; the positive is the distinct things in the environment (people, authorities, norms, etc.) in relation to which the individual defines himself, and which constitute the orientation points for the self's self-understanding. "The standard of measure for the self is always the thing vis-a-vis to which the self is itself. But this thing is in turn the definition of what 'the standard of measure' is. Because one can only add like quantities, everything is thus qualitatively that by which it is measured; and that, which qualitatively is its standard of measure, is ethically its goal.[45] And the standard of measure and the goal are qualitatively that which something is. . . ." The self is thus not simply the sum of the individual's properties, for such a sum cannot be totalled up in and for itself, but only with the help of a given standard of measure outside of the individual. The self is therefore the individual's representation of these properties, such as is brought about by means of the comparison with the adopted or inherited norm. I have earlier pointed out the significance of the fact that for Kierkegaard the self does not merely "relate itself to itself," but that "in relating itself to itself, [it] relates itself to an Other" (above, Chapter IV: 3: 2). The function of comparison itself has also been discussed (Chapter IV: 3: 1), but will be illuminated more concretely in Chapter VII: 1. Here it is only a matter of the short, formulaic statement about the standard of measure in *The Sickness Unto Death*. Kierkegaard illustrates the idea by giving brief descriptions of a couple of standards of measure and of the degrees of intensity of consciousness which correspond to them: "A shepherd who (if it were possible) is himself vis-a-vis cows is a very low self; likewise a ruler who is himself vis-a-vis slaves; they are really no selves, for in both cases the standard of measure is lacking. The child who has hitherto had the standard of measure of his parents, becomes a man by receiving the state as his standard of measure; but what an infinite emphasis is placed upon the self in receiving God as the standard of measure!" [XI 216, SD 210]. One may dispute how well-chosen or tasteful these examples are, but the idea is at least quite clear. More important than the examples themselves, however, is the use Kierkegaard elsewhere makes of the idea of the standard of measure.

The self-perception, however, is not only the totality of the individual's characteristics, as these are evaluated in sum by the individual himself with the help of the standard of measure, but it is also these abilities and attributes as the individual subjectively represents them to himself with the help of that ability to form syntheses which Kierkegaard in *The Sickness Unto Death* calls "the ability *instar omnium*,"[46] i.e., fantasy. Fantasy is the infinitizing medium, Kierkegaard says, and explains this as follows: "The amount of feeling, cognition, and will a person has ultimately depends upon how much fantasy he has, that is, how he reflects himself, i.e., in fantasy." "The abilities" are not simply given quantities, but possibilities which can be developed or inhibited, and that which conditions this development or inhibition is fantasy, or, more accurately, the self-perception which is arranged with the help of fantasy. Fantasy is a mirror or canvas upon which the individual projects his own image, and in this mirroring (reflection) lies the possibility for developing "the abilities" — feeling, cognition, will: "The self is reflection, and fantasy is reflection, the reproduction of the self, which is the possibility of the self. Fantasy is the possibility of all reflection; and the intensity of this medium is the possibility of the self's intensity" [XI 162, SD 164].[47]

The self-image acts retroactively as a motivational system upon the given abilities and contributes to forming (developing or inhibiting) them. It is undoubtedly with the help of the concept of fantasy that one comes to the most precise formulation of what Kierkegaard understands by the self as a psychological concept. "The self is the conscious synthesis of infinity and finitude," he writes, [XI 161, SD 162], and shortly thereafter the statement is varied: "The personality is a synthesis of possibility and necessity" [XI 172, AD 173]. If one understands finitude and necessity as the given, innate characteristics and abilities, then the self is the conscious synthesis of these factual characteristics, on the one hand, and of infinity and possibility on the other; the self is the individual's conscious image of himself — the individual's represented, experienced image of himself, an image which is brought about with the help of synthesis-forming fantasy (i.e., infinity and possibility) — as that which has these characteristics and contains these possibilities.

9:3. *The Representation and the Represented*

Kierkegaard thus differentiates between the representation (the image) and that of which it is a representation (that of which it is an image). The problem lies in this distinction, that is, in the possible incongruence between the representation and the represented. The incongruence is the misrelationship in the relationship of the synthesis, which constitutes despair. Although fantasy is "the ability *instar omnium*," this does not mean that it sovereignly and without preconditions creates man's actual self. *That* is "idealism's" (Fichte's) idea, which Kierkegaard labels as desperate.[48] The self-perception is the self, but it is not given that it is the true self. The true self is not unambiguously a product of fantasy's autonomous mastery over the given characteristics, but is the synthesis of the given and the possible, a product of the interplay between the factual characteristics and fantasy. The true self is not simply the static and given (finite, necessary) self. But the false self is the self which is torn loose from the given elements, the self which fantasy alone invents. Kierkegaard, however, has no unambiguous *a priori* criterion for his differentiation. The answer — and the problem — lies in the fact that the self is a becoming (cf. above Chapter IV: 3: 4). But the self is a becoming precisely by virtue of fantasy, in which man projects himself, and by means of which the relationship between the given and the possible, the finite and the infinite, is made problematic.

Fantasy, like anxiety, is an ambiguous phenomenon, which can have a positive or a negative effect. In the statements cited above we heard of the positive effects, of fantasy as the possibility of the self's intensity. But the fact that these sentences are an insertion in a longer explanation, which deals with the diffuse volatilization of the self into the realm of fantasy, is enough to make it clear that fantasy also involves other possibilities. In the section on "Time" (Chapter V: 4), where this entire line of reasoning was adumbrated from another perspective, it became clear that the future, understood as a product of fantasy, can also act in the present moment in other ways, as a blocking, enervating, or energy-transforming factor. The fact that the self and fantasy are reflection implies that they alone can take on the mirroring function; where in the normal case this self-perception comes into being by means of a mirroring in the surrounding world, this phenomenon can now be replaced by pure, solipsistic self-mirroring. Naturally, this is not a normal or healthy phenomenon, but one which is described by Kierkegaard under the special category of "The Despair of Possibility." When the self is posited, "it reflects itself in the medium of fantasy, and infinite possibility thereby manifests itself." Still, this is not yet sickly, but on the contrary is completely normal. But if self-mirroring emancipates itself from that which is factually given, this fantastic self-perception can become an autonomous and uncontrollable system of motivation, which reacts upon the entire form of the individual's life, so that he is no longer capable of identifying himself. "Even in relation to seeing *oneself* in a mirror, it is necessary to know oneself, for if one does not, then one does not see *oneself,* but simply a man. But the mirror of possibility is no ordinary mirror; it must be used with the greatest of caution. For this mirror is untrue in the highest sense of the term. That a self appears in the possibility of itself in such and such a way is only a half-truth. . . ." Here we have opened up a small insight into a particular, pathological form of despair, which in a way comes too early in our presentation, but this is unavoidable, as it is in connection with this that Kierkegaard puts forth his thoughts on self-perception. I wish to proceed a bit more slowly. The half of the truth which is lacking in the self that has volatilized itself in fantasy is the understanding of its own actuality, or, as Kierkegaard here prefers to express it, its necessity. "What is lacking is really the power to obey, to bow before that which is necessary in one's self, which might be called one's limit" [XI 167-69, SD 168-70]. Later in *The Sickness Unto Death,* this idea is taken up again during the description of another, but closely related form of despair, "defiance," which is characterized by the individual's desire to create or invent himself autonomously, to "determine what he will and will not include in his concrete self. His concrete self or his concretion has of course necessity and limits; it is this quite definite thing with these abilities, talents, etc., in this concretion of circumstances, etc. But with the help of the infinite form, the negative self, he wants first to undertake the re-shaping of all this in order to produce out of it a self which he wants. . . . " [XI 203, SD 201-02].

We are here confronted with the question of how Kierkegaard determines the relationship between the self-perception and the factual self. It has become clear that they do not always coincide with one another. But now it has also become clear from what has just been developed, that man is always in a certain sense left to "hit upon" whom he is, because the self is not a statically given, objectively measurable sum of characteristics, but an identity which is the represented aynthesis of these characteristics, subjectively established by the standard of measure and fantasy.

The problem is thus that the characteristics and the possibilities do not exist for the individual in an objectively available form, for they form themselves in his self-perception. The characteristics (understood ethically and psychologically) are developed, and in a sense first come into existence, in and with the coming-into-being of self-perception — "for, 'we do not yet know what we will become,' " as it was expressed with a biblical citation in the edifying discourse on acquiring the soul [IV 73, ED II 84; cf. above, Chapter IV: 4: 2]. There is no objective criterion for what belongs and what does not belong to the self, so to speak, of what one must accept as an essential part of the self and what one must reject as alien elements or perhaps as the products of a morbid fantasy. The "true" self is the self-understanding which stands in an adequate relationship to the given ("created," innate) characteristics. But, of course, according to Kierkegaard's anthropology, fantasy belongs among these characteristics as the ability *instar omnium,* as does consciousness as that which relates itself to, or posits, its standard of measure. Thus it is likewise impossible to guarantee the "choice" of a correct self-perception by the specification of unambiguous norms, and, at the most, one can make the general statement that the self has the task of developing all sides of its being: "The development must thus consist in coming infinitely away from oneself in the infinitization of the self, and in coming infinitely back to oneself in finitization" [XI 161, SD 162-63, cf. above Chapter IV: 3: 3].

Judge William, in whose writings the germ of most of Kierkegaard's fundamental problems lie, has also discussed this question. He, too, can speak of the self as something definite: in the choice one becomes conscious of oneself "as an individual, who has these abilities, these passions, these tendencies, these habits, who stands under these external influences, who is influenced this way in one direction, that way in another" [II 283, E/O II 266-67, cf. Chapter III: 1]. This sum of innate characteristics is "the individual's concretion," he says, in complete agreement with Anti-Climacus. And it is true that this concretion is "the actuality of the individual; but, because he chooses it in accordance with his freedom, one can also say that it is his possibility," or to use a more ethical expression, it is his task, the potential he is to develop [II 272, cf. 274; E/O II 256, cf. 258]. The problem is again how one is to become clear about which of these abilities and tendencies are really a part of one, and which are not.

It will perhaps be objected that this is a very artificial way of posing the question, for ordinary people do not ask this at all. To this Kierkegaard would not *only* answer with the well-known reply that that is because ordinary people are generally very thoughtless and spiritless, but he would also answer that every person does ask this, or rather, that every person makes his answer to the question — except it is not always clear to him that he does so. It is really this psychological point which I will track down here, but in order to understand it, it is necessary to remain for a little while with the Judge's ethical idea of the existential choice. It does not depend as much on "choosing what is right, as upon the energy, the seriousness, and the pathos with which one chooses," and therefore the choice is not primarily a disjunction between good and evil, but an acceptance of the validity of these concepts. That is, when the individual has obligated himself in the choice, then the subjective and concrete understanding will follow of itself, so that the person who chose what was wrong will be capable of correcting his choice [II 181 ff., E/O II 170 f.], much more so than if he had a normative, universal catalogue of duty by which to guide himself. He becomes acquainted with himself in the choice, and his continuing task is thus "to order, form, temper, enflame, suppress" his characteristics and passions [II 283, E/O II 267]. He distinguishes between what is essential and what is accidental in himself; he is "his own editor," but, be it noted, he is "officially responsible," so that the responsibility and consciousness also include that which the editor censors: "[H]e takes possession of himself in his entirety, with everything equally essential; but . . . having done that, he differentiates, though in such a way that, when he excludes that which is accidental, he takes upon himself an essential responsibility for having done so" [II 281 f., E/O II 265].

9:4 *The Unconscious Choice*

Judge William is an ethicist; what he describes is the "ideal" personality development. But he does this against the background of a solid psychological understanding of the self. The possibility of a continued, constructive development without the arbitrary exclusion of sides of the personality, which the choice emplies, is precisely what comes into being when the choice takes place consciously. Therefore, his depiction of self-perception is not only ethical and edifying, but also psychological, and as such also essential to the understanding of what happens when the choice takes place unconsciously: "In the individual's intercourse with himself, the individual becomes pregnant with himself and gives birth to himself. The self which the individual knows is at once both the actual self and the ideal self, which the individual has outside himself as an image, in the likeness of which he must form himself, and which, however, he at the same time has within himself, because it is himself. It is only in himself that the individual has the objective after which he is to strive, and yet he has this objective outside of himself, in that he is striving after it. . . . Therefore, the ethical life has this duality, that the individual has himself outside himself and within himself. The typical self, however, is the imperfect self, for this is only a prophecy, and therefore not the actual self. However, it accompanies him constantly; but the more he realizes it, the more it goes down inside him, until at last, instead of standing before him, it lies behind him as a faded possibility . . ." [II 279-80, E/O II 163-64].

What is described here is thus the ethicist's self-perception or simply his self-projection — an I-ideal one could say, though not in the narrow Freudian sense ("ego-ideal" = "super-ego"). That the self exists ideally or typically does not mean *primarily* that it is exemplary in the ethical sense, but that it is represented, thought, a product of the synthesis-forming fantasy, or, to use another expression from Anti-Climacus, it is the conscious synthesis of finitude and infinity ("at once the actual self and the ideal self" etc.). The I-ideal motivates the individual's actions, and is thus, *to that extent* actually "exemplary."

It is very doubtful that the Judge's description of his better I gives any correct impression of Kierkegaard's view of the ethical-religious sphere. Kierkegaard does not indeed view this pseudonym as Christian in the stricter sense, but as the representative of precisely that ethical idealism which must be broken by the Christian judgment upon man [see Pap. IV B 59, p. 214, and especially VII 243 f. and 254 f., CUP 230 f. and 239 f.]. It is therefore not so much the ethical as the psychological side of the Judge's notion of the ideal self which has significance for the understanding of Kierkegaard.

The fact is, indeed, that a self-perception, an ideal-I, also arises when the choice is made unconsciously. The Judge's line of reasoning is ethical, but it presupposes a psychological understanding of what happens when a person excludes sides of his being by forming himself a self-image without taking what the Judge calls conscious responsibility for the exclusion. This is precisely what the aesthete does. The ethicist William is also a psychologist. It is he who puts forth the idea of the unavoidable choice: "If one thinks that one can keep one's personality clear and empty for an instant, or that, in the strict sense, one can stop and interrupt personal life, one is in error. The personality is already interested in the choice before one chooses, and when one delays the choice, the personality, or the dark forces within itself, choose unconsciously" [II 179, E/O II 168].

The idea of the unavoidability of the choice is a consequence of Kierkegaard's anthropology. Man is never neutral, but always "interested," concernedly engaged in his own existence, whether he makes this clear to himself or not (cf. above, Chapter IV: 3: 1). The theological expression of this is that man is dependent upon the power which posited him (Chapter IV: 3: 2 and Chapter V: 1). In one of the religious discourses which deals with man's position in the point of conflict between God and Mammon, it is thus written that "if a man does not choose, then it is the same as the presumptuous position of choosing the world" [VIII 342, GS 229]. Man is never in a neutral position, but he makes himself unavoidably dependent, and finds himself a "god." The question is thus not whether the individual chooses or does not choose a self-image, but only how he chooses it.

In the aesthetic individual, "the personality chooses unconsciously." This does not necessarily mean that the choice takes place without any form of self-reflection. The extremely conscious, intellectually refined aesthetic pseudonym in *Either/Or*—just like the ethicist who describes him—observes "himself in his concretion and distinguishes *inter et inter*.[49] He sees one thing as belonging to him accidentally, another thing as essential." Just as the ethicist does, he, too, edits or makes a selection: "He says, I have talent to paint; that I regard as an accident; but I am witty and insightful, and this I regard as the essential, which cannot be taken from me without my becoming someone else" [II 280 f., E/O II 264-65]. The Judge refers to this selection as an illusion, because it is an arbitrary choosing of one striking and flattering characteristic at the expense of others. But this does not prevent the aesthete from in fact forming himself a self-image; he identifies himself with his wittiness and his insightfulness, and this self-perception motivates his life-style. Even if this is perhaps not exemplary in the ethical sense, it is in the psychological. The wittiness and the insightfulness become his I-ideal or the role which he attempts to live up to. Superficially seen, the self-perception does not even need to be wrong, for Aesthete A actually is both witty and insightful. If it is inadequate all the same, this is not due to his leading characteristics being less sterling than those of many other people, but because of the way in which he forms and looks after his role-self. As a conscious relativist, Aesthete A is capable of living different roles, depending upon the circumstances. But he is unable to stop playing a role for very long at any time, and role-playing serves precisely the purpose of the continuing confirmation of the self-image [II 174 and 209 ff., E/O II 164 and 198].

In the Judge's letter, the aesthete is depicted in connection with a series of less refined and less conscious aesthetic views of life. What is common both to the highly developed and to those at a lower level of consciousness is precisely the I-ideal. "Every man, however poorly gifted he is, however subordinate his station in life is, has a natural need to form for himself a view of life, a notion of the significance and purpose of life. The person who lives aesthetically also does so . . ." [II 194, E/O II 184]. Mentioned as examples are notions which are dominated by ideals of health and beauty (novelistically expressed: "Both the Count and the Countess had much education and yet the Countess' view of life was concentrated in the idea that they were the handsomest couple in the land"), views in which "riches, honor, nobility, etc., are made into life's task and content," and views in which the personality is "defined as talent," e.g., in the mercantile, mathematical, artistic, or philosophical areas [II 197 f., E/O II 186-87].

9:5. *To Despair "Over Oneself"*

Among the Judge's esthete-types we meet a young, infatuated girl whose self-understanding is dominated by the idea of her affiliation to her lover, and we also meet a Roman emperor whose life is his power. The two types appear again in *The Sickness Unto Death,* but in new situations, as an unhappy mistress and as a youth with disappointed dreams of empire. Using them as examples, Anti-Climacus explains the meaning in the expression to despair "over oneself." The young girl loses her beloved, and despairs. Apparently she despairs over the loss, over the fact that he dies or was unfaithful. But in actuality, she despairs "over herself," that is, over the fact that her self "shall be a self without 'him.' " She has formed for herself an image of herself as the person who belongs to the beloved, and what she despairs over is therefore not the loss itself, but the notion of herself as the person who has suffered this loss. The other example is clearer, perhaps; an ambitious young man has taken as the motto for his life the phrase "either Caesar or nothing at all." He does not become Caesar, and now he despairs over it. "But this means something else — that he, precisely because he did not become Caesar, now cannot bear to be himself. He thus does not really despair over the fact that he did not become Caesar, but over himself, for the fact that he did not become Caesar. . . . In the deeper sense, what is intolerable to him is not that he did not become Caesar, but this self, which did not become Caesar, is intolerable to him. Or, still more correctly, what is intolerable to him is that he cannot be quit of himself" [XI 149 f., SD 152].

The girl and the youth do not react to the factual happening, but to the break in their self-perception. Each has in advance identified herself or himself, respectively, as "his" fiancee and as a potential Caesar, and the frustration of these hopes now involves the loss of this possibility of identification. Without this advance identification, they would not have had reason to despair, but only (in the case of the young girl) to sorrow; but that is something entirely different. (I will later come back to Kierkegaard's distinction between sorrow and despair; cf. also the distinction between sorrow and melancholia, above, Chapter V: 3.) This is the reason that Kierkegaard can assert that they were also in despair before their hopes were disappointed, for the disappointment was only the occasion by which despair became manifest. If they had had their wishes fulfilled, they would merely not have had the opportunity to become aware of their despair: "He is essentially just as much in despair, for he does not have his self; he is not himself. In having become Caesar he would not have become himself, however, but would have become quit of himself; and in not becoming Caesar, he despairs over not having been able to be quit of himself" [XI 150, SD 152]. One sees that Kierkegaard does not label the "objective" fact of being Caesar or being married to the person one loves as despair. These roles only become despairing when the individual identifies himself with them in an unambiguous way, is absorbed by them, and thereby makes himself dependent upon them.

In *Works of Love* the same idea is formulated as follows: "It may be said of despair that only that person can despair who is in despair. . . . Despair lies in relating oneself to an individual person with infinite passion. . . . Despair is a misrelationship in the innermost part of his being—no fate and no event can penetrate so far and so deeply, they can only make it manifest that the misrelationship was there. . . . Despair is thus not the loss of the beloved; that is misfortune, grief, suffering; but despair is the lack of the eternal" [XI 53 f., WL 54-55].

Just as despair "about the eternal" is a diagnostic formula, so, too, is despair "over oneself." For the despairing person no more understands that he does not really despair over one or another particular occasion, but over the breach of his self-understanding, any more than he normally has a clear awareness of the fact that what he is really in despair about is the possibility of recovery. It is this breach of self-understanding which makes the given despair manifest in the experience of despair and the outbreak of despair. This holds as the diagnostic formula for "all despair."

However, the experience and the outbreak of despair are of course not what Kierkegaard really understands by despair. On the contrary, consolidated despair is what comes into being in the attempt to evade this experience — "in order to bring about obscurity." Despair's reaction to manifest despair is the attempt to forget it, though not with simple forgetting, but by the formation and defense of a reactive self-image, which is to repress the self-image which one despaired "over."

More about this in the next chapter.

Chapter VI

"THE CONTINUITY OF SIN"

1. The Formulae

Kierkegaard's linguistic genius celebrates some of its greatest triumphs in the formulae concerning "all despair" in *The Sickness Unto Death*. As he — and we, with him — moves from considering despair as a general category to viewing the various forms of despair, he must at the same time vary the basic formula which has been examined up to this point: "Despair about the eternal and over oneself." And yet it is an important point that the variations of this formula also lay claim to universality at the same time that they describe the particular forms of despair. "To despair over oneself, despairingly to will to do away with oneself, is the formula for all despair," he writes at another point in *The Sickness Unto Death,* and adds, "so, therefore, the second form of despair, despairingly to will to be oneself, can be traced back to the first form, to will despairingly not to be oneself, just as in the previous sections we broke down the form of despairingly willing not to be oneself into the form of despairingly willing to be oneself (cf. Section A)" [XI 151, SD 153]. Kierkegaard's reference to himself concerns the introductory section of the book, in which the dialectical antithesis of the cited formula is put forth (dialectic is, indeed, precisely the ability to be at variance with oneself without coming into contradiction with oneself): "Yes, so far is it from being the case that this second form of despair (despairingly to will to be oneself) is a mere designation for a particular sort of despair, that, on the contrary, in the final analysis all despair can be broken down and traced back to it" [XI 144, SD 147].

Thus: *a*) to despair "about the eternal" = *b*) to despair "over oneself" = *c*) "despairingly to will not to be oneself" = *d*) "despairingly to will to be oneself." These four formulae can be mutually dissolved into one another; each of them lays claim to being the predominant formula, and is, but each in its own dimension. They express the same thing, but not in the same way, i.e., they express different sides of the same matter.

The first two parts of the equation are the diagnostic formulae which are treated in the preceding chapter (but which are not therefore superfluous to the understanding of what follows). The two latter portions are both descriptive and diagnostic. They are descriptive to the extent that they—formulaically—reproduce the individual's self-understanding in the two basic forms of despair. Where c is the formula of a predominantly passive, weak, self-surrendering type of posture, with a low level of consciousness, d is the formula of a predominantly active, self-confirming type, with an intensified consciousness of himself. We will discuss these two basic types in the next section, where it will also be shown how the active forms can develop themselves on the basis of the passive. But this demonstration contains in itself the beginning of an understanding of c and d as diagnostic formulae.

As the descriptive formulae for two different basic postures they cannot be equated. Philistine spiritlessness (c) is simply not the same as intense, demonic, titanic defiance (d). When Kierkegaard all the same traces each of these two formulae back to the other, he is making an important diagnostic point. If the formula "despairingly to will to be oneself" (d) can lay claim to being of superior importance, this is due to the fact that it expresses the anthropological aspect of every form of despair, including the passive form: "This formula is the expression of the whole of the relationship's (the self's) dependence, the expression of the fact that the self cannot by its own efforts come to or be in equilibrium or peace, but only, in relating itself to itself, to relate itself to that which posited the entire relationship" [XI 144, SD 147]. This is the theological expression of the matter; regardless of whether it is active or passive, despair is rebellion against the will of the creating power. This rebellion—i.e., the individual's failure to realize his created possibilities for authentic self-realization—manifests itself psychologically as an inner dialectic in despair, a double-mindedness, which can be pinned down, among other ways, in the formulae "passivity-activity" or "activity-passivity." The idea is that in every form of despair, both the passive and the active, there are two counterposed tendencies which assert themselves: an active (conscious, striking) and a passive (unacknowledged) tendency. Thus understood, an equality can be asserted between formulae c and d, as is confirmed by the following quotation, where d is reduced to c, just as c was dissolved into or encompassed by d; where c is the straightforward, passive self-surrender, d is simply a more active variant of the same phenomenon: "The self which he despairingly wills to be is a self which he is not. . . . But, thus, however, he wills to do away with himself, to do away with the self which he is, in order to be the self he himself has thought up" [XI 151, SD 153].

This inner contradiction and its further consequences will be discussed later in this chapter. We must first come to the descriptive subdivision of despair into its principal forms.

2. "The Degrees of Consciousness about the Self"

One can find the beginning of a psychological typology as early as the Judge's descriptions in *Either/Or* when a differentiation is made between a "conquering" and a "possessing" fundamental posture [II 142 ff., E/O II 133 ff.]. It is this division into a predominantly passive and a predominantly active form of despair which is found again in *The Sickness Unto Death,* and in a slightly modified form also in *The Concept of Anxiety.* In Chapter III of this latter book are discussed the low-consciousness attitude types in which the individual reacts immediately to anxiety with a particular formless or ritualized behavior. Chapter IV, on the other hand, deals with the conscious forms ("anxiety about the evil" and "anxiety about the good") in which the individual is aware that his situation is critical, and he therefore reacts to it more intensely. However, it is in *The Sickness Unto Death* that Kierkegaard first implements this division more systematically, and for the sake of gaining an overview, it will be useful to begin the presentation of the different manifestations of despair with the almost schematic classification which can be derived from this book.

When Kierkegaard is to divide despair into various forms in *The Sickness Unto Death,* he employs three criteria of division, of which one, however, the criterion of consciousness, is psychologically the most important.

The first criterion which is employed is static and descriptive: "The forms of despair may be discovered abstractly by reflecting upon the elements of which the self, as a synthesis, consists" [XI 160, SD 162]. The self is a synthesis of finitude and infinity, of necessity and possibility, and the criterion is thus employed in the book in sketching two pairs of despairing states, namely, on the one hand, those of infinity and possibility, and on the other hand, those of finitude and necessity, or in other words a rootless fantasy-life lacking in character, vis-a-vis a narrow conventionality. The whole of this section was summed up above (Chapter IV: 3: 3) as a part of the illumination of Kierkegaard's concept of the self, whose task it is to be *both* finite *and* infinite, so that the development of fantasy is delimited and placed under concrete obligation by particular tasks of the present, while the present, on the other hand, is not allowed to engulf the individual in complete triviality. The static criterion is thus used to describe the situations in which despair manifests itself as the one-sided (unambiguous) development of particular sides of the personality at the expense of others.

Thus, on the basis of the first criterion, a differentiation is made between a predominantly passive and predominantly active sort of posture. But this distinction corresponds exactly with one which is produced with the help of the other basic criterion of division: "Chiefly, however, despair must be viewed under the category of consciousness. Whether despair is conscious or not is the qualitative difference between one despair and another. All despair must certainly be seen as conscious in principle, but it does not follow from this that the person who has this despair, and who may correctly be said to be in despair—it does not follow that this person is himself aware of this. Thus consciousness is what is decisive" [XI 160, SD 162]. In accordance with this, the basic distinction which is employed is between "the despair which is ignorant that it is despair" and "the despair which is conscious of being despair" [XI 174 ff. and 180 ff., SD 175 ff. and 180 ff.], or, thus, between a more passive form without the consciousness of crisis (acknowledgement of sickness) and a more active form with crisis consciousness.

This does not imply that Kierkegaard only concerns himself with the two extreme forms of despair. The actual forms of despair are distributed between them on a continuous scale. Kierkegaard himself draws attention to the fact that it is not the extreme forms, but the mixed forms which have special psychological significance, when he says in *The Sickness Unto Death* that life is too multifarious to contain simply the abstract antithesis between a total ignorance and a total consciousness of despair [XI 181, SD 181]. The consciousness criterion therefore not only forms the basis for a division into two forms, but for the setting up of a scale: "The degree of consciousness about the self" [XI 215, SD 210].

It is these gradations which will be sketched in outline of the pages which follow. But it is precisely in connection with them that Kierkegaard introduces a third criterion of division. This criterion is of decisive theological significance, but psychologically it is subordinate to or derived from the criterion of consciousness. It has to do with the specific contents of consciousness. *The Sickness Unto Death* is divided into two principal sections, of which the first deals with "the human self, or the self whose standard of measure is man," while the second deals with "the self vis-a-vis God" [XI 215, SD 210]. In the first section of the book, despair is described with respect to the individual's consciousness of himself and his reactions to this consciousness. In the second section it is described with reference to a definite, religious notional content, which intensifies the consciousness of crisis and the individual's reactions. In the conclusion of *The Sickness Unto Death* this criterion of content is permitted to dominate completely, so that the presentation here moves away from the psychological way of presenting the problem and develops into a lengthy polemical and theological argument which is incidental to the psychological point. But prior to this, a concise psychological sketch is given of the forms which despair can assume in the specifically Christian dimension of understanding. This sketch reveals itself to be a close analogy to that which is given in the first part of the book. Schematically expressed, the second principal section describes the development: sin → despair over sin → offense. This corresponds to the development in the first section of the book: weakness → consciousness of weakness → defiance. The two parallel sketches supplement one another very closely in psychological respects. In both cases it is a matter of a dialectical-reactive sequence of despairing states, from the "lower" to the "higher," from the more passive, unconscious states to the more active, intensely crisis-conscious forms of despair.

"Thus, consciousness is what is decisive. In general, consciousness, i.e., self-consciousness, is what is decisive in relation to the self" [XI 160, SD 162], because the self is the self-perception, and because the different principal forms of despair are different reactions to a given self-perception. On the basis of this criterion of consciousness, Kierkegaard operates with four fundamental forms of despair, among which there is a dialectical relationship of development: 1) a given self-understanding, which is uncontested, and which therefore has not come to consciousness; 2) a break with the given self-understanding which has been occasioned by external circumstances, and a partial coming-to-consciousness and reaction to the break; 3) a total coming-to-consciousness about the break in the self-perception, i.e., an altered self-understanding; and 4) a reaction to this altered self-understanding. With the assistance of Kierkegaard's own terms, the four forms can be arranged as shown in the chart on page 205.

I will later attempt to populate the columns of the diagram with some of the "pale, bloodless, nocturnal" (in a couple of cases, however, also bloody) figures from Kierkegaard's gallery of types; they cannot all be placed with equal unambiguousness, but an overview may be useful for the present. The arrows → between the four forms indicate that each form can be a concluded state in itself, in which the individual installs himself, but it can also be the transition to the subsequent state [cf. XI 182, SD 182]. Point 3 also ought to be supplied with an arrow which points out of the diagram, because it is precisely "despair over oneself" which is the crisis point, which contains the possibility not only of consolidated despair, but

		1 ⟶ 2 ⟶ 3 ⟶ 4		
"the human self" (1st part of *The Sickness Unto Death*)	"the despair which is ig- norant about the fact that it is despair"	"the despair which is aware that it is despair"		
		"despairingly not to will to be oneself, the despair of weak- ness"		"the despair of despair- ingly willing to be one- self, defiance."
		"despair over the earthly, or over some- thing earthly"	"despair about the eternal, or about oneself"	
"the self vis-a-vis God" (2nd part of *The Sick- ness Unto Death*)		sin	"the sin of des- pairing over one's sin"	"offense"

also of recovery or salvation. If we had been discussing *The Concept of Anxiety,* the lower left-hand box in the diagram would have contained the word "innocence," but in the meantime, Kierkegaard had given up the belief in man's state of innocence in the ethical-religious sense (cf. above, Chapter V: 7: 2).

At first glance it is not easy to see the difference between the two first categories in the diagram, the low-consciousness forms. They both deal with spiritlessness, and in a peculiar slip, which seems almost a thought, Kierkegaard writes of each of them that it is precisely that form which is "the most common" [XI 177, 191; SD 178, 190]. Thus, in both cases, the standard of measure for self-perception is the social milieu, the social role or the individual talent, as it develops itself within this framework. In the first case (1) it is stated that the individual "reposes obscurely in and is taken up into something abstract and universal (state, nation, and the life), or, in the obscurity about himself he takes his abilities simply as active forces, without becoming conscious in the deeper sense of the source from which he has received them; he takes himself as an inexplicable something, if this is to be understood inwardly" [XI 178, SD 179]. In the second case (2) it is written that the individual does not know himself, or that he literally only knows himself "by his costume" [XI 187, SD 187]. But in both forms of despair (1 and 2) it is a matter of a self-perception, and it is precisely by means of the self-perception that the difference between the two forms can be expressed.

Under the heading "the despair which is ignorant about the fact that it is despair . . .," Kierkegaard tries to depict what one could call the unfrustrated, and in the most real sense, fate-less and uncontested happiness. He differentiates between the usual, aesthetic concept of spiritlessness and the concept he himself employs, according to which the category of spiritlessness does not rule out the possibility of "amazing achievements," taste, intellectual accomplishments, art, science, and other good things. Kierkegaard is clearly not thinking only of the philistine way of life. Ignorance of being in despair can reveal itself as "a complete deadness, a merely vegetative life, or as an intensified life, whose secret, however, is despair." Thus one is not meeting only the common philistines here. Spiritlessness also has its aristocrats and its giants, and when I use the expression about fateless and uncontested happiness, it only means that what is being described is the spiritlessness which is too solid or too smooth to enable unhappiness to gain a firm hold. In *The concept of Anxiety,* the spiritless are called οἱ ἀπηλγηκότες [ol apelgekotes] that is, those who have lost the ability to feel pain [IV 401, CD 85; cf. Ephesians 4: 19]. The only example delineated in The Sickness Unto Death is a philosopher who constructs an all-encompassing system, but does " not personally take up residence in this enormous, high-arched palace, but in an outbuilding outside, or a doghouse, or at the most the concierge's apartment" (Xi 176-78, SD 177-78(. That it is the person of Hegel who here appears as an illustration is a surprising emphasis of the fact that for Kierkegaard spiritlessness does not mean dullness and a lack of talent, but is the designation for an absence of self-knowledge, which has nothing to do with the intelligence quotient.

In *The Sickness Unto Death,* all this is only just hinted at, because the section under discussion functions almost as an introduction to what follows. The piece about unconscious despair dealt with the unbroken and unmodified development of the given aptitudes and talents in accordance with a given (weak or strong, philistine or intense) role identification, and within the framework of a given and not radically doubted understanding of life. The section on conscious despair, on the other hand, (diagram categories 2, 3, and 4) deals with the reactive forms. That to which the person reacts, or what he despairs "over," is precisely the break in the given understanding of life or self-understanding, in spite of the fact that the despairing person perhaps does not make this clear to himself. The so-called immediate person also forms himself a notion about himself. But this self-understanding only becomes the object of conscious attention when it is broken. What happens when "something *befalls* (falls upon) this immediate self" is that he becomes aware of his self-perception, because that in which he "has his life or . . . the part of it to which he is especially attached, is taken from him 'by a blow of fate' " [XI 184 f., SD 184-85]. The individual is apparently reacting to this happening, but the correct explanation — cf. above Chapter V: 9: 5 — is that he is reacting to his own self-perception, which has now come partially to consciousness, which as part and parcel of the frustration also contains the notion of the critical condition. Now the despairing individual may by various means have the fortune to get on well with this trauma, and thus remain stuck in this condition. This will be discussed later. The individual certainly has a self-understanding which he seeks to preserve and render harmless, but "he has no consciousness of a self which is won by means of infinite abstraction from everything external; this naked, abstract self — in opposition to the clothed self of immediacy — is the first form of the infinite self, and is that which urges onward the entire process by which a self infinitely accepts its actual self with its difficulties and advantages" [XI 189, SD 188]. This self — cf. Judge William's "ideal self" (above, Chapter V: 9: 4) — is the system of motivation which effects the transition to the next form of despair, number 3 in the diagram above.

The transition takes place precisely by virtue of the abstraction from external things, not by means of an intellectual abstraction, but when "the self, with infinite passion, in fantasy," broadens its self-understanding, so that the despair is not something which applies merely partially to this or that unfortunate occurrence, but applies to "the earthly *in toto.*" "The category of totality lies within and belongs to the despairing person," in that one cannot, of course, in fact lose "everything." But by virtue of this act of consciousness, the individual has also gotten the possibility of comprehending what the person more devoid of fantasy and passion could not understand, namely, that he does not despair over this or that, but "over himself." The difference is "that the preceding form has the consciousness which belongs to weakness as its final consciousness, while here, consciousness does not stop at that, but intensifies itself into a new consciousness, a consciousness about its weakness." It is thus to this consciousness that the individual reacts. "Despair about the eternal or over oneself" is indeed in a certain sense the salient point in the whole line of reasoning which is outlined here, because this is "the formula of all despair," which is why the despairing person's self-understanding thus coincides with the diagnostic point of view (above, Chapter V: 8: 2 and 9: 5). If one calls spiritlessness a depot, then despair about the eternal and over oneself is a complicated and extended change of tracks, which can send the traveller into new dead-ends — but with a built-in turntable, to the extent that it can also be a place of "conversion."[1] Thus, the despairing person can "genuinely swing away from despair and toward faith, humbling himself under his weakness before God"; for "at every moment that despair is held open, there is also the possibility of salvation." However, it is not this path which engages Kierkegaard's psychological interest here, but the wrong paths which pave their own way when the despairing person will not hold the despair open, but, in spite of his changed self-understanding, still "does not will to be himself," but retreats into an escape position: "That which is called *encapsulation*" [XI 194-97, SD 193-97].

We shall return to the condition of encapsulation. For the present it is enough to mention the reactions which are enumerated by Kierkegaard in *The Sickness Unto Death* as being characteristic of consolidated despair on this level. The encapsulated person can remain "standing at this point, merely marching in place," attempting to isolate his problem, and for the rest living as most people do. We will later come to see that this is not a stable solution. But this fact is already clear in that his "incognito" can be exploded, so that he "breaks through to the outside and destroys his external costume" in order to cast himself into life as a restless spirit, who uses strong remedies in his attempt to drown out the noise inside himself; we are presented with a variant of Judge William's conqueror-type, a Don

Giovanni who seeks forgetfulness in sensuality and debauchery. But we only see him rush past in *The Sickness Unto Death,* for in this book Kierkegaard renounces all picturesque devices and concentrates almost ascetically upon the conflicts in the internal theatre. The real reaction-formation against despair, and the genuinely active form of despair, arise when despair intensifies itself into a new encapsulation and becomes "defiance" [XI 200, SD 199].

Defiance is thus the final and "highest" of the principal forms of despair. The previous despair "was over its weakness; the despairing person did not will to be himself. But if another dialectical step is taken, the person in this sort of despair comes to consciousness about why he does not will to be himself, and then there is a reversal; then defiance is present; for then it is precisely because of this that he despairingly wills to be himself" [XI 202, SD 201]. This transition is not difficult to understand for the person who understands, for example, Alfred Adler's psychology. But Kierkegaard's point is that that against which the reactive energy is thus invested is not the weakness (in Adler, the inferiority) itself, but against the consciousness of it. But this also reveals the despair of weakness as well; it is not *only* weak: "[I]t is now becoming clear how much untruth there was in the talk about weakness; it becomes clear how dialectically correct it is that the first expression of defiance is precisely despair over one's weakness" [XI 200, SD 199].

The despair of weakness is latent defiance, and defiance is implicit weakness. This dialectic is precisely the dialectic of reaction-formation.

3. "Activity-Passivity or Passivity-Activity"

In this section we will look more closely at the transitions between the states of despair which have been described, and thus also at the inner contradictions which constitute despair. In the despair "about the eternal and over oneself," the conscious form of the despair of weakness, "a significant progress" [XI 195, SD 194-95] has taken place, inasmuch as the despairing person's self-understanding here actually coincides with the diagnostic point of view. But to understand and to understand are two different things. It is one thing that the despairing person, in his pious intentions, consciously reflects upon his weakness and incorporates the notion of this into his self-understanding. It is another matter whether this consciously shaped self-perception is adequate, or whether it is precisely the conscious reflection over weakness which contains the possibility of self-deception. Encapsulation is the sign that this is the case. Kierkegaard illustrates the problem with a little psychological portrait sketch of a man who knows in himself that he is "weak," and who cannot escape again from this notion in the same convenient, superficial way as the spiritless person. He is humble; he is conscious of his humility, and this humility benefits those around him. His image as a "learned man . . . an unusually capable official, a respectable father, pleasant company, very sweet to his wife, carefulness itself with his children," corresponds with his private self-understanding, which he keeps to himself in privacy. He isolates his consciousness of the crisis, and his occasional need to withdraw in order to return to "his self's relationship to himself" is the only visible sign of his despair. The despair is not constituted by the making-conscious of this self-understanding, nor simply by the contradiction between the private despair and the bourgeois role-self, but by a contradiction which he develops in his lonely hours, without himself wanting to understand it.

If he had a confidant, that person would be able to explain the matter: "You are really proud of yourself, you know"; it is "pride which puts such an enormous stress upon weakness," and it is "because he wants to be proud of his self, that he cannot stand this consciousness of weakness." In his encapsulation, the humble person has become impressed by his own humility. Therefore he is unable to accept the explanation, for his self-image has become his self-defense, an unrelinquishable notion which must not be contested. "When he was alone with himself, he would certainly admit that there was something in this explanation, but the passion with which his self had understood his weakness would soon get him to imagine, once again, that it could not possibly be pride, for it was of course precisely over his weakness that he despaired." Therefore he must elaborate and intensify his consciousness of crisis, instead of giving it up in the upheaval which would lead him "forward to faith." The consciousness of his weakness and impotence, which could be the presupposition for his own conquest ("the self must be broken in order to become itself"), becomes for him a goal in itself, developing in him a need for the confirmation of this self-perception. Therefore he must unavoidably oppose the revelation of the pride in his notion of weakness: "[I]f one spoke like this to him, he would understand it for a passion-less instant, but soon passion would again see falsely, and then he would again take the wrong turn, into despair" [XI 198-200, SD 197-99].

The despairing person cannot let go of the self-image he forms for himself. In the despair characterized by the consciousness of weakness, this self-understanding still has much to do with the facts, but the self-understanding is not an unreserved acceptance of the weakness. It is reactive. "For when earthly things are taken from the self, and he despairs, then it is as though the despair came from without, even though it always comes from the self; but when the self despairs over this its own despair, then the new despair comes from the self, indirectly-directly from the self, as a counter-pressure (reaction), differing in this from defiance, which comes directly from the self" [XI 196, SD 196].

The point in reaction-formation is the hidden dialectic between the reaction and that against which it reacts. In the despair characterized by the consciousness of weakness, the reactive component in the self-perception (pride in weakness) is unnoticed by the despairing self; it is "passive," while the consciousness of weakness is "active." The situation is reversed with defiance, where the reaction-formation becomes manifest, because the despairing person refuses to incorporate the consciousness of weakness into his self-understanding: "Here despair is conscious of itself as an action which does not come from without as a suffering under the pressure of externality; it comes directly from the self. And thus defiance, in relation to despairing over one's weakness, is still a new qualification" [XI 202, SD 201].

In order to illuminate this, it will be useful to leave Anti-Climacus for a moment to see what Kierkegaard says elsewhere about psychic reaction-formations. "The main imperfection of everything human is that one first comes to possess the object of one's desire by way of its opposite. I will not speak of the multiplicity of formations which can provide psychology with plenty to do (the melancholy person has the most comic sense; the most exuberant is often the most idyllic; the most debauched is often the most moral; the doubter, often the most religious), but merely recall that it is first through sin that blessedness is espied" [I 5, E/O I 20]. The voice here is that of Aesthete A, but the idea is also Anti-Climacus', right down to the detail that the psychological observation is placed in a parenthesis as subordinate to the religious dialectic. Here we will remain with the psychological: "When one reads Luther, one certainly does get the impression of a sure, a certain spirit who speaks with a decisiveness which is 'gewaltig'. . . . And yet it seems to me that this certainty has something tumultuous in it which is precisely uncertainty. It is well-known that the opposed psychic state often seeks to conceal itself in its opposite. One builds up one's courage with strong words, and the words almost become even stronger because one is vacillating oneself. It is no deception, but a pious attempt. One does not wish to let the uncertainty of anxiety speak; one does not even want (or dare) really to mention it, and one compels the antithesis to come forth, precisely in the confidence that it will help. Luther thus makes such predominant use of the sin against the Holy Spirit, which is used so moderately in the New Testament. In order to force himself and the believer forward, he uses this phrase immediately and draconically about everything . . ." [Pap. VI A 108, Hong 2460]. This journal entry from 1845 contains one of the clearest formulations of a line of reasoning which plays a decisive role in both of Kierkegaard's principal psychological works. That it deals with just Luther is of no importance in this connection; Kierkegaard has many comments on Luther in his journals, including many critical notes, but there the criticism tends in another direction. The entry here could just about as well have dealt with Kierkegaard himself, as can be seen from another note in the same journal, a literary draft about "The Police Agent": "A demonic figure, who just as well could have been a dissolute figure, indeed, a murderer, etc., but who is now the servant of righteousness (a failed childhood and youth has filled him with hatred toward the human race). . . . There would be something uncertain in his behavior, which was rooted in his inner uncertainty, but which he has lyingly explained to himself and to others as cunning. His uncertainty was not a lie, but the fact that he afterward explained it as cleverness was a lie. It was true that he sometimes said what he did not wish to say, but afterwards he lied and explained that he had done so in order to spy on others" [Pap. VI A 10 f., Dru 508-09].

One does not need to know especially much of Kierkegaard's papers to see that this is a bit of self-analysis, a fantasy about a part of Kierkegaard himself. Here, however, I will let the private individual Kierkegaard remain in peace for the time being and return to psychology. The point in reaction-formation is its unconscious dependence upon its antithesis: " . . . the greater the need for striking decisions in external things, the less inner certainty," Kierkegaard notes. "The fact that the external is not always the internal is not only true with respect to ironists, who consciously deceive others with a false exterior, but it is also true quite often with respect to immediate natures, who unconsciously deceive themselves, yes, sometimes have almost a need for self-deception" [Pap. VII 2 B 235, p. 186].

The idea is crucial in *The Sickness Unto Death*. Defiance, we heard, is a "new qualification" in relation to weakness. And, correspondingly, despair over oneself is "a quality deeper than the previous" form, namely, despair over something earthly. But this is apparently true only in one sense, for shortly before this Kierkegaard has said that it is only a matter of "a relative difference" [XI 196 f., SD 195-96]. In an introductory remark, the relation between weakness and defiance is defined in the same way: "if this form of despair is called that of weakness, it thus already contains in itself a reflection of the other form . . . ., despairingly to will to be oneself. It is thus only a relative antithesis. No despair is entirely without defiance; there is indeed also some defiance in the expression itself: not to will to be. On the other hand, even despair's greatest defiance is never without some weakness. The difference is thus only relative" [XI 182, SD 182-83]. Regarding the despair of finitude versus that of infinity, it is similarly written: "That things are this way is rooted in the dialectical fact that the self is a synthesis, which is why the one thing is always its opposite. No form of despair can be straightforwardly (i.e., undialectically) defined, but can only be defined by reflecting upon its opposite. One can straightforwardly describe the state of the despairing person who is in despair, as a poet does, by letting him speak. But one can only define the despair by means of its opposite" [XI 161, SD 163].

We get the most systematic presentation of this idea in *The Concept of Anxiety,* in a subdivision of the section on the demonic, with the heading *"The Schema for the Exclusion or Absence of Inwardness":* "The absence of inwardness is always a determination of reflection, and therefore every form will be a double form." Here it is written with definitive pithiness: *"Every form of the absence of inwardness is thus either activity-passivity or passivity-activity, and whether it is the one or the other, it lies in self-reflection."* Every form contains it own antithesis: "The phenomena which begin with activity are more striking, and therefore they are most easily perceived; thus one forgets that a passivity also comes forth in this activity, and one never includes the opposite phenomenon when one speaks of the demonic" [IV 451-53, CD 126-28].

It ought to be unnecessary to "translate" this into modern psychological terminology. One feels tempted to ask whether the translation might not better go in the other direction. For it is certainly this same dialectical relationship between surface and underground which in differing linguistic variants appears among the psychoanalysts (cf. Chapter V: 6: 3). In *The Concept of Anxiety* Kierkegaard illustrates the schema with a brief analysis of three paired sets of complementary attitudinal types, in which each half of each pair corresponds to the other half as an active to a passive attitude, in such a way that the active is also revealed as passive and the reverse: "Unbelief—Superstition," "Hypocrisy—Offense," and "Pride—Cowardice." As an example, "pride [is] . . . a profound cowardice," while "cowardice is a profound pride." They can therefore also appear in mixed forms; indeed they do so invariably, because the antitheses are negatively determined in common by a negative (i.e., reactive) relationship to a third thing. "Unbelief and superstition both have anxiety about faith"; hypocrisy and offense "lack inwardness and dare not come to themselves"; and pride and cowardice are "identical" in the same way.

The point of this analysis is, among other things, its relation to the dialectic of weakness-defiance in *The Sickness Unto Death.* This relation is seen most clearly in the last pair of concepts, cowardice-pride, but also in the first pair, where unbelief contains "defiance, pride, and arrogance," while superstition contains "weakness" and "indolence, cowardice and pusillanimity" [IV 454 f., CD 129-30].

The point is the duality: that to a given demonic or despairing attitude corresponds a "'profound'' opposing tendency. It is this duality which constitutes the double-mindedness of the despairing person. The attitude is his attempt to establish himself unambiguously. If one asks for an explanation of this contradiction, the answer is that it is rooted in self-reflection, i.e., in the self-perception, which is that "over which" the person despairs. But if one asks why this contradiction continues, the explanation ultimately lies, in turn, in the "about what" of despair.

4. "The Consistency of Evil"

4:1 Oblivion

I have elucidated above what happens when the reaction takes place (double-mindedness), and I will now clarify in more detail how the reactive life-style makes its attempt to establish itself (unambiguousness). But, because double-mindedness and unambiguousness are categories of reflection, an examination of the latter will recall the former. This is because it is double-mindedness which intensifies the need for unambiguousness, while on the other hand, unambiguousness continually increases double-mindedness. We have an explanation of this theme in the confessional discourse about "Purity of Heart": whether the weak person despairs over his weakness or the defiant person despairs in defiance, they still resemble one another; "neither of them, in truth, wills one thing, however, desperately they seem to be willing it," for the despairing person is double-minded, and has "two wills, one which he vainly wants to follow quite entirely, and one of which he vainly wants to be entirely quit" [VIII 159, PH 61, cited above Chapter V: 5: 2]. We will now seek to arrive at a more exact understanding of why despair's attempt to follow the one will is in vain.

In despair "over oneself"—whether it has been made conscious of being what it is, or whether it is only known as a partial despair "over something earthly"—the crisis-struck person seeks to avoid the consciousness of himself in defeat. The contradiction is that it does not succeed. One cannot throw off the eternal; one cannot avoid having a self-perception. In despair, "something has caught fire which cannot burn, or cannot be burned up, in the self," and therefore despair—the manifest experience of despair—cannot "consume the eternal, the self, which forms the basis of despair, whose worm does not die, and whose fire is not extinguished." Despair can thus be defined as "a *self*-consumption, but an impotent self-consumption, which does not achieve what it wants. What the self wants is to consume itself, which it does not achieve, and this impotence is a new form of self-consumption, in which, however, despair again fails to achieve what it wants, to consume itself; this is the intensification or the law for the intensification . . ." [XI 149 f., SD 151-52].

The person in despair cannot forget. This naturally does not mean that he is always going around thinking about the great defeats of his life. Despair is constituted precisely by the *attempt* to forget, but if this attempt is characterized as impotent, it does not mean that the despairing person all the same comes to think of his youthful sorrows now and then, as it were. Oblivion means something different and something more to Kierkegaard than the opposite of memory. The idea can be isolated by means of a brief excursus to a couple of the aesthetic pseudonyms who have made observations upon the phenomena of memory, recollection, and oblivion. In spite of the fact that these aesthetes do not simply represent Kierkegaard's own view of the matter, their considerations can still illuminate his conception.

Memory, as opposed to recollection, concerns what is definite and delimited. "Thus, one can very well remember an event in every detail without therefore being able to recollect it," William Afham writes in the preface to *Stages;* what one has remembered, one can also forget, but this oblivion is not the genuine thing. Recollection is less precise, not directed toward details, but toward the total impression; it is the "ideality," which "wishes to vindicate to man the eternal continuity in life, and to guarantee that his earthly existence remains *uno tenore,* one breath, and can be expressed in one word." In spite of the fact that William Afham's rumination is a part of a completely different context than Anti-Climacus' rumination on the self, the two lines of reasoning are nevertheless closely related. Recollection is the individual's total self-understanding in relation to the past, and "one cannot forget what has been recollected. What is recollected is not a matter of indifference to memory. One can throw away what has been recollected; it returns just like Thor's hammer. . . . " Thus, recollection excludes oblivion, and to this extent we have here a confirmation of Anti-Climacus' idea of the vanity of the attempt to forget. But William Afham hints at the dialectical point by adding "but to recollect and to forget are not opposites" [VI 21-25, SLW 27-30].

"Oblivion and recollection are thus identical," says another of the pseudonyms, seconding the above notion: "When one speaks of 'writing something in the book of oblivion,' one is suggesting that it is at once both forgotten and yet retained." The speaker here is Aesthete A, and the text is "The Rotation Method" in *Either/Or,* the demon's cynical and eudaemonistic self-portrait. Aesthete A consciously and methodically cultivates oblivion as an art. Therefore it is not entirely correct to maintain that Kierkegaard has here given a description of repression in Freud's sense of the term, for of course repression takes place unconsciously and automatically. But "The Rotation Method" is a literary arrangement, and it is only by virtue of this arrangement that Aesthete A's self-portrait has become a portrait of a despair which is fully self-conscious of being in despair. The psychological error in the text is thus that the pseudonym describes a process which the despairing person himself is not normally capable of seeing through. The ethical error, the despair in the aesthete's life, is that he asserts that in oblivion he has found the "the Archimedean point with which one can lift the whole world." On the other hand, there can be no doubt about the agreement between the aesthete's and Kierkegaard's "own" psychological understanding of the phenomenon of oblivion. Also the aesthete makes the differentiation between recollection and memory. Oblivion in the significant sense is not identical with "forgetfulness." Therefore the aesthete is also of the opinion that the art of forgetting cannot be successfully practiced by the person who simply resolves to forget an impression or an experience: "If one behaves as many of those do who dabble in the art of forgetting, and strike the unpleasant entirely away, one will soon see what good it does. In an unguarded moment it often surprises one entirely with the whole force of suddenness." If oblivion is to be—demonically understood—effective and successful, something must be substituted for the forgotten, and this is where recollection is helpful. According to the wisdom of the aesthetic life, recollection is poetic memory. "The more poetically one remembers, the more easily one forgets, for to remember poetically is really just an expression for forgetting. When I remember poetically, then a transformation of what had been experienced has already taken place, and it thereby loses all that is painful."

Thus oblivion does not consist in simply removing a given unpleasant experience from consciousness, but in letting another, a "recollected" experience of the whole, repress it. "Oblivion is the scissors with which one cuts away what one has no use for, though, be it noted, under the careful inspection of recollection. Oblivion and recollection are thus identical" [I 306-08, E/O 289-91].

"The Rotation Method" confirms the fact that what interests

Kierkegaard psychologically is not especially the specific forgetting of particular past traumatic experiences, but the process in which one excludes "what one has no use for" in one's whole picture of oneself, by putting some other thing in its place. We will meet this idea again in *The Sickness Unto Death,* and see that this other thing is another picture of the whole. It is the notion of "obscuration" formulated in a new way. But first we must hear Vigilius' opinion.

4: 2. *The Impotence of the Demonic*

The fact that it is not the specific forgetting of past experiences which especially concerns Kierkegaard is clear from an example of the demonic in *The Concept of Anxiety,* where just such a situation is discussed. In his encapsulation, the demonic person can hide something which can "be so frightful that he dare not say it, not even to himself, because it is as though he committed a new sin in the mentioning of it, or as though it tempted him again." This can occur when it is a matter of an act committed in drunkenness or during an attack of madness, so that the individual has only an obscure recollection of it, "but nevertheless knows that it was so wild that it is almost impossible for him to admit it to himself." What is decisive for Kierkegaard, however, is not the critical experience itself, but "the individual's attitude to the revelation, whether he will penetrate this fact with freedom, appropriate it in freedom. As soon as he will not do this, the phenomenon is demonic. This is something one must maintain very strongly; for even the person who desires revelation is still basically demonic. He has, namely, two wills: one is subordinate, impotent, and desires revelation, and the other is stronger and desires encapsulation; and the fact that this will is the stronger of the two shows that he is basically demonic" [IV 437, CD 114-15].

Here we are back to our point of origin: double-mindedness, which is the pre-condition for the understanding of unambiguousness. There are thus reasons to hold firmly to the idea. In *The Concept of Anxiety* it becomes clear that this ambivalence is a constitutive characteristic of anxiety about the good. Just as a "profound" cowardice corresponds to pride, so, in the case of anxiety about the good, does the "stronger will" have a "weaker will" which corresponds to it and which wills the opposite of what the strong will wants: "One must hold fast to this, for otherwise one will go and think about the demonic more abstractly than it ever occurred, as if the will of unfreedom were unalloyed in its constitution and the will of freedom were not also continuously present, if ever so weakly, in the self-contradiction" [IV 453 note, CD 127 note]. It is not merely that the demonic has certain self-contradictory characteristics in its behavior, but the condition of the demonic itself is a self-contradiction. And the double will concerns this condition itself. Anxiety about the good is indeed described in *The Concept of Anxiety* precisely as a reaction to the fall into sin, thus — to use an expression from *The Sickness Unto Death* — as a form of despair "over" the consciousness of weakness. And, just as the despair characterized by the consciousness of weakness consisted in the reaction of encapsulation, which wishes to isolate itself with the crisis-laden self-understanding, so does the demonic person attempt, according to Vigilius Haufniensis, to establish himself in the crisis and to protect the unambiguousness by excluding alternative possibilities of self-understanding. It is the stronger will, the will to unfreedom which wants to consolidate itself. "The demonic is unfreedom, which wishes to terminate itself. However, this is and remains an impossibility; it always retains a relationship, and even if this has apparently disappeared entirely, it is nevertheless present, and anxiety reveals itself immediately at the moment of contact" [IV 431 f., CD 110]. The "relationship" which is mentioned is the relationship to that which is excluded (that with respect to which the individual terminated himself): "the good." The weaker will is thus that which maintains communication with this good. The idea is not that the demonic once in a while considers becoming good, so to speak, but decides not to (!), but rather that the reactively determined self-understanding can never be consolidated neatly and unproblematically in the unambiguousness which it aspires to establish. "If, on the one hand, unfreedom was capable of terminating and hypostatizing itself entirely, and if, on the other hand, it did not continually will to do so (which is where the contradiction lies, namely, that unfreedom wills something, when it has precisely lost its will), then the demonic would be anxiety about the good." The conflict between that which is consciously intended and the contrary term which renders compliance impossible, is thus also a part of the definition of the condition. The crisis is permanent and self-reinforcing. Kierkegaard adds in a note that the relation between the two wills can also be the reverse of this, so that the demonic person consciously wishes to change his condition; but this reversal is illusory, even if here the will of freedom is apparently the stronger, i.e., the more conscious: "Even when unfreedom says in the strongest terms that it does not will itself, it is an untruth, and there is always a will in unfreedom which is stronger than the wish [IV 444, CD 120].

Vigilius is thus clearly in complete agreement with Anti-Climacus' definition of despair as "an impotent self-consumption, which does not achieve what it wants." Despair, just as the demonic state, is the crisis-conscious person's vain attempt to obliterate his consciousness of the crisis.

In *The Concept of Anxiety* this is more closely defined as his attempt to arrange matters with this consciousness of crisis, and so reject the possibility of recovery. It is the attempt to establish oneself in the sickness unto death, to forget that it is a sickness. The attempt can succeed, but it can never succeed completely.

4:3. *The Power of Evil*

If one is to summarize this line of reasoning, it could hardly be done better than by calling demonic possession or despair "an impotent attempt to constitute itself." This formula is from *The Sickness Unto Death*—but it is, be it noted, a formula which Anti-Climacus rejects as superficial and speculative [XI 244, SD 236]. We are in the second part of *The Sickness Unto Death,* where it is "the self vis-a-vis God" which is being discussed, and thus where the definitively Christian view of despair as sin is being put forth. And apparently this view is not merely a disavowal of Vigilius' description of demonic possession but also of Anti-Climacus' own definition of despair in the first part of the book. I will attempt to demonstrate that this self-contradiction is only apparent, and that in actuality we are only dealing with a further development and elaboration of the views with which we have concerned ourselves up to this point.

The disagreement with Vigilius has to do with the theological question about what one really understands by sin. Is sin in the strict sense really the individual action, the individual transgression of the commandment, or is it the fundamental posture of which these actions are merely the products? Where, in the interest of ethics, Vigilius maintained the former view (but also hinted at the latter in his formulations), Anti-Climacus, for his part is not in doubt: "The state of being in sin is the new sin; it is sin" [XI 243, SD 236; cf. above Chapter V: 7: 2]. The theological formulation reads: *"Sin is not a negation, but a position"*—"which message thus, quite consistently, must be believed, for it is a dogma" [XI 234, SD 227]. But, even though this is said, the dogma is not merely a formula of damnation which lacks understandable relevance for human life; rather, it also implies an anthropological understanding: "Here it can only be a question of showing from one side that sin is a position," and this demonstration has to do precisely with consciousness in its relationship to the notion of God as the standard of measure [XI 237, SD 230].

But using this standard of measure as a tool, Kierkegaard can make his diagnosis of despair as a condition: *"The continuation of sin,"* or "the continuity of sin." Here, then, is the corrective to Vigilius: "But, 'the continuity of sin'? Is not sin precisely the *dis*continuous? See, here it is again, the idea that sin is simply a negation, to which one can never acquire title, just as the title cannot be won to stolen property, a negation, an impotent attempt to constitute itself, but which nevertheless, suffering all the torments of impotence in desperate defiance, does not succeed in doing so. Yes, such is sin, speculatively understood; but Christianly understood, sin is a position (this must be believed, for it is indeed a paradox which no man can apprehend), a position which develops out of itself a more and more positive continuity." Thus Kierkegaard draws the psychological consequence of a dogmatic postulate. "The continuity of sin" is a life-style. And what Kierkegaard is interested in are the inner dynamics or automatic principles of this life-style, not its expression in particular actions, which are merely ventings of the high internal pressure. To overlook "the intermediate area between the individual sins is just as superficial an observation as if one thought that a railroad train only moved every time the locomotive puffed. No, that puffing, and the forward jolt which follows upon it, are not really what ought to be observed, but rather the even speed with which the locomotive goes and which calls forth that puffing."

The railroad metaphor was carefully chosen, for it expresses not only the relationship between condition and symptom, but also the rigorously one-tracked, inflexible, and compulsively self-accelerating character of the movement: "It is splendid psychology when Shakespeare has Macbeth say (Act III, Scene 2): "Sündentsprossne Werke erlangen nur durch Sünde Kraft und Stärke.'[2] That is, sin has a consistency within itself, and in this consistency of evil within itself, it also has a certain power," but this does not exhaust the locomotive metaphor. The person who lives in such a consistency "in turn has an infinite fear of every inconsistency, because he has an infinite notion of what the consequence might be: that he could be wrested from the totality in which he has his life. The least inconsequence is an enormous loss, for of course he loses the consistency; at the same instant perhaps the enchantment will be undone; the secretive power which bound all the forces in harmony will be diminished; the tension spring will be relaxed, and the whole situation would perhaps become chaos, in which the forces fight one another in a rebellion, in which the self suffers, but in which there is no internal agreement, none at all, no speed, no impetus. The enormous machinery, which during the time of consistency was so compliant in its iron strength, so flexible in its power, is in disorder; and the more excellent and grandiose the machinery was, the more frightful is the mess."

Thus despair makes itself a marked feature of the individual's entire posture and makes the life-style into an end in itself, a detailed defense of itself against every alternative. That which is defended as irreplaceable is the despairing person's self-understanding, "the totality in which he has his life." And what motivates this defense and explains the rigorism and narrow range of development of this life-style is the anxiety about the loss of identity, about the chaos of role-collapse. The object of anxiety is inconsistency in the life-style or self-understanding, i.e., an alternative understanding, and the function of the defense is to keep this alternative out of consciousness: "One single moment outside of his consistency; one single dietary indiscretion; one single sidelong glance; one moment of seeing and understanding the whole situation, or even a part of it, in another fashion; then he would perhaps never again become himself, he says." But, the more the alternative is excluded from the self-understanding, the greater becomes the dependence upon it, i.e., the greater the need for further confirmation of the despairing person's own self-understanding, which therefore becomes more and more unambiguous and narrow. As a drinker keeps up his intoxication out of anxiety of becoming sober, so does the demonic state continue in itself. And as the morally conscious person avoids the temptation to sin, so does the demonic individual flee from "the good," if anyone wishes to confront him with it, because that sort of talk would weaken his self-understanding. "Precisely because the demonic is consistent within itself and within the consistency of evil, precisely for that reason he also has a totality to lose." This totality is his self-image, his identity: "Only in the continuation of sin is he himself; only in that does he live, does he have the impression of himself" [XI 244-47, SD 236-40].

The demonic state thus is anxiety about the good—also according to *The Sickness Unto Death*. The new element which is added here is that the demonic state can constitute itself. This is Anti-Climacus' corrective to Vigilius, and to his own earlier definition of despair as an impotent self-consumption, a tantalizing attempt to slip past or to endure despair's self-understanding. The corrective, however, is not a disavowal, but a completion of the idea, and without the "speculative" definition, the psychological interpretation of the Christian definition of sin as a position would be unthinkable. The two definitions supplement one another, because the point in the demonic state's constituting itself is the relationship of negative dependence to that which is excluded. The reactive self-understanding of unfreedom is only upheld by virtue of the repressed surface contact with freedom. Vulnerability grows along with dependency, and the defense grows along with vulnerability. The description of the continuity of sin thus does not disavow the definition of despair as an impotent self-consumption, but it modifies it so that it is really possible for the despairing person to forget, to ignore his weakness—

as long as the machinery functions with its iron strength and the self-image remains intact. But impotence betrays its presence in the compulsive character of the affirmation of identity.

Despair is thus: to be unable to forget ("consume oneself"), but despair is also to forget—that one cannot forget. But the forgetting is not a deliberate exclusion of a particular, traumatic content of consciousness. It is the total suppression of a given, intolerable self-perception with the help of another self-understanding, which must be defended at all costs. The self-perception is at one time that which is defended and at the same time the means of establishing the defense: "In order despairingly to will to be oneself, there must be consciousness of an infinite self. This infinite self, however, is really only the most abstract form, the most abstract possibility of the self. And it is this self that he despairingly wills to be, wresting the self from every relationship to the power which posited it, or wresting it from the notion that such a power exists. With the help of this infinite form, the self despairingly wants to be its own master, or to create itself, to make itself into the self he wants to be, to determine what he does and does not wish to include in his concrete self" [XI 202 f. SD 201]. The "infinite self" is the same as Judge William's "ideal self," which is the progressive force in the development of the personality (above Chapter V: 9: 4), but with the difference that the I-ideal now becomes more and more fantastic and autistic, because it serves only defensive (or defensive-offensive) purposes. It is no longer shaped according to some external standard of measure or any given "concretion" as a corrective, but in a solipsistic, reactive relation to the consciousness of weakness or crisis which is to be excluded.

"Defiance" is the most pronounced and striking form of despair. Autism is its specific characteristic, about which we will later hear more. But just as weakness is latent defiance, so is defiance a profound weakness, and the one form is merely a more active, the other a more passive, variant of one and the same despair. "The continuity of sin" is at once defiance and weakness. In the view of the dialectical psychologist, they are the easily penetrated disguises of descriptively different attitudinal types, which are disguises of and reactions to one and the same fundamental conflict.

One must therefore not be surprised that, in his description of this apparently so abnormally developed and rarely occurring phenomenon, "the continuity of sin," Kierkegaard also claims to have said something about the life of ordinary people. In order to make striking what is unnoticed, he must employ the striking example to illustrate his idea. It is his method and his conscious pedagogical intention to illuminate the universal with the help of the exception, as it is explained in the draft of the section on anxiety about the good in *The Concept of Anxiety:* "I speak here both about the significant phenomenon and about the many lesser and lesser, and in the end even apparently insignificant approximations" [Pap. V B 60, p. 133]. I have reminded the reader of this method on a number of occasions, but there is reason to do so again, in that this understanding is the precondition for following Kierkegaard's thought. In *The Sickness Unto Death,* he characterizes his definition of sin as a sort of "algebra," and adds that "the definition encompasses all forms like a net," which is why the individual forms will not be described in concrete detail [XI 219, SD 213]. Also the analysis of "the continuity of sin" will shed light upon the universal. For even if the everyday man does not make it clear to himself, the continuity of sin is an everyday phenomenon, which simply does not always assume forms which are dramatic enough to be used to illuminate anything. This, however, does not make the phenomenon any the less despairing. Most people are "only momentarily conscious of themselves, conscious in the great decisions, but in daily life they do not strike this chord," for the sinner "is in the power of sin in such a way that he has no notion of its total category": "In his perdition he is blind to the fact that he is blind to the fact that his life—instead of having the essential continuity of the eternal, by existing for God as grounded in faith—has the continuity of sin" [XI 243 f., SD 236].

5. Encapsulation

5:1. *The Methods of Defense*

Encapsulation is the word which Kierkegaard uses in *The Concept of Anxiety* as the designation of the life-style which corresponds to demonic anxiety about the good. In *The Sickness Unto Death* the word is used in connection with the despair of weakness and in connection with defiance.

Encapsulation is a self-defense. It is most pronounced and easiest to observe in the conscious despair "over oneself," because the experience of despair is most manifest here. But "above" and "below" it on the scale of consciousness there are similar defense methods which characterize the other forms of despair.

The most primitive "weapon or means of defense" is that which immediacy employs when misfortune strikes: "It despairs and swoons, and then lies quite still as if dead." If fortune changes, the immediate person revives again; otherwise he gets by by learning to imitate the others. "This form of despair is despairingly not to will to be oneself, or, even lower, despairingly not to will to be a self, or, lowest of all, despairingly to will to be someone other than oneself, to wish for a new self." Thus, here, as a parallel to the conventional understanding of life, flourishes cheap escapism, the wish to change identity, but the daydream does not collide with reality, because it is too lacking in passion, too superficial [XI 186 f., SD 186]. And yet this dream behind the reality is the rudimentary form of encapsulation, as it were. Kierkegaard does not use the term here, but it can be seen in the transition to a slightly more active variant of immediacy's despair, in which the occasion of despair is not merely a misfortune which comes from without, but can also be connected with a certain amount of independent thought and fantasy. Then the individual is not satisfied with "playing dead," but makes a more active "attempt to protect himself." His defense consists of a sort of temporary abstraction from the self, an experimental ignoring of the self. Kierkegaard expresses it with a metaphor. The same thing happens to a person who is in despair about his self as happens to a person whose house becomes uninhabitable for a time because of a bad odor: "[T]hus he leaves, but he does not move away; he does not take new lodgings; he continues to regard the old place as his dwelling"; therefore, as long as the unpleasantness continues, "he only comes once in a while, on a visit to himself, so to speak, in order to see whether a change has taken place. And as soon as it has, he moves home again; 'he is himself again,' he says . . ." [XI 188 f., SD 188-89].

The despairing person will forget a given self-understanding, but this can only happen when it is repressed by another. The role which corresponds to this can be entirely acceptable in the bourgeois sense. It is precisely the bourgeois self-understanding which Kierkegaard wishes to analyze as a sort of "Psychopathology of Everyday Life." When this despairing person, whose self was depicted in the image of a dwelling, does not quickly get rid of the unpleasantness which occasioned his despair, he can get rid of it by another means. In this connection, Kierkegaard sketches a portrait of the perfect philistine and his shrewdness about life, which consists of "good advice and clever turns of phrase, and wait-and-see, and taking things as they come, and writing things in the book of forgetfulness." He succeeds in wrapping himself up entirely in his role, but the motive behind his impeccable facade is anxiety about coming into contact with his other self. Kierkegaard explains this with a broadening of the image of the self as a dwelling: "The entire question about the self in the deeper sense becomes a sort of blind door in the background of his soul, a door behind which there is nothing. He takes possession of what he in his language calls his self, that is, whatever abilities, talents, etc., have been given him; however, he takes possession of all this in an outward-oriented direction, directed towards, as it is called, life, the actual, the active life; he is very careful in his dealings with the bit of reflection he possesses within himself; he fears that what is in the background could come up to the surface again. Then he gradually succeeds in forgetting it . . ." [XI 190 f., SD 189-90].

Kierkegaard uses the image of the closed door again in the following section, where it is no longer a matter of spiritlessness, but of the genuine encapsulation in despair "about the eternal and over oneself." The blind door "is here an actual, but certainly a carefully closed door, and behind it sits the self, as it were, and watches out for itself, busy with, or filling time with, not willing to be itself; and yet it is enough of a self to love itself. This is called *encapsulation*" [XI 197, SD 196]. It is naturally not true that there is nothing behind the blind door of the spiritless person; behind it is the self which he disowns and excludes. The difference between him and the person in conscious despair is that the latter focuses his attention upon that which the spiritless person ignores. Each is on his own side of the door. But what they have in common is that they each isolate that part of the self-perception which they will not acknowledge. The spiritless person isolates part of his self-perception simply by excluding it from his sphere of attention, which he can do by virtue of his bourgeois activity and his philistine wisdom about life. The more consciously despairing person isolates the unacceptable part of the self-perception by keeping it separate from the rest of his understanding of life and hidden from his fellow men, while his own attention circles precisely around the part thus isolated. This incongruence between the hidden and the public image is present in despair, regardless of whether it is the one side or the other which captures the despairing person's own attention.

Therefore this is also the case in defiance. Encapsulation is the same, and it is precisely a reactive symptom: "This hiddenness is precisely something spiritual, and is one of the ways of guaranteeing oneself that one has, as it were, a little enclosure behind actuality, a world exclusively for oneself, a world in which the despairing self is restlessly and tantalizingly engaged in willing to be itself" [XI 208, SD 206-07].

Thus, according to *The Sickness Unto Death,* encapsulation is an isolation of that part of the self-perception which is found to be unacceptable. The isolation can have varying grades of intensity and varying degrees of obscuration and distortion of the original self-understanding. The gradations denote an "ascent from the defensive to the offensive" [XI 264, SD 256]. What is decisive for the distinction between the various forms is whether or not the individual's attention is focused in front of or behind "the door in the background." There is always something behind this door, but the question is how well the door is shut, whether it is shut for the individual himself or only for those around him;

and the question is also the degree to which that which is hidden behind the door is forgotten, obscured or transformed into something else.

5:2. "*Everything is Self-Defense for Him*"

Thus, what the despairing person hides or isolates is a consciousness of the fact of his weakness, a consciousness about his weakness, or (in defiance) a reaction against this consciousness. This is what Kierkegaard says in *The Sickness Unto Death*. In *The Concept of Anxiety*, the delineation of "the contents of encapsulation" [IV 438, CD 115] is illustrated with more detailed examples, but is basically less clear, because the principal concepts are lacking here. There is one example in particular which—against the background of the line of reasoning in *The Sickness Unto Death*—may appear misleading. Vigilius speaks of a criminal who will not go to confession, but is compelled to by a sort of silence torture. It is true that the analysis quickly turns from the criminal to the inquisitor and his motives for employing this form of torture [IV 433-35, CD 111-13], but the example itself leaves the impression that the content of encapsulation is a definite knowledge, which the encapsulated person, for understandable reasons, wishes to keep secret.

And yet this does not seem to be the meaning. Immediately previous to this, Vigilius differentiates between demonic encapsulation and the encapsulation which is due to the fact that one shuts oneself up with an idea in order to realize a definite plan. The latter form can be "a pact with the good." As such it is the free, and what makes it into the opposite of the unfree is precisely its definite content?: "The demonic does not shut itself up with anything, but shuts itself up, and in this lies the profundity of existence, that it is precisely unfreedom which makes itself into a prisoner" [IV 432, CD 110]. Unfreedom is thus not this or that distinct secret, upon which the demonic person broods, but unfreedom is the vicious circle itself, which forces the demonic person to brood over himself. The content is thus relatively indifferent, for in *The Concept of Anxiety* the accent lies on a formal definition of encapsulation itself. Kierkegaard's idea is thus not merely romantic literary psychology's notion of the demon's secret dark spot in the past, which must be concealed from the surrounding world.

To continue to follow this line of reasoning, one can even go back to the idea of the primary crisis out of which consolidated despair can develop. For the present I am resting my argument upon a couple of the pseudonyms. "Infinite resignation is that shirt of which they tell in the old folk tales," writes Johannes de silentio in *Fear and Trembling* with respect to this crisis: "The thread is spun under tears, is bleached with tears, the shirt sewn in tears, but then it protects better than iron and steel." It is the first phase of encapsulation which is depicted. Johannes de silentio is interested in this because it is the precondition of faith (which is not self-protective resignation, but confident receptivity). But he also mentions in passing "the various misunderstandings, the reversed positions, the sloppy movements," and adds that it is important that the movement does not become "a one-sided result of a dire necessity" [III 108, FT 56]. As a defense against existence, Johannes de silentio's resignation is halfway demonic, but according to Kierkegaard's line of reasoning, it only becomes really demonic when self-protection becomes his fixed self-defense. Judge William depicts a similar transition from a slightly different perspective in a deliberation upon the expression "to lose one's soul." In a moment of despair, i.e., in the primary crisis, man is in danger of fastening onto something which is merely the external occasion of despair, and of choosing finitude; it is a variant of the idea of the unconscious choice. "Despair is there, but it has not yet attacked his innermost being; only when he hardens himself against it in the finite sense does he lose his soul. His soul is anesthetized in despair, as it were, and only when, upon awakening, he chooses a finite way out of despair, only then has he lost his soul; then he has closed himself; then his reasonable soul is smothered, and he is transformed into a beast of prey who eschews no methods, for everything is self-defense for him" [II 239, E/O II 226].

5:3. *Anxiety about Communication*

It is ideas such as these which are developed in *The Concept of Anxiety* and *The Sickness Unto Death,* but in less dramatic expressions. In the chapter in *The Concept of Anxiety* on anxiety about the good, it is particularly the closedness and its function as self-defense which are described. What the individual defends himself against is "the good," salvation, recovery. But the "good" which is the object of anxiety is more closely defined as "revelation" [IV 435, CD 113] and "continuity" [IV 439, CD 115]. "Language, the word, is precisely what saves . . . for in language lies communication." It is thus these categories which are decisive, not the different examples of the contents of encapsulation. Encapsulation is defined as "the mute" who will not "come out with language" [IV 432 f., CD 110-11] because it speaks in monologues [IV 437, CD 114]. The meaning is expressly not that the encapsulated person is hiding a particular secret, which he is simply refusing to communicate; in a footnote, Kierkegaard requests that his reader not misunderstand the word "revelation," "as if it were always a matter of something external, a tangible, obvious confession, which, however, as it is external, would do no good," and he explains that he could just as easily have chosen another expression: "Transparency" [IV 435 f., CD 113 note]. The explanation of anxiety about the good is that there is "something which freedom does not want to penetrate" [IV 439 f., CD 116], but the encapsulation is not merely the result of a particular denial of one or another fact, but is in a broader sense "the effect of the individual's negative relationship to himself" [IV 438, cf. 432 and 436 f. note; CD 115, cf. 110 and 114 note].

From these definitions arises a question which I have also touched upon earlier. Does Kierkegaard presuppose that the encapsulated self possesses an understanding of the fact that the object of his anxiety is "the good" (alias linguistic communication)? It is one thing to put forward abstractly the formula "anxiety about the good," and it is something else to assume that the anxiety-ridden person himself relates more or less consciously to this good, and is himself clear about the fact that language is that which will help him. I have previously compared Kierkegaard's line of reasoning with the psychoanalytic doctrine of resistance to recovery, but in that same connection I also pointed out the difficulty, in that such an understanding certainly presupposes either a therapeutic situation or a strongly analytic self-understanding (above, Chapter V: 8: 3). It is not particularly difficult to see the affinity between the psychoanalytic theory of resistance and Kierkegaard's depiction of the encapsulated person's ambivalent relationship to revelation: "Encapsulation can desire revelation, that it may be obtained from without, that it might happen to it. (This is a misunderstanding, as it is a womanish relationship to the freedom which is posited in revelation and the revelation which posits freedom. Unfreedom can thus well remain, even though the encapsulated person's condition becomes happier.) Encapsulation can will revelation to a certain degree, but retain a little remnant with which to begin afresh upon encapsulation. (This is the case with the subaltern spirits who can do nothing *in toto*.) It can will revelation, but incognito. (This is the most sophistical contradiction of encapsulation. However, examples of it are found in poet-existences.) The revelation may already have conquered, but in the same moment encapsulation makes its last daring attempt, and is clever enough to transform revelation itself into a mystification, and encapsulation has won" [IV 436, CD 113-14].

Thus the question is only by what psychological right does Kierkegaard assume that the encapsulated person is so aware of his own condition that he understands that language is "that which saves from the empty abstraction of the encapsulated" [IV 433, CD 111]. In a literary draft in the journal from 1845, which contains one of the rudiments of *quidam's* story in "Guilty?"/"Not Guilty?" Kierkegaard discusses an encapsulated person "in a third element, when he himself discovers that his guilt is nothing other than the fact that he has been encapsulated"; his task is thus revelation, but "he keeps this discovery . . . to himself again in encapsulation" [Pap. VI A 61, Dru 528]. But can this dialectic justifiably be presupposed in many other people besides a *quidam* and a Søren Kierkegaard?

Part of the answer lies in the fact that Kierkegaard operates with the idea of interpersonal situations. The entire section on the demonic in *The Concept of Anxiety* is cast in the form of an exegesis of the New Testament accounts of Jesus' meeting with the man possessed with demons. When he wanted to drive out the unclean spirits, they ask him to go away and leave them in peace. "The demonic therefore only becomes quite clear when it is contacted by the good, which thus comes to its boundary from without" [IV 427, CD 106]. Concepts such as language, communication, and revelation indeed concern precisely the individual's relationship to other people, and it is thus from this relationship that the understanding of the demand for openness emerges. Thus, to this extent, Kierkegaard's analysis of the demonic is based precisely upon the understanding of man's unavoidable relationship to other people which Kierkegaard is often criticized for lacking. The idea is put forth explicitly in the beginning of *The Concept of Anxiety*. Man is not merely man, but fellow-man. "Every individual is essentially interested in all other individuals' stories, yes, just as much as in his own. Completion in oneself is thus the perfect participation in the whole," and if the anthropologist does not hold firmly to this, he will end "in the Pelagian, Socinian, philanthropic number one, or in the fantastic" [IV 332 f., CD 26]. Kierkegaard's definition of anxiety about the good is the proof of the fact that he is not merely postulating this idea, but maintains it himself, and uses it as the basis of his most significant psychological analyses.

The demand for openness emerges from the situation of being with one's fellow men, but naturally it comes particularly from the situation in which the encapsulated person is confronted with the directly formulated demand or the expectation of communication, thus, for example, in the therapeutic situation. Therefore, it is in this situation that the inaccessibility of the encapsulated person is most dramatically revealed. In the prelude to one of his edifying discourses, Kierkegaard writes about the worry which pushes so deeply into the soul that the soul must see comfort as its enemy: "And who has not experienced what powers worry can give a person! How he knows how to protect himself from consolation with both cunning and strength! How he manages what no military commander manages, to lead worry's same defenses fresh into battle again in the very instant that they have been disarmed! Who has not experienced how passionate worry can give a person strength in thought and expression, of which the comforter himself is almost afraid! Who has not experienced the fact that scarcely any importunate person can speak so flatteringly to win over another person, as a worried person can speak rapturously in order to convince himself and the comforter that there is no consolation!" [VIII 336, GS 222].

5:4. *"Pseudo-Continuity"*

But the defense against the good does not only manifest itself in the present, interpersonal situation. It grows and dominates the entire self-understanding and life-style. That was the point of "The Continuity of Sin." The demonically encapsulated person, in the narrower sense of the term, comprehends his critical relationship to the surrounding world and thus also to openness and to communication, because he fears exposure, both in relation to others and to himself. He no longer has need of any particular interpersonal situation in order to become aware of his secretiveness and hiddenness. From within "the consistency of evil," he fears the good, i.e., the alternative to his unambiguous self-understanding, in which alone he can confirm his identity, and he therefore breaks off communication with others and with the possibility of recovery, and communicates only with himself. The analysis is continued in the following section of *The Sickness Unto Death,* which deals with "The Sin of Despairing Over One's Sin," which is "an attempt to give sin firmness and interest as a power, by supposing that it is now eternally decided that one will hear nothing of repentance and nothing of grace." This posture is thus not only an ideology, but a form of life. "Sin has become or wants to be consistent with itself. It will have nothing to do with the good; it will not be weak enough to listen to a different voice once in a while. No, it will only listen to itself; it will only have to do with itself, shutting itself up with itself, indeed, shutting itself up within yet another enclosure, and in despair over sin, secure itself against every assault or persecution by the good. It is aware that it has burned its bridges behind it, and is thus inaccessible to the good, as the good is to it. . . . This naturally extorts from sin the most extreme forces of the demonic, and gives sin an ungodly toughness and perversity, which must consistently regard everything that bears the name of repentance, and everything that bears the name of grace, not merely as empty and meaningless, but as the enemy against which one most of all must protect oneself. . . ." As has been mentioned, in *The Sickness Unto Death* Kierkegaard describes the demonic formations of defiance with a slightly different emphasis than in *The Concept of Anxiety.* Vigilius called demonic possession an unsuccessful attempt to hypostatize oneself, while Anti-Climacus maintained that sin is more than simply this impotent attempt, because it is a position in itself. I have attempted to demonstrate that, from a psychological point of view, this contradiction is only an apparent one, and here again it is revealed that the attempt to make sin powerful only succeeds because its strength is drawn from its own unsuccessfulness and emptiness: "At the same time, however, despair over sin is aware of its own emptiness; it is aware that it has nothing at all on which to live, not even its own self in the perception of this" [XI 247 f., SD 240 f.].

The unwillingness to communicate (encapsulated self-communication) and the experience of emptiness thus characterize the continuation of sin as a defense against the good. The corresponding categories in *The Concept of Anxiety* state that the demonic is "'the sudden" and *"the content-less, the boring"*; together with the category of *"the encapsulated,"* they express three aspects of the same condition [IV 438 and 442, CD 115 and 118].

The meaning of the three concepts is determined in relation to the concept of "continuity." In *The Sickness Unto Death,* "the continuity of sin" is stressed; in *The Concept of Anxiety* the discontinuity, but as has become clear, these two points of view support one another dialectically, because sin is only capable of establishing itself as a position by virtue of its relation of negative dependence on its opposite. In *The Concept of Anxiety* the good was more precisely defined as communication (revelation, language), but also as "continuity." The demonic also has continuity in its life, but it is a "pseudo-continuity," as is explained by means of a mechanical metaphor which expresses the same thing as the railroad metaphor in the analysis of "the continuity of sin": "The continuity which encapsulation has can best be compared with the dizziness which a top must have as it continually turns around on its point" [IV 439, CD 115].

The word dizziness itself suggests that this pseudo-continuity is closely connected with anxiety as an experienced quality. Boredom, which is connected with this, is a concept or a psychic reality which grows formlessly and illimitably in the demonic state. "The continuity which corresponds to the sudden is what one could call extinction. Boredom, or extinction, is namely a continuity in nothing." In *The Concept of Anxiety* Kierkegaard speaks briefly of this "terrible emptiness and absence of content" and of its more comic sides [IV 442, CD 118]. But the mood itself, or the interest in it, dominates his psychology so strongly that one could cite a whole series of descriptions and phenomenological definitions drawn from this area of experience, which lead us from the earliest journals forward to *The Sickness Unto Death.* Here I will be satisfied with a brief foray. Boredom applies not only to what is banal and trivial, but also to the intense, stifling mood which underlines aesthetic nihilism. Aesthete A differentiates between two sorts of people, those who bore others and those who bore themselves [I 301, E/O I 284]. It is the latter sort who have the greatest psychological interest. *"Boredom* is the *only continuity* the ironist has," Kierkegaard writes in his master's thesis in settling accounts with romantic ("ironic") philosophy and poetry, which lacks continuity and dissipates itself into nothing but noncommittal moods: "Boredom, that eternity lacking content, that blessedness lacking in enjoyment, that superficial depth, that famished satiety. But boredom is precisely the negative unity which is incorporated into personal consciousness, and in which opposites vanish" [XIII 386, CI 302]. The absence of differentiation which characterizes boredom is experienced in apathetic ambiguousness, the declining "demonic pantheism," which "reposes upon the nothing which meanders throughout existence; its dizziness is infinite, like that brought about by looking down into an infinite abyss" [I 302-04, E/O I 286-87]. The quotation, which again confirms the similarity between anxiety and boredom, is from Aesthete A's essay on "The Rotation Method"; the art of forgetting which he describes in his protection against boredom, just as diversion and elegant pastimes are motivated by his anxiety about repetition and time. The consciousness of time is the correlative and the condition of possibility for boredom, and in the "Diapsalmata," boredom is the substratum for all of the moods which move within the aesthete. "I die the death," one of the formulae reads, in an entry where he describes precisely his condition of anesthetized, emotionally-paralyzed boredom [I 24 f., E/O I 36]. The expression points forward to *The Sickness Unto Death,* where despair is phenomenologically defined as "this painful contradiction, this sickness in the self, to die eternally, to die and yet not to die, to die the death. For to die means that it is over, but to die the death means to experience dying" [XI 148, SD 151]. For Kierkegaard, even the word despair has a close connection with the experience of boredom. One of the earliest rudiments of *The Sickness Unto Death* is this journal note from 1839: "That which we in one sense entitle 'spleen,' and what the mystics knew under the name of 'lifeless moments,' was known by the Middle Ages under the name 'acedia' (ἀκηδία [akedia], apathy). Gregory, *moralia in Job,* XIII, p. 435: *'virum solitarium ubique conitatur acedia . . . est animi remissio, mentis enervatio, neglectus religiosae exercitationis, odium professionis, laudatrix rerum secularium'* "[3], Kierkegaard remarks that "the sickness is extremely well described," and adds: "It is what my father called: *a quiet despair* [Pap. II A 484 f., Hong 739]. Whence the name.

To keep from losing myself in moods, I will return to *The Concept of Anxiety*, where boredom was designated as a continuity in nothing, which corresponds to the sudden. By continuity, one is to understand both temporal continuity, the coherence in the individual's own self-understanding, and the individual's own "continuity with the rest of human life." These aspects of meaning are closely interconnected, for the dizzy pseudo-continuity of boredom with its own emptiness is the correlative of the discontinuity in relation to the surrounding world. It is this discontinuity which Kierkegaard calls "the sudden": "Encapsulation continually shuts itself off more and more from communication. But communication is the expression of continuity, and the negation of continuity is the sudden." In an inserted aesthetic analysis of the leap of Mephistopheles in the ballet *Faust,* Kierkegaard wishes to put forth an impression of "the abrupt" and the unpredictable, unmotivated, and unarticulated as a symptom of the demonic state: "However brief they may be, words and speech nevertheless always have a certain continuity, seen quite abstractly, because they are spoken in time. But the sudden is the complete abstraction from continuity, from what came before and what will follow after."

But what is here perhaps more important than the break in the temporal continuity is that the sudden also designates the break in continuity with the surrounding world; Kierkegaard thereby suggests a final perspective behind his analysis: the total autism of madness, as the most extreme consequence of the demonic self-defense. "Thus while the life of the individual is carried on in a certain continuity with life, the encapsulated person preserves encapsulation within himself as an abracadabra-continuity, which communicates only with itself, and therefore continually exists as the sudden" [IV 438-41, CD 115-18].

6. Madness

Kierkegaard has nowhere put forth anything which claims to be a coherent theory of madness in the strict sense, and if I wish to cite some of his remarks on the subject anyway, it is not in order to take sides with respect to the various theories of madness, particularly schizophrenia, which are on the market in our day. Kierkegaard's remarks do not give any material for this, in my opinion. In saying this, I have already expressed reservations about Ludwig Binswanger when he says that he knows of no other book which is more capable than *The Sickness Unto Death* of making a contribution to the Dasein-analytic interpretation of schizophrenia.[4] It is particularly the formulations about the self—to will and not to will to be oneself—which Binswanger regards as relevant to the problem of schizophrenia, and it cannot be disputed that Kierkegaard is used here in a meaningful fashion which is rich in perspectives. Like various other modern psychologists, Binswanger uses Kierkegaard loosely, citing individual passages which are striking, but he is not interested in Kierkegaard's total project. One must therefore object that it is too narrow to view *The Sickness Unto Death* purely and simply as a book about schizophrenia. Nor did Kierkegaard himself understand it in this way.

Nevertheless, the idea is obvious and fascinating, and some of his statements can contribute to the description of the schizophrenic process. Whether it is technically defensible to read Kierkegaard in this way is a question which researchers into schizophrenia must consider. Without pretending to know all about a problem about which the most intelligent specialists admit that they know very little, and without hinting that Kierkegaard has supposedly contributed essentially to its understanding, or that this is at all an essential side of his thinking, I will simply put forth a couple of views.

The precondition for saying that Kierkegaard's deliberations on madness are of interest at all is the assumption that psychic factors play an essential role in the schizophrenic development. As is well known, this is precisely the problematic point, but Kierkegaard cannot be used to support an exclusively psychogenic view. At one point in *The Concept of Anxiety,* he mentions in passing that madness is a purely somatic phenomenon [IV 439, CD 116], and in a journal entry he embraces an old distinction between two sorts of madness, a corporeal and a mental [Pap. VII 1 A 47, Hong 3896]. He also expresses himself cautiously: "In those cases when madness does have a mental cause," it is remarked parenthetically in *Either/Or,* "it always lies in a hardening at one or another point in the consciousness" [I 75, E/O I 81].

It is thus only mentally-caused madness to which Kierkegaard has given thought, or madness to the extent that it is mentally caused. It is not only Binswanger who has adopted psychological views of madness in modern times. Freud suggests something similar when he says that there must be an identity or at least a great similarity between the conditions of sickness in neurosis and in psychosis, while the difference is that the psychotic's I is too disorganized to be able to cohere with the external reality against the alien forces which press upon him from within: "When the ego is detached from the reality of the external world, it slips down, under the influence of the internal world, into psychosis" [Freud XXIII 173].

If the view is tenable that psychosis is a condition that can be understood by extension from more well-known, neurotic conditions, but with the difference that in psychosis the personality surrenders itself entirely to its inner world and lets go of contact with the external world, then the following sentence from *The Concept of Anxiety* must be called an especially accurate description of this transition: "If encapsulation does not push things to the point of complete madness, which is the sorrowful perpetual motion of monotony, then the individual will still maintain a certain continuity with the rest of human life" [IV 439, CD 115-16]. To the extent that some of Kierkegaard's earlier mentioned descriptions from *The Sickness Unto Death* are able to illuminate the problem of schizophrenia, they must be understood in a similar perspective, as a suggested final possibility of despair. *The Sickness Unto Death* does not describe any clearly psychotic conditions, but it does describe conditions which certainly make Binswanger's interpretation and use of the book understandable, particularly in view of the fact that Binswanger is especially interested in the phenomenological description of the premorbid psyche. In the despair which is that of infinity and of possibility, the individual is in the grip of his own uncontrollable, solipsistic fantasy, and in defiance and the continuity of sin the despairing individual will only listen to himself, while he makes himself inaccessible by cutting off communication, so that in his autistic enclosure he can cling tormentedly to a particular posture and self-understanding out of anxiety about the chaotic collapse of identity which threatens if contact is made with any alternative. In *The Concept of Anxiety* a similar view is suggested in the description of the encapsulatedness which continually communicates only with itself. It is precisely the total discontinuity of autism in relation to the surrounding world, the dissolution of the normal identity and of stable contact with external reality, which is indeed probably the most important characteristic of schizophrenia.

Kierkegaard's scattered remarks on the matter seem, like so much else in his psychology, to have a close connection with his attempt to understand himself. Johannes de silentio thinks that genius and madness are related phenomena, and he suggests that genius is a sort of mastery of a latent madness; the idea is formulated as a question: "In what relationship does madness stand to genius? Can one construct the one from the other? In what sense and to what extent is the genius master of his madness? For it follows of itself that he is master of it to a certain extent, for otherwise he would of course really be mad" [III 171, FT 116]. For Judge William it is also the dissolution of mastery over oneself in the purely psychiatric sense which characterizes the breakthrough of madness and its difference from the encapsulation which still preserves a certain continuity: "I have seen people in life who deceived others for so long that their true being was finally unable to manifest itself; I have seen people who played hide-and-seek for so long that finally madness forced their secret thoughts upon others with just as much disgustingness as there had previously been pride in their concealment. Or can you imagine anything more frightful than ending up with your being dissolving itself into a multiplicity, so that you really became many, so that you became legion, just like that demon, and so that you had lost that innermost, holiest thing in a man, the binding power of the personality?" [II 174, E/O II 164].

In his diaristic novel, *quidam* discusses the problem of madness at a couple of points. The inserted piece "A Possibility," which resembles a short story, is a symbolic fantasy about the closed universe of autism. Quiet, provincial Christianshavn, separated from the busy reality of the capital by a bridge[5] which really is not long, but which does, however, separate two very different worlds, is the symbol of this foreignness — "far, far away, out of the way in another world," which is silent, and empty and purposeless. "The great warehouses conceal nothing and produce nothing; for although Echo is a very quiet tenant, no landlord could be satisfied with his occupation or the rent he pays" [VI 291 f., SLW 258 f.]. A few pages earlier *quidam* had put forth a little theory of madness, which in his opinion can either come about suddenly, by means of a sudden vicissitude in which reason is lost and petrified, or by means of a gradual, creeping development, in which the individual slowly sinks down into insanity: "The suffering individual does not become petrified, but mad in a sum of impressions which displace one another with natural necessity, but which are not in any relation to the freedom which once freely called up these impressions, until they now call themselves forth in unfreedom" [VI 284, SLW 252-54]. In such an enclosed world of impressions lives the mad bookkeeper, who is situated in the symbolic Christianshavn in "A Possibility." The most interesting thing about the text is not the bookkeeper's case history, but the symbol of the person who is cut off, and yet so close to the world in which he lives; the text ends much as it began: "Long Bridge has its name from the length; as a bridge it is rather long, but as a road its length is not very significant, of which one can easily convince oneself by walking the length of it. When one then stands on the other side, in Christianshavn, then it again seems as though the bridge must nevertheless be a long road after all, because one is far, very far away from Copenhagen" [VI 304, SLW 268].

The case history itself is perhaps not so important. But in it Kierkegaard touches upon the question of how madness arises. In his youth, the bookkeeper was lured into bad company, went to a bordello when drunk, and now has the *idée fixe* that he is perhaps the father of a child. What is most interesting from a psychiatric point of view is certainly the description of the premorbid psyche, which shows that Kierkegaard does not simply find the explanation in one particular psychic trauma. Before the fatal visit to the bordello, the bookkeeper is a modest, intelligent office worker who lives a retiring existence, "and as year after year went by he became more and more foreign to the world. He himself did not notice it so much, for his time was always occupied. Only once did a presentiment arise in his soul; he became foreign to himself, or he seemed to himself like the person who suddenly stops and reflects upon something, which he must have forgotten, without being able to grasp what it is—though something it must be" [VI 297, SLW 263].

The feeling of being foreign to oneself, of being unable to be on familiar terms with oneself, but, rather, being split into a suffering (acting) and an observing I, has been discussed by Kierkegaard a number of times for personal reasons. "The common boundary of melancholia and madness is . . . becoming objective to oneself" [Pap. X 1 A 642, Hong 2692]. It does not seem to be his opinion simply that the cause of madness is a particular experience, such as an unclearly remembered visit to a bordello. "No, the matter is: in the [case histories which seem] more important, more unusual, more interesting, etc., one is concerned and interested in paying attention to the fact that the man went mad; it has a sort of novelistic interest, and one's concern is quite certainly egoism. In a case in which a person becomes mad over something insignificant, as it is called, the situation is different; and yet, here we forget something which a psychologist would consider right away, that it is precisely this [becoming mad over something insignificant] which certainly has a part in the constitution of madness, as if it were a reflection; thus the man lost his reason, became furious over the fact that 'such an insignificant thing had such power over him, that others should believe that such an insignificant thing had power over him' " [Pap. X 2 A 322, Hong 4552]. It is thus from this sort of insignificant thing, that is, from the reaction to it, that Kierkegaard apparently thinks madness develops itself: "for madness never has the inwardness of infinity," Climacus writes in a footnote (which has been especially emphasized by Ludwig Binswanger): "Its *idée fixe* is precisely a sort of objective thing, and the contradiction of madness is precisely in willing to encompass it with passion" [VII 179 note, CUP 174 note]. Here and later in the *Postscript,* as with other of the pseudonyms, a close connection between the pathology of normality and of madness is suggested by subjecting them to a common formula, so that the mad person's passionate adherence to his *idée* becomes a sort of extreme, caricatured form of the despair of finitude: "Vanity, avarice, envy, etc., are thus essentially madness, for it is precisely the most ordinary expression of madness to relate oneself absolutely to what is relative . . ." [VII 412, CUP 378].

If Kierkegaard's remarks on madness are so much more fragmentary than his other psychological theories, it can with good reason be interpreted as an expression of respect for the puzzling nature of the problem. "Such an observer must have cunning to a great degree, and love," writes Johannes de silentio in dealing with the relationship between madness and genius, but adds that if one will attentively "read through various of the authors of the greatest genius, it might nevertheless be possible, one single time, to discover a little, even if with much effort" [III 171, FT 116]. The preferred method of modern psychiatry in exploring schizophrenia is certainly not to read through authors of genius, and perhaps the yield is also modest. But precisely in view of the fact that in the present, despite enormous efforts, we have hardly come much further in our understanding than did Kierkegaard — when one gets to the root of the matter — precisely because of this, the reading of the authors of greatest genius could be thought to yield a sort of return, certainly not in the form of tangible knowledge, but in the form of stimuli, which might perhaps exert influence not so much upon theories as upon the attitude toward the problem and toward the patients ("cunning to a great degree, and love"). All knowledge begins in wonder, Kierkegaard writes. What one could learn from him in this area is not knowledge, but a sense of the closeness of madness, of the short distance from reason to unreason. This sense is especially useful, in Kierkegaard's view at any rate, because it promotes engagement and fantasy. "The physician at an insane asylum who is stupid enough to believe himself clever for all eternity and to think that his bit of reason is insured against all harm in life — he is indeed in a certain sense smarter than the mad, but he is also stupider, and he will certainly not heal very many" [IV 359, CD 48-49].

Thus, Kierkegaard's observations on madness also include the rudiments of a criticism of the science which concerns itself with it. Is the "reasonable" sicence more reasonable than the unreason it treats? It is this question which is hinted at in Climacus' distinction between subjective and objective madness. The exemplar of subjective madness is Don Quixote, whose passion encompasses a fixated, finite impression, which becomes his subjective reality, while for other people it has no validity. The syndrome which Climacus calls objective madness, on the other hand, can be recognized by the fact that a person completely ignores subjective human truth and reality in his impersonal, scientific search for the truth: "This sort of madness is more inhuman than the other; one shudders when one looks into the eye of the first sort of mad person, for one does not wish to discover the depth of wildness; but one dare not look into the eye of the second type for fear that he has no real eyes at all, but glass eyes, and hair of gold thatch, in short, an artificial product. If one accidentally meets such a mad person, whose sickness is precisely that he has no mind at all, one listens to him with cold horror . . ." [VII 181, CUP 175].

Chapter VII

"THE FORMS OF DESPAIR"

1. Spiritlessness: The Social Complex

We should be far enough along by now to have mapped the more important provinces and crossroads of the kingdom of sin, and we can now direct our attention to becoming better acquainted with the native inhabitants of the various regions. But as has become clear, the boundaries between Kierkegaard's various descriptive categories are not always sharply defined, and it would inhibit understanding if these boundaries were emphasized more than necessary. The psychological theme which will be presented in this chapter is really only a broadening and a concretizing of what has been discussed more schematically in the previous chapters. Even if one uses "the degrees of consciousness about the self" as a gauge, the chain of problems winds its way in and out of the boxes in the diagram, because we are no longer dealing with formulae here, but with Kierkegaard's psychology in living action.

The "lowest" form of despair is "spiritlessness." In order to avoid a very obvious misunderstanding it is important to recall that in Kierkegaard spiritlessness is not synonymous with low social status or a lack of education or intelligence (cf. above Chapter VI: 2). The simple, common man is not spiritless, or he can only become so after coming into contact with the bourgeoisie's norms of culture. In *The Concept of Anxiety* it is clear that it is the bourgeoisie which is the target, not the underclass of society. If one wishes to characterize spiritlessness from a literary point of view, one must not simply present it as unintelligent, it is stressed. Spiritlessness is not "stupid" in the ordinary sense of the word, but "it is 'stupid in the sense that it is said of salt: 'when the salt becomes stupid, what shall we salt with?' "[1] Therefore the language of spiritlessness is "cultured" language; its vocabulary is that of the enlightened bourgeoisie, or perhaps more exactly, that of the academic class. "Spiritlessness can say exactly the same thing that the richest spirit says, except that it does not say it by virtue of spirit. Spiritlessly determined, man has become a talking machine, and there is nothing to prevent him from learning a philosophical jingle by heart just as well as a confession of faith and a political recitation" [IV 401 f., CD 84-85].

If one restricts oneself to *The Concept of Anxiety* and *The Sickness Unto Death,* one might get the impression that spiritlessness is the form of despair which Kierkegaard finds least interesting. It is stated somewhat negatively in *The Sickness Unto Death* that "the lowest forms of despair" lack inwardness, or that at any rate there is nothing to be said about their inwardness, and one is therefore reduced to describing the externals of this despair [XI 176, SD 177].

Nonetheless, it is precisely for this reason that spiritlessness is an interesting category in Kierkegaard. Indeed, it becomes clear upon closer inspection that he has in fact a great deal to say about it, and it is important because it reveals that his psychology is not purely and simply a psychology of inwardness, but a psychology which also is capable of concerning itself meaningfully with "externality," with social and historical aspects of human existence.

One quite often gets the opposite impression, but one of the things one discovers when one occupies oneself extensively with Kierkegaard is precisely the fact that he is very concerned with the social and historical aspects of life as conditions for human existence. This is not clear from his best known principal works. The *Postscript,* for example, is exclusively concerned with "that individual," in a polemic against Hegel's interest in mankind's world-historical fate, and it is particularly from this polemic that Kierkegaard has gotten his reputation as the philosopher par excellence of individuality. But in reality his reflections upon the society and the social and cultural norms with which he was acquainted play a much greater role in the authorship than is usually understood — also a much greater role than appears from his most important psychological writings, *The Concept of Anxiety* and *The Sickness Unto Death.* In these books Kierkegaard's interests show a preference for the "inner" conflicts and the states of despair in which the individual's self-understanding is solipsistically disengaged from every concrete affiliation with outer circumstances. His concern with "externality" must be found for the most part in other writings and in the journals.

And yet it is precisely in *The Concept of Anxiety* and *The Sickness Unto Death* that the formulations are to be found which show that the "inner" does not stand in any chance or superficial relationship to the "outer." It is in *The Concept of Anxiety* that one finds the criticism of the "Pelagianism which leaves every individual unconcerned about the race to play out his story in his little private theatre" [IV 338, CD 31], and it is here that one finds the assertion that "every individual is essentially interested in the story of every other individual, indeed just as much as he is in his own" [IV 333, CD 26]. And, as I have attempted to demonstrate earlier in this book, these views are far from being without consequences for Kierkegaard's psychology. It holds true "in love just as much as in a man's birth, that the situation, the environment, with its psychological disposition, has a great influence upon what is born," it is stated programmatically in another connection [VIII 54]. The quotation is from a little book which Kierkegaard published in 1846, *A Literary Review* (partially published in English under the title *The Present Age*). The book contains a detailed review of a contemporary Danish novel, *Two Ages* by Thomasine Gyllembourg, which interested Kierkegaard because it juxtaposed the revolutionary period of the 1790's with the more petty restoration period of the 1840's. The latter half of Kierkegaard's book contains his independent analysis and criticism of spiritlessness, viewed as an epochally and sociologically determined phenomenon. Of one of the characters in the novel under review, he writes that "the author must motivate the romantic in Claudine psychologically, and then it can be the age which decides the particular direction it will take" (VIII 46).

However, it is especially in *The Sickness Unto Death* that we find the brief formulations which make it theoretically possible to consider the connection between the "outer" and the "inner," between the surroundings, society, and the historical epoch, on the one hand, and the individual's self-understanding and posture, on the other. Here I have in mind a central definition of the self as "a relationship, which relates itself to itself, and in relating itself to itself, relates itself to another" (above, Chapter IV: 3: 2), and the equally summary remarks about "the standard of measure," which give the explanation of what the "other" is to which the self relates itself in comparison (above, Chapter V: 9: 2).

We will here examine more closely this comparing function, which forms the basis for the shaping of the identity. "One sees very clearly here the great extent to which evil and sin exist in a vain relationship of comparison with the world, with other people," it is written in *Works of Love* [IX 323, WL 265]. In anticipation of this we have discussed the function of comparison previously in Chapter IV: 3: 1, where we encountered the fundamental distinction between knowing oneself "in relation to something other" and knowing oneself "in relation to oneself." It is the distinction between "spiritlessness" and the "higher" forms of despair, which are indeed determined by external relationships and circumstances, but which also have a conscious self-reflective relationship to these. The spiritless person, on the other hand, is "like a mirror, in which he captures the world, or, rather, in which the world reflects itself," as it is written in one of the edifying discourses [V 99, ED IV 23]. As will be clear by this point (cf. above Chapter VI: 2), spiritlessness is not identical with defects of intelligence or dullness. The spiritless person can be socially effective, just as his self-understanding is socially determined. He lives "in close acquaintance with an in clever calculation of his own powers, abilities, presuppositions, possibilities, and is likewise conversant with what knowledge of mankind and of the world has to teach to the initiated," while, on the other hand, he never "comes to himself in *self-knowledge*" [XII 444 f., JY 121].

All this is hinted at in *The Sickness Unto Death,* for example, when it is stated that the spiritless person only knows himself "by his costume" or by "externality" [XI 187, SD 187], i.e., by his social role. The section on the "despair of finitude" is a caustic critique of this form of life, but it also contains the rudiments of an analysis. It deals with the person who permits himself to "be tricked out of his self by 'the others'," who has "achieved perfection in all that he does," who is normally adjusted ("just as a person ought to be"), "praised by others, honored, and respected," etc. These are all social ("worldly") categories, and by means of the relationship of comparison to the system of social differences, the individual identifies himself and achieves his self-understanding — "for worldliness consists precisely in attributing infinite worth to what is indifferent. The worldly view always clings fast to the difference between man and man" [XI 164-66, SD 166-68].

The consciousness of social differences is the basis of the individual's identification with his social role, which becomes his only "self." For example, the role identity can appear as follows: "Like the foxfire of rotten wood, like the will o' the wisp of the swamp which glows in the fog, so, in the glimmer of his earthly greatness, he exists for others. But his self does not exist; his innermost being is consumed and hollowed out in the service of nothingness; as the slave of vanity, lacking power over himself, in the dizzying grasp of the world, God-forsaken, he ceases to be a man; in his innermost being he is as though dead, but his greatness walks ghost-like among us — it lives. It is no man with whom you are speaking when you speak to him; in his search for greatness he himself has become the sought-after, viewed as a man, a title" [X 73, Ch D 60].

A modern social psychologist would not express himself so emphatically, partly because he must be careful with respect to his own role-identity as an "objective" scientist — a caution which Kierkegaard disregards. But Kierkegaard knows very well that no man can simply avoid having a social role. What can be avoided is the absolute identification of oneself with the role. However, it is not simply the system of social differences, but also man's misunderstood anxiety about not having an identity, which forces him into a role identity. "Jehova says: 'I am that I am; I am.' This is the highest sort of being," Kierkegaard notes in his journal, and continues: "But such a way of being is much too high for us humans, much too serious. Therefore we must be sure to become something; it is easier to be something . . . . Most people, or, indeed, nearly every person would die of anxiety about himself if his being were—a tautology; they are more anxious about existing like that, and for themselves, than about seeing themselves. So things are toned down for them. What gives comfort is, for example, that I am a privy councillor, a knight of the realm, a member of the cavalry commission, a civic representative, a director of the club." Kierkegaard makes it clear that it is not the social functions themselves that he is criticizing, but their tendency to absorb the individual completely [Pap. XI 1 A 284, Hong 200]. In *Works of Love* social identity is discussed as "the outer garments of differentiation," which the individual binds firmly about himself, and in which he mimics all his life, like an actor in his costume [IX 104-06, WL 95-97].

The fact that the standard of measure of self-perception in role-identification is the relationship of comparison to the given system of social differences also involves the fact that this standard of measure is subject to historical change. It is of particular importance in this area that Kierkegaard has had insights into contexts which are rarely connected with his name, but which are of the greatest significance as a corrective to the exclusive "inwardness" which has most often been associated with his thought. It is important to note that Kierkegaard's basic anthropological definitions do *not* imply any assertion that man's essence is ahistorical and unchanging. The fundamental anthropological structure which is named in the definitions and concretized in the analyses of anxiety is precisely the potential structure, which is realized differently under different historical and social conditions. And in various connections Kierkegaard concerned himself intensely with these conditions, and, naturally, particularly with the conditions of his own period and his own society. And, be it noted, he did so with a very great awareness that the society in which he lived was anything other than unchangeable and static. This is perhaps most strikingly seen when one concerns oneself with Kierkegaard's view of his times and his intense sense that this was a transitional society, an unstable balance between a different past and an alternative and problematic future. In this respect, Kierkegaard was no less conscious of the demonic dynamic of bourgeois society than was his contemporary, Karl Marx.[2]

In *A Literary Review,* Kierkegaard attempts to diagnose what one could call his period's social character as the product of its total experience. In order to understand clearly the meaning of Kierkegaard's considerations, one must note that the period with which Kierkegaard concerns himself, the 1840's, was the beginning of Denmark's process of conversion to a modern, capitalistic society. Since 1660, the country had been an absolute monarchy, conservative or moderately "enlightened." It was a static, hierarchical, closed and comprehensible little society, in which the King and the Bishop of Zealand were the highest and almost uncontested authorities in a closed system of universally recognizable and acknowledged representatives of authority (the clergy, teachers, jurists, and other officials of the state). After the Napoleonic wars, the country was in a condition of poverty and stagnation for a long time, but after the mid-1830's economic growth began in the bourgeois professions, and in the wake of this came the beginnings of public discussion about the social situation, which culminated at the end of the 1840's and — with the inspiration of the French revolution of 1848 — resulted in the democratic constitution of 1849 after a nearly bloodless "revolution." (The newly-installed king was indifferent to power, if he were merely allowed to retain his title, his popularity, and his mistress.) A few years later came a liberal trade act, which abolished the corporate and guild privileges of the medieval and mercantile periods. The "free" society of liberalism was established, and the "cultured," property-owning haute bourgeoisie were the real possessors of power, despite the fact that the "unenlightened" peasants were also represented in parliament.

It is with this process of conversion that Kierkegaard concerns himself in his analysis of the times in the 1840's. The bourgeois revolution had not been completed in the political sense, but in the norms, value judgments, and morals of the society, it was already a reality. In this development Kierkegaard sees an unfortunate atomization of society. The political and religious bonds which "invisibly and spiritually hold states together," have been dissolved or weakened, and the result is isolation and abstract subjectivism, it is written in *Either/Or* [I 138 f., E/O I 139-40], where the period is compared to the dissolution of the Greek state: "Everything continues to exist, and yet there is no one who believes in it" [II 23, E/O II 19]. It is precisely the dissolution of the Greek state with which Kierkegaard concerns himself in detail in *The Concept of Irony,* where Socrates symbolizes the transition from the ancient Greek, cosmically-anchored world order to the modern, reflective and individualistic consciousness. In pre-Socratic Greece, "the laws had for the individual the venerableness of tradition, as that which had been sanctioned by the gods" [XIII 263 ff., CI 188 ff.]. Modern Socratic reflection, on the other hand, wrests the individual free of the state and shared religiosity, and throws him upon himself, because the individual learns that "what was supposed to be absolutely certain, what is determinative for man (laws, customs, etc.) brings the individual into contradiction with himself," so that he must accept the fact that the received norms are invalid [XIII 305, CI 227].

In his journal, Kierkegaard compares Socrates with the Renaissance figure Faust, who comes after the "naive" and "universal" ("catholic") wholeness of the Middle Ages, and signifies "the individual who has been left to himself after the disestablishment of the Church and after having been wrested from the Church's guidance" [Pap. II A 53, Hong 1968]. It is obvious that these studies of the dissolution of the traditional, meaningful whole, and of the isolated individual's emancipation from this whole, were written by Kierkegaard with a view to his own times, and it is also clear that according to the thesis, Socratic irony has its modern, extreme parallel in "irony after Fichte." With the acosmic idealism of Fichte— "*subjectivity to the second power,* subjectivity's subjectivity, which corresponds to reflection's reflection" [XIII 342, CI 260]—the substantial totality is completely denied on the philosophical plane. This tendency was continued by the German romantic school in a negation of all historical and present reality, while on the plane of fantasy it juggled consummately with the given reality, positing and suspending realities according to arbitrary principles. Kierkegaard's sketch of the romantics is noteworthy in that he stresses so energetically—and criticizes—the worldless, reality-denying, and traditionless aspects of what can briefly be called romantic and modernistic poetry, and the polemic against existence which it contains: "It is the finite, subjective person, who applies the lever of irony in order to tip the whole of existence off its joints. The whole of existence now becomes a *mere game* for poetic circumstances, which disdain nothing, not even the least thing, but for which nothing stands firm, not even the least thing" [XIII 403, CI 317].

This nihilistic romanticism is at once both the refined expression of the process of separation, and also one of the most recent preconditions of Kierkegaard's own time. However, this does not mean that such a literary high point of substantiality-denying arbitrariness and intensified subjectivism is simply identical with the movement of the times. It is merely a symptom of such movement. In one of the essays in *Either/Or,* "the ancient tragic" and "the modern tragic" are juxtaposed. The difference between the ancient Greek and modern tragedy is bound up with the special character of their respective historical periods. The ancient tragedy of fate is the expression of a world and a society which "did not have subjectivity reflected in itself. Even if the individual moved freely, he still reposed in substantial categories, in the state, the family, in fate," and the tragic hero was a tool for these forces, while the modern tragic hero's suffering is due to his own free action. He "is subjectively reflected in himself, and this reflection has not only reflected him out of every immediate relation to the state, the race, and to fate, but it has often even reflected him out of his own earlier life" [I 139 f., E/O I 141]. This represents a fundamental annulment of the essence of tragedy—but no real liberation, because "when the times lose the tragic, they gain despair." The tendency to isolate the individual is so characteristic that it can be shown to be present in "the general consciousness of the entire present time" [I 141, E/O I 142-43], however, be it noted, not as an uncompromising, strict insistence upon the responsibility of the individual, but rather, in a weakened and toned-down form as ordinary bourgeois morality. "In a certain sense, it is therefore a very proper rhythm of the times that it wishes to make the individual responsible for everything; but the misfortune is that it does not do this deeply or passionately enough, and from this comes the period's inadequacy" [I 143, E/O I 144].

The emancipation from the ancient substantial morality and the rebellion against the traditional, common norms and institutions is in Kierkegaard's opinion not the only characteristic of the modern epoch. The other characteristic is the fact that this development is concealed and disavowed. Herein lies the "inadequacy" which he mentions, the contradiction between reality in modern society and the general consciousness of this reality.

Kierkegaard also delineated this contradiction in historical dress in *The Concept of Irony*. Socrates is here the striking symbol of the change from the ancient to the modern consciousness, but the precondition for Socrates is the decay of the Athenian state, and the appearance of the sophists is a sign of this dissolution. "The sophists represent *knowledge which is wrenching itself loose* from substantial morality by means of a dawning reflection," but their culture is a superficial culture which does not reveal the crisis of consciousness, but conceals it. "In its first form, this culture makes everything vacillate; in its second form, on the other hand, it makes the honest disciple capable of making things firm again"; it awakens reflection, but it lulls it back to sleep again with argumentation and *loci communes*[3] [XIII 303-06, CI 225-28].

Kierkegaard's age—bourgeois society—is the zenith of modern sophistry. The highpoint of romanticism is one symptom, among others, but reality belongs to the epigoni, and romanticism only lives on in trivialized forms whose task it is to conceal that which had been the actual background of the most distinctive romantics, namely, the factual dissolution of traditional norms and values. In *A Literary Review*,

Kierkegaard speaks of his age as the age of reflection—a self-satisfied, cautious time, lacking in enthusiasm—and he sharply and wittily describes its conventionalism, its empty cultivation of form, its lack of originality, its pretentious and affected superficial culture, its external and ambiguous morality, its spinelessness and apathy, its narrow-minded small talk, and its great words and petty deeds as attempts to create security as a replacement for the inner certainty and naturalness of self-understanding of which change had deprived it. This is Kierkegaard's most detailed analysis of spiritlessness as a psychological phenomenon which is colored by its times: the ability to adapt, the smoothness, the lack of character, the cleverness, the superficial culture, the self-satisfaction, the officiousness, the irreproachable facade, the social role identity—the fear of acknowledging its own emptiness. The communication of the spiritless person with the surrounding world is talkativeness (the same thing which Heidegger calls *Gerede* [gossip]): "what is it to *chatter?* It is the abolition of the passionate disjunction between talking and remaining silent. Only the person who is essentially capable of remaining silent is essentially capable of speaking," but spiritlessness is capable neither of the one nor of the other. It is incapable of speaking, because its speech broadens itself diffusely and attempts to touch upon everything in an uninterrupted stream of gossip, pointless "private-public talkativeness" and "completely reliable" information about what so and so has done and said. Nor can spiritlessness keep silent: "chatter dreads the moment of silence which would make the emptiness apparent" [VIII 105-08, PA 69-72].

What is of interest here is that it is not merely the literary and philosophical currents of the period which are sketched, but its social character as well, which is explained in the context of the real changes in society. Here, too, Kierkegaard characterizes his period by its oppositional relation to older periods. In the sharply-defined class structure of ancient times, the relationship between the lone individual and the mass could be described in the formula: "the individual great man—and then the many; one free—and the rest slaves"; the great man meant everything, the individual member of the crowd, nothing. Later, in the history of Christianity, this situation was replaced by a representational one, where "the majority views itself in the representative, and is liberated by the consciousness that it is itself whom he represents, in a sort of self-consciousness" [VIII 92, PA 52]. The representative individual is the bearer of authority, (the clergy, official personages, the king) and the individual commoner, the layman, identifies himself in relation to them as a member of an organic whole, "himself supported by and supporting the whole" [VIII 115, PA 80].

The French Revolution marks the dissolution of these social forms of hierarchic and organic subordination and rule. The French Revolution is in the political and social sphere what German romanticism is in the philosophical and literary spheres. Kierkegaard speaks of the revolution with noteworthy respect and straightforward admiration. He speaks of "the idea of freedom and equality" and its results in various areas such as marital norms and the norms for the relationship between parents and children. But, just as "the present age" is not the time of romanticism, but of trivialized post-romanticism, so too is it not the age of a revolutionary, spontaneous manifestation of energy, but a distorted watering-down of this. And thus, in sketching bourgeois society, Kierkegaard refrains from using the ideological concepts of freedom and equality but uses instead the sociological concept of leveling.

The great French Revolution of 1789 was justified as an open, spontaneous rejection of a petrified hierarchy. The leveling of "the present age," on the other hand, is a disguised, unspontaneous, unprincipled weakening of the institutions and symbols of patriarchal society. It is not an open rebellion, but a gradual hollowing out of the meaning of the institutions and symbols. The work of art of the present age is "to allow everything to continue, but cunningly to cheat it of significance: instead of culminating in rebellion, it culminates in the emasculation of the inner reality of things, in a reflective tension, which, however, allows everything to continue to exist and changes the whole of existence into something ambiguous, which exists in its factuality, while a dialectical deception privately substitutes a secret interpretation — that it does not exist" [VIII 84, PA 42-43].

Kierkegaard traces the social-psychological essence and effects of social and cultural leveling, particularly the process of cunning and concealed leveling. In the older, hierarchical social formations, man was naturally identified by his place in the social whole, his social role, his calling and station in relation to his superiors and subordinates. It is this possibility of natural identification which leveling takes away from man. Feelings of comparison are universal, but the form they assume is determined by the age in which one lives. In the old "representative" social order, the characteristic feelings of comparison which form the basis of individual self-understanding are static, and give security and meaning: admiration, loyalty, respect, faithfulness, and the like; these feelings are occasioned by socially vertical relations of comparison. The roles are unchangeable, and individuals have no incitement to abandon or doubt them; they do not discover that the role is a role.

Leveling, on the other hand, means that the individual becomes conscious of himself and his social status, at the same time that he becomes aware of the possibility of changing these things. When "the enchantment of sensory deception ends, when existence begins to vacillate, then despair reveals itself as that which was fundamentally present all the time," it is written in *The Sickness Unto Death* [XI 176, SD 177]. When the old pattern of roles and norms is dissolved and leveled, despair manifests itself at the same time that the role identity becomes problematic and is made unstable by means of vertical comparisons. In the vacuum which follows upon the hierarchical structure, individuals seek new points of connection and possibilities for orientation. The feelings of comparison conditioned by this, and which constitute the basis for identification, are laden with rivalry: envy, suspicion, and disloyalty. These are feelings which thus are not only the products of social change, but also themselves contribute to changing society.[4] But at the same time, the fear of the superior authority in the hierarchical structure is replaced by a "horizontal" fear of differentiating oneself from the average. Conformism takes over the place of faith in authority.

Conformity and rivalry are two variants of the envious way of life. Conformity is stagnant rivalry, and rivalry is egoistically competitive conformism. Leveling is itself a product of envy, because the possibility of touching or transgressing social and intellectual class divisions is here within reach. In a reflective time it is not a case of a spontaneous revolutionary envy which "elevates and overthrows, raises and depresses," but of a stagnant envy which "strangles and inhibits" [VIII 91, PA 51]. In a time of reflection, envy is not merely the principle which seeks out differences and promotes competition, but is also "the negatively unifying principle." Mutual suspicion and individual fear of violating the compulsion to conform are the only factors holding individuals together. Nor is it merely in interpersonal relations that envy reveals itself as rivalry. It is also shown in the individual's relation to himself. "The idea of reflection, if one can speak of it as such, is envy, and envy is therefore a duality; it is that which is selfish in the individual and also the selfishness of the surroundings against the individual." The two forms of envy support one another. The individual's selfish, reflective envy is his fear of non-conforming action (but rivalry and competition in such a society are not non-conforming action). It is a prison cell, which is surrounded by "the great prison building which is formed by the reflection of the surroundings," i.e., which is constituted by the view which the social environment has of the individual [VIII 88, PA 47-48].

Kierkegaard, who has been used to support so many different ideologies in the 20th century, also has given us a long series of passages which support a theory of social envy as the key concept in the theory of the social order. The German sociologist Helmut Schoeck has stressed this little known side of Kierkegaard's thought in a very interesting fashion in the book *Envy: A Theory of Social Behavior*.[5] It ought to be emphasized, however, that Kierkegaard *cannot* be enlisted in support of Schoeck's extremely conservative version of the capitalist ideology.[6] It is quite true that one can find a great many remarks of a conservative, anti-democratic, indeed, anti-socialist character in the Kierkegaard of the 1840's.[7] And these remarks are far from being unconnected with the social-psychological views which have been summarized here. However, Kierkegaard is a very unreliable ally for conservative ideologues. What he wishes to "conserve" is something completely different from that which is the goal of modern conservatism, which, on the contrary, in its alliance with liberalism, has served as the ideological guarantor for what is perhaps the greatest revolution in society which the world has ever seen, namely, the complete restructuring of the world by capital. Moreover, Kierkegaard himself realized that the old-fashioned conservatism which he espoused in the 1840's had become antiquated and rendered impossible. He can be seen leaving conservatism quite expressly behind in his journals in 1852-53 [Pap. X 4A 563, Hong 1000; X 5 A 125, 126, 147, et al.].

There are a number of reasons for this about-face, and they show that the revolutionary events of 1848 in France made a deep impression on Kierkegaard, while the counter-revolution of Napoleon III disgusted him. But the most important theoretical reason can be seen as early as *A Literary Review* from 1846. Leveling is an evil, it is true, but Kierkegaard is at the same time realistic enough to realize that it is an unavoidable one. Therefore the old-fashioned conservative objections to it are to no avail. Just as envy itself is not merely an individual and moral matter, so, too, is leveling a more-than-individual development, which has powerful psychological consequences, but is also in itself more than a mere psychological concept. "The leveling is not the action of an individual, but a play of reflection in the hand of an abstract power. Just as one can calculate the diagonal in a parallelogram of forces, so can one calculate the law for leveling. For the individual who levels several others, also includes himself, and so on. While each individual egoistically seems to know what he is doing, one must say of them all that they do not know what they are doing, for just as enthusiastic solidarity produces a surplus which is not that of any individual, so, too, is a surplus produced here . . . No age can stop the skepticism of leveling, and neither can this time, the present age; for at the moment it wishes to stop it, it will develop its law still further" [VIII 93 f., PA 54].

Therefore, in spite of his own conservative views, Kierkegaard had to reject conservatism's attempt to stop the development. The person who wishes "to hold back his age" behaves just like the railroad passenger who wishes to stop the train by holding firmly to the seat in front of him, not understanding that both himself and the seat are moving away with the speed of the entire coach. "No, the only thing to do is get out of the coach and hold oneself back" [VII 150, CUP 147].

However, this "solution" of society's problems does not imply that Kierkegaard ceases to interest himself in the affairs of the world and the developing tendencies of society. And parallel to his conservative criticism of the leveling, bourgeois society, we also see a dialectical appraisal that it is just this new society which signifies "a progesss" in relation to older social forms [VIII 117, PA 82]. In itself, the leveling is an evil, but at the same time it is a crisis which can become the precondition of something radically new. The present age "wins in extensiveness what it loses in intensiveness. But this extensiveness can in turn become the precondition of a higher form, when a similar intensity again conquers the area which is held extensively" [VIII 104 f., PA 68].

This view becomes clear in the journal, when it is stated, in a summary of many deliberations, that: "In ancient times, only a single individual lived; the mass, the thousands, were squandered upon him. Then came the idea of representation. The people who really lived were again only individuals, but nevertheless, the mass saw itself in them, and participated in their lives. The final situation is this: the single individual, though understood such that the single individual here is not in opposition to the mass, but that every person is equally an individual" [Pap. X 2 A 265, Hong 2019].

It is with respect to the realization of this "final situation" that Kierkegaard understands his entire authorship, and it is also in connection with this that one must understand his attack upon the Danish State Church in 1855. Despite the fact that the optimistic tone had disappeared by that time, the viewpoint was the same, and the fight with the Church is precisely an attack upon "the idea of representation" and an attempt to reach the individual in the mass. This is not the place to give an account of this truly revolutionary project with all the problems if involves.[8] The attack upon "Christendom" was an attack upon bourgeois spiritlessness, as it had installed itself in the institution of the Church. It is important to recall here that "spiritlessness" is not Kierkegaard's designation for the lowest and unenlightened class of society, but precisely the cultured bourgeoisie. "It has always been a source of indescribable delight to me that before God, it is just as important to be a serving girl, if that is what one is, as to be the most eminent genius. From this comes my almost exaggerated sympathy for the simple class of people, the common man," it is written in one of the many journal entries which prepare the attack: "No, it is the cultured and well-to-do class—if not the notables, then at least the notable bourgeosie—who must be the target; the salons must be made to pay" [Pap. X 1 A 135, Hong 236].

It is from this point of view that one can best see the psychological perspective of the attack on the Church. It cannot be seen as clearly in the violently polemical pamphlets which constitute the attack itself as in the journal entries which precede it. We have a key to this complex of problems in the programmatic entry: "Seen as a whole there is an entire area for psychological observation here: the cunning with which human selfishness seeks to guard against the impression of life's wretchedness by making a show of sympathy, so that one's greediness for the pleasures of life is not disturbed." Kierkegaard here illustrates his idea with a brief analysis of a sermon by the Bishop of Copenhagen, which dealt with the problems of the poor, but which in reality contained not a consolation to the poor, but "a phrase extremely welcome to the rich," because it makes the entire problem trivial and idyllic [Pap. X 3 A 135].

The "area for psychological observation," which Kierkegaard here points out, is much broader in scope than what one would ordinarily expect of a Kierkegaardian or modern "existentialist" psychology, but it is not necessarily irreconcilable with it. Kierkegaard has only made a beginning, but it is pronounced enough to enable his modern readers to extend his fundamentals by broadening the analyses and rendering them topical. Kierkegaard is especially interested in the socially oppressing effect which the content of religious belief can have when it is reshaped into an institutionalized bourgeois and clerical ideology. The Church has allied itself with the state and the ruling class in society, and the Christianity of "Christendom" is therefore not only a deception directed against Christianity, but at the same time also against the people to whom Christianity especially addresses itself, "the proletariat" [Pap. X 1 A 669, Hong 4164], "the suffering, the poor, the sick, the lepers, the mad and so forth, the sinners, the criminals" [Pap. X 2 A 27, Hong 386].

In connection with his attack, Kierkegaard calls attention at many points to the close connection between the power of the Church and the power of capital, and the transformation of Christianity from the gospel into a commercial product. Here I will only mention, as an example, his analysis of how the religious idea of Providence really functions in bourgeois society. The religious faith in Providence is most often found in "people who own something or who have amounted to something in the world," but "if you analyzed this piety a bit more carefully, you might perhaps sooner tremble for this sort of cruelty and selfishness." The idea of Providence serves the personal vanity of the owner of property, because he can conceive of himself as the object of divine Providence's special attention, and of God as "the guarantee" of his continuing possession of his property. One understands one's social status as "Providence's reward, because one has made wise and pious use of life." But, in addition to this, this form of religiosity helps the well-off person to protect himself against receiving the impressions of other people's sufferings; it functions as "a defense of the fact that one does not do any more for the suffering than one does, for one is afraid of interfering with Providence's intentions for the individual." Thus, cosmic toryism moves into the place of Christianity, and transforms it into the opposite of what it originally was. And if the reference to Providence is insufficient, the religious notion of guilt is also made a part of the ideology of oppression: "If the suffering individual becomes impatient, then perhaps one goes a step further, and explains that his sufferings are self-deserved, that they are punishment — for there is a divine governance, a Providence, which apportions rewards to the good (charming!) and punishment to the wicked" [Pap. XI 1 A 267, Hong 3632].

This notion of guilt is thus nothing other than a legitimation of the desire of the possessing class to preserve its status and ignore the wretchedness upon which it is based: "See, this is how much we people love to enjoy life, so much so that we protect ourselves against finding out about the misfortunate and the wretched people, whose sufferings would disturb us and our pleasures in life by giving us another impression of God than that he is happiness; so we protect ourselves against these people by saying, "it is their own fault," and then we rejoice in life and in the notion that we have God on our side" [Pap. X 4 A 573, Hong 4683]. In this way, the gospel has been transformed into "an injustice against the suffering people which cries out to heaven," because the official ideology explains that wealth and power are signs of piety, and sees capital accumulation as a direct consequence of the fear of God. This explanation is produced by the Church in exchange for a suitable payment. "but with this the old cruelty comes forth once again, namely, that the condition of the misfortunate and the poor is their own fault, because they are not pious and true Christians" [Pap. X 4 A 578, Hong 4685].

This entire complex of problems — which quite definitely is no less contemporary in the 20th century than it was in the 19th, in spite of the fact that those who think along these ideological lines would naturally deny it — is a legitimate "area for psychological observation." Its connection with the rest of Kierkegaard's psychology is obvious enough, and it is only the more concrete application of the idea which is new in the context of the fight with the Church. According to Kierkegaard's psychological writings, it is precisely the need for self-protection, security, and the exclusion of the consciousness of conflict which characterizes spiritlessness. Spiritlessness is anxiety, but its anxiety is concealed and cannot be directly observed, because it "is known precisely by its spiritless certainty" [XI 176, SD 177]. It is just the safeguarding of the self — socially and existentially — which is the symptom of anxiety. The anxiety of spiritlessness is "hidden and disguised," but this is exactly why it is so unpleasant for the observer, because that which is frightful manifests itself precisely in that "it finds it necessary to disguise itself, in order not to appear as what it is, in spite of the fact that this nevertheless is what it is." Even though anxiety "is excluded, just as the spirit is, anxiety is nevertheless present; it is merely waiting." This anxiety is what manifests itself in the religiously disguised social and economic self-protection of the bourgeoisie. In *The Concept of Anxiety* Kierkegaard notes that it can also manifest itself in the authoritarian worship of idols or political leader-types; the phenomenon corresponds to "heathen fetishism. There is nothing which spiritlessness recognizes as authority, for it of course knows that there is no authority over spirit. But because spiritlessness itself is unfortunately not spirit, it is, in spite of its knowledge, a complete idolator. It worships a fool and a hero with the same veneration, but above all, its real fetish is for charlatans" [IV 402 f., CD 85-86].

With these passages we have led the investigation back to Kierkegaard's principal psychological writings. That spiritlessness is the "lowest" of the forms of despair means that it is the most directly dependent upon external social circumstances. The "higher" forms are characterized by a more "internal," complicated, conflict world. But the anxiety is the same, only in a different form. The difference between spiritlessness and the more pronounced "demonic state" seems to be in large measure a difference in social adjustment. Spiritlessness develops itself in an unbroken and undoubted continuity with the social environment, while the individual conflicts of which we will hear in the following sections are all concerned with one or another form of social deviation, abnormality, or encapsulation. It is this difference which determines the degree to which the individual is conscious of the crisis.

2. The Antigone Complex

2:1. *Aggression Directed Inward*

As a transitional form between spiritlessness and the more complex forms of despair, one may mention the Roman despot, Emperor Nero, as he is imagined by Judge William in a short, brilliant analysis in *Either/Or*. Strictly speaking, Nero belongs to the category of spiritlessness, but an intensified spiritlessness, which simultaneously reveals a new aspect, aggressiveness, which is associated with the anxiety of the spiritless person. If Nero were really to go beyond the boundaries of spiritlessness, his reflection would have to turn itself to the critical consideration of his social role function, his imperial dignity. The moment would have to come when "the glory of the throne, of his might and power, would pale, and he has not the courage for this." All the same, by means of its intensification, his spiritlessness points beyond itself.

The Judge notes that Nero's essence, the motive behind his desire to destroy, is melancholia. In Anti-Climacus' terminology this would be called despair. One recalls, in this connection, the passage in *The Sickness Unto Death* about the spiritless philistine who shuts up his despair behind a blind door in the back of his soul, while he appropriates his own talents and directs them outward toward the active life (above, Chapter VI: 5: 1). The same is the case here. Kierkegaard imagines Nero as a blasé hedonist, rather past his prime, tired of pleasure and yet unable to do without it, finding it dull when it reaches its culmination, and yet always chasing after new, cruel entertainment. It is a consequence of "the hysteria of the spirit" which is delineated above (Chapter V: 3), a state of consolidated despair in which the movement of the personality toward maturity has been effectively "suppressed," because the decision of the crisis is always averted, "pressed back" by new, ferocious pleasures. "Then the spirit gathers in him like a dark cloud; its wrath broods over his soul, and it becomes an anxiety which never ceases, not even in the moment of pleasure. Look, that is why his eyes are so dark that no one can stand to look at them; that is why his look is so electrifying that it gives one anxiety, for behind those eyes lies the soul like a darkness. They call that look an imperial glance, and the whole world trembles before it, and yet his innermost being is anxiety." This anxiety manifests itself in an aggressiveness which is directed outward. "He burns up half of Rome, but his torment is the same." He also specializes in exercising psychological terror upon his surroundings by allowing his own anxiety to propagate itself in others, making them insecure or torturing them in order to find enjoyment at the sight of their reactions.

And yet the point is that it is not merely Nero who causes anxiety in others, but that it is also (and especially) the others who cause him anxiety, and his hatred is only his means of concealing this fact. "He does not possess himself; only when the world trembles before him is he made calm, for then there is no one who would dare to seize him. Hence, this anxiety about people, which Nero has in common with every such personality. He is as though possessed, unfree in himself, and therefore, it is as if every glance would bind him. He, the Emperor of Rome, can fear the glance of the most wretched slave." This anxiety is thus the driving force behind his aggressiveness and his bloodlust, which only increases the anxiety [II 199-204, E/O II 190-91].

In addition to the suppression, the point of the analysis of Nero is his anxiety-laden, and therefore aggressive, dependence upon his surroundings. His life consummates itself in a vacillation between impotence and cruelty. Here spiritlessness has its culmination, but at the same time it has its point of contact with the more conscious forms of despair. In *The Sickness Unto Death* Kierkegaard describes a contradiction which is similar to that of Nero without being identical with it. Here it is a case of an encapsulated individual. If the encapsulation is preserved absolutely, it is written, there is a danger that he will commit suicide. If, on the other hand, the despairing person has a confidant to whom he opens himself, the tension is reduced enough to minimize the risk of suicide. It does not remove this risk, however, for it can happen that the encapsulated person reacts in precisely the opposite way, and despairs over the fact that he has opened himself to the other person. "We have examples of this, of an encapsulated person being brought to despair just by having gotten a confidant. Then a suicide can be the consequence. Poetically conceived (assuming, poetically, that the person was, for example, a king or emperor) such a catastrophe could also be formed so that he had the confidant put to death. One could imagine such a demonic tyrant, who felt the need to talk to a person about his torment, and thus consumed quite a number of people in succession; for to become his confidant was certain death; as soon as the tyrant had spoken to him, the individual was put to death. To present in this way such a resolution to this tormenting self-contradiction in a demonic person who could not do without a confidant, and who could not have a confidant—this would be a task for a poet" [XI 201, SD 200].

With this passage we have again made the transition from unconscious to conscious despair, because the encapsulated individual under study represents exactly the despair about the eternal and over oneself. It is he who is busy with his weakness-dominated self-perception, which he keeps behind the closed door in the background of the self, while externally he is "clad in the usual outer clothes" [XI 197, SD 197]. The king or emperor who appears as his poeticized stand-in could easily be Nero. In *Either/Or* it was quite appropriately written of Nero: "If he were not the emperor of Rome, he would perhaps end his life with suicide; for when Caligula wishes that all of humanity's head was upon one neck, so that he could obliterate the world at one blow, and when a man takes his own life, these are really only two expressions of the same thing" [II 203, E/O II 192].

The interesting thing about these two passages is that they both suggest a connection between murder and suicide, or, thus, between aggressiveness which is turned outward toward others and that which is turned inward toward the individual himself. The encapsulated person in *The Sickness Unto Death* takes his own life, but the catastrophe could also be formed in such a way that it was his confidant whom he put to death. Nero is aggressive toward others, but if he committed suicide, it would only be another expression of the same thing. Is conscious, intense despair an aggressiveness which is directed inward, then, or how are we to explain the despairing person's ambivalent relation to his surroundings at all?

Man clings to life, Freud says, and to this extent it seems inconceivable that a person could decide to take his own life. This also has a special explanation. We know, he continues, "that no neurotic harbours thoughts of suicide which he has not turned back upon himself from murderous impulses against others, but we have never been able to explain what interplay of forces can carry such a purpose through to execution. The analysis of melancholia now shows that the ego can kill itself only if, owing to the return of the object-cathexis, it can treat itself as an object — if it is able to direct against itself the hostility which relates to an object and which represents the ego's original reaction to objects in the external world" [Freud XIV 252].

The quotation is from a small but weighty essay from the period when Freud began the serious study of ego psychology. It deals with "the self-tormenting in melancholia, which is without doubt enjoyable," and which is due precisely to the fact that melancholia contains an unconscious satisfaction of unconscious tendencies to hate, which were originally directed toward others, but which now are turned inward upon the individual himself, because the real object of hatred has disappeared from the field of vision or the reach of the melancholy individual. The disappeared person, who serves as the occasion for melancholia, is the beloved who has been lost as a love object. Freud mentions "the case of a betrothed girl who has been jilted" as characteristic in this connection. But in order for melancholia to arise, the sick person must not be clearly conscious of what he has lost, or perhaps he knows whom he has lost, but not what he has lost in this person. The melancholy individual has been the object of an indignity, a disappointment, or slight — and now he despairs. Yet he is not despairing over the loss of the beloved itself, but over himself. And this is what differentiates melancholia from sorrow, despite the fact that sorrow is also caused by the loss of the beloved: "The analogy with mourning led us to conclude that he had suffered a loss in regard to an object; what he tells us points to a loss in regard to his ego." Thus arises weakness's despair, which is a consciousness of its own weakness. In contrast to the person who sorrows, the melancholy person displays "an extraordinary diminution in his self-regard, an impoverishment of his ego on a grand scale. In mourning it is the world which has become poor and empty; in melancholia it is the ego itself. The patient represents his ego to us as worthless, incapable of any achievement and morally despicable; he reproaches himself, vilifies himself, and expects to be cast out and punished" [Freud, XIV 245-52].

The article is entitled *Mourning and Melancholia*. Kierkegaard treats exactly this theme in two articles in *Either/Or:* "The Ancient Tragic Motif as Reflected in the Modern" and "Shadowgraphs." I will take the second of these two articles first. In the summary of Freud's article, I inserted a couple of Kierkegaardian phrases from *The Sickness Unto Death,* the meaning of which has been explained earlier in the present book. They fit into the context without much difficulty, and the similarity is unmistakable.[9] The transition which is depicted in "Shadowgraphs" is parallel to the one which is exemplified in *The Sickness Unto Death* by the young girl who did not get her beloved, and who now despairs over herself, i.e., becomes aware of her despair and weakness (above, Chapter V: 9: 5). We are thus at one of the central points of Kierkegaard's psychology, and we will now illuminate it from a somewhat different angle than previously.

2: 2. Reflected Sorrow

In "Shadowgraphs," Kierkegaard's pseudonym Aesthete A differentiates between "objective" sorrow and another phenomenon which resembles it without, however, being identical with it, reflected sorrow. The three case histories which are to illuminate the matter deal with three female literary figures, whom Kierkegaard poetizes a bit further: Marie Beaumarchais, who is abandoned by her fiance (in Goethe's *Clavigo*); Donna Elvira, who is deceived by her lover (in Mozart's *Don Giovanni*); and Margaret, who loses her Faust (in Goethe's drama). They share a common situation, which is not, however, identical in all three cases, but which is the situation which typically gives birth to reflected sorrow. Here Kierkegaard speaks only of the situation "in which the objective sorrow, or the occasion of sorrow in the individual, itself gives birth to the reflection, which makes the sorrow into a reflected sorrow. This is the case wherever objective sorrow has not been completed, wherever a doubt is left behind, irrespective of whatever other characteristics that sorrow might have." The typical occasion is thus one in which the situation is due to a deception, or in which there is some doubt as to whether or not it is due to a deception. Unhappy love is not enough in itself to give birth to reflected sorrow. "Thus, when her beloved dies, or perhaps when her love is totally unrequited, or when circumstances in life make impossible the fulfillment of her wish, then here there is certainly an occasion for sorrow, but not for reflected sorrow, unless the person in question herself was already sick . . ." [I 172 f., E/O I 170].

Here Freud is so much in agreement with Kierkegaard that the agreement is almost word for word: "The loss of a love object is an excellent opportunity for the ambivalence in love-relationships to make itself effective and come out into the open. . . . In melancholia, the occasions which give rise to the illness extend for the most part beyond the clear case of a loss by death, and include all those situations of being slighted, neglected or disappointed, which can import opposed feelings of love and hate into the relationship or reinforce an already existing ambivalence. This conflict due to ambivalence, which sometimes arises more from real experiences, sometimes more from constitutional factors, must not be overlooked among the preconditions of melancholia" [Freud, op. cit., p. 251]. The precondition enabling the melancholia's ambivalence conflict to arise is that the choice of object took place "on a narcissistic basis," and this also means that the love cannot be given up, in spite of the conflict with the beloved person [ibid., p. 249].

Kierkegaard assumes that the basis of the reflected sorrow "can lie partially in the individual's subjective nature, and partially in the objective sorrow or in the occasion for sorrow. An individual who is madly reflective will transform every sorrow into a reflected sorrow; his individual structure and organization make it impossible for him simply to assimilate his sorrow without further ado" [I 171 f., E/O I 169]. When Judge William and Anti-Climacus stated that the despairing person was in despair before he became conscious of his despair, this meant that the individual had previously identified himself with a particular object, for example, a love object. This immediate identification also contains a latent ambivalence. In Aesthete A's essay it is explained in such a way that love can be seen to contain both "egoistic" and "sympathetic" elements. One or the other of the elements can be the dominant one, but in general, "love contains both moments in itself," and this duality explains why the love permits itself to be assailed by doubt in a situation in which it is deceived or betrayed [I 180 f., E/O I 177-78].[10]

Thus the greatest likelihood that a deception will produce reflected sorrow arises when the deception "does not concern anything external, but a person's entire inner life, the innermost core of his life" [I 172, E/O I 170]. It is just such a betrayal of the individual's identification with the beloved which is sketched in the essay, and at this breaking point, the antithesis between the egoistic and the sympathetic elements becomes manifest. The three abandoned girls are depicted at the moment of the breach of identity. "Accustomed as she is to being supported by him, she does not have the strength to stand when he pushes her away, but sinks impotently into the arms of her surroundings," it is written with respect to Marie Beaumarchais [I 182, E/O I 179]. For Donna Elvira and Margaret, a life is lost in a more complete sense. Before her meeting with Faust, Margaret is an insignificant and simple young girl, whose identity and faith were literally built up by him. Faust is the more intellectual counterpart to Johannes the Seducer. He enriches Margaret intellectually and religiously; "her soul binds itself to his with increasing firmness," without really understanding what it is that he is developing for her, but in complete confidence: "At last, he himself becomes an object of faith for her, a God, not a man." She owes him the contents of her life and her faith, and is therefore bound to him, "disappearing completely in him"; and "imperceptibly, without the least bit of reflection, he becomes everything to her"; "she is nothing and only exists in him"—and then he leaves her [I 214 f., E/O I 208-09].

Donna Elvira is much more independent in relation to Don Giovanni, but here, too, an existence hangs in the balance. Her identity is not created by Don Giovanni, but is lost by means of their brief encounter. She is a nun, disciplined in the peace of the cloister, which, however, has not managed to tame her wild, passionate nature. Don Giovanni excites her passion, and she renounces her past. "The more significant that which she abandons, the more tightly she must cling to him" [I 193 f., E/O I 189]. Thus after the deception she is left without an identity: "She lost everything, heaven, when she chose the world, and she lost the world when she lost Giovanni. Therefore, she has no place to seek refuge, except in him . . ." [I 198, E/O I 193].

Thus the three women remain; Cordelia of "The Diary of a Seducer" is the fourth. And just as Cordelia's substantial love-anxiety vents itself openly as love-hate after the break (above, Chapter II: 4: 3), so does Elvira react with passionate hate, which is held in check by an equally passionate, egoistic love. If she found the faithless Don Giovanni, "then hate would arm her to murder him, but her love would forbid it, not out of compassion, for he is too great a figure for her, and thus she always wants to keep him alive; for if she killed him, she would be killing herself." She is only identified by her ambivalent bond with him, and therefore she would "prevent the lightning itself from striking him, if it were possible, in order that she herself might be the one to take revenge, and yet she would never be able to take revenge" [I 194, E/O I 189-90]. But this spontaneous reaction which is a completely adequate response to the loss, is still not reflected sorrow. She understands her situation clearly, and her feelings are given energetic expression and direction: "It flows through her with a single pulse-beat, and it streams outward; the passion shines through her with a flame, and becomes outwardly visible. Hatred, despair, revenge, love, everything breaks forth to reveal itself visibly" [I 196, E/O I 191].

Reflected sorrow arises when these aggressive feelings can no longer be directed outward, toward the other, because the object disappears or dissolves itself into ambiguousness. So the current of emotion is turned inward, toward herself. She is still not in doubt about the deception and about the vileness of Don Giovanni, but her complex of feelings also includes a hope of being reunited, and this indicates "that the elements of reflected sorrow are present, but they have not yet had time to gather themselves internally." As long as she pursues the faithless Giovanni and re-examines the proofs of his unfaithfulness, she is still clinging to that hope, and she is avoiding "the inner unrest of quiet despair." The feelings change, but they have a goal, and "her soul has not yet turned back upon itself to brood over the observation that she has been deceived" [I 198 f., E/O I 193-94]. How, then, does reflected sorrow get its hold upon her? For, after a final, passionate encounter, Don Giovanni's deception is so patent that it does not leave any room for doubt. Aesthete A half ironically suggests the possibility that she could become religious, but adds that the way back to the cloister would be via repentance. In order, then, "to save herself from this despair, she must cling to love for Don Giovanni." She has lost everything, and now discovers that her whole life is ahead of her, and the content of this life must be the memory of him: "It is self-defense which offers her this," and she thus must take refuge in thoughts of him, so that he becomes not a deceiver after all [I 202 f., E/O I 196 f.]. She turns herself inward with her sorrow, learns to control its expression, refuses any condolences; the sorrow inside her lacks nourishment and outer impulses, and yet she cannot give up her love, for it is her salvation—"and thus she can never come to sorrow coherently and healthily, because she continually seeks to know how she ought to sorrow." Kierkegaard reproduces her formless, confused, ambivalent inner monologue, which vacillates between various avenues of escape. She wishes to forget him in order to protect herself—but "what is this self of mine, wretchedness and misery; I was untrue to my first love [i.e., the cloister], and should I now set things right again by being untrue to my second?" Or she wishes to curse him, dedicate her life to hatred—"but do I really owe nothing to him when I hate him? Do I not live off him? For what is it that nourishes my hatred except love for him?" Thus he is idealized: "He was no deceiver," but was greater than the Olympian gods, and "I will honor him by making myself into nothing." Thus she turns the hatred and degradation toward herself. When she is reminded of him she feels anxiety, "an anxiety like that I felt in the cloister when I sat in my lonely cell and waited for him, and was terrified by the thought of the harsh contempt of the prioress, the terrible punishment of the cloister, and my crime against God." Thus it is in this guilt anxiety that she devotes herself to the memory. She is like a person who remains on board a wreched ship in order to save something, but without knowing what it is: "She is in distress at sea, her doom approaches, but it does not worry her; she does not notice it; she is confused about what to rescue" [I 206-08, E/O I 200-02].

Variants of the same development are sketched in the lives of Marie Beaumarchais and Margaret, but here the shift from aggression which is directed outward to that which is directed inward is less striking, because the point of departure was more ambiguous and the first hate reactions are therefore less energetic. Margaret is the weakest, the least independent of the three. What she is she has become by means of Faust, and now he reveals himself as the faithless doubter who leaves her. Her first reaction is a feeling of total powerlessness, but she gradually comes to the question of how she can now believe, when it was only by means of him that she had believed, and it was "by means of him that she came into being." Her moods do not take on form or expression, but gather themselves unclearly and "are dissolved in the general feeling that she is nothing." The exhaustion and impotence of this fundamental mood become the sounding board of her entire emotional life, and her inner monologue thus becomes more vague, yielding, and self-effacing, if not less capricious than Elvira's [I 216-19, E/O 209-12].

In Marie Beaumarchais' case it is the circumstances of the breaking of the engagement itself which occasion the reflected sorrow, because it remains in doubt whether Clavigo really deceived her or whether he had noble motives. The doubt makes it impossible to give up the thought of him; it is "the unrest in the perpetual motion of sorrow" [I 180, E/O I 177], and when Marie's family tries to help her by calling Clavigo a wretched deceiver whom it is not worth thinging about, she agrees in this devaluation of him, and bursts forth with declarations of hatred, but at the same time is gripped by a hidden anxiety about the humiliation of having been deceived. She begins to defend him to herself; she isolates herself with the thought of him, and so, here too there is an internal judicial hearing in progress, with its mitigating judgements and self-contradictory evaluations and curses which end in self-accusations: "Cowardly, wretched heart, despise yourself; learn to be great, learn it from him; he loved me more than I have understood to love myself. And should I be angry with him? No, I will continue to love him, because his love was stronger, his thoughts prouder, than my weakness and my cowardice. And perhaps he loves me yet; yes, it was out of love for me that he left me"; the curse flares up again; she feels that she has faded, is ugly and careworn. He has taken everything from her — and yet perhaps he was not a deceiver? "She will never be finished with the judicial hearing, because recesses continually occur, nor with the judgement, because it is only a mood." Nor is the end reached when she eventually forgets Clavigo, for he was only the object, but reflected sorrow is sorrow which has been wrenched loose from external reality and basically has no object other than itself: "Thus will time pass for her until she has consumed the very object of her sorrow, which was not identical with her sorrow, but was the occasion of her continual searching for an object of sorrow" [I 189-92, E/O 184-88].

With this, despair has worked its way in completely and has lodged itself firmly where no one can see it. This is emphasized in the essay by the fact that its announced, so to speak, official theme is the purely aesthetic question of what admits of artistic presentation. In contrast to joy and objective sorrow, reflected sorrow cannot be pictorially reproduced, because it is exactly in itself that its essence must be sought, and the external must be made indifferent. Sorrow has no adequate expression, and is at most recognizable by a pallor [I 169 f., E/O I 167-78] or by "a certain sickliness" [I 179, E/O I 176]. It is essential to the reflected sorrow to be inaccessible to direct observation. The real theme of the essay is the movement from the outer into encapsulation, and corresponding to this, the inner, self-obsessed movement of reflected sorrow: "It runs about inside itself as a squirrel in a cage, though not as uniformly as that animal . . .As the sick person who is in pain tosses first onto one side and then onto the other, so does reflected sorrow toss about in order to find its object and its expression." But the more the object disappears from sight and the more the sorrow works its way into its expressionless enclosure, the greater the monotony becomes: "Now it begins its uniform movement. It swings back and forth like a pendulum in a clock, and can find no rest . . . In the course of time, uniformity has something anesthetizing about itself. Just as the uniform dripping of water from the eaves anesthetizes, as the uniform whirring of the spinning wheel, as the monotonous sound of a person pacing back and forth with measured steps in the room upstairs, do does reflected sorrow finally find solace in this movement, which, as an illusory motion, becomes a necessity to it." Finally, the need to reveal itself ends completely, "and sorrow lives deep inside in its little cranny, like a well-guarded prisoner in an underground prison . . ." [I 170 f., E/O I 168-69]. But then the occasion, the object, and the situation are obliterated from memory, and all that is left is sorrow as a mood, which lives its autonomous, mute, incommensurable and unexplained life: "If a person possessed a letter, which he knew or believed contained information about what he must regard as his life's happiness, but the letters of which were fine and pale, the handwriting almost illegible, then he would read and re-read, in passion and with anxiety and unrest, and one moment he would get one meaning out of it, the next another, all in accordance with his belief that, having made out this word with certainty, he could interpret the whole letter in harmony with it; but he would never come further than to the same uncertainty with which he had begun. He would stare, with increasing anxiety, but the more he stared, the less he would see. Sometimes his eyes would fill with tears, but the more often this happened, the less he would see. In the course of time, the writing would become paler and less clear; finally the paper itself would disintegrate, and he would have nothing left but a tear-blinded eye" [I 192 f., E/O I 188].

In order to keep the rest of Kierkegaard's psychology in view, the three things which are especially important to note at this point in the presentation are: the ambivalent relation to one's fellow man, whose significance becomes fainter and fainter for the encapsulated person; the notion of the outward directed aggressiveness which is turned inward toward the subject himself and causes melancholia; and lastly, the statement that reflected sorrow finally finds solace in its movement, which becomes a necessity for it. It was concerning this last phenomenon that Freud spoke of the melancholy person's "self-tormenting in melancholia, which is without doubt enjoyable" — and with this we are again out of tear-blinded tenderness and over into the obstinately self-deceptive demonic state, for the melancholy person's self-condemnation was — according to Freud and according to Kierkegaard — basically a distorted condemnation of the other person, and from this he derives enjoyment.

Does Kierkegaard retain this insight when he ceases to speak brilliantly of literary ladies and speaks searchingly of himself? He is very well acquainted with the notion of a self-enjoyment which is connected with a generally critical, depressive condition. I have previously cited the journal entry from 1848, where he states that he has loved his melancholia [Pap. VIII i A 641, Dru 748; cited above, Chapter I: 1:2]. But even if the idea has a special, personal sting at this point — because Kierkegaard is now confronted with the definitive task to "break through" and abandon his encapsulation — still, on the psychological plane, the insight itself is nothing new to him; on the contrary, this is a case of a theme which is omnipresent, which is sounded as early as the "Diapsalmata": "My melancholia is the most faithful lover I have known; what wonder then, that I love in return" [I 5, E/O I 20]. In the midst of his sadness and his self-loathing, the aesthete will still not give up his depression, for it is a substitute gratification for him, and a protection against joy which must not be surrendered, and he can only tolerate joy in very small doses. Therefore he says of his sorrow what the Englishman says of his home: "My sorrow is my castle" [I 6, E/O I 21], and therefore he describes his sorrow as "my knight's castle, which is high up amid the clouds upon the tops of the mountains like the nest of the eagle; no one can take it by storm . . ." [I 30, E/O 141]. Of course it is precisely this surrogate enjoyment and this defensive function which make the phenomenon demonic, and it should certainly be clear from the earlier portions of the present book that this notion makes itself felt *everywhere* that Kierkegaard describes the demonic state and despair as a defense against the good. Thus the question here is not about this self-adhesive tendency, but about the relation between despair and agressiveness. Freud thinks that it always turns out that the melancholy person's self-accusations are tailored for other people: "their complaints are really 'plaints,' " and the sickness is the method whereby the melancholy person avoids showing this hostility to others or becoming aware of it himself; therefore his humiliation and self-effacement are not genuine [Freud XIV 248 f. and 252]. This, of course, is about the same line of reasoning as in "Shadowgraphs." We will later come to see how Kierkegaard develops this line of reasoning further. But first we must examine some other sides of the matter.

2:3. *Sorrow and Grief*

In the second essay from *Either/Or,* "The Ancient Tragic Motif as Reflected in the Modern," Kierkegaard's pseudonym also attempts to differentiate between objective sorrow and another phenomenon which resembles it without being identical with it: "grief." The topic of the essay is thus the tragic. It takes its point or departure in Sophocles' Oedipus trilogy — and if the agreement between Freud and Kierkegaard in the previous portions of the present book has perhaps seemed suspiciously great, it will certainly placate some people to see that it is not total. In opposition to psychoanalysis, in his understanding of the Oedipus situation Kierkegaard stresses: " . . . Oedipus has murdered his father, married his mother, and *Antigone* is the fruit of this marriage. This is how it is in the Greek tragedy. I deviate here. Everything is arranged the same with me, and yet everything is different" [I 151 f., E/O I 151].

What Kierkegaard describes could appropriately be called the Antigone complex, but it is not Sophocles', but Kierkegaard's own, modern Antigone who personifies the thought. In what does the difference consist between the ancient and the modern tragic, between sorrow and grief? One can say that it consists in self-reflection, and one can add that the difference thus described corresponds more or less to the difference in *The Sickness Unto Death* between "weakness's consciousness" and the intensification of this in "a new consciousness, which is about its weakness" [XI 196, SD 195; above, Chapter VI: 2]. Let me first tell the story of the life of the modern Antigone. King Oedipus lives happily married to Jocasta, and only Antigone, his daughter, knows that Jocasta is his own mother; at an early age she had a presentiment of this terrible secret, and later she came to a sudden certainty and was cast into the arms of anxiety. With this her life becomes forfeit, for she must live as a dead person with her hidden knowledge, with which she shuts herself in, not even daring to confide in Oedipus himself, for she does not know whether or not he is aware of the true state of things. Thus, she alone knows of his disgrace, and she becomes proudly conscious of being the one who has to conceal this knowledge, and thus save the honor of the family. It is particularly after her father's death that the secret becomes a painful burden to her, for she does not know whether he knew of it, and this uncertainty is the unrest in her soul which makes her alien to people. The dramatic collision comes when she falls in love, for her love is doomed to be unhappy. She cannot confide her secret to her beloved; the more he pleads with her to open herself to him, the more she shuts herself in, and so he continues to drive the arrow into her heart—the arrow of melancholia without which she cannot live, but which in another sense prevents her from living [I 152-63, E/O I, 152-62].

How, then, does the grief of the modern Antigone differ from the sorrow of the ancient Antigone? And how does Kierkegaard's Antigone complex differ from Freud's Oedipus complex? The second question is answered when the first one is answered. In the essay on the tragic, sorrow is the mood which is the definitive expression of Greek tragedy, while grief is the corresponding modern tragic mood. "Sorrow always contains something more substantial in itself than does grief. Grief is always an indication of a reflection upon suffering, which sorrow does not know" [I 144 f., E/O I 145-46]. That Greek sorrow is substantial means that man is understood as firmly and unreflectedly anchored in wholes which were larger than the individual himself, "in the state, the family, in fate." In contrast to this, the hero in the typical modern tragedy is subjectively reflected, and is beyond his immediate relationship to these super-personal forces, indeed, beyond even his own past. "If one wished to present an individual who had been so disturbingly influenced by an unfortunate childhood that impressions of this childhood caused his downfall, this sort of thing would not appeal to the present . . ." But in this attitude, the present is superficial, and in connection with this Kierkegaard comes to the defense of the ancient vision of man, and stresses that the individual is "the child of God, his times, his people, his family, his friends; only in all this does he have his truth . . ." [I 140-42, E/O I 141-44].

This view is not only that of Aesthete A. One might perhaps expect that Kierkegaard would place himself at a greater remove from heathen determinism, but in anthropological matters the aesthete is in complete agreement with Judge William, when the Judge speaks of the individual as the product of a particular environment, and with Vigilius Haufniensis, when he says that the race participates in the individual and the individual in the race, and criticizes the Pelagianism which ignores these connections. Aesthete A also calls this view Pelagian [I 140, E/O I 142], and thus expresses his criticism of it.

What he retains from the Greek tragic view of man is "the queer dialectic which places the crime of the race in relation to the individual. This is what is inherited," an "objective dialectic," which presupposes a connection between the guilt of the individual and that of the race [I 157, E/O I 157]. Greek tragic guilt is "something more than merely subjective guilt, it is inherited guilt,"[11] and as such is a "substantial determination" [I 147, E/O I 148].

In Sophocles' tragedy, guilt and fate are inseparable. The guilt is not something of which each individual is conscious, but is a fate which "rests upon the whole race like an impenetrable sorrow." The real guilt of the Greek Antigone — understood in the Greek sense — is not that she defies Creon's prohibition on her own initiative, for the only thing which gives this conflict tragic interest for the Greek is Oedipus' fate, which echoes forth in hers, "branching out into the individual members of his family, and "moving forward in its own frightful consistency like a force of nature; and Antigone's sorrowful fate is like a reverberation of her father's, an intensified sorrow," not so much the product of a free action as "the fateful necessity which visits the sins of the fathers upon the children," and which "encompasses not only the life of Oedipus, but also that of his family" [I 153 f., E/O 153-54].

The deterministic view of man, that the sins of the fathers are visited upon the children, is thus just as much a Greek as a Jewish notion [I 148, E/O I 148-49]. And it is thus also an important ingredient in Kierkegaard's own anthropology, as was clear from *The Concept of Anxiety* [IV 379, CD 65]. The diametric opposite of this is "modern" Pelagianism, which views the individual in isolation, and which "has lost every substantial category of family, state, and race" [I 146, E/O I 147]. The intention of the essay, however, was not to describe the ancient and modern tragic, respectively, but to connect the two views in the definition of what is truly tragic. What interests Kierkegaard in the modern tragic is that it makes guilt into something individual and ethical, and thus into the object of conscious reflection. In the Greek tragedy, guilt is "something half-way between acting and suffering"[12] [I 140, E/O I 142]. It is not abolished, for then there could be no talk of the tragic. The tragic depends precisely upon the ambiguousness which makes it unclear whether the hero is guilty of his fate, or whether the fate is the cause of his suffering. In the absence of this unclarity, the spectator's sympathy for the hero, which is the special characteristic of the tragic, disappears.

Now it is naturally not the concept of guilt and its relation to fate which interests Aesthete A most. The antithesis is developed only in order to illuminate the dialectic between sorrow and grief. The element of the "modern" tragic which he can use in his theory about the "truly" tragic is the notion of something individually experienced and lived through: "The hero suffers the whole of his guilt; he is transparent to himself in the suffering of his guilt" [I 145, E/O I 146]. This is grief, as opposed to the ancient sorrow. But in order for grief to possess tragic interest, the transparency in the acknowledgement of guilt must not be total, for if this were the case the aesthetic ambiguousness would be abolished [I 148, E/O I 149].

And now we have come to Kierkegaard's Antigone.

2:4. *Antigone's Secret*

The tragedy of the Kierkegaardian Antigone is substantial, that is, it is motivated by natural and hereditary relationships, but, in contrast to her ancient namesake, Kierkegaard's Antigone reflects upon her sorrow, and makes it the object of intellectual and emotional processing. The guilt is a part of her consciousness, and it has to do with substantial things, with her father's sin, which is visited upon her, but her reflection upon the guilt is indistinct and ambiguous. This reflection will thus convert her sorrow into grief, into an experienced sorrow, which she works upon and to which she reacts [I 151, E/O I 152]. One can easily see that it is this conscious processing of the conflict material which separates the Antigone complex from the Oedipus complex, and it is particularly this processing which Kierkegaard regards as psychologically significant. Kierkegaard regards the processing this way precisely because it is ambiguous and indistinct. The story of Antigone's life, which was told above, concentrates itself upon a secret, a hidden knowledge of the incestual relationship between Oedipus and Jocasta. What is of decisive significance, however, is *the fact that* she conceals something, and that "within this knowledge there is nevertheless an ignorance which can always keep sorrow in motion, always transform it into grief" [I 159, E/OI 159]. It is this transformation which is the theme of the sketch. Her sorrow is "not a dead, inviolable possession; it moves constantly." It is as if she were consecrated to the idea of keeping things secret and to sacrifice; "the great inspiring idea transforms her, and the garland of sacrifice is like a bridal garland. She knows no man, and yet she is a bride; she does not even know the idea which inspires her . . ." [I 156 f., E/O I 156 f.]. In contrast to the situation with the Greek Antigone, the modern Antigone's idea of her father's guilt and suffering is not "an external fact, an unshakable fact," and her own suffering beneath her father's guilt has no "external factuality." Thus, in order to explain the unreal and object-less nature of her suffering, Kierkegaard assumes that Oedipus is dead, and that "the amphibology in her grief" is due to the fact that she does not know whether or not Oedipus himself was aware of his crime [I 158 f., E/O I 158 f.]. Her "certainty" is anxiety-laden, and this means that the factual data are of subordinate importance. It is transformed into a perception of anxiety, and only as such does it set off the movement of grief. Anxiety's relationship to its object is inadequate, "because I always say 'to have anxiety about something,' by which I differentiate anxiety from that about which I am anxious; and I can never use anxiety in the objective sense; while, on the other hand, when I say 'my sorrow,' this can just as easily express that about which I sorrow as it can the sorrow itself."

Kierkegaard continues by discussing anxiety's relationship to time, and in this connection, anxiety's central position in the developmental course which he has sketched is summarized in the following pithy formula: "Anxiety is the organ by means of which the subject appropriates sorrow unto itself and assimilates it." Antigone desires sorrow as a person in love desires her beloved; she busies herself with it as a lover busies herself with love, and yet this anxiety contains within itself a duality "which causes it to cling all the more tightly to its object, for it both loves and fears it" [I 152 f., E/O I 152 f.]. Thus she makes the grief into a part of herself which must not be surrendered, and it is this impossibility of surrendering it which is revealed in the "tragic collision," the test-situation, when Antigone falls in love. She cannot surrender her grief, but can she belong to her beloved with her grief intact? Can she confide in him? "Can she defend this action to the deceased person?" For of course it was exactly the shame of the deceased person which she was supposed to keep secret. She struggles with herself, and the encapsulation wins; she cannot open herself, but must sacrifice her love. The beloved, who knows that she loves him in return, notices her resistance and reserve, but tries to conquer it without understanding that it is just by this means that she is locked shut, for his declarations of love push the arrow of sorrow deeper into her heart and make openness more and more impossible for her. This conflict only intensifies her grief, because she really loves him, but cannot express it or meet him halfway. "Thus our Antigone bears her secret in her heart like an arrow which life has driven in deeper and deeper, without killing her, for as long as it rests in her heart she can live, but the instant it is removed she must die" [I 160-63, E/O I 159-62].

Thus ends the story, but how is it to be explained? At the conclusion of the essay, which has been summarized, no real explanation is put forth. It is Antigone's own experience of the situation and her own explanation of the conflict with which we are presented: she cannot explain; she must hold on to her secret, and the more she is confronted with the demand for openness, the more she must retreat into herself and make herself inaccessible in her grief. But of course it is not Antigone herself who has written the essay, but Aesthete A. Does he, then, have another explanation of her conflict?

If we—as good psychologists—try to unmask the characters in this pseudonymous masquerade, it is not difficult to recognize Kierkegaard's features behind Antigone's mask. It is probably not even indiscreet to do this, but, on the other hand, it is perhaps a bit premature, for in so doing one easily overlooks the fact that the essay is not (only) an autobiographical document, but a literary text with two characters, the heroine and the narrator, or, as one could say, patient and physician, "case" and analyst. If Antigone is Kierkegaard himself, then who is Aesthete A who writes of her? Kierkegaard himself. But consequently neither of them is Kierkegaard. Antigone is the experiencing and suffering heroine, Aesthete A (in this essay) the psychologically analysing narrator. The question is, does he have an explanation of her melancholia and anxiety which differs from the experience of the conflict which she herself can describe?

He does, but it is only adumbrated. For the whole explanation is not to be found in the fact that Antigone's reflection is ambiguous because of her ignorance about the extent of her father's knowledge of the secret. Nor does her anxiety explain everything, but only the way in which sorrow works itself into her. But how is this anxiety motivated, why is it just this secret which is anxiety-laden, and why does just this secret develop an inexhaustible melancholia and a tragic collision with another person and with other people at all? For, even before she fell in love, Antigone was "alien to people" and "in conflict with her surroundings," though not openly [I 159, E/O I 159]. Despite the fact that her real, innermost life is hidden, she manifests herself externally as blooming and healthy, not as "a weak and sickly woman; on the contrary, she is proud and powerful."

Weakness-pride, that was the dialectic of despair according to *The Sickness Unto Death,* and the formula for the absence of inwardness according to *The Concept of Anxiety.* We will read further in Aesthete A: "there is nothing, perhaps, which so ennobles a person as keeping a secret. It gives his whole life a significance—which, however, it only has for him alone—which preserves him from every vain consideration with respect to the surrounding world, so that, sufficient unto himself, he reposes happily in his secret, one could almost say, even if his secret were of the unhappiest sort. Likewise with our Antigone. She is proud of her secret, proud of the fact that she was strangely chosen to save the glory and honor of the family of Oedipus; and when the grateful crowd applauds Oedipus with thanks and praise, then she feels her own significance, and her secret sinks deeper and deeper into her soul, more and more inaccessible to every living being . . .She is proud of her sorrow; she is jealous for it, for her sorrow is her love" [I 155, E/O I 155-56].

This, then, is Aesthete A's explanation, in spite of the fact that in the essay it is not presented as an explanation, but only as a part of the general description of an interesting young lady. If I say that it is the explanation all the same, it is because it is in agreement with the explanation which Kierkegaard puts forth in *The Concept of Anxiety* and *The Sickness Unto Death.* The reason for Antigone's grief is not that Oedipus married his mother, nor that Antigone came to know of this disgrace, but it is that she is proud of her grief, that she becomes significant to herself in her suffering, that the sorrow is not a straightforward sorrow, but a sorrow in which she conceals an enjoyment of herself, and a sorrow with which she therefore gradually comes to identify herself. This, then, is Antigone's secret, which she herself does not know. She conceals her pride from the others, but in the collision with her beloved she also conceals it from herself; she is left with the grief alone, the arrow in her heart, but she will not part with it, and the fact that she will not part with it and that she does not understand why she will not part with it, reveals that she has now also concealed the pride from herself, despite the fact that the pride is there and exerts its influence.

With this, then, the similarity between Kierkegaard and Antigone stops, for if Kierkegaard had known himself as poorly as she, he could never have written in *The Concept of Anxiety* that cowardice is a profound sort of pride, and pride a profound sort of cowardice. Antigone's anxiety is an anxiety about the good, i.e., about openness and communication with her surroundings, and particularly with her beloved. The connection with Kierkegaard's psychology as it is developed in the other works is obvious. The two texts from *Either/Or* which have been examined in this section should have helped shed light upon some of the problems in this psychology, but the result is probably that more questions have been raised than have been answered. In any event, there is still quite a bit to be said about fate and guilt, about pride and cowardice, about self-enjoyment and self-degradation, and thus about anxiety about the good.

3. The Problem of Guilt

3: 1. *Guilt-Feeling and Guilt*

As opposed to the Greek Antigone, the Kierkegaardian Antigone has an individual experience of guilt, which is part of her total complex of feelings. It is not associated with any particular action, but "she feels her guilt the more she loves her father; only in him can she find rest; they will sorrow with one another as equally guilty" [I 159, E/O 159]. Aesthete A does not wish to have his ideal creation of fantasy disturbed by any ethical reflection, but wishes to enjoy the sight of her in wistful aethestic indifference. Therefore he ascertains the presence of the guilt-feeling, but he does not directly pose the question as to whether she is guilty or not-guilty in her melancholia and her encapsulation. The feeling of guilt was also hinted at in "Shadowgraphs" when it was stated that, in her thoughts of Don Giovanni, Donna Elvira felt the same anxiety as she did in the cloister when she feared punishment for her crime against God. But neither of these "aesthetic" essays commits itself to the distinction between the psychological experience and feeling of guilt and the ethical problem of guilt. It is stated that Antigone and Donna Elvira experience guilt, but not whether they are guilty. This is not an aesthetic or a psychological problem — and yet there is indeed a connection between guilt-feeling and guilt.

The point of departure for this problem is in the article I have cited on *Mourning and Melancholia* by Freud, and in this article it was stated that not only is melancholia an inward-oriented feeling of hatred, but that this inward orientation presents itself as "a conflict between one part of the ego and the critical agency" [Freud, XIV 257]. The critical agency is the same thing which is called the super-ego in Freud's later writings, and the essay is important in the history of psychoanalysis because it is one of the first texts in which this concept is incorporated. The inferiority feelings of the melancholy person are chiefly of a moral sort, and this reveals the conscience as one of the great ego-agencies which "can become diseased on its own account" [*ibid.*, pp. 245 and 247]. The core of melancholia is thus the guilt conflict. Kierkegaard does not express himself like this, or, rather, he expresses himself more subtly. If one were to translate his line of reasoning into modern terminology — as has already been attempted — one might say that reflected sorrow is an inward-oriented, ambivalent feeling of hatred, into which guilt-feelings enter; and similarly, grief is a conscious — but dictated by anxiety, and therefore inadequate — unclear processing of the guilt-laden conflict material, which is why guilt-feelings naturally also enter into it as well. But thus far we have still not said anything about guilt — neither for nor against.

Freud's formulations seem to imply a reduction of guilt-feelings to a purely psychological problem, and not an ethical one. And to the extent that Freud does think this, he is in disagreement with Kierkegaard. But in the article *Mourning and Melancholia* there is an amusing intimation which points in another direction. When the melancholy person directs moral accusations against himself, it is fruitless to contradict him; it is stated: "He must surely be right in some way," and despite the fact that his self-understanding is not in straightforward agreement with the factual circumstances, it is nevertheless true when he depicts himself as petty, selfish, dishonest, and lacking in independence — cf. the girls in "Shadowgraphs" — "and we only wonder why a man has to be ill before he can be accessible to a truth of this kind" [*ibid.*, p. 246].

Here Freud does what the psychoanalyst generally does so rarely: he takes the patient at his word, respecting his own statement about himself. In this passage he is just as impolite to his patients as Kierkegaard is to his readers, but this impoliteness expresses, in fact, a respect for the patient's or the reader's independence and right to be guilty, and thus not to be an automatic product of unconscious mechanisms and the sins of the fathers. The fact that it is precisely in sickness — namely, the sickness unto death, despair — that a person becomes accessible to the truth about himself and his guilt, is an idea which is fleetingly intimated in Freud, while in Kierkegaard it is a dialectical theme which overshadows the psychology — without, however, rendering it superfluous.

3: 2. *Ritualism*

In *The Concept of Anxiety* the problem of fate and guilt is taken up again, but in a slightly different fashion than in the Antigone essay. The problem is posed both psychologically and ethically-religiously, and in order to make the psychological side of it clear, we must first direct attention to a phenomenon which plays a varied role in Kierkegaard's psychology: compulsive ritualism.

One could call Nero's burning of Rome a gigantic ritual for the alleviation of his anxiety. For ordinary, philistine spiritlessness, convention is the ritual, but it can also assume more striking forms. Kierkegaard notes in an early journal entry: "Philistinism is really the incapacity to elevate oneself above the absolute reality of time and space, and which therefore can devote itself to the highest sorts of objects, for example prayer at certain times of the day and in certain words" [Pap. I A 290, Hong 217].

This observation is employed in varied forms in *The Concept of Anxiety*. Kierkegaard's idea, of course, is that it is precisely faith which as a form of existence is liberated with respect to rituals and ceremonies in the widest senses of these words. Faith must not manifest itself principally in particular actions or meditative moments outside of daily existence, but if it is genuine it must be capable of being converted into, or be present in, every form in which life manifests itself, without differentiating itself as something special. It is not only the particularly religious functions which must be transformed by faith, but every function [IV 413 f., CD 94-95].

The most striking psychological illustration of the idea of ritualism is a couple of sketches in *The Concept of Anxiety* of religious individuals for whom the ceremonial becomes defense and self-defense. As an example, Kierkegaard mentions "an adherent of the stiffest sort of orthodoxy . . . He knows the whole thing; he bows before the holy; the truth for him is a sum of ceremonies; he speaks of meeting before God's throne, and he knows how many times one must bow; he knows everything just like the person who can prove a mathematical proposition when he uses the letters A, B, and C, but not when he uses D, E and F. Therefore he feels anxiety as soon as he hears something which is not word for word the same" [IV 449, CD 124].

The orthodox figure does not appear under the label of spiritlessness, but in the section on the demonic. The parallel figures are the unbeliever and the superstitious person; the "holy one," who is unfree in his religiosity; the mocker of religion who is unfree in his mockery, and therefore dependent upon the approval of the moment; and the speculative thinker with his proofs of immortality upon which he is also dependent. The dividing line between these phenomena and real spiritlessness is much less sharp than Kierkegaard's chapter subdivisions lead one to believe, and this may be intentional. The speculative thinker or the orthodox person — according to Kierkegaard's presentation — does not live in a permanent and intense consciousness of crisis or a permanent reflection upon his relationship to "the good" any more than does the philistine, but he makes himself comfortable in his position, and only differs essentially from the philistine in being more vulnerable and exposed to criticism. And thus Kierkegaard gives particular attention to ritualism itself in two sections of *The Concept of Anxiety,* which are placed between spiritlessness and the demonic state: "Anxiety Dialectically Determined in the Direction of Fate" and "Anxiety Dialectical in the Direction of Guilt." The one deals with heathendom and the immediate genius, the other with Judaism and the religious genius.

"Heathendom" — i.e., Greek antiquity — has "a relationship to spirit, without, however, in the deepest sense positing spirit *qua* spirit. But precisely this possibility is anxiety" [IV 403, CD 86] — and this anxiety is the explanation of the ritual. Kierkegaard speaks of fate as the "nothing" which is the Greeks' perception of anxiety. Here fate means something other than in the aesthete's essay on the tragic. In *The Concept of Anxiety,* fate is something in the future, something imagined, and as such not a posited, external actuality, but a merely psychic reality. For the Greek, fate — as a notion — is at once something unavoidable and something incalculable ("the necessary" and "the accidental"). It is therefore ambiguous, and when the Greek seeks to explain it, the explanation is just as ambiguous as that which it is supposed to explain: "The *oracle* was also like this. . . . The heathen's relationship to the oracle was also anxiety. Here lies the profound and inexplicable tragic element in heathendom. The tragic element, however, is not to be found in the fact that the oracle's pronouncement is ambiguous, but in the fact that the heathen dare not neglect consulting it. He is in a relationship to it; he dare not refrain from consulting it; even at the moment he consults it he is in an ambiguous (sympathetic and antipathetic) relationship to it. Consider the explanations of the oracle on the basis of all this." [IV 404 f., CD 87].

Thus it is not the "objective" forces — fate or the oracle — which create the bond, but the heathen's own anxiety, which makes itself dependent upon the notion and the institution which it itself has produced in order to procure security and mastery over the unknown. Kierkegaard naturally is not writing his analysis with a cultural-historical intent, but out of psychological interest: "What has here been briefly intimated in the context of world history repeats itself in individuals in Christianity" [IV

412, CD 93]. Consulting the oracle was depicted as a collective, institutionalized ritual for the alleviation of the anxiety of the heathens. But rituals can also appear individually. True to his custom, Kierkegaard illuminates the universal with the exceptional, and chooses for this purpose a genius in whose life "the phenomenon shows itself most clearly." From a literary point of view, the fantasy upon Napoleon's military career, which Kierkegaard now writes, is every bit the equal of the analysis of Nero, with which it also shares similarities. the genius is "immediate spirit in the eminent sense"; in his impressive ability to act, the genius becomes great to the world, "but what I might call the planetary core, which radiates forth everything, does not come into being. The genius' significance to himself is nothing," and his existence is determined in relation to such concepts as "good fortune, misfortune, glory, honor, power, immortal renown." Thus, the only thing which differentiates the immediate genius from trivial spiritlessness is intensity and omnipotence, and it is precisely for this reason that Kierkegaard chooses the genius as an example, so that the inner contradiction might show itself all the more clearly. The dialectic between pleasure in destruction and anxiety, which characterized Nero's life, finds its counterpart in the antithesis between omnipotence and impotence in the sketch of Napoleon. "The genius is capable of everything, and yet this is dependent upon something insignificant, to which the genius in turn, by virtue of his omnipotence, imparts an almighty significance" [IV 405-09, CD 88-91].

What Kierkegaard wishes to take hold of in his Napoleon analysis is the *idée fixe* which is the product of the individual's own anxiety. "The faith which subjugated the kingdoms and lands of the earth under his mighty hand, while people thought they were viewing a fairy tale, this same faith overthrew him, and his fall was an even more unfathomable fairy tale." But this faith was superstition. Napoleon was in league with secretive forces, and was dependent upon them. No more than the Greeks, did he dare to refrain from consulting his oracle. He "reads the will of fate" in an invisible writing which only he understands, but when he finds a "dubious commentary" he collapses in impotence. He cannot do without this private ritual, and his frightful wrath is directed at the person who "interferes with him at the moment when he must perform his augury." The armies are arranged in battle formation; everything is ready; the situation is favorable, and yet he must wait until June 14th, for that is the lucky day on which he won at Marengo. The legions await their battle orders; the morning sun dawns splendidly upon the field of battle, but Napoleon hesitates, "because the sun did not rise this splendidly at Austerlitz, and only the Austerlitz-sun inspires and gives victory." Thus it is not "fate" which lifts him up or traps him, for fate is "nothing," and "it is he himself who discovers it" and gives it meaning. Therefore, his judgement of situations is idiosyncratic and his anxiety is incommensurable with the objective danger; he has "anxiety at other times than ordinary people do," because his anxiety itself produces its own object — and therefore the anxiety becomes his fate. "In general people admire his greatness when he wins, yet he is never greater than when he falls before himself. This must be understood as meaning that fate does not proclaim itself in an external way. When, on the other hand, just at the moment that everything is won, humanly speaking, when he then discovers the dubious interpretation and collapses, then one might indeed exclaim: 'What a giant it must take to overthrow him.' But therefore there was no one who was capable of it, excepting himself" [IV 406-08, CD 89-90].

The two sections in *The Concept of Anxiety* which deal with the relationship of anxiety to fate and to guilt are constructed in a parallel fashion. To the Greeks' faith in superstition corresponds the Jewish sacrificial ceremony; to the immediate genius, Napoleon, corresponds "a religious genius." But the section on guilt is not just a repetition of what had come before, for the problem of guilt is far more ramified than the problem of fate.

Judaism is "the standpoint of the law," which can also be expressed as "Judaism reposes in anxiety." With this the dimension within which the analysis takes place has been indicated. The Jewish sacrificial ritual is an analogy to the Greek faith in oracles, and Kierkegaard understands both these phenomena as attempts to reduce anxiety about super-personal forces, which really are simply projected perceptions of anxiety. But, while fate in this (prospective) sense is a psychic phantom, which only comes into being in "the heathen's" worried fantasy, guilt is more than simply a psychic reality for Kierkegaard. It is also an ethical reality. "And yet it is true that as long as it is the object of anxiety it is nothing," i.e., it remains a psychological problem. For the Jews, guilt is "a power which expands everywhere, and which, nevertheless, no one can understand in a deeper sense, while it broods over the whole of existence. That which is to explain it must be of the same character. . . . Therefore, no one can understand the sacrifice either. In this, there is in Judaism a deeply tragic element which bears analogy with the relationship to the oracle in heathendom. The Jew resorts to the sacrifice, but it does not help him, for that which would really help would be annulment of the anxiety's relation to guilt, and a real relationship posited. When this does not happen, the sacrifice becomes ambiguous, which is expressed in its repetition. . . ."

The explanation of this compulsion to repeat lies in the ambivalence of guilt anxiety. Guilt not only deters, but fascinates, and therefore the sacrificial act must be repeated as a preventive action, directed against the continuing, but unconscious, fascination of guilt. "The relationship is, as one of anxiety, always sympathetic and antipathetic . . . for while the anxiety frightens, it keeps up a cunning communication with its object, and cannot ignore it; indeed, it does not want to, for if the individual wants to do this, then remorse will set in." The propitiating sacrifice is thus the Jew's defense against the acknowledgement of guilt. With the help of the ritual, he excludes the consciousness of the ambivalent relationship to the guilt-incurring action which motivates the ritual. It is easy for the psychologist to point the cases "in which the individual, in his anxiety, stares almost desiringly at guilt, and yet fears it" [IV 410 f., CD 92; see above, Chapter V: 7: 3].

3: 3. The "Suppressed Consciousness of Sin"

In continuation of the guilt anxiety of the Jews, Kierkegaard depicts "a religious genius," whose relationship to guilt is analogous to the relationship of the immediate genius to fate. Guilt is an anxiety-laden perception, a "form" which the genius "discovers" by himself. He "projects the guilt," "posits it by himself," but because guilt only exists for him as a perceived possibility, he is obsessed by the perception with the same ambivalent bond which the Jews had: "But when freedom stares at itself, wishing with all its passion, and wants to keep the guilt away, so that one cannot find a speck of it in freedom, then it cannot stop staring at guilt, and this staring is the ambiguous element of anxiety, just as self-denial itself, when it is within the realm of possibility, is a desiring."

The genius is without stain or blemish, the knight of the clean conscience. The question is whether Kierkegaard here wants to describe a religious self-deceiver, a puritanical soul whose moral compulsion for cleanliness prevents him from seeing the beam in his own eye, or whether the religious genius is a sort of paradigmatic figure for him. The answer is: both. The genius is innocent, we learn; he is not afraid to acknowledge that he is guilty, but he "fears to become it." Thus he fears individual actions — in accordance with the train of thought in the rest of *The Concept of Anxiety,* where guilt is the individual action which cancels innocence. All the same, it is exactly in a sketch such as this that the casuistic notion of guilt is dissolved. But the religious genius understands things casuistically, and can thus regard himself as innocent. It is precisely from "the standpoint of the law" that the problem of guilt becomes acute. The religious genius does not judge himself to be guilty, but in his fantasy-occupation with guilt, "sin's anxiety [is] upon him in the condition of possibility." He has guilt-feelings and notions of guilt, not a personal acknowledgement of guilt, for his feeling has no distinct, present sin with which to associate itself; but just for this reason the notion overwhelms him and presses him firmly into the thought of guilt, so that it is "as if the whole world's guilt united itself in making him guilty, and, what amounts to the same thing, as if he, in becoming guilty, became guilty of the guilt of the whole world."

Judging by all appearances and according to Kierkegaard's psychology, this tension ought to be released by means of anxiety about sin producing sin. However, we will allow the genius to remain in his tension while we ask how Kierkegaard conceives him. The text betrays the fact that Kierkegaard is not a little bit impressed by his hero's uncompromising disavowal of spiritlessness's pedestrian homeostatic solutions to the question of guilt. In his development of this situation, Kierkegaard comments with several more general observations upon the concept of guilt, and this contributes to the impression that Kierkegaard is allied with his hero. But, as in other texts (the Antigone essay), here, too, there seem to be two people present, the experiencing individual, the genius himself, who expresses his self-understanding in an intimated inner monologue, and the pseudonym, Vigilius, who allows him to speak, while he himself comments discreetly and sporadically. The problem is simply to keep the two voices separated, and Kierkegaard has not made the matter easy for his reader. It is necessary to insist upon the idea that the religious genius is presented as the analogy to the immediate genius and to the Jews. In these analyses there is no doubt about the ritual externality or about the diversionary function of ritual. The chapter heading for all these sketches, including the depiction of the religious genius, is "anxiety as the Consequence of That Sin, Which is The Absence of the Consciousness of Sin." The author expressly distances himself from his hero in a footnote, where he reminds the reader of the psychology of innocence which had appeared earlier in that book: "However, one must not forget that the present analogy is invalid to the extent that we are not dealing with innocence in the later individual, but with the suppressed consciousness of sin."

Thus, the genius is not innocent, but thinks that he is. His method of suppressing the consciousness of sin is not a sacrificial ritual, but his own fantastic notions about a guilt which he has outside himself, while in his own freedom from guilt, "not a speck of it is to be found." His ritual is less resistant than the Jewish sacrifice, but it has the same function, to ward off the acknowledgement of guilt as personal consciousness. An overwhelming, ambivalent, and emotionally colored, directionless guilt anxiety is a part of the notion of personal innocence. But anxiety about sin produces sin, we know: "[I]f guilt were actually posited, [the genius] posits it by himself." The guilt anxiety seeks out an object to which to fasten itself: "[A]s soon as . . . remorse breaks through with the actual sin, then it has the actual sin as its object." However, this is not the real point here. On the contrary, the story of the religious genius is the story of a recovery, not a report of a guilt anxiety which makes a man into a transgressor of the law, but an account of the suppressed consciousness of sin which breaks forth and topples over the genius' fantastic notions. A tension is built up; the genius is at the point where his consciousness of freedom only relates itself to the anxiety-laden notion of the whole world's guilt which threatens to overwhelm him—until finally the notion is punctured and he understands that he is guilty: ". . . and this is the moment of culmination, the moment when he is greatest, not the moment when the sight of his piety was like an extraordinary festivity of a holy day, but the moment when, by his own devices, he sinks before himself into the depth of the consciousness of sin" [IV 415-18, CD 96-98].

The story of the religious genius does not merely point beyond the pathology and toward recovery, but *eo ipso* beyond the legalistic understanding of guilt as well, and toward the Christian understanding, where guilt is not this or that transgression, but man's total misuse of his created life, and where the repentant individual must therefore surrender himself and his remorse in order to receive, in faith, the forgiveness of sins which is offered to him.

But recovery is not the only possible consequence of the anxiety-laden notion of guilt. Another possible consequence is when the frantic anxiety about sin compulsively produces sin time after time. Before we come to "anxiety about the evil," however, it can be enlightening to acquaint ourselves with what Freud has to say about guilt.

3:4. *Excursus on Freud.*

"It was a surprise to find that an increase in this *Ucs.* [unconscious] sense of guilt can turn people into criminals. But it is undoubtedly a fact. In many criminals, especially youthful ones, it is possible to detect a very powerful sense of guilt which existed before the crime, and is therefore not its result, but its motive. It is as if it was a relief to be able to fasten this unconscious sense of guilt on to something real and immediate." This is Freud's formulation of the idea that anxiety about sin produces sin. But the entirety of the section in *The Ego and the Id,* from which this passage is taken, is interesting in relation to Kierkegaard, because Freud here suggests a continuation of the idea of the repression of guilt which had been experimentally put forth in *Totem and Taboo* (above, Chapter V: 7: 3).

What is noteworthy is that at this point Freud does not limit his discussion to the genesis of the guilt-feelings, and to their well-known, violent expression in melancholia, where the sick person abandons himself to the guilt-feelings; the guilt-feelings can also manifest themselves in the compulsive neurosis, where the patient, in spite of his overwhelming sense of guilt, tries to convince himself and the physician of the fact that he has no reason to feel guilty. Perhaps, Freud writes, guilt-feelings not only play a role in these neuroses, but in all the more severe neurotic situations, and perhaps it is precisely this factor which determines the degree of severity of the neurosis. It is not the conscious guilt-feelings which present the greatest difficulty, but the unconscious. It concerns "what may be called a 'moral' factor, a sense of guilt, which is finding its satisfaction in the illness and refuses to give up the punishment of suffering." This is therefore a very important hindrance to the therapeutic treatment of neurosis, because it causes the patient to oppose recovery. The task of the analyst here is not to explain the causes of the manifest guilt-feelings, but to make an unconscious guilt-feeling conscious. The task is difficult, perhaps insoluble for the psychoanalyst, Freud explains in an important footnote, because the analyst cannot do anything directly for the patient, and "nothing indirectly but the slow procedure of unmasking its unconscious repressed roots, and thus gradually changing it into a *conscious* sense of guilt." Freud does not say that the neurosis is caused by the absence of a recognition of guilt or that the way to recovery must go through the needle's eye of repentance, but this must be more or less what he means. But it is difficult for the analyst to bring about this recovery (unless we are dealing with an artificial, "borrowed" guilt-feeling), because the rules of analysis normally forbid him to play "the part of prophet, saviour and redeemer" [Freud XIX 50-52].

As far as I can see, Freud did not elaborate on the idea of the repressed consciousness of guilt in his later writings (where, on the other hand, there is often mention of the origins and inhibiting effects of the conscious guilt-feelings). However, Freud did not completely repress the idea, for he later notes that this form of resistance evades psychoanalytic recovery: "The fifth [resistance], coming from the *super-ego* and the last to be discovered, is also the most obscure though not always the least powerful one. It seems to originate from the sense of guilt or the need for punishment; and it opposes every move towards success, including, therefore, the patient's own recovery through analysis" [Freud XX 160, from *Inhibitions, Symptoms and Anxiety*].

This admission comes close to being what is perhaps the most "Kierkegaardian" element in Freud's theory of this problem, for the idea that the repressed guilt can only be uncovered indirectly, and the warning against posing as a prophet or saviour of souls is in complete agreement with Kierkegaard, who says, for example: "But to what end does the speaker speak so terrifyingly? For only in himself does a person understand that he is guilty. The person who does not understand it in this way, misunderstands" [V 227, TCS 34]. But this will be discussed in more detail later. Kierkegaard begins about where Freud leaves off, but perhaps Freud's understanding of the problem of guilt can contribute to the understanding of why Kierkegaard must refer to an authority beyond the patient-physician relationship, and outside interpersonal relationships in general, who has the authority to speak personally to the individual about sin and about the forgiveness of sins.

Freud's suggestion of the repressed realization of guilt has been followed up by modern psychologists, who, in sharp polemic against Freud, maintain that it is not "the id," but "the super-ego" which is being repressed. I will not offer an opinion as to whether this psychoanalytic neomoralism has any connection whatever with Kierkegaard.[13] Nor shall I attempt to coordinate Freud's suggestions unambiguously with Kierkegaard's theories, but I will satisfy myself with putting them forward for consideration. Of particular interest is the idea of the need for suffering punishment, which causes the individual to find satisfaction "in illness"; the idea of unconscious (or unclearly perceived) guilt-feelings; and the idea of the necessity of making them conscious.

3:5. *Insane Remorse*

The "anxiety about the evil" which is described at the conclusion of *The Concept of Anxiety* strongly recalls the earlier description of the anxiety about sin which "produces sin." And with this the similarity is also demonstrated both to "Jewish" guilt anxiety, which produces ritual, and also to the anxiety of the religious genius. In all these situations, the individual relates himself to guilt as an imagined, future possibility, and the factual action is a product of the anxiety. This is the case regardless of whether the perception of guilt is merely something imagined or whether it has a definite, completed individual action with which to associate itself— "for a longing after sin can even conceal itself in remorse," as it is written at one point in the journal [Pap. III A 85, Hong 3783].

All the same, "anxiety about the evil" is not simply a repetition of the earlier analyses. I cite the central passage, in which Kierkegaard allows the rhythm of the sentences to dramatize the psychological description of the climax: "The sin which is posited is an illegitimate actuality; it is actuality and is posited by the individual as actuality in remorse, but the remorse does not become the freedom of the individual. The remorse is reduced to being a possibility in relation to sin; in other words, the remorse cannot annul the sin; it can only sorrow over it. Sin goes forward in its consistency; remorse follows step by step, but always a moment too late. It forces itself to look upon what is frightful, but it is like the insane Lear ('O thou shattered masterpiece of creation!')[14] who has lost the reins of government and has only kept the power to grieve. Anxiety is here at its highest point. Remorse has become insane and anxiety has been intensified into remorse. The consistency of sin goes onward; it drags the individual along with it like a woman whom the executioner drags by the hair, while she screams in despair. The anxiety goes in advance; it discovers the consistency before it comes to pass, just as one can feel that a storm is approaching; it comes nearer; the individual trembles like a horse who comes groaning to the place where once it was frightened. Sin conquers. Anxiety casts itself despairingly into the arms of remorse. Remorse dares its ultimate effort. It conceives of the consistency of sin as a penal suffering, and of perdition as a consequence of sin. It is lost; its judgement has been pronounced, its condemnation certain, and the increased severity of the sentence is that the individual is to be dragged through life to the place of execution. In other words, remorse has become insane."

In the present context it is not of decisive significance to fasten one or another modern psychiatric label to this description. The characteristics which connect anxiety about the evil with Kierkegaard's other sketches of ritualism are clear enough: the stereotype; the catathymic character; the unfree, compulsively accelerating course which evades control by the will, because the over-sensitive individual is governed by the anxiety which is outside of him like an alien force, and which automatically translates itself into action when it discovers the inescapable perception of guilt. Here it is the remorse itself which functions as the ritual, as it were. That remorse "is reduced to being a possibility in relation to sin" means that it serves the same purpose as the Jewish sacrifice: to avoid the real admission of guilt. Its function is to avert a repetition of the sinful action ("annul the sin"). But where the Jewish ritual functioned in a stable fashion, insane remorse is ineffective as preventive action, and instead of the sacrifice it is the sin which is repeated compulsively, because the anxiety overwhelms the individual and takes the place of remorse. As concrete examples of phenomena which can be the object of this compulsive repetition, Kierkegaard mentions, among other things, drinking, the taking of opium, and debauchery, as well as various sorts of emotional outbursts. The individual could, for example, feel remorse about an outburst of anger in order to avoid a repetition. "But the remorse cannot make him free; in that he is mistaken. The opportunity comes; anxiety has already discovered it; every thought trembles, and anxiety sucks the blood out of the strength of remorse and shakes its head; it is as though the anger had already conquered; he already suspects the crushing of freedom, which is reserved for the next moment; the moment comes; anger conquers" [IV 423-25, CD 102-04].

The remorse is impotent, but why? Both here and in the section on the Jews and the religious genius it is a case of individuals with strong moral consciousness who fight against sin. But, while a cunning desire for the object of anxiety, unacknowledged by the people involved, was what lay behind the Jewish ritualism and the guilt anxiety of the genius, there must be another explanation of the anxiety about the evil. The individual relates himself to a definite, completed action as the object of remorse; he conceives of his sin as illegitimate and tries to escape from it. When this does not succeed, this ought — according to what we have heard earlier in that book — to be due to the fact that in spite of everything he has placed the sin in a relationship of possibility to himself, and "in one or another deceitful way prevents it from becoming something past and done" [IV 398, CD 82]. But the deceitfulness does not consist in the fact that he cunningly desires the sinful action itself. It consists, on the contrary, in the fact that he desires the guilt-feeling, the anxiety, and the self-degradation. Therefore he cannot let go of the sin. In remorse he conceives of his sin as a penal judgement, and the feeling of being the damned person who must be dragged throughout existence to the place of execution is the terror of his life. But it is also a feeling, or a self-understanding, which he defends passionately, and with which he will not part at any price. In the sketch of this defense lies the explanation of the deceitfulness of insane remorse. In addition, we also get here a more detailed commentary upon the adjective "insane," for in the final phase of the development, when the guilt-burdened individual fights for his right to feel himself condemned, Kierkegaard describes him in a state of autistic and paranoid obsession, in which he is inaccessible to arguments and sound reason: "The sophism which insane remorse manages to produce every moment cannot be conquered by any dialectic. Such a remorse possesses a contrition which is much stronger in its passionate expression and in its dialectics than is true remorse. (In another sense, it is naturally much weaker, but it is still remarkable what people who have observed cases such as this have noted, what gifts of persuasion and what eloquence such remorse possesses with which to disarm every objection, to convince everyone who approaches it, in order then to despair over itself once again, when the diversion is past.) It is a waste of time to wish to stop this terror with words and phrases, and the person who attempts it can always be sure that his preaching is like the babble of children compared to the elemental eloquence which such remorse has at its command" [IV 424, CD 103].

Thus, as Freud also saw, the resistance to recovery which stems from the consciousness of guilt, or from the need for punishment, is the most difficult of all to deal with. To explain Kierkegaard's concept of anxiety about the evil it is not sufficient to place it in relation to his other analyses of guilt anxiety and guilt anxiety's cunning and sympathetic relation to sin. It must be placed in relation to the dominant concepts: "anxiety about the good" or "despair about the eternal and over oneself." On the other hand, "anxiety about the evil" can then reveal a hitherto unnoticed side of the demonic anxiety about the good, the unconscious guilt-feeling.

3: 6. *"Anxiety About the Evil" and "Anxiety About the Good"*

In *The Concept of Anxiety,* Vigilius differentiates very carefully between "anxiety about the evil" and "anxiety about the good." Anxiety about the evil is the guilt-conscious person's sin anxiety, while perceptions of guilt apparently play no special role in anxiety about the good, which, on the other hand, is characterized by the attempt to install oneself in the state of crisis.

Nevertheless, the relationship of opposition is perhaps not the only relationship between the two conditions. "The evil" and "the good" in this arrangement are not simply opposites, for "the evil" here means the distinct individual action or the notion about it, which is the object of anxiety, while "the good" is not simply the individual moral action, but is freedom, redemption. Nor, according to *The Concept of Anxiety,* is the antithesis of sin virtue, but faith. A closer analysis of Kierkegaard's texts thus shows that the person who has anxiety about "the evil" (the definite sinful action) also has anxiety about "the good" (freedom, recovery). But Vigilius does not express himself to this effect; on the contrary, he emphasizes the difference between the two states. I have asserted earlier that *The Concept of Anxiety* is not especially clear on certain points, as if it had not been thought through to completion. Descriptively it naturally makes sense to differentiate between the very guilt-laden conflict in "anxiety about the evil" and the conflict in "anxiety about the good," where notions of guilt apparently are not of decisive significance. However, a closer, textual-critical analysis, which includes, among other things, Kierkegaard's manuscripts, shows that it was first during the writing of the book itself that Kierkegaard differentiated sharply between the two conditions, and that in so doing he forgot an older plan which employed guilt anxiety and anxiety about freedom as two aspects of the same conflict.[15]

However, in this descriptive separation the book loses a diagnostic point which is suggested in Kierkegaard's manuscripts, but which first becomes clear in *The Sickness Unto Death*—although there it appears under a different terminology. Thus when I maintain, in opposition to Vigilius' statement, that anxiety about the evil is *also* an anxiety about the good (freedom, recovery, communication), it is not because I am a better psychologist than he, but because Anti-Climacus is, and it is also because Vigilius himself hints at this connection in his sketch of the elemental eloquence with which insane remorse manages to disarm every objection against its self-understanding.

"Anxiety about the evil" is one of the sections in *The Concept of Anxiety* which most clearly anticipates the thinking of *The Sickness Unto Death*. This affinity is decisive, because it is Anti-Climacus who first makes possible the final interpretation. When Vigilius here speaks of "the consistency of sin," it is natural to place this expression in connection with Anti-Climacus' description of "the continuity of sin" and "the consistency of evil." But in *The Sickness Unto Death*, "the continuity of sin" was indeed not characterized by any overwhelming guilt-feeling and anxiety about the evil, but was on the contrary a further development of Vigilius' concept of anxiety about the good, in which the despairing person encapsulates himself in order to be able to harden himself against the recognition of guilt (above, Chapter VI: 4: 3).

The two conditions—on the one hand, anxiety about the evil; on the other hand, anxiety about the good, and the corresponding phenomena in *The Sickness Unto Death*—show themselves to be very closely related when one says that they relate to one another as weakness is related to defiance, or as that which is reacted against is related to the reaction-formation. The difference is relative, the antitheses are dialectical, such that defiance is a "profound" weakness and weakness is a "profound" defiance. Anxiety about the good is self-assertion in the face of the possibility of recovery. Anxiety about the evil is passionate self-degradation and self-condemnation. But in self-degradation there is also the self-assertive element that it *wants* to be condemned. It is in this dialectic (cf. above, Chapter VI: 3) that the point of coincidence lies for these formations: for the "weak" and the "strong" forms, for cowardice and pride, for anxiety about the evil and anxiety about the good. They are variants of one and the same conflict model, whose key forms are Vigilius' "anxiety about the good" and Anti-Climacus' "despair about the eternal and over oneself."

Anxiety *about* the evil is a despair *over* oneself, and thus a despair *about* the eternal (the good, communication, recovery) as well. Or, using the corresponding language from the latter portion of *The Sickness Unto Death,* anxiety *about* the evil is a despair *over* sin, but thereby also a despair *about* the forgiveness of sins [cf. XI 252 note, SD 244 note].

Thus, sin anxiety is a hardening of the self against the good, a resistance to recovery. But if it is correct that anxiety about the evil is a "profound" anxiety about the good, then the reverse must also be the case: "anxiety about the good" must be a "profound" sin anxiety; it must contain an unconscious guilt-feeling, and this repressed guilt-feeling must be the explanation of its resistance to the good.

In *The Concept of Anxiety* it is only suggested in individual, scattered remarks that the demonic anxiety about the good also contains an unsolved guilt problem. No conscious, articulated experience of guilt is to be found here, although a sense of unfreedom or that the situation is "illegitimate" may well be present. However, a bit earlier in that book one finds a short, pithy passage about the transition in which the individual succeeds in forgetting the problem of guilt, and in which the manifest ("notable") anxiety about sin and its consequences "more and more disappears": "The more anxiety abates here, the more it means that sin's consequence has entered into the flesh and blood of the individual, and that sin has acquired the right of citizenship within the individual." But the important point, which Kierkegaard here summarizes in a short, concise formula, is that guilt anxiety does not disappear, but on the contrary is strengthened, when it is excluded from consciousness and is thus no longer recognizable as guilt anxiety: "But seen from outside such an individual, and from the point of view of spirit, this anxiety is greater than any other" [IV 422 f., CD 101 f.].

If one compares this with Kierkegaard's original manuscript, one sees that it was originally the introduction to his section on "anxiety about the good." The explanation of this formation is thus repressed or disguised guilt anxiety. Anxiety about the good is a "profound" anxiety about guilt and about the recognition of guilt, and here as elsewhere what is profound is what is of decisive significance. Vigilius does not say this directly or clearly, for he is too busy with his descriptive differentiation between guilt anxiety and the demonic state to do so. But Anti-Climacus confirms this to excess. What is common to the forms of despair — which according to him are the positive consequences of anxiety about the good — is indeed precisely the relationship of negative dependence upon what has been excluded, the reaction's active-passive, offensive exclusion from the self-perception of the recognition of guilt: the despairing person must "consistently regard everything which goes under the name of repentance, and everything which goes under the name of grace, not merely to be empty and meaningless, but as his enemy, as that from which he most of all must defend himself . . ." [XI 248, SD 240].

Thus "anxiety about the good" is motivated by a repression of the consciousness of guilt, which in "anxiety about the evil" is manifest — and insane. In his "madness," the person with this guilt anxiety is lost to the world, and in any case, the comparison with *The Sickness Unto Death* must make it clear how closely related reaction-formation, formations of defiance, and autism are. But Kierkegaard's assertion is that anxiety about the evil is nevertheless the condition of possibility for its own conquest of itself. The advantage of guilt anxiety is that it is manifest. Therefore anxiety about the evil, "seen from a higher standpoint, [is] in the good," because, in contrast to anxiety about the good, it has not excluded the recognition of guilt, but has "only" misunderstood it. Guilt anxiety is a crisis; it is sin, but it is not by definition a perpetual motion, for it contains the possibility of change. Its misunderstanding of guilt is serious enough and pathogenic enough. We have already seen it suggested in Freud that the melancholy person must in one or another misunderstood way be correct in his self-accusations, while the question to be answered was "why a man has to be ill before he can be accessible to a truth of this kind." In this way — more or less — Kierkegaard believes that, in addition to being pathogenic, manifest guilt anxiety also contains the possibility of truth and of recovery, if it will surrender its latent self-assertion and, thereby, its anxiety — just as, according to Anti-Climacus, despair is not only the sickness unto death, but also the means of recovery [XI 134, SD 143]; because, "for every moment that despair is held open, there is also the possibility of salvation" [XI 197, SD 196].

"The only thing which truly can disarm the sophistry of remorse is faith, courage to believe that the condition itself is a new sin, courage to forsake anxiety without anxiety, of which only faith is capable — without, however, annihilating the anxiety, but remaining eternally young, and continually extricating itself from the moment of death in anxiety." The added phrase is important, because it expresses the fact that recovery does not consist merely in a repression or a superficial decision to ignore the problem. The situation does not call for the simple obliteration of the recognition of guilt, but for "getting the individual properly situated in relation to sin," that is, to place the individual in his relation to "the atonement." As something ambiguous, anxiety cannot annul itself, but must be annulled by means of the relation to a power which can command the individual to believe in the forgiveness of sins. In this situation, remorse will thus finally "annul itself by means of new remorse . . . when it then collapses" [IV 425 f., CD 104-05].

Or, as it is written in connection with the "Jewish" sacrificial ritual: "[I]t is first in sin that the atonement is posited, and its sacrifice is not repeated" [IV 411, CD 93].

4. The Richard III Complex

4:1. *Hypocrisy*

A short summary of the reactive beginnings of despair is contained in this passage from *The Sickness Unto Death:* "[F]irst a man sins out of frailty and weakness; and then — yes, then perhaps he learns to flee to God, and to be helped to come to the faith which saves from all sin; but we are not speaking of this right here — then he despairs over his weakness, and becomes either a pharisee, who despairingly pushes things to a certain legal righteousness, or he despairingly hurls himself into sin again" [XI 218, SD 213].

As far as faith is concerned, "we are not speaking of this right here." As for the amoralism which hurls itself into sin — alias the defiant formations of despair — they have been discussed above and they will be discussed again later on. Here, however, it is pharisaism with which we first must acquaint ourselves. In *The Sickness Unto Death,* Kierkegaard presents the pharisee under a heading which is connected with anxiety about the evil: "The Sin of Despairing Over One's Sin." The portrait of the pharisee is not without similarities to the portrait of the remorseful individual in *The Concept of Anxiety,* who had gotten himself stuck firmly in his notions of guilt and punishment. Kierkegaard himself alludes to the problem of guilt which was contained in the earlier book when he compares his pharisee-type with "the anxiety about sin, which sometimes nearly worries a person into sin, because it is self-love to want to be proud of oneself, to be without sin" [XI 251, SD 243]. The reference applies perhaps best to the religious genius. Pharisaism in *The Sickness Unto Death* differs from anxiety about the evil in being more quotidian and unimpressed. The situation is otherwise about the same: the sophistical remorse gets firmly stuck and subsides into depression. Pharisaism is less deep, is less violent in its manifestations, than insane remorse, and it is more untrustworthy and dishonest. Vigilius' insanely remorseful person was indeed really convinced of his guilt, while the pharisee hardly is, even though he also despairs over his sin. The example is a man who early in life became addicted to one or another form of sin, but who has gradually conquered the temptation, until one day he has a relapse, which causes him to despair. But, says Anti-

Climacus, one must not always accept the expression "despair over sin" at face value: "In a confused unclarity about himself and his own significance, or with a touch of hypocrisy, or with the assistance of subtlety and sophistry, which is present in all despair, despair over sin is not without a tendency to give itself the appearance of being something good. Then it is supposed to be an expression that this is a profound nature, which is therefore so very sensitive to its sin." When he assures us in emphatic language that his relapse is a source of great pain to him and brings him to despair, so that he can never forgive himself, the converted sinner in his double-faced attitude after the relapse betrays the fact that his remorse is artificial. What he overlooks in his grief is, from a theological point of view, that "if God now wants to forgive him, then he could at least have the goodness to forgive himself," and, from a psychological point of view, that he is not sorrowing over his sins, but about his injured self-understanding, about the blot upon his sense of moral honor. "The matter is this: during the time that he successfully resisted the temptation, he became better in his own eyes than he really was, and he has become proud of himself," whence comes the grief. His depression can no more annul the sin than insane remorse can; it can only grieve about it. However, the pharisee in *The Sickness Unto Death* has more control over the situation; he does not go mad, but only becomes depressed: "It is possible that his sorrow could plunge him into the darkest melancholia, and a foolish spiritual counselor might be close to admiring him for his deep soul and for the power of the good in him — as if this were of the good. And his wife, yes she feels herself deeply humbled in comparison with such a serious and holy man, who can sorrow about sin like this" [XI 249-51, SD 241-44].

Kierkegaard's pharisee differs from his New Testament colleagues in that he not only praises himself for his goodness, but also for his badness. In the *Postscript* pharisaism is cited as an example of what is involuntarily comic: ". . . [T]hree 'awakened' pietists carry on a dispute of honor among themselves as to which one is the greatest sinner" [VII 502, CUP 458]. For Kierkegaard this is a specifically Christian phenomenon, pride in self-degradation, dishonesty in grief. In a religious discourse which was published shortly after *The Sickness Unto Death,* Kierkegaard has given a description of the specifically Christian form of hypocrisy, the cunning which employs and which is determined by Christian notions of humility and the consciousness of sin. The Gospel condemned the moralistic pharisees and justified the honest publican. "But there is also another sort of hypocrisy," namely that in which the hypocrite takes the publican as his exemplar, and yet remains a hypocrite, placing himself self-effacingly in the background, but only in order to "have contempt for others" and pharisaically thank God that he is not—like the pharisee! "Oh yes, this is certainly the way things are; Christianity came into the world and taught humility, but not everyone learned humility from Christianity; hypocrisy learned to change its mask and remained the same, or rather became even worse. Christianity came into the world and taught that you must not proudly and vainly seek a place at the head of the table at the banquet, but sit at the foot of the table—and soon pride and vanity sat vainly at the foot of the table, the same pride and vanity, yet no, not the same, but even worse" [XI 293 f., ChD 371]. Indeed, the only thing which separates Kierkegaard from Nietzsche in this piece is the fact that, having said this, Kierkegaard simply writes his discourse on the publican, who confessed his sin before God and went home having been justified.

The pride of the pharisee is a feeling of comparison which makes it possible for him to set a higher value upon himself than upon his surroundings, even when he formally degrades himself. In the pharisaism which appears in Christian disguise, one not only impresses one's fellow man, but one is impressed by oneself. Self-assertion in self-degradation is not merely a conscious deception of the surrounding world, but a thoroughgoing self-deception. With the assistance of his analyses of what—to use an Hegelian expression—might be called the moral forms of the evil, Kierkegaard gets on the track of hypocrisy not only as a moral-philosophical, but also as a psychopathological problem, not simply as a conscious notion, but as an impenetrable illusion about life. Vigilius has formulated it briefly: "Therefore all hypocrisy ends with being hypocritical to oneself, because the hypocrite is offended in himself or is an offense to himself. Therefore, all offense, when it is not annulled, ends in hypocrisy toward others . . ." [IV 454 f., CD 129].[16]

4:2. "Against Cowardice"

In an edifying discourse from 1844 with the title "Against Cowardice," Kierkegaard discusses the moral hypocrisy which cunningly feels better about itself than it will admit, and he briefly places it in context with some of the problems which also have occupied us in this chapter: the inwardly directed aggressiveness of reflected sorrow; self-enjoyment in self-effacement; and pride in weakness. The discourse was published shortly after The Concept of Anxiety and it elaborates upon a theme from that book: "Pride and cowardice are one and the same" [V 145, ED IV 83]. Melancholia is very pithily defined here in good agreement both with the two essays on sorrow and grief from Either/Or and with the analysis of the self-condemnation of insane remorse—as follows: "Here we are not speaking of hypocrisy, which wishes to seem better than it is, but of the opposite, of a hatred of oneself, which is unjust to the man himself, so that he is merely being inventive in finding ways to increase his torment. But yet hatred of oneself is nevertheless also self-love, and all self-love is cowardice" [V 165, ED IV 109].

The edifying discourse can help us get a bit further along in the understanding of these problems. Apparently the subject is very special and "private," for it apparently has to do with a Kierkegaardian self-analysis and self-criticism. And, while I have hitherto attempted to keep the private person Kierkegaard out of these matters, I can see no possibility of doing so any longer. However, the intent still remains that this should not be an analysis of Kierkegaard, but an excursion into the area which we might call his personal self-understanding, in order to bring forth a couple of viewpoints which do not obligate us to any particular conception of him. This will only be done to the extent that it serves to illuminate his psychological thinking. It is certainly impossible to separate this thinking entirely from its originator unless one wishes to leave parts of the thinking untouched. Therefore, some portions of the pages which follow will be a mixture of psychological biography and a summary of Kierkegaard's psychology, but the intent is not to direct attention upon the biography. Self-analyses are also analyses, and to the extent that I cite several passages in which I think that Kierkegaard has been superficial and dishonest in his analysis, this is only done to serve as a background for the understanding of other passages where this does not seem to me to be the case. I will not offer any opinion as to whether it is the superficial, self-glorifying, rationalizing, mythologizing analyses, or the deeply revealing, de-mythologizing, intensely honest settling-up with himself which is correct from the historical-biographical point of view.

On to "Against Cowardice." In order to link this with what has gone before, there is reason to recall that Antigone was indeed a sort of idealist; she had an idea, the idea of Oedipus and the honor of the family, for which she chose to sacrifice herself and her happiness. And even if this idea were perhaps an irrational product of her own anxiety, still, according to Aesthete A, there is nothing which ennobles a person more than just such a possession of a secret and an ideal consistency in one's life. And there is no doubt that Kierkegaard is in agreement with his pseudonym in this judgement. "Every decision which is good in its most profound roots, is silent; for it has God as its confidant, and it goes in to him in its secret chamber," we read in the edifying discourse. But just as Antigone became proud in her secrecy and was therefore unable to give up her melancholy idea, so is this also the case in this discourse. The point of departure for these deliberations is the scriptural warning against hypocrisy, which says

that the person who fasts must salve his head and wash his face in order not
to display his piety to people. But we have just seen Kierkegaard draw
attention to the fact that there is also another, more cunning form of
hypocrisy than the sort which wishes "to seem better." This, then, is the
theme of the discourse. The person who wishes to avoid hypocrisy toward
others by avoiding the display of his piety risks ending in hypocrisy toward
himself. The anti-hypocrite comes into an oppositional relationship to the
world; he is misunderstood. To that extent, he thus receives no reward for
his good works—outwardly. "Let us see, however. When he suffers from
the misunderstanding, he easily becomes self-important; he does not
indeed judge others, but wants his works to judge others, and in a cunning
manner he builds up a credit balance with God, if I dare say it" [V 161-67,
ED IV 103-11].

It is a case of a very particular psychological type, an ironizing, moral
self-righteousness which prides itself in its imagined problems instead of
opening itself to the tasks presented by reality and his fellow man. And yet
the theme is perhaps not quite so specialized as might appear. In any case,
Kierkegaard has sought to elevate the problem out of its private seat by
asking what motives underlie this behavior. The discourse does not provide
any unambiguous answer, but it is satisfied with suggesting what motives
could be underlying or involved in this behavior. The person who is in a
position such as this, the discourse says, must ask himself, "[1] whether it
might not be that a defiance, an anger, is bitterly involved in his efforts.
Does not the wrong road lie close at hand? Oh, perhaps there was even a
person who called down a curse upon himself, yet who was right; whose
conscience was saved by the thing for which he was judged, but who was
wrong in keeping silent, wrong, perhaps, [2] for the reason that he lacked
the courage to acknowledge his weakness to himself, that he would rather
appear bad and he hated than be loved and have his weakness become
apparent to others. Oh, perhaps there was a person who bore useless
sufferings which were so heavy that they could inspire a poet, and who thus
[3] sometimes became self-important in the pain of being misunderstood,
and who, if he would but be honest, would have to admit to himself that he
could have mitigated his sufferings with a little admission! Oh, perhaps
there was a person who went for days and for years under the yoke of
misunderstanding, who did not become self-important, because he
suffered under it as a punishment, and who yet [4] had permitted himself a
revision, so that he was not being punished for that for which he should
have been punished, but for something else, and who accepted people's
mistaken judgement of him as a judgement from the hand of God, but
allowed the people to be mistaken, [5] because silence and rashness can

also indeed conceal a melancholic who loves the good in melancholy fashion. This must be very strenuous, and what is worse, the melancholia is nourished and strengthened by it. And silence and indifference to everything can indeed also conceal a bad conscience which nevertheless takes from the good the expression that it wishes simply to suffer its punishment [6]" [V 164 f., ED IV 108].

This is indeed an entire catalogue of problems, and I have therefore assigned numbers to several points: 1) aggressiveness; 2) fear of the revelation of weakness; 3) self-involvedness in suffering; 4) disdain for men with the help of the relation to God; 5) the role, and 6) the fact that this is written by Kierkegaard himself. The last point is not the least in significance. What we are here presented with is the register of Kierkegaard's specific sins, and what makes the strongest impression, perhaps, is the fact that it is he himself who reels it off. He hereby frees his reader from a lot of trouble with settling accounts with Kierkegaard, for it has already been done — in 1844. But it is true that Kierkegaard lived all the way to 1855, and various things might perhaps give the indication that this list is not merely a settling of accounts, but also a prophecy of what was to come. Even in the settling-up with his own hypocrisy, we have no guarantee of his own honesty, for — according to Kierkegaard's own psychology — one can of course also be proud of the settling-up; one can become interesting to oneself as the person who manages to undertake this excellent settling-up.

We have come to the line at which a balance must be struck between the presentation of Kierkegaard's psychology and the analysis of his psyche, this latter only to the minimal extent necessary. The point is that Kierkegaard is his own interpreter, and that my own combinations build upon his self-interpretations. Therefore, we must also take account of the self-interpretations in which he does not seem to come up to his own standards. If Kierkegaard had never misunderstood or interpreted wrongly or dishonestly, he would never have understood or interpreted correctly either.

4:3. *The Fear of Being Found Out*

The list of problems from the discourse "against Cowardice" will form the theme for the pages which follow. Points 2 and 5 are particularly related to one another. Silence and rashness can conceal melancholia, functioning as roles or masks which cover the weakness which the melancholic will not reveal to others at any cost. "From my childhood I was in the grip of an enormous melancholia, whose depth finds its only true expression in the equally enormous ability, granted to me, to conceal it under an apparent merriness and joy in living—my only joy, almost from as far back as I can remember, has been that no one could discover how unhappy I felt; this situation (the equally large dimensions of melancholia and the art of dissimulation) means, of course, that I was referred back to myself and the relationship to God," it is written in the autobiographical section of *The Point of View for My Work as an Author*. "That which reconciled me to my fate and my suffering was the fact that I—alas, the unhappy, tormented prisoner—had received the unlimited freedom to be able to deceive, that I had become, and had received permission to become, unconditionally alone with the pain . . ." [XIII 604 and 606, PV 76 and 78-79].

Kierkegaard does not want to be found out. He has his melancholia; it is an established institution, world-famous in our times ("the melancholy Dane"), but in his own times was known only by himself— *The Point of View* was only published after his death, among other reasons, because the book said too much about himself—because no one might know about it. In the edifying discourse it said "that he lacked the courage to acknowledge his weakness to himself, that he would rather appear evil and be hated than be loved and have his weakness become apparent to others." This is not said quite as directly in *The Point of View*, but one does not need to look far to get the message. The role does not necessarily have to be that of the hated person. In personal relations I am a light and merry fellow, it is written in the journal in 1850: "It is not noticed that this is a form of melancholia, and just a sign of how deeply I suffer, just as I of course also shudder at being made the object of other people's pity. Perhaps this is pride; however, I understand it as the grace of God, that he, in not freeing me from sufferings, has given me the consolation of being personally able to hide them" [Pap. X 2 A 433]. The theme of pity is characteristic of Kierkegaard, and no less characteristic is the fact that it is combined with the relation to God. One should also take note of the question of whether this is pride. Kierkegaard has never said a word to anyone about how he really suffers—"I cannot. God is my only refuge" [X 3 A 488]. His odd appearance is "a cleverly invented deception, under which I conceal my misery" [Pap. X 2 A 61, Dru 970]. Particularly when he broke with Regine, he suffered so much that anyone "could be moved to the deepest pity if he really found out, quite literally, how I suffered. It was precisely this that intensified the pain, that I knew that I was a sure victim of pity—therefore I did everything, everything of which I was capable, and it was granted to me to be able to conceal it entirely" [Pap. X 2 A 105, Dru 982]. "I have been wronged indescribably when people have continually thought that it was pride, when it was only calculated to preserve the secret of my melancholia. But I understand this; I have really achieved what I wanted; for hardly anyone has ever felt pity for me" [Pap. VIII 1 A 179, Dru, 683].

This is not completely true. There was one person who did have pity for Kierkegaard, and it was she who least of all was permitted to have it, Regine. Therefore he also denies this energetically, at the same time that he himself talks about it. This happens in a detailed retrospection upon the story of their engagement, which was recorded in the diary in 1849 under the title "My Relationship to 'Her'," with a marginal note labelling it as "rather poetic," that is, not a little bit retouched, though undoubtedly correct in the details and only wrong in interpretation. Kierkegaard records how the engagement was entered into; he did nothing to captivate her; "I even warned her against myself, against my melancholia" [Pap. X 5 A 149, p. 160]. But to warn against oneself in that situation is of course really to appeal to her sympathy, and as far as I can see that is the point in the entire story, but Kierkegaard will not hear of it. They become engaged, and Kierkegaard sees immediately that it was wrong; he was, of course, a melancholic penitent whose life was consecrated to the idea. "She did not seem to notice anything. On the contrary, at the end she became so insolent that she once declared that she had taken me out of pity; in short, I have never known such insolence." One must take note of the phrase "on the contrary" and of the irritated portion at the end of the cited passage. In spite of the fact that in a certain sense this was a relief, still "I confess my weakness that she did make me angry for a moment" [Pap. X 5 A 149, p. 160 f.]. From the beginning, and later as well, Kierkegaard revealed himself. It is reported from another source that he often sat crying with her.[17] He has fallen out of his role, betrayed himself, and this is intolerable. Therefore he must disparage her love and understand it as a purely selfish devotion. The fact that there were strong, ethical pity feelings present in her love for him is confirmed by some of her remarks, which Kierkegaard himself repeats in his retrospection. But he denies that she had this motive, and especially that her pity should have been the reason that he broke with her. His famous letter of termination to her — which according to his own statement was cited word for word in "Guilty?"/"Not Guilty?" — also appeals, though unintentionally, to her more ideal feelings: "[F]orgive a person who, even if he was capable of something, was nevertheless incapable of making a girl happy" [VI 347, SLW 304]. But Regine does not want to be happy at all; she wants to make him happy. And he does not want to be made happy, that is, the object of her compassion, and therefore reacts violently to her attempt to hold on to him after the break: "[N]ow my nature reared up gigantically in order to shake her off. There was only one thing to do: to push away with all my power" [Pap. X 5 A 149, p. 163]. Thus does he protect himself against being found out in his weakness, or rather, against the admission that his weakness has been found out. He flees, because he does not want to be inferior and to receive. In the flight he is consciously looking after her future happiness. She tries to hold on to him out of conscious concern for his happiness. Each refuses the concern of his/her counterpart for his/her respective happiness.

Regine was perhaps a poor psychologist, precisely because she struck him at his tender spot, which was that he did not want to be dependent upon her, of less worth than his fiancee. But her motive was ideal enough (or was it just that which was wrong?), and this he will not admit. After the breach he immediately falls back into the role, concealment. "I spent the nights crying in my bed. But by day I was my usual self, more fresh and witty than ever; it was necessary" [Pap. X 5 A 149, p. 165]. It is important for him to reduce her in order to assert his own superiority: "I was old as a dotard; she was as young as a child, but I had the powers — alas, it is almost the worse for it! — to enchant her, and when I had a glimmer of a hope I could not deny myself the joy of enchanting her, she who was a lovable child, remained a child and in spite of everything she had suffered, was still as a child when we parted" [Pap. X 5 A 150, p. 174-75]. Therefore we must disparage her idealism and her understanding of the situation, and imagine that her motive was selfish [Pap. X 5 A 150, p. 171-72]. "In order to defend my behavior to her, I must always be reminded of my fundamental misfortune" it says at one point in the journal [Pap. VIII 1 A 100, Dru 655]. This is probably the basis for the gigantic dimensions which the fundamental misfortune assumes, precisely because it serves as a defense of his actions. The conscious reasons for the break — the obligation to his father's memory, marriage's requirements of openness, the secret note, etc. — comprise the mythology which comes into being in order to enable him to escape from the recognition of inferiority in relation to the girl. To this also belongs the entire literary production, the self-dramatization in the novels (which, of course, be it noted, is not the *only* point of view which can be applied to these!), which is also noticeable in the retrospection from 1849. "But what a pattern of unhappy love! It is not as with, e.g., Goethe's Frederikke . . ." One could enumerate many statements which demonstrate that this collision is precisely the most interesting and most Christian of all. To this literary production also belongs the self-idealization which situates Kierkegaard on the superior side, the side of genius, even in defeat — so superior that he can generously grant her the justice which she is due, if only it is maintained that he is the sovereign power who directs the course of things: "For my part, it is the law for my whole life; it returns at every decisive point: like that general who, when he was shot, had commanded it himself, so has it always been I myself who has commanded when I should be wounded. But the fencing itself, which she had to perform, was in fine form and worthy of admiration. In a way, I put in her hand the bow; I myself strung the arrow on it, and showed her how to take aim. . ." [Pap. X 5 A 150, p. 172]. Thus, Kierkegaard not only gives us a theory of the melancholia, which becomes so self-important in its impotence, and so proud in its weakness, but he also gives us illustrative material for the theory, and does so involuntarily. One could cite many more examples, but here it is just the point itself which is of importance, that Kierkegaard can both live in his melancholy, self-assertive animosity (cf. Antigone) and interpret it (cf. Aesthete A). Also a part of this mood is the latent aggressiveness which Kierkegaard himself interprets, among other places in "Against Cowardice," when he speaks of hidden anger and defiance, and in *The Sickness Unto Death,* when he writes about the encapsulated person who cannot do without and cannot have a confidant, and who therefore can poetically be imagined to have his confidants put to death after he has opened himself to them.

4: 4. *Melancholia's Self-Understanding*

We could continue the account of Kierkegaard's inferiority complex for many more pages, but this is surely a sufficient suggestion of it, for we are not interested in the complex itself, but in Kierkegaard's own understanding of it. The moral which he draws out of the matter for himself in these notations on "her" is the following: "As for myself, I have learned that I have more than a little of the self-torturer in me. Now this will certainly be changed" [Pap. X 5 A 149, p. 170]. I will not answer the question of whether the change did indeed take place. We have been moving in a border area. On the one side lies the world of Kierkegaard's moods, where he suffers, and disdains, and rationalizes; on the other side lies the world of his thought, where he analyzes. But the two worlds meet and integrate; the rationalizations intervene in the analysis, but the analyses also affect the moods and keep them in check, and from this syncretism come new formations of thought which are valid in themselves, which it would be unspeakable narrowmindedness simply to reduce to psychopathological symptoms. Kierkegaard is correct in insisting that his inferiority complex is not a completely banal case, and he is correct because he himself understood very well what was involved.

"As a youth I went forth confidently into life," he writes in *The Point of*

View, "with an almost foolhardy and proud bearing; I have never for an instant in my life been devoid of the faith that one can do what one wills to do — excepting only one thing, though otherwise everything, unconditionally; but not one thing, I could not remove that melancholia in whose power I was held. It has never . . . occurred to me that there was anyone alive, or anyone who might be born in my time, who was my superior — in my innermost being I myself was the most miserable of all. . . . This, however, must be understood as meaning that I was very early in life consecrated to the idea that to win is to win in the infinite sense, which in the finite sense is to suffer; so this, in turn, was in agreement with my melancholia's comprehension in my innermost self, that I was really suited (in the finite sense) for nothing" [XIII 605 f., PV 78]. Here both the inferiority and superiority feelings are maintained. All the same, an impartial psychologist would hardly call this confession an adequate self-analysis, because here Kierkegaard apparently overlooks the dialectical relationship between the extremes, which he described so clearly in *The Sickness Unto Death* and other places.

Nevertheless, we must not prematurely dismiss Kierkegaard's self-understanding as superficial. We will gradually come to see that he actually understood the relationship between inferiority feelings and compensation very well, but that, *with* this understanding as a background, he did not wish to give up the conflict. This is why he depicts it as ineradicable, and this is why he uses it as the substratum of his thinking ("the idea that to win is to win in the infinite sense, which in the finite sense is to suffer"). One can call this maintaining of the conflict demonic, and one can be moved to pathos at the thought of Kierkegaard's almost cynical (because the level of consciousness is so high) rejection of the possibility of recovery; he ought to have seen through the conflict entirely, and thus given it up. Such an objection would not even be in conflict with his own descriptions of the person in the demonic state who at the last instant leaps away, back into the sickness. But Kierkegaard also has another viewpoint which can be applied to melancholia. It is not important to be healthy and sound at all costs, because sickliness contains a possibility of knowledge for him, a possibility from which the healthy and conflict-free person is cut off. "Melancholia's perspicacity" is an expression he uses at one point.

Thus, in *The Point of View,* the melancholic conflict between superiority and inferiority is viewed as a given precondition, and the problem is not how this conflict can be dissolved, but how it can be reacted to: "When this is given (such a pain, and such a concealment), how it is dealt with depends upon the differences which the individual possesses:

whether this lonely inner pain demonically finds its expression and its satisfaction in hating people and cursing God, or just the reverse. The latter was my situation. As far back as I can remember, I was in agreement with myself about one thing, that for me there was no comfort or help to be sought from others; satisfied with the great deal which had been granted me in other respects, as a man longing after death, *qua* spirit desiring the longest possible life, it was my idea, that, loving in a melancholy way, I could help others, find consolation for them, find for them above all clarity of thought, specifically about Christianity" [XIII 606, PV 79].

This passage from *The Point of View* contains in compressed form both the self-analysis and the ethically reflected superstructure. First we will bring forth one aspect of the analysis.

4:5. Universal Aggression

In the passage cited there is mention of two possible reactions to the inner suffering, either "hating people and cursing God, or just the reverse." Common to both of these reactions is the feeling of inferiority, the consciousness of one's own weakness. The difference between them is the reaction to this consciousness. The first of the two types, the aggressive type, is the type whose encapsulated monologue is registered thusly by the greatest of poets:

> I, that am rudely stamp'd, and want love's majesty
> To strut before a wanton ambling nymph;
> I, that am curtail'd of this fair proportion,
> Cheated of feature by dissembling nature,
> Deform'd, unfinished, sent before my time
> Into this breathing world scarce half made up,
> And that so lamely and unfashionable
> That dogs bark at me as I halt by them;
>   . . .
> And therefore, since I cannot prove a lover,
> To entertain these fair well-spoken days,
> I am determined to prove a villain
> And hate the idle pleasures of these days.

I have cited Gloucester's monologue from Shakespeare's *Richard III* in English, where Kierkegaard cites the German translation, and I have cited four lines more than he includes in *Feat and Trembling* [III 169, FT 115]. The context is as follows. In order to illuminate the figure of Abraham, Johannes de silentio sketches a series of literary themes, and among these he ventures into the border area of the demonic and of sin. Among the examples is Sarah in *Book of Tobit,* of whom it has been prophesied that if she marries, an evil demon will kill her husband on her wedding night. Tobias wishes to marry her all the same. Tobias is heroic, but fundamentally it is really Sarah who is worthy of respect. If one does not understand this point, one has "not even comprehended the little mystery that it is better to give than to receive, and has not an inkling of the great mystery, that it is much more difficult to receive than to give." Sarah is the heroine, because she has the faith which makes it possible to permit herself to be healed, to receive the help: "What humility vis-a-vis another person! What faith in God that she should not in the next instant hate the man to whom she owed everything!" [III 168, FT 113].

The demonic person lacks this humility and faith. Richard III (Gloucester) is in approximately the same situation as Sarah, but he hardens himself and cannot receive, that is, he cannot stand to be found out as a person who has use for the sympathy of others. "The proud, noble nature can stand everything, but one thing it cannot stand, it cannot stand pity. It contains an affront which can only be given him by a higher power, for, by himself, he could never be the object of pity. If he had sinned, he could bear the punishment without despairing, but to come forth innocently from his mother's womb predestined to be the object of pity is a sweetish smell in his nostrils which he cannot endure. Pity has a queer dialectic; at one moment it requires guilt; in the next it will not have it; and therefore the person who is predestined to be pitied becomes more and more frightful, according to the degree to which the individual's unhappiness has a spiritual tendency." Richard III thus becomes demonic in order to avoid being pitied by others. He encapsulates himself, disdains the pleasure of love: "I can of course become a Bluebeard who has the joy of seeing the girls succumb on the wedding night" [III 168 f., FT 113-14].

Kierkegaard returns to the figure of Richard III a number of times. What was the motive behind this man's erotic and political conquests, *quidam* asks: "[I]t was hatred of existence; it was by means of the power of the spirit that he wanted to mock the nature which had mocked him; he wanted to make it ridiculous together with its invention of love and of loving the beautiful, because he, the wronged person, the cripple, he the despairing person, he the devil, wanted to show that he, in spite of language and in spite of all the laws of existence, could be loved." Whence his lies and intrigues, his hatred, which made him himself into a seducer and his life into an insane revenge, by which means he wanted to save his pride and assert his honor [VI 371 f., SLW 324].

Richard III also appears in *The Sickness Unto Death,* without his name being named, but clearly identifiable, when it is stated that the sort of despair under discussion really only occurs in the pure form "in the poets, that is to say, the real poets," that is, Shakespeare [XI 207, SD 206]. The section on "the despair of despairingly willing to be oneself, defiance" is divided into two parts, and the second and more important of them is an amplification of the Richard III theme of compensatory hate. Defiance is the form of despair in which the despairing person wishes to create himself with the assistance of a fantastic self-perception, wishes to determine who he himself will be instead of respecting his created concretion. Kierkegaard speaks of an "experimenting self, which despairingly wills to be itself," but is prevented from doing so by one or another "fundamental injury," a "thorn in the flesh (whether it is really there, or whether his passion makes it there for him)." The self focuses its attention upon this real or imagined injury, but instead of humbly coming to terms with it or hoping for recovery, it is adopted in its self-perception, where it comes to dominate. "For, to hope for the possibility of help, and particularly by virtue of the absurd, by virtue of the fact that everything is possible for God—no, he will not do that. And to seek help from another—no, he will not do that for all the world; he would rather, if it should come to that, be himself with all the torments of hell than seek help." It is not the case that a suffering person is always glad to be helped, for help means humiliation. This is true both religiously, when the task is to become as nothing before God, and humanly, when the condition is to bow oneself before another person and "as long as one is seeking help, to have to give up being oneself; oh, there are surely many sufferings, even long and painful sufferings, from which the self does not shrink like this, and which the self therefore fundamentally prefers, while retaining itself." It is the theme of pity which is developed. In his rejection of help, the defiant person identifies himself with his suffering in a hate-filled, compensatory rebellion against existence. Even if every power of the good offered him its assistance, he must protest that the error is not his but the world's, and he must "rage against everything, being the one person in the whole world who is wronged by existence, to whom it is precisely of importance to watch carefully to make sure that he has his torment ready to hand, and that no one takes it away from him—for then he could not prove to himself and convince himself that he is right." This despair thus not only wants to deify itself, but it wishes to turn its aggressiveness outward in its self-degradation; "it wills to be itself in hatred of existence, to be itself in accordance with its misery; it does not even will to be itself in defiance, or defiantly, but out of defiance." Thus, in the religious dimension, the despairing person becomes a living anti-theodicy, and just because he conceives of himself as a personified proof, a conscious, existential denial of the goodness of God and of existence, just because of this he cannot receive consolation: "[P]recisely this consolation would be his downfall — as an objection against the whole of existence" [XI 205-09, SD 203-07].

4: 6. *Moral Reaction-Formation*

Universal hatred, cosmic aggression, is Kierkegaard's evil possibility, just as Richard III is his *alter ego* — with emphasis upon the *alter*. This is the meaning in *The Point of View* where it was stated that the lonely, inner torment either can find expression as hatred of God and man, "or just the reverse." In the journal from 1854 he can sum things up: "alas, in earlier times I felt all too deeply the pain, [the pain] that it had been made impossible for me to come to enjoy life, this beautiful human life. In a Richard III this has the effect that he then decides to embitter life for others. With me this has not been so: I have intended to keep my suffering hidden and to beautify life for others . . ." [Pap. XI 1 A 210, Smith 90]. It is precisely a resume. In an entry from 1847, the Gloucester analysis from *Fear and Trembling* is repeated almost word for word. The beginning of the demonic is that one is situated in life in such a way that everyone wants to have pity upon one, and what decides the matter is whether the person who is thus situated is evil, like Gloucester, and hates and curses, or whether he is good — like Kierkegaard! — and chooses to be sacrificed for other people. One cannot maintain that Kierkegaard puts his light under a bushel when he chats with himself about himself, and it is tempting to ask whether perhaps this light also flickers and smokes a bit. Even the person who sacrifices himself like this, it is stated, still does pose one condition, and thanks God when it is fulfilled: "to conceal his misery, to avoid becoming the object of pity. Oh, of all sufferings, none, perhaps, is so torturing as being chosen to be the object of pity; there is nothing which so tempts one to rebel against God. People generally think that such a person is dull and limited; alas, it would not be difficult to show that this is precisely the secret which is concealed in the existence of many of the most eminent world-historical spirits. But it is kept hidden, and it can be done, for it is as if God wanted to say to such a person, if this person uses his other remarkable gifts in the service of the good, 'I do not will that you should be humbled before people in this way, that you should be at the mercy of this, your undeserved misery; but your misery must help you to remain aware of your nothingness in relation to me' " [Pap. VIII 1 A 161, Hong 4599; cf. VIII 1 A 650, Dru 754].

Experimentally, one can give the following form to the matter: God protects Kierkegaard's feeling of inferiority, helping him to avoid being found out by his fellow man, while, in return, Kierkegaard is found out totally in his relationship to God, becoming nothing, or becoming conscious of his nothingness, before God. This then is the precondition for Kierkegaard's productivity in the service of love of his neighbor, for his activity as an author. If this formulation is correct, then one can further ask whether God is thereby acting as a good psychologist, or whether he is not more likely making himself available as a defense mechanism for Kierkegaard's despair and legitimizing his demonic encapsulation. If one finds these words blasphemous, they can be translated into the question of whether Kierkegaard is not using this religious interpretation to procure himself a religious alibi which makes it possible for him to maintain the illusion that he is unconditionally superior in relation to the common humanity of his surroundings, that he has no real weakness to admit, but that he then, in return, is willing to confess his wretchedness and impotence before God? " . . . [M]y suffering is my superiority," he writes in an entry on the problem of pity, which we cited earlier [Pap. X 2 A 105, Dru 982].He himself does not simply understand the sentence straightforwardly according to the wording, e.g., as meaning: my suffering is that I, the intellectually superior person, must associate with people and be exposed to their misunderstandings and envy. The context shows that the statement also means that his superiority is a product of his suffering, his intellectual wealth as an author is a consequence of his defeat as a person. We will return to this, but the question is whether an impartial psychologist might not also understand the sentence in a third way, i.e., that his sufferings are due to the fact that he will not acknowledge his inferiority, his purely human insufficiency in the face of his surroundings, but will only admit his religious guilt before God. This is the same question which Kierkegaard suggested in the discourse "Against Cowardice": "[W]hether he has permitted himself a revision, so that he was not being punished for that for which he should have been punished, but for something else, and accepted people's mistaken judgement of him as a judgement from the hand of God, but allowed the people to be mistaken." Is Kierkegaard being punished for that for which he ought to be punished, i.e., is his grief connected to his actual relation to his fellow man, or is it a case of a self-created torment which makes it possible for him to ignore the authority of his fellow man and the guilt which he takes upon himself in relation to his fellow man?

If I ask these questions without proceeding toward a definite answer to them, it is because the answer, to the extent to which it concerns Kierkegaard's private existence, is irrelevant to my purposes. On the other hand, the questions can contribute to creating a profile of some of the themes in his psychology.

I return to *Fear and Trembling,* where Kierkegaard first expresses the idea of the two paths which stand open to the person who has come into existence in so warped a manner as Richard III and Kierkegaard himself: "Such natures are placed in the paradox from the very beginning, and they are in no way any less perfect than other people, except that they are either lost in the demonic paradox or saved in the divine paradox" [III 170, FT 115]. The question which now makes its appearance — and which I will attempt to answer, because it does not (only) concern Kierkegaard as a private person, but also Kierkegaard the psychologist — concerns the person who does not turn his aggressiveness outward in the cursing of God and the world, but who consciously appropriates his own presuppositions and chooses to serve the good. Will he be capable of conquering the Richard III-nature, the aggressiveness in himself, and will he be capable of conquering the melancholia which was his presupposition, the product of the aggressiveness which had been turned inward? When all is said and done, it does indeed seem to be a case of a sort of reaction-formation in the "good" direction: "I was so deeply shaken," Kierkegaard writes about himself in *The Point of View,* "that I came to a fundamental understanding that it would be impossible for me to succeed in striking the tranquilizing middle way, where most people live; I had either to hurl myself into despair and sensuality, or absolutely to choose the religious way as the only way — either the world, to a terrifying degree, or the cloister. That it was the latter which I would and must choose was fundamentally decided; the eccentricity of the first movement was only the expression for the intensity of the second . . ." [XIII 561, PV 18].

But the reaction-formation never vanquishes its opposition entirely, Kierkegaard has taught us. His fundamental meaning must be that to the extent that an individual really sees through his conflict and, as surety, admits it to himself and appropriates it as his own, then it is no longer a case of reaction-formation, but of a recovery. But, to the extent that one merely develops oneself upon the basis of the suffering, this development is more or less suspect, more or less demonic, even if it is consciously placed in the service of an ethical intention.

We are thus back in the area of moral hypocrisy and the ideal self-deception, from which we came earlier. In connection with Richard III, as early as *Fear and Trembling* there is mention of the example of a demonic person who "does the good. Thus the demonic can also manifest itself as a contempt for people, a disdain which, however, be it noted, does not cause the demonic person himself to act contemptibly; on the contrary, he has his strength in knowing that he is better than all those who judge him" [III 170, FT 115]. Carping, which can well be regarded as a sort of occupational disease in authors who concern themselves with ethics, is the moral form of aggression, and Kierkegaard has both known of it and admitted to it, even if, naturally, in a somewhat reversed form. In his younger days, he writes in *The Point of View*, it satisfied him to deceive people, so that they thought him a worldly, piquant personage, while, deep inside, he was profoundly religious; the danger which awaited him was "an almost obsessive ecstasy at the thought of how the deception succeeded, which so indescribably satisfied the inner resentment which I had had from my childhood onward, because, long before I had ever seen it, I had learned that lies and wretchedness and injustice ruled the world" [XIII 587 f., PV 52]. The documentation of this moral theme of revenge in the young Kierkegaard can be found, among other places, in the "Diapsalmata": "When I see myself cursed, loathed, hated for my coldness and heartlessness, then I laugh, then my anger is satiated. If indeed the good people could really cause me to be wrong, to act unjustly — yes, then I would have lost" [I 28, E/O I 39]. It is the demonic aesthete who is speaking. Whether the same motive also plays a role in the older Kierkegaard is a question which need not concern us here; this is possible, but it is also possible that his understanding and criticism of hypocrisy argues for the more sterling character of his own notorious indignation which is the background of his polemics. It is enough that he himself has described the sickness. The question of whether he also suffered from it cannot concern us.

5. "What is a Poet?"

5: 1. *The Poet-Existence*

Kierkegaard's private melancholia has to do with what one could call his psychology of the poet — a special topic which for various reasons occupied him intensely. "What is a poet?" it is asked in the famous prelude to Aesthete A's papers, and the answer is that a poet is an unhappy person whose work is a beautified sublimation of his torments [I 3, E/O I 19]. One could call Kierkegaard's psychology of the poet Freudian, to the extent that Freud, too, tends toward viewing the work of poetry as a pure and simple symptom of an unclarified inner conflict, a text which can be studied according to the same principles as the dream. This means that the interest is not directed principally at the text, but at that which is revealed in and behind it, the poet-existence. This does not prevent Kierkegaard from expressing his admiration for the text, but after the outburst of admiration follows the analysis: "[F]or a poet purchases the power of the word which can speak of everyone else's burdensome secrets, for a little secret of which he cannot speak. And a poet is not an apostle: he can only drive out devils by means of the power of the devil" [III 125, FT 72].

Here we will not discuss Kierkegaard's opinions of the art of poetry in general, its significance and its limitations, nor will we discuss the question of the extent to which and the sense in which his own pseudonymous books are a part of that art, in spite of the fact that both of these questions are stimulating enough. When in his later years Kierkegaard commonly describes himself as a poet, the word has a quite distinct meaning. "The poet" is precisely the person whose personal existence is not congruent with that about which he writes [e.g., Pap. X 1 A 11, Dru 861]. It can also be expressed by saying that his poetic work is a compensation for a lack of existential realization. The poet can state everyone else's secrets, but not his own. His productive fantasy originates in his absence of clarity about his own existence. Unclarity is the condition of growth for the productivity. Nothing is thereby said about one or another particular poet, Judge William explains, but "a poet-existence as such is situated in the obscurity which is a consequence of the fact that a despair has not been carried through, that the soul continually trembles in despair, and the spirit cannot win through to its true transfiguration" [II 227, E/O II 214]. Therefore, writing becomes a surrogate reality and a condition of life, a refuge for the melancholic: "[I]n grief himself, he seeks the consolation of song" [V 248, TCS 60]. This is the case for the romantic poet, but it is also the case for Kierkegaard himself: "[A]s Scheherazade saved her life by telling fairy tales, so do I save my life or keep myself alive by producing" [Pap. IX A 411, Dru 841]. From my earliest age I have been in the grip of melancholy, he writes in one of the innumerable journal entries which deal with himself, "but on the basis of this pain an eminent intellectual existence as an author developed itself" [Pap. X 2 A 619].

5: 2. *Ways of Viewing Suffering*

The question for Kierkegaard is which point of view he will apply to this suffering and to the productivity which originates in it. One possibility is to view the suffering as an inherited and ineradicable, psychosomatic suffering which was simply his lot in existence, for which he could not be made personally responsible, and which he therefore must be permitted to sublimate, though, be it noted, only when its impetus is placed at the service of the universal and the ethical and of Christianity. This self-understanding receives very clear expression in some of his journal entries. Certainly melancholia is a sin, the sin *instar omnium*,[18] which is why the physician cannot cure it. We have Judge William's word for this and the later pseudonyms indeed agree with him. And yet, in *The Sickness Unto*

Death, Kierkegaard himself opens the possibility of another interpretation of his own melancholia, namely, when it is written in the introduction that "the sickness unto death" does not include "earthly and temporal suffering, want, illness, misery, adversity, difficulties, torments, psychic sufferings, sorrow, and grief" [XI 138, SD 145]. It could indeed be the case the Kierkegaard's melancholia was not despair at all, but a psychic suffering, a sickness pure and simple. Vigilius Haufniensis, who is almost more strict on this point in his rejection of the understanding of sin as "an illness, an abnormality, a poison, a disharmony" [IV 320, CD 14], also leaves the door open a crack for another understanding of the demonic. I will dwell upon his thinking in a bit more detail.

In the course of time, the demonic has been viewed in three different ways, "aesthetically-metaphysically," "ethically-judgementally," and "medicinally-therapeutically," Vigilius writes and concludes in his psychosomatic, or rather pneumato-psycho-somatic thesis (cf. above, Chapter III: 1). This thesis itself contains an interesting corrective to a tendency in Kierkegaard to choose the "spiritual" and the "internal" sides of a problem and to treat as bagatelles the remaining aspects. In doing this Kierkegaard seeks to avoid distracting attention away from what seem to him to be the essential aspects in the analyses. The reflected sorrow in "Shadowgraphs" was invisible or at most discernible only in "a certain sickliness" which is not described in any more detail [I 179, E/O I 176]. But in any case, some of the forms of despair are also sickly in the clinical sense, which is clear simply from the fact that they can be viewed "medicinally-therapeutically." Despite the fact that Vigilius criticizes this form of treatment, the matter under discussion is thus a condition which it could seem natural to report to a physician. Vigilius thinks—just as Judge William—that it is inconsistent to go to a physician with a demonic condition, because the demonic is not "something somatic," which belongs "to the natural phenomena, but is a psychic manifestation, a manifestation of unfreedom" [IV 439, cf. 444 note; CD 116, cf. 120 note]. The medicinal view is therefore superficial and one-sided, even if its methods of treatment perhaps can seem effective enough: ". . . [N]aturally! My powder and my pills—and then enemas! Now the pharmacist and the physician joined forces. The patient was isolated so that the others would not become afraid. In our heroic times one does not dare to say to a patient that he will die; one does not dare to send for the priest, for fear that the patient will die of fright. . . . The medicinal-therapeutic view regards the phenomenon as purely physical and somatic, and does what physicians often do, and in particular a physician in one of

Hoffman's short stories; they take their snuff and say: 'This is a serious case' " [IV 430, CD 108].[19]

With this Kierkegaard has not absolutely rejected the somatic point of view, but only criticized it as subordinate to the psychological and the "pneumatic." But his confidence in the art of the physician is of moderate proportions. "And when all is said and done, in the medium of actuality, of becoming, what do the physician and the physiologist really know, then?" he asks in the famous or notorious general settling-up with natural science in his journal from 1846. And yet, perhaps the question is not *only* rhetorical: "But in the situation of actuality, where, then, shall a beginning be made? Must the sufferer first take the medicine, or must he first believe?" [Pap. VII 1 A 186, p. 127, Hong 2809]. The alternative is perhaps not entirely as vulgar as it looks, for "the situation of actuality" in 1846 was for Kierkegaard, among other things, the situation in which he posed himself the question of whether it is a sickness in the spirit, the sickness unto death. Which way of viewing it should he adopt?

According to Vigilius, the demonic condition also admitted of being viewed "ethically-judgmentally." This is not simply Kierkegaard's own view, but the mediaeval view, represented by the Church Fathers, who recommended the death penalty for heretics. Kierkegaard clearly takes' exception to "the contradiction in the strict behavior of that ancient time," which presupposes the fantastic notion of totally giving up evil. The only part of this view of which Kierkegaard approves is the ethical view which makes the demonic person responsible for his suffering: "[I]t is not fate; it is guilt," the consolation reads, and it is precisely the consolation when it is said "honestly and seriously" [IV 429-31, CD 107-09].

The guilt viewpoint is excluded by the third possible way of viewing the demonic which Vigilius enumerates: "One can view the demonic aesthetically-metaphysically. Then the phenomenon belongs to the category of misfortune, fate, etc., and admits of being viewed in analogy with having been born mad, etc." Naturally, this view is not simply adopted by Kierkegaard either, but on the other hand it is not a view which he dares to reject without further consideration: "If the demonic is a fate, then it can happen to everyone. This cannot be denied . . .," he writes, and continues with an attack upon the people of his wretched times who are too busy to be interested in lonely thoughts and spiritual scruples. And it is exactly here that Kierkegaard's personal scruples lie. What matters, he writes, is to "clear up how much of it is fate and how much guilt. And this distinction must be drawn with the concerned, as well as the energetic, passion of freedom, so that one would dare to maintain it even if the whole world collapsed, even if it seemed that one would cause irreparable injury by one's firmness" [IV 428 f., CD 107].

This is more easily said than done. This last sentence, for all its stalwartness, could be viewed as Kierkegaard's attempt to convince himself. Is melancholia fate or guilt? Is it a medicinal or an ethical-religious problem? The apparent inconsistency lies in the fact that, according to Kierkegaard himself, there ought not be any contradiction between these two categories. As early as in Judge William, Kierkegaard elaborates the idea of repenting oneself back into the race and of including in one's repentance the sins of the fathers, i.e., of making oneself responsible also for that which one might view as one's hereditary taint. Vigilius expresses the same idea when he speaks of the fall into sin as the qualitative leap in which the individual shows that he is guilty, regardless of what psychological presuppositions and catenae of natural events can be enumerated as motives. Elsewhere in the book he expresses this in the fate-guilt terminology by saying that heathendom — Greek antiquity — had not come to the concept of guilt in the deepest sense. "If this had emerged, then heathendom would have foundered upon the contradiction that a person became guilty by fate. This is indeed the highest contradiction, and in this contradiction Christianity breaks forth" [IV 405, CD 87; cf. above Chapter V: 7: 2].

But, then, is the alternative — "how much of it is fate and how much guilt" — a false alternative, or an expression which Kierkegaard moreover leaves behind as "aesthetic-metaphysical"?

5: 3. *Sickness and Sublimation*

There is no doubt that Kierkegaard views himself as "guilty by fate," that is, that he makes himself the bearer of the responsibility for the melancholy sufferings which he considers to be the product of an hereditary and environmental taint. It is this self-understanding as an author which he expresses in *The Point of View* and in the journals: "Thus I felt myself to be sacrificed, because I understood that my sufferings and torments made me resourceful in exploring the truth, which could then help other people" [Pap. IX A 130]. "I have understood my task as being that of a person who himself became unhappy, and who, if he loves people, wishes to help others who are capable of being happy" [Pap. VII 1 A 126, Dru 600].

This is Kierkegaard's self-understanding, or, if you will, the ideology with which he keeps away the possibility of Richard III. According to this understanding, the demonic is not the suffering itself, the heterogeneity, the natural category, the inheritance, but the demonic is only the evil, destructive reaction to this suffering. "the original natural or historical situation in which one is placed outside the universal is the beginning of the demonic, in which the individual himself, however, has no guilt," he writes in the analysis of Richard III in *Fear and Trembling* [III 170, FT 115]. The idea is that the demonic state only arises when the individual reacts "demonically" to this condition, by an open aggressiveness or by contempt for mankind. Kierkegaard thinks he has vanquished this demonic possibility by virtue of his ethical-religious (but also psychological) self-understanding, which makes him capable of converting his melancholia into literary productions which become a joy for others. Whether we, as his readers, want to believe him or whether we will find in this a new, pharisaical self-deception, is another question. One might tend to think that Kierkegaard's "guilt" is not simply identical with his "fate," that is, with the given melancholia which was inherited or implanted at an early age, but that it is connected with something which Kierkegaard himself regards as completely legitimate, indeed God-sanctioned, namely, his concealment, his roles, which serve as a protection against the pity of others. One could assume that if he, like Sarah in *Fear and Trembling*, had had the humility vis-a-vis another person which is necessary in order to permit oneself to be healed, he would also have been healed. But, having said this, one must admit that these suspicious assumptions have been inspired precisely by his own formulations, not only by the definition of encapsulation as anxiety about communication, but also, for example, by the discourse "Against Cowardice."

It is in a context such as this that one must understand Vigilius' question: "[H]ow much of it is fate and how much guilt?" If Kierkegaard's melancholia is guilt, then the task must be to escape from it, to renounce it, to annul it or to have it annulled in the assurance that the guilt has been forgiven him, and thus to turn back to the universal, to complete life instead of writing books about the completion of life (and its opposite). If, on the other hand, it is fate, "in analogy with having been born mad, etc.," then it is an unchangeable fact, and the task is to remain in the position of the exception and to utilize the possibilities of melancholia as the impetus which is behind, and as the fertile soil which underlies, an authorship which is in the service of truth. In that case, the melancholia is not a sickness of the spirit (despair) but a physical-mental suffering whose treatment belongs to the province of medical science — if it can be and if it is to be treated.

This is how Kierkegaard understands the matter in this journal entry from 1846, as well as in other places: "I am an unhappy individual in the deepest sense; from my earliest childhood onward I have been bound fast to one or another suffering which bordered upon madness, and which must have its deeper cause in a misrelationship between my mind and my body; for (and this is what is strange, as well as being my infinite encouragement) it does not stand in any relationship to my spirit, which on the contrary has achieved an unusual degree of elasticity, perhaps as a result of the strained relationship between mind and body." Here, as elsewhere, it is the clearly and consciously expressed ideology of sublimation. Spiritual superiority corresponds with suffering. It is not difficult to state what Anti-Climacus would think of the diagnosis. He would object that it is a case of the aesthetic use of the word "spirit" in the sense of talent and genius. But this is in 1846, and inasmuch as this is the diagnosis, it is consistent that Kierkegaard goes to a physician with his suffering. Here he comes, formal and buttoned-up: "Despite the fact that I am not in favor of confidants, despite the fact that I have absolutely no inclination to speak with others about my inherent being, I do think, and have thought, that it is a man's duty not to bypass the authority which consists of consulting another person; only it must not become a foolish confidence, but serious and official communication. I have therefore spoken with my physician about whether he thought that this misrelationship between the physical and the psychic in my construction admitted of being removed, so that I could realize the universal. He doubted that this were possible; I have asked him whether he thought that the spirit, together with the will, was capable of transforming or reshaping such a fundamental misrelationship, and he doubted that this were possible. . . ." From that moment onward he has chosen, he continues, chosen to accept the suffering as an unavoidable and indissoluble condition which makes it possible for him to "assert the universal and make it lovable and accessible for all others who are capable of realizing it . . ." [Pap. VII 1 A 126, Dru 600].

Kierkegaard carefully arranges his question to the physician so that he is certain of getting the desired answer. The visit to the physician is an alibi with which he provides himself. A couple of years later, after a new consultation in 1848, he explains just how formal and huffy he had been, how little desire he really has had to inform his physician or to permit himself to be helped, and how little confidence (rightly or wrongly) he has had in this help: "It does, however, give me comfort that I have spoken with my physician. I have often been afraid about myself, that I might perhaps be too proud to speak with anyone. But, as I have done it earlier, I have now done so again. And what did the physician really have to say? Nothing. But it is important for me that I have respected this human authority." And then follows the customary self-interpretation: "Thus I can also understand my life: that I proclaim consolation and joy, even though I am bound in a pain for which I see no relief" [Pap. VIII 1 A 645, Dru 749]. The visits to the physician were a pure matter of form, for in reality Kierkegaard is not at all interested in being healed. Even if it were possible to remove the thorn in the foot, am I permitted to do so, he asks, when it is just with the help of the thorn that I leap so high? [Pap. VIII 1 A 156, Dru 670]. The justification of the torment is that it is the precondition for my eminent spiritual existence: "In any other case I would have seen to it to repair the damage a bit" [Pap. VIII 1 A 185].

In 1849 this view has been fully formed: "Yes, if my suffering, my weakness, were not the precondition for the whole of my spiritual activity — yes, then I would naturally still make an attempt to approach the matter quite simply in medical fashion. What is the point of suffering as I suffer, and not doing anything about it at all, when one's life is devoid of significance all the same? But here is the secret: my life's significance corresponds precisely with my suffering" [Pap. X 2 A 92, Dru 981].

5:4. *"Poet-Existence With a Religious Tendency"*

Here again we are moving in the boundary area between the presentation of Kierkegaard's psychology and the analysis of his psyche. The resistance to recovery, the anxiety about the good, the fear of "what Socrates says at one point, to permit oneself to be cut and burned by the physician in order to be healed" [IV 430, CD 108], are of course the central themes in Kierkegaard's psychology. Is this anxiety not only described by him, but also typically exemplified by him as well? If that is the case, he himself has managed to analyze his own resistance, and it is exactly his own analyses which can be used to support another view: that this is not a case of an unfree, demonic anxiety about the good, but of a conscious, ethical decision upon the basis of an adequate self-understanding and an understanding of the special possibilities which melancholia provides to "explore the truth." It is not certain that Kierkegaard has anxiety about recovery, but it is certain that his concept of recovery differs from the customary concept of psychosomatic health. Is it Kierkegaard's melancholia and encapsulation which rule him, or is it not more likely he who rules over the melancholia and the encapsulation by utilizing them as a springboard, at the same time that he disciplines himself as an author to preserve the connection with the earth? As I have said, I will not decide the matter, because my investigation is not biographical, even if it unavoidably must utilize biographical material.

Ultimately, of course, the question is an ethical one. The section about anxiety about the good in *The Concept of Anxiety* is one of the Kierkegaard texts which — implicitly — most powerfully formulates the requirement of confidence, openness, and communication. And yet even here Kierkegaard does not condemn encapsulation under all circumstances, but differentiates between a freely-chosen, purposive, and content-filled encapsulation and an unfree encapsulation, which does not encapsulate itself with anything, but encapsulates itself and becomes a prisoner of itself [IV 432, CD 110; cf. above, Chapter VI 5:2]. The antithesis of concealment-openness is important in Kierkegaard's pseudonymous writings (particularly *Fear and Trembling*), and one of the problems is the relationship between justified and unjustified concealment. The problem is posed dialectically, so that neither the hidden nor the open is opted for unambiguously. But sometimes dialectical ambiguousness and unclarified ambiguousness can scarcely be distinguished from one another. At one point, Vigilius formulates the problem of the free encapsulation as follows: "One must always bear in mind that according to my linguistic usage one cannot be encapsulated in God, or in the good, for that encapsulation means precisely the highest sort of expansion. Thus the more definitely the conscience is developed in a person the more expanded he is, even if, in other respects, he shuts himself off from the world" [IV 443, CD 119]. Is this the demonic Kierkegaard's private denial of his own teaching about openness, the expression of his own escape from the reality of his fellow man into an anxiety-laden monologue with God? Or do the words express precisely the opposite, that the relationship to God liberates man, also in relation to his fellow man, that is, liberates him from anxiety about communication with his surroundings, so that his possible social isolation has other, more objective motives than the escape from an intolerable confrontation with reality and his neighbor? This latter is evidently the meaning. The core of Kierkegaard's personal problem is the question of whether he dare regard his own isolation as freely chosen and willed by God, or whether he must regard it as demonically unfree. In any case, he has been forced into isolation [Pap. X 2 A 61, Dru 970; X 3 A 499, Hong 1300; XI 3 B 68, and many other entries]. However, freedom is of course not an autonomy without presuppositions, but the conscious appropriation of the given presuppositions. Here the hunting is best for the person who wishes to trap Kierkegaard in his own contradictions. But to the person who finds this method of hunting banal and condescending, Kierkegaard's vulnerability reveals itself as his strength. It is scarcely possible to put forward any qualified criticism of him, which he himself has not anticipated in his self-analyses. I daresay this is the point which makes the work of the critics into the productions of epigones, and the analyses into genuine psychology.

A good example is the objection, repeated countless times, that Kierkegaard and his thought ends in a pure, one-sided abstract spiritual existence, which draws its strength from indifference to concrete temporality and its conditions. In *The Sickness Unto Death* Kierkegaard grants that the critic is right: "Much of that which is decked out under the name of resignation in the world is a sort of despair, which despairingly wills to be its abstract self, despairingly wills to have enough in the eternal, and thereby to be able to defy or ignore suffering in the earthly and temporal sphere." He is also ready with a psychological explanation of the phenomenon: "The dialectic of resignation is really this: to will to be one's eternal self, and thus, with respect to something particular, in which the self suffers, not to will to be oneself, comforting oneself with the knowledge that after all this must cease in eternity, and therefore thinking oneself justified in not appropriating it in temporality; the self wills, in spite of the fact that it suffers under it, nevertheless, not to make to temporality the admission that it is a part of the self; that is, the self will not, in faith, humble itself under it." This resignation is thus no elevated piety, but a masked variant of defiance [XI 205 f. note, SD 204 note].

The analysis of the despairing resignation which suffers, but which utilizes the suffering as the boost for the spring into an incorporeal spiritual existence instead of confronting the suffering, is carried further a few pages later in *The Sickness Unto Death,* in the sketch of "what one might call a poet-existence with a religious tendency." it is precisely because the suffering has this function that it becomes impossible to give it up. The religious poet relates himself to God, but he is unhappy in his religiosity, and this is exactly why his description of the religious sphere is more intense than that of other people, and his presentation is his better I. "He loves God above all, God who is his only consolation in his secret torment, and yet he loves the torment; he will not let go of it." I have above suggested the possibility of a psychological interpretation of Kierkegaard in which his concept of God could be a sort of defense mechanism, a rationalization by the help of which he procures religious legitimation for the retention of the melancholia and the encapsulation which he loves and will not get rid of. And quite rightly—Kierkegaard understands this himself: the religious poet relates himself to God, "it would be the greatest terror for him to have to do without God; 'it would be something to despair about'; and still he really does permit himself, though perhaps unconsciously, to poetize God a little bit into something different than what God is, a bit more in the style of a loving father who indulges the child's one wish altogether too much." The wish is to retain the torment, and the god whom the poet "perhaps unconsciously" poetizes for himself is a god who allows him to do so.

But the poet is also a bit of a psychologist; he is in the process of seeing through his own rationalization. "He understands obscurely that what is required of him is to let go of this torment . . .," but he does not do it; he evades with a new manoeuvre. To let go of the torment means "in faith, to humble himself under it and appropriate it as belonging to the self." This means the opposite of thrusting the problem away from oneself, and thus the opposite of what the poet does in relation to his torment: "[F]or he wishes to hold it away from himself and precisely thereby to hold on to it firmly, despite the fact that he really does think — and this, as every word from a despairing person, is true in a backwards sense, and thus is to be understood in reverse — that this means to separate himself from it, as far as possible, to let go of it, as far as it is possible for a person to do so. But he cannot appropriate it in faith, that is, in the final sense he will not; or, his self ends in obscurity here" [XI213 f., SD 208 f.].

It is a self-portrait, and yet it is not, for by virtue of the analysis itself, Kierkegaard has distanced himself from the religious poet, and his self-understanding is clearer than that of the poet. The poet wishes to keep the torment away from himself, but the dialectic of despair makes sure that this means just the opposite. When he makes the attempt he prevents himself from letting go of the torment, and that is what he wants, for he loves his torment. Kierkegaard's analysis is presumably an indication of the fact that privately he did get out of this vicious circle. Whether this was in fact the case historically will not be discussed here. To know one's soul is not identical with acquiring it in patience, but at the most a precondition for this acquisition: "Therefore, every knowledge which will not stand in relation to an acquiring is incomplete and lacking, because he of course does not yet know what he will become; because he becomes it only in the acquiring; and even in the company of an acquiring, knowledge is lacking, because 'we do not yet know what we will become' " (cf. above, Chapter IV: 4: 2).

Neither for Kierkegaard himself nor for his curious reader does the analysis of the religious poet contain any guarantee that he is now saved and eternally secured against the demonic state. The religious poet "will" not come out of despair. Kierkegaard analyses his will, but as is known, the will is something dialectical, and the analysis which is committed to paper is not a secure bastion against this dialectic. If one turns from *The Sickness Unto Death* to the journal entries from which the description of the religious poet has been distilled, one could write a very lengthy account of the development of Kierkegaard's self-understanding as a private person and as an author, about decisions which were given up and decisions which were maintained, about conflicting motives with respect to a mass of factors: Kierkegaard's financial situation; his literary plans; his plans to seek a parish; his relationships to the people and institutions of his times; his attempt to determine what sorts of challenges the Christianity of the New Testament contained for him in particular and for contemporary man in general; his observations about how this challenge could best be brought to bear upon Christendom's use of the message of grace as the guarantee of safety for the idyllic egoism of the bourgeoisie; and his discussion with himself about whether it is he who must take upon himself the task of doing this.

The dilemma of the religious poet is pre-eminently to be found in these questions: "[I]s he the person called, is the thorn in the flesh the expression of the fact that he is to be used for the extraordinary, is it perfectly in order with God that he has become this extraordinary being? Or is the thorn in the flesh something under which he must humble himself, in order to achieve that which is universally human?" [XI 215, SD 209]. This is the *posing* of the problem, and as so often in Kierkegaard, it is perhaps more important than the attempts at solutions. I will not follow Kierkegaard's development historically, but will simply attempt to note the most important positions of principle.

5:5. *"But Now God Wants Things Otherwise"*

The analysis of the religious poet demonstrates clearly enough what is dubious about the ideology of sublimation. When Kierkegaard can maintain that the melancholia is an inherited suffering of the psychic and somatic sort, he is not in doubt that his utilization of its impetus in the service of the authorship is legitimate. But the substratum of melancholia also admits of being understood as despair, with the assistance, namely, of *The Sickness Unto Death.* Johannes de silentio's analysis of Richard III in *Fear and Trembling* is not carried through. Viewed with Anti-Climacus' glasses it is superifical, and it is this superficiality which forms the basis of Kierkegaard's ideology of sublimation, i.e., for the viewing of the melancholia as an undeserved, non-demonic suffering. Johannes de silentio differentiated, as we saw, between the undeserved suffering, conditioned "by the natural or historical situation," on the one hand, and the open aggressiveness or contempt for mankind, on the other, and he thought that only the aggressive reaction was demonic. What he overlooks is the psychological middle term. It is Anti-Climacus who makes it clear how important this is. The despairing person never despairs "over something earthly," even though he himself thinks he does, but always "over himself." He does not despair over the given, objective condition, but over the self-perception which he forms for himself, for which this condition serves as the opportunity—"whether it is really there, or whether his passion makes it there for him" [XI 205, SD 204]. Despair, that is, is not a straightforward consequence of the misrelationship, but of the relationship which relates itself to itself, i.e., of the self-perception which fantasy produces. "This means that every time the misrelationship reveals itself, and every moment that it exists, it must refer back to the relationship" [XI 147, SD 149; cf. above, especially Cahpter V: 9: 1 and 9: 5]. It is this that Johannes de silentio overlooks, and therefore he also overlooks the fact that the demonic state is not simply the aggression of a Richard III, but also the inwardly-directed aggressiveness (melancholia) of a Soren Kierkegaard, for both are reactions to a despairing self-perception. But Anti-Climacus does show this; this analysis is not my own and the product of someone outside the situation who is safely situated, but it is Kierkegaard's own in *The Sickness Unto Death*.

But when Kierkegaard has to grapple with his existential problems at close quarters, it does not take place merely with the help of a more precise psychological self-analysis, but by virtue of a new, religious self-interpretation, in which God no longer appears in the role of the protector of melancholia.

The substratum of melancholia admits of being interpreted as anxiety about the good, as sin, the sin of despairing about the forgiveness of sins. It may be understood not only as mental suffering, but also as unbelief, for melancholia is the self-loving hatred of oneself, which manifests itself as guilt-feelings, the same insane remorse as that which Vigilius described, the remorse which must ultimately have itself as its object and annul itself. "Perhaps unconsciously," the religious poet makes God a bit different than he is, a bit more of an indulgent father who lets the child have his wish, to retain the torment. "Had I lived in the Middle Ages I would probably have gone into a monastery," it is written in Kierkegaard's journal from 1847, "and have offered myself to penance. In our times I have understood this need of mine differently. All self-torment in the monastery leads only to fantasy; but then I have chosen something else. I have chosen to serve the truth, and at one of the points where it is the most thankless of tasks. Here I have a unity of penance and doing good." This is the ideology of sublimation again, but now in a new key. The idea of penance—which plays a much greater role in Kierkegaard's self-understanding than can be recounted here—is the core in, or at least a very important part of, the psychological substratum of the authorship, and the authorship is a method of subduing guilt-feelings by doing something beneficial in return. What is fantastic is that here it is again Kierkegaard himself who says it. The lack of appreciation and the mockery to which he has been exposed as an author and a public personality "satisfies me in another sense, precisely as a penitent," he writes. He applies a purely psychological viewpoint to himself as a person who has a need for degradation, and he characterizes this need itself not as sickly, but as unpleasing to God, and justifiable only to the extent that the possibilities of knowledge which the melancholia contains are consciously utlized in the service of Christianity: "I know well that God does not desire that a man torture himself in order to please Him, and that this is precisely unpleasing to God; but God will either permit or forgive my practice of this sort of doing penance, when I do not attribute to it any merit, but do it only because I cannot do otherwise. The penance of the Middle Ages was wrong in itself, and then wrong again, in that it was supposed to be meritorious. No, penance, when it is to be tolerated and permitted, must be a need in man, and he must therefore be willing continually to ask God for forgiveness for doing it" [Pap. VIII 1 A 116, Dru 660].

This is what Kierkegaard in *The Sickness Unto Death* calls poetizing God a bit. Another entry, written several months later, begins by recapitulating the position. The poet ideology is put forth again, but now in order to be made the subject of debate. With the help of his literary productivity Kierkegaard has kept the suffering at arm's length, has helped himself, diverted himself, forgotten himself, and the authorship is the symptom, a diversionary tactic — which, however, can be of benefit to others. The suffering is psychosomatic, which the physician really ought to deal with, if he could, and if Kierkegaard would allow him to do so. And it is God who has approved of this and has helped him by protecting the melancholia.

The entry then continues: "But now God wants things otherwise. Something moves within me which is a sign of a metamorphosis. . . . I must therefore now remain silent, must not work too strenuously, indeed, scarcely strenuously at all, not begin any new book, but see to it that I come to myself, *in order properly to think the thought of my melancholia together with the presence of God.* In this way my melancholia might be annulled, and *that which is Christian might come nearer to me.* Hitherto I have protected myself against my melancholia with intellectual labors which keep it away. Now I must see to it — in the faith that God, in forgiveness, has forgotten the element of guilt there is in it — to forget it myself, but not by means of any diversion, not by means of any distance from it, but in God, so that when I think of God I must think that He has forgotten it, and thus teach myself to dare to forget it in forgiveness" [Pap. VIII 1 A 250, Dru 694].

Then the story goes no further. Historically, of course, the story is much longer, for Kierkegaard lived eight more years, and much happened, both in the outer and the inner theatres. But in the entry which has been cited, the position and the tendency have been indicated, or rather, the position has been surrendered, that is, the defensive position. In this entry Kierkegaard is transparent to himself. Certainly the melancholia is a suffering, but it is not only a physical-mental abnormality with which he is afflicted, of course. It is a despair, because he has used the suffering as the substratum for his accomplishments and has used the accomplishments to abstract himself from himself and from his given actuality and concretion. Now the melancholia is understood in connection with the thinking of *The Sickness Unto Death* and the message which supports the conclusion of that book: "You must believe in the forgiveness of sins" [XI 254, Sd 246]. Kierkegaard must no longer bear his melancholia, endure it, love it, sublimate upon it; he must give it up, die away from the dearest thing he possesses, his "self-tormenting in melancholia, which is without doubt enjoyable," not by reflecting himself out of it, but by believing that it has been forgiven him. It is what Johannes de silentio called the great mystery: that it is much more difficult to receive than to achieve, even if it were the most remarkable thing one achieved.

Kierkegaard achieved no little bit in the years until his death, a handful of books, several thousand pages of dilemma-filled journal entries, and a frontal assault upon Danish Christendom's bestial exploitation of the Gospel. Viewed purely ideally, the motive behind these accomplishments should be indicated in the formula: "[T]he infinite humiliation and grace, and then an effort which comes from thankfulness" [Pap. X 3 A 734, Hong 993]; and: "Here again is reduplication! That the most strenuous human effort is after all foolery, a waste of time, a laughable gesture, if it is supposed to be an attempt to merit blessedness — and yet still (and if I were right, this is still what is infinitely inspiring!) to exert oneself as much as anyone who believed in all seriousness that he could acquire blessedness by means of his efforts!" [Pap. X 4 A 640, Hong 1431].

Whether a biographical-psychological investigation would reveal that there were also other motives at work will not be discussed here. Merely a study of the dates of the passages I have cited on the previous pages will show that Kierkegaard's thought moves forward in a retrograde motion, backwards and zig-zag, not on a straight line toward a fixed result, but with a continual revision of the attained results and the hard-won resting places, as a unity of result and striving, ends and means. Whether this style of thinking is to be called dialectical or ambivalent; whether Kierkegaard's actions — externally and internally — in the final years, are an expression of critical reflections on the basis of a personal "transparency," or whether we should understand them as the products of the religious poet's last, fantastic self-deception; whether the attack on the Church is to be understood as a clearly thought-out and correctly mounted unveiling of the clergy's insidious treachery against the Gospel it was supposed to administer, or whether it should be understood as the aggressive release of a life-long condition of neurotic convulsion; whether it is the story of a runaway religious madness, developed in the brain of a man who could not, i.e., would not, believe what he himself said: all these are irrelevant questions in this context. But for the purpose of the present investigation, it is enough to establish that he said this.

Chapter VIII

"THE FUNDAMENTAL RECOVERY"

1. Kierkegaard's Problem and the Problem of Kierkegaard

What is it that Kierkegaard is trying to do in writing his psychology? Why did he write it? What is its function and intention and its significance? And what is implied by the fact that the psychology is developed within the framework of a Christian understanding of existence?

Christ's message is the message of the forgiveness of sins; the psychology is a penetrating analysis of sin, and especially of the sin of refusing to allow oneself to be healed. "It is indeed easy enough to receive everything with the help of a Gospel — were it not for the fact that its being the Gospel is the most difficult thing of all" [VII 419, CUP 384]. This is the problem in Kierkegaard's work: to receive. Man does not want to receive (to open himself), but wants to be his own master. This is why "all despair can ultimately be dissolved and referred back to" the formula: "despairingly to will to be oneself" [XI 144, SD 147]. But, because Kierkegaard is a psychologist, this is not understood to be merely the external sort of offense which explicitly "declares Christianity to be untruth and lies" [XI 271, SD 262], but it is understood with reference to the implicit offense with regard to the paradox, which reveals itself in all the forms of despair. The Gospel is "easy enough," but it is also "the most difficult thing of all," because the Gospel is the message that man must receive his life, instead of encapsulating himself in the attempt to save himself. This is where the problem lies.

Just as Christianity here is both the easiest and the most difficult thing, so is everything in Kierkegaard understood under the sign of duality: existence as the intersection of finitude and infinity; the moment as the concrete contemporaneity of the temporal and the eternal; the self as owning and acquiring; communication as the art of unifying qualitatively antithetical things; power as the renunciation of power; weakness as strength; obedience as freedom; gift as task; [1] man's greatest perfection as achieving nothing, yet achieving everything by virtue of the absurd; the relation to God as distance and nearness, as suffering and blessedness, as degradation and elevation; faith as fear and love, as obligation and thankfulness; the believer as sinner and justified; God as infinite reduplication; Christianity as a good which hurts, mildness and strictness; Christ as God and man, a sign of antithesis which reveals and forgets, judges and forgives, requires totally and atones unconditionally, demands man's life and gives him the possibility of living — to put it briefly.

One can understand this thought as dialectical or as ambivalent. Dialectic can be defined — in Kierkegaard's case — precisely as the bringing to consciousness of the thorough analysis of an ambivalence, which has sufficient dialectical awareness to avoid rejecting that in which it originates and which nourishes it: duality. One can find this insistence upon paradoxality excellent or offensive. One can call Kierkegaard's thought the overwhelming indication of the health of faith, because it is capable of maintaining the conditions of its coming-into-being without ever stagnating in unambiguousness, or one can call his work a compendium of sado-masochistic thought complexes, a product of the vain attempt of an authoritarian personality to revolt against its own chains. One can call the ambiguousness which is Kierkegaard's element a nihilistic vacuum, or one can call it the space of simplicity which never encloses itself, because simplicity opens itself simply outward, towards the existence in which it has its origin, receiving its elasticity from this openness. One can understand his work as an honest man's attempt to articulate an interpretation of existence and a proclamation of Christianity in relation to an inescapable condition; and one can thus understand this condition as a challenge to take up this given life in an obligated openness to its possibilities, by giving oneself away in unreserved and undefended confidence, to a life task which can be realized when the self obediently grounds itself in the power which posited it, a life in which the self gives up its I-centered, anxious demand to control and seize possession of its life in an unambiguous, secure comprehensibility. Or one can understand his work as the glorification of a form of life which binds itself in an eternal, monomaniacally fixed, and in the end, compulsively repetitive circular movement around an insoluble and unreal complex of problems, offering no exit and no vista, no holding point and no resting point, no solution before the dissolution of death, but only an aimless back-and-forth motion in air which continually becomes thinner, an endless and unceasing rotation among possibilities which each have several meanings, moving forward toward total acedia and a total longing for death.

Kierkegaard's authorship is ambiguous enough to permit both interpretations. Therefore, when I separate out several comprehensible, and therefore answerable, individual problems in the pages which follow, I do not thereby pass any judgement upon Kierkegaard *in toto*. He has not become so irrelevant to me that I am capable of labelling him either as the incarnation of the festering spiritual sore of our culture or as its conquerer. His contradictions are not a matter of indifference to me, and I can use him neither as a whipping boy nor as an infallible source of truth.

2. Settling-Up With Kierkegaard?

2:1 *Reductionism*

The first, and perhaps also the most important, objection which can be raised against Kierkegaard as a psychologist has to do with his indubitable penchant for speculative, systematic thinking. The objection is made much more obvious by the fact that it was of course Kierkegaard who won fame as the fearless campaigner against every speculative or scientific system of existence.

Kierkegaard's older friend and teacher, Poul Møller, remarked in an aphorism that "of all the sorts of presumption, the most intolerable is that which lays claim to a knowledge of human nature." The remark is not a rejection of every form of psychology, not of the form which takes its origins directly from the psychologist's ability to make observations and "peer into himself"; but it is a rejection of the psychology which takes this as its starting point and loses itself in the abstract and rigorous formulation of theories and in pretentious speculation: "That which is universally true about man reveals itself in infinite modifications in the individual actions. As a necessary consequence of his contemplative nature, the theoretician is much more easily deceived than the daring practical man, who is not supplied with rules according to which he must proceed." The theoreticians are those who are rigid in their systematics, but who succumb to any compulsion which their own system exercises, because the system is an obstacle to the most elementary, human understanding of the living beings which they make the objects of their study: "The essence of the soul becomes clear to them by means of profound self-observation, by means of the ease with which they abstract that which is general from the characters with which they are familiar; but when they meet something unknown in life, they hastily refer it first to one category, then to another."[2]

Poul Møller's objection was scratched down on a couple of scraps of paper at the point when Kierkegaard first entered school and brought upon himself the nickname of "The Fork" because of his attitude of being the ironic observer and his sarcastic way of keeping himself at arm's length from life. A bit more than twenty years later he published *The Concept of Anxiety* and dedicated it to the memory of his late teacher and friend, "my admiration, my loss" [IV 307, CD 3], or, as it is written in the draft, "the reader whose loss I feel" [Pap. V B 46]. The question is what Poul Møller as a reader and critic would have said about Kierkegaard's psychology, which is undeniably more abstract and less spontaneous, more schematic and less warm-hearted than his own scattered observations. No one need have any doubts as to Kierkegaard's ability to come to a psychological understanding of himself personally. But it is not this which is being questioned, for his psychology claims to be other and more than autobiography; it claims nothing less than universal validity. Such a claim must be met and always will be met with Poul Møller's objection: is it not presumption, a potential encroachment against that which it is claimed fits into the system? The question is not whether Kierkegaard knows himself, but whether he knows, and whether he will know, the unknown which meets him in life, or whether he does not rather, precisely with the assistance of his psychology, hasten to liquidate the unknown reality in order to assign it to one or another category in his ready-made framework.

The formalism and schematization are most clearly present in *The Sickness Unto Death.* To define is to delimit, to conclude, to determine, and the definition must always be a latent threat to openness, regardless of how capacious it is. Vigilius himself says that "refraining from definitions in matters involving the concepts of existence is always a sure sign of tact," because when a living, beloved reality is cast into the form of a definition, it "so easily becomes something alien and different" [IV 457, CD 131]. But he himself makes definitions, and Anti-Climacus excels in making definitions of the self, the spirit, despair, sin, and faith. Is this linguistic alienation? While Vigilius can still speak of "the vegetative lushness of the spiritual life," and maintain that "spiritual conditions are more numerous in their varieties than the flowers" [IV 436, CD 113], Anti-Climacus permits this luxuriance to stiffen into a rigorous pattern. It is true that there is a variety of forms of despair, but the varieties "must admit of abstract discovery by means of a reflection upon the moments of which the self, as a synthesis, consists" [XI 160, SD 162]. He deduces from the framework to reality, so that "that which is intellectually correct, and which thus will and must suffice, does suffice . . ." [XI 182, SD 183]. One can be in despair in thus and such ways: 1, 2, 3, and 4; but every form can be referred back to one and the same abstract formula: man is constructed in such and such a manner, and there can be so and so many variants. And if reality does not accord with the system, so much the worse for reality (as Hegel said). Kierkegaard's strong point from a psychological and scientific point of view is his enormous ability to objectivize, his *unum noris, omnes,* his level of abstraction, but, seen from an ethical point of view, this strength can show itself as an unforgivable error. Existence is cast into formulae; everything is reduced. Humankind is viewed in the image of Sóren Kierkegaard, i.e., in the image of despair. What is problematic is the reductionism itself. In his earlier writings Kierkegaard certainly did attempt idiographic descriptions of characters, fully-rounded images of people, but behind the fullness of the individual, the framework is everywhere noticed, and in *The Sickness Unto Death* there is not much left besides the framework. Doesn't Kierkegaard reduce "that individual" to a "case," one example among others of the universality of despair? Doesn't he make the living, real — and *qua* real, also "inconceivable," irreducible — individual into a manageable object, which can be labelled and put to one side?

In order to discuss these questions, it will be necessary to clarify several problems: what function does a psychological statement have? Where is psychological analysis relevant, and where is it not? What is the epistemological status of psychology? Into what situation can it be thought to enter, and what functions does it have in this situation? These questions will be discussed in what follows. But first we must raise a new objection which is related to that already mentioned.

2: 2. *Expertise and Contempt*

Anti-Climacus is an expert in psychology. As a writer he knows more about the despairing person than the despairing person knows about himself. As a physician makes his diagnosis without relying upon the patient's statement, so, too, is "the psychologist's relationship to despair" [XI 155, SD 156; cf. above, Chapter V: 8: 2]. By virtue of his psychological expertise he can point to the happy and healthy individual and say that he is in despair, that his sickness is the sickness unto death, and that it is all the more dangerous because the individual himself does not realize this. "It is true that all despair is in principle conscious, but it does not follow that the person whom it is conceptually correct to call despairing, is himself conscious of it" [XI 160, SD 162]. But the psychologist knows the situation, and Anti-Climacus is not one of the sick, but the expert who is concerned about the sick: "In its presentation, everything Christian must resemble a physician's discourse at the sickbed," we read in the Foreword to *The Sickness Unto Death:* "Even if only the medical expert understands it, it still ought never to be forgotten that it is at the side of the sickbed" [XI 133, SD 142].

Expertise is an ethical problem. If my physician discovers that I suffer from a highly dangerous illness which at this point can only be ascertained with X-rays, there is scarcely any reason to object to this. If, on the other hand, the psychologist, with his self-proclaimed X-ray vision, claims that I suffer from the sickness unto death, which indeed has not revealed itself, and which I perhaps will never recognize or acknowledge as such, then there is reason to ask with what right does he say this, and to ask whether his statement might not be based upon a disrespect for me, and might not contain a latent assault upon my integrity.

The problem can be viewed in various ways. I will approach it by means of a short detour which also points forward to new questions. Despair is not only sickness and sin; it is also the means of recovery, Anti-Climacus says [XI 134, SD 143]. Only in the crisis, in the sickness unto death, does man become accessible to the truth about himself. There is no immediate health of the spirit, for immediacy and spiritlessness are also in despair, but do not know it, do no experience despair as despair, But it is only in manifest despair that despair can be conquered. *The Sickness Unto Death* demonstrates this thought, and to this extent it is not entirely correct when it is stated in the Foreword of that book that the book only deals with despair as a sickness and not as a means of recovery. Without the crisis there is no recovery, for without the crisis there is no revealing of the unavoidable despair. "The person in despair who is ignorant of the fact that he is in despair, is, compared with the person who is conscious of this, simply one negativity further away from the truth and salvation"; in the ignorance of despair, the despairing person is "quite securely in the grasp of despair," and therefore this can be "the most dangerous form of despair," even if, from an ethical point of view, it is not as reprehensible as the more intense forms [XI 176 f., SD 177-78]. But the way to recovery goes precisely through the intensive, i.e., the manifest, despair, in which the despairing person can "turn smartly away from the despair and in the direction of faith" [XI 196, SD 195]—in spite of the fact that he does not always do so.

What does this imply? Well, it implies the idea that the crisis is not merely a negative phenomenon which must be avoided at all costs, because it is also the precondition of genuine renewal, recovery. *Per aspera ad astra,*[3] the road to salvation, is just as ancient as the camel's way through the eye of the needle. Modern psychologists also know this, e.g., Jung, when he says that the neurosis can be the way to a better, more profound integration of the self. The self must be broken up and struggled with before it becomes itself. The Christian formulation is the one which Kierkegaard uses, the most radical: "[B]y means of the eternal, the self has the courage to lose itself in order to win itself" [XI 202, SD 201].

But behind this lurks contempt and intellectual arrogance. Contempt and intellectual arrogance are perhaps not unavoidable consequences of the idea, but they are consequences which lurk behind *The Sickness Unto*

Death. Kierkegaard loses sight of οἱ ἀπηλγηκότες [oi apelgekotes][4]; spiritlessness seems to be lost beyond helping. The ballast which he here drops from his balloon is the idea of equality.

Viewed ethically, Kierkegaard's idea of equality is the idea that every person, by virtue of the fact that he is human, has humanity's possibility of realizing the task of existence. Salvation is not reserved for the gifted and the socially well-protected, for it has nothing to do with innate or socially conditioned "differences." If one comes ultimately to speak of the difference between the simple, common man and the learned, thinking man, it is the latter who has the more difficult problem; he must first become what the simple person is, simple. This is the case in the *Postscript* and many other places. Kierkegaard is apparently uncompromising in his criticism of "that distinguished sickness," the "intellectual importance" which has contempt for "the poor, or for the person who laboriously works for a miserable return for himself and his family"; the criticism applies to the intellectual class division which is socially conditioned: "[W]ho could be impudent and presumptuous enough to attempt to introduce earthly differences especially into divine matters instead of having compassion upon the differences of this earthly life" [V 232 f., TCS 41].

The Sickness Unto Death builds upon this idea of equality in speaking about "the person" in the definite form. But, when, on the other hand, Anti-Climacus presupposes the anthropological idea of every person's "fundamental" equality, he at the same time introduces a new, psychological distinction by the back door. The people who "say that they are in despair are generally either those who have a nature which is so much deeper that they must become conscious of themselves as spirit, or those who have been helped by difficult circumstances and frightful decisions to become aware of themselves as spirit" [XI 158, SD 159]. But to "say" that one is in despair is the condition of possibility for ceasing to be in despair. In order to get free of despair, one must become aware of one's despair, but this movement is reserved for the "deeper nature." In order to become spirit one must have a deep nature. The shallow-natured people are left behind and lost beyond helping, not because of their badness, but because their nature—or is it the Lord himself—has equipped them with less passion, or failing that, has exposed them to less difficult circumstances and less frightful decisions.

Sometimes the fact that Kierkegaard comes to unreasonable conclusions has an explanation which is hardly so unreasonable. We are approaching the problem of what he understands by recovery, and it can first be posed negatively: what isn't recovery?

I return to the problem of expertise. "The absence of insight into illness means that the individual cannot himself experience the symptoms which have been established by an expert as being present, and/or that the individual cannot understand what measures ought to be taken to change the situation." The quotation is from Joachim Israel's book *Alienation: From Marx to Modern Sociology*[5]. Israel uses the example from psychiatry to illustrate the phenomenon which Marx and Engels called "false consciousness." The absence of insight into one's own situation, which is revealed, for example, when the alienated person does not experience his own alienation, must, according to the Marxist line of reasoning, be interpreted as an extreme stage of psychological alienation.[6] The problem is precisely the same as that which we have previously encountered in Kierkegaard. The expert possesses the criteria and norms according to which he is able to characterize an individual as alienated or despairing, and which permit him to ignore the individual's own possible statements to the effect that he is not. The problem of expertise is the same for the two views. The mere assertion that a number or a majority of people are alienated or despairing without themselves being conscious of this is enough to show the radicality of both views. But the assertion that man does not know himself is not only Marx's and Kierkegaard's, but also that of Freud and psychoanalysis. The only question is which norm the expert acknowledges, and what practical consequences he draws from his superior knowledge. For that superior knowledge is of course present, and the assault, therefore, is always latent, just as it is latently present in every religious preaching which demands that you and I ought to convert ourselves; here, too, it is "the expert" who knows the truth about me, and in virtue of this tries to wrest me out of my false consciousness.

The fact that the problem is present is the criterion of radicality, for radicality is precisely the assertion of superior knowledge, to the extent that this knowledge is used to unmask given norms and to bring to consciousness the latent sickliness behind established facades.

The expert is not always and necessarily radical in this sense, for he can also place his expertise at the disposal of the norm. No long argument is needed to maintain that this is what the majority of 20th-century psychologists (and others) have done. "Today the function of psychiatry, psychology, and psychoanalysis threatens to become a tool in the manipulation of man. The specialists in this field tell you what the 'normal' person is, and, correspondingly, what is wrong with you; they devise the methods to help you adjust, be happy, be normal."[7]

Where the norm of normal psychology is the social (in Marxist terms, "the reified"; in Kierkegaardian terms, "the spiritlessly despairing") self — a commercial product which is capable of performing effective repression and sublimation — Kierkegaard's norm is the simple and transparent self which defenselessly surrenders itself to its existence. Where normal psychology's standard of measure is the demand for stable adaptation to the given social structure, Kierkegaard's standard of measure is the relationship to God, by virtue of which "the individual, as the individual, is higher than the universal, is justified over against it, not subordinated, but in a superior position . . ." [III 119, FT 66].

This is Kierkegaard's radicality, or one expression of it. He draws no political consequences from it. It is only in his final struggle, the settling-up with the Church, that he comes to the view that the inner revolution can be supported by an outer one: "If I were to compare the task with anything," he writes in *The Moment* no. 2, "I would say it resembles the medical treatment of a mental patient. We must work with the psyche, the physician says, but it does not follow from this that there is not also something physical to be done" [XIV 122, AC 97].

It is the expert who is speaking, the expert who knows the situation and who knows what the others do not know, who reveals what the others dare not look in the eye. We must leave the problem of the attack on the Church and the entire question of the individual's relation to society (including the religious society) at this point. But it is Kierkegaard's radicality, his rejection of the existing social and ecclesiastical order as the supreme giver of the norms for the individual's self-understanding, which dictates this attack, just as in large measure it dictates his psychology. And it is a symptom of this radicality that in *The Sickness Unto Death* he does not worry very much about the idea of equality, and leaves spiritlessness (which thus is not simply a sociological category) behind as lost beyond helping. *The Sickness Unto Death* is just as much a polemic as a psychological work, just as much a forerunner of *The Moment* as a continuation of *The Concept of Anxiety*. And because the ideology of adaptation is so massive, the attack against it must be total and without nuance. The attack must not ascertain academically that it is, unfortunately, only the deep natures which can be saved, while the passionless types are condemned to perdition, but the attack must create passion.

3. Possibility, Actuality, and Communication

3:1 *The Problem of Knowledge*

On the preceding pages, several problems have been raised in connection with Kierkegaard's psychology. The dilemma of radical expertise is, among other things, that it may show disrespect for the statement of the non-expert about himself. It does this precisely by virtue of its radical, superior insight, and the result can be a theoretical or practical contempt for the *other* individuals who are the "object" of this insight, or a theoretical or practical assault upon the integrity of these people.

It is not my intention to write an apology for Kierkegaard in this book. Therefore, I will not explain away or ignore the fact that such consequences are latently present in his thinking, but, on the contrary, I find it important to take note of this fact. It is, however, an important point that Kierkegaard himself was also extremely aware of this problem. For the non-radical expert—the advertising psychologist, the strategist of revival, etc.—this would only be a problem in the sense that it would be important to find the most effective method of utilizing his desrespect for the object of his strategy of influence. For Kierkegaard, on the other hand, the problem is a genuine dilemma, because he himself is aware of the problematical aspect of his superior knowledge and his latent repudiation of the other person's self-understanding. Upon closer inspection, the dilemma is whether he must give up his radical insight, possibly reserving it for himself, or whether he can communicate it in such a way that the insight is passed on, but the assault is avoided.

But in connection with this we must also ask what is the epistemological status of psychological statements and the statements about sin, despair, etc. Kierkegaard speaks abstractly about sin and despair as concepts, and in many connections he also describes the forms of despair in more detail: spiritlessness, guilt anxiety, the demonic state, etc. On the other hand, he never makes any definite statement about any particular person's spiritlessness or sin. *The concept* is the middle term between Kierkegaard and his reader, and if what Kierkegaard is saying is to be a statement about the reader, then it is the reader's statement. Therefore, it is perhaps not so much contempt as respect which is expressed for this reader.

The preceding pages have served only to point out these problems. In order to come to a more precise answer, it is necessary to consider the questions about what relevance for reality Kierkegaard attributes to his psychological and theological conceptual statements, what theoretical validity and what practical applicability they have—and do not have. In other words, we must look more closely at several main points of Kierkegaard's epistemology and his theory of communication, in order by this route to come to the question of the "maieutic therapy" which he suggests.

We will begin with the epistemology. "Immediate sensation and cognition cannot deceive," we read in the inserted "Interlude" in *Philosophical Fragments* [IV 274, PF 101]. In this respect the *Fragments* are building upon the Climacus fragment from 1842-43, where it says: *"Therefore, immediately, everything is true."* This does not mean that sensation is cognition's most reliable fundament, but it does mean that the question of truth and untruth does not exist at all for immediate sensation and cognition, and therefore: *"immediately, everything is untrue."* As long as one only senses, the question of the truth or actuality of what is sensed does not exist. "In immediacy the most false and the most true are equally true; in immediacy the most possible and the most impossible are equally actual" [Pap. IV B 1, p. 145-47] [8] Kierkegaard shares this point of departure with Greek skepticism, he explains in the *Fragments*. A so-called sensory deception is not a deception. "If, for example, sensation shows me at a distance that an object is round, which close up appears to be square, or if it shows me that a stick in the water is broken, even though it is straight and whole when it is taken out of the water, sensation has not deceived me at all. . . ." Both sensations are correct, or rather, the problem of correctness does not exist. It only comes into existence when I ask. One must understand that it is not a naively empirical epistemology for which Kierkegaard is setting the stage, but the opposite of this. The problem of correctness and the problem of actuality do not belong to sensed phenomena or to sensation, but to the individual who wishes to interpret what has been sensed. The phenomena exist only in uninterpreted concretion, and the contradictions they contain are not given in the mere registration of them, but only in the attempt to interpret: "I am only deceived when I conclude something about the stick or that object." Thus does Kierkegaard summarize the view of the Greek skeptics, but even here he deviates from the skeptic. "The Greek skeptic does not deny the correctness of sensation and immediate cognition, but, he says, error has a completely other cause; it comes from the conclusions I draw. If I could only stop drawing conclusions, I would never be deceived." Kierkegaard agrees, but he does not draw the skeptic's conclusion that it is a matter of remaining with uninterpreted, unmediated cognition alone. This is indeed impossible. When the skeptic *"wants* to doubt," this is already a sort of conclusion [IV 274, PF 102]. Man cannot avoid interpreting. "Cannot consciousness, then, remain in immediacy? This is a foolish question, for if it could, then there would be no consciousness in existence at all" [Pap. IV B 1, p. 146]. [9] Consciousness is indeed the unavoidable function of questioning (cf. in this connection above, Chapter IV: 3: 1).

The thesis that immediate sensation cannot deceive is thus not the expression of an empirical view, but of an assertion that empiricism is an illusion, or at best a matter of indifference. From pure experience one learns "nothing, or a merely numerical knowledge. As soon as I form a law on the basis of experience, then I am putting into it something more than is in the experience" [Pap. IV C 75].

The view does not imply any disrespect for facts, but rather a reflection upon the relationship between the merely given and sensed actuality and the understanding of it. Cognition is never a merely neutral reproduction of reality, but always a subjective interpretation of it. This point of view does not render scientific cognition impossible, but precisely renders it possible by recalling its conditions. "As a science, psychology can indeed never be concerned empirically with the details which are subordinate to it, but yet these details can receive their scientific representation in proportion with the concreteness which the psychology attains" [IV 327, CD 10]. It is thus not a matter of a rejection of "faithfulness to actuality" or of a legitimation of the arbitrary, but of a reflection upon the fact that scientific cognition is unavoidably an abstract cognition. Cognition never grasps its object, but only its linguistic representative, the concept, the sign. As a system of signs, language is at once both the precondition of cognition, and the reason that cognition is not identifiable with the thing known. An apple is not an apple, but only becomes so when the language and my use of language makes it into an apple. "As soon as I speak the immediate, then this statement is first and foremost an untruth, for I can say nothing immediate excepting mediately" [Pap. IV B 10 a 1, printed as a supplement in Pap. XIII, p. 36] it is written in the draft to the Climacus fragment. In the fragment itself this is expressed in slightly different words. Actuality is always only present to the knower in a linguistic interpretation, and therefore the knower does not have direct access to actuality (with one exception, which will be discussed below). Mere sensation is not genuine cognition, but an undifferentiated registration. Cognition unavoidably involves an organization of the merely sensed, thus an abstraction from the concretion of sensation. But this does not mean that language's reproduction of actuality stands in an arbitrary relationship to it. The word annuls actuality by speaking of it, but it does so "by *pre*supposing it . . ., for that which is spoken of is always *presupposed*." Actuality exists prior to consciousness's linguistic interpretation of it, and yet linguistic interpretation is cognition's only access to actuality. Kierkegaard does not make any attempt to go behind language into a preverbal or pre-conscious, pre-symbolic cognition of the surrounding world, which he regards as illusory, but he clings fast to language as the condition for and the boundary of cognition. "Immediacy is the reality; language is the ideality; consciousness is the contradiction. At the instant that I speak of reality, the contradiction is present, for what I say is ideality." Language in itself can indeed no more deceive than can actuality in itself. "In ideality, just as much as in reality, everything is true." Language can be used naively, as identical with actuality, such as the immediate person (the child) uses it—or such as speculative idealism imagines itself to do, when it assumes that thought is identical with being, that consciousness is identical with actuality. Post-Kantian idealism ignores the antithesis which Kierkegaard cites in the beginning as an example: the incongruence between reality and ideality, between what is factually given and the consciousness of it, between the concrete and the abstract, or, as he expresses it in another connection, between actuality and possibility—or between knowledge and belief (cf. below). In themselves and each one by itself, both reality and ideality are free of contradiction and contain "no possibility of doubt." But neither reality nor ideality exists "in itself" for consciousness, which of course is precisely the unavoidable juxtaposition of them, and which therefore conditions the way in which the problem arises, and thus the cognition: "[F]or only at the instant that ideality is brought into relation to reality does *possibility* come forth. . . . Reality is not consciousness, no more than ideality is, and yet consciousness does not exist without both of these, and this contradiction is consciousness's coming-into-being and its essence" [Pap. IV B 1, p. 146 f.][10]

Kierkegaard maintains this thought throughout the authorship. In 1850 he summarizes in his diary: " 'Actuality' does not admit of being conceived. Joh. Climacus has already demonstrated the correctness of this quite simply. To conceive is to dissolve actuality into *possibility*—but then it is indeed impossible to conceive it, for to conceive is to transform it into possibility and thus not to cling to it as actuality. It is a retreat, a backward step, not a step forward to conceive in relation to actuality. It is not as though 'actuality' were without concept, not at all; no, the concept which is found by dissolving it conceptually into possibility is also in actuality, but there is of course something extra—that it is actuality" [Pap. X 2 A 439, Hong 1059].

The reference to Climacus does not (only) concern the early fragment, but particularly the *Postscript,* where he ramifies this line of reasoning. As soon as there is talk of actuality, it is no longer actuality which is under discussion. In *The Sickness Unto Death* it is stated briefly: "The concept posits a position, but the fact that it is conceived is precisely the fact that it is negated" [XI 234, SD 227-28]. The designation relates to that which is designated as a map does to a landscape, or, to remain within Kierkegaard's terminology, as the navigational chart to the 70,000 fathoms of water. "What actuality is cannot be indicated in the language of abstraction. Actuality is an *inter-esse*[11] between the elements of abstraction's hypothetical unity of thought and being. Abstraction discusses possibility and actuality, but its conception of actuality is a false reproduction, for the medium is not actuality but possibility. Only by annulling actuality can abstraction get hold of it, but to annul it is precisely to transform it into possibility. Everything which is said in the language of abstraction and within abstraction about actuality is said within the realm of possibility. In speaking the language of actuality, the whole realm of abstraction relates itself to actuality as a possibility, and not to an actuality within the spheres of abstraction and possibility" [VII 302, CUP 279].

One can read this passage as a criticism of Hegelian speculation, which of course it is. But one can also read it as a sketch of Kierkegaard's own method of speaking about actuality, his attempt to come to a clear understanding of this. The fact that Kierkegaard speaks "the language of actuality" does not mean simply that he speaks "actually." He himself acknowledges this when he says that in a certain sense the subjective thinker speaks "just as abstractly as the abstract thinker" [VII 342, CUP 316; cf. above Chapter I: 1: 2]. The similarity is that they both "speak about" something; the difference is that only the subjective thinker understands clearly what this implies. Kierkegaard speaks abstractly about the concrete and admits his "interestedness in existing" [VII 302, CUP 279]. "The language of actuality" also makes use of abstraction, and it is thereby subject to the same conditions as the most abstract speculation. But the difference is that the language of actuality allows abstraction to relate itself "to actuality as a possibility, and not to an actuality within the spheres of abstraction and possibility." Actuality is concrete existence. "If I think it, then I annul it, and then I do not think it. It might seem correct to say that there is something which does not admit of being thought, namely, existence. But the difficulty is again present, in that existence juxtaposes these things in the fact that the thinking individual exists" [VII 296, CUP 274]. The subjective thinker exists. In addition he thinks about existence. The fact that he thinks can be called a part of his subjective actuality (cf. below), but what he thinks (the result of his thinking) is not actuality, but only possibility, that is, abstraction from actuality: "If existence does not admit of being thought, and yet the existing individual is thinking, what does this mean? It means that he thinks momentarily; he thinks in advance and he thinks afterwards" [VII 317, CUP 293]. This is Kierkegaard's sketch of himself; he thinks abstractly. No thought can do otherwise, because it is the essence of thought, of the medium of language, and therefore it is an illusion when speculation "assures us that what is thought is what is actual, that thinking is not only able to think, but also to give actuality" [VII 307, CUP 283].[12]

3: 2. *Conclusion, Decision, "Belief"*

"If by being . . . one understands empirical being, then the truth itself is transformed into a desideratum and everything is placed in becoming, because the empirical object is not finished, and the existing, cognitive spirit itself is indeed in becoming. Thus truth is an approximation, whose beginning cannot be absolutely fixed, precisely because there is no conclusion, a fact which has a retroactive effect. While on the other hand, every beginning (if it is not something arbitrary because it is not conscious of this fact), when it *is made,* does not take place by virtue of immanent thought, but it *is made,* by virtue of a decision, essentially by virtue of belief"[13] [VII 174 f., CUP 169].

With this quotation from the *Postscript* we are back at the point of departure for these epistemological observations. Mere sensation cannot deceive, for doubt about the validity of what has been sensed arises only when the cognitive subject wants to draw conclusions on the basis of what has been sensed. The conclusion is not a part of the phenomenon but of the knower; the interpretation is not given in and with the thing, but when the conscious individual poses questions. "Empiricism is the false sorites which continually repeats itself, both in the progressive and the regressive sense" [Pap. II A 247, Hong 2254]. A "pure" science of experience is unthinkable, because it would lack a point of view and thus a beginning. The point of departure for the cognitive process is not an indifferent conclusion, but a decision — regardless of whether the knower is clear about this or not (in exactly the same way that the individual always "chooses himself," regardless of whether this takes place consciously or not). The knower himself structures his understanding of what is given. He does so by virtue of language, but language contains many possibilities of understanding, and therefore the knower establishes his interpretation by virtue of a subjective use of language, i.e., "essentially by virtue of belief." The quotation from the *Postscript* merely repeats the idea from the "Interlude" in *Philosophical Fragments,* where Climacus points out for the sake of good form that the word "belief" is used "in the straightforward and ordinary sense," and not "in the quite eminent sense" [IV 279, PF 108]. The idea is otherwise the same. "The conclusion of belief is not a conclusion, but a decision"; it is not "a cognition, but an act of freedom, an expression of the will" [IV 275, PF 103-04]. In the *Fragments* the idea is used in an argument against a deterministic conception of history.[14]

But it is not only Kierkegaard's idea of the freedom of coming-into-being, which comes into being by virtue of belief. Every cognition begins by virtue of a decision or belief, not by virtue of immanent thought, it was stated in the *Postscript*. In *Works of Love* this is explained in more detail, in a purely edifying context. (It is characteristic of Kierkegaard that he does not present his epistemology in itself, but always in connection with something else, which it is to be used to explain.) Here it is confirmed that "belief" is to be understood in an "ordinary sense," about an attitude, "a believing," which can also be un-belief or superstition. But this does not change the meaning. Kierkegaard wants to say that one should not believe evil, but good, about one's neighbor, and he expresses this by saying that the knowledge one has about another person can always be interpreted—and always is interpreted. Therefore one should be very slow to judge and patient in believing the best about one's neighbor. The mere fact is neutral, and judgement is never made upon the basis of it alone. To overlook this is to abandon oneself to an illusion: "What indeed is the discerning secret of mistrustfulness? It is a misuse of knowledge, a misuse which wishes straightforwardly and simply, in one breath, to connect its *ergo* to something which *qua* knowledge is quite true, and which only becomes something quite different when, turning things backwards, something else is believed by virtue of this knowledge, which is just as impossible as it is backwards, for one does not believe by virtue of knowledge. What mistrustfulness says or presents is really just knowledge; the secret and the falsity lie in the fact that it then simply converts this knowledge into a believing, acting as though it were nothing, as though it were something which did not even need to be mentioned—'for, of course, everyone who has this same knowledge must *necessarily* come to the same conclusion'—as though it were eternally certain and decided, that when knowledge is given, then how one decides is also given. The deception is that it is *from* knowledge (for the illusion and the falsity claim that it is by virtue of knowledge), *in virtue of* the unbelief which is present in the mistrustful person that mistrustfulness concludes, assumes, and believes what it concludes, assumes, and believes, while *from* the same knowledge, *in virtue of* belief, one can also conclude, assume and believe exactly the opposite" [IX 259, WL 214-15]. "Knowledge, as such, is impersonal and must be communicated impersonally. Knowledge places everything in possibility and is to that extent outside of the actuality of existence and in possibility; only with the *ergo,* with *believing,* does the individual begin his life. But most people take no note of this at all, take no note of the fact that in one way or another, in every minute they live, they live in virtue of an *ergo,* of a believing—so carelessly do they live. In knowledge there is no decision; the decision, the definiteness and determinedness of the personality, come first in the *ergo,* in believing. Knowledge is the infinite art of ambiguity, or the infinite ambiguousness, which reaches its highest point precisely in placing equally opposed possibilities in equilibrium" [IX 263, WL 218].

To live is to interpret the uninterpreted given, not in an arbitrary pleasing of itself, but in a continuing interpretation of the ambiguous. This last quotation deals with communication. The meaning is naturally not that the ideal is to communicate indifferent, neutral knowledge. On the contrary, the line of reasoning means that all real understanding is subjective. In his authorship, it is precisely interpretations which Kierkegaard communicates. But what is "interpretation" from Kierkegaard's own viewpoint is "knowledge" for his reader, who is therefore directed to interpret. Or, to return to what was discussed above, what is personal "actuality" for Kierkegaard is "possibility" for the reader.

What, then, is actuality? This is, as Climacus would say, a foolish question, for the answer would not of course be actuality, but only possibility; it would not be an answer to what is being asked about, but an abstract statement by virtue of the fact that it is a linguistic statement. The answer is that actuality is always *my* actuality, and as soon as I communicate it to another person it is something else: "[T]he individual subject . . . can know what dwells in him; [this is] the only actuality which does not become a possibility by being known and which cannot only be known by being thought, because it is his own actuality . . . ." [VII 308, CUP 284].

Actuality is thus always "my" actuality. This does not mean that no actuality exists outside of me, but for me this alien actuality is possibility, that is, I only have access to it via language, the symbol, the concept, cognition, or via *my* use of language, etc. My actuality also encompasses my understanding of the alien actuality. Therefore my use of language is a constituent part of my actuality. Language (the symbol, the concept, etc.) is the medium between me and the alien actuality, which prevents me from grasping it concretely and immediately. Therefore language (my use of language) is in a certain sense my actuality, because it contains my interpretation of actuality.

But "my" actuality is not only conceptual and verbal. "All knowledge about actuality is possibility; the only actuality about which an existing thinker is more than knowing is his own actuality, the fact that he exists; and this actuality is his absolute interest." I have my actuality in virtue of my self-understanding, my "belief." That I am "more than knowing" about it means that it is more than merely thought. Kierkegaard calls this actuality the "ethical" actuality [VII 303 f., CUP 280], i.e., my total engagement with existence in understanding and action, and this engagement, this "absolute interest" is the more-than-conceptual total interpretation of the actuality which is my actuality.

"This world of inwardness, the reproduction of what other people call actuality, it is actuality" [IX 432, WL 354]. This does not mean only — I am tempted to say "in the external sense" — that Kierkegaard challenges his reader to "turn himself inwards" in introspection, but it means that man always lives by virtue of this interpretation or this "belief." The conclusion of *Works of Love,* from which this last quotation comes, explains the matter edifyingly. Kierkegaard interprets the saying of Jesus, "Be it done for you as you believe," as follows: "[W]hat is done for you, is what you believe" [IX 426, WL 349]. "For God is really this pure measure for measure, the pure reproduction of how you yourself are," an infinite echo of man — whether man is aware of this or not [IX 433 f., WL 355 f.]. Man's actuality is his belief, his total, realized self-understanding in interpretation and action: "If you have the faith to be saved, then you are saved" [IX 426, WL 349-50]; if you forgive your enemy, then you are forgiven, "for it is one and the same thing," and if you accuse your neighbor, you accuse yourself [IX 429, WL 352].

This ethical actuality is the only actuality I have; it is my identity, my "belief" — which can also be unbelief or mistrust. Anti-Climacus is the one who says it most precisely: "What is done for you, is what you believe, or, as you believe, so you are; to believe is to be" [XI 230 f., SD 224].

3: 3. *The Incommunicable—and the Effect of Communication*

It is not in spite of, but in virtue of, his epistemology that Kierkegaard can speak abstractly and schematically as a psychologist about the self, despair, sin, faith, etc. It is not in spite of his idea about actuality as "my" subjective, untranslatable, irreducible actuality, that he applies formulae to man, but it is in virtue of this idea, because the idea is that "my" actuality is under *all* circumstances an indescribable and incommunicable actuality. An attempt at an idiographic, phenomenological description of an individual's universe of experience is therefore in principle erroneous and futile, if it pretends to reproduce this individual's actual, subjective world, for self-consciousness "is so concrete that no author, not even the one richest in words, the one most masterful in exposition, has ever managed to describe a single one, while every single person is such a one" [IV 453, CD 128]. Instead of the illusory attempt to pin down actuality in a linguistic description, Kierkegaard therefore chooses in *The Sickness Unto Death* and other writings to formulate the possibility, the abstraction. Scientific discourse about the self and the selfish unavoidably tends toward tautological, content-less statements, Vigilius writes, and this remark also applies to his own statements. No science can say what a self is, while "every person who pays attention to himself knows what no science knows, for he knows who he himself is." Science can only speak "quite generally" about this, that is, abstractly [IV 383-85, CD 69-71]. And this is just what Kierkegaard does. Thus when he reduces the irreducible to abstract formulae — instead of producing in minute detail a phenomenological registration of the life of the individual psyche — it is not a symptom of a linguistic alienation [Entfremdung], but a conscious effect of estrangement [Verfremdung]. "The unconditioned does not lie in an approximation, but is a repellent point; that which is nearest the truth is not that which straightforwardly lies nearest to the truth, if you will; no, this latter is precisely that which is the most dangerous deception, the most dangerous, precisely because it lies so near the truth without being the truth" [Pap. XI 1 A 146]. The definitions and the descriptions are and must be abstraction, possibility. The formulaic reduction is not an expression of disrespect for the other person's — the reader's — actuality, but rather the reverse. As a psychologist Kierkegaard can understand other people, but he cannot have any other person's self-understanding [cf. *inter alia* Pap. VII 2 B 235, p. 176-78; AR p. 143-44]. In spite of all his psychological expertise and all his capacity for sympathetic insight, he cannot, strictly speaking, identify himself with the other person or say anything definite about him, because, strictly speaking, the other person's self-understanding is incommensurable with formulations. And it is precisely this situation which is respected in the abstract language of possibility. "It is the case, with respect to every actuality outside of me, that I can only get hold of it by means of thinking. Were I actually to get hold of it, I would have to be able to make myself into someone else, into the acting person in question; I would have to make the alien actuality my own actuality, which is an impossibility. If I do indeed make this alien actuality my own, this does not mean that I, in becoming knowing about him, become him, but it means a new actuality, which belongs to me as opposed to him" [VII 308 f., CUP 285]. The psychological understanding of the surrounding world has not been made impossible by this, not even made suspect, for it is precisely the intention of the argument to mark off the boundaries which keep it from becoming suspect. The existing individual has only his own actuality, and "he is merely knowing about every other actuality; but the true knowledge is a translation into possibility" [VII 303 f., CUP 280].

The idea of the incommunicable, subjective actuality is the core in Kierkegaard's teachings about genuine communication. His theory about and attempt to realize indirect communication is an attempt to bring abstract language in relation to concrete actuality, not an attempt to reproduce that actuality. "Language is indeed something abstract, and always gives one the abstract instead of the concrete," and therefore the user of language is misled into "the delusion that he actually knows something, which is why he has the word [for it]" [Pap. X 2 A 235, Hong 2324]. "Language is an abstraction" [Pap. XI 2 A 106, Hong 4056], a "thieves' argot," and this is so not merely by virtue of the individual misuses of language, but by virtue of "human nature" [Pap. XI 2 A 37, Hong 2333]. The difficulty in communicating adequately about actuality is therefore not merely accidentally caused by a particular historical period's stilted use of language (though this is also the case). "Here we are not speaking of an error which can be cleared up at the wave of a hand, so that it is gone. We are here discussing errors which have rooted themselves firmly from generation to generation, errors in which we are brought up, with which we have grown together entirely, errors by virtue of which we have formed the whole of our linguistic expression," Kierkegaard writes in his lectures on communication; "I know this from my own experience, quite apart from the fact that I have concerned myself with this matter for a long time" [Pap. VIII 2 B 82, p. 157; Hong 650]. The medium of communication itself, as a medium, blocks the way for direct communication. "Existential actuality does not admit of being communicated" [VII 347, CUP 320]. Linguistic communication always takes place by means of the abstract mediation of possibility, and it therefore always involves the risk of becoming abstract, that is, unreal. The existence of the problem does not cause Kierkegaard to give up every thought about communication, but rather to reflect all the more upon the dialectic of communication. The idea does not result in a monological solipsism, and it does not imply any contradiction of Vigilius' conception of language, of the word as that which delivers one from encapsulation and the demonic state (above, Chapter VI: 5: 3). "The word," in the eminent sense, is the deliverance in its eminent sense. It is also true in the ordinary sense that "the word and the expression and the inventions of language can be a way of recognizing love, but this is not certain," it is written in *Works of Love,* for the word can both reveal and conceal; it can be the expression of honesty or of hypocrisy: "[T]he same word in one person's mouth can be like the 'blessed, nourishing grain,' and in another person's mouth it can be like the barren splendor of the leaves." But it does not follow from this that one should hold back, in envy or self-importance, from expressing oneself, for the person one loves also has a right to the verbal expression of love: "[T]he expression is his credit balance, for in your emotion you belong to him who moves you, and you become conscious of the fact that you belong to him" [XI 21, WL 29].

The presupposition for Kierkegaard's theory of communication is the assumption that the recipient of the communication (Kierkegaard's reader) possesses an individual potential of understanding which makes him capable of transposing the communicated "possibility" back into the medium of actuality, i.e., to react to the communication by virtue of his own "actual" self-understanding. Therefore, it is not the intention of Kierkegaard's abstract statement about the self, sin, etc., to say anything definite and unambiguous about any particular individual, but to offer the potential reader a framework for orientation which can take on meaning in a functional, situational context of communication and in a context of individual understanding. Kierkegaard's writings are all calculated to fit into a process of communication. They are all written for and to a recipient, just as the edifying discourses are addressed to that individual, whom Kierkegaard with joy and thankfulness calls *his* reader, "who, in receiving this [i.e., the communication, the book], by himself and in his reception of it, performs for it what the chest in the temple did for the widow's mite: it hallows the gift, gives it significance, and transforms it into much" [IV 7, ED II 5], i.e., into actuality. The abstract formulation—and it is abstract, indeed, even in the edifying discourses—thus has the purpose of giving the recipient the possibility of placing what has been communicated into *his* context. It is for this reason that *The Sickness Unto Death* was published pseudonymously. "This book is written as if by a physician, it is true. But he who is the physician is a person who is no one; he does not say to a single individual: 'You' are sick—and neither, thus, does he say this to me; he simply describes the sickness. . . . It is thus left to the individual, to the reader, to decide whether he feels touched by it" [Pap. X 5 B 23]. Kierkegaard has expressed this intention in many places. The communication must not prescribe one particular reaction or aim at one particular effect, but situate the recipient freely in his appropriation of what has been communicated. "Yes, even when it is something spoken, you are of course the person who speaks to himself with the voice of the speaker. Only you know what the speaker has to say precisely to you; he does not know how you understand what has been spoken; only you know that," it is written in the confessional discourse from 1845 [V 203, TCS 3]. Therefore, the preacher of damnation and awakening, who points out the individual as sinful, is a religious deviate, who can certainly make his listener fearful and superstitious, but who cannot acquaint him with sin, for sin is something which the individual only knows by himself [V 217-22 and 227 f., TCS 21-27 and 34 f.]. But neither can the psychologist and the theologian speak of sin as other than a possibility. "How sin came into the world is something which every individual understands only in himself; if he wishes to learn this from another, he will *eo ipso* misunderstand it," Vigilius writes [IV 355, CD 46], and this idea is varied at many points in the authorship, especially in the edifying works. "For, the effect which the true discourse is to produce depends entirely upon who the listener is. . . . It is not the discourse which frightened the one person; and it is not the discourse which has calmed the other; it is the one person and the other person, who have understood themselves in the discourse" [X 236, ChD 209; cf. e.g., VII 521, CUP 473; VIII 293 f., 298, 316, GS 170 f., 176, 198; X 19-22, ChD 13-15; XII 284, TC 252].

Kierkegaard's intention is thus clear enough. The psychology and the religious writings contain no statement about the actuality of the individual person, but are hypothetical speech, an offer of an opportunity for understanding, which the other person can use or refrain from using. The abstract formulations are one of the linguistic agents which serve to counteract the misunderstanding that what has been communicated is actuality. The statement is possibility, "knowledge," and the recipient must not have any particular conclusion forced upon him.

However, it is one thing that it is Kierkegaard's intention to situate the reader of his writings freely in the appropriation of them, and thus avoid every form of assault or condemnation by virtue of his expertise; whether this intention is realizable at all, and whether Kierkegaard's practice as an author does not counteract precisely this intention, is another matter. Viewed ideally, the maieutic method of communication is liberating, in that it consciously takes into account the independence of the recipient in relation to what has been communicated. Viewed realistically, the maieutic method can just as easily cover the opposite phenomenon, the manipulation of the recipient's self-understanding, a psychological strategy which, under the pretense of respect for the other person's integrity, indeed builds precisely upon disrespect for it.

I will discuss some aspects of Kierkegaard's theory of communication, partially by way of extension of what has just been said, and partially because it is a precondition for the later discussion of the question of whether, and in what sense, one person can and may help another in his psychological and existential despair.

3:4. *Indirect Communication*

The person who communicates has an effect upon the person to whom he communicates. Calling attention to this simple fact must be the point of departure for every discussion of the matter. If one wishes to avoid influencing, and thus avoid the potential assault, one must refrain from communicating, or avoid coming into any sort of contact with others. For even silence is an influence, and "the despotism and torture of encapsulation," which exercises compulsion upon its surroundings by being itself silent, is far from the weakest form of influence [IV 433 f., CD 111]. The interdependence is unavoidable, and for Kierkegaard the word "communication" is not merely the designation for a written or spoken statement, but for a functional whole. It does not mean static information, but a process of communication. "As soon as I think about communicating, I think about four things: 1) the object, 2) the communicator, 3) the recipient, and 4) the communication" [Pap. VIII 2 B 83, Hong 651]. By the object, one must understand that which really is to be communicated, in this case "actuality," which, however, cannot be communicated, in this case "actuality," which, however, cannot be communicated directly, but only via the medium of language ("the communication") as the abstract middle term between the communicator and the recipient. What is particularly decisive is the recipient's role as the integrating link in the process of communication; and in the lectures on communication from 1847, Kierkegaard draws attention to the fact "that 'recipient' is an active word, that we have no passive word"[15] [Pap. VIII 2 B 81, p. 146; Hong 649]. He presupposes a many-valued potential for reaction in his reader. As an ethical-religious communicator Kierkegaard takes upon himself the responsibility of communicating, but not the responsibility for the adequate reaction of the reader. Kierkegaard can prepare the condition of possibility for the authentic reaction of the reader, but the inauthentic reaction ("the falsification of the didactic") neither can nor should be prevented [Pap. XI 2 A 270, Hong 3595; cf. X 3 A. 474]

How Kierkegaard practices the art of indirect communication in his books, and how he theorizes about this concept, will only be suggested here in a brief overview which is to form the prelude to the continued discussion of the concept of the maieutic.

Indirect communication may be defined as a communication which—in contrast to straightforward communication—always contains an inner contradiction on one or more levels. When "communicating" is "four things: 1) the object, 2) the communicator, 3) the recipient, and 4) the communication," the contradiction can thus be between two or more of these parts (A), and/or it can consist of an internal contradiction in one or more of these parts (B). There are an infinite number of possibilities of combinations and variations and degrees of many-valuedness. Below is merely a schematic overview.

A 1, incongruence between the object and the communication (i.e., the text); e.g., the intentional misunderstanding [VII 58 note and 71 f., CUP 65-66 note and 77] or the intentionally negative, ironic communication which denies everything [XIII 160 ff., CI 91 ff.; and many other places], which the young Kierkegaard attributes to Socrates, while he himself feels that the contradiction must not lead to a total impossibility of understanding; in that case the symbol of contradiction is no longer a symbol [XII 146, TC. 125].

A 2, incongruence between the communicator and that which is communicated produces the intended, but not the totally impenetrable contradiction. The communicator (e.g., the pseudonym, or in the Anti-Climacus writings, the editor) places himself "lower" than that which is communicated, declares himself to be a non-Christian, a poet, without authority, etc. (examples are found everywhere). The communicator must be "a Proteus" [Pap. VIII 2 B 81, p. 151; Hong 649], "no one, a person absent, an objective something, no personal man" [XII 155, TC 133]. The reason for this is, for example, that "there can in the straightforward sense be absolutely no teacher of the art of existing. . . . [There is only] one teacher: existence itself" [Pap. VI A 140, Hong 1038]. The intent: "Thus, when I lack authority and become extremely unreliable in people's eyes, then I say the truth and thereby place people in a contradiction out of which they can only be helped by appropriating the truth themselves" [Pap. IV A 87, Dru 432].

A 3, incongruence between that which is communicated and the recipient, who is assumed to be "in untruth" — for, of course, otherwise the communication would be superfluous [Pap. X 6 B 135, p. 183]. The communication must act as a hypothetical challenge in relation to the unambiguous understanding of life which the recipient has; it is to attack the invulnerability itself, which must first be rendered vulnerable with the assistance of the many-valued alternative contained in the communication, which must at the same time also contain the points of orientation for a new self-understanding. It must not "move him to go the same way, but precisely urge him to go his own way" [VII 264, CUP 247].

B 1, internal contradiction is always present in the object, to the extent that the object is existence in its ambiguousness and Christianity in its paradoxality.

B 2, internal contradiction in the communicator is the characteristic of the specific and definite Christian communication, which is in itself "a simple apodictic statement" [XI 122, PA 102], while the contradiction exists between the authority of the preacher and his total renunciation of the exercise of power and of any demonstrable institutionalized legitimation of the validity of the statement [XI 114-25, PA 93-105; the article "On the Difference Between a Genius and an Apostle"]. Christ as "the sign of contradiction" (Luke 2: 34) is the highest example of indirect communication, by being at once both God and—in an "omnipotently maintained incognito"—an individual person [XII 144-66, TC 122-44].

B 3, internal contradiction in the recipient, whose unclarified doublemindedness is supposed to manifest itself and thus be brought to consciousness by means of its reaction to the confrontation with the ambiguousness of the communication.

B 4, internal contradiction in the communication (the wording, the text) is present in the built-in deceptions in the pseudonymous writings; the reciprocal corrections of the pseudonyms; equivocality on many levels; the "intensive dialectical tension and coyness" [Pap. X 6 B 121, p. 157] which is also present (and intended) in many of the non-pseudonymous writings, and which also manifests itself in the style, whose function is always to recall the communication situation; and the internal contradiction is also present on the merely verbal plane of communication, by breaking the "ideal" character of language. What constitutes the style is the breach of style, the unprepared shift from soporific circumlocution to a stringent lapidary style, from pathos to mockery, from anecdote to analysis, from spoken language to narration, from sublime rhetoric to vulgarisms, etc. Even the punctuation has a conscious function: "Abstract grammatical punctuation does not suffice at all in rhetorical matters, particularly when there is an admixture of the ironic, the epigrammatic, the cunning, the evil (in the sense of the idea), etc." [Pap. VIII 1 A 33; cf. VII 57 f., CUP 64-65, on Lessing's style; and VII 261 note, CUP 245 note, on the function of style in the *Fragments*]. Compare, with this, the criticism by the somewhat older Kierkegaard of his own elaborate, rhetorical sermon-style in the edifying authorship, "an art of eloquence which stems from the evil" [XII 347-50, SE 35-38].

4. Maieutics and Anthropology

4: 1, *Maieutics*

Kierkegaard's method of indirect communication is a sort of literary maieutics. I have sketched several aspects of the idea, but the concept of maieutics can also be viewed from other angles. In *Works of Love* Kierkegaard differentiates between the relationship of communication which he himself, as an author, attempts to establish with his reader, and that which may exist mutually in a personal relation between two people. The written presentation of Christianity is always, because of the nature of language, a decorated untruth in comparison with actuality, and therefore the author must express himself as sharply and uncompromisingly as possible, he writes. He who writes "as a guide" must not attempt to ingratiate himself with his reader. "If one were to speak of his own relation to the world, that would be another matter; then it is a duty to speak as mildly, as apologetically, as possible. And even when he does so, it is his duty to remain indebted to love" [IX 225, WL 190]. Private communication must develop itself differently from public communication. The distinction is not a sharp one, nor is it unambiguously carried through, but it indicates a tendency in Kierkegaard, which can also be expressed with the assistance of another, related distinction. In the manuscripts for the lectures on communication from 1847, Kierkegaard sketches two methods. It is not a question of a sharp or unambiguous differentiation here either, but of two tendencies within the realm of the maieutic.

The first method is negative: "To what extent the recipient must first be cleansed—the negative element in maieutics. To communicate can thus mean to trick someone out of something, and this sort of communication is very dangerous for the communicator, for Socrates indeed says that people could become so angry with him that they would gladly have bitten him— when he tricked them out of one or another stupidity" [Pap. VIII 2 B 81, p. 152, Hong 649]. The other method is called upbringing: "The real communication and instruction in relation to the ethical and the ethical-religious is *upbringing*. By means of upbringing one becomes what he is essentially regarded to be (a horse, when it is brought up and the teacher is understanding, becomes precisely a horse). Upbringing begins by observing the person who is to be brought up as being κατὰ δύναμιν [kata dynamin][16] that which he shall become, and by directing his attentions at the person with this observation in mind, the teacher brings it forth from him. He *brings* it *up*, thus, it is present already—(to nurture up a plant, to bring up a child)" [Pap. VIII 2 B 82, p. 156, Hong 650].

What will be illuminated in the remainder of this chapter are these two methods, the relationship between the two of them, and their communicational and anthropological implications.

In both instances it is a matter of a relationship between two people, one who can help and one who is to be helped, the insightful person and the person who is to be the object of his insight, the upbringer and the person brought up, etc. The relationship of influence is one-sided, and the problem of expertise comes forth again. In a certain sense what is problematic is the fact that Kierkegaard involves himself at all with thinking that one person can be capable of helping the other in the existential situation, in relation to "belief." In a way it would be less problematic if he had simply held himself to the well-known view that it is precisely "yet another glory of faith that no person can give it to another"; for "every person has [the highest good] if he wants to have it; and this is precisely what is glorious about faith, that it can only be had on these terms . . . " [III 26 f., ED I 15]. If this passage, from Kierkegaard's first edifying discourse. "The Expectation of Faith," was the only thing he had to say about the matter, there would be nothing to add to the assertion of the encapsulated *quidam* about the relationship to one's neighbor: "The highest truth concerning my relationship to him is this, that I cannot benefit him in any essential way," because "essentially the individual only has to do with himself" [VI 361, SLW 316]. Were this all there is, then there would be no problem, and perhaps precisely this would be what is problematic. However, "essentially" does not mean literally, but fundamentally and in principle. In "The Expectation of Faith" Kierkegaard therefore has an addition to the theme that no person can give faith to another: "And if he is not in possession of it, then I can indeed be very helpful to him, for I will accompany his thoughts and force him to see that it is the highest good, and I will prevent him from slipping into any hiding place, so that it does not become obscure to him, whether he can comprehend it or not; I will penetrate every irregularity in him until he has only one expression — if he does not already have it — with which to explain his unhappiness, that he *will* not . . . as I presuppose that he does possess it, I will bring him to will to possess it" [III 28, ED I 16-17].

This is called psychological therapy (care, service, cure). To believe is to will to believe, but belief is not simply to will, it is to be able to will. And if he is not in the possession of this, then I can indeed be very helpful to him.

4: 2. *Therapy*

Kierkegaard was his own spiritual counselor and physician, and if one is to have an impression of what he understands by therapy, one of the points of departure must be the self-therapy which he describes in the final chapter of *The Concept of Anxiety*, "Anxiety as Saving by Means of Faith." The principle in self-therapy is in part the same as that in the therapeutic relationship between two people.

"Anxiety is the most frightful sort of spiritual struggle — until the point is reached at which the same person is trained in faith, that is, in viewing everything reversed: to become full of hope and confidence when things happen which previously would almost have brought him to sigh and swoon in anxiety; to go cheerfully into situations from which he previously knew only one means of salvation, to flee, and so on" [Pap. X 2 A 493, Hong 1401]. This quotation from the journal from 1850 summarizes the

fundamental idea of the little chapter about "Anxiety as Saving by Means
of Faith." This text deals with the conquest of anxiety. However, just as the
earlier text about guilt anxiety said that only faith is capable of forsaking
anxiety—"without, however, annihilating anxiety, but, eternally young,
continually wresting itself free from the death throes of anxiety" [IV 425,
CD 104]—so, too, is it the case in the present passage that anxiety can only
be forsaken by being persisted in. The background for the text is the prior
chapters of *The Concept of Anxiety,* where Vigilius has sketched the more
or less demonic effects of anxiety, and the disguises in which it appears
(spiritlessness, ritualism, encapsulation, etc.), while the individual himself
perhaps does not notice anxiety directly, or only notices it sporadically. On
the other hand, guilt anxiety is manifest in the religious genius and in
anxiety about the evil. The anxiety which is sketched in the final chapter
has similarities with guilt anxiety. It tortures the anxiety-plagued person
like the Grand Inquisitor, explores him like a spy, "and no keen judge
knows how to examine, yes, to examine, the accused as does anxiety, who
never lets him go, not in diversion, not in tumult, not during labor, not in
the day, not at night" [IV 466, CD 139]. Anxiety is manifest, conscious, a
plague and a suffering, and it is precisely by being this that it can be
"saving." Where, in the earlier chapters of the book, Kierkegaard spoke of
anxiety's more or less life-destroying, confining effects, here he concludes
dialectically with its healing function, which it has, or *can* have, when it
appears without disguises, as intensely experienced anxiety. The
experience is the condition of possibility for the transformation of anxiety,
and therefore every person must "learn to be made anxious, in order that
he not be lost by never having been anxious, or by sinking down in anxiety;
therefore, the person who has learned how properly to be made anxious,
he has learned the highest thing" [IV 465, CD 139]. To be made anxious
properly is to live through anxiety instead of retreating in the face of it:
"he remains with anxiety; he does not let himself be deceived by its
numberless falsifications; he remembers exactly what has happened in the
past; finally, anxiety's attacks, though frightful, are not such as to cause
him to flee. Anxiety becomes a serving spirit for him, which leads him,
against its will, where he wants to go. When it then shows itself, when it
cunningly behaves as though it had now found an entirely new means of
terror, which was far more frightful than ever, then he does not shrink
back, and even less done he seek to keep it away with noise and confusion,
but he bids it welcome, he greets it festively, as Socrates festively hoisted
the cup of poison; he encapsulates himself with it; he says as a patient says
to a surgeon when a painful operation is to begin: 'Now I am finished.'
Then anxiety goes into his soul and searches everywhere; it chases what is

finite and narrow out of him in anxiety, and then it leads him where he wants to go" [IV 469, CD 142].

Therefore, the person who is in the grip of anxiety should not exclude anxiety, but encapsulate it and get anxiety in his grip, and thus continually wrest himself free of anxiety. He must be formed by anxiety in order to be healed of his narrow egoism and his ceaseless self-concern. Instead of collapsing in anxiety about fate and guilt, he must, through and by means of anxiety, learn to repose confidently in Providence and redemption [IV 471 and 473, CD 144 and 145].

He who is brought up by means of anxiety is at once both an "autodidact" and a "theodidact" [IV 472, CD 145], i.e., he is his own therapist. It is very easy and obvious to make objections to Kierkegaard's line of reasoning, and the objection must precisely concern the autodidactics, for it is the idea of autodidactics which is responsible for the fact that the chapter "Anxiety as Saving by Means of Faith" not only demonstrates the therapeutic principle that anxiety must not be repressed, but lived through, but also that this is done in a way which may seem insufferable and depressing. The fundamental tone of the chapter is loathing for banal, external actuality, and contempt for the wretched souls who permit every day to be sufficient in its tangible suffering, and who are therefore incapable of imbibing stimulation for the soul from the self-created plagues of the power of the imagination. Here again, the idea of equality is brushed aside, and salvation seems to be reserved for the athlete of anxiety who has no other considerations than "internal" ones. There is a question whether one will acknowledge at all the notion of "salvation" with which Kierkegaard is operating here, for the text can very well be read such that "salvation" means the anxiety-laden person's emancipation from having anything to do with intolerable external reality. And Kierkegaard is not satisfied with saying that the man who is now plagued by anxiety must go through "possibility's course in unhappiness," but he also says that this course must be gone through by every person who does not want to be classified as vermin, lost in spiritlessness. The text is excellent as a sketch of the pathological course of crises, and the text is characteristic as a demonstration of the principle that passion must be worked through before one becomes free in relation to it, but the text has a tendency to prescribe precisely this particular experience as normative. It can be read as a morbid glorification of what Anti-Climacus called "the despair of possibility," the autistic, depressive, or fantastically euphoria-laden melancholia.

Therefore, if Kierkegaard had nothing other than this to say, one might lose patience with him and devote oneself to tracking down the mad consequences of his extremist thinking. Here it must suffice to point out these consequences, and thus to point out that the interpretation of Kierkegaard which is put forth here is not the only possible one. But Kierkegaard has of course also described "the despair of possibility," for example, precisely as something which was despairing, and he has described other forms of therapy besides self-therapy. With these other forms it is also true that the suffering (anxiety, despair, guilt-feelings, etc.) must be suffered through before it can become the means of healing, for when one keeps the torment away from oneself one clings fast to it.

Kierkegaard himself acted as a spiritual counselor, namely for a Mrs. Spang, the widow of an acquaintance who had died in 1846. The philosopher Hans Brochner was familiar with the case, and reports, apparently in Kierkegaard's own words: "He consoled, not by means of covering the sorrow over, but by first bringing it properly to consciousness, by clarifying it entirely, and then by recalling that it was a *duty* to sorrow, but precisely therefore it was also a duty not to permit oneself to be crushed down by sorrow, but, in sorrow, to preserve the strength for one's task, indeed, to find in it the incitement to perform this task even more completely."[17] The principle in the spiritual counsel described here is in profound agreement with Kierkegaard's psychology, and particularly with his distinction between sorrow and melancholia. For it is indeed precisely when sorrow cannot find an expression and an object that it is transformed into a reflected sorrow, i.e., when it is not brought to consciousness and completely clarified (cf. above, Chapter VII: 2: 2). The meaning is the same when Kierkegaard writes in *Works of Love* that the sorrow which commences at the death of a beloved person, for example, must be lived through in order that it not become despair: "I must not be allowed to harden myself against the pain of life, for I *must* sorrow; but neither am I allowed to despair, for I *must* sorrow; and yet neither am I allowed to cease to sorrow, for I *must* sorrow" [IX 56, WL 57].

Suffering must be suffered. That is Kierkegaard's counsel, also to the physician who is to help patients. In our time, as is well-known, it is "the physician [who is] the spiritual counselor" he writes at one point; people are (without reason, really) afraid to call the pastor, "so they call the physician." But in this little parody of the modern psychiatric interview, Kierkegaard does not betray more confidence in the spiritual counsel of the physician than in the others. A patient suffers from guilt anxiety; "the struggle of an anxious conscience," Kierkegaard calls it. The physician is called. He prescribes a trip to the spas, exercise, recreation, healthy hobbies, a light diet, and frequent ventilation of the bedroom. The patient objects that this will scarcely help much with his problem, an anxious conscience. The physician: "Oh, be gone with that sort of prattle! An anxious conscience. Things like that do not happen any more; they are a reminiscence from childhood of the race. Nor is there any enlightened or cultivated pastor who would think of such a thing," and the physician eagerly assures his worried patient that he, for his part, would throw out any member of his household, his servant or his own child, if the person in question went in for having an anxious conscience, for otherwise the whole house would of course soon be a madhouse. The patient: "But, Doctor, sir, that was a frightful anxiety [you just displayed] for something you say does not exist, 'an anxious conscience'; one might nearly believe that it revenges itself, if one wants to abolish the anxiety of conscience—this anxiety [of yours] is indeed like a revenge!" [XII 542, f., JY 210].

In this case it was thus not the patient, but the physician who was analyzed; the physician and not the patient suffered from repressions. "But with respect to this entire aspect of psychiatry it is so deeply true," Kierkegaard comments in his journal with reference to the problem of madness, "that to be the physician is to be willing, oneself, to suffer. The person who does not possess this humble devotion, patience, and love to will to endure the suffering, to want to serve (as a servant, as the lesser, in the form of a servant) and to become acquainted with the other—he will heal no one; and if the physician is willing, in this way, to suffer more than the sick—then he will heal many" [Pap. X 2 A 322, Hong 4552].

This is the true therapeutic relationship, "the secret in all of the helping arts" as Kierkegaard describes it in *The Point of View for My Work as an Author* in illustrating his own method as a writer. All true teaching, unbringing, therapy, maieutics, etc., begins with the teacher listening to the person he is to instruct, and allowing that person's conception and understanding of the situation to serve as the point of departure. "For, being a teacher is not to say: 'This is the way it is.' Nor is it to give lessons and the like. No, truly to be a teacher is to be a learner. Instruction begins with you, the teacher, learning from the pupil, acquainting yourself with what he has understood, and how he has understood it, if you yourself have not understood it before. Or, if you have understood it before, then you are to let the pupil listen to you recite, as it were, so that he can be sure that you know your lesson. This is the introduction; then a beginning can be made in another sense." The helper has a "greater understanding," an expertise, but if he makes it take effect immediately he is vain or proud, and does no good. The sufferer must have the possibility to live out his suffering. If the helper cannot transform himself into a "benevolent and attentive listener," if he cannot speak with the suffering person in such a way that the sufferer "finds a true consolation in speaking with you about his sufferings, so that, in the additional comments you make concerning his suffering, you almost enrich him with poetic conceptions — you, who are nevertheless not in that passion and would precisely like to get him away from it — if you cannot do that [i.e., situate yourself in his passion] then you cannot help him. He will close himself away from you; he will shut himself up into his innermost self — and then you only preach at him. Perhaps you should force him, by means of your personal power, to admit to you that he is wrong — oh, dear friend, in the next instant he will steal away by another secret path to a liaison with the hidden passion, for which he now only longs all the more; indeed, he is almost afraid that it could have lost some of its seductive charms. Now with your behavior you have only helped him to fall in love yet another time, namely, with his unhappy passion — and then you just preach!" The method is thus to humble oneself, "not to rule, but to serve," and "for the present to learn to live as one who is wrong" [XIII 568-70, PV 27-30].

This is precisely a method, a strategy, and herein lies the problem. A modern psychologist easily sees how advanced Kierkegaard's idea is, but what is advanced about it is at the same time what is problematic about it. The strategy, the trick, if you ´will, consists in avoiding awakening resistance in the person who is to be influenced. "If you in any way cause the ensnared person to set his will against it, then everything is lost. And one does this by a direct assault . . ." [XIII 567, PV 25]. The willingness to let the other person speak and be right is not a spontaneous devotion to and acceptance of the other, but it is teleological, goal-defined, and the goal is to find a way in which to alter the other person's self-understanding.

It is this method which Kierkegaard calls deceiving another person into the truth.

4: 3. *The Deception*

The intention of Kierkegaard's method of indirect communication in the authorship is to liberate the recipient and to make him independent: "[N]ot a single person alive has the same task as I, and, in turn, among the millions there is not a single one — according to my view — who has the same task as any other. And it is precisely this which I must proclaim. . . . My message is the reduplication of the proclamation of individuality. . . . And my task is this: while being myself an individual, and preserving my status as an individual (which God in Heaven also watches out for in infinite love), to proclaim what infinite reality every person has in himself when he becomes himself before God" [Pap. XI 2 A 19, Smith 189-90].

The liberation and the making independent of the recipient is also the idea of the maieutic method: ". . . lovingly to help a person to the point at which he becomes himself, free, independent, his own; to help him to stand alone — that is the greatest benefaction," to teach him "to stand alone — with another's help," it is written in *Works of Love,* with reference to Socrates [IX 311 f., WL 255-56].

But, as has been mentioned, Kierkegaard's proclaimed intention is one thing; the question of whether the intention is realized or is capable of being realized is quite another matter. The problem in the maieutic practitioner's personal relationship to another person is here analogous to the problem of the relatiohship of the author to the reader. According to *Works of Love,* the art which Socrates practices consists in "concealing his help," and this art is "clever and cunning," but in the good sense, Kierkegaard feels. It consists in "deceiving the other person into the truth," "taking his foolishnesses from him and obtaining the truth for him by means of trickery" [IX 312-14, WL 256-58].

The expression "to deceive a person into the truth" is used by Kierkegaard in a number of places, including *The Point of View for My Activity as an Author,* to designate the plan of his authorship [XIII 577, PV 39; cf. the lectures on communication, Pap. VIII 2 B 85, p. 166; Hong 653]. The expression is suspect according to every criterion of decency, also including Kierkegaard's. If the truth is the way and not the result, then it seems that to deceive a person into the truth means to deceive him out of the way to the truth, and thus out of the truth, or, in other words, to make oneself his guardian. There is therefore reason to inquire more closely into what Kierkegaard means.

In "The Diary of a Seducer" we get a strong impression of the deception, i.e., of the psychostrategy which depends upon an illusory giving of independence and a factual depriving of authority, and the question which must be asked concerns whether the only thing which separates Johannes the Seducer from Kierkegaard is the goal of the seduction, the sexual and the religious climaxes, respectively. In that case there would be nothing besides the ends to justify the means, and that is hardly sufficient. I have examined the seducer's strategy in Chapter II, and in that connection I quite provisionally mentioned a difference between him and Kierkegaard. But the question must be posed again. Johannes the Seducer liberates Cordelia and makes her independent, for he only wants her as a free person. The initiative must come from her, despite the fact that in reality it is he who gives her this initiative and this freedom, so that she is in a merely apparent independence and is actually directed by his intrigues. His method is the deception. He does not make his intention known from the start, but feigns having other intentions. In erotic respects he places himself lower than she, and influences her indirectly and ambiguously with the assistance of repulsion and attraction, but in such a way that he is continually learning from her how the deception is to be put into effect, until she finally, irresistably, in chimerical freedom, succumbs before the manipulation, or before the maieutics, which is the same thing in this case.

Johannes the Seducer speaks of his battle plan for the campaign against Cordelia. In *The Point of View* Kierkegaard speaks of a "new military science . . . which is completely saturated by reflection," and adds: "The method must be indirect" [XIII 576, PV 38]. The strategy is the same. The whole of Kierkegaard's aesthetic authorship is a deception, which consists in the fact "that one does not begin *straightforwardly* with that which one wants to communicate; one begins by taking the other person's fantasy as genuine. Thus one does not begin . . . like this: 'I am a Christian. You are not a Christian.' But like this: 'You are a Christian. I am not a Christian.' Or, one does not begin like this: 'It is Christianity I proclaim, and you are living in merely aesthetic categories.' No, one begins like this: 'Let us speak about the aesthetic sphere.' The deception consists in the fact that one talks like this precisely in order to come to the religious sphere" [XIII 578, PV 40-41].

This is really the method of the seducer, the bait-method, the Jesuitical method, or, in other words, the expert-method. Now it must certainly be maintained that what we are presented with in *The Point of View* is not Kierkegaard's actual authorship, but his own retrospective interpretation of it, about which he himself explains that this first became clear to him in the (provisional) conclusion of the authorship. He had not been clearly conscious of the plan from the beginning [XIII 534, 601 f.; PV 150, 72 f.]. And from a purely factual point of view, the authorship cannot be said to have functioned seductively, either in Kierkegaard's time or since then. An author's relation to his public is more impersonal than a seducer's relationship to the seduced, and he does not have the possibility which Johannes the Seducer had in relation to Cordelia, of keeping an eye on his reader and of assuring himself that the strategy is taking effect without the disturbance of any other influences. And furthermore, one does not have to nose about in Kierkegaard's books—even the "aesthetic" books—for very long before one catches the scent of Christian blood and gets the opportunity of backing out. Kierkegaard himself is aware of the fact that his deception is not impenetrable; the mystification does not exclude the fact that "the true explanation is there to be found for the person who honestly seeks for it" [XIII 560, PV 16]. Thus, in practice the problem of seduction in the relationship between Kierkegaard and his reader is of manageable size.

What is suspect, then, is not Kierkegaard's practice as an author, but the fact that in *The Point of View* he himself can use the viewpoint "deception" with regard to his works at all—apparently without finding it suspect. This indicates that as a communicator and maieutic practitioner he accepts a method whose point of departure is dishonesty. The tendency of the deception is the opposite of Kierkegaard's proclaimed intent, for the tendency is to deceive the recipient out of his decision, because it deceives him out of the understanding of what the conditions are upon which the influence takes place and what the intention of that influence is.

The question is whether this is really Kierkegaard's tendency, thus whether his method is maieutic or whether it is manipulative. Is the deception an actual deception, or does it mean something else? The question can also be formulated in another manner, which will provide the criteria for an answer. In *Works of Love* it was stated, with respect to the method which consists in deceiving the other person into the truth, that the help which is given in order to get the other person to stand alone, must be given in such a way that *"the gift looks as though it were the property of the recipient"*[IX 320, WL 255]. It is here that the problem lies. If, indeed, the gift only "looks" like the property of the recipient, but is in fact a gift which the helper gives him by means of trickery, then the method, in spite of all good intentions, is really a deception, a form of manipulation (suggestion, indoctrination). Manipulation must, of course, be defined precisely as that method of influencing in which the influencer first disarms the influenced person's ability to make resistance against the influence, preventing him from coming to clarity about the fact that he is being influenced—and then influences him. if, on the other hand, one assumes—as other of Kierkegaard's formulations indiciate—that what is "given" *is* in fact the property of the recipient, which he simply has not acquired, then the help does not consist in the helper's forcing upon the other person an understanding which is foreign to his being, or tricking the other person into it, but it consists of helping him to acquire what he himself already owns in advance.

Maieutics and anthropology are indissolubly bound to one another (and in this respect Kierkegaard is surely but one example of a quite general problem). For the person who finds Kierkegaard's anthropology unacceptable, the maieutics will also be unacceptable. Whether a given method is to be called maieutic or manipulative is ultimately a question of what understanding of man one has. If one is in disagreement about the anthropology, then what looks to one person like genuine maieutics will appear to the other as illegitimate manipulation—and vice versa.

4:4. *The Analogy to Socrates*

The question of whether "the gift" is the property of the recipient leads us back to the center of Kierkegaard's anthropological deliberations, as they were presented in the previous chapters. At the conclusion of Chapter IV I examined the edifying discourse "To Acquire One's Soul in Patience." The precondition for this acquisition was that the soul (the self) is owned in advance as a possibility which can be actualized. In Kierkegaard the idea of this potential self was formed in analogy with the Socratic-Platonic idea that the individual himself possesses the truth in himself, and only needs to bring it forth by means of recollection. Thus, the idea of the potential truth which is realized in repetition, which is his conscious parallel to the idea of anamnesis, and the existential instruction and upbringing, do not consist in teaching the learner anything new (the communication of knowledge), but in luring forth that which is within him (the communication of capability).

However, this fine idea runs into difficulties as soon as Kierkegaard definitively puts the Christian understanding of man in the place of the Greek-inspired notion. The conflict model is the same as the ethical-anthropological model, and yet it has another aspect which is qualitatively different, for Christianly understood subjectivity is untruth, and the individual is not on the road to acquiring the truth about himself, but is turned away from it, more and more deeply involved in the passage into untruth, and is therefore incapable of withdrawing from the vicious circle of sin. He cannot escape the consistency of sin by himself, but only by means of the person who has the power to forgive sins, Christ. However, with this formulation the concrete problem is not solved, but only posed. Regardless of the so-called "objective" aspect of Christianity (that it is the forgiveness of sins) the "subjective" problem (that the individual himself must believe in it) still remains [cf. e.g., Pap. X 2 A 301, Hong 4551].

But the relation between the ethical-anthropological model and the conflict model is not simply that the latter disavows the understanding of man which the former contains. In the *Fragments* Climacus explains that there is one analogy between the Greek and the Christian conceptions. According to the Greek conception, the teacher is the occasion for the disciple to discover the truth by himself. This is not so from the Christian point of view, for the learner is untruth and thus cannot discover his own truth. He can, on the other hand, discover his untruth — "in respect to which act of consciousness it is the case, Socratically, that the teacher is only an occasion, whoever he is, even if he is a god; for I can only discover my own untruth by myself, because only when *I* discover it is it discovered. . . ." This is the "only analogy to the Socratic" [IV 208, Pf 17], but this analogy is particularly important, because it involved the fact that in this respect one man can be the occasion for another man's self-understanding, thus, a maieutic practitioner.

To illuminate this in more detail there is reason for us to remember that Kierkegaard also operates with another, but closely related, analogy between the Socratic and the Christian views, even though he himself does not formulate the matter in this way. In *Philosophical Fragments,* where the passage is to be found, he lets Socrates represent the Platonic doctrine of anamnesis, according to which man himself is in possession of the truth and only needs to reflect upon it, and thus Kierkegaard establishes the antithesis between the Socratic-Platonic and the Christian doctrine of sin. In the *Postscript* this view is made problematic by letting Plato be the real representative of the doctrine of anamnesis, while Socrates continually takes leave of the idea in order to maintain objective uncertainty (cf. above, Chapter IV: 4: 1). But the most definitive expression of the Socratic in its opposition to the Platonic is ignorance. Therefore, in his master's thesis Kierkegaard depicts Socrates' method of questioning as purely negative. Its real idea, which the Socratic questions are to reveal, is the idea of ignorance, that the only thing man knows is that he knows nothing [XIII 144 f., CI 76 f.]. It is this understanding of Scorates which forms the basic framework when Kierkegaard attributes to the Greek ironist "the negative element in the maieutic," which consists in tricking other people out of their imagined knowledge.

The Christian analogy to this Socratic ignorance which has been made conscious, is the consciousness of sin. In the *Postscript* Kierkegaard uses an expression about the sinner, that he "achieves nothing before God," but Kierkegaard adds that he does, however, achieve one thing, namely, "to become conscious of this fact" [VII 451 note, CUP 413 note; cf. V 100, ED IV 25]. In an edifying discourse it is said, with respect to the woman who was a sinner in the Gospel that *"she understood that with respect to finding forgiveness she was capable of doing nothing by herself"* — and yet, she does do something, of course; she seeks out Jesus, for even though she is capable of nothing, she is nevertheless capable of understanding that she is capable of nothing [XII 301, TC 266]. "the highest thing of which a man is capable is to let God be able to help him" [Pap. V B 198, Hong 54], but this means precisely to become as nothing before God. That man "is capable of nothing" in sin must naturally not be understood literally, but precisely in relation to the notion of the consistency of sin, which the sinner is not himself capable of breaking. The highest thing which man can achieve is to acknowledge his incapacity, and in this acknowledgement to open himself to the forgiveness of sins. The idea of this bringing-to-consciousness is Kierkegaard's analogy to the Socratic idea of making a

man conscious of his non-understanding. The analogy is of significance for
the understanding of the negative element in maieutics. When
Kierkegaard attributes to Socrates this method, which consists in indirectly
unmasking and seeing through illusory knowledge, fancies, and
foolishness, this maieutics thus also has its elaborated, Christian analogy.

This will be seen when we ask what role Kierkegaard's psychology plays
in relation to Christianity.

4: 5. *The Significance of Psychology*

There are two things to be said about Kierkegaard's psychology in this
connection. Its most genuine task is to help bring forth the negative
understanding which is the contents of the consciousness of sin—and the
consciousness of sin is in turn the most definitive expression of self-
knowledge. Further, Kierkegaard's psychology demonstrates that this
knowledge of sin and of oneself is real knowledge, an understanding, and
thus not merely a blind experiencing of nothing.

If the knowledge of sin were not real knowledge, why would Kierkegaard
have occupied himself with the writing of psychology? Certainly
Christianity did not arise out of any human heart, which is why man is not
to "conceive" it, but "believe" it—or be offended by it. One does not come
into relationship to Christianity in virtue of any philosophical reasonings.
But it does not simply follow from this that faith is blind and without
understanding, in Kierkegaard's view. "In an—admittedly clever—logical
argumentation, he wrests knowledge and action from one another, in
order to give Platonism knowledge which is devoid of action and
Christianity action which is devoid of knowledge, both halves being
constructs pure and simple," writes L.E. Logstrup.[18] I think it is Logstrup
and not Kierkegaard who is constructing. What separates Kierkegaard
from "speculation" is not that speculation speculates while Kierkegaard, in
an ascetic denial of knowledge, batters his readers with slogans such as
choice, responsibility, duty, will, and ought, for he knows very well that
the most radical statements tend toward meaninglessness when they are
employed "baldly and simply." "Therefore, from a psychological point of
view, it is quite noteworthy to see the absolute disjunction used deceptively
precisely for purposes of escape," he writes, with a friendly greeting to his
zealous, "existentialist" epigones, for the subjective thinker must quite
definitely have the disjunction ready at hand, "but not in such a way that
by abstractly resorting to it he is able indeed to hinder existence" [VII 339
f., CUP 313]. Inwardness is a "deed," but also an "understanding,"
Vigilius writes, but quite certainly with the addition which we have also

encountered in Anti-Climacus: "To understand and to understand are two things. . . . Inwardness is an understanding, but *in concreto* it is a matter of how this understanding is to be understood. To understand a discourse is one thing; to understand the element in it which points to one personally is something else. To understand what one says, is one thing; to understand oneself in what one has said, is something else" [IV 452 f., CD 126-27]. But the reservation about knowledge is just that, a reservation, not a rejection, and in *The Sickness Unto Death* Kierkegaard even takes it upon himself to "prove the eternal element in man" upon the basis of his theory about despair [XI 151, Sd 153]. Naturally it is not a proof in the stricter sense, but an interpretation, faith's exegesis of and argumentation for its understanding of existence.

The consciousness of sin is thus not simply a lived-through and suffered-through experience of impotence, for the experience also contains a possibility of knowledge, and it is helped forth and supported by an understanding which can be purely psychological. It is clear from *The Concept of Anxiety* that psychology is "in the service of another science," namely, dogmatics, so that psychology serves the doctrine of sin and of the forgiveness of sins [IV 327, CD 21].

What is its function, then? "Psychology must remain within its boundaries; then its explanations will always have significance," writes Vigilius [IV 343, CD 35-36]. The pseudonymous books "have their significance," writes Climacus, with particular reference to *The Concept of Anxiety,* and adds that "on this point a communication of knowledge could be necessary, before it is possible to go over to the appropriation of things in inwardness" [VII 256, CUP 241]. "And even if this knowledge can have its significance, it nevertheless has often deceived man, precisely as the world often does, so that the man thought he possessed it, while it was his knowledge which possessed him," Kierkegaard writes in the edifying discourse about acquiring one's soul in patience [IV 73, ED II 84]. Taken together, these three passages give an impression of the role which Kierkegaard assigns to purely psychological understanding. What is most striking in his warning against superfluous knowledge, against, as it is stated in *Works of Love* "devoting oneself to observation or to exploratory self-observation which only 'makes the spirit sad' and delays growth" [IX 19, WL 28]. The edifying discourse about acquiring the soul warns against the intellectualization of self-understanding, which only hinders the work of existential patience. "The knowledge of one's own soul, if one views this as an acquiring, is therefore, a self-deception, because in its greatest completeness it is only a hint of what reveals itself distincly during the acquisition." "Knowledge as such" does not help at all, but, adds psychologist Kierkegaard, the man who truly knows his soul, knows it "as a thing which he can indeed describe well and accurately" [IV 74, Ed II 85]. This latter passage is a surprisingly strong emphasis of the fact that, despite all existential and psychological reservations about intellectualization, pure psychological understanding can nevertheless "have its significance."

In the narrower sense, Kierkegaard's psychology belongs to what he calls the negative element in maieutics. It is analyzing, unmasking, breaking-down, and critical, and what holds for the religious address also holds for psychology: it "intrudes searchingly into the interior of a man. . . . [I]t pushes through, trying him, in order to show the double-mindedness in him . . ." [VIII 155, PH 56], and "it must travel every path, know about where the errors dwell, where the moods have their hiding place, where the passions have their lonely self-understandings. . . ., know where sensory deceptions tempt, where the paths divide, etc."—and here Kierkegaard also suggests that "in this respect the one person [can] do something for the other . . ." [VII 417, CUP 382-83]. Kierkegaard's psychological and his edifying writings are a maieutic offer of "help" to the person who might find the help relevant. To the extent that it is unmasking, the help is a negative help, not an unmasking of the reader, but of the reader's possibility for unmasking himself. What is unmasked is the despair behind the facade, the emptiness and the misery, the self-deceptions, the illusions, the sin; and what is helped forth in a negative and maieutic manner is the consciousness of sin.

The negative element in the maieutic "can thus mean to trick something away," and Kierkegaard shares with Socrates this negativity, the art of deceiving the other by "taking his foolishness from him and obtaining the truth for him by means of trickery." From a Socratic point of view the truth is ignorance; from a Christian point of view it is the consciousness of sin. At the instant that the maieutic practitioner wants to go further and obtain, by means of trickery, any positive truth for the other person, then it would no longer be a matter of maieutics, but of indoctrination, inasmuch as the presupposition is that the truth about man is that he is untruth (or, Socratically, ignorance).

But *is* this the truth, the only truth, about man?

4: 6. *The Anthropological Question*

In *Works of Love,* Kierkegaard presents and praises the Socratic method, which consists in fooling the other person out of his fancies and foolishness and obtaining the truth for him by means of trickery. But he also puts himself at arm's length, not only because the Christian maieutic practioner is more serious and more concerned than the ironic, smiling Socrates, but especially because he knows that he cannot liberate the other person, however much he tries. "Therefore, thanking God, he says, 'now this man stands alone — with my help.' But there is no self-satisfaction in this latter, for the loving person has understood that, essentially, every person nevertheless stands alone — with God's help . . ." [IX 315, WL 259]. Even the Socratic who is most self-denying with respect to power cannot free his fellow man entirely, and therefore maieutics must point beyond itself negatively in order to be completed [cf. Pap. VII 1 A 181, Hong 1251, cited above, Chapter IV: 3: 2]. The completion of the task of the maieutic practitioner is not done by the maieutic practitioner himself. In *Training in Christianity* Kierkegaard describes Christ as an indirect communicator; but this indirect communication is the genuine maieutics. Christ wants to draw everyone to himself, it is written, and this can "not mean to draw man away from being himself, to draw him in such a way that he loses all existence by being drawn into that which drew him. . . . No, when the person who is to be drawn is a self in himself, this truly means that to draw means first to help him truly to become himself, in order then to be drawn; or it means: in and as a part of being drawn, to help him to become himself" [XII 182, TC 159]. In *Philosophical Fragments* it is expressed as follows: that man does indeed become "nothing" in the forgiveness of sins, but he does not become "annihilated" [IV 224, PF 38].

This is the theological expression of the matter. The question which is to be discussed here is whether the faith of the believer contains anything other than the naked postulate, devoid of understanding, or whether faith also contains an understanding. Are the forgiveness of sins and grace abstract assertions without any foothold in anthropological reality, a cramp-like self-defense against the despairing knowledge that man is "without God in the world," and thus in despair only because this despair functions as a defense against this knowledge?

Perhaps. In any case, this is a very common way of understanding Kierkegaard. But precisely because it is so common, it is tempting to try another explanation, which is, if not the real one, at least a possible one.

Let us first sum up the situation. Originally, from the hand of God, the human synthesis is in the proper relation [XI 146, SD 149], and faith is "the original element" in every person [III 26 f., Ed I 15]. But in the fall into sin, when God lets man go free, the relationship becomes a misrelationship, and freedom first manifests itself as unfreedom (the positive is recognizable by the negative). Man despairs; he obscures his self-understanding at the same moment that it begins to come into being; he twists and distorts the possibility of his life, turning himself away from the truth, and burrows into the consistency of sin (regardless of whether the consistency is more closely defined as being that of spiritlessness, defiance, etc.). The created glory is lost, and man has been excluded from it by himself. The task of preaching is to proclaim this loudly and to call man back to the point of conversion, in which his despair is transformed into a total, manifest consciousness of sin, thus becoming the means of recovery, "a mortal illness, which, however, is so far from being unto death, that it is indeed unto life . . ." [XII 298, TC 264]. Psychology is in the service of this proclamation, and its task is to penetrate, to break down and dissolve the despairing person's defenses of his despair, to lay bare, to unmask, to reveal the despair which is fundamentally present. The specifically Christian task is namely a negative, passive act, a giving-up, but thereby it is also a receiving, an opening of oneself. "It is not a matter here of adding something to the soul, but of taking something from it, that is, something which it apparently possessed," it says in the edifying discourse [IV 71, ED II 82]. And this movement is the same when Kierkegaard speaks "edifyingly" and when he speaks in a definitively Christian way. "The act of inwardness is a suffering, for to re-create oneself is something of which the individual is not capable; it becomes foolishness, just as affectation does" [VII 423, CUP 388]. "The I chooses itself, or rather, it receives itself" [II 192, E/O II 181]. "But to repent is . . . not an action, but a letting something happen to oneself" [VI 499, SLW 430]. "Christianity . . . presupposes in the person in question a resolve — to resolve, to open up — which is always required in relation to a radical cure" [Pap. X 2 A 461, Hong 3612]. This little group of quotations must be enough to suggest the idea. To pursue it in every detail would not only be unmanageable, but also futile because it is a case of something which is strictly speaking incommunicable.

The task of psychology is thus primarily to help forth this negative action in a negative, maieutic fashion. It reveals the despair which is fundamentally present: unfreedom, guilt, sin. Is this unmasking then, the most fundamental and final disillusioning truth about man? "How does Kierkegaard know that a person *only* can become a self, only can live genuinely, in guilt? Why is it excluded that a person can become himself in confidence, mercy, love, honesty, and faithfulness? How does he know that it is *only* in anxiety that man's fundamental conditions emerge? How does he know that there is not a fundamental condition which emerges in the individual's joy, so that it, too, is a fundamental mood?" asks K.E. Løgstrup.[19] The questions are rhetorical; it is not asked whether, but only why, Kierkegaard thinks one thing and not another.

As for the first of the rhetorical questions quoted above, according to my editions of Kierkegaard's collected works, it is not in guilt, but in the forgiveness of sins, that man "genuinely" lives. Kierkegaard calls the forgiveness of sins "fundamental recovery" [Pap. VIII 1 A 558, IX A 176]. What is the fundament to which he refers? Or, in other words: How does Professor Løgstrup know that according to Kierkegaard man's fundamental condition cannot emerge in joy, or, for example, in love? He certainly cannot know this upon the basis of Kierkegaard's edifying discourses, especially not those which deal with the lily and the bird. Could it be from *Works of Love* that Professor Løgstrup has this idea?

4: 7. *"Works of Love"*

I return to the maieutic, to the question of whether the one person has the possibility of helping the other. We have heard about the negative element in the maieutic, which consists in fooling away and stealing away from the other person his fancies and his lies about life by giving him the possibility of seeing through them himself. This is the task which Kierkegaard takes up when he writes his psychology of despair. Let us now instead see what he says when he speaks of love and of the works of love. Love also possesses a sort of maieutics, but a different sort than that which we have discussed up to this pont. And if one asks what love has to do with psychology and psychotherapy, Judge William already has the beginning of an answer. The Judge knows very well that Aesthete A is an excellent psychologist, and he also attributes to him abilities as a practicing therapist: "You are undeniably a good surgeon. You understand how to penetrate into the most secret enclosures within sorrow and worry. . . . Well, I assume that you have succeeded in healing your patient. You do not take any true or deep joy from it, because the whole thing bears the stamp of arbitrariness, and you have no responsibility. It is only when one takes responsibility that blessing and true joy come, and they come even if one cannot do it half as well as you. It often gives a blessing when one can do nothing at all" [II 95, E/O II 87-88]. Deep psychological exploration and analytic technique can thus be very fine, but it is more important to be obligated. In *Works of Love* Kierkegaard dares to use a stronger, more precise word: love. One might wish that the person who is to help another would have "insight and knowledge and talent and experience," but it is more decisive that he be loving [IX 254, WL 211].

The idea is very straightforward and reliable. We can take several examples. *"Love hides the multiplicity of sins, for love presents sin from coming into being, smothers it at birth."* Kierkegaard knows that the prohibition is sin's opportunity. "The commandment, the prohibition, tempt, precisely because they want to compel evil; and now sin takes its opportunity; it *takes* it, for the prohibition *is* the opportunity" (cf. above, Chapter III: 3: 2). In the same fashion it is concretely true, with respect to man's daily surroundings, that sin is the opportunity for sin. If, on the other hand, the surroundings are loving, then they become the opportunity for love. The individual's sin cannot hold its own against the love of its surroundings, and therefore the milieu of a prison or a hospital is of decisive significance. "Oh, the authorities must often think up very ingenious means to keep the criminal captive, and the physician must often employ great inventiveness to discover means with which to compel the madman. But with respect to sin no surroundings are as compelling, but also, no compelling surroundings are as full of salvation, as love." Love smothers anger; it lets wickedness perish; it mitigates resentment, reconciles the defiant and unjustly treated spirit; it takes away from evil plans the stimulus to be fulfilled. "Oh, how many crimes have been prevented, how many evil intentions destroyed, how many desperate decisions brought to forgetfulness, how many sinful thoughts stopped on the way to becoming deeds, how many intemperate words stifled in time, because love did not give them the opportunity!" [IX 337-40, WL 276-78]. One should notice the verbs: prevent, destroy, bring to forgetfulness, stop, stifle, plus the most important one, to hide—and one will thus get an impression of the communication situations in which Kierkegaard makes use of the idea of confronting, penetrating, persisting, making manifest, unmasking, etc., and of the situations in which these words do not adequately cover his view.

Love hides the multiplicity of sins. It does not seek curiously after other people's sins, nor listen to gossip, but remains silent about things and mitigates and forgives [IX 318 ff., WL 261 ff.]. Kierkegaard naturally knows very well that one can forgive another person in a way that "noticeably, strikingly increases the guilt instead of diminishing it"—but love forgives lovingly [IX 335, WL 274]. Love is the acceptance of the other person in his particularity; it renounces all narrow intolerance and desires of domination; it respects what is different because it possesses "pliability in understanding others," and it therefore does not wish to recreate the other person [IX 306 ff., WL 252 ff.]. Love does not love the other person in spite of his errors and weaknesses, but loves him with his errors and weaknesses, just as the true portrait painter does not need to travel around the world to find a face which is beautiful enough to paint, but finds the beauty in every face [IX 181 f., WL 156-57]. Love accepts. It does not select, but accepts; it does not apply any skeptical double standard to the beloved, but loves the person it sees in front of itself. "When it is a duty to love the people one sees, *then it is important that one love the individual actual person, and not substitute an imagined notion of what one thinks or could wish that this person should be"* [IX 188 ff., WL 161 ff.]. Love does not love for its own sake, but for the sake of its neighbor, and therefore the difficulty is not to find a worthy object for one's love, but to be, oneself, loving [IX 33, WL 38]. "The neighbor is the first You" [IX 72, WL 69], and love "turns outward, encompassing everyone, and yet loving each one individually" [IX 82, WL 78]. Love does not dwell upon itself, does not become self-important in self-observation or in comparing its own works with those of others, for love is sheer activity, and thus beyond comparisons [IX 116 ff., 204 ff.; WL 105 ff., 174 ff.]. Its motives in action are the sorrows of the poor, not its own; its work is the relieving of poverty, not to seek relief for itself [IX 23, WL 30], all of which can be summarized in the statement that "in all its manifestations love turns outward toward people, where it has its object and its tasks . . ." [IX 216, WL 183].

This is the message of the book, or at least its most important ethical idea, and it is difficult to dispute with Kierkegaard when he says that this is so easy to understand, that the problem is not the further, theoretical understanding of the commandment of love, but the problem is the simple one, to act according to it.

But naturally neither does this imply that Kierkegaard's message is devoid of understanding, a "Thou shalt" which is empty of thought. Thus the message raises problems enough, and the first and greatest of them is that man does not indeed act accordingly. Kierkegaard speaks of "love" and "the loving person." Who is it? We have Kierkegaard's own word for it in the book that it is not he [IX 74, WL 71]. He leaves it to his reader to determine if it applies to the reader himself. Kierkegaard himself knows of only one man who "was love," in whom love is sheer activity, uninterrupted, without thinking of itself, pure spontaneity. This man is the historical Jesus of the Gospels, who rendered the Law superfluous by being himself the fulfillment of the Law. For the unloving person, on the other hand, the Law is his downfall, because it lays bare the lack of love and acquaints the person with sin [IX 118 ff., WL 106 ff.]. But because the Law is man's standard of measure for knowledge of himself, it does not mean that the Law has thereby ceased to be the Law. It is both in one: judgement *and* requirement, proof *and* instructions—both/and.

The requirement is to love, and to love is to accept the other person, not to criticize but to accept, not in words, but in works. Then the next problem is: how is this idea related to "the negative element in the maieutic." to Kierkegaard's psychological unmasking of the person (not of this or that individual person), to the idea of stealing away from the other person his errors, foolishness, self-deceptions, his despair? Is it sheer unlovingness? What is it to love one's neighbor? What is the *content* of this requirement?

4: 8. ". . . the Consistency of the Good"

At one point in *Works of Love* Kierkegaard puts the content of the requirement—and naturally the requirement *has* a content—into the following formula: *"For to love God, that is truly to love oneself; to help another person to love God is to love another person; to be helped by another person to love God is to be loved"* [IX 126, WL 113]. It is clear from this that to help another person to love God is identical with helping him truly to love himself. To conclude the formula yet another quotation must be added: "If you wish to show that your life is determined to serve God, then let it serve men, yet continually with the thought of God" [IX 185, WL 159].

The formula is thus: to love God = to love oneself = to love the other person. The one is the formula for the other; the one does not exist without the other. It is a circle, not the vicious one of sin, but the circle of love and of faith, and the commandment to love one's neighbor bids us to help the other person into this "consistency of the good," as it is called in *The Sickness Unto Death* [XI 246, SD 238].

What have been cited are just formulae, not concrete and detailed instructions for particular actions. I will comment briefly upon the three parts of the equation.

Truly to love oneself is to love God and one's neighbor. The commandment to love my neighbor commands me to love my neighbor as myself, and thereby presupposes that I in fact do love myself, indeed commands me to do so: *"You must love yourself in the proper way,"* for the person who does not do so can "not love his neighbor either." The two expressions "are fundamentally one and the same." The Law does not require egoism; on the contrary, it begins by taking from me my self-love by requiring me to love my neighbor as myself, but to take away my egoism is precisely to teach me "the proper self-love." Egoism is misunderstood self-love. The melancholic also loves himself (we also know this from other of Kierkegaard's analyses, cf. above, Chapter VII: 4: 2, and other places), and so does the nervously officious person, the reckless person, the self-torturer, and the suicide; in brief, the despairing person, who wastes his life, and who therefore, if possible, must learn to give up self-love and to love himself truly. The idea is important, because it connects *Works of*

Love with Kierkegaard's other writings on despair and faith. Believing is naturally precisely to love oneself, "in the way that you love your neighbor when you love him as yourself" [IX 27 f. and 33 f., WL 34 f. and 39 f.].

To love God is to love oneself and one's neighbor. "God is not a part of existence in such a way that he requires his part from you. He requires everything, but when you bring it to him, you immediately get, if I may put it thus, a note written on it which explains the destination to which it is to be forwarded, for God requires nothing for himself, regardless of the fact that he requires everything from you." To say that the requirement originates with God is therefore, on the level of content, the same as saying that it originates with one's fellow man, for it is the interests of the fellow man which are to be looked after. God manages without help; he is not "envious" but "merciful." Yet the part of the equation entitled "to love God" is not thereby reduced to an empty repetition of the other two parts. The three parts say the same thing, i.e., they express one thought, but three different aspects of it, which are all indispensable for the understanding of it. To love God is not a partial action or an isolated religious mood, but a more detailed definition of the other two parts of the equation, and — because the book does indeed deal with the relationship with the neighbor — especially of the part about loving one's neighbor: "[T]he more he loves the invisible, the more he will love the people he sees. Not the reverse, that the more he rejects the people he sees, the more he will love the invisible, for if this were the case, then God would be transformed into an unreal something, a fantasy" [IX 184 f., WL 158].

To love one's neighbor is to love God and oneself. The one does not exist without the other. If man's relationship to himself is not also a relationship to God then it is despair, i.e., a relationship to unknown, alien forces, which have the individual in their grasp. If man's relationship to his neighbor is not also a relationship to God, then it is not a relationship to his neighbor, but a relationship of mutual dependency, a latent or manifest assault, the egoistic attempt by the isolated subjectivity to exploit the other person for the confirmation and expansion of his own selfishness, and thus not love's acceptance of and respect for the other person in his particularity.

In presenting Kierkegaard's thinking we have thus met two circles, a vicious one and a good one, the consistency of sin and the consistency of the good. It is true of both of them that each presupposes itself and strengthens itself. In the circle of sin, man *simultaneously* cuts himself off from an adequate relationship to himself (the obscured or demonically idealized self-perception), from the relationship to God (despair is hidden or perhaps open offense), and from the relationship to his fellow man (encapsulation, etc.). The one part presupposes and conditions the other, and the tendency reinforces itself, so that the person more and more profoundly turns away from the good. In the circle of love, man *simultaneously* loves God, his fellow man, and himself—"in the proper way." For the rest, the circle has the same properties as the circle of sin. This must be the meaning of Vigilius' statement that, according to his linguistic usage, one cannot "be encapsulated in God, or in the good, for that sort of encapsulation means precisely the highest sort of expansion" [IV 433, CD 119; cf. above Chapter VII: 5: 4]. To be encapsulated in the circular course of love is to be expanded and open.

Each of the two circles is an autonomous, closed system, as it were, which takes the person captive and makes itself master of the person and of the manifestations of his life. It is not the individual himself who encapsulates himself within the consistency of sin by this or that individual sinful act, but it is original sin, as the presupposition which stretches beyond the consciousness of the individual (this, at any rate, is all that psychology can ascertain). It is not the individual who procures for himself access to the consistency of love by means of some independently produced (performed) loving action, but it is the love which is "fundamentally" present. I will return to this later.

But does this imply that the two circles are unbreakable, unchangeable, super-individual mechanisms, predestined to remain within its consistency forever more? It goes without saying that this is not the case. Kierkegaard is an adherent of the doctrine of original sin, but an opponent of the doctrine of predestination [VII 573, CUP 516; Pap. X 2 A 301, Hong 4551; X 4 A 180, Hong 3550]. Neither of the circles are unbreakable. The consistency of the good is not guaranteed; "goodness" is not automatically its own consequence, for "if it is true that a person is not in despair, he must at every instant destroy the possibility" of being in despair [XI 145 f., SD 148]. Kierkegaard can therefore say that "the believing person, who thus reposes in, has his life in, the consistency of the good, has an infinite fear for even the least sin, for he has infinitely much to lose" [XI 246, SD 238]. Salvation is unsecured, not a concluded state but a continuing movement. To "approach" God is in another sense to remove oneself from him: " 'He must increase, but I must decrease,'[20] this is the law for all approaches to God" [Pap. X 5 A 23, Dru 1282]. Kierkegaard's system of salvation is therefore not an unambiguously progressive movement out of contradiction and toward unambiguousness and religious homeostasis, but a movement toward being able to live in contradiction: "[S]een *qua* spirit . . . man's condition is always critical" [XI 156, SD 158].

In another sense it is also true of the consistency of evil that it can be broken and that a transition can thus be affected between the two circular courses. The idea has been touched upon above: the "objective" precondition is Christianity's promise of the forgiveness of sins; the subjective is the individual's opening of himself to this message, as happens when despair manifests itself in self-recognition, the consciousness of sin, in repentance's "letting something happen to itself." It is the fundamental thought, and this surrendering and receiving is what is called the great mystery in *Fear and Trembling·* "that it is much more difficult to receive than to give." The further theological consequences of this thought will not be debated here. Instead I will point out another side of the matter which is discussed less frequently, namely, the fact that even though one person cannot "essentially" benefit another or give him faith, still, here, too, the one person can help the other from the circular course of sin over into that of love. The definitive expression of this help is not the indirect revealing of sin and despair, but love's revealing of love.

In a communion discourse from 1851 Kierkegaard writes: "Righteousness looks judgementally upon a man, and the sinner cannot endure its gaze; but love when it looks upon the man, indeed, even if he withdraws from its gaze and casts his eyes downward, he still perceives that love is looking at him; for love penetrates much more intimately into life, into life itself, into the place from which life issues forth, than does righteousness, which repels and establishes a yawning chasm between the sinner and itself, while love, of course, stands on the sinner's side, does not accuse, does not judge, but forgives and pardons" [XII 320, JY 12]. Thus is love the deepest and most irresistable unmasking of man in his despairing unlovingness. But at the same time that love unmasks unlovingness, it also uncovers love.

Love unmasks, but the deepest thing which it reveals is love in the other person which is fundamentally present, behind the despair. From this perspective, despair is not the fundament, but the surface, which covers up, while love sees through in order to uncover the fundament.

This is the fundamental thought in *Works of Love*. However, in order to uncover it we must first concern ourselves with some of the book's more superficial and therefore perhaps more striking strata.

4:9. *Many Sorts of Love*

We have already seen that love is an acceptance of and respect for the other person. But we have also seen that the part of the formula entitled "to love God" contained a more detailed definition of the part which was entitled "to love one's neighbor," In what does this more detailed definition consist? The fact that unreserved acceptance is the work of love *par excellence* does not simply imply that it is under all circumstances an uncritical approval of the other person's self-understanding. Kierkegaard expresses the idea with the help of the relationship to God, and he does so in a manner which would perhaps be open to misunderstanding if the fundamental idea of the book were not so clear. One can get the impression from individual quotations, torn from their context, that the relationship of love which is man-God-fellow man is not a circle in which each part presupposes and conditions and augments the others, but a regular triangular relationship, in which God and the fellow man are rivals who contend for the loving person's love, while Kierkegaard decides the issue to the advantage of one of the parties, so that love of God excludes love of the neighbor.

It has already become clear that this is *not* Kierkegaard's meaning, and when he says, for example, "that God thus does not become the third figure in every love relationship, but really becomes the only beloved object, so that it is not the husband who is the wife's beloved, but it is God, and it is the wife who is helped by means of her husband to love God, and vice versa, and so on" [IX 141, WL 124]—it must thus mean something other than it appears to mean when one isolates it from its context. Unless the interpreter takes refuge in the emergency explanation that Kierkegaard is contradicting himself, he will see that throughout the book it is not God who, as a lover, is envious, jealous, and exclusive in his demands upon the beloved, but it is the "merely human" love which is characterized in this fashion. The essence of "merely human" love is exclusiveness, the demand for the exclusive possession of the beloved; the delimiting of love, by intolerance, to one's own social class and one's own level of culture [IX 73 ff., WL 71 ff., *et passim*]; the exclusive selection of the object of love, which includes a latent criticism of the beloved, latent skepticism, suspicion, dependence upon the attributes of the object, and the lovers' mutual dependence in domination or subjection [e.g. IX 146 f., WL 128 f.]; and finally it is the romantically idealized superstructure of this bourgeois individualistic conception of love, with its sublimated fantasy and its spiritualized cultivation of the erotic, the poetic culmination of fastidiousness and contempt for mankind [IX 185 ff., WL 159 ff.]. It is in order to break up this exclusiveness which adheres to itself that the relationship to God commands man, by means of the commandment to love his neighbor, to love "all people" and to do so "equally." But in order for a person to be able to love all people equally, the relationship to God must be superior to the relationship to the neighbor in the sense that the criterion of what love is is not taken from the other person's notion of love, but from the relationship to God, i.e., from the commandment to love one's neighbor, Indeed, it must be presupposed that the other person's notion of love can be self-loving in the bad sense, so that he does not know what is best for himself. In the relationship to God a person must conduct himself worshipfully with unconditional obedience, but unconditionally to obey and worship another person is idolatry, not love [IX 30, WL 36]. Despite the fact that the other person is the object and the task of love, the other person is not the authority which is to pronounce the final decision on the extent to which the behavior displayed toward him is loving [IX 216 f., WL 183 f.], for the beloved might demand to be loved exclusively and in opposition to others, to deify or be deified, or to bind himself in an unfree relationship of dependence. Love of one's neighbor is therefore not always and unconditionally identical with complying with the other person's demands and wishes. With a careful, restrained, and harmonizing exegesis of Jesus' statement about hating those closest to one,[21] Kierkegaard expresses this idea as meaning that in a given situation love *can* be forced to express itself in a manner which will be understood by the beloved as hatred, because the beloved, precisely because he is dependent, must understand the loving action as the opposite of love [IX 126 ff., WL 112 ff.]. The idea is that when a love relationship between two people develops in such a way that the one person is irremediably cutting off the other person's coming to independence and freedom, then the task and the duty is to rescind the relationship.

The party who takes the initiative for the separation — in this very special, even if also very illuminating, case — at the same time takes upon himself the responsibility for the other person's fate, to the extent that this is within his power. He does so upon the basis of his understanding of the commandment of love and upon the basis of his conviction of what is best for the other person — regardless of whether the other person has another opinion. In a certain sense it is the problem of expertise and of the negative element in maieutics which we here encounter again, even if here it is not the psychological expert who is pronouncing his judgment upon the basis of superior insight, but the one person who unprofessionally assesses the other person's situation in virtue of what he must understand as his better, more correct, conviction. He takes the responsibility for the other person, influences his fate. This is what is problematic in the notion, and Kierkegaard does not circumvent the problem.

Thus, just as in one situation the requirement for one person can be: "[D]evote yourself," so can it be for another person in another situation: "[G]ive up this devotion" [IX 70, WL 68]. In that sense the requirement can be said to be "without content," i.e., in the sense that its content always stems from the situation and from the acting person's understanding of the situation. "The Law" is, precisely because of its many provisions, undefined, and therefore definable, full of possibility, susceptible of interpretation. It relates itself (to use Climacus' expression) as possibility to actuality, and love is the fulfillment of the Law, its actualization [IX 123 ff., WL 110 ff.]. There is much room for interpretation between requirement and action, and love is "a matter of conscience," which is why there is not one, definite type of action which is *the* Christian action—not even "hating" the beloved [IX 170, cf. 22; WL 146, cf. 30, *et passim*]. "The one person can do just the opposite of the other person, but if they each do their opposite action in love, the opposites are edifying" [IX 243, WL 202].[22]

4: 10. *Love is Maieutics*

How, then, is the requirement to love one's neighbor realized? We have heard several formulations and examples, and we have heard that these are examples among others. The requirement can be realized in many ways. But Kierkegaard can also express it such that there is only one work of love, "one and the same thing in all the multiplicity": "*Love builds up by presupposing that love is present.*"

In this statement, and in Kierkegaard's interpretation of it, all the strands are brought together, not only his doctrine of maieutics, but the fundamental notion in his anthropology, which is that love is present.

"*Love builds up.*" The section of *Works of Love* which bears this title [IX 239 ff., WL 199 ff.] deals with maieutics, not especially in the physician-patient relationship or the relationship between an author and his reader, but in every relationship between people, and thus also in the relationship between physician and patient, etc. It is not one special action which is the loving action, but every action can be this (unless in its content it directly negates love), and every relationship can be a relationship of love. Love does not have any "being in itself on a par with other things"; it does not exist in and for itself, but can be present in everything.

Love differentiates itself from every other attribute a person can have. A person can have wisdom, power, talents, etc.; these are "properties which exist in themselves" which a person can possess. There is no logical (though certainly a factual and ethical) contradiction in saying that I am wise and all others are stupid. But if I say that I am loving and all others are unloving, then it is a logical contradiction, a self-denial. "Love is not a property which exists in itself, but a property by means of which or in which you exist for others." Love is only *in* the individual person when it is *between* him and the other person.

As communication (in the sense of making something shared, to share something with someone, share-with),[23] love is different from all other communication. A teacher presupposes that his pupil is ignorant; a moralist assumes that he is addressing himself to corruption which has need of moralizing. But love presupposes that the other person is loving. This does not mean that the teacher's communication of knowledge is necessarily unloving, for, of course, every action can be carried out lovingly; but it is not loving in virtue of being the communication of knowledge. The moralist is unloving, because he will not be satisfied with presupposing love in the other person, but, corrupted and confused himself, wants to tear down and split apart. "It is therefore unloving and in no way edifying if someone presumptuously imagines that he wants to and is capable of creating love in the other person. All busy and conceited zeal in this regard neither builds love up nor is itself edifying."[24] Love builds up, and thus does not tear down. Perhaps one discovers faults and frailties in the other person and attempts to remove them. But even to discover the fault is unloving, and even when the other person seems totally corrupted the loving person must not tear down, not even "for the sake of salvation," but presuppose love. It is a temptation for the selfish person to tear down, and it is also a temptation to build up when it means "that one does something with the other person." The loving person does not do anything with the other person, i.e., he does not make any attempt to re-create him, but he "does something with himself, he presupposes that love is present in the other person." Nor does he require any proof that the method is effective, or a result to which he can point; he does not arbitrarily choose a day "on which it will now be clear what comes of this." And yet this is the only way in which to build up. To be loving is to be "the serving person," and love therefore resists the temptation to be the master builder, the teacher, the chastiser, and thus "to rule over others." Love labors; however, it does not work directly by means of compulsion, persuasion and admonition, but unnoticed, "as though it did nothing at all." And yet it labors, and its work is to presuppose love. Kierkegaard interprets St. Paul's hymn to agape in I Corinthians 13. Love is long-suffering in its presupposing and in refraining from passing judgement; it seeks not its own by "pushing everything else aside"; it endures everything, just as a healthy organism "extracts nourishment even from what is unhealthy"; it believes everything and hopes everything, i.e., it presupposes love even in the most corrupted, hate-filled and lost people. "See, the prodigal son's father was perhaps the only one who did not know that he had a prodigal son, for the father's love hoped everything."

In this way, love builds up by presupposing that which is to be built up, love, and "the more perfectly the loving person presupposes love to exist, the more perfect is the love which he loves forth." Love requires no proof of its effectiveness as a maieutic method, but is satisfied with believing. "Thus does he lure forth the good; he nurtures love; he builds up. For love can and will only be dealt with in one way, by being loved forth. To love forth is to build up. But to love it forth is of course precisely to presuppose that it is fundamentally present." Love is not a demonstrative individual action, but a labor which is hidden in every action, "and yet the forces of eternity are in movement," not only in the loving person, but in the relationship and in the person who is loved. "We can therefore only compare this task of building up which is performed by love to the hidden labor of nature. While man sleeps, nature's forces sleep neither at night nor by day; no one gives thought to how they endure, while everyone finds enjoyment in the loveliness of the meadow and the bounty of the field. Thus does love conduct itself; it presupposes that love is present, like the sprout in the grain, and if love then succeeds in making it grow, love has hidden itself, just as it was hidden while it labored both early and late" [IX 243-55, WL 202-11].

4:11. ". . . *Like the Sprout in the Grain*"

Kierkegaard does not pamper his reader with metaphors of organic growth and "natural observations" about man, and there is therefore reason to ask why he uses the image — "that love is present like the sprout in the grain" — precisely in this extremely important context. Is it rhetoric which has no underpinnings? In itself the idea is quite certainly as radically thought out and as pithily put (thus, not *only* beautifully put) as one could wish, but is it not in glaring contradiction with the rest of Kierkegaard's thought, with his talk about man as spirit, and about love as a duty? Is it not in contradiction with the idea of the negative element in maieutics, of the repulsion, of the love which takes the form of hatred in order to help the other person love God — and in general with Kierkegaard's indisputable talent for revealing, tearing down, dissecting, and reducing?

There is nothing to prevent one from maintaining that Kierkegaard is in contradiction with himself, that his practice denies his theory, and that the theory consequently is only rhetoric, one of the despairing roles which it pleased Kierkegaard to adopt in order to escape being himself — to use an obvious expression. For the benefit of the skeptics I cite a passage from the draft of one of the writings from the attack upon the Church in 1855: ". . . I have annihilated myself as an edifying author, for, by the living God, I was not destined to build up but to tear down" [Pap. XI 3 B 216, p. 358].

Thus the objection has ground under its feet; the dialectical antithesis enters the scene; the rhetoric is broken — and we can pass on to seeing what it is that Kierkegaard says. The objection points in the direction of the question: What is Kierkegaard's real, personal view, and is this view acceptable to us? In the final analysis the question is: Who was Søren Kierkegaard, was he good or evil?

It is with precisely this question that Kierkegaard concludes the final discourse of *Works of Love* — but only to reject the question. Oddly enough, the discourse deals with the work of love of writing a book about works of love, and it concludes: "Thus when a person takes it upon himself to praise love, and it is asked whether the fact that he does so is really love on his part, then the answer must be: 'No one else can decide this with certainty; it is possible that it is vanity, pride, in brief, evil, but it is also possible that it is love' " [IX 422, WL 343]. This is irony in operation. On the previous pages Kierkegaard has with (apparent?) seriousness discussed the question of how one can lovingly describe love, and thereby (apparently?) presented himself as "the loving person" — to the unspeakable irritation of the reader, an irritation which is mixed with curiosity about knowing whether Kierkegaard is really naive enough or clumsy enough to strike such a pose in so transparent a fashion. Is it naive braggadocio? It is precisely this question which is worked up — and then comes the point, that it is possible, very plausible, that it is vanity and pride. One can never know.

The question — the real question for Kierkegaard's reader, and thus for Kierkegaard research — is not who Kierkegaard was or what he believed, nor what we should think about his opinions, but what his reader can learn about himself — with Kierkegaard and his various opinions as the occasion. Therefore, the protest against Kierkegaard is just as adequate a reaction as the loyal disciple-relationship to him — provided that the protest is a loyal one. Kierkegaard speaks of maieutics, but he also practices maieutics. "For that reason you will not come to know about yourself, then it is by means of yourself" [V 221, TCS 26; cf. above Chapter VIII: 3: 3].

Even when they deal with the subject of maieutics, the views of the maieutic practitioner are of subordinate significance in relation to the total project of communication. They are and remain opportunities, and if Kierkegaard can provoke an honest protest, then he has achieved what he wanted: honesty. The views are possibility, even when their originator casts off his mask of pseudonymity and personally acknowledges them. But thereby they do not of course lose their character as views, and what he can do as an interpreter is thus to put forth his understanding of them. In themselves they are subject to interpretation. Thus the interpretation presupposes itself. Just as love presupposes love in the other person, while unlovingness presupposes unlovingness, so does the interpreter presuppose either that Kierkegaard is a consistent, dialectical thinker, or that he is a scatterbrain who gets tripped up in his own contradiction-filled opinions. The interpretation comes about in virtue of this presupposition. [25]

Is Kierkegaard in contradiction with himself when he says that love's most genuine (not its only) task is to presuppose love? This theme is elaborated in several of the latter sections of *Works of Love*. Love believes everything; this is not due to ignorance or naivete, but love chooses to believe the good about others upon the basis of the same ambiguous knowledge which the mistrustful person also possesses [IX 257 ff., WL 213 ff., cf. above, Chapter VIII: 3: 2]. Love hopes for everything and is not disappointed by the result [IX 280 ff., WL 231 ff.]. Love is the victory of reconciliation, which wins what has been vanquished; "the vanquished" is the person whom love has vanquished by means of returning good for evil, but this person must also "be won" for the good. However, it is an offensive infringement to "win" the person for the good by letting him feel that he is in the wrong, and therefore it must be done "adroitly," by means of the loving person humiliating himself instead of the other [IX 375 ff., WL 306 ff.]. Even here it is perhaps doubtful whether Kierkegaard is persisting in the notion of unconditionally regarding the other person as loving. It is written earlier in the book that one must not be blind to the faults and weaknesses of the other person, nor should one make a one-sided attempt to root them out, but instead let "the relationship itself . . . fight with united strength against what is imperfect," and precisely for that reason, make the relationship more intense and loving [IX 191, WL 164].

To presuppose love in the other person is thus a formal definition, not a definition of content. The action does not receive expression in definite, verbal statements, but can be expressed unspokenly in every word and every action [IX 243, WL 203]. The only word and the only action which is excluded by this definition is that which directly expresses a negative judgement, a condemnation of the other person, with the intention of moralizing. Every other action can be done, every other word can be spoken "lovingly," thus without the need of stating love directly. This must thus also be true of the act of "tricking away" something from the other person, "to take from him his foolishness and obtain the true for him by means of trickery," that is, the negative element in maieutics, "the deception," etc. Love does not exclude criticism, for criticism, too, can be carried out lovingly, for example by an author's presenting his criticism as possibility, and leaving it to the reader to decide if it is actuality.

But that is not all. To presuppose love in the other person is in itself a form of negative maieutics. On the basis of Kierkegaard's manuscript on the dialectic of communication, I have differentiated above between two forms of maiutics, the negative ("to trick away".) and what was called "upbringing," which is clearly the same as what is called "building up" in *Works of Love*. This distinction is important in several respects, but upbringing/building up is also a negative, ironic method — naturally not in the sense that the person who builds up is to adopt an ironic tone or be dishonest or feigned in his belief that the other person is loving "in his fundament." But *Works of Love* does indeed deal precisely with the fact that by means of the Law man does not come to know his own excellent love, but sin. Thus when Kierkegaard presupposes that the other person is loving, then it is irony in the sense that he presupposes the other person's love as a possibility, not unconditionally as an actuality in the other person.

But what does irony do? It reveals. By means of his irony Socrates reveals the other person's ignorance by posing his questions in such a way that the other person himself must see through the fact that his knowledge is imagined. In his psychological works and many of his edifying writings, Kierkegaard indirectly reveals his reader's existential incapacity (sin), not by pointing out the reader as sinful or despairing, but by analyzing self-deceptions purely abstractly and ideally, with himself as the primary object of observation ("*unum noris, omnes*"), and thus leaving the judgement and the unmasking to the individual who is reading. "Now he judges. But how he judges is not within my power. Perhaps he judges just the opposite of what I wish" [XIII 574, PV 35]. This is also true with respect to *Works of Love,* for example: "Yet we do not say this in order to judge; let us not waste time on that. These deliberations only seek to penetrate illusions with the help of thought and a little knowledge of mankind. . ." [IX 145, WL 127]. But it must similarly be true that by presupposing love in the other person the loving person indirectly contributes to revealing unlovingness.

Nevertheless, this is not what is of the most decisive significance. Love indeed reveals something deeper. In an unmasking what is unmasked is always what is presupposed; it is the hermeneutic circle. "The negative element in maieutics" reveals a negativity, a nothing: that in actuality man knows nothing (in the Socratic sense), or that he "is capable of absolutely nothing before God." Kierkegaard's psychology reveals the despair behind the facade. But love reveals love. "Of all the relationships of the world there is none which contains a measure-for-measure in which the result corresponds so exactly to that which was presupposed" [IX 250, WL 207].

Man's self is plastic, a possibility which can be actualized in many different ways. Johannes the Seducer takes aim at a childish schoolgirl with the gaze of a seducer, and he gets out of it what he presupposes, an erotically-charged beauty. "The loving person" in *Works of Love* takes aim at the other person with the view that he is loving, and he gets out of it what he presupposes. They share the method and the principle. I have discussed the parallel above and have established that if the intention (the sexual and religious climaxes, respectively) were all that separated them, then there would be no decisive difference between them, then Kierkegaard would also be a seducer, merely religious instead of erotic. In a certain sense he is this, too, for the reason that *every* relationship between people is to a greater or lesser degree a relationship of influence and of dependence, because people always have expectations of one another. The special characteristic of Johannes the Seducer is that he is aware of this and exploits it to his advantage. The special characteristic of "the loving person" in *Works of Love* is that he is aware of this and exploits it to the advantage of the other person. The difference between Johannes the Seducer and "the loving person" is not that the one influences another person by presupposing something about him, for they both do this; it is unavoidable. Nor is the difference between them merely the intention, but the difference is what they presuppose. Where Johannes the Seducer presupposes eroticism, "the loving person" presupposes love.

To presuppose something in the other person is to take responsibility for a part of that person's life—without, for that reason, taking from that person responsibility for his own life. Johannes the Seducer ignores the responsibility, but could make himself responsible if he wanted to. Man is not only responsible for himself, but also for his relationship to his fellow man. But the responsibility of loving one's neighbor (to presuppose love) is not borne by the individual himself; it is God's responsibility [IX 30, WL 36]. This means that the influence which is a part of presupposing love in the other person, and in general in every form of maieutics, is legitimate *only* under the precondition that what is presupposed and nurtured, namely, love, is not merely assumed to be present in an experimental and fictive fashion, but really *is* "in the fundament"—and thus is not merely something which the one person suggests or indoctrinates into the other person. But according to Kierkegaard's Christian anthropology—the idea of creation—love *is* in the fundament. This idea, then, is the legitimation of the influence. If one disagrees with Kierkegaard about this anthropology, one must also find his psychology and his maieutics suspect.

We return to the text: "Love builds up." Maieutics is help in giving birth, but the caricature of maieutics is suggestion (manipulation, indoctrination). "Thus when it is a matter of the work of love in building up, this must mean *either* that the loving person inplants love in another person's heart, *or* that the loving person presupposes that love is in the other person's heart, and builds up love in him precisely by means of this presupposition — builds him up from his fundament, inasmuch as the loving person indeed lovingly presupposes love to be in the fundament. To build up must mean one or the other. But, now, can the one person implant love in the other person's heart? No, this is a superhuman relationship, an unthinkable relationship between man and man; human love cannot build up in this sense. It is God, the Creator, who must implant love in every person, He Who himself is Love. . . . The first sort of upbuilding relationship was unthinkable, then, so we are thinking of the second relationship" [IX 247, WL 205-06].

Love *is* present, then. It is "present, like the sprout in the grain" i.e., as possibility, and it is made to "grow," i.e., becomes actuality, when another person presupposes love in the person in whom love is present as a possibility.

Kierkegaard's psychology aims at helping the individual who cares to occupy himself with such matters come to clarity about himself, to become transparent to himself in self-understanding, i.e., in self-revelation. However, this is not the whole of the matter. At a couple of points in *The Sickness Unto Death* he touches upon the question of whether "complete clarity about oneself, about the fact that one is in despair, can be united with being in despair" [XI 180, SD 180]. His clearest answer to this question can seem surprising. The answer is in the affirmative. Clarity and despair can very well be thought of as united: "The devil's despair is the most intense despair, for the devil is pure spirit, and to this extent absolute consciousness and transparency" [XI 174, SD 175]. The statement places Kierkegaard's talk of transparent consciousness in a strange light, and forces us to put the question more precisely. What does Kierkegaard mean by this? He clearly means not *only* that the task of existence is to become aware of all of one ̓s motives in self-reflection. To be "pure spirit" is on the contrary the most intense, devilish despair — and furthermore a superhuman ideal, an illusion. Transparency of consciousness is certainly an ideal for Kierkegaard in the sense that it is the honest person's task to permit consciousness to penetrate his own self-deceptions again and again, but it is not an ideal in the sense of an achievable state. Judge William notes that "no person can become transparent to himself" [II 205, E/O II 194], and Kierkegaard persists in this thought, for example in a journal entry from 1854: "No religious person, not even the purest, is such refined, purified, subjectivity, pure transparency, in willing only what God wills, that there is not a residue of his original subjectivity, a portion which is not yet quite penetrated, not yet quite conquered, a portion which is perhaps not yet even discovered in the depth of his soul: this is where the reactions come from" [Pap. XI 2 A 132, Hong 4384]. It is true in both the psychological and the ethical-religious senses that man cannot become completely transparent to himself. Kierkegaard explains this in some detail in his confessional discourse from 1845, and places it in connection with original sin—just as did Judge William in the cited passage—which is indeed "an unfathomable connection"; but he adds that this is not a theme upon which we need to enlarge, so that it might not come to serve as an excuse for man in the attempt to become honest in his self-understanding [V 224-26, TCS 30-33; cf. above, Chapter V: 7: 2]. The Christian analogy to Socratic ignorance was the acknowledgement of sin, the idea that the highest thing of which a person is capable is to come to the understanding that he is capable of nothing. But, Anti-Climacus corrects, in actuality the sinner does not even understand this: "What you understand least of all is how far you are from perfection and what sin is" [XI 233, SD 227]. Man cannot indeed do the accounting and understand how far he is from achieving anything [IX 156, WL 136]. As it is written in *Christian Discourses,* no one knows himself, and honest self-examination reveals precisely this lack of knowledge. "And when a man examines his relationship to Christ, who is the man who knows his faithlessness entirely; who is the man who dares think that there could not be faithlessness even in this self-examination! Therefore you will not find rest in this fashion. So rest, then, so seek rest for your soul, then, in the blessed consolation that even if we are faithless, He is nevertheless faithful" [X 343, ChD 294].

This is more than an edifying phrase; it is a fundamental anthropological notion. Faith was not indeed defined in *The Sickness Unto Death* as becoming transparent to oneself, but the formula was: "[I]n relating itself to itself, and in willing to be itself, the self grounds itself transparently in the power which posited it" [XI 145, SD 147, *et passim*]. That is something different. Introspective self-knowledge can reveal the depths and catch sight of despair, but what it cannot catch sight of is "the power which posited it." Anti-Climacus does not explain this expression in any more detail, for his book deals, of course, with the revealing of despair, not with what else is revealed in this process. One must therefore find the more detailed explanation in *Works of Love.* What is revealed is love, which is "in the fundament," created by the power which posited man. But it cannot be observed.

What is it, then, to "ground"[26] in love? What does it mean to say that love is present in man "as the sprout in the grain"? Man penetrates into

himself in self-observation, but what man sees in this manner is his own—
i.e., despair's—mirror image, and not love, for it is not seen. "As the quiet
lake invites you to observe it, but forbids you by its mirror of darkness from
seeing through it, so does love's mysterious origin in God's love forbid you
from seeing its ground. When you think you see it, it is a mirror-image
which deceives you, as if it were the ground, that mirror-image which only
conceals the deeper ground. The ingenious cover of a treasure chest looks
like the bottom, precisely in order to conceal what is hidden. In the same
way, that which conceals the depth of the ground looks deceptively like the
bottom, only to hide what is still deeper." The life of love arises in a place
in man's interior which no one can see; "however far you penetrate, the
origin withdraws into distance and concealment," just as the light and the
rays of the sun blind the person who observes the light and the sun, but
invite him to observe the world which is illuminated. Or, to use another
metaphor: just as the physician can dissect and anatomize the innermost
and most hidden parts of the body by destroying it, "so is it also the most
painful and also the most corrupting suffering, when someone, instead of
taking joy in the manifestations of love, wants to find joy in fathoming it,
that is, by disturbing it." It is scarcely accidental that here Kierkegaard
again uses comparisons with nature (sunlight, spring water, the body). The
analyzing gaze "forces inward," but "the life of love" forces outward, it
"goes out" from the innermost region, and this "hidden life" is only present
in its manifestations, just as, according to the Gospel, the tree can only be
known by its fruits. "Every life, and thus also that of love, is hidden as
such, but is revealed in something else. The life of the plant is hidden; the
fruit is the manifestation. The life of thought is hidden; the utterances of
speech are the manifestation" [IX 17-19, WL 26-28].

This "life" is thus an hypostatization, to the extent that it does not exist
in and for itself as a fixed, demonstrable object, but exists only in its
manifestations. Love in and for itself, apart from the works of love, is not a
provable fact, and Kierkegaard can therefore begin *Works of Love* by
saying that if one were to believe what the sensory eye can see, then one
would first and foremost have to stop believing in love. But love must
indeed be believed in, and the person who does not believe in love deceives
himself, it is said, with an allusion to the notion of the vicious circle:
"[T]he self-deceived person has excluded himself and continues to exclude
himself from love . . . the self-deceived person has prevented himself from
winning the eternal," for "eternity does not permit itself to be mocked" [IX
13-15, WL 23-24]. We are in the center of Kierkegaard's anthropology (cf.
above, Chapter V: 1), but it is a new aspect of it which is developed here.
To "believe in love" is to interpret its manifestations as manifestations of

love, for it is true here as elsewhere that the sign, the action, the manifestation, must be the object of interpretation, in that love is not directly recognizable by its fruits. Even the demonstratively loving action can be unloving, and even the most meagre fruit can be a fruit of love: "[T]here is nothing, no 'like this,' of which it can unconditionally be said that it unconditionally proves the presence of love, or that it unconditionally proves its absence" [IX 23, WL 31].

And yet love is to be known by its fruits, and Kierkegaard takes the opportunity to reject the misunderstanding that his ethics is purely a so-called ethics of temperament, a soulful sensitivity which is too dignified to manifest itself in action [IX 24, WL 31]. Love is not a static property which is demonstrable in itself, for it exists only in the need to manifest itself, and therefore the fruits of love "can be said to push forward when the situation is right . . ." [IX 20, WL 28]. Love is a need. A need (a requirement, an instinct) is indeed, from a psychological point of view, an hypostatization, not observable in itself, but only in its manifestations. Kierkegaard speaks of this need at a number of places in *Works of Love*. He is not satisfied with saying negatively, as a concession, that the commandment to love one's neighbor does not involve any frustration of man's naturally given social needs. Christianity is no cloistered piety; it allows the instinct, the inclination, and the feeling to remain in force, and it expels neither romantic love nor friendship [IX 166 ff., WL 144 ff.; cf. above, Chapter III: 2: 6]; nor does it require that man must love his neighbor *in contrast* to his nearest surroundings, which would be just as much an "affected predilection" as the reverse situation [IX 76, WL 73].

But the social need and the need for love must not merely be tolerated, they must be lived. They are deeply grounded in man's nature, willed and created by God, and Kierkegaard explains in detail that the historical Jesus, the exemplar, "a true human being, tried in everything human," not only pitied the hungry in the desert, and not only was capable of "sharing with mankind in this need to love and to be loved, sharing in a purely human way," but that He Himself, to the confusion of the disciples, had a need to be the object of the special devotion of a chosen group of people: *"So deeply is love grounded in man's being, so essentially is it a part of man"* — while unloving people withdraw from this blessedness, "making themselves unhappy" by isolating themselves socially in self-pity, dissatisfaction, pride, self-sufficiency, and fastidiousness [IX 177-81, WL 153-56].

The need to love and to be loved is the shared, God-created (psychobiological) basis both of the love which Kierkegaard proclaims and of the love he criticizes as "merely human." In spite of the fact that

Kierkegaard also uses the word "natural" in connection with it, "merely human" love is not simply the love of need, instinct, and requirement, but is the elaboration of the need, or is its superstructure in the form of the ideology of bourgeois-romantic individualism. Love of one's neighbor is another, essentially different, elaboration of the *same* need. Kierkegaard describes "self-love's inconsolable independence, which became independent because it did not have the courage to form commitments, thus because it became dependent upon its own cowardice." True independence is not emancipation from the need; on the contrary: "To have a need is the expression of the greatest wealth," and freedom is only won when one commits oneself. "The person in whom love is a need certainly feels himself free in his love, and it is precisely the person who feels entirely dependent, so that he would lose everything in losing the beloved person — it is precisely this person who is independent. Though upon one condition, that he not confuse love with possession of the beloved." There is no contradiction between this statement and Kierkegaard's saying that God must be the "only beloved," but there is an affirmation that this latter formulation is a purely formal definition, not the expression of a situation of rivalry between the relationship to God and the relationship to other people. The lover has "the law of his existence" in the relationship to God, in the obligation to live in agreement with the need. True love "certainly feels a need to be loved, and this need, with this 'thou shalt' is therefore an eternally unanimous agreement; but it can do without being loved, if things *must* be this way, while it nevertheless continues to love. Is this not independence?" — while the false, "proud independence," is that which thinks itself elevated above the need to be loved, despite the fact that it is perhaps in these very words that it betrays that it "still *needs* someone to love," i.e., someone to admire its pride [IX 50-52, WL 52-54]. "The need of love" can be the need to love exclusively and in contrast to something else, and is thus conditioned by the properties of the exclusively chosen object. But the need can also be to "love all," i.e., to love independently of "the particular characteristics of the object," and the need thus becomes "an expression of wealth": "a need, the deepest need; he does not need people merely in order to have someone to love, but he needs to love people" [IX 82 f., WL 78].

Love, then, is not something that the person himself produces, though it is indeed something to which he gives form and direction. But love itself is a pre-individual and pre-moral force, which neither the maieutic practitioner nor the person in whom he presupposes love can produce. It is spontaneous and inexhaustible; its source can never run dry, and therefore it also cannot be compelled. Its need is a need to express itself, a need to manifest itself, "a need in love [to] be recognizable by its fruits," and this need cannot be suppressed. If "the plant which sensed the luxuriance of life and blessing in itself did not dare to let it become recognizable," then the blessing would be a curse. "Therefore this is not the case. For even if a single, particular manifestation of love, even a main stem, were, out of love, suppressed into a painful secrecy, the same life of love would nevertheless find itself another manifestation and become recognizable by its fruits" [IX 19 f., WL 28].

In exactly the same manner as original sin, but with the opposite arithmetic sign and in an even deeper sense, love is a presupposition which extends beyond the consciousness of the individual. And, just as original sin is "an unfathomable connection" between the individual and the entire race [V 226, TCS 33 cited above Chapter V: 7: 2], so is love's hidden life in the innermost part of man "unfathomable, and is thus again in an unfathomable connection with the whole of existence" [IX 18, WL 27]. Love is the original blessing. "Love is the source of everything, and spiritually understood love is the deepest ground of the life of the spirit" [IX 246, WL 205]. It "exists before everything, and remains when everything is past" [IX 15, WL 24], and thus does not belong to any individual person as his possession, because it is grounded in "God's love" [IX 18, WL 27]. Therefore, Kierkegaard can conclude the section of *Works of Love* which is entitled "Love Builds Up" by saying: "To build up is to presuppose love. To be loving is to presuppose love. Only love builds up. For to build up is to erect something from the ground up, but, spiritually understood, love is the ground of everything. No man can lay love's ground in another person's heart. Yet love is the ground, and one can only build up from the ground up; thus one can only build by presupposing love. Take love away, and there is no one who builds up, and no one who is built up" [IX 256, WL 212].

NOTES

Introduction

1. Hjalmar Helweg, *Søren Kierkegaard, En psykiatrisk-psykologisk Studie* [Søren Kierkegaard. A Psychiatric-Psychological Study], Copenhagen: Hagerup, 1933.

2. Especially John Björkhem, *Søren Kierkegaard i psychologisk belysning* [Søren Kierkegaard in the Light of Psychology], Uppsala: Nyblom, 1942.

3. Especially Fanny Lowtzky, *Søren Kierkegaard, Das subjective Erlebnis und die religiöse Offenbarung, Eine psychoanalytische Studie einer Fast-Selbstanalyse.* [Søren Kierkegaard. Subjective Experience and Religious Revelation. A Psychoanalytic Study of a Near Self-Analysis], Vienna: Internationale Psychoanalytische Verlag, 1935; F.C. Fischer, *Die Nullpunkt-Existenz. Dargestellt an der Lebensform Søren Kierkegaards* [The Zero Point of Existence, as Shown by the Life Form of Søren Kierkegaard], Munich: C.H. Beck, 1933; Arnold Künzli, *Die Angst als abendländische Krankheit. Dargestallt am Leben und Denken Søren Kierkegaards* [Anxiety as a Western Sickness as Shown in the Life and Thought of Søren Kierkegaard], Zurich: Rascher, 1948.

4. By E. and K. Shinhøj, *Acta Psychiatrica et Neurologica Scandinavica,* XXX, Copenhagen, 1955, p. 315-25. On the other hand, it is embarassing to note that at that time it would not have been possible to write many sentences on Kierkegaard in Danish or Scandinavian psychology. This deficiency has recently been corrected for the first time in a searching and inspiring work by the Danish psychologist Boje Katzenelson, *Angstteorier* [Theories of Anxiety], Copenhagen: Munksgaard, 1969, a systematic and original discussion of theories of anxiety, which very much deserves to be translated into English.

5. Rollo May, *The Meaning of Anxiety,* New York: Ronald, 1950, especially p. 32-45. See also Rollo May's introductory articles on existential psychology in *Existence: A New Dimension in Psychiatry and Psychology,* R. May, E. Angel, and H. F. Ellenberger, eds., New York: Basic Books, 1958 (and later editions).

6. J. Preston Cole, *The Problematic Self in Kierkegaard and Freud,* New Haven and London: Yale University Press, 1971.

7. But this does not prevent me from feeling that the psychological approach to Kierkegaard is equally as relevant as the literary-critical, when this latter is practiced strictly, as is the case in some of the newer American Kierkegaard research, especially that of Louis Mackey (*Kierkegaard: A Kind of Poet,* Philadelphia: University of Pennsylvania Press, 1971) and Josiah Thompson (*The Lonely Labyrinth: Kierkegaard's Pseudonymous Works,* Carbondale: Southern Illinois University Press, 1967, and *Kierkegaard,* New York: Alfred Knopf, 1973; cf. also Josiah Thompson, ed. *Kierkegaard: A Collection of Critical Essays,* New York: Doubleday, 1972). The present book was written without knowledge of these works, but certainly contains an implicit, relevant critique of their points of view and results.

8. Kresten Nordentoft, *Kierkegaards psykologi* [Kierkegaard's Psychology], Copenhagen: G.E.C. Gad, 1972.

Chapter I

1. "If you know one, you know all," cf. Terence, *Phormio* 256: "unum cognoris, omnes noris"—Translator's Note.

2. "The crux of the matter"—Translator's note.

3. "The grand total," "the ultimate result"—Translator's Note.

4. This is especially true with respect to the fictional writings, for example, *Repetition,* where Constantine Constantius finally informs us that he has invented "the young man," and hints that there is no sharp boundary between his own identity and that of the young poet [III 290, R 154].

5. *"Sub una specie"* means "under one form" or "seen from one side"; *"sub utraque specie"* means "under two forms" or "seen from two sides". The expressions are used particularly in the Roman Catholic Church with reference to the forms in which Holy Communion is enjoyed, *sub una specie* meaning only the bread, *sub utraque specie* meaning both the bread and the wine—Translator's Note.

Chapter II

1. I will later attempt to explain the contradiction present in the fact that Kierkegaard at once maintains that each individual has had a state of innocence, and nevertheless speaks of original sin. This matter is connected with the ethical-religious view of innocence and not the psychological view, with which we are presently occupied.

2. The Danish word for "original sin" is "Arvesynd," which literally means "inherited sin"—Translator's Note.

3. Karl Rosenkranz, *Psychologie* [Psychology], Konigsberg: Börnträger, 1837, especially pp. 5-10.

4. *Ibid.,* p. 106.

5. It goes without saying that this has nothing to do with Kierkegaard's later doctrine of the stages.

6. Kierkegaard's Mozart essay, as it is reproduced here, will perhaps seem unrecognizable to a reader of Kierkegaard—the subject of the essay is music after all! Yes, but it is more than that. Here in the American edition I have omitted most of the analytical textual argumentation, which is not of importance for Kierkegaard's psychological concerns, even though it is indeed relevant to the question of *whether* the essay can be interpreted as it is here. I must refer the sceptical Kierkegaard specialist to the more detailed documentation of the Danish edition. This is also the case for the pages which follow.

7. Later in the essay it is stated that all the characters in Don Giovanni stand "in a sort of erotic relationship to Don Giovanni." This is also the case for the male characters (excepting the Commendatore): "There is also something erotic in Leporello's relationship to Don Giovanni; there is a power by which he is captured against his will" [I 121, E/O I 124].

8. That which is alogical and without center in this form of experience is alluded to in Pap. I C 125 [Hong 4397], among other places, where it is stated that it is "precisely because the I is not given, that, from the highest level of approximation, the following question could be its own answer: Since the earth is, after all, a heavenly body, why does one not see it in the heavens?" [Pap. I C 125, Hong 4397].

9. Kierkegaard is in fact the source. This of course does not exclude the fact that there were historical and philosophical preconditions. The interest in contradictions and doubleness themselves was certainly inherited from Hegel (among others), whom Kierkegaard criticized so sharply for his speculative, harmonizing treatment of these themes. Psychology, the doctrine of the "subjective spirit," is a part of the weakest sections of Hegel's system. The subject was taken up by the rather independent pupil of Hegel, Karl Rosenkranz, whose *Psychologie* is mentioned above. Rosenkranz and Sibbern, who is also mentioned above, both concerned themselves with the phenomenon of "mixed emotions." Kierkegaard noted this in his diaries, but he was unable to learn anything of essential importance from these academic psychologists, who smartly and elegantly enumerated the individual emotional states, but let the "mixed emotions" remain isolated as special variants, while Kierkegaard placed sympathetic antipathy and antipathetic sympathy in a central, dynamic functional context. Furthermore, "anxiety" is not only a manifest emotion, but equally much the name of a double tendency, which precisely has to do with the indefiniteness of the emotion.

But the intention here is not to track down systematically Kierkegaard's historical preconditions. The perspective forward toward our own time seems more fertile and hermeneutically proper. And, at any rate, it is scarcely in technical psychology that one must look for the most important and profound literary inspirations behind Kierkegaard's psychology, but in his extensive, not especially systematic reading of fiction, drama, poetry, and aesthetic writings, which, together with theology, constitute the tonal background from which he takes now an example, now an impulse, or an idea. Shakespeare's importance is inestimable, as we shall come to see, but in addition to this must be reckoned German and Danish romantic literature and various folk tales and legendary literature, which Kierkegaard's earlies journals show that he especially devoured with relish and with psychological profit.

10. "And reveals itself hovering in the air," cf. Virgil, *Georgics* I 404—Translator's Note.

11. What follows is not an exhaustive literary analysis of "The Diary of a Seducer." However, we do not focus *only* on Cordelia, but also upon the structure and the main character of the novel. This is due to a number of things. One does not understand Cordelia without having a notion of whom her seducer is. Furthermore, a description of the seducer's maieutic technique is essential for the discussion of Kierkegaard's own method of communication, which will come in the last chapter of this book; and the pages which follow, therefore, have the additional function of preparing the way for this discussion. Finally, it can certainly be of interest—particularly for psychologists—to see the high degree to which psychological analysis and literary fantasy fertilize one another in

Kierkegaard. If Kierkegaard had not been "a kind of poet," he would never have become exactly the psychologist he became. On the other hand, if he had been *only* a poet and not a thinker as well, he would never have become a psychologist at all.

12. The sexual and human impotence of the Seducer, as well as the potency of his ability to sublimate, is hinted at in figurative language. His dinghy does not bore its prow down into the depths of the sea, because he sits on watch in the mast, lifted over the dash of the waves [I 342, E/O I 320]. When they play ring-toss and Cordelia daringly casts two in the air, he is unable to catch them on his stick [I 465 f., E/O I 428], but he has complete control over the process of sublimation: the horses in front of his carriage are "wild and ungovernable as natural forces . . . The horses rear up; the carriage lifts into the air; the horses stand almost vertically over our heads; we drive through the clouds into the sky; it is whistling all around us. . . . If you become dizzy, my Cordelia, then hold tightly to me; I do not become dizzy . . . if our light carriage disappeared from under us, we would still hold and encircle one another, hovering in the harmony of the spheres" [I 421 f., E/O I 391]. On the other hand, many of the book's particularly erotic passages are fundamentally only the products of a forced, worked-up fantasy (cf. also Bradley A. Dewey, "The Erotic-Demonic in Kierkegaard's 'Diary of the Seducer,' " *Scandinavica*, X, No. 1 (London and New York, 1971), p. 1-24).

13. "Something worthy of respect." In the Roman Catholic Church it is used in connection with the Host — Translator's note.

14. Cf. the section [I 46-65, E/O I 422-28] about woman as a category. I take this opportunity to point out that the special part of Kierkegaard's psychology which deals with woman will not be presented separately here. In my view, the topic has no great psychological interest, though certainly a sort of cultural-historical interest, to the extent that Kierkegaard can be said to express the period's general conception. What he says is most often not very original, even if it is expressed with such complexity that one senses that the matter was of personal significance to him. But he only rarely transgresses the boundaries of decency, which is something he had in common with the whole period. One can also learn from Karl Rosenkranz, for example, that woman is "psychologically determined as *feeling* and as *unity with herself and the world,*" a passive, unthinking bundle of feelings which cannot produce art or science, but only children, while man is determined "as thought," etc., (*Psychologie,* p. 65 f.). In Kierkegaard this sort of outpouring is generally followed by an assurance that "in another sense" woman is more important than man [I 464, IV 351; E/O I 426, CD 42]. Regardless of whether or not this is reasonable, it is in any event not original. Moreover, I believe that "in another respect" Kierkegaard had a genuine respect for woman, but had it according to the ideas of a past which is distant from us. But even when he lets his aesthetes mock woman in *Stages on Life's Way,* he is basically unprovocative and trivial, and he also immediately has Judge William pour oil on the troubled waters. Incidentally, Kierkegaard is very close to an incisive analysis of the matter when, in the symposium on woman in the *Stages,* he has Victor Eremita say that woman's misfortune is "that her life has become meaningless in the Romantic consciousness, so that at the one moment she means everything, at the next nothing at all, without

ever coming to know what she really does mean"; woman enjoys the attentions of galantry, and this means that she is understood in fastastic categories; galantry is a mockery upon her, a mockery by which she is deceived into a delusion. "If I were a woman, I would first and foremost forbid all wooing of me, and be satisfied with being the weaker sex, if that is what I am, but keep careful watch—and this is the main thing if one is to retain one's pride—that one does not go beyond what is true." However, Victor does not set forth any program for emancipation with this, because he is convinced that women will always prefer galantry and the status of children, and builds his cynical male philosophy upon this expectation [VI 67 ff., SLW 67 ff.].

15. Cf. the Hegelian J. E. Erdmann's distinction between a *"richer and more concrete"* and a *"(by definition) poorer* and *more abstract"* level of development, which Kierkegaard may have had in mind here: "Das Abstracte ist immer, was nur eine einzige, das Concrete, was eine Veilheit von Bestimmungen, zusammengewachsen gleichsam, enthält" [The abstract is always that which contains only one thing, the concrete, which has a multiplicity of determinations, grown together, as it were] (*Leib und Seele* [Body and Soul], Halle, 1837, p. 21).

16. See Chapter I, Note 5—Translator's Note.

17. In a journal entry from 1847, it is noted that "the forbidden tree could also have a name other than the tree of knowledge; it is a matter of indifference which it is, but it is firmly maintained that Paradise has a tree which is the forbidden tree" [Pap. VIII 1 A 69, Hong 3012].

18. The word "passively" in Danish is "lidende," which also means "suffering"—Translator's Note.

Chapter III

1. When Kierkegaard speaks of Greekness here and elsewhere, one must not allow oneself to be bothered by the fact that the idea is perhaps historically unsatisfactory, marked, in part, by classicistic ideas of noble simplicity and quiet greatness. "Greekness" in Kierkegaard is not to be seen as a contribution to classical research, but more as a construct, which is to illuminate Christianity by its opposition to it. Only when he discusses particular Greek thinkers are his conceptions more subtle.

2. Kierkegaard here inserts the German "Widerspruch" apparently to remind his reader that the Danish word for "contradiction," "Modsigelse," also has the literal meaning of something which "speaks against" itself—Translator's Note.

3. When Kierkegaard writes that something is a "determination" of spirit, or that man is "determined" as spirit, the word he uses is "Bestemmelse" (related to the German "Bestimmung"), for the noun form, and the appropriate form of "at bestemme," for the verb form. These words have generally been translated here, as by Lowrie and others as "determination," "determined," etc., not, of course, in the sense of "doggedness" but in the sense of "defined," and, indeed, there are places in this translation where "defined" has been preferred to "determined." However, the Danish "Bestemmelse," etc., a very key term for Kierkegaard, has more richness

and nuance than can easily be translated into English, and often carries the additional sense of "destined," "destiny," etc. Thus, for Kierkegaard, man is not only "determined" or "defined" as spirit (which is all that an English translation can convey), but he is also "destined" (that is, by God) to be spirit—Translator's Note.

4. It should be noted that the Danish word which occurs here and throughout the book is "Menneske," which literally means "human" or "person." It is a neuter noun and the pronouns used in referring to it are likewise neuter ("det" and "dets," meaning "it" and "its"). The Danish word for "individual," "Individ," is also neuter and takes the same "it" pronouns. Standard English usage, as well as the inappropriateness of most applications of "it" to human beings, have compelled the translator to use the somewhat misleading "man" for "Menneske," and to use masculine pronouns where the Danish uses neuter pronouns. It is important to note that the "masculinity" of many passages it not in the Danish original, but is an inescapable by-product of translation into English—Translator's Note.

5. In addition to his use of words compounded from "Eros," Kierkegaard uses two distinct Danish words for "love," "Elskov," which is applied to the ordinary romantic and erotic senses of love, and "Kjerlighed," (from the Latin "carus"), which is the higher and spiritual form. Thus, for example, "works of love" are works of "Kjerlighed," and "love's victory" is "Kjerlighed's" victory—Translator's Note.

6. According to *Works of Love* the erotic is a passion which as such completely takes over the individual, engages him and prevents him from relating himself to himself and the beloved in a disinterested, indifferent manner. To this extent, erotic love can be "an image of faith"—but precisely only an image, because faith's "Thou *shalt* love" gives the passion a fundamentally different form than that which it has in romantic love. It is "as if love lost everything by this, even though it gains everything" [IX 38-40, WL 42-44]. Christian love relativizes the passionate absoluteness of the erotic. It does not (necessarily) negate erotic love, but it wants to make room for love of one's neighbor "surpassing even the first and highest moments of romantic infatuation" [IX 163, WL 141]. Seen deeply, romantic infatuation is infatuation with the self, intensification of the self, "the pinnacle of self-esteem," because the lover is "intoxicated in the second I," which at root is simply "the first I over again." The compounding of the first (loving) I and the second (beloved) I into "one self, one I" is the result of a "self-love which can selfishly unite the two in a new, selfish self." Love of one's neighbor, on the other hand, does not make the lover "one with the neighbor in a united self," because "the neighbor is the first You" [IX 70-72, WL 68-70]. Love presupposes "a You and an I," but it excludes "mine and thine (these possessive pronouns)." In romantic infatuation, on the other hand, where the difference between "You and I" is abolished, the difference between "mine and thine" has only apparently disappeared. In actuality it has only been transformed into an "ours" which "is exactly the same thing for the fellowship as 'mine' is for the single person." The exclusiveness is thus the same, an "ennobled and ramified self-love." But because "mine and thine" is not radically vanquished here, this difference is also latently present ("though it sleeps as a possibility") in romantic love's uniting of "You and I"

Romantic love is fundamentally a trading relationship, and the custom of exchanging rings is a "completely appropriate symbol of romantic love." But in spite of the fact that the trading relationship seems to abolish individuality and the difference between individualities, it does not abolish the individual *property* relationship, "for the thing for which I exchange myself then becomes mine" [IX 302f., WL 248f.]. The requirement of erotic love is love in return, "precisely as in the world of money": "One does the business of love; one gives one's love away in order to trade," and if repayment is not made, one has been deceived. This deception is a reflection of the self-deception of romantic love, when it thinks "that one can only love one person," and that this one person is presumed to be one who will repay [IX 270, WL 223].

The property relationship which is fundamental to erotic love is not obvious and, therefore, not conscious either—"for an infatuated person seeks his own in a certain unconscious sense, and thus also has a 'mine.' " The difference between "mine and thine" is not abolished by doing away with the concept "thine," but it is abolished when "self-denying love" does away with the concept of "mine" and makes everything into "thine." However, "sacrificing love" cannot by itself make "all" into "thine," for even the concept "thine" contains an unspoken contradiction, but "in all there is no contradiction." The radical abolition of the difference between "mine and thine" thus happens only when "all becomes his, his who had no 'mine' at all, he, who in self-denial made all his to thine" [IX 304 f., WL 250-51].

7. *Love Without Stockings,* a very popular farce written by the Norwegian-Danish playwright J.H. Wessel in 1772—Translator's Note.

8. Among modern psychologists there is disagreement about the extent to which modesty's anxiety awakens of itself or whether it does so only by means of some external influence. Among those who would find Kierkegaard correct is Anna Freud (*The Ego and the Mechanisms of Defence,* Cecil Baines, trans., 2nd ed., London: Hogarth Press, 1942). The question could seem to be of little practical significance, in that anthropological instinctual anxiety normally enters into complex connections with environmentally conditioned anxiety. However, the problem has the consequences for upbringing which are mentioned by Anna Freud, namely that with her "pessimistic" view one must remain rather sceptical about the belief of the more hopeful Freudians that all possibilities of neurosis can be removed with the help of reforms in child-rearing. One can assume that Kierkegaard would be in agreement on this point as well, in spite of his criticism of puritanical strictness, for genuine ignorance about the sexual, according to him, is "reserved only for the animal, who is therefore a thrall to the blindness of instinct, and walks in blindness," while modesty is the characteristic of that which is specifically human [IV 374, CD 61].

9. "The story tells of you," Horace, *Satires,* 1, 1, 70—Translator's Note.

Chapter IV

1. The Danish contains an important pun here, of which Kierkegaard often

makes use: "gift" is "Gave," and "task" (or "problem") is "Opgave" — Translator's Note.

2. "κατ᾽ ἐξοχὴν [kat exochen]" means "in the eminent sense" — Translator's Note.

3. "πρώτη φιλοσοφία [prote philosophia]" means "the first philosophy" — Translator's Note.

4. The fragment has been published separately in English as *Johannes Climacus or, de omnibus dubitandum est*, T.H. Croxall, trans., Stanford: Stanford University Press, 1958. The portions cited are from pp. 150-153 — Translator's Note.

5. *Ibid.*, p. 149.

6. The Latin word *interesse* means both "to be between" and "to be a matter of concern," cf. *Johannes Climacus* translation, p. 152 note — Translator's Note.

7. *Ibid.*, p. 147-51 — Translator's Note.

8. Readers of Heidegger can associate this with the concept of care in *Being and Time* (trans. from the 7th German ed. by John Macquarrie and Edward Robinson, New York: Harper, 1962) — and consider whether on this and other points Heidegger has allowed himself to be directly inspired by Kierkegaard.

9. And in many cases it is precisely Kierkegaard's edifying and religious discourses which furnish the more detailed commentaries and illustrations to the theses which are put forward — sometimes in completely summarized form — in his principal psychological works.

10. The same thought is expressed in a journal entry from 1846 with the assistance of the concept of conscience, which, for Kierkegaard, is not merely a particular moral authority, but an expression of creation: "It is really the conscience which constitutes a personality. Personality is an individual certitude established by being known by God in the possibility of conscience. For conscience can slumber, but its possibility is what constitues it. Otherwise the certitude would be a transitory moment. Not even the consciousness of the certitude, self-consciousness, is what constitutes it, inasmuch as the consciousness is only the relationship in which the certitude relates itself to itself, while God's co-knowledge, on the other hand, is the fixation, the consolidation" [Pap. VII 1 A 10, Hong 3214].

11. Poul Møller, *Efterladte Skrifter* [Posthumous Writings], Copenhagen: Gyldendal, 1856, vol. III, p. 163 ff.

12. "κατὰ δύναμιν [kata dynamin]" means "according to its possibility" or "potentially" — Translator's Note.

13. "Μαιεύεσθαι [maieuesthai]" means "maieutics" or "midwifery" — Translator's Note.

14. The Danish word for "repetition" is "Gentagelse," meaning, literally, "to take again."

15. The Danish word "erindre" can mean "recollect," but it can also mean "to make internal," cf. the German "er-innern."

16. The Danish word is "maa," which can express both possibility ("may") and necessity ("has to," "ought to") — Translator's Note.

17. The citation is from I John 3 : 2 — Translator's Note.

Chapter V

1. Cf. Freud XIV 15. For what follows, see Patrick Gardiner, *Schopenhauer,* Harmondsworth: Penguin, 1963, especially pp. 161 ff. and 174 ff. Schopenhauer may also have been of significance for the early Freud via Edouard von Hartmann's *Philosophie des Unbewussten* [Philosophy of the Unconscious] from 1868.

2. Arthur Schopenhauer, *The World as Will and Representation,* vols. I-II, E.F.J. Payne, trans., New York: Dover, 1966.

3. *Ibid.,* vol. II, chapter XIX, p. 201 ff.

4. *Ibid.,* p. 201.

5. *Ibid.,* p. 206.

6. *Ibid.,* p. 209.

7. *Ibid.,* p. 218.

8. *Ibid.,* p. 208.

9. *Ibid.,* p. 202.

10. *Ibid.,* p. 207.

11. *Ibid.,* p. 201 ff.

12. When Kierkegaard became acquainted with Schopenhauer's writings in 1854, he also expressed his opinions on him in his journal. The relationship between the two of them has often been discussed in general by Kierkegaard researchers. Kierkegaard finds a kindred spirit in Schopenhauer, but he also has very serious objections to his philosophy. But this entire problem complex does not concern us here, as Kierkegaard's remarks on Schopenhauer in his late journals do not deal with Schopenhauer's psychology of the will, but with other aspects of his thought.

13. For one or another reason, in his translation of *The Sickness Unto Death,* Walter Lowrie has omitted what is perhaps the most important sentence in the quoted passage: "The will is something dialectical, and under it, in turn, is the whole of man's lower nature."

14. In Kierkegaard's Copenhagen, this "second floor" was where the better class of people lived, and in the Danish text of *The Sickness Unto Death,* Kierkegaard refers to this second floor with the French "Belle-Etage"—Translator's Note.

15. The word which here is translated as "mind" (also "mental," etc.) is "Sjel" in Danish, a cognate of the English "soul," which is indeed the word which Walter Lowrie commonly uses for it. In the opinion of the present translator, the word "soul" easily gives rise to the misunderstanding that Kierkegaard means a divine, immortal part of man, whereas he actually means man's ordinary mental functions, while "spirit" ("Aand") is normally reserved for the higher, immortal part. The present translator has thus used "mind" (and occasionally "psyche") for the Danish "Sjel," and has avoided using the word "soul" except where it would not cause confusion—Translator's Note.

16. CF. e.g., *Brett's History of Psychology,* R. S. Peters, ed., London, 1953, p. 61 f.page 397

17. Cf. Chapter II, Note 1—Translator's Note.

18. Schopenhauer, *op. cit.,* p. 226.

19. "Before"—Translator's Note.

20. This is not to deny that intellectual material from Hegel and idealism has in various ways played an important role for Kierkegaard. Kierkegaard was not *only* an anti-Hegelian, but has also learned from his great opponent. Quite a number of the developmental ideas and dialectical points with which we make an acquaintance in the presentation of ·Kierkegaard's psychology would be unthinkable without inspiration from Hegel and other German philosophers. But we have to leave this question of influence out of this account. We will simply note here that the notion that Kierkegaard purely and simply thinks in opposition to Hegel, or independently of him, cannot be confirmed when one examines Kierkegaard's psychology.

21. "Which is as important as all [of them]"—Translator's Note.

22. "Under the aspect of eternity"—Translator's Note.

23. Cf. e.g., A.O. Lovejoy, *The Great Chain of Being: A Study in the History of an Idea,* Cambridge: Harvard University Press, 1936, and subsequent editions.

24. It may again be necessary to note that this unconcerned confidence does not concretely involve any passive indifference to the world. The simple person gives up self-concern, but not engagement. Kierkegaard's own revolutionary engagement in the settling of accounts with the established church in 1855 is the best proof that his "simplicity" means neither naiveté nor indifferentism.

25. See, *inter alia,* A.C. Oerlemans, *Development of Freud's Theory of Anxiety,* Amsterdam: North Holland Publishing Co., 1949.

26. The more detailed argumentation for this interpretation of Freud can be found in Boje Katzenelson's *Angstteorier* [Theories of Anxiety], Copenhagen: Munksgaard, 1969, p. 156-69. The book has unfortunately not—yet—been translated into English. Katzenelson himself has reservations about his interpretation. I would think it is correct, but one-sided. It is a contribution on the side of the neo-Freudian environment point of view, and a criticism of the view that instinct in itself is supposed to be a conflict-causing factor. The presentation of the problem can seem a bit abstract, in that the instinct certainly never appears "in itself," but always in relation to an environment. The separation which Katzenelson emphasizes is of course a general human condition. And the situation is probably this, that neither Freud nor Kierkegaard operates with an exclusively environmental or with an exclusively intrapsychic point of view, but with an interplay between the individual's innate potential for anxiety and the relationship to the surrounding world which develops the potential and gives it form as manifest anxiety. In the potential lies the possibility that the fact of separation itself can call forth separation anxiety at all. In one way or another, the possibility of being anxious must be a part of the fact that man is man. It is this possibility which Freud has attempted to explain with the help of his theory of the inherited basis of anxiety and the birth trauma [cf. Freud XXII 94 f.], while Kierkegaard explains it by saying that man is created as a synthesis, a relationship which relates itself to itself (and he supplements this explanation with a sort of inheritance theory, cf. above Chapter III: 3: 1). Katzenelson apparently accepts this, for he himself differentiates between a common, human "normal" anxiety, and a pathological anxiety, which

can develop upon the basis of normal anxiety; the same distinction is found in Rollo May and, for example, in Karen Horney.

27. Ruth L. Munroe, *Schools of Psychoanalytic Thought,* New York: Dryden, 1955.

28. New York: Norton, 1939.

29. It is not the dividing line between "libido schools" and "non-libido schools" which has been decisive for my choice of Adler, Horney, and Fromm for the illustration of the dialectic. I think that this difference has been overemphasized in discussions about psychoanalysis, at the expense of other, more important problems. I would think that a markedly libido-oriented analyst such as Wilhelm Reich could illustrate the same dialectic, namely, with his early theory of character armor, which in some respects reminds one more of Adler's "neurotic life style" than of Freud's theory. What is decisive for the present is not so much from *what* one escapes, as the rigid blocking which the escape brings about. It is often said that "neo-Freudian revisionism" is a superficial dilution of Freud's teachings; however, Herbert Marcuse's criticism in the epilogue of *Eros and Civilization* (Boston: Beacon, 1955) seems all too brief and not very just. Certain parts of their productions are not of any interest in connection with Kierkegaard. But where they make a real analytic effort, they are relevant. Other names could be mentioned, but the intention here is only to sketch a frame of reference which is meaningful to a 20th-century reader.

30. Anna Freud, *The Ego and the Mechanisms of Defense,* Cecil Baines, trans., 2nd ed., London: Hogarth Press, 1942, p. 73-74.

31. Cf. Rollo May, *The Meaning of Anxiety,* especially pp. 191 ff. and 223-26.

32. Cf. Lewis Way, *Alfred Adler: An Introduction to his Psychology,* Harmondsworth: Penguin, 1956.

33. *New Ways in Psychoanalysis,* New York: Norton, 1937; *The Neurotic Personality of Our Time,* New York: Norton, 1937; *Our Inner Conflicts,* New York: Norton, 1945.

34. New York: Rinehart, 1941.

35. I refer the reader also to Philip Rieff, *Freud: The Mind of the Moralist,* New York: Viking, 1959; cf. also the conclusion of Erich Fromm, *Sigmund Freud's Mission,* New York: Harper, 1959.

36. Cf. also Ernest Jones, *The Life and Work of Sigmund Freud,* Penguin ed., Harmondsworth: Penguin, 1964, pp. 231 ff. and 278 ff.

37. K. E. Løgstrup, *Opgør med Kierkegaard*[Settling-Up with Kierkegaard], Copenhagen: Gyldendal, 1968, p. 136 f. [German edition: *Auseinandersetzung mit Kierkegaard,* Munich: 1968]; and by the same author, *Kierkegaards and Heideggers Existenzanalyse und ihr Verhältnis zur Verkundigung* [Kierkegaard's and Heidegger's Analysis of Existence and its Relation to the Preaching of the Gospel], Berlin: E. Blaschker, 1950, p. 64-69.

38. Cf. Chapter II, Note 2 — Translator's Note.

39. The same is the case where Freud says at one point that psychoanalysis confirms "the habitual pronouncement of the pious: we are all miserable sinners" [Freud XIII 72]. His pronouncements cannot simply be attached to Kierkegaard's.

But when, for example, Freud presents his theory of the death instinct and of constitutional aggressiveness [*Beyond the Pleasure Principle*] or when he rejects faith in man's natural goodness as an illusion [*New Introductory Lectures on Psycho-Analysis,* Freud XXII 103 f.], then it is natural to call his psychology an attempt at a scientific charting of original sin—even if the idea here is incidentally not in agreement with Kierkegaard's view of it (cf. Will Herberg, "Freud, the Revisionists, and Social Reality," in Benjamin Nelson, ed., *Freud and the 20th Century,* New York: Meridian, 1957, p. 155 f.).

40. The similarity between Fromm and Kierkegaard is quite easily seen (cf. *inter alia* Rollo May, *The Meaning of Anxiety,* p. 170 *et passim*). Fromm's principal neurotic type, the authoritarian character, is driven, just as the despairing individual in *The Sickness Unto Death,* by the wish not to be himself: "*to get rid of the individual self, to lose oneself;* in other words, *to get rid of the burden of freedom,"Fear of Freedom,* London, 1960, p. 131. More areas of agreement could easily be pointed out. The fact that Fromm surely deviates greatly from Kierkegaard when he develops his ordinary, humanistic philosophy of life in his later writings is quite another matter.

41. Kierkegaard himself was clear about the fact that *The Sickness Unto Death* abounded with subdivisions and definitions, but was relatively impoverished in details and nuances: "But the fact is that the task is all too large for a rhetorical design in which every individual form would also have to be depicted poetically. It is done better with dialectical algebra." The book contains "an excellent schema," but Kierkegaard seems for a time to have found it *too* schematic, and he therefore had plans to rework it into a series of religious discourses [Pap. VIII 1 A 651 f.].

42. The point that Kierkegaard is making is reinforced by a Danish pun which cannot be rendered in English. The English preposition "about" has been used to translate the Danish preposition "om," which Kierkegaard uses when speaking of the deeper sort of self-knowledge of despair. The first syllable of the Danish work for "conversion" is "*Om*vendelse" (which, incidentally, literally means a "turning around"), which Kierkegaard italicizes in order to stress the inner connection between the deeper form of self-knowledge of despair and the religious conversion—Translator's Note.

43. The "eternal blessedness" of which Kierkegaard speaks in the *Postscript,* is "the absolute good," which "*absolutely and only admits of definition by its mode of acquisition,"*in contrast to all other goods, which "must be defined in terms of the good itself" [VII 416, CUP 382].

44. Need I recall that the fundamental book of classical psychoanalysis, Freud's *Interpretation of Dreams,* came into existence according to the same principle? In Kierkegaard the principle was called relating oneself objectively to one's own subjectivity (above, Chapter I: 1:2). "Psychoanalysis begins with a heroic exception to the rule that the self may not know the self, the subject not be its own object," but "Freud's self-exposure becomes exemplary only as it becomes impersonal" [Philip Rieff,*op. cit.,* p. 65 f.].

45. Kierkegaard strengthens his point here with a play upon words which cannot be rendered in English. The Danish word which has been translated as "standard

of measure" is "Mallestok", while the Danish word which has been translated as "goal" is "Maal"—Translator's Note.

46. Cf. Note 21 above—Translator's Note.

47. Kierkegaard refers to J.G. Fichte's doctrine of the productive power of the imagination: Fichte assumed correctly, "even in relation to cognition, that fantasy is the origin of the categories." However, one must not allow oneself to be misled by this insertion into thinking that Kierkegaard is hereby setting forth his own epistemology. The passage is purely psychological.

48. The reference to Fichte is not found at this point in *The Sickness Unto Death,* where he is only mentioned in passing, but in *The Concept of Irony* [XIII 372 ff., CI 289 f.].

49. "Between the one and the other"—Translator's Note.

Chapter VI

1. See Chapter V, Note 42—Translator's Note.

2. Kierkegaard used the Schlegel-Tieck German translation of Shakespeare. In English, Kierkegaard's German "Shakespeare" reads: "Works which have sprung from sin gain their power and strength only through sin." This Englishing of the German conveys Kierkegaard's meaning better than Shakespeare's original English, namely: "Things bad begun made strong themselves by ill."—Translator's Note.

3. "Wherever acedia surrounds the solitary man . . . is a lowering of the soul, an enervation of the mind, a neglect of religious exercises, a hatred of profession [of religion], a praise of things secular"—Translator's Note.

4. Ludwig Binswanger, "The Case of Ellen West," translated in May, Angel and Ellenberger (eds.), *Existence: A New Dimension in Psychiatry and Psychology,* New York: Basic Books, 1958, p. 297.

5. Even today, downtown Copenhagen is connected with the Christianshavn section on the island of Amager by a bridge which is called The Long Bridge.

Chapter VII

1. Matthew 5: 13 (also Luke 14: 34) used the word "μωρανθῇ [moranthe]," which is derived from "μωρὸς [moros]," which means "foolish" or "stupid." The Revised Standard Version reads: "If the salt has lost its taste, how shall its saltness be restored?"—Translator's Note.

2. I have investigated the whole problem complex suggested here in the book *"Hvad siger Brand-Majoren?"—Kierkegaard's opgør med sin samtid* ["What Does the Fire-Chief Say?": Kierkegaard's Settling-Up With His Times], Copenhagen: G.E.C. Gad, 1973. The book has not been translated into English, but some of its most important conclusions will be summarized here in the American edition of *Kierkegaard's Psychology,* because they are of decisive significance to the understanding of the full dimensions of Kierkegaard's psychological insight. The more detailed documentation for that which will be discussed here will be found in the Danish book. Relatively little has been written in English on this problem complex, and here I will content myself with referring to Werner Stark's article "Kierkegaard on Capitalism" (reprinted in Lewis A. Lawson, ed., *Kierkegaard's*

Presence in Contemporary American Life, Methuen, New Jersey: Scarecrow Press, 1970).

3. General propositions or arguments—Translator's Note.

4. "In his financial worries, the worried man is not satisfied with being human, but wishes to be or to have a difference, wishes to be rich, affluent, well-off . . . he looks, comparingly, at the others, at the differences, and his financial worries are a relationship of comparison," it is written in one of the edifying discourses [VIII 313, GS 194].

5. *Envy: A Theory of Social Behavior,* Michael Glenny and Betty Ross, translators, New York: Harcourt, Brace and World, 1969.

6. A theory about envy as that which is created by society and which creates history could probably be better incorporated into a socially-critical theory of society.

7. These—and only these—sides of Kierkegaard's view of political development are emphasized by, among other people, Howard A. Johnson, in the essay "Kierkegaard and Politics," in Johnson and Niels Thulstrup, eds., *A Kierkegaard Critique,* New York: Harper and Row, 1962, p. 74-84.

8. On Kierkegaard's religious thought, particularly in the last years, English-speaking readers can be referred to Bradley A. Dewey's book *The New Obedience: Kierkegaard on Imitating Christ,* Washington: Corpus Books, 1968.

9. Even if it was involuntary revelation which made such a strong impression upon Kierkegaard, Freud also includes this when he mentions that, in contrast to the sorrowing or remorseful person, the melancholy individual can display a pressing desire to communicate, "which finds satisfaction in self-exposure" [Freud XIV 247; cf. IV 438, CD 115, on the demonic ventriloquism which can begin at the slightest opportunity: "The ventroloquism itself can proclaim directly or can be indirect, as when a mad person betrays his madness by pointing at another person and saying 'He seems most unpleasant to me; he is probably mad.' The revelation can manifest itself verbally, when the misfortunate person ends by forcing his own hidden secret upon everyone . . ."].

10. In *Works of Love* Kierkegaard explains in a bit more detail how immediate, romantic infatuation is fundamentally a form of narcissistic identification, and therefore fundamentally ambivalent. Mere infatuation is not a devotion to a "you," but to "the second I, the second self"; it is essentially self-infatuation [IX 68 f., WL 66-67; cf. above Chapter II:2:6]. But, because this self-infatuation has as its object another person, it also becomes dependent upon this object. Therefore, this infatuation is also a latent hatred, because it can reverse itself into its opposite, though, be it noted, without ceasing to be love. It is only hatred to the extent that it is love: "Deep down, love is still burning, but the flame is that of hatred; only when the love is burnt out is the flame of hatred also extinguished . . . it is the same love which loves and hates" [IX 46, WL 49].

11. The Danish word which has been translated as "inherited guilt" is "Arveskyld," which is a closely related variant of "Arvesynd," which means "original sin"—Translator's Note.

12. The Danish word which has here been translated as "suffering" is "Liden,"

which also means "suffering" in the less usual English sense of "being acted upon." Both the usual and the less usual senses are intended here— Translator's Note.

13. O.H. Mowrer's theory about this is summarized by Rollo May (*The Meaning of Anxiety,* p. 102-12). If I remain with Freud throughout this presentation it is due to the fact that, like the angels, I rejoice more over one sinner who shows signs of conversion than over the 99 righteous psycho-moralists.

14. Here, as elsewhere, Kierkegaard cited his Shakespeare in German from the Schlegel-Tieck translation. The translator has re-translated the German into English in order to reflect Kierkegaard's text as precisely as possible. — Translator's Note.

15. The detailed textual-critical analysis, with references to Kierkegaard's manuscripts (volume V in the Danish edition of his *Papirer*) is omitted in the American edition of the present book due to considerations of space. Only the results of the investigation are summarized here. Kierkegaard specialists must be referred to the Danish edition. On the pages which follow a great deal of the "philological" argumentation for the reconstruction of Kierkegaard's thinking has also been omitted.

16. The word "offense" is not used here in the special sense of man's protest against Christianity, but in the ordinary sense of moral offense. The projection mechanism of the moral pharisee is transfixed in the formula that "an offended individual ultimately uses this offense as a fig leaf for something which could well use hypocritical clothing" [*ibid.*].

17. Hjalmar Helweg, *Søren Kierkegaard,* Copenhagen: Hagerup, 1933, p. 146.

18. Cf. Chapter V, Note 21— Translator's Note.

19. The tone is the same as Freud's, when he remarks that the analyst's insight makes it difficult for him "to give the kind of opinion another doctor would— 'There's nothing wrong with you'— with the added advice: 'You should arrange for a mild hydro-pathic treatment' " [Freud XVI 246].

Chapter VIII

1. Cf. Chapter Iv, Note 1— Translator's Note.

2. *Efterladte Skrifter* [Posthumous Writings], vol. III, pp. 21 f. and 10.

3. "Through difficulties to the stars"— Translator's Note.

4. "Those who have lost the ability to feel pain"— Translator's Note.

5. Boston: Allyn and Bacon, 1971.

6. *Ibid.,* p. 80 ff.

7. Erich Fromm, *The Sane Society,* London: 1963, p. 168.

8. *Johannes Climacus or, de omnibus dubitandum est,* T.H. Croxall, ed., pp. 147-49.

9. *Ibid.,* p. 148.

10. *Ibid.,* p. 149-50.

11. Cf. Chapter IV, Note 5— Translator's Note.

12. Cf. VII 321 (CUP 296), where Kierkegaard appears to designate his own thinking as "concrete thinking"; the meaning, however, is the same as elsewhere: that "there is a thinking individual and a definite something (in the sense of

something individual) which is being thought, in which existence gives the existing thinker the thought, the time and the space." On the other hand, it is not the case that the product of thought as such is concrete, for he is inquiring about actuality "in the language of abstract thinking" [cf. VII 320, CUP 295].

13. The Danish word which has here been rendered as "belief' is "Tro," which can also have the specifically religious sense of "faith." When the more general context is intended, "belief' has been used, while when the religious sense is intended "faith" has been used. The verb and gerund forms—e.g., "at troe," "troende," etc.—have been dealt with in the same way—Translator's Note.

14. "All coming-into-being takes place by means of freedom, not by necessity" [IV 267, PF 93]. I will not examine Kierkegaard's argument in more detail, but will merely point out that he is not a spokesman for indeterminism here either (cf. Johannes Sløk, *Die Anthropologie Kierkegaards* [Kierkegaard's Anthropology], Copenhagen: Rosenkilde and Bagger, 1954, p. 36 ff.). He does not contradict the idea of "a consistency of natural law" (*ibid.*), but maintains that the necessity, with which the determinist operates in the explanation of the transition from one state to another, cannot be empirically ascertained, but only assumed hypothetically. (Slok points out the affinity with David Hume's epistemology.) Determinism is an hypothesis which has utliity in the explanation of otherwise inexplicable connections—and we have seen that Kierkegaard himself utilizes the hypothesis in his psychology. The hypothesis is the scientist's, the psychologist's, interpretation of the given situation. Freedom is faith's interpretation, and from a scientific point of view it is neither more nor less legitimate than the deterministic hypothesis. The deterministic hypothesis is a framework of understanding which the psychologist establishes *before* he interprets the individual phenomena, not an understanding which he derives from a neutral, unbiased observation of the phenomena. This is the case whether the scientist is aware of it or not. One finds an amusing example of the latter situation in Freud's *Lectures*. He says that if one studies a particular phenomenon (errors) "really thoroughly and without prejudice or preconception, and if one has luck, then, since everything is related to everything, including small things to great, one may gain access even from such unpretentious work to a study of great problems" [Freud XV 27]. I wonder which comes first, the absence of preconceptions or the unproblematically presupposed faith in the universal coherence of things, in the fact that "everything is intimately related"[*ibid.*, p. 224], alias "the universal concatenation of events," alias the unbreakable "determinism of natural events," which is fundamental to "the whole *Weltanschauung* of science" [*ibid.*, p. 28]? The theory is no less speculative than the romantics' faith that "for itself everything is nothing, but in everything, everything is all" (Adam Oehlenschlager, *Jesu Christi gientagne Liv i den aarlige Natur* [The Life of Jesus Christ Repeated in the Seasons], Copenhagen, 1805). Freud can properly maintain that his emphasis is not upon the thesis of the universal coherence of things, but upon the material of empirical verification which supports this. The situation is of course that all his material would fall to pieces as a mare's nest of curious and inexplicable data if it were not for the fact that precisely this speculative hypothesis about the coherence of things had

organized it into a thought-out whole—just as Kierkegaard's psychology would collapse into individual autobiographical observations if he had not presupposed his *unum noris, omnes* and the daring hypothesis to which that principle gives rise. The difference between Freud and Kierkegaard is not that the one is a scientist and the other an exclusively "unscientific" thinker, the one an empiricist, the other a speculative philosopher, the one a determinist, the other an indeterminist, but that Kierkegaard, in contrast to Freud, has methodically reflected upon the conditions and the status of his knowledge, and can therefore imagine other interpretations of existence than "the whole *Weltanschauung* of science."

15. The Danish word which has here been rendered as "receiver" is "Modtager," which has the active, literal meaning of "one who takes in (or takes toward)"—Translator's Note.

16. Cf. Chapter IV, Note 12—Translator's Note.

17. *Erindringer om Søren Kierkegaard* [Recollections of Søren Kierkegaard], edited and with notes by Steen Johansen, Copenhagen: Gyldendal, 1953, p. 51 f.

18. *Opgør med Kierkegaard* [Settling-Up With Kierkegaard], p. 164 f.

19. *Ibid.,* p. 168.

20. John 3:3; — Translator's Note.

21. Luke 14:26.

22. While the collision which commands the lover to express his love as hatred is a *possible* consequence of the commandment to love one's neighbor, the collision between Christianity's love and the world is *unavoidable,* "because, from a Christian point of view, the resistance of the world stands in an essential relationship to the inwardness of Christianity" [IX 221, WL 187]. The collision is essentially unavoidable because it is a collision between two essentially different attitudes. When Kierkegaard maintains that love is and must be love of one's neighbor, he cannot admit that an injustice is perpetrated against a person's nearest surroundings when he loves his neighbor, for the person who loves his neighbor naturally also loves his nearest surroundings—as his neighbor. But to the extent that its conception of love is not the Christian concept of love, the nearest surroundings do not want to be loved as a neighbor, but want to be loved preferentially and at the expense of others. Whence the collision. The fact that this is not often seen in daily experience does not disprove its inevitability, but merely shows that love of one's neighbor is rarely practised in daily life. The inevitability manifests itself paradigmatically at the only point in history at which love of one's neighbor was practised paradigmatically, in the life of Jesus, the ignominious conclusion of which, according to Kierkegaard, cannot be an accidental ending to an otherwise successful career of a preacher of the commandment to love one's neighbor.

23. The Danish word which has here been rendered as "communication" is "Meddelelse" (verb form: "at meddele") means literally "sharing-with"—Translator's Note.

24. The Danish adjective "opbyggelig" (verb form: "at opbygge") is here rendered "edifying," in accordance with most translations, particularly of the "edifying discourses." However, "opbyggelig" and its related forms literally mean

"up-building," "to build up," etc. When, as in the latter portions of this chapter in the discussion of the section of *Works of Love* entitled "Love Builds Up," Kierkegaard clearly works with the "constructive" senses of these words, they have been translated by the appropriate forms of "building up." "Building up," et al., if somewhat clumsy, conveys the meaning of the Danish far better here, while the more standard (if somewhat cloying) "edifying" has been used in the other contexts—Translator's Note.

25. I can easily be seen that I am moving in the inevitable hermeneutic circle in this case, when I adopt Kierkegaard's doctrine of interpretation and use it to interpret him. "Be it done for you as you believed" [Matthew 8: 13] is also true in a limited sense in relation to Kierkegaard research, and it is in any case true of the present piece of Kierkegaard research, but only in the sense that I could also be capable of adopting completely different points of view (as hinted here and there), for Kierkegaard is no object of faith for me, and I could produce a settling-up with him in a fraction of the time it has taken me to produce the present exposition— except that I would find it a bit undialectical and self-righteous to do so. Kierkegaard is probably the most vulnerable writer we have in Danish; one can defeat him with one's left hand, while one must use both hands and one's head as well in order to get him to appear in his whole stature. But the suggested hermeneutic principle naturally does not mean that the interpretation is hermetically sealed off from criticism, etc. On the contrary it means that the interpreter is aware of other possibilities of interpretation, and is aware of his own interpretation as one among a number of possibilities, taken (chosen) out of an actuality which has many meanings ("actuality" used in the Kierkegaardian sense, because the word "Kierkegaard" is indeed not the designation of the historical person, nor of the corpus of printed matter which bears the inscription "Kierkegaard's Works," but of "my" consciousness of all this). One can find this "arbitrariness' unfortunate, to the extent that it is neither willing nor able to guarantee its own correctness, but merely seeks a reasonable degree of decent loyalty toward its subject. But one can also find this gratifying, not only because it does not in principle exclude other possibilities of interpretation, but also because, according to its limited abilities, it respects Kierkegaard's intentions by *not* making a claim to represent the one incontestable truth about him and his "real" opinions, and about what we consequently can "learn" from him. In humanistic research, the results are worthless in the final analysis, and one cannot "essentially" learn anything from a maieutic practitioner. This is Kierkegaard's literary testament. "Whatever the one generation learns from the other, no generation learns what is genuinely human from the previous one. With respect to this, every generation begins primitively, has no other task that every preceding generation, and comes no further, to the extent that the previous generations did not abandon the task and deceive themselves" [III 185, FT 130].

26. The Danish word which is rendered as "ground" here and subsequently in this chapter is "grunde" (noun form "Grund"), which literally means "ground," but also "basis," "fundament," etc. Earlier in this book, as in the title of this chapter

("Fundamental Recovery"), variations of "fundament" have been preferred to "ground" as being less clumsy, but in the latter portion of this chapter, where Kierkegaard so clearly depends upon "construction" metaphors, variations of "ground," "grounding," etc. have been preferred—Translator's Note.

INDEX OF NAMES

407